Henry J. Kaiser
Western Colossus

An Insider's View By Albert P. Heiner

HALO BOOKS
San Francisco, California

Library of Congress Cataloging-in-Publication Data

Heiner, Albert P., 1915 -
    Henry J. Kaiser, Western colossus : an insider's
view/ by Albert P. Heiner.
       p.   cm.
    Includes index.
    ISBN 0-9622874-3-1
    1. Kaiser, Henry J., 1882– . 2. Businessmen –
United States – Biography. I. Title.
HC 102.5.K3H46 1991
338. 092–dc20
[B]   91-28070
                                  CIP

Excerpts from *The Secret Diary of Harold L. Ickes* by Harold L. Ickes reprinted by permission of
Simon & Schuster, Inc. Copyright ©1953 by Simon & Schuster, Inc.
Renewed ©1981 by Harold M. and Elizabeth Ickes.

Halo Books
P.O. Box 2529, San Francisco, CA 94126

Cover Design By Susan Larson

To my wife, Dora,
whose wise counsel, constant inspiration (and endurance)
have made this book possible.

ACKNOWLEDGMENTS

From the time I decided (years ago) to write a book on Henry J. Kaiser, my Kaiser associate, Barney Etcheverry, has consulted with me. He shares my conviction that Kaiser was not only an industrial giant, but a high-principled champion of the American way of life.

It is with special gratitude that I acknowledge the permission granted by the Bancroft Library at the University of California in Berkeley, California, to quote from the Kaiser archives on deposit there.

I also wish to thank Shelia Young and Judith Lyons for their counselling and secretarial assistance throughout the life of this project.

Credit must also be given to Jay Nitschke of Fifth Street Computer Services for his always prompt and accurate typesetting.

CONTENTS

FOREWORD

This interesting and comprehensive biography of Henry J. Kaiser by Albert P. Heiner has brought alive personal memories of this dynamic man. He was quite as Mr. Heiner depicts him and as I knew him—an incredible business genius and fascinating personality.

I have never seen so many telephones in any room as in Mr. Kaiser's Oakland office. One rested by every chair and on every table. Wherever he happened to be at a given moment he had a telephone nearby. And his conversations were national and international, for so were his interests.

He bought me my first Hawaiian shirt and took my wife and me to our first dinner at Trader Vic's Restaurant. Few people ever did so much for Hawaii as Henry Kaiser. He left an indelible mark on the islands.

Once the churches of New York decided to ask laymen to give the Sunday morning sermon instead of pastors. I invited Henry Kaiser to take this assignment at my church. He gave a memorable message.

I view him as one of the greatest positive thinkers I ever knew. A workman once told me of the day he arrived at a construction site following a violent storm which almost buried earth moving machinery in a sea of mud.

"Whatever are we going to do?" the workman said glumly to Mr. Kaiser. "Just look at this mud."

"What mud?" Kaiser asked, "I see only that big sun shining down. It will soon turn that mud into solid ground."

And the workman added, "That is why Mr. Kaiser accomplished so many seemingly impossible things."

Mr. Heiner has written a captivating story of one of the strongest personalities ever to dominate the American scene and he has done it with skill.

—Norman Vincent Peale

THOS. J. WATSON
590 Madison Avenue
New York 22 N.Y.

January 25, 1949

Dear Henry:

I always have been fascinated by anything I have heard, read or observed about your amazing career. This time it is the recent article in Forbes magazine that recalls to mind your exceptional achievements. I notice at least one major omission in the enumeration of your activities; the chairmanship of the clothing drive.

It seems to me that your life typifies exceptionally well the sort of thing we mean when we refer to the American Way. Abounding energy and courage, ability and good judgment, initiative and inventiveness, personal integrity and character—all compounded with a goodly portion of adventurousness—have brought you a degree of success in many fields that most men would have been happy to achieve in one.

I want to congratulate you on your accomplishments and express my personal appreciation of your great contribution to the American standard of living.

With kindest regards, I remain
Sincerely yours,

Tom
(Founder and Chairman of the Board, IBM)

PREFACE

by Kevin Starr

In writing the biography of Henry J. Kaiser, Albert Heiner has fashioned a narrative of significance on many levels. The story of Henry J. Kaiser, among other things, constitutes an almost representative fable of American individualism. It is also a story of self-instructed, idiosyncratic talent. The master of an emerging American institution, the diversified corporation, and an impresario of corporate culture, Kaiser was also a pioneer in the field of social thought and social responsibility in the private sector. He was, in short, an industrial genius whom future historians, basing themselves in this eye-witness memoir and in subsequent scholarship, will eventually give the recognition that has strangely, until the appearance of this biography, been withheld.

Through a good portion of Henry J. Kaiser's career, Al Heiner was there—as a public relations officer for Kaiser Steel, but also as an eyewitness to many of the events that make this biography such lively reading. Over the years, Heiner kept notes, remembered conversations, stored impressions. He then supplemented these first-hand experiences with months of research in the massive Kaiser Archives now on deposit at the Bancroft Library at Berkeley. The combination of eyewitness account and well-researched inquiry confers on this biography an authority that will keep it used and cited in years to come. Heiner also writes in the vivid, straightforward manner of the practiced journalist and public relations practitioner. This biography teems with vivid, frequently tumultuous anecdotes, each of them set-pieces of skilled narrative. Under Heiner's guidance, Kaiser's story becomes a storehouse of significant events—the building of Boulder and Grand Coulee Dams, the mass-production of Liberty ships, the premature introduction of the small car to America—which illumine not only the Kaiser story but add to our understanding of how American corporate culture emerged and operated in the mid-twentieth century.

American society and hence its folklore and literature are replete with examples of men and women who were fundamentally the products of their own determined self-invention. The boy heroes of the Horatio Alger stories, Carrie Meeber, Jay Gatsby—

the list is endless in American folklore and literature of men and women who, seemingly coming from nowhere, fashion onto an identity and a vision and then proceed to externalize it for better or for worse. Henry J. Kaiser was such a figure. In body, mind, and will, he seemed to his contemporaries (even those who disliked him) a figure of folkloric dimension, a demiurgic force of nature, on the telephone at all hours directing vast and complicated enterprises like a character in a novel by Theodore Dreiser.

In later years, Kaiser created for himself a mythologized past—poverty, a lack of opportunity, a saintly but exhausted mother dying in her son's arms—that was not so much fabrication (although it was not exactly true either!) as it was just another instance of Kaiser's lifelong habit of seizing upon opportunities and making them work. Kaiser left school after the eighth grade, not because upstate New York or his own family could not provide future educational opportunities, but because he was anxious to get on with it, to seek the main chance, and school had little to offer in this regard. He became a photographer because that seemed handy and later, when roads needed paving, he got into the paving business with equal aplomb. He later entered the worlds of dam-building, ship-building, steel-making, cement-manufacturing, automobiles, hotel and real estate development, broadcasting and prepaid comprehensive medical care with equal virtuosity. In each case, Henry J. Kaiser merely imagined himself in the midst of these activities, and somehow this imagining came true. The man who had to look up ship terms in the public library in 1940 was a few short years later the greatest mass-producer of ships in our nation's history.

All this, of course, took talent; and Henry J. Kaiser had talent to spare—although exactly what was the precise nature of his talent is difficult to ascertain. The very ability to project himself into the midst of a situation and to start performing on its terms gave a quasi-chimerical Wizard of Oz quality to Henry J. Kaiser's talent. It was not so much what Kaiser himself knew or could do personally that made him so effective but, rather, what he could convince others they could do. The history of American talent is filled with self-instructed tinkerers, Wizard figures, ballyhooers and boosters. There seems to be, in fact, a distinctly American capacity for invention as in the Latin root <u>invenire</u>, to come upon, to discover. Henry J. Kaiser possessed this American talent for exploratory tinkering, although in his case the material he worked with was not just mechanical but new and bold combinations of technology, corporate organization and finance, labor, and marketing. Like his fellow Californian, the horticulturalist Luther Burbank of Santa Rosa, Kaiser grafted and spliced, repotted, fertilized and pruned, and as a result new varieties of fruits and flowers flourished.

Henry J. Kaiser possessed both vision and a capacity for action. In certain cases—the small car most dramatically—he ran too far out ahead of his time and hence lost out. In others—prepaid comprehensive medical care, for instance—he ran out ahead of his time and won. Building Liberty ships at an unprecedented rate during the war, he also dreamed of devising and manufacturing giant cargo and passenger planes, moving tons of freight and hundreds of soldiers into the war zones. Given government approval, he most likely would have made such visions happen. This is how Kaiser worked. He imagined it—a dam, a road, a car, an airplane, steel, cement, hospitals, television stations, hotels—and it happened. Salesmanship provides the key. Quintessentially American, Henry J. Kaiser had a quintessentially American talent for sales. He loved to sell, to pitch, to convince, to make others believe. This was the Wizard of Oz side to his character and personality.

If Kaiser had one metier, it was the corporation. He had a genius for getting the most out of other people's talents, cooperatively organized, and then giving them credit as well. Strong in ego, he was not egotistical. He shared the credit. Kaiser encountered the American corporation in the 1920s, when it was still teetering from the assaults and corrective action of the Progressive era and he refashioned and re-energized it with a vision and a creative action that proceeded from his own uniquely American personality and point of view. Kaiser found the corporation a family factory and a company store, and he left it in theory, at least, and frequently in the practice of his own companies—a fully diversified and integrated social and economic environment. In this he brought to the United States a sensibility once thought to be exclusively Japanese, a concern, that is, for the totality of the work environment. Kaiser pioneered the vertical and horizontal integration of allied industries. Building dams, he manufactured cement. Building ships, he made his own steel. Of more importance, he paid attention, magnificent attention, to human creativity in both labor and management. Surrounding himself with talented young executives, he thrust upon them responsibilities infinitely beyond their years. When his son Edgar was still in his early twenties, he thrust major responsibilities on him and on Edgar's fraternity brother Eugene Trefethen, Jr. The two of them became an effective team. Clay Bedford was barely into his thirties when Kaiser had him building Grand Coulee Dam and, later, Liberty ships. Liking young people, he had a habit of making sons of his top (and very young) executives. This largesse extended to other members of his executive team as well. The Kaiser executive dining room was part conference room, part club, part family gathering. Kaiser understood labor as well, and his successful dealings with unions was part of the total pattern of his creativity as a corporate impresario.

In the area of the social and ethical responsibilities of the corporation, he was a true pioneer. His willingness, among other things, to provide comprehensive prepaid medical coverage for his workers, the Kaiser Permanente system, which today sees to the health needs of five million members, helped lay down the foundations for the current HMO movement. Indeed, towards the end of his life, Kaiser said that his efforts in medical organization and economics would be the accomplishment by which he would be most remembered. Today, sadly, many of the industries he established have been disestablished or have passed into other hands; but the Kaiser Permanente medical program remains.

Lest we go too far, however, in the direction of hagiography, it must also be said that Henry J. Kaiser was frequently domineering, an obsessed workaholic who tended to devour even the private schedules of his top executives, a strangely dependent man with streaks of infantilism in his nature, a much too exuberant lover of good food, and a frequently over-demanding parent. As in the case of Jay Gatsby, Kaiser's self-inventions, the grand dream he pursued, frequently contained in it an element of delusion. The Wizard of Oz was by and large capable of making the Emerald City a glorious place, but behind the curtain Henry J. Kaiser was also another young fellow from upstate New York on the make, never fully believing in the stability of his accomplishment and hence determined to push it further and further and further. But then again, this too is, as Emerson would say, a very representative American trait. Dreaming, struggling, cajoling, inspiring, prophesying—and sometimes deluding, sometimes pushing it to the point of collapse—Henry J. Kaiser played out a representative American life which Albert Heiner now presents to us for our enjoyment and interpretation. In life Kaiser took his risks. Al Heiner now takes risks as well. Most biography these days seeks to debunk its subject. Al Heiner, by contrast, truly liked the Boss (as Kaiser was called by his staffers) and in this vivid biography he has the courage to let his admiration shine through. This book has the exuberance of life and experience. Critical studies of Kaiser will one day fill the shelves, true—but they will all begin their inquiry with this celebratory account.

Fortune Favors the Bold

Audentes Fortuna Iuvat

Vergil 70-19 BC

CHAPTER 1

MEET THE MAN WITH A SMILE

"I am certain that I was less than an average boy to everyone but my mother."

How can we account for Henry J. Kaiser? What made him rise from obscurity to stand out from all other people?

Was his greatness born into him? Did it come from his early training? From his devotion to his mother? Or from a childhood of happy experiences? Was he all that much smarter than other people? Did he have such robust health as to motivate him into a lifetime of activity? Did his early successes feed the fire of ambition? Did he have a strong sex drive that sparked his energies? Was it his religious bent that carried him to such heights?

In this day and age of genetic enlightenment we can say with assurance, "It all started with, or spun off from, his genes." There were forces inside him that would carry him to the top no matter where he was born or what the circumstances of his life were. All of the experiences that came to bear on the shape of his life were unconsciously, automatically tempered and influenced by the makeup of his inner, natural gifts. Heredity blessed him with greatness outright, guided him toward greatness instinctively, and prepared him for greatness when it came his way. His life was the fulfillment of Shakespeare's words: "Some are born great, some achieve greatness, and some have greatness thrust upon them."

What we can't say is that his greatness could have been foretold. Even though his name was Kaiser, which is German for Caesar or Czar (and for a long time the emperors of Germany were called Kaiser), there were no kings or emperors or famous names in his long Germanic bloodline. His was not a "pedigree" family where a genius might be expected. Rather, it would have to be said his gifts at birth came from one of those rare match-ups of genes that happen every so often in the human family—like a David, the shepherd boy in the Bible who became king, or an Abraham Lincoln, who rose from his log-cabin background to become president.

Kaiser's father, Francis John Kaiser, was born in Steinheim, Germany in 1842 where he lived on a dairy farm with his father, Frank Kaiser, Jr. There is an amazing paucity of information about the activity of the family in Steinheim, but we do have an excellent photograph of the family—mother and father, 4 sons, 1 daughter. Kaiser's father was indeed a handsome, impressive young man. He first found work as a skilled mechanic in a shoe factory in Steinheim.

Considerably more information is available about the family of Kaiser's mother, Mary Yops. She, too, was born in Steinheim, Germany, the second child and first daughter of John and Wilhelmina Wolfert Yops, in 1847. Two more children were born there, and then when Mary was only six years old the family emigrated to Canajoharie, a tiny village in upstate New York, where five more children were born.

In 1873, at age 31, Francis John Kaiser emigrated to America and went to live at the Yops' home in Canajoharie where he soon fell in love with the beautiful Mary Yops, who was five years younger than he. Soon thereafter they were married in a Protestant ceremony in the family homestead. Their first two children were born there, Elizabeth and Anna. In the meantime, the father had been busy building an impressive two-story home in nearby Sprout Brook, including a connecting barn where he would begin his work as a shoe cobbler. They moved into their new home in 1877, and a year later their third daughter, Augusta, was born there. It was in this home that Henry J. Kaiser was born May 9, 1882.

As a young woman, Mary had worked in a cheese factory in Starkville, New York, not far from Fort Plain. Later she became manager of this plant and worked there at various times after she was married. Along the way she took up part-time practical nursing as something she could do without too much interference in the raising of her own children. She had a good background for this, having been the big sister in a family of nine children.

We are indebted to the oldest daughter, Elizabeth (called Lizzie by the family) for a better understanding of her father and mother, in a family reminiscence she wrote April 25, 1943:

> Before father married mother, both her parents had died and their property was divided among the nine children. Mother had a bank account. She had what in those days was a nice savings for a home for her family, so the newspapers and magazines have been wrong and misconstrued the facts in regard to our being in poverty, for as I remember it, we were far from poverty. Father and mother were just hard working, honest, thrifty people, and very, very ambitious to accumulate, as, after all, most of the older German families in those days were.

> Dad was an honorable, good living citizen, and always very industrious and pious. We were never allowed when we all were at the table to ever start eating without first asking blessing for the food. We would get a talking to if

we did from Dad. I, being the oldest, it fell to me to ask the blessing, which I was taught to say in German when we were small, and later as we grew older in English. Dad was most particular about all those things.

With this happy family beginning—so typical of early American families—it becomes difficult to comprehend the different relationship that seemed to develop between Henry Kaiser and his mother, and Henry Kaiser and his father. Kaiser virtually worshipped his mother—one is reminded of Abraham Lincoln who said of his mother, "All that I am or ever hope to be I owe to my angel mother"—yet for some unexplained reason Kaiser never seemed to maintain a close contact with his father.

All of Kaiser's executives and close associates heard him recount on innumerable occasions the principles his mother had taught him. Several times in major speeches he listed the ideals he had gained from her. It was her concern for the welfare of people, and the fact that she herself had died in his arms at age 52 "because of lack of proper medical care," as he so often stated, that he was determined to make such a growing success out of the Kaiser Permanente Health Plan. Surprisingly, he always spoke of his mother dying in his arms when he was only sixteen, yet she actually died December 1, 1899, which would make him seventeen years old. There are other unanswered questions: Where was the father at the time of the mother's death? Where were his three older sisters at the time? Shouldn't the death of a mother be acknowledged as a tragedy shared by the family, not just a death occurring in the arms of one of the children?

A clue as to the relationship between Kaiser and his father might be found in one historical notation that said that sometime after 1884 (two years after Kaiser had been born) the mother and father had separated. It was indicated that a Catholic priest had told the father, who was Catholic, that he was not married in the eyes of the church because the wedding was a Protestant service. No further reference is made to a separation, so if it did occur, it must not have been for long. And very possibly it had little or no bearing on Kaiser's relationship with his father.

The one thing that seems to be definite is that Kaiser seldom, if ever, spoke about his father to his associates, including his long-time personal secretary (Edna Knuth) who came to know all about the sisters and the mother. She said Kaiser never asked her to write letters to his father or send money to him. He was never known to praise his father or to tell stories of any kind about him. None of the Kaiser executives, even from earliest days, nor his secretary, ever met the father. None was ever aware that the father had come to visit Kaiser or that he had ever visited his father. Some of them even labored under the assumption that the father must have died when Henry was in his teens. Actually, the father lived till October 18, 1929, long after Kaiser had been successful enough to help him generously, yet there is no record of that. Kaiser had taken on a $20,000,000 contract for road building in Cuba in 1927 and it wouldn't have been much out of his way to stop by and visit with his father who at that time was living with Kaiser's sister, Mrs. R. H. (Augusta) Le Sesne in Daytona Beach,

Florida, but there is no record of such a visit.

Kaiser did mention that his father had gone blind along the way (again, "for lack of proper medical care"). This had to be very late in the father's life because pictures of him in his early eighties didn't show him to be blind, and indeed the pictures portray him as a very pleasant, kindly person. His condition in later life was best described by Mrs. Bess Kaiser, wife of Henry, who made this family record about her father-in-law:

> HJK's father developed cataracts. HJK brought him east for operation, which was not successful.

> The father then went to live with daughter in Florida. Could see very little. As work lessened before this near blindness, he read a great deal, turning more and more to his Bible.

> Died because he could probably do nothing. Was not allowed to read, and finally not even allowed alone on beach—all this because family was protecting him and caring for him, but it broke his spirit, and undoubtedly caused his death.

The death certificate of the father in Daytona Beach was signed by his son-in-law R. H. Le Sesne indicating the father's age at 86 years, 11 months, and 15 days. He was buried in Whitesboro, New York, alongside his wife Mary, with an impressive single, stand-up headstone reading:

FRANCIS J. KAISER
1842 - 1929
MARY HIS WIFE
1847 - 1899
KAISER

There is no record that Kaiser attended whatever graveside services might have been conducted. Obviously, however, Kaiser and/or his sisters must have planned and financed the fine headstone.

One event that raises some questions took place in Chicago in February 1929, nine months before Kaiser's father passed away. The July 1929 issue of The Communicator, official publication of the Associated General Contractors of America, describing the February convention, had a headline reading "Fathers and Sons Receive Speech by Henry Kaiser with Enthusiasm." The article goes on to point out there are few industries in the world which compare with the construction industry in the fact that they are "Father and Son" enterprises where the sons can go into the business on the ground floor, learn the game from the bottom up, and then qualify to carry on the father's work to still greater heights. Kaiser gave one of his typically inspiring, optimistic talks with messages for both fathers and sons. He said,

I, too, have a son—one of 11 years due to arrive in Chicago this morning at nine, and another, 20, in California in school . . . He is now just in preparatory school eventually hoping to enter the school you boys are now enjoying.

I, like the majority of fathers, fully feel the pangs of paternal love, and I, at this moment, turn to a worn envelope, a worn Thanksgiving card which I treasure much and carry with me always. It was sent to me by my older son on Thanksgiving Day with a very personal greeting on it which I shall not read . . .

. . . To the fathers I want to leave one thought; namely, as fathers our lives can never be called complete until we have lifted up our sons to be better and greater men than we have been. They, to be free, even to disappoint us, be certain to allow our sons to choose their own paths of life and define for themselves their own good—trying only to influence them for good by the example that we ourselves set for them.

There is not one bit of doubt that Kaiser meant every word he said, not one bit of doubt that he was giving of himself lovingly and enthusiastically in the upbringing of his two sons. However, the questions that arise are: Had he taken the time to build the same kind of bond with his own father, who was still alive, that he was now doing with his two sons? Did he ever send a Thanksgiving Day greeting, or other day greeting, that would be treasured by his father as much as the one that was so near and dear to him?

Over the years Kaiser did try to keep in touch with his three sisters—Lizzie, his older sister who had become Mrs. Cummings and was living in Santa Monica, California; Anna Kaiser who was a milliner living in Portland, Oregon; and Gussie Le Sesne of Daytona Beach, Florida. They weren't drawn into company activities, so they had only a slight acquaintance with a few of Kaiser's older executives. He tried to extend them birthday and Christmas greetings each year, often sending along money. On Anna's 70th birthday, October 23, 1946, Kaiser sent her a $500.00 check with a warm, personal letter signed, "As ever, your loving brother, Henry." Two months later when his brother-in-law, Richard Le Sesne, passed away Kaiser wired his sister Gussie:

Your telegram was such a shock to me that we both know how it must affect you. Words at such a time can so inadequately express our deep feeling for you in this, your hour of darkness. That you will bear it bravely only your brother can fully know. He knows though far away, his sister can meet any crisis, and that through the years to come sunshine will come again. Write me when you can so I will know your future plans. With deep consideration and much love. Bess and Henry.

In the summer of 1955, he did bring his three sisters for a family reunion with him at his Lake Tahoe, California estate.

Christian Background

At various times some people would speculate that Kaiser was Jewish. Amazingly, one of his earliest and most important executives believed that might be true. In the twenties and thirties it was sometimes assumed that a German background was equated with a Jewish background. That was certainly not the case with Kaiser. To begin with, he was so incredibly frank and open about everything he did he would have been the first to express his pride at his Jewish heritage if such had been the case. Actually, the family had deep Christian roots going back several generations. As already noted, his father was Catholic, the mother Lutheran. Kaiser was christened Henry John in St. John's Lutheran Church, Canajoharie, New York on February 24, 1884. He and his sisters were raised as Protestants, regularly attending the Methodist Church in Sprout Brook.

When he was only 9 years old, young Henry first experienced the joys of work and his first hard lesson in responsibility by pumping the organ in the Methodist Church. As he later recalled,

> As I pumped away one Sunday, I was stricken with boyish curiosity as to what would happen if I stopped pumping. I did stop—right in the middle of a hymn by the choir—and lost my job right then and there.

Since that unhappy day he made it a point never to "stop pumping."

At age 15 he became involved in activities of the Presbyterian Church and took up membership there. Later when he moved to Lake Placid he became a lay reader at the local Episcopal Church.

It was not long thereafter he got so immersed in a host of other activities that he ceased being a regular church goer. By the time he got all steamed up over the contracting business he rarely took time to attend church even though his appreciation for Christian principles kept mounting year by year. None of his closest associates in business can recall that he spent very many Sundays going to church. The one exception might be his attendance at the outdoor Chapel of the Transfiguration, a charming Episcopal church at Lake Tahoe, California just a few miles from his home there. Nearly every weekend when he was at the lake he would attend this church. He became a very close, personal friend and admirer of the Rt. Rev. Noel Porter, D.D., Ph.D., Bishop of Sacramento, who presided over the church. Kaiser was many times invited to preach the sermon which he enjoyed doing because he seemed to be doubly inspired by the beauty of the natural setting. Also he welcomed the opportunity most Sundays to carry around the collection plate. This never failed to impress those in attendance, seeing this fat, wealthy, older man cheerfully invite their financial support, however small.

On March 14, 1943, Bishop Porter wrote to Kaiser:

. . . Henry, you are the Bishop's Warden at the outdoor Chapel of the Transfiguration, Lake Tahoe, that is, the Bishop's right hand man, counsellor and friend in behalf of the interests of the church there. And you know we deeply appreciate the friendship of you and Bess. God bless and keep you day by day.

On February 9, 1945, Dr. Paul Cadman, then Executive Assistant to Kaiser, wrote to Reverend Shires, Church Divinity School of the Pacific in Berkeley, California:

You may or may not know that Mr. and Mrs. Kaiser, with their two sons as well as a daughter-in-law, were confirmed as Episcopalians July 30, 1939 by Bishop Porter in the outdoor cathedral at Tahoe.

The younger son, Henry J. Kaiser, Jr., was a particularly devoted Episcopalian who ended up having a very lovely, specially designed Prayer Garden at his home in the Oakland hills which he used every day when he was in town.

Like everything else he got involved in, Kaiser was not content to be a listener. He wanted to help out in any way he could think of. So it was that on July 29, 1946 he wrote this letter to Charles C. Wilson, Chairman of the Board of General Electric Corporation:

For your personal information, Charlie, I am Senior Warden of a little church in the Sierra Pines at Lake Tahoe. There is an outdoor chapel, and they have built a wall of stone around the chapel. . . .

At the dedication ceremonies in the chapel, I am making a short talk. The theme is God's Garden and the security which comes from such a garden being surrounded by walls of stone. . . .

Yesterday I heard the choir on your Hour of Charm program singing "Thank God For A Garden." It was beautifully done, and I knew then that the selection should be a part of our service.

I thought it might be possible for you to send me a transcription of that particular portion of your program. We could use it effectively as a part of the ceremony. The service is held outdoors and the congregation will be between five hundred and a thousand. . . .

One of the warmest, longest-lasting friendships Kaiser ever enjoyed was with Dr. Norman Vincent Peale, D.D., Minister of the Marble Collegiate Church in New York City. Mr. and Mrs. Kaiser attended Dr. Peale's services quite often when they were in New York City, including many Easter Sundays. He also gave generous financial support to Dr. Peale. There is a long string of letters between the two men, with each seemingly trying to outdo the other in expounding Christian principles and in expressing love and admiration for the other.

On Sunday, October 16, 1949, Kaiser gave a sermon at the Marble Collegiate

Church entitled, "Philosophy of a Happy, Successful Life." In December Dr. Peale wrote Kaiser:

> Scarcely have I ever seen such a popular reaction to a Layman's talk as to that delivered by you.... The 30,000 copies that were printed for our use are practically exhausted.... We feel we should have at least 10,000 additional copies on hand.

The Early Taste of Success

It's the genes that make the difference, all right.

But one more ingredient should be added—a childhood of successful and happy experiences that whet one's appetite for life. More and more, modern behavioral psychology is telling us that impressions gained in our early years shape our thoughts and actions throughout the rest of our lives.

Henry Kaiser was lucky. He was a healthy, vigorous boy who was bright, curious, outgoing, pleasant, self-assertive, fine-looking, and happy most of the time. He found life an exciting game that challenged the best in him. He never suffered from poor health, nor did he encounter that defeat or series of defeats that might have taken the edge off his thrill at being alive. He came through his early years unscarred, free from negativism, all charged up, ready to make the rest of his life as much fun as his boyhood had been. The early taste of success was sweet and he wanted more of it.

An early clue to what was in store for him was reported in the New York City Journal American of August 9, 1942, datelined Canajoharie, NY:

> When Henry was only seven his family moved to Whitesboro, but he continued to spend many of his summers here at the farmhouse of his uncle, Casper Yops, it was recalled today by Mrs. Daniel Luther, a cousin.
>
> If Henry ever thought something could be done, you could be sure it would be done no matter how many insisted that it couldn't.
>
> I remember the time he spent a summer here and asked his uncle for some chickens to take back to Whitesboro. Mr. Yops knew there were no facilities to take care of a flock of chickens in the small Kaiser place in Whitesboro, and so he wrote Henry's mother and asked her what he ought to do about the boy's request.
>
> She wrote that if Henry had decided to raise chickens, 'You might as well give them to him, because he'll find a way.'
>
> He got them, set up a chicken business, made it pay, and sold it to begin another venture which everyone said just couldn't be done.

Another insight into his early years was provided by some thing he wrote later in life when he was in the midst of doing so many seemingly impossible things:

When I was young I used to skate to school. It seemed to me that the wind was blowing against me when I went to school and when I came home, too. I mentioned this a few years ago and someone told me 'That's the story of your life. You're always skating against the wind.'

His skating was not confined to roller skating. In another of his letters written later in life to a friend he said, "Many a time I skated on the ice of the Erie Canal from Whitesboro to Utica."

What happened when young Henry turned thirteen has been written up hundreds of times. He quit school. Most of the stories have made him out to be a rags-to-riches hero who was forced to leave school to look for work to help support his family. Not so, according to his sisters. Here's how Lizzie told the story in a reminiscence she wrote April 25, 1943:

> When Henry reached the age of 13, he wanted to go to work, and was very determined to. We all realized he should go to school longer and was too young to leave school. I felt terrible about it and I said, 'Henry, you don't realize now, but you will later when your opportunities have slipped away, and another year or two would help you much.' But he felt he wanted to earn money and get started. He borrowed $5.00 from his sister Anna and hit out for New York City where he tramped the streets for three weeks looking for a job, but to no avail. When he returned I was worried about getting him started among the right influence, so I myself started out to find the right position with good influence for the dear brother I worshipped, and I secured a position for him at J.B. Wells Dry Goods Store, and he went to work as cash boy. Soon he worked up to the home furnishing department. His environment was good and he began to realize after a few years the great value of an education as I told him. He made fine, influential friends, and he began to study and read fine books, both educational and upbuilding for fine character which he really had within himself, and at the age of 16 or 17 years he thought he was qualified to take a position as traveling salesman on a small scale, which he had been studying up on, and therefore step by step rose to higher things. Henry was and is very open and frank, and in his youth seemed like a sister among us and came to us with all his social affairs, for instance, when he came east to be married and to take his bride, he and I sat up all night and had our heart to heart talk together before his going on to Boston, and I feel I can remember every detail of his life up to the time he was married.

Another insight into Kaiser's qualities as a youth was provided in a letter his sister, Anna, wrote him June 1, 1943. Just a week earlier Kaiser had given the Baccalaureate address, at Washington State College in Pullman, Washington, not far from Spokane. On that occasion the college awarded him a Degree of Doctor of Laws. Here's what

Anna who lived in Portland, Oregon wrote to him:

> Just previously heard thru' Oregonian 'Dr.' Kaiser was on his way to Wn State College to deliver address. It meant more to me than anyone else. I thought of the long tireless midnights you read and studied when so young. To me was assigned the task of awakening you with so little sleep—and you were keeping your promise to mother to study, if she'd consent to your leaving school. You had learned the struggle without schooling. Am glad that educators find the great need of your assistance, and grand to have the award in your home state as you who have been self-educated, can better understand the workingmen you enjoy as their leader.

On his eighty-fifth birthday, May 9, 1967, Kaiser reminisced about his childhood:

> In my very early years, as soon as I was strong enough to do a good job at it, I pitched hay from morning till night. Then when I left school I walked the streets of New York City hunting for a job and being turned down. Later when I had my job at the dry goods store I used to walk four miles from my home to the store until I made a deal with the operator of the horse-drawn streetcar that I would hitch up the horse at 5:00 a.m. and drive the car to his house. That way I earned the nickel fare.

These childhood experiences made impressions on him that would stay with him throughout his lifetime. On June 16, 1952 he answered a friendly letter he had just received from Mrs. John Schroeder of Baldwinsville, New York, part of his reply stating:

> When you wrote that your late husband, John Schroeder, used to bicycle with me to Canajoharie, and also that he worked in the J.B. Wells Dry Goods Store for $3.00 a week, it brought back many memories to me. In fact, I was visiting Utica at the time of the historic anniversary, and I retraced some of my boyhood steps at Sprout Brook, Canajoharie, Whitesboro and Utica. I well recall riding a bicycle up the long hill to the farm where I would work. I also went to the Wells Dry Good Store, where, incidentally, I started at the age of 13 at $1.50 per week.

It was in the Wells Dry Goods Store where young Kaiser learned a lesson that would stay with him all his life. He recounted the experience in an interview with the Utica Observer Dispatch, November 18, 1947.

> I'll tell you about a lesson I learned from Edward Wells, I never forgot. When I worked in the drapery department I had to unfold them on racks for customers to inspect. When the customers were through looking, I had to fold them up again.
>
> One day after the customers had seen the curtains I decided it was too

much bother to fold them up again. Ed Wells walked into the department and saw the lace curtains still hanging on the racks. 'Henry,' he said, 'You haven't folded up the curtains.' 'No, Mr. Wells. I thought another customer might be around to look at them.'

'And there may not be another customer right away,' he replied. Then he paused and looking squarely at me, said slowly, 'Henry, when you go home tonight I want you to tell your mother not to make up your bed for you—because you might want to sleep in it the next night.'

Orderliness was next to Godliness with Ed Wells, and I always remembered that lesson about neatness. When I go through some of my offices and see something that is on a desk that is out of place, I usually call it to the attention of the one in charge.

With his overflowing energy, young Kaiser was always ready for youthful "horseplay." He was reminded of this in a letter he received from Mrs. Abbie M. Wright of South Hero, Vermont dated December 15, 1949. In that letter she said:

. . . I have a photo of you taken at Mirror Lake. I had three finished from it. I am sending you one, the others I gave to Martha Davis and her daughter Myra, as they and I visited Wallace. He was her brother—my cousin for whom you were working at that time. One day as work was stacked at the studio you came to the house full of fun, went to the bedroom and came out with one of Wallace's night shirts which was in rags. Wallace's wife, Flora, says, 'Let's take his picture!' You ran out of the house up a hill back of the house. You stopped when you were at the top, nicely posed. We got a good picture of you.

Another clue to Kaiser's youthful exuberance was contained in a letter from Robert C. Elliot, Executive Assistant to Mr. Kaiser, who wrote to Hiram K. Smith of Detroit, January 4, 1952, answering questions about Kaiser's involvement in speed boat racing. The letter stated,

First, you ask how did Mr. Kaiser happen to get into boat racing. About the turn of the century, when Mr. Kaiser was not yet twenty years old, but was in business in Lake Placid, New York, he rigged up a one-horse-power naphtha engine with make-and-break ignition, installed it in a light weight Adirondack lake skiff and achieved speeds of six to eight miles an hour. The thrill of boating that he gained as a young man has always remained with him and it has always been his hobby when he could spare the time for the sport.

In his book, Inside U.S.A., John Gunther has a short section on Kaiser. He reported on an interview in which:

He [Kaiser] told me that the deepest emotion of his life—the joy of achievement—was rooted in his childhood experiences. "I'm doing now all the things I swore I'd do when I was thirteen."

His introduction to the photography business came when he got a job doing general work at T. E. Colwell Co., wholesale and retail dealers in photographic supplies in Utica. This soon led to a job as shipping and billing clerk, later salesman, for W. A. Semple, wholesale and retail dealer in photographic supplies in Utica. After hours he boosted his meager income by taking pictures.

The contact with W. A. Semple was much more than an employer- employee relationship. They developed a genuine respect for each other and their friendship lasted for many years. On October 26, 1901, Semple wrote this typewritten letter:

To Whom It May Concern:

The bearer, Mr. Henry Kaiser, has been in my employ for the past few years and he has proven himself a very capable and trustworthy man in every respect. As a salesman, both travelling and inside, he is very proficient, being attentive to all details pertaining to a merchantile [sic] business. He has also served me as shipping and billing clerk with entire satisfaction. I can faithfully recommend Mr. Kaiser as a steady and industrious man, always busy with business, and I feel confident that he can and will fill any position to which he may aspire.

Nearly thirteen years later, Semple wrote Kaiser congratulating him upon his first paving contract in far-away Vancouver, B.C. Using his new letterhead, "Henry J. Kaiser, Paving Contractor, Vancouver, B.C.," Kaiser wrote to Semple in longhand under date of April 27, 1914:

It certainly was good to hear from my old friend and employer. You know I attribute what little success I have attained to the splendid training, knowledge I received from you and your asscociation [sic] and particularly the recomendation [sic] you gave me which I still have.... You yourself know that the impressions a young man gets when he first starts in life have much to do with the shaping of his life success. The contract I secured covers thirty-two blocks of paving which I have now partially completed. I am completing it well within my estimate, but of course I don't expect to retire on the profits. It means a great deal to me however to finally get started. It's my first start in business for myself since I left the photo business, and if the country prosperity remains only normal I feel sure I will continue successfull [sic].... I wish I could see you and have a good talk with you. You ought to manage to take a trip West soon. You should visit the Panama exhibition and make us a visit. I often think of you driving that Stanley steam car, the first auto in existence.... I hope this finds you and yours in the very best of health and with kindest regards to all from Mrs. K and myself believe me. Ever your friend, Henry

As important as Semple's friendship was for Kaiser in getting started in the photographic business, there were other contacts that Kaiser was busy making. His swirl of activities at that time was delightfully described in an article published in the <u>Lake Placid News</u> of May 24, 1979 written by Mrs. Mary McKenzie, Lake Placid Historian. She carefully researched all of the available records in the area, and interviewed as many people as possible who could recall Kaiser's activities around the turn of the century. With her permission the following is taken from that article:

In 1900, as a traveling salesman of photo supplies in upper New York, he checked into the pleasant summer resort of Lake Placid. It was a case of love at first sight. The mountains and lakes had a strong appeal for young Kaiser. He must live in this enchanted land.

Visiting W. W. Brownell, owner of a modest photo shop on Main Street, he offered to work as a helper without pay. The hook, however, was baited, and with a lure that was to become a Kaiser trademark. Without pay, yes— but only until he doubled the store's business, at which time he wanted 50 percent of the profits. For Mr. Brownell, the come-on was irresistible.

Mr. and Mrs. Brownell took a fancy to the young Horatio Alger hero, providing meals and a cot in the back room. Henry did not double the business. He tripled it within a year. A new sign, 'Brownell and Kaiser,' went up outside, along with another of Henry's creations: 'Meet the Man with a Smile.' And people did. Profits continued to soar. It was all too much for Mr. Brownell.

'I can't stand the pace, Henry,' he cried. 'It's too hectic. Buy me out!' And Henry did. Scarcely 20, he was the sole proprietor of a thriving little business.

Henry had moved to the more solid comforts of Lakeside Inn, boarding and rooming in style. He was popular in the village, and his high spirits and joy in living were infectious. A lay reader at the local Episcopal Church, he also swam, boated, danced and mountain-climbed. Snapshots from this period portray a handsome and charismatic young blade, usually surrounded by a bevy of pretty girls.

The small world of Lake Placid was Henry Kaiser's oyster. Here he had plumbed the secrets of success—a little luck, a lot of hard work, and a willingness to gamble—and set the pattern of his life. There was one hitch. The village rolled up its plank sidewalks in the fall. A local businesswoman persuaded Henry to winter in Florida. And so it was that he began dividing his time between north and south.

This very act of breaking free from the world of Lake Placid would open his eyes to the potential for adventure that lay in every direction. Florida, of course, had a charm all its own and he was quick to fall in love with it. But he was not there to vacation, he had to make a living, so he faced the challenge of setting up a photographic business. This was not an easy thing to do for a stranger to the territory, but immediately good fortune opened the way for him. Here's his own account of how he got started:

When I arrived at Daytona Beach with photographic equipment and my total cash savings of $500, I discovered there wasn't a single store building to be rented.

A total stranger on a hotel porch noticed I was upset, and asked me, "What's the matter, young man? Things can't be as bad as you look." I told him I had to find a way to build a store. The stranger volunteered to loan me $4,000 and we built the store!

Next year the tourist business dropped to a mere fraction, and I had to figure out a way to get enough work to keep the photographic business going. It happened that every tourist who did come to Daytona Beach would take a scenic boat trip on a little boat called 'Uncle Sam.' So I got the job of being purser and narrator on the sightseeing boat.

Did I give service! I told the sightseers where the scenic wonders were to snap. I sold them the film and helped them load their cameras. I even had to dive to the bottom of the river to recover a lost lens. When we returned to port from the sightseeing trip I'd collect the film, get their hotel and room number, then take the film with me to develop and print. The next morning, before my customers had breakfast I would have the developed film in their hotel box. I learned the fine lesson of serving people. So whatever photographic business there was that lean year came to my store and the business survived and grew.

That kind of service obviously paid off. Soon he proceeded to expand into Palm Beach and Nassau with each store front proudly proclaiming, "Meet the Man With a Smile." It was indeed a flourishing business. He had visions of a great future balancing out his winter-time success in Florida with his solid summer-time business in Lake Placid.

Then something unexpected happened in the spring of 1906 that would dramatically change all his plans and start him on a totally different career. It was when a young lady from Boston came into his Lake Placid studio to sit for a portrait. Before the session was over, Kaiser knew this was the one he had been waiting for. Lovely Bess Hannah Fosburgh felt the same way.

Enter Bess

Up till that time Bess had not known what it was like to live in normal, stable family conditions. She was born in Cadillac, Michigan April 9, 1886 and within two weeks her mother died. Immediately her mother's mother from Wilkes-Barre, Pennsylvania came and brought her back to live with her. From that time forward Bess had an itinerant family life, hardly knowing what the word "home" truly meant. With this kind of background it is really quite remarkable she retained her poise and charm to attract Henry Kaiser so completely. In a way, the variety of challenges she encountered as a young girl helped prepare her for the ever-challenging life she would have to put up with as Kaiser's wife.

Bess lived with her strong-willed grandmother (and an aunt and an Uncle Howard whom Bess adored) for six years.

Following the death of the grandmother Uncle Howard took Bess along with him to Chicago where his business affiliation had been transferred. He was not married at the time and arranged for governesses to help him raise Bess. She went to kindergarten and the first grade in Chicago. Then from the age of eight to eleven years she lived with another uncle (a brother of Howard) and aunt in Indiana. By that time her favorite uncle, Howard, had gotten married and wanted to bring Bess back to live with him and his new wife. Unfortunately, the wife resented having to put up with Bess. As Bess later recorded:

> She turned out to be hard and dictatorial, even relentlessly depriving my uncle of all freedom of personality and restricting me to the severest, plainest regime imaginable—clothes, hair, food, friends—everything.

> Punishment was meted out for much, and my uncle was never permitted to show affection of any kind for me—not even to come into my room when I was ill.

Where was Bess' father, Edgar Charles Fosburgh, these early years of her life? He was, of course, grateful that his mother-in-law would take the baby as soon as his wife died. Then when he remarried three and a half years later in Cadillac, Michigan, he and his new wife sought to bring Bess with them, but by this time the grandmother was determined to keep the child. For the next ten years he kept in close touch with Bess living with the grandmother and the various aunts and uncles that she did.

Within a few years after the father's remarriage he moved to Norfolk, Virginia where he established his own successful business, the Fosburgh Lumber Company. Although it was distant from where Bess was living, it was nearly always possible for her to spend Christmas with her father and stepmother.

> On one trip to Norfolk when I was thirteen, he sighed when he saw this poor ugly duckling. 'Oh, Bess, your mother was so tiny, dainty, and lovely, and you are so fat with such hands and feet, and oh, such clothes.' It was then he found out that the money he had been sending had been used in part by

my aunt. Also, when I told him how restrictive my aunt had been, not only to me but to my uncle, Howard, he made the decision to take me away from Chicago and put me in a school near Boston, the Howard Seminary.

Her studies at the seminary continued for two years, then at age 15 she entered Dana Hall in Boston where four years later she graduated. After that she lived another year at West Newton, near Boston, with a family who acted as her chaperons, where she studied music. Fortunately, all these experiences seemed to be pleasant enough and, of course, she was learning a great deal. Nevertheless, after a rather hectic childhood it was a test of her character that she was living away from any of her own family during the school portion of these seven years.

The big event in Bess's life came when her father took her to Lake Placid in the spring of 1906 for a few weeks vacation. To say the unexpected happened is an understatement. Here was a 20-year-old lady who had bounced from one home to another in her early years and who just 7 years earlier had been told by her father, "you are so fat with such hands and feet", posing for a portrait in the studio of Henry Kaiser. Here was a 24-year-old, virile, dashing photographer who had courted all the beauties which Lake Placid and Florida had to offer. One look in the camera and "zing went the strings of his heart." Within a few weeks they had become engaged, but Bess' father had his own very definite ideas about marriage. Notwithstanding the fact he had never provided a home for Bess, he stood firm in his disapproval of the kind of "gypsy" life she would have to lead if Kaiser continued in his photo business spending five summer months in Lake Placid and seven winter months in Florida. The father had often told her, "I can give you everything but a home, and I can never give you that." So he gave his consent to her marriage on three conditions: (1) that Kaiser go west and establish himself in a stable business; (2) that he be earning at least $125.00 per month; (3) that he have a home built before their marriage. Reports often cropped up that the father also insisted that Kaiser must have $1,000 in the bank. This was not true, and both Henry and Bess often repudiated that.

A big order indeed for a twenty-four year old at that time, but Kaiser didn't bat an eye. Here was a chance to break away from the photography business which he had begun to tire of, because he said,

> I couldn't do what people wanted in portrait photography. They all wanted to look like actors or actresses, not like themselves, so I went to landscape photography. I took a photo of a landscape—all natural—and it didn't sell at all. Then I took another—everything fake—and it sold wonderfully, so I decided to get out of that, too.

Nevertheless, Kaiser always maintained fond recollections of his days in photography, and throughout his life he could always be found taking pictures. For a long time he carefully packed away in Oakland the original photographic equipment with which he made his first commercial success.

And he always remembered the people who inspired and helped him during his photographic career. He once recalled," I used to get as high as $25 for some of my pictures. It was great fun."

Go West, Young Man

Kaiser immediately took up the challenge, thereby opening a way of life he may have never ventured into if he had remained in Lake Placid. It is interesting to speculate just what business he might have ended up in if he had not left for the west. In all probability he would never have started out in the construction business because at no time in his childhood activities nor in his working experiences once he got his first job at age thirteen did he get involved in building things. There just wasn't a lot of building activity going on around Lake Placid. If he had remained in the photography business, or any other business that offered prospects in the Lake Placid area, he would have no doubt cut a big figure, perhaps a national figure, in his chosen field. But by July he had sold his photography businesses in New York and Florida and was heading west for a totally unknown and unpredictable career. Bess returned to West Newton, Massachusetts to continue her study of music while waiting for her fiance to make good on his commitments.

Again, fate took a hand in shaping Kaiser's future. On his way west he became stranded in Lewiston, Idaho where he made every effort to find a job. Being unsuccessful there, he went on to Spokane, where after a great deal of fruitless searching he finally stumbled onto a job, or rather an opportunity, in a hardware store owned by James C. McGowan. McGowan actually had no openings, and did his best to discourage the young man. But the persistent Kaiser went back for the 13th time and on this occasion he spotted a stock of silverware which had been badly tarnished in a fire. He had the bright idea to polish the silverware and sell it. With nothing to lose, McGowan agreed. From that time forward Kaiser considered 13 to be his lucky number.

To McGowan's surprise, Kaiser hired extra girls to do the polishing. He was then able to sell the silverware, make enough to pay the girls and himself, and end up with a tidy profit for McGowan. He was put on the payroll at $7.00 per week.

McGowan, who remained a friend of Kaiser for life, would later reminisce,

> Kaiser speedily showed at that time that he was not a $7.00 a week man. He was a go-getter, fired with faith, enthusiasm and hard work, a great believer in giving his customers service over and above their expectations. I made him a city salesman, but that was not enough, because even then he had begun visioning for himself a position in the field of contracting. I remember one time I happened to overhear him talking to a prospective customer for belting, pulleys and sawmill equipment. He was using technical terms in explaining about the size of belting and pulleys required to transmit a certain amount of power. After the customer left, I asked him where he had secured

the information he was giving the customer. He immediately stepped back of the counter and pulled out a book he had secured from the public library which treated of the subject and promptly turned to the particular page containing that information. Thereupon, I marked him as an exceptional boy, because not many young men of his time of life would think about going to the public library to secure information which would better fit him for his work.

The hardware store had been an ideal training ground for the ambitious young Kaiser. It was a crossroad of sorts for everyone in the construction business. People building their own homes came there for a wide variety of tools and building materials. Large-scale contractors had to supplement their equipment and supplies with purchases from the hardware store. Then, too, anyone working there would keep abreast of nearly all the construction going on in the area. In the process, Kaiser developed a reputation for knowing every single item carried in the store, the supply and location of each—the kind of work which modern day computers perform. It got to the point where others working in the store would simply turn to Kaiser to find out what the price was on each product.

Once Kaiser became a salesman he had an opportunity to visit the actual job-sites. Without any doubt the romance of field construction from these first-hand contacts captured his imagination. His dreams about getting into the construction business began firming up.

Notwithstanding, with all of his enthusiasm in getting started in the hardware business, Kaiser didn't lose sight of his commitment to have a home for his bride-to-be. Naturally, to him it wouldn't be a matter of buying a home, but rather an opportunity to build his own home. He chose a lot with a fine view and land enough on which to build a large home. For someone starting out on a shoestring as he was, it was quite incredible he went forward in building the size home he did. It ended up with so many outstanding features that the Spokane Review newspaper of Sunday morning, June 14, 1908 had a long article about it, with both exterior and interior pictures and the architect's design for the first and second floors. The article was headlined "Unique Residence Has Roof Garden." The article started off,

> Something wholly unique and original has been obtained in the effective design of the residence which Henry J. Kaiser has just completed on the east side of Grand Street at the head of Sumner Avenue. The house plan is strikingly adapted to the unusual site, which is near to and high above the street, and which commands an exceptionally fine view, even in Spokane, the city of beautiful views.

The article didn't spare any superlatives in describing the livability and artistry of the home, room by room, with emphasis on the charming color effects. It stated the roof garden "is to be furnished as a lounging room . . . especially delightful for summer evenings with its superb view in all directions." It even put in a good word about the basement with its "cement floor and walls, a chauffeur's room, the furnace room, fuel rooms, fruit room, and laundry."

The article ended with the sentence, "The cost of the house was about $6,500." In 1908 this was a considerable sum of money.

A few observations are appropriate.

1) From the start, Kaiser always thought "big."

2) He always sought the aesthetic.

3) His roof garden of 1908 was a harbinger of a magnificent 3-acre garden, open to the public, which he would insist upon for the roof of the garage adjoining his 28-story Kaiser Center office building in Oakland as it neared completion in 1959.

It is regrettable indeed that this unique Spokane home was torn down some years ago.

In less than a year Kaiser had a good start on his new home and had met the other two conditions for his marriage, so he proudly headed east to claim his bride. Bess' father, Edgar Fosburgh, would have liked to have the marriage at his home in Norfolk, Virginia. However, after his second wife's offer to take Bess with them when they were first married, which the grandmother refused to have her do, the stepmother (even as good as she had been to Bess in her direct dealings with her) chose to live a sham, never telling anyone that Fosburgh had been married before. It was for this hypocritical vanity that Bess had been forced to live away from home in the years when she attended school and before her marriage, only going to Virginia for short visits at Christmas and during vacation periods. Even for something as important as the wedding, the stepmother didn't want her secret to be known by her friends in Norfolk, so she refused to have the marriage at her home.

The father had never been active in a church, therefore, he decided the marriage should take place in a hotel, his two favorites being the Astor in New York and the Touraine in Boston. He finally chose the Touraine and it was on Monday, April 8, 1907 that Henry and Bess were married.

It was written up in the newspaper a few days later:

HENRY KAISER MARRIED
SPOKANE MAN WEDS SECRETLY
IN BOSTON
BRIDE IS MISS BESSIE FOSBURGH
NEWS OF CEREMONY IS BETRAYED
BY RECORDS

Boston, Mass., April 13. News of the secret marriage here last Monday at the Hotel Touraine of Miss Bessie H. Fosburgh of Norfolk, VA., leaked out here today by the filing of the marriage record at the city registrar's office. The ceremony was performed by Rev. Edward H. Rudd of Dedham, Mass. The bride is a daughter of Edgar C. Fosburgh of Norfolk, VA. As far as can be learned there was no elopement nor any special reason for secrecy beyond the desire of the contracting parties to avoid publicity.

Once the ceremony was performed there was no time for the ecstatic bride and groom to go on a honeymoon as such. As Bess later described it,

> Business called of course and we started immediately for the west. I have spent my life traveling with men who have never known just quite what to do with me.

Kaiser had made a happy choice. Bess became his almost constant companion—a helpmate with whom he could discuss all his dreams and business plans for the next 44 years until her death in 1951.

CHAPTER 2

A ROUGH-AND-TUMBLE BUSINESS

"It is always good to get on high ground and see the vision. But I can never escape the urge to do something about it."

"I've ruined my brand-new suit," A. B. Ordway said in disgust as he picked himself up and began examining how badly his hands and knees had been skinned. He had just swung off a moving train that wouldn't stop.

"Ord" had swung off because his impetuous and impatient boss, Henry J. Kaiser, had jumped off right ahead of him. "I had to find out if he had broken his neck," Ordway said many years later as he recounted the story.

Ordway was Kaiser's first employee, and in 1921 Kaiser didn't have many, because highway jobs were hard to come by. Thus, when Ord happened to be in Red Bluff, California, where he fortuitously overheard competitors discussing a big road-building job between Redding and Red Bluff that was coming up for immediate bid, he wrote Kaiser in Mount Vernon, Washington.

We are indebted to Kaiser's wife, Bess, for her recollection of how her husband reacted to Ordway's letter. In a birthday remembrance she later wrote in longhand:

The Mount Vernon work about completed, Ord left on a vacation to California (his first in seven years) traveling in his old Chandler. Hearing of a sizable amount of work coming up down there which looked very interesting he wrote to you and then started homeward. His letter aroused considerable thought in your mind; so that night you sat by the fireside in our home and continued thinking. Suddenly, out of a clear sky you decided Ord had about reached Roseburg, Oregon, so you picked up the phone to try to locate him there at the old Umpquah Hotel. In less than five minutes you and he were talking. He had just happened in; thus the result. You asked him to meet you in Portland on the Shasta, the fast train to California at that time.

The two did meet in Portland, Oregon, and then took the southbound Shasta Ltd. Ord recalled:

> After we boarded the train, we discovered that it didn't stop at Redding, but that didn't faze Henry. He wanted to jump off at Anderson from the observation car, but the brakeman wouldn't let us, so we went up to the middle of the train where there wasn't any brakeman, and we opened the vestibule to jump off. I used to do a little hoboing in my time and was pretty good at hopping off moving cars, but Henry was a little heavy and we both had suitcases. The next town was Cottonwood and I learned the train would slow down a bit just long enough for the engineer to snatch his orders off a pole while the train was moving.
>
> That's when Henry decided to grab his suitcase and jump. He let go near the little Cottonwood station house and tumbled head over heels, skidding head first into a pile of railroad ties. When I jumped I rolled over my suitcase and came to a stop right in front of the station door. The stationmaster came out just as we got to our feet and were examining our skinned hands and legs. 'You damn fools,' he said, and of course he was right. We lost a little skin and ruined our suits (which I never got reimbursed for) but we did get the job, at $527,000, our biggest one up until then, and we've been in California ever since.

A rough-and-tumble business, indeed. No more revealing prologue to the life of Henry J. Kaiser could have been dreamed up by any writer. This one incident was so typical of the hundreds of times he would go plunging ahead, full of confidence as to the outcome, sure of his ability to overcome any problems, and unafraid of the inevitable risks.

Consider these elements:

(1) The minute Ordway mentioned the upcoming bid, Kaiser grasped the potential.

(2) He took the fastest possible means to get to the destination, although in his hurry he failed to discover that the train did not stop at Redding. No matter.

(3) He didn't let the risk of bodily injury, or damage to his clothing, or possible embarrassment of any kind, interfere with reaching his goal.

(4) He put together the winning bid on short notice, and sold himself as being reliable, even though he had not done any previous roadwork in California.

Of course, he had been in the thick of the rough-and-tumble construction business long before 1921. After his return to Spokane with his bride in 1907 he continued with the McGowan Hardware store, primarily responsible for calling on customers. One time he sold some shaker screens to a man who owned a sand and gravel business. The owner installed the screens, but they didn't work satisfactorily. Naturally, he complained that he had been sold the wrong kind of screens. Young Kaiser replied: "The screens are all right; you just don't know how to make them work properly." The customer then challenged Kaiser to get the screens in working order. With the permission of McGowan, Kaiser spent nearly two weeks solving the problem, during which time he had to do a lot of improvising, an experience which convinced him that a little ingenuity and a lot of hard work could overcome almost any mechanical problem. From that time forward, even though he had never been trained as a mechanical engineer, he was constantly tinkering with every piece of equipment he ever worked with, trying to find a way to get it to do the job faster and more efficiently.

By 1909 he could see a greater opportunity in the construction business than in the hardware business. He went to work for the Hawkeye Fuel Company of Spokane, dealers in gravel and cement, for about half what he'd been getting at McGowan's. Then within two years he transferred over to one of Hawkeye's customers, the J. F. Hill Company (which owned Canadian Mineral Rubber Company) where he began inching closer to setting up his own business. At this plant, production was erratic, failing to live up to the promises he had made as a salesman. So at night he worked with both men and equipment to improve the output of the plant.

By early 1912 he was on the payroll of the subsidiary, Canadian Mineral Rubber Company. On February 3, 1912, his new boss in Victoria, B.C., wrote the following memo to him at the Empress Hotel in Victoria:

> I take pleasure in advising you that commencing January 1, 1912, your salary will be at the rate of $4,000 per year. The allowance of $75 per month which you have been receiving since you located in Victoria will continue as long as you remain there.

A year later he was confronted with a kind of challenge that would convince him the time had come to get in the construction business on his own. His employer, the Canadian Mineral Rubber Company, was low bidder on a $167,000 Vancouver, Canada paving job but went out of business before the work could begin. Kaiser was determined to hold on to the contract, so he took it upon himself to get the necessary financing. He went straight to the president of a Vancouver bank and asked for $25,000. He frankly listed his knowledge of road building as his only asset. That, plus his personal persuasiveness, prompted the banker to write to his cashier: "Please honor the credit of Henry J. Kaiser for $25,000."

The banker wasn't soft-hearted. While Kaiser was only 31 years old he already had a good reputation as one who knew a great deal about building roads in the Pacific Northwest. Kaiser posted the required $40,000 bond, accompanied the bid with an $8,300 cash deposit, and was ready to take on his first road job as his own boss. When the job was completed in 1914 with a profit of $19,000 he knew he was in the construction business to stay.

He was entirely on his own in preparing a bid for another paving job in Vancouver. In the Vancouver World of December 30, 1913, under the heading, "Permanent Bids Are Considered," it was reported,

The city engineer stated that in almost all the cases the Columbia Bitulithic Company and Mr. Henry J. Kaiser were the lowest tenderers, the latter being the lowest on the biggest item on the programme, the paving of Victoria Drive from Powell to Twelfth, for $133,922.33.

This was significant not only because of Kaiser making the lowest bid, but it was the first time his name was published in a newspaper in connection with his own construction work. He savored the publicity, and from that time forward he never hesitated in any of his undertakings to have his name appear in publications of all kinds. From the early 1930's when he was one of the partners building Boulder Dam, right on through World War II, and continuing till his death in 1967, Kaiser's name would be before the public more often than any other industrialist in the country.

Kaiser was finally awarded the Victoria Drive contract in early January, 1914, but for some unexplained reason, possibly adverse weather conditions as well as time required to line up equipment and supplies, construction was not actually started until late March. After that, Kaiser got into his stride and on June 4, 1914 the Vancouver World reported:

Well on its way to establishing a record in pavement construction in Vancouver, the contract for the paving of Victoria Drive between Powell and Twelfth Avenue, in the hands of Mr. H.J. Kaiser, is approaching completion, and if the work is finished as anticipated by the end of June, the task of paving about 30 blocks will have occupied but a bare three months.

It is the largest undertaking, so far as pavements are concerned, ever let by the city in one contract, and opinions have been freely expressed that it would not be through before the fall, but aided greatly by excellent weather for the most part, the contractor has set a splendid pace and will finish at the end of the month, if all continues to go well.

It was at this same period Kaiser was learning that jobs in the construction business crop up at the most unpredictable times. A contractor can never rest on any one job—he must always be looking ahead to the next one so he can keep his people and equipment busy. Thus it was that right in the middle of his hurry-up job on Victoria Drive bids were called for new surfacing of other roads in Vancouver. Once again the story is best told by another article in the Vancouver World dated May 5, 1914:

A proposition was made by Mr. H.J. Kaiser, paving contractor, to the civic Board of Works on Tuesday afternoon to put in a 3 inch bituminous base and 1 inch bituminous surface for the sum of $1.35 a square yard, and he backed up his offer by guaranteeing to furnish a bond to maintain the pavement for five years without extra charge.

Mr. Kaiser explained that he had a $130,000 plant and as this bituminous pavement was but a side issue of the paving business he could manufacture it cheaply.

It was therefore decided to lay some of this material on Fourteenth Avenue between South Cambie and Manitoba, likewise the north side of Pender Street east, between Victoria and Lakewood, and the work was recommended to be given to Mr. Kaiser.

Kaiser had to step in the breach in behalf of Canadian Mineral Rubber Company in another instance—this time in the City of Nanaimo, British Columbia. This was reported in the Nanaimo Herald newspaper of June 27, 1914:

At last evening's meeting the City Council released Canadian Mineral Rubber Company from its street paving contract and awarded it to Mr. H J Kaiser, contractor of Vancouver. The amount of paving covered in the contract is 100,000 square yards, and the approximate cost will be $250,000. Mr. A B Ordway, who is already well known in Nanaimo, will superintend the work for Mr. Kaiser, and under his practical supervision the city should get a good job done.

That was a good send-off for Ordway who had become Kaiser's first employee in 1912 when Kaiser was still with Canadian Mineral Rubber Company. As Ord later put it, "I walked up and asked for a job. Been with Henry Kaiser ever since." Ord quickly caught on to Kaiser's way of doing business and never hesitated working almost as long and as hard as Kaiser himself. One early experience drove home to Ord just how relentless Kaiser would be in getting work finished as quickly as possible. It was on the first paving job in British Columbia, and as paving was new there, the crew was made up of Americans. July 4th was coming up, so Ord asked Kaiser if it was to be a holiday. The answer was, "no—because American holidays don't apply in Canada." Then not long thereafter a Canadian holiday came along, and Ord asked if it would be a holiday. "Of course not," Kaiser replied, "Americans shouldn't celebrate Canadian holidays."

From that time forward, Ord was a trusted, capable, intimate associate of Kaiser's. He was not only Kaiser's first employee but he stayed with the company until he died at age 89 in 1977, nearly ten years after Kaiser himself had passed on. Ord was so respected by Kaiser and so revered by all who knew him, the second large, 28-story building built by the Kaiser companies in Oakland in 1970 was named the Ordway Building. Ord had such warmth, such wisdom, such good humor about him people somehow felt closer to Kaiser just by knowing Ord. There will be a great many occasions in this biography to bring out the invaluable role Ord played during the 65 years he worked for the Kaiser companies. See Chapter 8, page 186.

Having successfully bid on important jobs in British Columbia, Kaiser decided it was time to incorporate, which he did December 14, 1914 in Vancouver, B.C., as the Henry J. Kaiser Company, Limited. He issued 20,000 shares at $1 each with half being owned by himself and half by his wife. The new company was located in a one-room, two-desk office with Henry Kaiser as president, A.B. Ordway as "Mr. Outside," primarily as job superintendent, and Stuart McWhorter as office manager, accountant, and "Mr. Inside." There were no other employees; foremen and laborers were not carried between jobs and the company was too small to warrant superintendents. On the job, the office was usually a tent. There were few assets in the way of equipment; horses, and most equipment were rented, and asphalt plants could be leased if the contractor used the manufacturer's asphalt. Only hand tools, like shovels, had to be purchased.

Bursting Into Washington

It was inevitable that Kaiser would start bidding on jobs in the state of Washington. On one of those paving contracts, Ord told Kaiser there was not enough money in the bank to meet the payroll. "How much is there?" Kaiser asked. "$600" was the reply. Kaiser told him to draw it out, then took it down the street of the small town, placing an order for a brand new Lincoln car. "It was beautiful," Ord often related, "black with red lining around the windows."

Kaiser then drove the Lincoln to the town bank, parking it right in front of the window where the president of the bank always sat because he liked to see everyone going by or coming in. Kaiser went to the desk of the president and was invited to sit down. When the president asked him what he wanted, Kaiser said that he needed funds to finance a new paving job that he had just been awarded. After being told the highlights of the upcoming contract, as well as Kaiser's record with other jobs, the president said, "How much do you need?" "It will require $10,000," Kaiser replied. The president studied the young man thoughtfully, then looked again at the brand new Lincoln right outside his window, and said, "Well, I think we can arrange that." So Kaiser took the $10,000, deposited it in his account at the bank, then went back to Ord and said, "Now you can meet the payroll."

Because he was superintendent on so many different projects, Ord tried wherever possible to have his wife, Wilma, live in the auxiliary tent at the job site with him. Being so intimately involved in all that was going on, Wilma practically became a member of the Kaiser family. She and Bess Kaiser became lifelong friends. She cooked many hundreds of meals with Henry and Bess as her guests. She was like a second mother to the two Kaiser boys, Edgar born in Spokane in 1908 and Henry Jr. born in Everett, Washington in 1917. Without any doubt few couples have ever had a closer lifetime relationship, both business-wise and socially.

Thinking back over the multitude of different construction jobs he had been involved in, Ord later recalled:

> We always made our money clear to hell and gone out in the desert or mountains. Whenever we took a job near the cities, we lost money. Everybody could go home at night—I guess that was the reason.

It was in one of those remote places that Kaiser contrived a scheme to pump water from a swift stream near the project. He anchored a barge in the stream and fitted it with a paddlewheel from a broken-down river steamer. The stream turned the wheel, the wheel worked the water pump, and Kaiser had his water.

"We don't need engine power for our pump," the exultant builder told his foreman. "The Lord does it for us."

But one day no water gushed from the pump. The foreman hiked to the stream and found it dry. He investigated further and learned that the stream was the overflow of city water supply, and the city had diverted all the water to its own use.

At another time when he was paving the Everett-Marysville Road in Washington, he lost 2,000 barrels of cement when the scow on which the cement was being towed from Bellingham sprang a leak. The captain of the tugboat, after discovering the leak, towed the scow to shore, but then the tide came in, flooding the cement and causing a loss of about $4,000. Kaiser immediately ordered another scow of cement from Bellingham for delivery to the point closest to where the work would be performed. However, he already had sufficient cement on hand to get started but as frequently happens in Washington he had to wait several days because rain came and softened the sub-base making it impossible to lay concrete.

If it wasn't one problem it was another. On that very same job Kaiser had to bring in a large supply of gravel by scow which would be unloaded into bunkers on the shore. As reported in the Everett newspaper of June 2, 1916:

> A section of the gravel bunkers of H.J. Kaiser, contractor on the Everett-Marysville road paving, caved down yesterday causing a slight delay in the work. It will be repaired today. A scowload of gravel had just been loaded and the structure came down with a crash. No one was injured.

Proving that troubles often came in bunches of three, Kaiser had another marine misadventure at Everett, only this time it was turned into an advantage. This is how Ordway recalled the incident:

> Again, enlarging on our water experience, we were paving a viaduct at Everett, Washington. Our asphalt plant was located on a dock and the materials going into the asphaltic concrete came alongside the dock in barges. The barges were unloaded with a floating clamshell rig. One evening the towboat delivered a barge of gravel, which we tied up to the dock and went home. The tide differential was about eight feet at that location. The next morning, when I came to work, there was no barge in sight. As I stood on the edge of the dock to see if it had broken loose and was out in the stream, I noticed that the hawsers were still taut on the dolphins. Further investigation showed that as the tide went out, the barge settled on a submerged pile which punched a hole in the bottom and the barge sank. In order to float the barge, we had to unload the barge by way of the clamshell through about eight feet of water. During this process, we found that the bottom on the channel contained a

very excellent asphalt sand, and from then on we bought no more sand but simply took it out of the stream, so the catastrophe made us some money. . . .

On February 15, 1918 the Mt. Vernon, Washington, newspaper, Argus, reported that Kaiser had been awarded a contract to build the Avon-Allen road of bitulithic material (bituminous, asphaltic). The cement people were fighting bitulithic "to the death." The largest landowner along the road joined in the fight by filing a suit, claiming it was an inferior roadbuilding material that would do damage to the value of his property. He asserted there was a conspiracy between Kaiser and the County Commissioners. The judge issued a temporary restraining order, but in the course of the hearing the complaining landowner became so troublesome the judge had to give him a severe "calling down."

In an attempt to prove conspiracy, the plaintiffs charged that Kaiser had paid all the expenses of a big junketing trip to Portland for the commissioners and other county officials to have them view how well a bitulithic road there was holding up. The steam was taken out of this complaint when Kaiser was able to prove that the cement people themselves had also financed a trip and big banquet in Portland. Kaiser felt his fight was well worth the effort when the court found "no fraud in the Avon-Allen contract." This early court experience convinced Kaiser that because he always conducted his business in an honest, "above-board" manner he need never fear of being drawn into a court battle. Over the years he would be involved in numerous lawsuits, most of which he would win through waging a vigorous case based on revealing all the facts.

Most of the roadbuilding jobs at that time involved relatively short distances. This meant that Kaiser was faced with the continuing necessity of coming up with one new bid after another, always trying to bid low enough to get the job, high enough to cover all costs including any unforeseeable complications. Miss out on too many bids and you're sure to go broke. This was made more difficult because of World War I at that time. Looking back, Kaiser commented:

During the first World War, we were faced, as today, with inflation. Each year, although I raised my bids trying to anticipate the constantly increasing wages and prices of materials, I never quite caught up with the soaring costs. The result was that, for five years, I made no money.

In preparing his bids for each new job, Kaiser would try to conceive every possible technique that might justify making a bid low enough to win the job. But his search never stopped there. Once the construction was underway, he was forever trying to come up with ideas that would expedite the work. His emphasis was always on speed. He had a conviction that the faster the project was completed the lower his costs would be, even though at times extra expenditures would be required to bring about the step-ups in speed. That was a way of doing business he would steadfastly adhere to throughout his entire life in every one of his ventures. It was why he was so often called "Hurry-up Henry."

This approach led to an invention in 1920 that seemed simple enough but which was a revolutionary concept. Hauling material in wheelbarrows was standard procedure in early roadbuilding work. On a highway job near Mt. Vernon, Washington, the iron wheels of the wheelbarrows kept sinking into the marshy ground and threatened failure of the job.

So Kaiser hit upon the idea of a two-wheel, two-man wheelbarrow with ball-bearing wheels and pneumatic rubber tires. It was built in his shop and consisted of a shallow steel box set in a frame and hinged so that the load could be released and dumped by gravity off the front end. He quickly improved the new rig by putting a motor on it.

The workmen considered it "the greatest invention since the paycheck." An engineer from the state, recalling the occasion many years later said, "Since then, Henry Kaiser has done several outstanding things, but the rubber tire for the wheelbarrow is a lot of glory for any one man."

Another of Kaiser's "outstanding" innovations was his early recognition of the efficiency and economy of the diesel engine. To him the arithmetic was clear: It cost $1.00 an hour to fuel a gasoline engine, but only $1.00 a day for a diesel. As early as 1923 he began trying to persuade manufacturers of heavy equipment to install diesels. When he couldn't convince Caterpillar Tractor Company to use diesels on their tractors, he then begged, pleaded and even cajoled the president of that company to sell him tractors without motors so he could install diesel engines himself. After the president flatly refused, Kaiser said, "All right, I'll buy 'em, but I won't use your damn engines." As each Caterpillar tractor was delivered to him, he ripped out the gasoline engine and substituted diesel in its place. The time eventually came when Caterpillar itself began installing diesel engines in its new tractors.

Even with the diesels it was not smooth sailing. Diesels have microscopic openings in the nozzles where the fuel is injected. That was fine for the Germans who invented the diesel and who used it for marine purposes where the air was clear. But on construction jobs, dust got in the diesel fuel which clogged these openings. On a Colma highway job just south of San Francisco, Kaiser's diesel-powered tractor kept stalling. Clay Bedford spent two months wrestling with the problem, sleeping under the tractors until he finally hit on the idea of using chamois skins to strain the diesel oil before it was injected into the nozzle.

Mack Trucks played a big role in early day road construction. A 1913 model was used for several years and then sold to an Italian gardener. One day in 1919 while working on the Leary Way job in Seattle, Kaiser saw the truck and decided to buy it at a cheap price. He then converted it into a mobile machine shop or traveling blacksmith shop, equipping it with nearly every sort of machinery to permit its use as an emergency field repair shop for road-building equipment, trucks and automobiles. Kaiser was using it on a Kelseyville, California job in 1921 when Mack Truck people became so struck by the novelty of the idea that they used it in their advertising to show how adaptable their trucks were, and, of course, how durable.

One of his early foremen said:

> Whatever Henry Kaiser bought, he had to put sideboards on it. Once when we got a beautiful new steam shovel and he started loading it with extras, I told him, 'Mr. Kaiser, you're going to break everything on that rig.' He smiled and said, 'But the contractor's profit is in the overload.'

From 1914 to 1927, the record of the Kaiser Paving Company primarily amounted to a succession of hundreds of little road jobs, with an occasional big one. A superintendent said:

> We usually had several jobs going at the same time, large and small, coming in and phasing out. We did one job for $737 with a profit of $26. Our general pattern of progression was, first, city streets; then short highway pieces for counties and states; and finally the longer highways.

One secret of success was to start so early that the steam from the horses' nostrils could hardly be seen, and then quit only when it became too dark to see the grade markers. As Ord put it:

> In those early days, we had construction business up and down the whole coast. When Mr. Kaiser and I would visit these jobs, we would drive nights, and many times I picked him up at his house after dinner and we drove all night to distant areas, spelling each other on the driving.

> We would go over the work the next day and again that night drive to the next job. By doing this, we did not waste any working hours in the daytime—and we sure saved a lot on the hotel bills.

It was in Seattle in 1919 that Kaiser lucked out in one of his new hires. Tom Price who had experience as a quarry superintendent in North Carolina had drifted west and fallen in love with Seattle. Someone suggested he apply:

> 'to a man named Kaiser who was just starting in the paving business in Seattle.' I found him in a one-room office. He was explaining something to two or three people and made no particular impression on me except that he was dark and even then fairly heavy. He gave me a minute or two and wrote a note in longhand as follows: 'Jim, a likely looking material man,' and directed me to give it to Jim Doyle, superintendent of work on Leary Way. Jim gave me a job as material man, receiving and spotting and generally taking care of sand and gravel being dumped by trucks on the sub-grade after it was prepared. I went to work at once, no salary or wages being set. I saw Mr. Kaiser occasionally but have no impressions as he usually just drove by and paid no attention to me. Three months later Mr. Kaiser came to see me and asked me if I would take a job as 'cashier' on the job near Marysville. I

said, 'no,' as I was just floating there for the summer. But I went to Marysville. I didn't know it then, but the die was cast. He asked me what I was being paid, and I told him I didn't know as apparently I had not been on the payroll. This made a real impression on him, to think I had been working three months without pay and had not complained. He immediately arranged for my back pay and then put me on the payroll. Thereafter he seemed to be much more aware of me.

If Kaiser was lucky to find Price, the luck would go double for Price who remained with Kaiser for more than forty-three years until his death in 1962 at age 71. Price was the third "permanent" hire by Kaiser, following after Ordway and Stuart McWhorter, and at his death was the second oldest employee in point of service, next to Ordway. Price could never have found another boss who would provide him the opportunities and the freedom to realize his potential that Kaiser did.

Price was a homespun, earthy, unaffected, uninhibited, chatty, "Southern boy," who made people feel as comfortable around him as an "old shoe." He had a way with words—written as well as oral. Entirely on his own, he became one of the company's best historians or recordkeepers. On nearly every project he ever became associated with, he took it upon himself to write a detailed report listing all the facts such as owner, date, location, description, volume, contractor, superintendent, and narrative highlights, including anecdotes, of what went on during the construction.

Here are a few random observations he chose to scribble, describing Kaiser's early days in the Northwest:

In the old days we had two very important policies --namely, "work" and "economy". There was always plenty of work, but we had to be economical because we had no money to do anything else. When we were successful bidders on a hundred thousand dollar job, once or twice a year, we were in clover. I averaged the 2nd to the 8th jobs the company acquired in 1914 through 1916—$23,000 each and the profit was $2,750 each. The winters in Washington State are either wet or cold, and we could not do much construction work; so we made up for it in the summer time—12 hour shifts and seven days per week. Hours of work meant absolutely nothing to either superintendents, foremen or laborers. No such thing as overtime existed. It was straight time for the laborer; and for the supervisor—the clock didn't exist. I suspect I built 20 or more gravel plants prior to Radum in 1930, and practically every one of them was built out of, and with, second-hand equipment. There were two exceptions—we bought a new 5-ton solid tire Mack Bulldog truck in 1920 and a new road paver in 1924. My, my, but they were beautiful. We didn't join anything in those early days. We couldn't afford it. Besides, Mr. Kaiser always had a feeling of being entangled in joining anything. In 1920-21 I was doing the engineering for the company; in fact I was the first engineering department. I had to furnish all the equipment consisting of a hand level, a rod, a plumb bob and notebooks. I needed a small leather bag in which to carry my engineering department, and I bought a little leather bag costing $3.25 and put it on my expense account. It brought a prompt visit from our one-man office force. A certain lovable character by the name of Stuart McWhorter, who was our office force, spent a day telling me that an employee simply could not do such a thing—so I paid for it myself.

Like Ordway, Price played such key roles with Kaiser for so many years there will be other occasions in this book to mention him. See in particular Chapter 8, page 184. However, it was in Seattle that Price did Kaiser a lasting favor—he introduced his friend from North Carolina, G. G. Sherwood, to McWhorter, who hired him. Sherwood later became Kaiser's top financial man, serving on the Boards of Directors for most of the Kaiser companies until his death in 1952.

Meeting A Giant

In that hectic, rough-and-tumble period Kaiser had the great good fortune of becoming acquainted with one of the giants of the western construction industry—Warren A. "Dad" Bechtel, founder of the mighty Bechtel organization.

It was in 1921 that they met. The story is best told by Kaiser himself in a speech he gave when Bechtel was inaugurated as President of the Associated General Contractors of America in 1928. Kaiser paid Bechtel glowing praise as a far-sighted leader and man of action, deserving of enthusiastic backing by all builders. In the course of his talk Kaiser said:

> I want to tell you of my first meeting with this man Bechtel. It was seven years ago on one of those hot, dry, dusty days in California such as the Sacramento Valley knew so well before hard-surfaced roads made it famous. I was standing alone surveying thirty miles of paving which we were constructing for the state at the time, when suddenly in a whirl of dust up rolled an automobile and out of it jumped a stranger. 'Your name Kaiser?' he asked. I answered, 'Yes.' 'My name is Bechtel, your competitor. I have been looking over your job and I have noticed many creditable things—your work is neat and trim, organization good, and I find only one thing wrong with you.' 'Well,' said I, 'out with it.' And he replied, 'You are not a member of our contractors' association.' 'That is true,' I said, 'but what is more I have considered it carefully, and decided not to be.' Bechtel hesitated—surveyed me carefully, and said, 'Well, you are just not a good sport, eh?' After a short silence, I answered, 'I've changed my mind, Bechtel. I will join your organization and sign the application right now.'

It was one of the most important acquaintances Kaiser would ever make. The friendship and mutual admiration which Kaiser and Bechtel felt for each other would lead to their teaming up in some of the West's biggest construction projects. To be associated with Bechtel would raise the stature of Kaiser in the construction world. Then there was the fact that Bechtel stood for the highest standards of quality construction and the highest standards of ethics and honesty. This would only reinforce Kaiser's commitment to these same principles.

It was "Dad" Bechtel who really opened the doors for Kaiser in California. "I was unwelcome when I first came to California. The other contractors banded against me," Kaiser later said. In time, Bechtel once said he liked Kaiser because he was a "hard worker, enthusiastic, with a lot of ingenious ideas."

In its article of August 1943, Fortune Magazine wrote:

> "Dad" Bechtel is perhaps the only man, living or dead, about whom Henry Kaiser speaks in the respectful tones of a junior partner. Kaiser says, 'There are two principles "Dad" followed. He hated to sign papers, on the theory that if you couldn't trust a man's word, you couldn't trust his signature. And his usual condition for entering any proposition was a fifty-fifty division. "Dad" had no patience with fifty-one, forty-nine arrangements. He used to say, 'No man with a sense of self respect wants to be controlled on that kind of percentage.'

The warm, personal friendship of "Dad" Bechtel for Kaiser was evidenced on Christmas 1932 when he gave him an exquisite silver goblet engraved, "To my dear friend, Henry, whose word is as good as his bond." That gift not only meant a lot to Kaiser, but it was especially treasured by his wife, Bess. She always shared her husband's admiration and affection for "Dad" Bechtel.

While on a construction mission to inspect the great Dnieprostroy Dam at the request of the Russian Government, "Dad" Bechtel, not quite 61 years old, died in Moscow, August 28, 1933, a little more than two years after the start of construction on Boulder Dam. Kaiser was one of the pallbearers at the funeral. Thereafter, Kaiser's dealings would be with "Dad's" three sons, Stephen, Warren, and Kenneth. In particular, Kaiser would have occasion to keep in touch with Steve who became the driving force in the Bechtel organization.* No better expression of Kaiser's affection for "Dad" Bechtel and the Bechtel family can be found than a letter which Kaiser wrote

---

*After World War II, Kaiser and Steve Bechtel took entirely different paths. Bechtel stuck to the construction business, building pipelines, refineries, power plants (particularly nuclear), transit systems, and even whole cities—all around the world. He chose to keep the company private, with ownership remaining in the Bechtel family except for small blocks of stock owned by key executives. He also worked hard at maintaining a low public profile so the company could concentrate on its construction business. By the seventies and eighties it had become the largest and most successful engineering and construction company in the world.

By contrast, Kaiser chose not to expand his engineering and construction division, although he personally directed a flurry of construction activities in Hawaii during the last nearly fourteen years of his life. The postwar story of Kaiser primarily involves his dramatic entrance into the industrial world where he became a major force in the production of steel, aluminum, cement, and even (temporarily) automobiles. At the same time his health and hospital program was growing by leaps and bounds. To finance his industrial ventures he went "public," which in time meant the loss of control by the Kaiser family. One other difference with Bechtel's way of operating was Kaiser's wide-open approach to the press—he reveled in publicity.

As divergent as their lives had become, Kaiser and Bechtel maintained their mutual respect and friendship till Kaiser's death in 1967.

on September 1, 1949, to the three sons:

> September 1, 1949
>
> Bechtel Corporation
> 155 Sansome Street
> San Francisco, California
>
> Dear Steve, Ken and Warren,
>
> Since you kindly sent me a copy of the book, "A Builder and His Family," I have been looking forward, before writing you, to the opportunity of reading this life story of "Dad" Bechtel and the prodigious construction works of "Dad" and his boys.
>
> The volume is a grand memorial with which to make the fiftieth anniversary of "Dad's" starting in construction. The pictures, as well as the text, brought back rich memories to me. I need not tell you how much I valued the friendship and associations with your Father—his honesty, courage and stalwart character.
>
> The book brought to my mind vivid flashbacks to my first meeting with "Dad" Bechtel, when the point of discussion was the Associated General Contractors of America, in whose activities I later shared with him a lot of interest . . . and then the teamwork that followed with him—from that first road job in 1921 near Redding, a rock plant at Oroville, the Continental Gas pipeline, the Dotsero Cutoff and other work in Colorado, insurance, Hoover Dam at Boulder Canyon, Bonneville Dam and the San Francisco Bay Bridge's east piers.
>
> I'm enclosing a copy of one of my favorite poems, "The Builder," for it seems to sum up the spirit to motivate great individuals of construction like "Dad", and to epitomize the tradition that you—Steve, Ken and Warren— were bequeathed.
>
> With warmest personal regards.
>
> Sincerely,
>
> Henry J. Kaiser

Huge Earthmoving Equipment

Another acquaintance of the 1920's that would have an influence on Kaiser's approach to life was the friendship he had with R. S. (Bob) Le Tourneau, inventor and builder of the world's largest earth-moving equipment. Kaiser had an obsession for finding bigger and better equipment, and here was the very man who was the leader in that field.

Here's how Le Tourneau recalled his first meeting with Kaiser:

It was in 1923, when one of my foremen came up to me on the job, real excited, and said, 'Henry Kaiser is down there watching your big scraper work.' I knew Kaiser was a big contractor, but I had never met him.

I went down and introduced myself. Boom! He was the fastest talking, hardest driving man I ever met in my life. I remember that out of that first rush of words he said, 'That's quite a machine you've got there.' I managed to say, 'We think so.'

'I'll buy three of those machines right now and pay you cash on delivery,' he rushed on. 'I understand you're going to sell the patents and work out a deal with some engineer. Right?'

I managed to say, 'Yes, we've been talking up a deal.'

'You're crazy if you sell to him,' said the blunt Mr. Kaiser. 'I'll do better. Now what do you say? Are you one of these men who can recognize a good thing when he sees it, or are you one that needs weeks to make up his mind?'

I didn't know what I was making up my mind to, but I didn't like the idea of waiting weeks to make it up. I've jumped into many deals like that since, most of which I learned to regret, but not that one.

'It's a deal,' I said, and so began a remarkable association.

In his book, <u>Mover of Men and Mountains</u>, Le Tourneau stated his construction creed:

There are no big jobs; only small machines. The Panama Canal and the Suez were big only because they were measured with a team of mules and a hand shovel. Today we have machines that could dig a canal across Nicaragua or Arabia so fast they would make most of those "big jobs" an exercise in ditch digging . . . In the 1920's the small machine attitude wasn't just strong, it was a set procedure. One man who didn't think that way was Henry Kaiser.

The first major, permanent Kaiser sand and gravel plant was erected at Livermore, in the Bay Area, in September, 1923. It was during the start-up of this operation that Kaiser and Le Tourneau first teamed up.

They worked several jobs together and built a factory on the Livermore site where new types of earth-moving equipment were designed and assembled. They often drove late into the night, or overnight, to reach jobs they were working on. Le Tourneau was a very religious man who greatly enjoyed singing religious hymns. No matter how intent the two men were in discussing the job ahead of them, Le Tourneau always managed to get Kaiser singing some of the religious songs as they were driving. It didn't bother Kaiser that he didn't know the words or the tunes as well as Le Tourneau; he was religious enough in spirit, and so totally uninhibited, he enjoyed singing as best he could.

One of the first big jobs where Kaiser used the Le Tourneau scrapers to good advantage was reported in the Sacramento Bee newspaper of May 7, 1924:

> The contractor of the Sacramento-Old Elk Grove and Galt jobs is the Kaiser Paving Company, one of the largest paving concerns in the country. The methods and machinery used are said to be the most modern employed on the Pacific Coast. Machinery replaces hand labor wherever possible, and all factors are on a large scale. The concrete mixer or paver as the whole outfit is known, is the largest highway outfit in the West and probably in the world.

But the big notoriety came two years later when Kaiser said to Le Tourneau:

> There's a big dam job up in the High Sierra near Philbrook. I'd been figuring on it, but I didn't see how I could tackle it without tying myself up for a couple of years. But with those scrapers of yours we can put that thing in like a boy damming a gutter.

In his book, Le Tourneau describes the project:

> The Philbrook Dam (in Butte County on a tributary of the Feather River) was a milestone in the engineering business and in my life. It was the first major project in which the new broke entirely away from the old. There was not a mule on the site. We were still using some men with shovels and pick-axes for clean-up work, but the heavy labor was done with power shovels, mechanized dump trucks, and, in the starring role, my scrapers. From the start it was clear that nothing short of an earthquake would stop us from setting an all-time record in dam building. For my part I was getting my first lessons from a master organizer. At one time we must have had a thousand men on the job in 57 varieties of work. Kaiser had that job timed to perfection. More, he knew how to get along with the men, even when the men didn't know how to get along with each other. The speed with which we completed the Philbrook Dam (from June through December) astonished the construction world. Kaiser was swamped with offers of even bigger jobs.

After that, Kaiser and Le Tourneau pretty much went their separate ways, because Kaiser kept plunging ahead in construction jobs (later in a myriad of industrial ventures) while Le Tourneau was everlastingly trying to build bigger and better earth-moving equipment. But they never lost their affection and admiration for each other. As late as December 5, 1958, when Kaiser was virtually working around the clock in his Hawaiian enterprises, he took time to write this letter to Le Tourneau in Texas:

The word has caught up with me in my travels that a host of your friends celebrated your 70th birthday on November 30.

Seventy still makes you just a youth—for one of your rugged stamina and energies and drive. I'm 76, but keep on discovering that a person ought to be as young at heart as he remains youthful in the zest for working and undertaking new things. Some of our mutual friends tell me you keep everlastingly engaged in useful new works.

Thinking of you, Bob, I am reminded of a favorite poem, "The Builder"— certainly not because you are the old man going the lone highway—but because it seems to me to give the answer as to why you never slacken in giving of yourself to your fellow men. The poet's words are these:

The old man going the lone highway
Came at evening old and grey,
To a chasm, vast and deep and wide.
The old man crossed in the twilight dim.
The sullen stream had no fear for him.
But he turned, when safe on the other side,
And built a bridge to span the tide.
'Old man,' said a fellow pilgrim near,
'You're wasting your strength with your building here.
Your journey will end with the ending day,
You never again will pass this way.
You crossed the chasm deep and wide,
Why build this bridge at eventide?'

The builder lifted his old grey head
'Good friend—in the path I've come,' he said,
'There followeth after my day,
The youth whose feet must pass this way.
This chasm that has been naught for me,
To that fair-haired youth may a pitfall be.
He, too, must cross in the twilight dim
Good friend—I'm building this bridge for him.'

Warmest personal best wishes to your health and happiness.

Le Tourneau was quick to reciprocate Kaiser's good wishes. Under a letterhead reading, "R G Le Tourneau Inc., Manufacturer of Heavy Duty Electrically Powered and Controlled Equipment," he responded on December 10, 1958:

I very much appreciate your letter of greetings for my 70th birthday and the fine poem. I seem to be going stronger than ever and putting in as many hours as I ever did. I don't feel like this human machine of mine is anywhere near worn out and I'm not making any plans to slow down yet.

It looks like this electric wheel is going to be the biggest improvement in construction machinery yet. You have probably heard about my new 8-wheel scraper that will load itself without a pusher to the tune of 150 tons.

I saw Edgar and Tom Price at the Beavers meeting in Los Angeles not long ago and Dusty Rhoades took wonderful care of me one day when I needed some aluminum in a hurry.

I trust the Lord is becoming more precious to you as the days go by. Isn't it wonderful that we can place our faith in the Christ that shed His blood for us and have the assurance of salvation in our heart.

If you ever come near Longview I would like to show you our plant and the steel mill I built even to the motors that run it.

An Association Man

Once Kaiser had accepted "Dad" Bechtel's challenge in 1921 to become a member of the Associated Contractors of America, he entered enthusiastically into the activities of that organization. By 1924, and again in 1925, he was president of the Northern California chapter. Its monthly letter dated January, 1924, had this front page greeting:

HAPPY NEW YEAR

Make this our motto: 'Modern equipment; modern methods; good construction. Skill, honesty, and responsibility.'

Henry J. Kaiser
President

The letter then goes on to describe a successful convention, December 14, 15, 1923 at the Whitcomb Hotel in San Francisco. At the meeting the directors went into executive session and within a few minutes had elected Kaiser as President. On Saturday night a stag party was held for the members and their close friends at Marquard's, where a "bountiful feast was served." The ladies were entertained at the Orpheum Theatre. "Mr. Henry J. Kaiser was toastmaster at the stag and presided with all his usual enthusiasm and pep."

This involvement in the leadership of the contractors' association would mark a significant turning point in Kaiser's career. For more than ten years he had "gone it" alone, bidding in competition with other contractors. He had proved to himself he could get more than his share of construction business by carefully making his cost estimates and by devising new techniques to get the job done faster and more efficiently.

Now he found himself in a position of influencing other builders, and, indeed, having an impact on the direction the construction industry would be going. He discovered that his persuasiveness and salesmanship abilities would work just as well in behalf of the industry as they had in winning for himself one construction job after another. He liked the taste of this new role of leadership. He pitched in heart and soul to do a good job for the industry just as he had done individually.

He gained a lot of stature by the leadership he provided in a campaign to convince the California Railroad Commission that it should require all public utilities to put their construction jobs out to competitive bidding rather than continue the practice of doing the work themselves. He concluded his appeal to the Commission on July 31, 1924:

> It is my earnest belief that if a ruling is made by the Railroad Commission requiring the public service corporations to advertise for contractors' bids for major construction undertakings, three definite results would be accomplished:
>
> First, the public service corporation officials would be grateful in the end that they had been induced or required to do their work by contract methods, as they would soon realize the amount which can be saved.
>
> Second, the public would enjoy lower rates on account of lower construction costs.
>
> Third, the contracting fraternity would generally become more efficient by reason of the greater variety of work offered, and the reasonable cost of all work would be materially reduced through this greater efficiency.

The successful culmination of these efforts was reported in the monthly letter of the Contractors' Association of Northern California for November 1925:

> The most progressive action ever taken for the betterment of the contracting business with respect to public works is the formation of the Clearing Bureau of Contract Investigation by the joint action of the principal surety companies doing business in Northern California, the Contractors' Association of Northern California, and the California Administration of Public Works . . . Mr. Henry J. Kaiser was the leader in the movement which terminated in the formation of this Bureau.

It was while Kaiser was still president of the Northern California chapter of the Associated General Contractors in 1925 that he advocated a toll road between San Francisco and Los Angeles. It was his idea that this would be the best way to finance the much better highway that was needed between these important metropolitan centers. He was laughed at and called visionary, and nothing ever came of his proposal. In looking back, it is interesting to note how many toll roads in the east came along at a later time as the most practical way to finance expressways between major cities.

Then Kaiser took the lead in recommending that all the contractors, equipment manufacturers, and others interested in highway construction work raise enough money to put an initiative measure on the ballot creating the first gas tax in California, the money from which would be used solely for highway construction. Incredibly, the automobile clubs of Northern and Southern California opposed the idea, using as an argument that those favoring the tax would benefit from the expenditure of the money. In his bafflement to understand the position of the auto club, Kaiser speculated that the opposition must have arisen because the clubs themselves had not first come up with the idea. There must have been some truth in Kaiser's surmise because at the very next session of the Legislature the two automobile clubs introduced a law creating the first gas tax and were successful in getting it passed, thanks to great amounts of expensive publicity.

Investing in Youth

It was during this era of feverish road and small dam building that Kaiser hired his third trained engineer. Kaiser himself had no formal engineering training, but he had hired two Civil Engineers—A.B. Ordway and Tom Price. The other three key people were not engineers—Stuart McWhorter, office manager, G.G. Sherwood, treasurer, or Joaquin Felix dos Reis (Joe Reis), bookkeeper. Guided by Kaiser's uncanny ability to look at a construction job from every angle, this small team had outdistanced the best engineers most other firms had to offer.

On the face of it, Kaiser's newest trained engineer didn't look like any threat to the rest of the industry. He was only twenty-two years old, fresh out of Rensselaer Polytechnic Institute in Troy, New York. His name was Clay Bedford. From the start Bedford insisted he wanted to be more than an engineer—he wanted to be a "contractor," a "businessman." Nevertheless, it was his engineering skills that made him stand out in every job he tackled.

His father was a graduate of Rensselaer, and since 1912 had been chief engineer of Northern California Division Number 2 for the California Highway Commission. As a youngster, Clay picked up a lot of construction savvy by just riding around with his father and looking at the various jobs. Once Clay said he wanted to go into the contracting business his father gave him two pieces of advice that would shape the rest of his life: (1) he should get his degree in Civil Engineering at Rensselaer, and (2) after graduating he should aim to get a job with Henry Kaiser, "the only honest contractor I know."

Clay had met Kaiser in the summer of 1922 when he was home from school. However, after graduation in 1925 he went directly to Ordway and asked for a job. As Ordway later said, "Here was a graduate engineer, the son of the chief engineer where most of our work was done—how could I turn him down?" Little did Ordway realize he was hiring someone who would turn out to be one of the top men of the Kaiser organization, someone who would set shipbuilding records in World War II at the

Richmond shipyards starting just 15 years later where he would head an organization of 100,000 workers.

One of the first field jobs assigned to Bedford was to serve as cashier for the Woodland, California "Y" construction project. He got a taste of how Kaiser operated, because every night Kaiser would phone him around nine o'clock and ask, "Well, what are the costs for today?" No matter how detailed Bedford tried to be Kaiser would keep pumping him for further information. As Bedford put it:

> We used to call Kaiser the 'suction pump' because he would extract every bit of information that anybody had. You had better be accurate, too, because he would ask everybody the same thing and if there was any discrepancy he would call you right back and say, 'Now, why did you tell me this and so-and-so tells me that? What's your explanation?' He wouldn't get angry if he found you in error, but he would sure correct you. However, if he found you were lying to him, he would really raise hell. Boy, I tell you, you better not try to mislead him in any way. He really would get emphatic! He wasn't interested in putting anyone down. He simply wanted the facts. If he thought you had a point, he would accept it; and if he thought you were wrong he would tell you, and tell you why. As a result I was never afraid to stand my ground when I thought I was right.

A short time later at the Livermore, California rock and gravel plant a bridge broke down as the narrow gauge dinky locomotive was pulling some loaded cars across. Kaiser made a routine call from his Oakland office to find out what was going on. Bedford had to tell him the bridge fell down. Bedford remembers:

> Kaiser said, 'Why in the world did the bridge fall down?' I had to tell him, 'Because Bill (Fudge) put a post under it.' 'My God!' Kaiser said, 'Do you mean to say that he put a post under the bridge to help support it, and that's what caused it to fall down?' I said, 'Sure. The post reversed the stresses on the top cord.' He said, 'Well, I can't believe that, but I'll come out and take a look.' We found the top cord and it had been pulled apart, because with the post under it there was no compression holding it together. This involved a construction principle that an engineer would know. Kaiser soon caught on and agreed with me. That's the way he always was—he wouldn't get mad, he'd just keep digging till he understood the problem.

The sequel to that story is that the county advertised for bids to clean up the wreckage. Kaiser put in a bid, got the job, and ended up using some of the steel from the ruined bridge to make an addition to his plant.

Another time Bedford's engineering expertise played an important role was in 1926, less than a year after his graduation. Kaiser had the contract to build the Gordon Valley Dam for the city of Vallejo, California. With his long experience in the use of trucks he sensed that the level of the dam was not being raised as fast as it should for the number of truckloads handled. He asked Bedford to find out what was wrong. After two days Bedford concluded that the city engineers were requiring that the fill be put in wider than the drawings called for. As Bedford recorded:

> When I told Kaiser what was wrong, he said, 'Well, do you think you're right?' I said, 'Come on out and I'll be glad to show you. You can hold the intelligent end of the tape and I'll hold the other end, and we'll measure out and then we'll measure how far down it is, and I'll run the level for you, and I'll show you that you are building more dam than you are getting paid for.' Once Kaiser understood the problem he asked to meet with the Vallejo City Council. The meeting was held in the City Hall. Kaiser left me on the outside steps but I could hear everything going on. Soon Kaiser and the Council got in a big shouting match and they asked him, 'Who told you the engineering firm was requiring the dam to be built too wide?' He said, 'My engineer, Mr. Clay Bedford.' They said, 'Where did he come from?' 'He's from Rensselaer Polytechnic Institute.' 'What year?' '1925.' So they said, 'Do you mean you take this kid's word against this important engineering firm in San Francisco?' Kaiser said, 'If he's right, I sure would, and he is right.' You know, they raised their voices and were raising so much hell, Kaiser offered one of the fellows out for a fisticuffs for calling him dishonest. Then, after the meeting was over, Kaiser said to me with a twinkle in his eye, 'Do you think I overplayed it?' He had sounded madder than the devil, but all the time he was playing a part, and inside was cool and calm. His performance was calculated for an effect. He had to get over the obstacle of some kid telling them that their dam was being built too wide against a firm of well-known San Francisco engineers. In any event, the dispute was later submitted to arbitration and we won out.

A Turning Point

"I have great admiration for Cuba, because you have blazed the trail of highway progress, enlightened by dynamic energy, foresight, vision, determination, for other nations to follow." He went on to point out that no other nation, not even the United States, had linked their country by highways as completely as Cuba was doing.

That was Henry Kaiser speaking to the delegates of the Sixth Pan American Conference held at the Hotel Camaguey in Camaguey, Cuba, February 26, 1928. Just a year earlier Kaiser had been awarded a subcontract to build 200 miles of highway in the Camaguey province for $20 million. The total project known as the Cuban Central Highway extended from one end of the island to the other, a distance of 755 miles at a cost of $75 million, the largest paving job ever put under contract at one time up until then. Warren Brothers Company of Massachusetts was the prime contractor. The $20 million subcontract awarded to Kaiser was more than three times the total business volume of the company during its first 14 years.

A. B. Ordway, who was in charge of the Cuban venture for a while, would later say:

> Cuba was the turning point in our history. We were successful highway contractors, work was increasing steadily, and the future looked bright. But our determination to go into Cuba gave us that one large job we had never had and always wanted. We finished a year ahead of schedule to enhance our reputation, and it provided the money that allowed us to go into big dam building and beyond.

The Cuban project confronted Kaiser with a host of problems he had never encountered before—the wide variety of soil conditions was not conducive to easy construction, sources of aggregate and other materials had to be continually improvised, more than 500 small bridges had to be built because of the heavy rains, 300 miles of fence were required, there was a language barrier in dealing with labor and government, frequent attempts were made by Cuban officials to get "under-the-table" bribes, getting progress payments from the government called for constant attention, and, of course, the whole undertaking was far removed from the home office in Oakland where Kaiser remained based.

Here's how Kaiser described the job:

> Cuba was a great adventure. But the job required an organization ten times as large as I had then, and that proved a real task, filled with headaches. I had to mobilize every experienced construction man I knew.

> It was rough pioneering, really tough. Training native workmen, getting sources of aggregate and cement, trying to use earth- moving equipment in a primitive land. Yet the biggest problem of all was to muster able management and supervision.

> We learned you can't get fine talent into your organization by simply offering high salaries. You and the men who work with you have to build yourselves up to the capacity to tackle bigger and bigger jobs.

The first superintendent for the challenging project was Harvey Slocum, who had done work for Kaiser on dams. However, he couldn't get along with the Cubans, so Kaiser asked Ordway to take over after a few months. Still, the progress payments from the government were slow in coming. It was then Kaiser decided his young engineer, Bedford, should get in the act. He told him he need only be in a Cuba a couple of months to "straighten out the engineering" and to speed up the progress payments, and then could come back to the states, but Bedford knew it would inevitably end up longer than that. In time he did get the engineering straightened out, so that the claims for progress payments were honored more rapidly. Kaiser then began plying Bedford with a flood of questions about the entire construction program. "How would you do this? How would you do that? What else would you do?" One time

Bedford said, "Mr. Kaiser, don't ask me that. Look in the mirror and ask that guy." Kaiser then said, "Okay, okay. I'll get out of here and quit bothering you." The next morning he came to Bedford and said, "Mr. Ordway, the general manager, is going back to the states with me, and you're the new general manager."

It was the summer of 1928 and Bedford was just approaching his 25th birthday! Kaiser asked if he should tell the superintendents of the change. Bedford said no, he would be able to establish his leadership more effectively if he could meet the superintendents one by one and go over their plans with them and present his ideas to them. Bedford had one important thing going for him—he knew the language reasonably well and could communicate acceptably with the Cubans.

It was typical of Kaiser's way of doing business once he got a project underway to turn the responsibility over to the person whom he put in charge. It was no surprise therefore that Kaiser only visited the Cuba work about twice a year. On one of his trips he and Bedford were taking a boat from Miami to Havana. Bedford recalls:

> We took the overnight boat out of Miami to Havana. I was tired, but he went up to the dance, so I had to go with him. Afterwards, we climbed in our bunks—he had the lower and I had the upper. About four o'clock in the morning when I was sound asleep, I was aroused by hearing him say, 'Clay.' I thought I would just wait a minute and see what he would do. He didn't say anything for a few minutes, then 'Clay,' a little louder. Then finally he took a shoe and banged on the bed: 'Are you awake?' My God, I would have been dead if I hadn't heard him, so I said, 'Sure, I'm awake. What do you want?' 'Well,' he said, 'now about that job,' and boom, he began telling me how he thought one problem after another should be handled. On the trip down we had talked over a lot of the ideas, what the problems were, what ideas I had for solving those problems—we'd gone through the whole package. Now here he was in the middle of the night rehashing them and telling me exactly what he thought should be done. When he finally decided he had mapped out the right course of action, he dropped off to sleep. This was only the first time of countless other nights when he would wake me in the middle of the night to discuss what he wanted to have done the next day.

Bedford had been warned that Cubans were accustomed to "under-the-table" payoffs, but that was one thing Kaiser absolutely refused to get involved in. One time a Cuban engineer inspector handed his hotel bill to Bedford who looked it over and said, "No es para mi es suyo" (It's not mine, it's yours). He said, "No, no, usted lo paga" (You pay it). I said, "No, no, usted lo paga" (I don't pay it. You must pay it).

It wasn't a big hotel bill but the inspector was so annoyed he ordered everything to be shut down—the concrete mixer, the gravel plant, and the road work itself. Fortunately, Bedford had earlier given some very valuable engineering assistance to one of the young Cuban engineers, who went to his boss urging that the work be restarted. If Bedford had complained to the boss about the inspector, this might not have set so well, but when one Cuban took on another one, the boss was free to overrule the inspector. Neither Bedford, nor any other person working for Kaiser, ever paid a single bribe, or "cumshaw" or "mordita" (the bite), even though there was reason to believe other subcontractors on the total highway project did at times get suckered into it.

It was in Cuba that young Joe Reis established himself as one of the key men who would eventually be a top officer for Kaiser. Reis was put in charge of the accounting in Cuba, and in accordance with Kaiser's policy he didn't report to Bedford but to the home office. Nevertheless, the two developed a smooth working relationship— Bedford would speed up production to insure early progress payments from the Cuban government, Reis would present such claims promptly and in proper manner to earn the cooperation of the government. Both of them knew that the Cuban government was building a $10 million palace in Havana, using money that had been raised to finance the highway. They, therefore, wanted always to be the first subcontractor to be paid before the money ran out.

This worked so advantageously that soon the financial officer for Warren Brothers, the prime contractor, complained to Kaiser that the only reason Reis was getting his payments ahead of Warren Brothers was that he was bribing the government officials. Kaiser talked with Reis saying he knew it wasn't true but he wanted his explanation anyway. Reis responded:

> Well, the auditors can examine the expense accounts that I have turned in which are very meager, and you know how much salary you are paying me, and I certainly can't do lot of bribing with my meager expense accounts and my salary. The answer is that we are getting paid on the basis of goodwill and friendship for the promptness and manner in which we are handling our claims.

What happened was that the government would keep running out of cash and Reis had a friend in Havana who would tip him off when the cash was running low, so instead of making his progress estimates on the 25th of the month he would work with the engineers to get the reports in on the 21st. Several times he had to go to Havana with two security guards with him, bringing back the gold payments in a suitcase, with the understanding that he would deposit the money with the National City Bank which in turn would transfer the gold back to the government treasury.

With 500 bridges to build, and with construction time being of the essence, which it always was with Kaiser, he found it expedient to subcontract many of the bridges. Most of the subcontractors did a responsible job, but there were others losing money, which led to trouble with their banks. Reis became aware of this, and asked his own engineering people to estimate what the actual costs of the subcontractors probably were. He concluded many of them were being underpaid. The next time Kaiser was in Cuba, Reis discussed the problem with him. Kaiser asked, "What do you recommend we do?" Reis said, "I recommend that we help them by renegotiating with them, giving them a fair break—taking their costs, comparing them with our own estimates, and paying them something like 10% more." Without much hesitation Kaiser said, "Okay, that's the thing to do. We don't want anybody to go broke as a subcontractor of ours."

Reis had already gained Kaiser's confidence by his use of figures in the California highway construction jobs. In his first work as a timekeeper in California it was his assignment to get the payroll daily cost report in to the Oakland office. He found he couldn't accomplish that because the foreman, and even the general superintendent, were carrying the time cards in their pockets, and wouldn't make them available to him on a daily basis. Here's how he recalls the shaping of his responsibilities:

> In frustration I went to the superintendent one day and said I was hired to do a certain job which I could not do without the time cards. I told him I would not turn in daily reports that were incomplete. So I asked him to please call the Oakland office and tell them to get a replacement because I was resigning. He called my boss, Sherwood, and somehow Mr. Kaiser overheard the conversation. He then got on the phone with the superintendent and asked what the problem was with me. The superintendent suggested he should talk with me. When I explained my problem, Mr. Kaiser asked to speak with the superintendent again. I could hear his voice, 'You get the foremen to turn in their time cards on a daily basis to Reis or he has my authority to fire them.' I could see the superintendent's face getting redder and redder. After that, I had no trouble getting the information I wanted, and I was nicknamed 'Little Kaiser.' Soon after that I was brought back to the home office to relieve Sherwood on the accounting end of the business. That's when I introduced budgets and cost accounting. Up until then Mr. Kaiser relied a great deal on graphic charts prepared by Tom Price. Mr. Kaiser soon became very fond of my cost figures. On the first or second day of each month he would come to my desk and say, 'Reis, do you think you can get me a rough estimate of what we did last month?' And I'd say, 'Yes sir, I'll try.' Then as he left he'd look back and smile and say, 'Not too rough, though, Reis.'

> In Cuba my budgets and forecasting proved to be indispensable. Years after that, when we were in shipbuilding and automobiles, Mr. Kaiser couldn't understand why no one could equal Joe Reis in estimating and preparing budgets, because I was never off more than 1/2 of 1% from the final result.

The Cuban job came along right at the time Kaiser was using Le Tourneau scrapers so successfully in California highway construction. Naturally, he assumed they would be equally efficient in Cuba, so he shipped ten of them there. It wasn't long, however, before he found out that Cuban labor was so cheap, the old-fashioned method of building highways with hands and oxen and burros produced lower costs.

Hence, the scrapers lay idle for a long time till Kaiser could find a buyer for them.

Kaiser had long since known that most people are willing to work hard if they feel a part of any given project, and if they feel they are in competition with someone else. It was no different in Cuba. Here's how Bedford expressed it:

Mr. Kaiser was an expert in the handling of people—a talent he was born with. Getting along with people is being able to understand what their problems are and taking the opportunity when you see it to give help. But you can't say, 'You do this and you do that.' What you do is to ask the kind of questions that will draw the response you want, and once you get that response you say, 'It's a great idea,' never indicating that you planted the idea. I made this work well in Cuba, along with promoting competition. Instead of working everybody in one group I separated them into seven different divisions and then I put them in competition to see who could do the most the quickest. I drove up and down the job letting each one know what the others were doing. No more than that. And, boy, they'd just break their necks to excel. That was one of the main reasons we finished the Cuban job a year ahead of schedule. It was a Kaiser technique which we later used in both dambuilding and shipbuilding.

One time Kaiser brought "Dad" Bechtel with him to Cuba. It was a great opportunity to brag about the progress being made. It was also a stimulus to the superintendents to show off to this prominent figure in the construction world what they were doing.

Another time Kaiser heard that Colonel Charles Lindbergh would be landing at Camaguey for a brief visit. Fortunately, on this occasion, September 20, 1929, Mrs. Kaiser was also in Cuba, so they arranged to be introduced to Lindbergh while standing near the cabin of his airplane. Actually Kaiser himself never flew in those days. He was one of the last to give up trains for airplanes, but once he got started using planes, especially when jets came along, he practically lived on them.

Bedford kept Kaiser informed on progress by sending a weekly report. One month he reported $998,000 of work had been done. The next time Kaiser came to Cuba he said, "For God's sake, man, why didn't you put something in there to make it a million, so I could tell everyone we had a million dollars of progress in one month?"

As infrequent as his visits to Cuba were, Kaiser made the most of every minute. During the day he would inspect the work going on, taking time to visit with superintendents, foremen, and even the lowliest of workers. He would pump them for their ideas, he would volunteer his suggestions (never giving any commands), and he would mostly commend them for the fine progress they were making.

After dinner at night he would review all phases of the work with Bedford, Reis and other top people. He was always trying to come up with a way to improve the use of both equipment and man power. But he seldom stopped there. More often than not, he would find time to talk about the future. Both Bedford and Reis recall how often

Kaiser would start that kind of discussion by saying, "Now let's talk about the future. I have been dreaming what lies ahead for us." Here's how Reis recalls a meeting held in his office with Bedford and Kaiser after the budgets and operations had been worked over:

> Mr. Kaiser said, 'Boys, there's a tremendous construction job to be built in the United States known as Boulder Dam. It will be the biggest construction project to date. No one contracting outfit will be capable of either financing the job or doing it. It will have to be a group or consortium of the best qualified builders. For example, we are tops in sand and gravel and concrete work, another outfit is tops in tunnel work [which later proved to be Shea Company], and another company is good on industrial buildings [which later turned out to be MacDonald and Kahn]. When I get back to the States I am going to try to get together a group that will complement each other and give us the experience and the organization and the capital to take on this tremendous job. I want you boys to be thinking about this, so we can end up with the best possible team.'

It was not generally known that as a result of helping Kaiser get going on his subcontract for $20 million, the prime contractor, Warren Brothers, owned 51% of Kaiser Paving Company, with Kaiser owning the other 49%. Sometime after the Cuban job was completed Kaiser went to Boston to buy out Warren. Along with him came Sherwood, secretary, and their train went through El Paso where Joe Reis, who had been working on a pipeline project there, joined them. Here's how Joe Reis recounts the story:

> On the train we talked over our plans for dealing with Warren and then retired for the night. For some reason I was roomed with Mr. Kaiser—he had the lower berth, I had the upper. About two o'clock in the morning I was sound asleep and suddenly I heard this voice, 'Reis, are you awake?' It gradually got louder, 'Reis, are you awake?' Finally, 'REIS, ARE YOU AWAKE?' At last I had to say, 'Yes, sir, I'm awake.' He said, 'Now about that meeting in Boston, this is what I think we should do.' He laid out what we had already discussed, together with his conclusions, and then eventually dropped off to sleep with his usual loud snoring. But that was his way—always thinking. That was not the last time he woke me in the middle of the night to tell me of his plans for the next day. Anyway, in Boston we found out Warren Brothers were stuck with about $12 million of Cuban bonds as a final settlement. We had no bonds in our settlement; we had cash all the way through. However, as part of our consideration in buying out Warren, Kaiser agreed to take $300,000 of the Cuban bonds, which we sold soon thereafter. The Cuban job had thrust Mr. Kaiser into the big time, and it had made him a millionaire for the first time in his life.

Ready For The Big Leagues

For seventeen years, from 1913 till 1930, Kaiser had lived a rough-and-tumble, tumultuous, challenging existence. He had built scores of roads—some small, some large, some in cities, some in the country—in British Columbia, Washington, California, Cuba. He had battled rain and mud and cold; he had endured drought and dust and heat. On each new job he had to scrounge for new sources of roadbuilding materials—gravel, sand, cement, asphalt. He built the nucleus of a small management team, but most often had to rely on new, local hires for his laboring crew.

At the start, horse-drawn equipment and hand labor did most of the work. With the on-rush of mechanically-powered equipment, Kaiser pioneered in its use, not only buying the newest power shovels, but constantly coming up with his own modifications to improve their efficiency.

Kaiser helped open up the West. It was an age when the automobile was revolutionizing the American economy, and his roads aided and abetted that revolution. If his construction career had ended at that time, he could have basked in the glory of his remarkable accomplishments. After all, he had become a millionaire, and that was no small achievement in those days.

But in those seventeen whirlwind years, he built much more than highways. As corny as it may sound, he built an approach to business that would set the stage for far greater achievements in the years ahead.

To begin with, he had become totally sold on the benefits of unrestricted competition. Every bid he won meant he had somehow "out-competed" his rivals. He liked the taste of that. It was stimulating, exhilarating, rewarding. It required that he devise every scheme he could think of to cut costs. Innovation therefore became a way of life for him. He became convinced—perhaps more than any other builder—that the faster a job gets done the lower the costs can be.

And he looked at competition from another angle—the benefit it brings to the buyer or user of the construction service. He took real satisfaction in bringing lower costs to his customers. He became one of America's most vocal proponents of the free, competitive enterprise system. Even when he lost out to another competitor, he would openly proclaim it was all to the good because of the benefits to the buyer.

He became obsessed with the rewards of hard work and long hours. He thrived on just a few hours' sleep each night. Once he was awake his mind was consumed with the challenge and the joy of what he was working on. Work was his pleasure, his therapy. As much as he loved his wife and his two sons, the greatest happiness with them always had a backdrop of hard work well done.

A third attribute that became firmly imbedded in his way of doing business was his total commitment to honesty. He traced it back to the training he received from his mother, but his roadbuilding experiences showed him he would be much more productive if he was not bedeviled by temptations to make a few extra dollars by cheating on anyone. It became important to him to have a reputation for complete honesty. This quality served as a firm undergirding for all the major enterprises he would be entering into during the rest of his life.

There were other business principles that became deeply rooted in Kaiser during his roadbuilding days—emphasis on quality work, commitment to good industrial housekeeping, boldness in delegating responsibility, reliance on young men, willingness to take risks. Over and over he had proved to himself that faith was indispensable, that it can be a very real and tangible force for success—faith in himself, faith in his co-workers, faith in the future of the American economy.

Kaiser was 48 years of age when he came to the end of his roadbuilding career. He was in vigorous good health ready to take on the world. He had proved himself in the minor leagues. Now he was eager to show what he could do in the majors.

CHAPTER 3

TOGETHER WE BUILD

"What man can conceive and imagine he can accomplish. Impossibles are only impossible as thinking makes them so."

Boulder Dam

"Then get your God damn feet off of my desk," Felix Kahn barked at Henry Kaiser. It was hardly the kind of talk expected between partners, but Kaiser was soliciting business.

It was 1933 and Kaiser had just returned from four days in Washington. His job had been to keep the money coming for the construction of the giant Boulder Dam (often known as Hoover). In the nation's capital, he had met with Secretary of the Interior Harold Ickes and various members of Congress involved in the funding of the giant project.

Kaiser was only one of a team of builders, called the Six Companies, who had taken on the challenge of constructing the largest dam in the world. It was so big no single contractor had the finances, the equipment, or the people to tackle it alone.

This was not the first time Kaiser was to team up. He had teamed up with other contractors before. The Bechtel family and the Kaiser family were particularly close in the 1920s. Ever since 1921 when "Dad" Bechtel and Kaiser had become acquainted, they had teamed up frequently on construction and pipeline jobs. Kaiser had also joined with other contractors on famous western projects. But Boulder Dam was a milestone in many ways, including the refinement of teamwork to a fine art between western contractors.

Kaiser was chairman of the Executive Committee because of his ability to get people to work together, and because of his persuasive sales powers. They were needed. Superintendent Frank Crowe, possibly the one man most responsible for successful construction of the dam, was once asked: "What in your opinion will be the hardest part in the construction of this dam?" He replied: "Getting along with the board of directors." It never turned out that way because the partners realized they were pioneering in cooperation on a grand scale, so they made a constant effort to work together and to give the construction crew itself as free a hand as possible.

On this particular occasion, Kaiser was so pleased with the progress he had made in Washington that on his return, he phoned Felix Kahn of MacDonald & Kahn, one of the major partners, and told him he would be happy to fill him in on the Washington discussions.

In his usual "timid" style, Kaiser barged into Kahn's office, sat down, tipped his chair back, put his feet up on Kahn's desk, lit a cigar, and started talking.

Fifteen minutes later, when the Boulder Dam developments had been updated, Kaiser said, "Felix, how about letting me furnish sand and gravel for the road you are building from San Jose to Pleasanton? My Radum plant is in an ideal location to serve you."

Kahn squinted at Kaiser with dawning suspicion.

"Henry, did you come here to tell me about your meetings in Washington, or did you come here to sell me gravel?"

"Well, of course I would like to sell you some gravel," Kaiser protested. Killing two birds with one stone seemed completely natural to him. It didn't to Kahn.

"Then get your God damn feet off of my desk," Kahn snapped.

For a moment Kaiser's jaw dropped, but a second later, both men laughed. Kaiser, however, promptly took his feet off Kahn's desk. He ended up, though, with Kahn's sand and gravel business.

A dam on the Colorado River had been dreamed about—and talked about—for many years. However, because of the immensity of the engineering problems, and because of the enormous costs, it was difficult to find the ways and means to take on the challenge.

The stampede of population to the West Coast in the 1920s and 1930s, particularly to Southern California, changed all of that. The rapidly expanding cities were hurting for both power and water. The thirsty farmlands in the far southwest held the promise of greatly increased crops if the supply of water, and the power to pump that water, could only be increased. Besides, harnessing the river would eliminate down-river destruction which the raging Colorado would cause in flood years.

What better time therefore "to bite the bullet" and get the dam underway than 1931, when the great depression was really beginning to pinch. It was an open invitation to President Herbert Hoover, a Californian who was himself an engineer by training. All of the activity incident to building the dam could be a shot in the arm to the economy. Furthermore, construction costs for labor, supplies, and equipment would more likely be held in check in a down period.

Actually, authorization for the giant project had been granted by Congress in late 1928 with the passage of the Swing-Johnson bill. Immediately, the Bureau of Reclamation set about drawing up plans and specifications for the "biggest and most challenging" dam ever built up to that time. It was said of the Colorado River that its waters were too thick to drink and too thin to plow. Dr. Elwood Mead, directing head of the Bureau of Reclamation, after whom the lake formed by the dam would be named, described the river's torrent of red mud as "roaring through Black Canyon with the speed of a railway train."

Not the least of the concerns was the impact the temperatures would have on the thousands of employees (4,400 at the peak) who would be needed to build the dam. In the summer the heat in the shade would hit 125 degrees F. for days on end; in the winter temperatures would drop to freezing. This would not only test the endurance of the workers, but would mean unpleasant living conditions for their families. (On one of his visits to Boulder, Kaiser would give Crowe a scare by keeling over from heat exhaustion.)

"Nonetheless, I was wild to build this dam," said Frank Crowe. "I had spent my life in the river bottoms, and Boulder meant a wonderful climax for me." He had been dreaming about it for a quarter of a century, ever since the late A.P. Davis, Director of Reclamation, had prophesied to him, an engineer fresh from the classroom, that not even the stupidity of man could keep a great dam from being built in the gloomy canyon where they stood. Crowe had in fact made a rough estimate of the dam for Davis as early as 1919.

At the point where the dam was to be built, the gorge was 970 feet wide at the top, narrowing to 370 feet at the bottom. The silt of centuries would have to be excavated before bedrock could be found to anchor the main dam, starting 140 feet below the river bed and rising 730 feet above it, nearly twice the height of any dam ever before attempted. At the base, the dam itself would be as thick as two city blocks—660 feet. Enough cement would be used in the dam to build a highway 2255 miles long, 6 inches thick and 20 feet wide.

This required that the canyon be kept dry. The first order of business, therefore, was to drill two huge mile-long tunnels, one on the Nevada side of the river, the other on the Arizona side. Each would start several thousand feet above the dam site, emerging nearly a half mile below. All of the river water would flow through these tunnels, leaving the construction area open for all the men and equipment.

Once the government had completed its basic plans for the dam, it sent out more than 100 sets to be sure to give every potential interested contractor an opportunity to bid.

Even the largest of the western builders knew the job was far too big and too expensive for any one construction outfit. So now a fantastic poker game began. What builders had the finances, and the willingness to risk those finances, to share in the undertaking? What builders could really bring something to the table in terms of manpower, know-how, and equipment? What contractors had the best chance of working together, or was there an advantage to rugged individuality?

Of course, it was necessary to have a surety company that would put up the bond to cover the project. The logical party was the Fidelity & Deposit Co. of San Francisco, headed up by Leland Cutler who knew most of the big contractors personally, and who was an old friend and schoolmate of Hoover. At first he said any group would have to have working capital of $5 million. As the time for bidding got closer he went east to sound out other surety companies. They told him it would be dangerous for any group of contractors to take on the job with less than $8 million in working capital. Notwithstanding this warning, Cutler had enough confidence in the builders to stand by his original figure of $5 million when it came close to bidding time.

The two contractors who first zeroed in on Boulder Dam were Utah Construction Co. and Morrison-Knudsen, for whom Frank Crowe worked. Utah even flirted with the idea of going it alone, but in time recognized the advantage of teaming up with M-K. After that, M-K took the lead in lining up the partners.

Kaiser had laid awake so many nights while building the highway in Cuba, trying to figure out how to take on Boulder Dam, that he wanted to play a leading part. On "Dad" Bechtel's trip to Cuba, Kaiser outlined his thinking. Bechtel was leery of it— "Henry, it sounds a little ambitious." Nevertheless, Bechtel's interest had been stirred to the point where they proposed to Warren Bros. of Cambridge, Massachusetts, that the three of them team up for Boulder. Warren Bros. had subcontracted the Cuban highway job to Kaiser.

Kaiser originally planned to fill out his group with several wealthy eastern contractors. But when he returned to California—in the late summer or fall of 1930—and learned how far Morrison and Utah had progressed with their plans he abandoned the idea of setting up a rival group in favor of making an alliance with them. Kaiser, Bechtel, and Warren Bros. came in as a unit although in the showdown Warren didn't actually put up cash, leaving it up to Bechtel and Kaiser to do so.

It would be a consortium without precedent—all hard-driving, risk-taking, independently-successful, fiercely-competitive contractors with different skills, several of whom had not met each other. Their headquarters were far apart—Ogden, Utah, Boise, Idaho, Portland, Oregon, Oakland and San Francisco, California, and even Boston (at the start), but, strangely, none from the Los Angeles area, the main beneficiary of the Boulder Dam. One or two were the whiskey-drinking, cigar-smoking, card-playing gambler types; some were deeply religious. That they could blend together so fast, work together so harmoniously, and continue as partners so long after Boulder was built, is one of America's great industrial stories.

After all the jockeying back and forth, here's how the Six Companies shared the $5 million working capital kitty:

Utah Construction	$1,000,000
Morrison-Knudsen	500,000
Kaiser-Bechtel	1,500,000
MacDonald & Kahn, Inc.	1,000,000
J.F. Shea Co., Inc.	500,000
Pacific Bridge Co.	500,000
	$5,000,000

Now the job was to come up with a bid that all could agree upon. Three cost estimates had been prepared independently—one by Crowe, one by Utah's engineer, and the third by Chad Calhoun of MacDonald & Kahn. (Calhoun would later become Kaiser's Washington man.)

These estimates were furnished to the partners at a morning meeting in mid-February 1931, held at the Engineers Club in San Francisco, just three weeks before the bids were to be made to the Bureau of Reclamation. Everyone was astounded to find that the high and low estimates were only $700,000 apart ($40,000,000 and $40,700,000) and the other was "right in the middle."

Interestingly, Kaiser's enthusiasm was such that he seemed to be the leader in the discussions. When lunchtime came the partners adjourned to the Palace Hotel, leaving behind some of the "working stiffs" to wrestle with some forecast figures that were on the afternoon agenda. Not long after reaching the hotel, it was realized there had been an embarrassing oversight—one of the men left behind was a Director of Utah Construction, Marriner Eccles (who later became Chairman of the Federal Reserve Board and a nationally prominent figure). They sent a messenger to ask him to join them, but he preferred working on the figures during the lunch hour.

It was automatically understood that the Board of Directors would be composed of the participating partners. However, it was necessary to settle on officers for the new company. Respect for experience and age played a part in this, and no dissent was voiced against this line-up:

W. H. Wattis, Utah Construction Co.	President
W. A. Bechtel, W.A. Bechtel Co.	1st Vice President
E. O. Wattis, Utah Construction Co.	2nd Vice President
Felix Kahn, MacDonald & Kahn	Treasurer
Charles A. Shea, J.F. Shea Co.	Secretary

Kaiser was appointed Chairman of the Executive Committee, "in recognition of his unique ability to get people to work together."

Some discussion was held concerning the amount that should be added to the $40 million cost estimate, to cover contingencies and profit. However, in order to keep the bid a secret until the very last hour, no definite figure was arrived at. This had the added advantage of giving each partner some time to ponder just what the profit factor should be.

Various names were proposed for the new combine, including Continental Construction and Western Construction. However, when Kahn suggested Six Companies, it was immediately adopted. The name had special meaning in San Francisco where it had long been used as the name of the famous tribunal to which the powerful Chinese tongs submitted their differences. A few days later Six Companies, Inc., was incorporated in Delaware.

Although W.H. Wattis had been chosen for President, everyone knew he was in precarious health, even then being hospitalized in San Francisco. Thus, it was that on several occasions important exploratory discussions were held around Wattis's bed. A scale model of the dam was built with movable parts for demonstrating crucial operations. It was wheeled into the hospital room so that Wattis could comment on the alternative plans.

Two days before the deadline the partners met in Wattis's room and at last agreed on a figure of 25% for contingencies and profit. A few hours later they left by train for Denver. Next night, at the Cosmopolitan Hotel in Denver, Crowe was up until dawn refining the estimate until the very last hour. His final figure—the one that went on the bid—was $48,890,995.50.

On Wednesday, March 4, 1931, the bids were opened in an empty store beneath the Bureau of Reclamation's Office. Interior Department officials from Secretary Ray Lyman Wilbur on down had been awaiting the opening of the bids with keen interest. As one newspaper article reported:

> The Six Companies stood out as the probable builder, as their low bid of $48,890.995.50 was $5 million below their nearest competitor and within $200,000 of Federal estimates. As an item favoring the bid of the Six companies, Dr. Elwood Mead, head of the Bureau of Reclamation, said Frank Crowe, former construction engineer of the bureau, would be in charge of the project.

In its story of March 4, 1931, the Oakland Tribune reported:

> Six Companies, Inc. was apparent winner of the Boulder Dam project with its bid of $48,890,995.50. Second lowest in bidding was Arundel Corporation of Baltimore, Maryland, at $53,893,878.70. Then came Woods Brothers Corporation of Lincoln, Nebraska at $58,053,107.50. Two other bids could not be considered because they were not in proper form and were not accompanied by the required performance bond—one at $200 million, or cost plus 10%, and another even higher. The bids were opened in a crowded room by Raymond F. Walter, chief engineer of the Bureau of Reclamation, who laughed uproariously at the two highest bids. Representatives of scores of building firms were present and the smoke from cigars and from photographic flashlight guns filled the room.

Kaiser's role in building Boulder Dam was primarily two-fold: (1) It was his responsibility to work out the method for handling the aggregates, (2) he was the Washington, D.C., contact man to be sure the necessary funds would keep coming during the deep depression period.

Tom Price, who had proved himself as an expert in handling aggregate since joining Kaiser in 1919, was placed in charge of designing and assembling the maze of equipment for "harvesting" the enormous volume of gravel from the stream bed, eight miles upstream from the dam site. This proved to be so efficient, Superintendent Crowe later said, "We never lost an hour on account of not having the materials."

Price later said his gravel plant was "not just a dream:"

> The gravel plant at Hoover Dam was most modern in every respect. One
> of the features was the control of the machinery. All the starting and stopping
> of the motors that powered the plant were by remote control. The push but-
> tons that controlled the motors were brought to one point in a small tower
> where the operator could see everything. This tower was the show place to
> take visitors. One day Frank Crowe had a high ranking dignitary visiting him
> and in the course of showing him around, decided to take him up to the
> gravel plant control tower. 'Now,' Frank said, 'this control board with its
> buttons is just like an organ. The man who works it can do anything he
> wants. The plant is really so easy to operate the man could do it in his sleep!'
> With that statement, the visitor was led up the steps to the tower. The plant
> was in full operation, and, by gosh, the operator was sound asleep.

Price was also in charge of the railroad network at the dam which, while in operation, carried the largest volume of material of any railroad west of the Mississippi. He
later described this interesting anecdote:

> When Boulder City was built there was no sewage system and it was
> necessary to use outhouses for every residence, which was an awful lot. Once
> the sewer system was completed, Crowe could not bring himself to destroy
> these metal 'sentry boxes' so he had them stacked up in a huge pile beside
> the shops. They really made a mountain that could be seen anywhere in town.
> Everyone kidded Frank unmercifully about saving them. Finally, Frank
> ordered all the various superintendents to use them up anyway they could.
> Being in charge of the railroad at the time, I conceived the idea of putting
> one at each end of every siding, and to install a telephone in it, for the train-
> men to use in taking orders. One day Charlie Shea, who was then Director of
> Construction, had his personal doctor, Dr. Joyce, and wife, from Portland
> down to see the job and asked me to show them around. I took them to the
> gravel pit, among other places, and after showing them how things worked
> there I asked them to excuse me a minute while I telephoned. When I came
> out of the telephone booth and back to the car Mrs. Joyce said, 'you didn't
> fool me a bit. I know what you went in there for.'

As busy as the partners were in carrying out their various responsibilities on Boulder Dam, they were careful to keep up their work on other fronts. Kaiser had been
active in the Associated General Contractors organization, following by a few years
in the footsteps of "Dad" Bechtel. Then, due to the unexpected death of the president
of AGC, Kaiser was elected national president at a meeting of the executive board
held in Washington May 2 and 3, 1932. This was reported in the Engineering News
Record of May 12, 1932, with the following comment: "Taking his new office at the
height of his business activity, Mr. Kaiser brings a wealth of energy and a close con-

tact with construction problems that will be of great value to the association of which he is now the head."

In August 1932, the Constructor, official publication of AGC, ran this story, along with a picture of Mr. and Mrs. Kaiser:

> Henry J. Kaiser, President of the Associated General Contractors of America, and Chairman of the Executive Committee of Six Companies, Inc., builders of Hoover Dam, completed a three months' stay in Washington, D.C., which began last April 20. Although one of the busiest construction executives in the United States, Mr. Kaiser took this time from his own business affairs to assist the Associated General Contractors in the conduct of its affairs. Mrs. Kaiser accompanied her husband during his work in the East which involved making numerous trips to other metropolitan centers in the interest of the construction industry. Both Mr. and Mrs. Kaiser became well-known figures in Washington before they departed July 20 for their home in Oakland, California.

Much has been written about the close friendship Kaiser enjoyed with President Franklin D. Roosevelt. In particular, Kaiser probably had as close, or closer, relationship with Roosevelt than any other industrialist during World War II. It was shortly after Roosevelt took office in 1933 that Kaiser had the door opened for him to meet the President. The immediate purpose was to pave the way for Kaiser to acquaint the President with construction activities on the San Francisco-Oakland Bay Bridge, but, of course, construction on Boulder Dam was in full swing at that time so he undoubtedly highlighted progress on the dam as well. Following is the letter Will F. Morrish, President of the Bank of America in San Francisco, wrote to Roosevelt April 21, 1933:

> I wish to introduce to you Mr. Henry J. Kaiser, President of Bridge Builders, Inc., one of the low bidders on the San Francisco-Oakland Bay Bridge. He is also Chairman of the Executive Committee of the Six Companies, who hold the contract on Boulder Dam. Mr. Kaiser is in Washington on matters pertaining to the Bay Bridge, and while there would like to consult with you. He is a man of outstanding ability, very highly thought of in this community, and has been a friend and customer of the bank since the first day he came to California. Any courtesies extended to him, I shall greatly appreciate.

If there had been any question in the minds of any of the partners at the start regarding what Kaiser could bring to the table those feelings were very early dispelled. Kaiser set up headquarters at the Shoreham Hotel in Washington and soon successfully lobbied a deficiency appropriation that would keep construction going.

Then, under the Roosevelt Administration, the new Secretary of the Interior, Harold L. Ickes, blasted the Six Companies by charging it with 70,000 violations of the eight-hour-day law and fining them $350,000. The government contract stipulated that no overtime should be paid except in emergencies; this was aimed at spreading the work in the depression period. The contractors felt that getting the job done quickly was in itself an emergency condition.

When the nation's newspapers played up Ickes's charges, Kaiser went to work in earnest. As he would do so many times in later confrontations he had a very professional booklet issued giving all the facts. The booklet, "So Boulder Dam Was Built," pointed out all the crises that had been encountered and how the obstacles had been overcome. Congressmen and high government officials, as well as newspapers and radios, were flooded with copies. Kaiser even went on the air to tell the story firsthand. In the end the fine was reduced to $100,000. It had been an excellent opportunity for Kaiser to get to know Ickes, and a mutual respect was generated which would be helpful to both of them in years ahead.

A final Washington victory that meant so much to the Six companies was Kaiser's persuasion of the government to take the dam off their hands with a minimum of argument. It's one thing to do a good job, it's quite another to get a government bureau to admit it's finished. Without unequivocal acceptance, you run the risk the government will keep adding one extra after another. It was a surprise and a relief to the partners when Kaiser cleaned up all the details with the government within six months. The government took over the dam in March 1936, almost exactly five years after the contract was first awarded—two years and two months ahead of schedule!

The profits reflected the fast construction time. After taxes, there remained $10,400,000 to be prorated according to the capital contributions. The individual shares, however, were actually larger than the original proportions would suggest because the interest of Warren Bros. and certain others had in the meanwhile been bought out.

As important as the profits were, there were other features of Boulder Dam that might have been more meaningful to Kaiser. He had once again—on a grand scale—demonstrated that the key to profit is the speed of construction. And, perhaps even more important, he had proved himself to be a master salesman, not just a construction wizard, in a big-league partnership commanding nationwide attention. He had experienced the thrill and excitement and rewards of speaking out boldly. From that time forward—for three full decades—he would become the most articulate and highly visible spokesman in American industry.

"No Man Will Ever Walk Across The Columbia"

Henry Kaiser was always looking ahead and preparing in advance to take advantage of upcoming opportunities. He once stated:

> Contractors are all alike. They start out broke, with a wheelbarrow and a piece of hose. Then suddenly they find themselves in the money. Everything's fine. Ten years later, many are back where they started from—with one wheelbarrow, a piece of hose—and broke. So, before you work yourself

out of the last job, line up a bigger one to pull yourself out."

It was this creed that led him, more than any other contractor, to start up rock, sand and gravel plants that could keep busy between his different jobs by supplying materials for other builders. In a sense, his later entrance into a variety of industrial operations was a means of balancing out the violent ups and downs he had experienced as a contractor.

That's why he was the one partner among the Six Companies who, right in the middle of the building of Boulder Dam, insisted a bid should be made on the Bonneville Dam to be built on the Columbia River, thirty miles upstream from Portland, Oregon. Bidding on Bonneville was scheduled for May 1934. Throughout that spring the partners had argued the pros and cons of taking on Bonneville.

The Columbia was treacherous—swift, deep, and with a normal flow about the same as the Colorado at flood. There was no convenient canyon of solid rock to form a bottleneck; the banks were soft and far apart. There was no way to build diversion tunnels as at Boulder, so cofferdams would have to be erected allowing water to be pumped out to provide areas dry enough to pour the concrete.

Kaiser was stubborn. The more hesitant his partners became, the more energetically he tried to convince them. He contended that the river could be harnessed, especially with the kind of men who were doing so well at Boulder. Further, he stressed that Bonneville would hold together a nucleus of experienced men. He was sure that a good profit could be realized on a project costing about one-third as much as Boulder.

One compelling motivation for Kaiser was his conviction that his 25-year-old son, Edgar, had proved himself at Boulder and was ready to head up the Bonneville project. Also, Kaiser had great faith in the engineering skills of 30-year-old Clay Bedford who had done such an outstanding job on the Cuban highway, as well as at Boulder Dam. Kaiser, always a believer in the ingenuity of young men when thrown into a challenging situation, considered it an advantage that these two young men, "didn't know why it couldn't be done."

To shore up his determination, he went to his banker asking for financial assistance. In accordance with his lifetime policy, he wanted all the facts to come out—he didn't want to sugar-coat any feature of the project. He told the banker flatly:

> Government engineers are doubtful if the dam can be constructed. Bonding companies refuse to take the risk of bonding this hazardous project. The raging waters of the Columbia can rise 20 to 30 feet within a day and rip out our work. Even the native Indians have a legend that no man will ever walk across the Columbia. But we have the faith that we can build the dam.

The bank's Chairman of the Board, in response to Mr. Kaiser's utterly frank analysis of the hazards of the project, turned to the President of the bank and said, "Get on your boots! We're going to wade the Columbia River with Henry Kaiser."

Looking back on the building of Bonneville, Kaiser testified before the Truman

Senate Committee July 30, 1942:

> My associates said, 'You are going to break your heart. That can't be done. It just can't be done.' Some of my most intimate associates sat up with me until 4 o'clock in the morning and said, 'Just don't try that one. It just can't be pulled.'

Kaiser won out, with Bechtel, Utah, Morrison-Knudsen, and MacDonald and Kahn joining him to form the Columbia Construction Co. However, Charlie Shea, Gorrill Swigert of Pacific Bridge, and Jack McEachern of General Construction—all based in the Pacific Northwest—teamed up separately to submit a competitive bid. The Kaiser group was low bidder at slightly more than $16,500,000. However, two months later Columbia Construction lost out to the Northwest group on the power-house which was to accompany the dam.

Edgar Kaiser would later say:

> Bonneville was without question the most difficult construction project we have ever built. At the start there were no specifications, not even a solid plan. Engineers had to improvise as we went along. There were constant changes. Nothing ever stayed put. One stormy, spring night when the water was high and really roaring, I was afraid we were going to lose our coffer-dam so I phoned a supervisor at the dam site, a short distance upstream. 'Everything is OK,' he reported, 'I think we're going to be all right.' Just then, I looked out the window and saw a dark mass approaching. It was one of our cofferdam cribs floating down the river. With it went the unlimited hours of work of hundreds of men. This was a real tragedy. But the will and determination of the men of the camp were unbroken. We could turn from that tragedy back to the drawing board, knowing that we would build again, and yet again, if it happened that way.

Bonneville took four years to build, but it was finished one year ahead of schedule, resulting in a net profit of $3 million. Considering the doubts of his partners at the start, and the vindication of his faith in young men, it was one of Kaiser's most satisfying monuments. He would repeat over and over during his life, "They said it couldn't be done, but my kids went ahead and did it."

Win Some, Lose Some—Grand Coulee Dam

The era of western dam building, which would abruptly come to an end with the start of World War II, was at its peak during the depression years of the thirties. Within one month after the bids were opened on the Bonneville Dam, bids had to be submitted in June 1934 for the excavation and foundation work for the mighty Grand Coulee Dam to be built on the Columbia River 467 miles upstream.

"A piece of cake," the Six Companies' partners agreed. Surely, with all their expertise they would know how to do the job more efficiently than anyone else, and hence should end up with the lowest bid.

In Spokane, the night before the bids were to be opened, the partners and their wives gathered for a big party at the Davenport Hotel. Kaiser was host. Harry Morrison of Morrison-Knudsen gave an account of the bidding:

> Everyone was very cheerful and hilarious. Toasts were drunk to our success on the biggest dam of all. I remember Felix Kahn promising that the next party he was going to put a hundred dollar bill under each lady's plate, because we'd all be in the money by then. The competition, incidentally, was staying at the same hotel; when they heard all the noise and cheering, they got kind of worried.

> Next morning at ten we all met for the opening of the bids. Us Six Companies were right up in the front row. There were only two bids. The competitive bid was opened and read first. It was $5 million under our bid of $34,600,000. We didn't wait to hear our own bid. We just got up and filed out. By noon there wasn't a Six Companies man to be found in Spokane.

That account was not quite true. One partner did stay around. It was Henry Kaiser who had previously been invited to speak to a meeting of the Spokane Chamber of Commerce that night. He decided not to duck out, but to use the occasion to "turn a problem into an opportunity." Here's how the newspaper reported his speech:

Didn't Lose;
Spokane Won

> Henry J. Kaiser, chairman of the executive board of Six Companies, Inc., Oakland, Cal., who began his career in Spokane as a $75 a month clerk in MacGowan's Hardware store here, gave probably the most effective speech made at the banquet.

> The Six Companies, Inc.'s bid was approximately $5,000,000 more than that of the Mason Company.

> 'They say we had lost,' Kaiser told the crowd of 400 at the banquet. 'But we haven't lost. We have won, because Spokane won.'

Three days later, Fred K. Jones, President of the Spokane Chamber of Commerce, wrote this letter to Kaiser:

> You will be interested in the attached clipping from last evening's Spokane Press.

> As stated in that article, I feel that you made the outstanding talk at the banquet Monday evening.

We all know that the world always acclaims a winner but we also know that the world loves a good loser.

You proved yourself to be a good loser and I am sure that by so doing you did much to increase the esteem in which you and your associates are held here in Spokane.

Some of these days, I am going to visit Bonneville and introduce myself to that son of yours. I surmise that he is a worthy son of a worthy father.

The winning bidder was called MWAK, consisting of the Silas Mason Co., Inc., of New York, Walsh Construction Co. of Davenport, Iowa, and the Atkinson-Kier Co. of San Francisco. They did a bang-up job on the foundation, even freezing a hillside to keep it from sliding by imbedding brine-carrying pipes. This feat, together with other imaginative and dangerous work they had to do, proved costly, so they just about broke even by the time the contract was completed.

When the time came for bidding on the Grand Coulee Dam itself (along with the foundations for the pumping plant, and the powerhouse on the left bank), in December 1937, the Six Companies' partners had become a bit more cautious. With rising costs on a project that would take four years, the group decided to spread the risk by inviting Tom Walsh of MWAK to join them. He was glad to accept, hoping to earn a profit to make up for his break-even on the excavation work. MWAK was given a 50 percent interest in the job.

Clay Bedford had been dispatched to Grand Coulee long in advance to study the upcoming dam project from every angle as a basis for making the bid. He became excited about a new technique of handling the sand and gravel and pouring the huge quantities of cement that would be required. He reviewed his innovative ideas in great detail with both Henry Kaiser and Edgar Kaiser. Once they agreed with him, the other partners in the group accepted the merit of his plan and submitted a bid of $40,800,000. Here's how Bedford recounts the opening of the bids:

Our competitor's bid was read first. It was over $46,000,000. Felix Kahn just looked a hole right through me; he was ready to kill me right there, because we had left on the table, so to speak, around $6,000,000. Then what happened was that they read the Reclamation Bureau engineer's estimate. Well, the government rule was that you could not be awarded the job if your bid was more than 10 percent above the engineer's estimate. Fortunately, our bid was less than 10 percent higher. So there was great relief when the engineer's estimate was read. Felix Kahn began settling down.

I was pretty sure we could make out on our bid, because I had timed the cranes, I had timed the various operations, and had calculated pretty carefully how fast we could pour the concrete. Also, I knew we could get agreement from the union to use every labor-saving operation we could devise.

The Grand Coulee Dam would produce a cataract over its spillway twice as high as Niagara Falls. It would not be as high as Boulder Dam, but would be three and one-half times wider (nearly four-fifths of a mile long) and would require twice as much concrete as Boulder.

The timing couldn't have been better. Edgar Kaiser, Clay Bedford, and their construction team were just finishing up their work on Bonneville Dam. It was unanimously agreed by all the partners that they were the logical choice to take command at Grand Coulee. Almost like at Boulder Dam, the assembling of a large group of workers, and the establishment of living quarters for them, in the relatively remote and undeveloped area of Grand Coulee, some 90 miles west of Spokane, would be no small undertaking. Also this would turn out to be the proving ground for the prepaid health plan which had been started in the desert of Southern California a few years before. It was at Coulee that Henry Kaiser first met the young founder of the health plan, Dr. Sidney Garfield (see Chapter 4).

Progress at Coulee went ahead even better than expected. On this job the combined organization borrowed from the experience of the Bechtel-Kaiser pipe-laying days earlier in the decade. Records had been set by breaking up the work force into several groups and encouraging rivalry. At Coulee, the successful strategy was to "cut the dam in parts" with three crews pitted against each other.

By mid-1940 the dam was far enough along that Edgar and his father agreed Clay Bedford could be spared to begin directing construction of a huge Naval Air Station at Corpus Christi, Texas. Edgar himself remained in charge at Grand Coulee through 1940 but in January 1941 he left to start up the Portland ship yards. It took a year after that for the dam to be completed but the remaining management and crew were so well organized that construction went forward without any hitches. As a result, the dam was finished a full year and a half ahead of schedule, with the partners sharing a profit of $7,200,000 before taxes.

Once more, Kaiser's kids had done the impossible.

Getting Burned—The Caldecott Tunnel

The meeting had become very tense. Each side felt it was caught in a crunch with no satisfactory way out. The stakes were high, and there was no room for bargaining.

It was a meeting in May of 1936 between officials of a joint district formed by Alameda and Contra Costa Counties, and the contractors who had won the bid to build the Caldecott twin-bore tunnels through the coastal range hills separating Oakland from eastern Contra Costa County. Just two years before, the Six Companies, builders of Boulder Dam, had bid $3,683,931 to do the job, some $700,000 lower than the next lowest bid. At that time the District had made it clear that the financing was strictly limited by the terms of state aid, a WPA grant, and a District bond issue. Their own engineers had estimated the cost of the job and the Six Companies knew their bid would have to be very close to that estimate or the construction would not even be undertaken.

The tunnels would be a much needed improvement in the East Bay, and Steve Bechtel, with his home in Oakland and his office in San Francisco, had a very laudable ambition, not only to do the job as a matter of home company pride but in the conviction that with the help of the home community engineers he could perform the work within the available funds.

It soon developed that the driving of the tunnels was far more difficult than anyone had anticipated. The ground was sedimentary in origin, largely composed of fractured shale, and had been tilted almost 90 degrees. It was situated on an earthquake fault. Three different geological formations were encountered, all of them bad for tunnel driving. In addition, considerable water drainage posed a constantly annoying problem—a veritable quagmire. Two serious cave-ins occurred on the job, one with the tragic death of three workers.

After about a year, Steve Bechtel came to the opinion that possibly he might not be doing everything that should be done to solve the problems, and, wanting to do whatever might help the work, asked Henry Kaiser, as an older man and a new face, to assume the sponsorship, which he agreed to do. But that didn't change things. Costs and delays continued running far ahead of estimates.

In good faith, the contractors felt that somehow additional funds could be found. The District, however, said its hands were tied, so Kaiser went to Washington, hoping to talk the WPA into providing $3 million, but he came back empty-handed. It became a stalemate where the lawyers of both sides began assuming control. In the meantime, the contractors had asked Frank Crowe, the construction genius behind the Boulder Dam to see if he could come up with an answer to the construction problems. He told them they were through the worst ground and that they should, "Stop lawin' and start diggin'."

At last the showdown meeting was held with lawyers doing most of the talking. Both sides refused to budge. Finally, Kaiser couldn't stand it any longer. He got up and reviewed the situation from beginning to end. As he waxed emotional, the head lawyer for the District rudely stood up, walked over to a window and opened it. "What's that for?" Kaiser demanded. "That's to let your tears flow out," said the lawyer, "so we won't all drown."

Under the circumstances, the attorneys for the Six Companies and the other contractor members themselves unanimously urged Kaiser to rescind the job to stop further losses. None wanted to do this, least of all Kaiser who had always prided himself in making good on every contract, but he finally gave in and announced recision of the contract.

Immediately, Kaiser met with representatives of the District and advised them that in his opinion the early completion of the job was more important than anything else. To that end, he offered them full cooperation in both maintaining the present work and assisting them in advertising and letting and performing the rest of the work. This offer was appreciated and accepted by the District. The job was then separated into several smaller units. By the time the contract had been rescinded, the opening up of the ground all the way through the tunnel had been completed, so that the finishing work of the several small contractors was not hazardous.

The District took its case to the Federal Courts and won. The loss to the contractors was a serious one, a total of $2,400,000. While such a loss might not have been borne by any one member of the group without most serious consequences, nevertheless when spread among many was not fatal to any. The reputation of the Six Companies, however, did suffer a setback. But the partners who had become a bit cocky after their success in building Boulder Dam learned a bitter lesson in the tunnel job which made them much more cautious in future bidding.

Notwithstanding all the construction problems and legal conflicts, Kaiser and his associates could look back with pride on the role they played in encouraging and building these incredibly difficult tunnels.

The tunnels were long overdue and long awaited, so when they were opened to traffic December 5, 1937, it was a time for celebration by the people of the East Bay. It was also a significant occasion for San Francisco, because just one year earlier the San Francisco-Oakland Bay Bridge had been put in service, and now people could drive between the City and most population centers in Contra Costa County east of the tunnels in much less than one hour. It was like opening a whole new frontier.

In 1964, another tunnel was completed (the Six Companies were not involved), providing two more lanes. This additional cost, together with all costs to date, including the expenses of a wind tunnel, tile, lighting, control offices, highway approaches, etc., came to a total of $24 million—more than six and a half times the cost of the basic tunnel driving bid of the Six Companies in 1934.

The six lanes, originally identified as the Broadway Low-Level Tunnel, were named Caldecott Tunnel after Thomas E. Caldecott, Chairman of the Board of Directors of the Highway District, and an Alameda County Supervisor who had spearheaded the drive to get the tunnels approved.

By 1988, 138,000 cars were moving through the tunnels as a daily average, and with the population exploding in Contra Costa County, agitation was heating up for another two-lane tunnel.

"The Best Thing We Ever Lost"—Shasta Dam

How could any hardened, ring-wise group of contractors find anything good about losing out on their bid to build the Shasta Dam? They couldn't. Not even the perennial sunshine partner, Henry Kaiser, could see any silver lining. That is, not at first.

The famous Six Companies, builders of Boulder, Bonneville and Grand Coulee dams, were confident in 1938 that after weeks of sweating out cost estimates, they had come up with the lowest bid to build Shasta—$36,200,000. At the last minute, one of the partners, Jack McEachern, suggested they knock off $500,000 more "to break the million"—but Frank Crowe, the construction genius behind Boulder Dam, said "No." That was the fatal error. When the bids were opened, Pacific Constructors, Inc., was under by $263,000.

Following past patterns that could have been the end of the Shasta story for the Six Companies. Will there be another construction project we can soon bid on?

But Kaiser seldom followed past patterns. There must be some other way to share in all that money being poured into Shasta, he reasoned. How about furnishing the cement? The sand and gravel?

He became excited. It didn't bother him that he did not at that time have a cement mill. It didn't bother him that a strong West Coast cement combine had dominated the cement business for a long time—extremely influential men such as George Cameron, publisher of the San Francisco Chronicle, Herbert Fleishhacker, the Cowell family, A. E. Wilson of Pacific Gas and Electric. As someone said at that time: "When Kaiser decided to go after the cement people, he didn't take on any corporals."

The huge cement contract for Shasta Dam (nearly six million barrels) presented Kaiser with an opportunity to attack this complacent group on the flank. He took an option on a large limestone deposit not far from San Jose. (It is still supplying the much-expanded cement plant in 1988.) From there to Shasta was only 300 miles, all of it over the Southern Pacific Railroad. Besides, the existing cement plants were mostly located in the San Francisco Bay Area so they would enjoy no lower freight rate than Kaiser.

Kaiser figured he had one thing in his favor—Harold Ickes, Secretary of the Interior, whose Bureau of Reclamation would have the final say on suppliers to Shasta, was an outspoken critic of controlled, uniform cement prices. The Bureau of Reclamation had long been exasperated by the industry custom of submitting identical bids on nearly all government jobs.

The limestone Kaiser optioned was of good quality, high on a hill above the spot where the cement mill would be located at a place soon to be named Permanente. The limestone would come down two miles by gravity to the mill. The brakes on the steeply inclined belt were generators which would produce the power to run the electrical scoop shovels digging out the limestone—an unusually favorable arrangement.

All well and good. But Kaiser had never produced cement before. And how could he possibly build a new plant in time to meet Shasta's needs? Kaiser acknowledged:

> I didn't know anything about producing cement—or at least not very much. Of course, I had been in the sand and gravel business, but never in cement. So I sent my boys off East to learn how it was done, how to go about building a plant, and how to get it done in a hurry.

He put his experienced estimators to work, and based on the information his engineers had brought back from the East, he felt prepared to bid on Shasta's total requirements of 5,800,000 barrels. It was unheard of for one supplier to provide the whole amount, but Kaiser finally persuaded the Interior Department he should be permitted to make such a bid.

This introduced the problem of getting a bonding company to back him up. Kaiser recounted:

> I couldn't find a bonding company unless I gave half of the business to the other cement companies. I soon found out they were very powerful. But there was a provision for a personal bond on such contracts. So I went to my five associates in Six Companies who had already indicated they wanted to participate in the new company. We all put up our personal bonds. It was taking a chance, but my partners believed I could do it.

It startled the construction world when the bids were opened:

	Per Barrel	Total Bid
Permanente (Kaiser)	$1.19	$6,902,000.00
Beaver, Calaveras, Monolith, Santa Cruz, Pacific, Yosemite joint bid	$1.482	$8,595,866.80
Savings to the Government		$1,693,866.80

The cement crowd protested that Kaiser's bid was illegal, since he obviously was without a plant to produce cement. The government actually held up the award for a month while it investigated whether Kaiser could reasonably be expected to make good. Kaiser even had to overcome an uprising of property owners in the Santa Clara Valley, reportedly stirred up by the combine, who demanded that the county refuse him a building permit on the argument that his plant would destroy property values.

Construction of the plant began in early June 1939. Setting the model for all the industrial construction he would later be doing, Kaiser and his men raced to a seven month's completion. It was said that the finest present Kaiser ever received was the first bag of cement handed to him by his "boys" that Christmas.

Completion of the facility in December was so far ahead of schedule the Shasta Dam contractor was not yet ready to receive cement. No problem. Kaiser would start selling cement commercially by hiring a bunch of salesmen. This raised another howl among the other cement producers who didn't want to see their market invaded at lower prices. Kaiser liked the taste, so he started building a third, and then a fourth cement kiln to service the commercial market once he had to start fulfilling his Shasta commitment. Then just before Pearl Harbor, Kaiser could see his entire output above his Shasta requirements could be sold to the government for Navy installations in the Pacific. This became a signal for the other cement companies to try to convince their commercial customers to commit any postwar business to them in consideration of taking care of their needs at that time. However, like all hard-headed buyers, the customers wouldn't fall for that, and insisted they would retain the right to buy their cement from any supplier who best served their needs at any given time.

Kaiser's entrance into the business of furnishing cement for the Navy in the

Pacific was far-sighted—and fortuitous. Use of bulk cement was at first opposed by the Navy, because it had never been done before in the tropics, and it was feared the moisture would cause the cement to deteriorate. Kaiser was so confident that would not be the case he guaranteed acceptable quality delivered right to the construction site, using compressed air to blow the cement in and out of the ship. When Pearl Harbor was attacked, 65,000 barrels were available in the Pacific area. Most of this was in Permanente's privately owned bulk facilities in Honolulu. That amount helped put Honolulu's airfields back into action fast, but it was a drop in the bucket to what became needed. In 1942 Permanente was given the contract to supply all bulk cement for Pacific airfields, fortifications, and other wartime installations. This was possible because the company bought and refitted two old ships—the Ancon and Cristobal— to transport the cement in bulk. Shipments averaged 5,000 barrels daily from the bulk silos in Honolulu during the critical 1942-43 war period, exceeding rated plant capacity in 1942.

The dollar volume of sales to the Pacific exceeded $15 million. The savings to the government from using this bulk cement as compared with sacked cement came to $7.5 million. This does not take into account the savings which bulk operations accomplished in ship-hours which were huge; nor does it take into account the man-hours necessary for handling sacked cement. The dollar value of the precious man-hours saved by this operation can be estimated at a minimum, as double that of savings to actual price of the product. No doubt about it, Kaiser's bulk cement—the only American company so involved—helped win the Pacific war.

The original cement plant near San Jose, designed and built by Kaiser engineers in 1939, and soon expanded, cost $10 million, of which $7 million was borrowed from Bank of America. The rest was put up by the partners, with no government money whatsoever being involved. Within the first two or three years, profits were running at better than $1 million a year.

But Permanente was much more than a tidy money-maker. It was really the turning point of Kaiser's career. Up until then he had been essentially a construction man (except for his small sand and gravel company which did sell to some customers as well as supply Kaiser's needs). Now Kaiser had successfully plunged into a significant industrial venture. In doing so he had licked a tough bunch. From that time forward, he wasn't afraid to spread out industrially in many different directions and on a large scale.

At Shasta he had turned defeat into victory and set the pattern for the rest of his life. Is it any wonder, therefore, that he was often heard saying, "Shasta is the best thing we ever lost."

The Flagship Company — Cement

The construction of a cement mill in 1939 not only catapulted Kaiser into the industrial world, it became a solid moneymaker that kept on growing year after year. It never reached the heights in sales or profits that his steel and aluminum companies did, but it was a backbone operation, a bread-and-butter business. In a way it became the "flagship" for the whole convoy of Kaiser companies.

It worked a special kind of magic in 1944. Samuel A. Perkins, 80-year-old owner of Standard Gypsum, headquartered in Tacoma, Washington, a $20 million per year business, suddenly startled everyone by offering Kaiser a 50-50 partnership deal to take over the operation of his company. His story was told in the Oakland Post Enquirer of July 28, 1944:

> 'I'm only 80 years old, just a kid trying to get along and during the last 40 years I've got hold of a mighty big pile of gypsum, the mostest and bestest supply of gypsum on earth, I guess—500 million tons—in my own town of San Marcos on the Gulf of California. But I got to figuring I was 80 years old, and I've lost my own boy, and here's Henry Kaiser who has a pair of fine boys who ought to go even further than he has with all the chances he's giving them. So I studied his organization for two months, and came to the conclusion that the very best thing for my estate was to put Henry Kaiser to work for it.' Thereupon, Perkins genially referred to Kaiser who was 62 as 'my new office boy,' which set the local Maharajah of Magnesium off into a vast rumble of mirth. 'Stick out your chest, Henry,' added Perkins, moving his chair closer to his new partner, 'because here you are sitting right along-side of ME.'

Kaiser responded by stressing that while there had been a lot of talk about private enterprise getting business going after the war this new partnership would start imme-diately doing something about it. He pledged:

> The Henry J. Kaiser Company is going to invest many millions in making light steel panels that'll make up a large part of a house, and in making gypsum wallboard panels that'll go on the steel panels. Under this system of mass production we plan, everyone can have a better house, and cheaper, than in the past. It is going to give labor and management a chance to work together for the good of all.

This was just another instance where luck would play a role in Kaiser's success. Of course, it was luck that had been earned, because Perkins was so impressed with Permanente Cement's progress, as well as other Kaiser achievements, he could visu-alize how under Kaiser's leadership, the cement and gypsum business could go hand-in-hand in attaining new sales peaks.

In time, Kaiser bought out Perkins' interest and the name of the company became Kaiser Cement & Gypsum Corporation. Over the years the gypsum business would prove highly profitable. The huge San Marcos deposit was of good quality and extremely easy to mine. Shipments in bulk carriers to the Long Beach, California, plant resulted in one of the most favorable raw material costs in the industry. Later, Kaiser opened highly successful gypsum plants in Florida and New Jersey. The warm friendship of the two men continued through the years, as evidenced by this letter when Perkins was 85 years old:

> I am in receipt of and want to thank you for the birthday greetings and good wishes.

> I hope this finds you in the best of health and my association with you has been one of great pleasure. I still maintain that anybody who sells Kaiser short is crazy. You can rest assured of my continued cooperation.

Just a few months before Perkins had made his unexpected offer to turn over his gypsum operations to Kaiser on a 50-50 basis, Permanente Cement had acquired ownership of the Glacier Sand and Gravel Company in Seattle. This established Permanente as an important factor in the construction field in the Seattle area, furnishing a large part of the aggregates and ready-mix concrete used in that major market.

Then a few years later Permanente Cement thought it had gained a strong foothold in the northwest cement business by buying Pacific Coast Cement Company. Litigation was immediately instituted by Superior Portland Cement, Inc., contending that Pacific Coast had committed to sell to them. The Court decision ran against Kaiser, and thereupon Superior took steps which Kaiser construed as trying to block Permanente Cement entirely from that market.

It was the kind of fight Kaiser enjoyed. He came out bellowing. He accused Superior of trying to gain a stranglehold on the northwest. He even referred back to the time when he was a young roadbuilder in that area how Superior had tried "to prevent me from securing the award of a contract for a highway job on which Superior had not sold the cement." In a long, two-page news release dated November 24, 1949, blasting Superior from every angle, he concluded:

> Competition has built America, and it will build a much greater future for the Pacific Northwest. Superior's efforts to stifle competition already have closed the plant and thrown employees out of work. But Permanente Cement is and will continue to be an ever-increasing force, contributing to the building of this area.

Kaiser Cement & Gypsum Corporation kept on spreading out and growing, not spectacularly but soundly. As brought out in Chapter 11, page 334, he even ended up building a cement mill in the Hawaiian Islands. When he died there in 1967 the cement company announced that the corporate sales for that year came to $94 million. It stressed that recent expansions had left the company in good position to take advantage of the large-scale growth that economists could foresee for the next decade. A Pacific-oriented company in the fifties, it had moved farther afield in the sixties with production plants in Montana and Texas and then overseas in Thailand and Okinawa. Served by its own steamship line, five manufacturing plants, and eighteen distribution plants, the company's markets extended from Alaska to Mexico, and from Texas to the Far East.

Kaiser Gypsum, which was born when S. A. Perkins decided on his own to let Kaiser share in his Standard Gypsum business, paralleled its parent cement company's expansion during the sixties by moving into Eastern markets with plants in Florida and New Jersey. It was the fourth largest maker of wallboard and other gypsum products in the United States by 1967.

It had been twenty-eight years since Kaiser turned defeat into victory at Shasta Dam by deciding to bid on the cement contract after losing out by a hair in securing the construction contract. It is interesting to speculate whether Kaiser would have ended up going into the cement business if he had not been frustrated at Shasta. He probably would have done so all right, but it would have been sometime later and it may have delayed his entrance into other industrial ventures.

Strange forces are often at play in determining the direction that some businesses take. Not even Kaiser with all his ebullience could have dreamed that one cement mill to supply one dam would turn out to be such a far-flung and successful business—and such a pace-setter for other large-scale industries.

A 9.6 Mile Conveyor Belt

Lost in the glamour of Kaiser's cement conquest, was the fact that he also made the winning bid in 1939 to supply the sand and gravel for the Shasta Dam. It really wasn't a side show. It was big business. It involved 11 million tons of aggregate, and Kaiser's bid came to $4.4 million.

Kaiser knew exactly where to get the aggregate. Nearly 20 years before, on a road job in the same area, he had found a gravel bank that looked so promising he bought it for the future. It was 1 1/2 miles from the Southern Pacific Railroad, and he asked the carrier to build a connection which they refused to do. Instead they suggested that he should build a conveyor belt for that distance to bring the aggregate to the railroad. They then offered a rate of 27 cents a ton, from there to the dam which he immediately branded "prohibitive." Then, as he would do so many times later in some of his industrial companies, he became personally involved in the freight rate negotiations, "cajoling, wheedling, threatening, and appealing to SP's pride in contributing to a project that would mean so much to the farmers of California." He got nowhere because SP felt its rate was at rock bottom, and presumably there was no other way to move the aggregate. That's where SP made its big mistake.

Kaiser later recalled:

> Then one of my boys said to me, 'Why don't we just build our own conveyor belt the whole distance across the mountain?' At first I didn't like the idea. Then he had the nerve to say to me, 'Are you chicken?' Well, I sure didn't like that either, so I said, 'I'm not chicken; we'll build it.'

It would be the longest conveyor belt built anywhere in the world up to that time—9.6 miles up and down rugged, sometimes steep, terrain. It would require two crossings of the Sacramento River, one over the main state highway, and others over five county roads, four creeks, and the main line of the Southern Pacific Railroad. Except for these crossings and ravine crossings where trestles had to be built, the belt was kept low to the ground. Attention had to be given to construct horizontal cross posts to discourage the hazardous practice of riding on the belt, with the top and sides of the belt being screened by wire mesh fencing when the belt passed near a school. A plank walkway extended the full length of the line as did a pipeline to provide wash water at each transfer station. A dirt roadway paralleled the belt and a 100-foot right of way was cleared of trees and brush as a precaution against fire.

Because of the range in sizes of the materials to be handled, each of which had a different trajectory at the 26 transfer points, special engineering was required. Also, this called for careful specifications in the belt which Goodyear Rubber Company manufactured.

Construction of the line was started November 20, 1939, with some 200 men, about half assigned to carpenter crews of five men each. Had it not been for a period of unusually heavy rainfall and floods, the work would have been completed March 1. As it was, the first aggregate was discharged into the dam's coffers May 6.

It was an engineering marvel, costing only $1.5 million. It delivered the aggregate at 18 cents per ton as compared with the railroad offer of 27 cents. It proved reliable from the time it started until the dam was completed.

Years later at a Kaiser Aluminum management and employee meeting at Baton Rouge, Louisiana, where serious operating problems were being encountered, Kaiser talked about building the Shasta conveyor belt. He said the banks all told him, "You're going to go flat broke. This conveyor is never going to work." "However," Kaiser went on, trying to bolster the spirit of his Baton Rouge people, "the conveyor never gave one minute's trouble, but we hadn't paid much attention to the gravel plant that was feeding it, and that almost broke me."

The conveyor was bold pioneering at its best, another proud feather in Kaiser's cap. It was one more reason Kaiser could say, "Losing out on construction of the Shasta Dam was one of the best things that ever happened to us."

CHAPTER 4

THE SHINING STAR—KAISER PERMANENTE*

"When I was a boy of 16, my mother died in my arms because of improper medical care. Then my father went blind because he didn't have proper medical care. Mrs. Kaiser and I lost our only daughter in childbirth owing to lack of medical care. Now I am searching for a cure for multiple sclerosis which has afflicted my son, Henry, Jr. I don't want to lose him for lack of medical care."

"Young man, if your idea is half as good as you say it is, it's not only good for this project, it's good for the entire country."

Henry Kaiser had been grilling Dr. Sidney R. Garfield for three hours on every detail of the prepaid medical care system Garfield was putting in on Kaiser's construction project.

And the project was a big one. It was one that some Army Engineers said couldn't be done. This was the Grand Coulee Dam. The year was 1938.

Kaiser was the sponsoring contractor for this $41,000,000 project to harness the mighty Columbia River in a rugged area some 90 miles west of Spokane, Washington.

Because of the remoteness of the region, hospital and medical care had to be built from the ground up for the 15,000 or more people who would be directly or indirectly involved. Edgar Kaiser, Henry's oldest son,—29 years old at that time—was in charge of the project.

Edgar had persuaded Dr. Garfield to tackle the challenge at Coulee. Garfield had developed a successful medical plan during the construction of the Los Angeles Aqueduct, starting some five years previously. It had worked well in the splendid isolation (and torrid heat) of Desert Center, a little water hole half-way between the

*Certain portions of this chapter rely on research and writings by John G. Smillie, M.D., who will soon be publishing a book exclusively on the Kaiser Permanente Medical Care Program.

towns of Indio and Blythe in Southern California.

But this three-hour session at Coulee was the first time Henry Kaiser had met Dr. Garfield, the first time he had heard the details of the prepaid medical care.

Garfield later recalled:

> His immediate enthusiasm for my program knocked me right off my feet. It was music to my ears, but at the same time it frightened me to think of the entire country when I was having such a tough job getting doctors and good medical assistants for Grand Coulee alone. But as Mr. Kaiser would do so often in the years I was to be associated with him, he took time to reassure me. With a laugh he said, 'Doctor, don't you worry. You won't have to do the job yourself. If you're any good, you're going to have a great deal of competition, and that'll help you do your job. You're going to be copied. Therefore, your particular job must be to make sure your model is the very best in the whole country and remains worthy of being copied.'
>
> I was amazed that in three hours he had grasped the essence of my plan, and had seen a wider application than I had ever dreamed of. He never lost that vision. For the nearly thirty years after that meeting, until he died, Henry Kaiser had a missionary zeal in his efforts to strengthen and broaden the health program.

In later years, Henry Kaiser came to like the designation, "Founder." It perfectly described the role he played in all his business ventures. He conceived the original ideas; he brought them into being; he founded the companies.

In time he gave his son Edgar the title of Chairman of the Board for all the operating companies. In turn, each of those companies had a separate President and Chief Executive Officer. By that time, Kaiser was generous in the titles he gave his top people. But there was only one Founder.

As above described, in the one enterprise he would later say he was proudest of, the one that had the greatest chance of perpetuating his name—Kaiser Permanente Medical Care Program—he could not be called Founder.

That designation would have to go to the young, soft-spoken, self-effacing surgeon, Dr. Sidney R. Garfield, just out of medical school who was groping for a way to make a living in the depression year of 1933. Even for him the title Founder could be subject to challenge. For the first five years when he was experimenting with his different approach to medical services, he never envisioned its long-run potential. And three times—at the end of the five year period in the Southern California desert; at the completion of the Grand Coulee Dam; and then when he was drafted into the service at the outbreak of World War II—he would start to walk away from the program, only to have other influences come to bear to keep him involved and to keep his idea alive.

But destiny seemed to ride on Garfield's shoulders from the very beginning. One job offered to him after leaving school was a medical position in Indio, California, at $125.00 per month working for the Metropolitan Water District of Los Angeles, just then starting construction of an aqueduct from the Colorado River to Los Angeles, the longest in the world. As desperate as the times were, he couldn't quite see getting along on such a low salary. However, that offer started him thinking about the great need for medical care that would arise in the desert area once the construction got underway. He talked it over with his longtime friend, Dr. Gene Morris, who was already practicing in Indio. They agreed to form a partnership.

As partners, Dr. Morris would continue to practice in Indio; Garfield would build a small hospital near Desert Center, about 60 miles east. There, a fee-for-service industrial medicine practice for on-the-job compensable injuries and illnesses could be combined with non-industrial medicine for about 5,000 workers on the aqueduct. There were about 20 contractors with jobs spread out across the desert in locations remote from any doctors or hospitals.

Luckily, Dr. Garfield's father was willing to loan him $2,500. That was enough for a down payment to build a 10-bed hospital in Desert Center. Arrangements were made with a surgical supply company to equip the hospital. Nurses were hired and a married couple came aboard for a reasonable fee whose duties included housecleaning, cooking, laundry, maintenance and ambulance driving.

But it was uphill from the start. Needing money, the doctor was eager to see sick and injured men come to the hospital. To his dismay he found the insurance companies haggling over fees and challenging his services. Also, once he had stabilized those patients seriously ill or injured, his payments were cut off when the insurance companies insisted on transferring them to more favored hospitals and doctors in metropolitan Los Angeles. For non-industrial care the income was disappointing because at the minimum wages the workers were getting, they weren't good credit risks. In time it became a struggle to meet the payroll. Payments to the contractor who had built the hospital and to the surgical supply house were dragged out as much as the creditors would allow. To make matters worse, Dr. Morris' practice in Indio was just barely covering costs. He suggested dissolving the partnership which would leave the challenge entirely up to Dr. Garfield.

This was the first brink, but not the last, on which Garfield's future would teeter. But at that time it was so serious he carefully weighed the possibility of closing down, going bankrupt. When word of this got to the contractors and insurance companies, they became alarmed. They knew they could not be without medical care near the work sites. Something had to be done to keep Dr. Garfield in business.

It was then that Harold Hatch, a manager for the major insurance company, the Industrial Indemnity Exchange, came up with the idea that in time would become the cornerstone of the Kaiser Permanente Medical Program: Prepayment. He suggested that the Exchange pay Dr. Garfield half of the part of the workmen's compensation premium that was allocated to medical and hospital expenses. The other half was to be set aside to pay the charges of doctors and hospitals caring for patients transferred to Los Angeles.

Now that a steady and predictable income was assured, remarkable things began to happen. It was possible to pay the nurses and assistants as well as the indebtedness to the contractor and surgical supply company. Based on the enthusiasm everyone seemed to have for the new concept, it was decided to offer medical care for non-industrial illnesses or injuries at roughly the same amount, or $1.50 per month per employee. The workers soon caught on that this was a nickel a day, and even in a depression period when they were only making minimum wages, they were willing to invest that much in their own health.

Then something quite unexpected occurred. Men who had previously put off coming to the hospital until they were desperately ill, which of course confronted Dr. Garfield with costly treatments, were coming in early enough that their illnesses could be reasonably controlled. Over the years, early treatment would prove to be one of the most important features of the health plan, not only in helping to keep costs down but in minimizing the trauma that comes from serious illness.

The next closely related idea that occurred to Garfield was to find ways to reduce the number of injuries among the workers. With regular monthly payments coming in from the insurance companies, clearly it would enhance the solvency of the program to cut down on injuries. Dr. Garfield launched a campaign to educate workers on how to avoid injuries, quite innovative at that time though universally practiced today. He even took it upon himself to visit work sites to point out how practices could be changed to reduce the risks of injury. Instead of hoping for new patients, he was determined to keep people healthy enough so that they would not need medical care.

Thus was born the other cornerstone of the Kaiser Permanente Medical Care Program: Prevention. In the desert of Southern California in the depth of the depression, almost by happenstance, a young doctor was learning the principle of health preservation that would be the same driving force behind the tens of thousands of Health Maintenance Organizations (HMOs) that would spring up throughout the nation in the 1960s and 1970s. And in the 1980s when nearly everyone seems to be swept up with the craze for health preservation through exercise and diets and stress avoidance, it is interesting to recall how actually revolutionary such an idea was in the 1930s.

Fortunately, as these new concepts were taking root, Dr. Garfield was not harassed—as he would be in later years—by local medical societies. They didn't even exist in the Godforsaken areas where he was practicing. Besides, there were no governmental constraints or regulatory requirements on building and equipping the hospitals as there are today.

Encouraged by the acceptance he was gaining with the insurance companies and the workers, Dr. Garfield decided a hospital should be built near Parker Dam for the aqueduct contractors working in that area. Parker Dam on the Colorado River was to create the source of water for the aqueduct to Los Angeles. It was about 100 miles from Desert Center.

A third hospital was built at Imperial Dam, the purpose of which was to store and provide water to irrigate Imperial Valley. Each hospital was staffed with at least one physician. Other doctors were located at some first aid stations between hospitals. But Dr. Garfield was the only fully qualified surgeon and was obligated to travel between the three to provide specialized surgical care. Nevertheless, the benefits of group practice were unwittingly being experimented with.

Not many plants or flowers spring up in a desert area. When they do, it is a challenge to stay alive long enough to bloom. But when they do they often are amazingly hardy and spectacularly beautiful.

It was in the desert that this new health program took root, later to be known as the Kaiser Permanente Medical Program. It survived a shaky beginning because of two fundamental forces:

(1) Prepayment, prevention, and group practice were ideas whose time had come.

(2) The professional skill and unmatched dedication of one young surgeon, barely out of post-graduate medical school.

The other doctors who joined Garfield in the desert were all young men who shared his dreams. Over the years the thousands of doctors who would become associated with this new health program would add their own expertise and dedication. Through all the troubled times faced by a rapidly expanding organization, through all the bitter opposition they would encounter from organized medicine accusing them of introducing "socialized medicine," they never lost sight of their mission—better medicine at lower cost through group practice.

Indeed, it was the opposition that gave unity and purpose to the whole program. The doctors knew they were on the right course. To them it was medicine at its best. And they were proud of their desert heritage. It became the bond to help hold them together. It was so often the rallying point for their efforts that over the years it would quite literally become known among them as "The Desert Song."

Enter Henry Kaiser

Everyone knows the State of Washington is deluged with rain. Right? No, only partly right. West of the Cascade Range it is a verdant garden because of all the rain. East of the Cascades it is another story. Surprisingly, it's an arid region, a large portion of which is accurately called desert. At Grand Coulee on the Columbia River, about 50 miles east of the Cascades the rainfall is only 3 inches more per year than in Palm Springs in Southern California. Actually, that was one of the main reasons the Grand Coulee Dam was being built—to provide irrigation water for the dry countryside around it. It was there the second verse of The Desert Song would be sung.

Dr. Sidney Garfield had wound down his activities connected with the Los Angeles Aqueduct when that project was completed in 1938. In five years time he had ended up with retained earnings of $250,000, an incredible achievement during depression years. Not being aware of any comparable construction project that might need his services, he was eagerly looking forward to using his earnings to finance a permanent situation as a practicing surgeon in Los Angeles.

Then he received a call from A.B. Ordway, President of Industrial Indemnity Exchange, the primary insurance carrier Garfield had dealt with. More than any other person, Ord had befriended and encouraged Garfield through the tough times. Kaiser was a major partner of Industrial Indemnity and Ordway was Kaiser's oldest employee in years of service.

"Sidney," Ord asked, "do you know Edgar Kaiser?" "No," was the reply. "Well, he's just taken over the Grand Coulee Dam job. He'd like to talk to you about the medical care end of it." "I'm not interested in another temporary job," Garfield said. "I want to get my roots down in private practice. There's really no chance in my wanting to go up to Grand Coulee."

Ord argued but made no headway. Finally he said, "Will you go up there as a courtesy to me? I promised Edgar you would at least talk to him." Reluctantly Garfield conceded, "Well, I'll go up there for your sake, but both you and Edgar Kaiser should know I do not intend to stay."

Garfield recounts:

> The next thing I knew I was at the Multnomah Hotel in Portland where Edgar had temporary offices. But he was tied up, and would I wait? Six hours went by, and I was getting mad. I started trying to get a reservation back to Los Angeles. Then word came that Edgar would see me in his room. As I was walking upstairs I was rehearsing how I was going to tell him I was not interested. I knocked on the door. Sue Kaiser, Edgar's wife, opened it. She was a charming gal. She said, 'Doctor, I'm so glad to see you. There's something wrong with my daughter Becky. Could you look at her for me?' Well, that was right up my alley. I soon determined she had the measles. I calmed down a little.

> I started to tell Edgar I couldn't take the job. But he said, 'Sue and I and our two daughters are driving up to Coulee tomorrow. Won't you ride with us and at least look at the job? Maybe you can advise us what to do.'

Charmed by Sue Kaiser and intrigued by the challenge, he agreed to go. It took six hours to make the trip to Coulee. In that time Garfield acquainted Kaiser with all phases of his operations in Southern California. In turn, Kaiser pointed out how the medical program at Coulee had gotten off to an unsatisfactory start, how the union was opposed to any company-sponsored medical services. Rather than discouraging Garfield it began to sound more and more like the kind of situation he would enjoy.

"Then when I saw Coulee itself, I realized I couldn't turn it down. It was too great an opportunity to take our little desert health plan, expand it into a family health plan, take care of not only the workers but the community around the dam."

Convincing the union was another problem entirely. They knew nothing about this young surgeon from Southern California or his health program. They had an instinctive distrust of anything sponsored by the company. They would rather have set up their own hospital program, but somehow they weren't well enough organized to do so. Reluctantly, they agreed to go along with the company plan, but their initial opposition was such that thereafter Dr. Garfield went out of his way to demonstrate that his first loyalty was always to the patient, not to the company.

The toughest problem of all at the outset was the recruiting of qualified physicians. Garfield's primary doctor friends were in Southern California, but to them Washington was too far away and the Grand Coulee location itself held no appeal. The one exception—and a most important one at that—was Dr. Wally Neighbor, himself a native of Washington state. Dr. Neighbor had been physician in residence at Arrowhead Springs Hotel in Southern California, not far from Dr. Garfield's desert practice. He was a medical school associate of Dr. Garfield's and was eager to rejoin his friend at Grand Coulee. He would end up one of the foremost physicians in the Kaiser Permanente Medical Care Program.

In Seattle, because it was nearest, Garfield talked with residents at the county hospital. They had heard of the poor reputation of the Coulee medical program during the first phase of the construction when Kaiser was not involved. They were not about to associate with a project with a tainted record. It was no different in Portland, Oregon.

However, fortune was with Dr. Garfield at San Francisco General Hospital. Dr. Cecil Cutting was about to complete his residency in general surgery and orthopedics. He became intrigued by the large volume of surgical and clinical experience he could gain in a short time at Coulee. He sought moral support of the Dean of Stanford Medical School, Dr. Chandler, under whom he trained. The Dean met privately with Dr. Garfield, heard him describe the opportunity and the proposed prepayment plan at Grand Coulee. Reflecting the almost universal feelings of the medical fraternity at that time, the Dean warned Cutting not to join with Garfield. The idea of prepayment was very suspect, and the Dean thought Dr. Cutting might later be blackballed from respectable practice. That Cutting made his own decision to team up with Garfield marked him as a courageous person. Events over many decades confirmed this quality because Dr. Cutting's influence in the medical program was second only to Dr. Garfield's. As Dr. Cutting would later say, "The doctors who were willing to go to Grand Coulee had to be pretty idealistic with a lot of intestinal fortitude, dedicated to the principles of prepayment and group practice."

Up to this time, Henry Kaiser had not met Dr. Garfield. But, about four months after Garfield had gotten started at Grand Coulee, Kaiser finally showed up. Everyone was looking forward to seeing the big boss. The royal carpet treatment was arranged. Front and center were the engineers, the management team. Surely that is what Kaiser, the builder, would be most interested in.

Off-stage, somewhat apprehensive, were Dr. Garfield, Dr. Cutting and others of the medical team.

A welcoming line was formed so that everyone could shake hands with Mr. Kaiser. Dr. Cutting was a little let down because Kaiser had a somewhat brusque manner—"He had a way of shaking hands and pushing you right off, he didn't want to stop and talk," Cutting would later say. "Over the years I saw him shake hands with thousands of people. A few times his hands even got bloody from shaking hands with people wearing rings. I had to patch up his cuts a time or two, so I can understand why he didn't want to keep pumping hands."

Then Mr. Kaiser went to work. To the surprise of everyone he soon cornered Dr. Garfield. He spent the best part of that first day grilling Garfield on every aspect of his medical program at the Los Angeles Aqueduct. He was still talking to Garfield when he had to pull away to take Mrs. Kaiser to dinner at the hotel. That's when he jolted Garfield with his words: "Young man, if your idea is half as good as you say it is, it's not only good for this project, it's good for the entire country."

In that remote location and under the limitations of the temporary construction job Garfield couldn't come up with a model hospital. He did, however, procure the most modern medical equipment and he did everything possible to make the existing hospital medically worthy—repairing doors and windows, painting walls, refinishing floors, putting up curtains. Based on his desert experience he knew how important air conditioning would be. He asked Edgar Kaiser for funds to make the installation but it was rejected as being a "luxury." Garfield knew that for patients it was a necessity not a luxury, so he purchased the units with his own money saved from the aqueduct project. Edgar Kaiser criticized him but arranged to reimburse him.

By this time the workers and their union had become sold on the medical care they were receiving. However, their wives and children could only receive treatment by paying for it. This meant that many of them put off seeking medical attention because of the cost. Now it was the union's turn to appeal to the company and Dr. Garfield to provide prepaid coverage for the families. At first Garfield dragged his feet. In the Southern California desert he had not ventured into a prepayment plan for families. The union threatened to strike. Reluctantly, Dr. Garfield agreed, "Okay, Edgar, let's try fifty cents a week for the wife and twenty-five cents for each child." Those figures were picked out of thin air because nobody could find any precedent for family coverage.

Once again, a new concept began to bring unexpected results. Up until then, wives and children had been brought into the hospital only when they were desperately ill— terminal pneumonia, ruptured appendixes, late stages of breast cancer. Within a short time that disappeared. Family members started turning to the doctors in the early stages of pneumonia, appendix pains, breast lumps and other ailments.

The next even more unexpected development was that fee-for-service income increased rather than decreased. How could that be? The answer was the more satisfied the workers' families became with the medical care they were receiving, the more they would talk about it over the back fence with their neighbors.

Dr. Garfield recalled:

> The way we found out, we had one patient in who was a family plan member, with a small tumor in her breast. We performed the mastectomy.

She went back home. The next week we got four cases of lumps in the breast. None was a family plan member. They were community people who had heard about our doctors.

That was an invaluable lesson. Whenever we got into trouble with medical societies, whenever they were afraid we were going to take away their income, we could answer, 'No, you're going to make more than you have ever made, because we're going to increase the medical consciousness of the community.'

Dr. Garfield had not crossed the bridge of offering prepaid medical care to the public, but he was getting closer. It was an idea that the doctors at Grand Coulee had plenty of time to kick around during the nearly four years they were there.

Altogether, there were about 15,000 people served by the doctors and their hospital. These included not only the dam construction workers and engineers, but also the government people associated with the dam, and the townspeople.

In the small community where activities were limited, it was natural that the medical people were almost like one family. They not only worked together, most of their outside activities were with each other. They became intimately acquainted with Edgar Kaiser's family and those of the other executives and engineers, including Clay Bedford, General Superintendent of construction. At the same time the doctors and their staff became well-known and well-respected throughout the community.

As frequently as they talked about the future, they couldn't quite see how to set up a prepaid group practice in a permanent community such as the Bay Area or Los Angeles. They were keenly sensitive to the opposition they would encounter from the American Medical Association and its local affiliates. Also, they couldn't figure out how to finance such an undertaking. They knew it would be almost impossible to attract a significant membership in an urban center. In temporary isolated communities like Grand Coulee and the Southern California desert, prepaid care was easily understood and accepted. In a large city people would have established patterns of getting medical and hospital care. Advertising was unethical and unthinkable. (It's ironical that by the 1980s advertising of hospitals, health plans and medical services was being plastered all over the country.)

So, once again, as construction of the dam began winding down, it looked like the last verse of The Desert Song had been sung. Garfield returned to the county hospital in Los Angeles to refresh himself in surgery and to teach surgery at the University of Southern California. The rest of the medical staff dispersed to various parts of the country.

But the roots of this medical concept were now deep. The doctors knew in their hearts that group practice was the right way to go. They had wintered and summered with it, and they knew that it could take hold with the general public if only some way could be found to get it launched. They knew that desert flowers have a way of springing up under the most adverse conditions. And they knew that Henry Kaiser was standing in the wings looking over their shoulders, with his lifelong interest in proper medical care, his outspoken enthusiasm for the group plan the doctors had been evolving, and his proven record for crossing new frontiers.

The Big Leagues

Like everyone else at that time, Dr. Garfield was soon caught up in the swirl of activities brought on by the oncoming war. He had become First Lieutenant Garfield in the U.S. Army Medical Corps ready to go overseas in case of war. Then came Pearl Harbor and he got his notice to report for duty—assigned to India to provide medical services along the Burma Road.

Things had also begun to explode at the Kaiser Shipyards in Richmond, California, on the San Francisco Bay. Workers were streaming in from all parts of the country, large contingents actually arriving by the trainloads. Since many of them were physically unfit for military service, they were often in need of immediate medical care.

Clay Bedford was Vice President and General Manager of the shipyards. He knew the medical problems at the yards were reaching crisis proportions and would get worse as the volume of workers expanded. He had gotten to know Dr. Garfield at Grand Coulee and was completely sold on his medical techniques and on his leadership qualities. He phoned Garfield in Los Angeles, asking him to come to Richmond to set up a medical program. "Look, Clay, I'm in the army too,' Garfield said. "I've just received orders to report for duty."

Clay used the same approach Edgar Kaiser had done three years earlier. He urged Garfield to spend one month in Richmond to get the program launched. Lt. Garfield acquiesced, and spent a busy month doing the best he could to line up doctors and hospital beds. Unbeknown to Garfield, his earliest friend in the Kaiser organization— and one of his strongest supporters, A.B. Ordway—went to Washington, D.C., pointed out to the Maritime Commission the medical crisis at Richmond, and returned with a letter signed by President Roosevelt, relieving Lt. Garfield of his military obligations.

Garfield was now in the big leagues of medicine, for he would be organizing medical care for hundreds of thousands of workers at Richmond as well as Portland, Oregon, and Vancouver, Washington, where Edgar Kaiser was opening up three major shipyards. From now on, Dr. Garfield's career and the fortunes of the growing number of Kaiser Companies would be linked inseparably.

The problems were mountainous—lining up able and willing doctors when the military services themselves were drafting doctors right and left; finding makeshift hospital facilities and planning the construction of new ones; and acquainting the workers with the availability of medical services and the need to avoid illness or injury whenever possible.

A starting point was an unoccupied four-story building, a cement shell on the corner of Broadway and MacArthur in Oakland, about 12 miles from the Richmond shipyards. It had one time been Fabiola Hospital, owned by Merritt Hospital. Merritt agreed to sell it to Dr. Garfield for $50,000 and to provide 20 beds in nearby Merritt for shipyard workers until Fabiola was refurbished. The sale was accomplished in early March 1942.

Dr. Garfield took Henry Kaiser on a brief tour of the Fabiola shell. Kaiser listened intently to the plans to renovate. Somewhat discouraged by Kaiser's silence, the doctor manifested nervousness as he awaited the older man's opinion. Kaiser smiled, put his arm around Garfield, and said, "What's the matter, Sid? Don't you think I have any vision?"

Renovation would cost about $250,000. Garfield thought he would approach his old friends at Industrial Indemnity Exchange for a loan. He asked Kaiser's permission, but the industrialist expressed disfavor and suggested instead they go together to see A. P. Giannini, founder of the Bank of America. Garfield felt confident about the loan. After all, he had built, equipped, and paid for three hospitals on the desert, and had operated the Mason City hospital at Grand Coulee in the black. Giannini, the bold banker who was known to take risks that other bankers wouldn't touch, somewhat stunned them. "Doctor," he said, "I would not lend you one red cent on a hospital. If something happens, there is no way our bank could foreclose. What would we do with a hospital? However, if Henry here will guarantee the loan, you can have the money." Kaiser guaranteed the loan, and renovation of the Fabiola Hospital was commenced. With all the changes and additions that would be made to it over the years it would become the "mother" hospital of the entire Kaiser Permanente medical program. And Kaiser's financial commitment at that time would only be the start of the backing that would be necessary in the years ahead.

Dr. Garfield and Dr. Raymond Kay had been the closest of friends ever since getting out of medical school, even though they hadn't practiced together. Now Dr. Kay was shipping out of San Francisco for overseas duty. He made it a point to stress with Dr. Garfield that the time had come to establish a foundation to conduct the medical activities.

This idea was promptly broached to Clay Bedford who agreed, and who suggested that Kaiser be consulted. Kaiser was so busy that it seemed questionable how soon anybody could see him. However, right at that moment he was on a train returning from Washington, D.C. Bedford hit on the thought that Garfield should board the train at Sacramento and spend the two hours riding to Oakland with Kaiser's full attention, discussing the foundation. Bedford furnished the auto and driver to take Garfield to Sacramento.

On the train with Mr. and Mrs. Kaiser was Paul Marrin, San Francisco attorney who had been Kaiser's top lawyer and who would remain so throughout Kaiser's lifetime. The Kaisers became enthusiastic about the idea of a non-profit foundation which could own hospitals and lease them to doctors. Marrin did not think it could be done. After some discussion, Kaiser chided him, "Paul, don't tell me what I can't do. Figure out a way to do it." That would become a theme song of Kaiser in his dealings with lawyers. Lawyers working with him came to realize it was always their responsibility not to point out why something couldn't be done, but to figure out a way to get it done legally.

The Permanente Foundation was established, with Henry Kaiser as Chairman of the Board of Trustees, Bess Kaiser as trustee, along with certain Kaiser Company executives and outside attorneys. Fabiola Hospital was deeded to a new entity, Capital Construction, which reimbursed Dr. Garfield for his $50,000 investment and which assumed the liability for the $250,000 bank loan. Capital Construction then donated its assets and liabilities to the Permanente Foundation, a non-profit, charitable trust. In turn, Dr. Garfield leased the hospital from the foundation.

Dr. Garfield ran a tight ship. Dedicated doctors worked for salaries in the range of $300 to $500 per month. Garfield himself took no salary, living on an expense account. Every purchase of furniture or equipment was carefully screened.

Millie Cutting, wife of Dr. Cecil Cutting, contributed enormously to the operation of the program. As an unpaid assistant to Dr. Garfield she filled many roles. She was often the director of personnel, hiring nurses, receptionists, clerks, and some times even doctors. She purchased supplies and equipment. She found housing and generally assisted newcomers to the staff. She even drove the truck between Fabiola and Richmond Field Hospital. She entertained the staff in her home and provided board and room often for bachelor Sidney Garfield.

On one occasion, it was decided to change the format of the medical records at Richmond from 3x5 cards to 8x11 sheets. The Cuttings and Dr. Garfield transcribed the records nightly after work until the job was completed. The single luxury that Dr. Garfield allowed himself during these years was dinner with the Cuttings, and occasionally others, at a new restaurant on San Pablo Avenue in Oakland called Trader Vic's (which itself became the "Mother Church" for all the Trader Vic's restaurants that would spring up around the country and even overseas).

As soon as the initial debt to the Bank of America was paid, another $250,000 was borrowed for the first expansion, again guaranteed by Kaiser. Later $1,500,000 was borrowed from the government for a major expansion. By 1945 the old Fabiola shell had become a first-class hospital with 300 beds.

During the 4 years the Richmond shipyards were in full swing employment reached a peak in excess of 90,000. They were a strange host, not only of the healthy but the half-sick, the half-alive, the halt, the maimed, the partly blind. Thousands were 4-Fs, rejects from the draft. Thousands were women not used to the kind of heavy work they were being called upon to do. Many were old, really too old to work at all, but this was war time and everyone's services were needed in one way or another. Dr. Cecil Cutting described them as a "walking pathological museum."

Yet none was denied coverage by the health program. No preliminary examination ruled out the unfit. There were no ifs, no buts, no embarrassing questions. Long-time chronic illnesses were ignored. The same was true when the plan was soon extended to permit family members to join. Basic to Dr. Garfield's medical philosophy—from the very start in the Southern California desert until his death in 1984—was the unqualified inclusion of everyone, because indeed it's the sickliest who need medical attention the most.

As swamped as Kaiser himself was with the shipyards in Richmond and in Portland, Oregon, and Vancouver, Washington; with his big new steel mill being built at Fontana in Southern California; with his exciting new plant to produce magnesium at Permanente, California (near San Jose), alongside his growing cement plant there; he opened up on his crusade for the health program—a crusade that would only grow in fervor as the years went by.

In November 1942, he gained nationwide headlines from his ringing appeal for more doctors, for more medical care—for everyone—at a United States Senate Committee hearing in Washington, D.C. Even though his own workers were already taken care of, he saw fit to take the time and trouble to plead the cause of millions of America's underdogs who were needlessly sick, who might needlessly die, for lack of proper medical care.

Shortly thereafter, he was the principal speaker at a meeting of the National Association of Manufacturers. In his customary free-swinging style he shared with the nation's industrial leaders his dream of a post-war America needing super highways, cheaper housing, cheaper automobiles, cheaper and better airplanes, and all the products the country would be hungering for after going without during the war. What a golden opportunity to talk about a subject the manufacturers didn't expect—medicine! He threw out the challenge:

> Will the manufacturers now dare to organize, finance and manage medical centers in every industrial community, where medical service could be purchased on an insurance basis at a cost which would bring not only the skill and facilities but all the advantages of research within the reach of the common man?

He was not preaching subsidized medicine. He was not preaching socialized medicine. He was calling for leadership in establishing medical centers that would pay their own way through prepaid fees the poorest could afford. In this day and age when medical insurance is available to every person regardless of his physical condition or his age, it is a little hard to believe that just forty years ago that same message was looked upon as "a voice crying in the wilderness."

It was in this period of time that Kaiser felt the operation of the hospital program should be an "open book" to everyone who might be interested. This was not an approach he reserved only for his medical activities. More than any other industrialist, he was committed throughout his lifetime to laying bare anything and everything about his companies' operations. Because of Kaiser's talks before the Senate Committee and the Association of Manufacturers, Paul de Kruif, colorful writer who spent a lifetime promoting more medical care for the masses, saw in Kaiser the one person who could break the barriers that were limiting the benefits of proper care. de Kruif took it upon himself to become acquainted with Kaiser, and thereupon began a life-time mutual admiration society. By 1943 de Kruif had written a book on the Kaiser health program, entitled "Kaiser Wakes the Doctors." In his 1949 book, "Life Among the Doctors," de Kruif repeatedly explored the techniques and the significance of the Kaiser plan.

The start of their friendship was in New York City in late November 1942. de Kruif pumped Kaiser endlessly. Kaiser devoted all the time required to cover the subject. Then Kaiser said:

> Paul, maybe there are bugs in this health plan. Why don't you come out to the west coast, and try to find out what's wrong with it? The hospitals, the medical staff, how the workers feel about it—all of it is open to you. You can see the books and accounts, the whole set-up. You can talk to the doctors of the San Francisco Bay Area who've looked us over. Ask them. Why don't you come out and go over the details with Dr. Garfield? He originated it, and is responsible for all of it.

While all of this was going on at Richmond, an equally big hospital program was underway in the Northwest. Two Kaiser shipyards in Portland, Oregon, and one across the Columbia River in Vancouver, Washington, had about the same ship capacity as Richmond and with roughly the same number of workers, 90,000. That area also became inundated with newcomers most of whom arrived by the trainloads.

Edgar Kaiser, by now all of 33 years old, ran the three yards. Naturally, he called on Garfield to set up a hospital program simultaneously with that at Richmond. Not only did Garfield get it launched in an amazingly short time, but he even found time to design a hospital to be built a few miles east of Vancouver. Garfield's new design placed the operating rooms around a central clean support area with an outside corridor for non-clean traffic. This was the start of Garfield's obsession for more efficient hospital layouts, not only for the convenience of the doctors, but more importantly for the comfort and cheer of the patients. He introduced numerous new concepts including direct access for visitors from the outside with sliding glass doors that provide airy, bright atmosphere for the patient. He gave a lot of attention to new designs that would make it possible for mothers to have their babies with them for longer periods of time than had been customary.

Portland would have been preferable to Vancouver as a site for the hospital. There were up to 50,000 workers on the Portland side and 40,000 in Vancouver. However, in the metropolitan area of Portland there was already such an undercurrent of opposition against prepaid medicine, it was decided to establish the main base of the program in Vancouver. As a result, care for industrial conditions only was provided for workers in Portland. Non-industrial care for workers in Portland was provided through a plan in which all Portland physicians participated—not under the auspices of Dr. Garfield.

Recruiting good and committed physicians was even more difficult than in California. Most of them were provided through the Federal Procurement and Assignment Service. They had heard very little about the prepaid plan and many of them were skeptical about it, willing only to go along with it because of the war.

Nevertheless, the medical needs of the peak 90,000 shipyard workers were served remarkably well for the 4 years the shipyards were in operation. But when the yards were shut down abruptly after V-J Day in August 1945, the medical staff expressed every intention of terminating the group and health plan. Fortunately, a newcomer to the staff recognized the post-war potential of the plan. Dr. Ernest Saward, an internist, had been director during the war of the medical program for the atomic bomb Manhattan Project at Hanford, Washington. His program provided both industrial and non-industrial care for the employees. It involved group practice, a company owned and operated hospital, and salaried physicians, with emphasis on preventive care. When the project at Hanford began to wind down in the spring of 1945, he several times visited Dr. Wallace Neighbor who was directing the shipyard medical care program. Dr. Saward joined the Northern Permanente staff in June 1945.

He shared the same commitment to the health plan that Dr. Neighbor did and together, they prevailed on a majority of the doctors to continue it and to open it up to the communities of Portland and Vancouver.

The curtain had come down equally as abruptly on the shipyards in Richmond. The membership of 68,000 workers at the war's end suddenly dropped to 10,000 who voluntarily continued membership. Notwithstanding this jolt, a corps of doctors was determined to carry the program forward. Based on their own convictions, and under the gentle persuasions of Dr. Garfield and Dr. Cutting, these doctors knew they were riding a wave of the future in the field of medical practice. The names of many of these doctors would become well-known because of their medical skills and because of their dedication—A. LaMont Baritell, Morris F. Collen, J. Paul Fitzgibbon, Robert W. King, Melvin Friedman, H. Donald Grant, Norman Haugen, Thurm Dannenberg, Philip Raimondi, and other highly qualified physicians.

Peacetime Adjustments

It was in April 1945, a few months before war's end, that Paul de Kruif received a wire that helped confirm his high regard for the quality of the Kaiser medical program. It was from Dr. Karl S. Meyer, Director, Hooper Foundation, University of California:

I am highly enthusiastic over possibilities to provide prepaid medical care of the highest quality at low cost through a group organized like the Permanente Foundation under the superb direction and honest leadership of Dr. Sidney Garfield. Last Wednesday I saw the ultramodern hospital with all its excellent facilities and its staff of sincere and capable young physicians guided by the highest motive of service and research. Every possible assistance should be given to this undertaking.

Sometime later this report was received by de Kruif from Dr. William J. Ken, Professor of Medicine, University of California Medical School:

> For the past few years I have had the opportunity to observe the development of the Kaiser Foundation hospital. I am prepared to state that the quality of service to the sick is of a very high order. The members of the staff are interested in the advances in medical science and practice. Their group contribution to our community is inspiring.

It had been a great team during the war—Dr. Garfield and his coterie of dedicated doctors pioneering in every kind of medical service, and Henry Kaiser speaking out on every possible occasion, including the halls of Congress, in behalf of prepaid medicine and group practice. What made Kaiser doubly effective was that he was not just trying to build up membership in his own health plan, he was a crusader trying to arouse the medical fraternity to the enormous benefits that would accrue to all if similar health plans were launched throughout the country. He looked upon health as one of the cornerstones of a strong postwar America. And although a chorus of voices would begin to swell branding the Kaiser health plan as socialized medicine, he was totally convinced it was just the opposite, namely, that privately organized prepaid medicine was the surest way of avoiding socialized medicine.

The more vocal Kaiser became in championing prepaid medicine the more the members of the American Medical Association felt it their duty to speak out for private practice by individual doctors. Once World War II was over, the storm clouds really began to gather. The rumblings were being heard in increasing crescendo. The deep-down resentment that had smoldered so long among private physicians against any form of prepaid group medical care was now out in the open.

In retrospect, it is quite astounding that the doctors equated the Permanente Plan with socialized medicine. Kaiser and Garfield and their doctors knew from the start that their program was the best possible method of forestalling government entrance into the field of medicine.

Few doctors knew anything about Dr. Garfield's activities in the depression in the Southern California desert, so that had not stirred up any opposition. Likewise, at Grand Coulee Dam, it was in such a remote area and was temporary, so there was no occasion for the independent doctors to be up in arms. The shipyards were a different thing because of the hundreds of thousands of patients who were involved. However, ships were desperately needed during the war, and besides, individual doctors were so busy taking care of their patients they had no time to mount an attack against the Kaiser Health Plan.

With the ending of the war, a flood of skilled and quite experienced doctors, mostly young, came back seeking to get established in their own practice. To them, and to the doctors who had remained at home during the war, the Kaiser program was a clear and present threat.

One of the first salvos fired was in early 1946 after Garfield had hired a new surgeon, Dr. Clifford Keene. Dr. Keene's credentials were unimpeachable; however, he did not have a license to practice in California. Once the County Society learned of this, they filed a complaint with the California Board of Medical Examiners. Following a hearing the Board suspended Garfield's license to practice. Dr. Garfield responded by pointing out that Dr. Keene had been hired as a resident physician in surgery. It was common practice in teaching hospitals to employ residents whose license applications had not yet been processed by the State Board of Medical Examiners.

Soon a superior court lifted the suspension. But the Society would not give up; they appealed it to an appellate court. The matter became moot in the middle of 1946 when Dr. Keene was appointed Director of Industrial Medicine for the Kaiser-Frazer automobile manufacturing plant in Willow Run, Michigan. (In 1955 Dr. Keene returned to Oakland and replaced Dr. Garfield as head of the Kaiser Permanente Health Plan. He remained in that capacity until his retirement in 1975, a period of rapid growth for the plan with ever-increasing public acceptance.)

Another flare-up occurred as a result of a misunderstanding over the license of Dr. Thomas Flint, Jr. The situation was soon clarified in favor of Dr. Flint who ended up having a most distinguished career with the health plan and as an author of highly respected medical books. But it was a clear indication that the Society was looking for every opening to expose Dr. Garfield.

In this atmosphere, Permanente physicians who applied for membership in the local county medical societies were regularly denied acceptance. Membership in the local county medical association was a prerequisite to membership in the California Medical Association and the American Medical Association. Thus, Permanente physicians were prevented from participating in state and national affairs that affected doctors. Naturally, it became difficult, but by no means impossible, to recruit reputable doctors of good quality.

This almost unbelievable ostracism of Permanente physicians was more damaging to their self-perceptions and professional pride than to their capabilities of earning a living from the practice of medicine. Membership in the medical society was desirable for physicians who charge for their services, since it was usually required for staff privileges in community hospitals. Permanente doctors did not need this "seal of approval" for their practice in the Permanente hospitals.

Despite all the friendly overtures made by Kaiser and his health plan doctors to the medical profession, the juggernaut of opposition kept rolling along. It was inevitable, therefore, that the medical association would take the matter to court. On June 8, 1948, this long-awaited suit was filed:

ALAMEDA COUNTY MEDICAL ASSOCIATION

VS.

DR. SIDNEY R. GARFIELD

This suit charged Garfield with unprofessional conduct, citing these accusations:

Advertising and solicitation of patients for the health plan,

Placing mass production ahead of the health needs of the patients,

Preventing patients from having free choice of physicians,

Rendering inadequate service because the hospital was inadequately staffed,

Medical services rendered under conditions which made adequate medical care impossible,

The Foundation and Health Plan directly profited from the professional services rendered by Dr. Garfield and his associates. (In effect, Henry Kaiser was being charged with fraud—he was accused of making money under the guise of philanthropy.)

If these charges were upheld by the California Medical Association and by the courts, Dr. Garfield could be stripped of his license to practice medicine, and the Permanente Foundation could lose all its assets.

The suit was a bold, actually foolhardy, thrust. In his book, Life Among the Doctors, Paul de Kruif who had given a life time extolling the dedication and skills of American doctors, expressed his shock at the action taken by the Society:

The charges were made out of whole cloth, without any examination whatever of the books and the financial arrangements of Permanente Foundation and the Permanente Health Plan. The Alameda County Medical Association doctors had not asked to see the books; they had invented the charges. Nor had they ever investigated the medical care that Permanente Hospital and Permanente Health Plan gave its patients; nor had they requested to be allowed to make such an investigation.

But in the media-happy world in which we live it is always the charges that get the headlines, not the painstaking and time-consuming efforts involved in ferreting out the rebuttal facts. Blood had been drawn by the Society; and the newspapers and radios splashed the story for all to read and hear.

How to fight back? Tod Inch, Kaiser attorney, suggested the possibility of fighting fire with fire. He said, "If, as we believe, a conspiracy to restrain the practice of medicine exists, the State of California is by law obligated to proceed with the dissolution of the medical associations themselves."

Fight these doctors? Dissolve their medical association? That was not what Kaiser wanted to do. All his life he had looked up to doctors for their service to mankind. "I do not believe," he said, "that wars are necessary either among nations or doctors. Physicians should use their energies saving human life, not fighting each other. We must sit down with them and reason together."

Dr. Garfield was the other cool head. He was a surgeon himself and had the profoundest respect for the integrity and good intentions of most doctors. The last thing he wanted in the world was to be at war with the profession he had given his life to.

But because of the seriousness of the Society's charges, a quick yet thorough study was made of the simplest and toughest criterion of medical care and hospital services—comparative mortality in disease conditions for which there is generally recognized effective treatment. What was the rate of dying among the patients in Permanente Hospital compared to the best hospitals in California? The investigation covered the overall mortality rate for pneumoccal lobar pneumonia, for cases of perforated peptic ulcer, for appendicitis with peritonitis, and for childbirth, including that by Caesarean section.

The results were exciting. Permanente was actually better than nearly all the hospitals. Yet Dr. Garfield was careful to point out this was understandable in part because his patients were prepaid and could go to their doctors and hospitals without hesitation, whereas most people dealing with individual doctors tried to put off their hospital visits because of the looming large medical bills. The earlier you treat any curable sickness, the greater the chance of cure, the less the chance of dying.

Meeting after meeting was held by Dr. Garfield and his team, along with Henry Kaiser and a few of his key people. Interestingly, they had invited the author, Paul de Kruif and his wife, Rhea, to fly from New York and spend two weeks counseling with them in this upcoming life-and-death struggle. Here's how de Kruif described those two weeks:

> On the 8th of June, 1948, the charges came, special delivery. They left Sid not much, if anything. Worse, they left Mr. Henry J. Kaiser next to nothing. Tough cookies, these doctors, when they are out to get you.
>
> All that week, off and on, Henry J. Kaiser had been reminiscing to us about Sid, and it was clear Sid was to him as a son is to a father. Henry Kaiser—he is generally described purely as a big, bold builder and high-powered supersalesman who shoves everybody around till he gets his way— is sentimental and gentle, though maybe a bit impatient about getting what the sentimentality and gentility tells him people should have. All that weekend, banging us about in his very fast speedboats on Lake Tahoe, sitting before the big fire in our guesthouse at Homewood, or the next week in E. E. Trefethen's office in Oakland—Gene Trefethen is Kaiser's 'alter ego'—the big man thought out loud, fumbling at the thorny problem of how we could get the doctors to lay off Sid Garfield. How could we fix it so that Permanente and solo medicine could live side-by-side...maybe even co-operating?
>
> 'You see, Paul,' Henry Kaiser told me privately, 'Sid's a genius at the organization of this pre-paid group medical care, but he's the poorest salesman in the world. He knows how to do it, but when he gets up to tell it, what comes out of Sid's mouth ain't music,' said the big builder, laughing.
>
> I have never seen the genial giant so serious or sad as he was that week

giving Rhea and me the story of what the care of the sick—and the lack of it had meant to him.

Then his massive face—Gabriel Pascal has noted it is grooved deep with the pain of years, pain not physical, the same grooves you see when you look close at Sid Garfield—Kaiser's face lighted up as he told us how he'd found Sid as a youngster, absolutely unknown among the big shots of medicine, operating a clean little hospital in the desert, saving the lives of construction workers. (Actually, Kaiser first met Garfield at Grand Coulee Dam.)

'They'd never before been given decent medical and surgical care,' he said.

Henry Kaiser was forever needling Sid to get along faster with his Permanente expansion, knowing well what Sid's hurdles were, and joshing Sid about his being such a poor salesman. Now Henry Kaiser said: 'No one knows the number of lives Garfield saved as he moved his services to the big job at Coulee Dam. And then to our shipyards when there weren't enough doctors to go round, in Eastbay.'

The giant was puzzled. Didn't the Eastbay doctors see that Permanente health plan was the hope against socialized medicine? Wasn't Permanente proving there are ways to provide medical care—greater and finer than any of the government could give?

Henry Kaiser was exasperated at all this smearing and knifing of Permanente. 'Won't all thinking doctors agree that methods of spreading the cost of health --for those who can't afford their own private physician—are sure to come?' he asked. 'What's wrong with a well-worked-out, privately operated system like Permanente?'

'If they kill a system like Sid's, if Sid fails,' he said, 'they'll get compulsory government medicine.'

It is worthy of note that all of this was taking place in one of the busiest times in Kaiser's always-busy life. The Kaiser-Frazer automobile production had reached its peak and was facing very challenging market competition. The refinancing of the steel mill at Fontana—one of Kaiser's knottiest problems of all—had not been solved. Kaiser Aluminum was growing so fast it continually posed new problems of how to bring it about. And yet here was Kaiser spending days on end making sure that his hospital program would survive.

Finally, a show-down meeting was held in the office of Gene Trefethen, Kaiser's top aide, and a person universally admired for his cool and detached judgment. Most participants, including surprisingly de Kruif, wanted to take the results of the study and blast the other hospitals. Here's how de Kruif described that meeting:

To my astonishment, Henry Kaiser did not want to take this action. 'I don't claim that Permanente is perfect,' Kaiser said slowly. 'I don't claim that Blue Cross is perfect or that the California Physicians Service is perfect or that numerous other kinds of plans are perfect. I only know,' he said gently, 'that encouraging them all will eventually prove which prepaid medical plan best for all. I only know this war between doctors can only force a delay in the ultimate correct answer.'

de Kruif went on to write:

That afternoon Henry Kaiser made me feel very small. While some of us wanted to strike back because of the unfairness of the charges, Kaiser reminded us that nothing would be gained by trying to damage the opposition.

Like all court cases, the suit against Dr. Garfield dragged on and on. Somehow the medical association was not inclined to press for prompt action. The doctors seemed content to let the court case hang over Dr. Garfield's head. After a year had passed Gene Trefethen would write this interoffice memorandum on June 19, 1949:

Today I called Dr. Barnard and he advised me that he had received a copy of James M. Neil, M.D.'s letter of June 13 to the Hon. William James, copy of which has been sent to you and is attached hereto.

He further stated that he felt that no decision would be made on this matter until such time as the proceedings were completed as set forth in this letter, and that he estimated that it would be approximately two months before such a decision was reached.

I then asked him how Permanente was getting along and he replied, 'I haven't heard of a single complaint against Permanente in months'; after which I asked him, 'Is that all?'. His reply was, 'As a matter of fact I have heard many good things about Permanente of late.'

I advised him that it was unfortunate that these proceedings had to be carried forward for otherwise we could be working more constructively with them on various matters of interest to the Medical Society and to Permanente—to which he made no comment.

Soon after that Sid Garfield's trial was postponed. Then a committee of Alameda County Medical Association physicians took Mr. Kaiser up on his suggestion for them to begin their own investigation of how the Permanente Hospitals were operated and how the books were kept. In that atmosphere the acrimony of most independent doctors began to fade. A few months later Superior Court Judge Edward P. Murphy ordered the State Board of Medical Examiners to rescind all action against Dr. Garfield.

Like any bitter battle, some scars remained. But the threat to Dr. Garfield's license to practice medicine was over. And the independent doctors, as well as the community at large, had learned that Kaiser would never do anything to hurt the medical profession, but would only seek to encourage and support it.

Over the years, Dr. Garfield had been in contact with Dr. Ray Lyman Wilbur, past president of the American Medical Association, and past president of Stanford University. During the pendency of the court case Garfield had once more turned to Dr. Wilbur. The friendly, kind veteran of a lifetime in medicine counseled Garfield:

> Young man, you are not wearing a crown of thorns. Nothing new or good has ever been achieved without strong opposition. If you were not opposed, it would be because you were not contributing anything worthwhile. You are very fortunate. Not only are you doing something new and good for the people, you are doing something new and good for the doctors of this country, and you should be very happy.

All In The Family

Kaiser's fascination with the medical world was born into him. Nothing was more natural to him than getting involved with doctors and hospitals and health care. If he had not early in life experienced the thrill of running his own businesses, if instead someone had encouraged him to study medicine and had suggested a way of paying for it, he could well have become a doctor himself.

His wife, Bess, shared his leanings. From the time she first met Dr. Garfield at Grand Coulee in 1938 she gave more attention to the health program than any of the other exciting new activities her husband was breaking into. She was always by his side encouraging him to do more and more to promote the doctors' efforts. She was the one who liked the name Permanente. That was the name of the creek in the hills near San Jose. The Spanish named it Permanente because, unlike most of the coastal range streams, it didn't dry up in the summer time. In 1939 Kaiser had built a cement plant near the creek due to the availability of limestone there, and since Permanente was synonymous with the long-lasting character of cement, that became the name of the company. Bess felt it would likewise be descriptive of the hospital program—a permanent, enduring activity that the public could depend on.

The doctors and nurses at the hospital became part of her family. She was closer to Dr. Garfield and to Dr. Cecil and Millie Cutting than almost anyone else in the Kaiser organizations. In a way, they filled the void in her own family. She was very devoted to her two sons, but she never really accepted her daughters-in-law in a warm, companionable way. She seemed to feel that they were somehow intruding upon the flow of attention she expected from her sons. Some of Edgar's children have frankly acknowledged that their grandmother didn't like their mother and for long periods of time would hardly talk to her. More surprising, Bess (and for that matter, Kaiser himself) spent very little time with her grandchildren. They hardly got to know her. She never became a second mother to them, as most grandmothers do.

This strange craving for center stage was not confined to her dealings with her daughters-in-law. She tried to be motherly to some of the key men working for her husband, but even then several of the wives felt she resented the fact that these men had first loyalty to their own wives. This quality never became generally known within the company, and certainly not on the outside. No doubt it was a matter of some concern to Henry Kaiser but he had such faith that things would always work for the best, and he was so incredibly busy, he couldn't allow himself to be weighed down by family differences. To him, and to the world, the far-flung Kaiser operations would always be one family.

Bess's attachment with the hospital people grew over the years. During the war her second son, Henry J. Kaiser, Jr., began suffering increasingly from multiple sclerosis, a disease first detected when he was a student at Stanford. This called for an all-out effort by the doctors to find some cure, so Bess was regularly in touch with them regarding her son's condition.

In time Bess herself began to need more and more medical attention. She was an extremely heavy woman, not very active physically, and numerous ailments began to show up requiring the highest priority of attention by the doctors and nurses. In the last year of her life ending March 14, 1951, it would become an almost around-the-clock challenge to try to keep her alive. Here's how Dr. Cutting described it:

> I happened to be lucky enough to hit her veins for intravenous treatments, which wasn't all that easy because of her weight, so she didn't want anybody but me to be her doctor. For close to a year, I practically lived at their apartment at the Bellevue Staten in Oakland. At least I went in and out every day. I'd draw blood, rush over to the hospital to test it, and then bring back the appropriate medicine to keep her chemistry balanced. It was a constant struggle. We'd get her feeling better, so she'd get up for a while. She loved to go to Trader Vic's for dinner, but at times we would almost have to carry her in. The next day she might feel worse and we would have to start all over. Naturally, during that time I came to know Henry Kaiser extremely well.

It was Millie Cutting who recommended the full-time nurse for Mrs. Kaiser. Alyce Chester was supervisor of the emergency department working closely with Dr. Don Grant. She was a thoroughly trained and competent nurse. Her natural good cheer and dedication made her the logical choice to take on the demanding job of caring for Mrs. Kaiser. Ale, as she was known, not only attended to Mrs. Kaiser's medical needs but became her constant companion, going out in the evenings with Mr. and Mrs. Kaiser whenever Mrs. Kaiser's condition permitted it. As Bess's health deteriorated, Mr. Kaiser was finding how much he was depending on the liveliness and sharpness of the 34-year-old nurse half his age. To those close to the scene it became apparent that Kaiser was developing a strong attraction for Ale.

After Mrs. Kaiser's death it was no surprise that Kaiser married Ale. What did surprise everyone was how soon the marriage took place—only 27 days later. This important turning point in Kaiser's life, and its impact on what he would do and what his relations would be with his key people, is covered in Chapter 12. For purposes of this chapter, it is sufficient to point out that the marriage to Ale only enhanced Kaiser's involvement with the hospital people because of the close ties that existed between them and Ale. Over the 16 years of their marriage, she would encourage him at every turn to expand the hospital program. Because of her experience and brightness she became influential in bringing about improvements in medical practices and hospital designs. The opening for this also arose in part because of her close relations with the Cuttings. Then the clincher came when shortly after Kaiser's marriage, Dr. Sidney Garfield (who had been married previously for a short time just a few years earlier) married Ale's sister, Helen. Kaiser was so pleased at the prospect of Dr. Garfield and Helen getting married he became a virtual cupid, doing everything possible to bring their marriage about. It had become one big, happy, hospital family and the Garfields were soon the most frequent evening companions of the Kaisers.

It almost seemed that Kaiser's marriage to Ale, a nurse, was foreordained. His own mother had been a practical nurse who cared for her patients in her home and theirs. She had symbolized everything tender and inspirational in his life. To him nurses were angels of mercy in the most real sense. Just the year before he married Ale he told the 1950 graduating class of the Kaiser Foundation School of Nursing:

> You who have entered nursing have chosen a profession of giving—giving always of yourself, your toil, your sympathy and human understanding, your knowledge of the medical and nursing science, forever giving to your afflicted fellow man. You are performing one of the greatest of all services to mankind.

The continuing illness of Henry Kaiser, Jr., created another strong bond between Kaiser and the hospital group. Kaiser was determined to track down every possible treatment that might arrest or even reverse the nerve disintegration that multiple sclerosis was bringing on his son. Word came that Dr. Herman Kabat, a neurophysiologist, working alone in his home in Washington, D.C., had been having success in treating MS through the use of prostigmin. Immediately, this was tried on Henry, Jr., with very encouraging initial results. The other therapy Dr. Kabat was having success with was vigorous physical exercise which helped to rebuild nerve-muscles.

Henry Kaiser would have nothing but that Dr. Kabat should join the Kaiser Permanente Health Plan. Kabat agreed and by 1946 he and Garfield established the Kabat-Kaiser Institute in Oakland. Later when the facilities in Oakland became crowded the center of rehabilitation efforts moved to the Vallejo, California, Permanente Hospital, about 20 miles away. Nothing was spared to make it possible for Dr. Kabat to achieve his hoped-for breakthrough in the treatment of multiple sclerosis victims. Another type of patient treated at the institute involved several hundred coal miners who suffered spinal cord injuries. These men, members of the United Mine Workers, were sent by train from their homes in West Virginia and Kentucky. To one degree or another, thousands were benefitted by the treatment provided by the institute, but in time, the other Kaiser hospitals could offer much of the same rehabilitation practices pioneered by the institute. Without doubt, Dr. Kabat had eased the suffering of Henry Kaiser, Jr., and had helped him maintain a degree of vigor that added to his enjoyment of life. In the end, however, the deteriorative process could not be reversed and, tragically, Henry Kaiser, Jr., died in 1961, at age 44. His father knew that he had done everything in his power to save his son; and Henry Jr.'s valiant struggle became an inspiration to all who knew him.

A Family Squabble

Some of the worst squabbles of all can be in the family. If you're in an argument with an outsider, you can call him all the names you want, or you can walk away from the controversy, or you can go to court.

But if you're having a donnybrook with someone in your own family, you've got to try to sweat it out. Your feelings can run just as strong, or stronger, but you have to hang in there until you resolve it.

A family squabble in Kaiser Permanente? How could that be, considering how all parties had stood together through some very tough times? The doctors knew their achievements would have been impossible without Henry Kaiser. He in turn knew the doctors were the very heart and soul of the whole program. Together, they had weathered, and were still weathering, bitter opposition from the medical establishment.

The schism was slow in taking shape, almost imperceptible at times, but it was really quite inevitable, and would keep the parties on edge for five years. There were two primary forces at the root of the problem:

(1) The rapid growth of the health plan with its myriad of new activities that had not been encountered before. Differences of opinion were bound to crop up as to how to handle all these new problems.

(2) On the one hand, the determination of the doctors to maintain the integrity of their medical freedoms and responsibilities; and on the other hand, the strong convictions of Kaiser and his associates that the program should be run as a business, with the doctors working for that business.

The growth after the war was not just surprising, it was phenomenal. Once the shipyards closed down, the membership dropped abruptly from more than 60,000 to less than 10,000. In less than two years, however, it had bounced back to 60,000; by April 1948 it had reached 72,000; and six years later, it was serving 400,000 members in the three west coast states.

To cope with this kind of growth, it was agreed early on there should be three separate entities:

1. The Permanente Health Plan. This was the business end of the operation. Its duties were to build membership and to administer financial affairs.

2. The Permanente Foundation Hospitals. This was to arrange financing for the growing number of hospitals and to oversee their operations.

3. The Permanente Medical Group. This was a partnership of doctors free to practice their medicine without answering to businessmen.

One reason for this separation was to build a defense against the harassment of medical societies. It was felt that the critics would have difficulties in creating problems for a partnership of physicians, particularly when the partners were persons who were known and respected in the medical community. It was also a way of saying to the world that the doctors were not employees of a health plan corporation or of Henry Kaiser.

At first, Dr. Garfield was the moving force in all three entities. Then it was realized that as Executive Director of the Health Plan and the Hospitals, he was tainted in his role as managing partner of the Medical Group. Thereupon, he resigned from the Medical Group hoping this would underscore the total freedom of the doctors.

One major project brought out in the open the differences between Kaiser and the doctors. With his marriage to the young nurse, Ale, in April 1951, Kaiser's interest in medical and hospital activities immediately spurted. For her part, Ale, sensitive to coolness she received from executives of the industrial companies, wanted to strengthen her ties with nursing and hospitals. Together they proposed building a Kaiser Permanente Hospital in Walnut Creek, California, not far from their new home in Lafayette. The hospital would be model for everything that was best in hospital design—attractive, efficient, and dedicated to personal service. This showplace hospital would serve some 5,000 health plan members from Walnut Creek and surrounding communities.

Kaiser personally supervised construction of the new hospital to insure that it would be the exemplary institution he intended. As usual with him, speed of construction was all important, with very little concern for costs. Kaiser donated $700,000 and Bank of America loaned $800,000.

The Permanente Medical Group Executive Committee was not consulted about building the Walnut Creek hospital. Although the Foundation Board had the right to build whatever and wherever it pleased, the Medical Group assumed that it would be responsible to provide care and should have been consulted. Some leaders of the Medical Group were of the opinion that it was inappropriate to allocate scarce resources to a "luxury and showplace" hospital in a community with only 5,000 enrollees. Meeting the needs of members in the other Bay Area Permanente facilities seemed more important.

Then the Medical Group was stung when Ale Kaiser took it upon herself to select Dr. Wally Cook to be Physician-in-Chief of the hospital, along with other doctors of her choosing. Now the Medical Group was convinced their responsibility and authority had been usurped.

Kaiser decided that the way to cope with the medical group was to establish a separate doctor's partnership at Walnut Creek. He even leaned toward that idea for each hospital. But this was anathema to the doctors. They sensed that this would be the means of splitting the doctors up and weakening their position in the whole program. They were convinced they had to stand together if they were to have any kind of balance of power in dealing with Kaiser. In that atmosphere Dr. Cook and his Walnut Creek colleagues decided to stick with the group. It could very well have been that if they had splintered at that time, the history of Kaiser Permanente could have been quite different.

Dr. Garfield was in the middle. He realized how terribly important it was for Kaiser and his new wife, the nurse, to be so deeply involved in the hospitals' activities, yet he knew in his heart that the medical people must remain independent. So he took it upon himself to try to win Kaiser over to that basic concept. It wasn't easy. Kaiser was accustomed to running whatever business he got into. And he was not quite able to see the distinction between the hospital program and his other businesses. To him it should be a matter of pride to be called a "Kaiser" doctor. But the doctors cringed at being called a Kaiser doctor. They are doctors in their own right who are proud of their professional skills and their dedication to their patients, and they justifiably want to be recognized as such.

Here's how the stalemate was described years later by Dr. Cecil Cutting:

> Mr. Kaiser felt strongly that he should run anything he was part of. He was so dynamic and powerful he could only feel comfortable when he had hold of the reins. On the other hand, we doctors felt we must not be employees of anyone. We didn't want lay domination of our practice. He held his ground, we held our ground, and it came to some pretty rough table pounding and pretty hot words for a while. It finally got to the point in 1955 where it looked like our whole program might be collapsing, where no agreement could be reached on current operations or plans for future growth. We all knew that something had to be done or we would soon be parting company. That's when Mr. Kaiser said, 'Come up to my place at Lake Tahoe, off campus from the hospitals. We'll work it out. We won't come back until we do.'

> We spent close to two weeks at the lake. We all had a chance to let off steam. We came to understand each other's point of view more clearly. The tone for the meeting was set by Gene Trefethen. He was the great compromiser. In the end we reached a working relationship that satisfied both sides. Indeed, we had laid a solid foundation that would insure a bright new future for our medical program.

A Lifetime Commitment

Kaiser never tired of working on hospital problems. It was a good change of pace from the corporate matters he wrestled with in his industrial companies. He knew and understood all phases of the hospital program more intimately than anyone else, save perhaps Dr. Garfield. He knew personally most of the doctors and many of the nurses. He was like a father to them. Above all, he believed in the importance of the hospital work with all his heart and soul. As a result, scarcely a day went by, certainly never a week, without his making phone calls, or writing letters, or holding meetings dealing with one phase or another of the health care program.

It was an ideal arrangement—the doctors absorbed in doing their best to offer advanced medical service, with Kaiser being their champion at every turn. There is no way this group of physicians could have captured the public interest without someone as well-known and as forceful as Kaiser speaking out for them.

Kaiser personally made phone calls and wrote letters to Charles Wilson, president of General Motors, and to Benjamin Fairless, chairman of the board of United States Steel, inviting them to visit Permanente Hospitals so that hopefully they would encourage their employees to become members of the health plan. He likewise importuned David McDonald, president of the United Steelworkers of America, to set up programs for union members to join the health plan wherever Kaiser hospitals were conveniently located.

He also kept up his contacts with Congress, freely offering to write letters and appear before committees in behalf of bills that would assist hospital programs all around the country, including those sponsored early by Senator Robert F. Wagner and later by Representative Charles A. Wolverton. Then on February 27, 1954, he wrote a detailed letter to President Eisenhower commending him for his involvement in health matters and requesting the opportunity to discuss the subject with him. He ended his letter:

> I agree with you we should carefully avoid the socialization of medicine. . . . I am sure that independent groups of doctors throughout the country, assisted by enactment of the Wolverton Bill, would themselves provide the needed voluntary health plans and facilities to meet what you have forcefully pointed out are the severe hardships imposed on families by rising medical costs.

Thereafter, Kaiser rallied all his forces to help bring about passage of the Wolverton Bill. He wrote personal letters to all the Congressmen who served in any of the districts where his various plants were located. He gave an important talk before the National Press Club on "The New Economics of Medical Care." He wrote to newspaper editors throughout the country, as well as radio and television stations. In all of these efforts he was careful to point out he was not just championing the case for the Permanente Health Plan, he was vigorously advocating that doctors, hospitals and private groups of all kinds should organize their own programs of health care for the benefit of as many people as possible.

Notwithstanding the numerous times various branches of the American Medical Association had attacked Kaiser and the Permanente Health Plan he never once ceased in his efforts to cooperate with them in any way he could. By 1954 he had transferred his base of operations to Honolulu where he looked forward to building a hospital there and opening up his health plan for the people of that city. He was careful, however, not to make any moves that would be construed as being antagonistic to the existing medical fraternity there. Indeed, he went out of his way to offer support to the Hawaiian Medical Association. They had written him on January 23, 1955, appealing to him "not to introduce" the Kaiser Foundation Plan in Hawaii. Within a week he responded with a comprehensive four-page letter urging the Association itself to initiate its own kind of prepaid medicine and offering to assist in getting such a program started. In this letter he volunteered:

> We respectfully suggest for your consideration the Hawaiian Medical Association itself take the leadership in assuring the doctors and the people of Hawaii a complete freedom of choice between two basic types of health plans. This could readily be accomplished if your association adds to your existing fee-for-service indemnity plan an alternate group practice, prepayment, direct care plan for all doctors and patients who desire it. You can call upon the Kaiser Foundation Health Organizations for every possible cooperation if you desire to add an alternative service type health plan to HMSA's existing coverage. We shall be glad to make available to you findings from more than 20 years of experience regarding facilities and health plan benefits and operations, as well as to assist in planning integrated facilities and other phases of the program. I shall look forward to meeting with your House of delegates, because I have been impressed by your declared desire to explore means of broadening health protection for the people, and I believe it is within your power to pioneer a medical care program that will make a tremendous contribution in this vital field.

The Association never took Kaiser up on his offer. Obviously, this meant the door was open for him to go forward with his own program whenever he felt the time was right. And there certainly couldn't have been any doubt among Association doctors that Kaiser would do just that, because he was so convinced of the benefits to both doctors and patients in prepayment and group practice.

Actually, Kaiser was so busy with his other projects in Hawaii it was not until three years later—January 1958—that he first broke ground for his Honolulu hospital. For the story on this, see Chapter 11, Hawaii Calls.

A New Job For Sid

Kaiser had a great talent for delegating authority—and responsibility. Once he judged a person's capability he never hesitated to pile work on him. He knew that in such a situation a person would strive energetically to live up to what was expected of him. At the same time, Kaiser had a "sixth" sense that would let him know if things were not coming along as they should. In such circumstances, he would never hesitate to step in and help out. He knew almost instinctively when it was time for him to use his experience and prestige to get something done.

He tried to encourage this same approach by the people who worked for him. He wanted them to free themselves from as much detail as possible in order that they might be more creative on more important matters. He wanted them to be developing capable people under them so that if anything happened to the top person there would be somebody ready to take over the job.

With these considerations in mind, Kaiser had begun wondering whether the time had come to give Dr. Garfield freedom from some of his daily pressures so he could do more long-range planning, possibly becoming a force nationally for the development of prepaid health plans. For the twenty years Garfield's health plan had been in existence it had been molded and shaped by him to the extent that it was virtually an extension of his own personality and his commitment to medicine. Garfield was still a young man—only 45 years of age at the time—yet Kaiser could see benefits both to Garfield and the health program by making some changes.

He was influenced along that line by reason of the fact that Dr. Clifford Keene who had done such an outstanding job as medical director of Kaiser-Frazer in Willow Run, Michigan, for nearly eight years was free to return to the West Coast by late 1953. Keene had become highly regarded by Edgar Kaiser, who was president of Kaiser-Frazer. Others shared Edgar's view that Keene could take over some of Garfield's duties. To bring that possibility into focus, Henry Kaiser wrote a letter to Dr. Garfield, December 5, 1953, stating in part:

If Keene is willing to accept such a position, and since it was agreed that it should be stated to him that such a position is open, it now becomes clear that if he is willing to accept it, and the trustees favor it, there should be no great harm in trying him out. Personally, I am certain there could be no harm if you would give every assistance possible to make him a success in such a position. There could be harm only if you are unwilling to indoctrinate another individual into the day to day detail work that you have been doing in the area.

It might be a good idea to call a meeting of all the heads of the different departments with the trustees and have a thorough discussion of this plan. . . .

You know and I have stated many times that I need you and your time to fulfill objectives which I have to develop you in a situation where you would become a national figure in the development of better medical care for more people at a lower cost.

Not long thereafter Dr. Keene was offered the opportunity to take over some of Garfield's duties. Although his work at Willow Run was winding down, it was not an easy decision for Dr. Keene. He knew many of the doctors working for Garfield would not take too kindly to the prospect of having someone placed over them who had not wintered and summered with the health plan itself. It was not enough for

Edgar Kaiser to urge him to take the job. He had to hear from both Henry Kaiser and Dr. Garfield that they genuinely wanted his services and would give the strong backing to insure his being accepted by the group of doctors.

It turned out to be a wise move. Dr. Keene was an experienced surgeon who understood all the ramifications of proper health care. He had a more outgoing and outspoken way about him than Dr. Garfield. At first, this became a source of annoyance to the doctors who had become accustomed to the soft-spoken, gentle persuasions of Dr. Garfield. In time, however, Dr. Keene won the confidence of the doctors and provided the kind of leadership that would greatly contribute to a period of remarkable growth in the membership of the health plan.

Long after Henry Kaiser's death in 1967 Keene would state that the two most powerful personalities that he looked up to in life were Henry Kaiser and General Douglas MacArthur. Partly because of this awe in which he held Henry Kaiser, and partly because Kaiser's natural affection was towards Dr. Garfield, Keene found himself struggling to win Kaiser's total confidence. By the time Keene had assumed his new responsibilities, Kaiser had become headquartered in Hawaii, and this meant special trips to seek approval on specific actions. It was not at all like the free-flowing relationship that Dr. Garfield had enjoyed with Kaiser when they were located near each other and could react jointly to problems as they arose. Because of this separation from Kaiser on a day-to-day basis, and because Dr. Keene wanted so desperately to earn Kaiser's favor, there were several trips to Hawaii where he ended up totally frustrated and personally piqued. This was not a sign of weakness—everyone agreed Dr. Keene was a strong person—it was only a measure of how much he wanted the kind of relationship with Kaiser that Dr. Garfield had enjoyed.

At the same time Dr. Garfield was finding it a little difficult to adjust to having someone else share in his leadership role. He would instinctively be inclined to interject himself in a particular situation, yet he knew some things should be turned over to Dr. Keene. Finally, he mentioned to Kaiser the difficulty he was having in delegating his responsibilities while still maintaining an active and meaningful role. Kaiser promptly wrote this letter to Garfield on January 28, 1955. One can just imagine how much fun Kaiser had in writing this masterpiece of goodwill and good humor:

> Last night I was disturbed when you remarked to me that you had nothing to do and no longer controlled anything. I looked up the records of the last hospital meetings on January 5, 1955, and find from the charts and resolutions adopting these charts that you are -
>
> 1. Executive Director, The Kaiser Foundation
> 2. Executive Director, Kaiser Foundation Hospitals
> 3. Regional Director, Southern California Region Kaiser Foundation Hospitals
> 4. Executive Director, Kaiser Foundation Health Plan
> 5. Regional Director, Southern California Region Kaiser Foundation

Health Plan
6. President-Trustee, Kaiser Foundation School of Nursing
7. Executive Vice-President, Kaiser Foundation Northern Hospitals
8. Executive Director, The Utah Permanente Hospital

and in addition Personal Physician to Henry J. Kaiser.

Too bad, Sid, you have nothing to do and don't control anything! It looks to me like I'll have to find something else for you to do as these duties apparently are not enough. I'll have you fix my foot in the morning.

All my love.
Henry J. Kaiser

P.S. Should you be neglecting any of these control responsibilities, you might advise me.

Best Years Ahead

The one thing that bothered Henry Kaiser most during his early days in the construction business was its temporary nature. You complete one project, then what do you do? That's why a lifetime goal of his was "to build a business that will never know completion."

While the doctors would balk at calling the health care program a "business," they knew there should never be any end to the kind of services they were providing the public. And of all the ventures Kaiser was involved in, the one that had the greatest chance to keep on growing and growing, was health care.

This had become evident before Kaiser died in Hawaii in 1967 at age 85. By that time the Kaiser Permanente Medical Care Program was already the largest HMO (Health Maintenance Organization) in the United States.

Members	1,683,000
Physicians	1,630
Hospitals	18

But that was only the beginning. The idea that Dr. Sid Garfield had chanced upon in the desert more than thirty years before was really taking off despite the fact that he had now become only a consultant, and despite the fact that Henry Kaiser was no longer looking over anyone's shoulder with his perpetual enthusiasm, and despite the fact that the original cadre of dedicated physicians who had stood shoulder-to-shoulder with Garfield in the early days had been replaced by a legion of highly skilled doctors. Clearly, it was that idea—prepayment, prevention, early treatment, comprehensive services, group practice—that would keep the program intact and would insure its inexorable growth.

Here's where the program stood in 1990:

Voluntarily enrolled membership	6 million plus

Regions served:
Northern California
Southern California
Oregon/Washington
Colorado
Ohio
Hawaii
Mid-Atlantic States
Texas
Connecticut/New York/Massachusetts
North Carolina
Georgia
Kansas/Missouri

Physicians, representing all specialties, who devote all their professional time caring for Kaiser Permanente members	8,000
Nonphysician health care professionals and administrative, clerical and technical employees	68,000
Medical centers	28
Licensed hospital beds	7,000
Medical office locations for outpatient services	150
Value of land, buildings and equipment	$5 billion

Kaiser Permanente is an epoch in American medical history; indeed, an epoch in American history. It was the forerunner of the countless prepaid and group practice medical care programs that have sprung up all over the country.

It is the story of thousands of skilled and dedicated doctors who stood firm in their commitment to provide the best possible medical services at the lowest possible costs. It is the story of tens of thousands of nurses who gave of themselves to bring comfort to those in need of care. It is the story of millions of patients who decided to entrust their lives to this revolutionary and sometimes embattled program of health care.

But most of all it is the story of two men: Dr. Sidney R. Garfield and Henry J. Kaiser. One a practicing surgeon just out of medical school. Shy, soft-spoken, self-effacing, idealistic, imaginative, tenacious. The other, America's foremost industrialist. Bold, visionary, optimistic, dedicated to the urgency of good medical care.

An unlikely pair. Yet a most likely pair. A father-son relationship. An old man-young man relationship. A doctor-patient relationship. Kaiser would never have impacted on the medical world the way he did if he had not met Garfield. In turn,

Garfield could never have made it to the big time without Kaiser's forceful backing.

If they could be taken back in time to stand on the dam at Grand Coulee, Washington, where they first met in 1938, they would share rich memories of what they did together. When their musing was over, their parting shot to each other would most assuredly be:

"Kaiser Permanente's best years are still ahead."

CHAPTER 5

"MIRACLE METAL"

"I always have to dream up there against the stars. If I don't dream I'll make it, I won't even get close."

Jesse H. Jones, Federal Loan Administrator, was in a hurry as he left the Shoreham Hotel in Washington, D.C., that February morning in 1941. He climbed into his car, but before his chauffeur could close the door an uninvited guest, Henry Kaiser, slipped in and sat alongside him. Jones graciously spread the lap robe over Kaiser's knees, and the conversation began.

Kaiser had been trying for days to win the hardheaded Jones' approval for a loan to build a magnesium plant on the West Coast. Finally, late one afternoon when Kaiser and his aides finished discussing their proposal, Jones said, "I'll think it over. I'll be working late tonight and you can call me about nine o'clock at my office."

When Kaiser called at nine, Jones was gone. He then phoned Jones' room at the Shoreham Hotel where he himself was staying. No answer. The next morning early, Kaiser called again. "Mr. Jones is sleeping and can't be disturbed," a voice chided him. Neither pride nor vanity ever stood in Kaiser's way. He called every twenty minutes until he got Jones on the phone.

"You told me to call you at your office at nine last night," began Kaiser. "I did, and you weren't there."

"I ran out on you, didn't I?" replied Jones. "I'll see you in the lobby in half an hour."

Kaiser was waiting downstairs when Jones swept out of the elevator. He rushed to greet Jones, but to his astonishment, the great Government banker swept imperiously past him without a flicker of recognition. Kaiser flushed. Then he streaked through the whirling door just as Jones was stepping into his limousine. Without hesitating, he piled in the car next to Jones. He was not about to miss this opportunity for a one-on-one conversation on a subject that was so near and dear to him.

It was quite surprising that Kaiser had become so fascinated with magnesium. It was not a metal like steel, or even aluminum, that he had worked with in his road-building and dambuilding days. But to him it was some kind of miracle metal because of its extreme lightness. He knew the Germans were dominating the air in Europe with their Stuka dive bombers, and he attributed this in part to the generous use of magnesium. He pointed to Germany's reported output of 100,000 tons of magnesium annually as compared with America's pitiful production of only 6,500 tons. By late 1940 he had convinced himself he was just the one to get America rolling in the manufacture of magnesium.

Three factors helped trigger Kaiser's determination to get into the magnesium business:

(1) Nevada had large deposits of magnesite, the primary ore from which magnesium is refined. One of the main sources was Gabbs which was less than 300 miles from Permanente, California, where Kaiser wanted to put up his plant.

(2) In late 1940 Kaiser had become acquainted with Dr. F. J. Hansgirg, Austrian scientist and a refugee from the Nazis. Hansgirg had successfully produced magnesium by a new "Carbothermic" process in a plant in Korea built for the Japanese, and another at Swansea, Wales, built for the British. After Kaiser and his men studied the process, they became convinced it would work.

(3) One main feature of the process was precipitation of the metal from vapor after the ore had been heated in kilns to 2,300 degrees Fahrenheit. At that point a terrific blast of cold natural gas would precipitate the metal in powder form. Amazingly, the natural gas did not lose any of its heating qualities and could be recaptured as the heating agent in the cement kilns. By building his magnesium plant next door to his cement mill, Kaiser would thus get double duty from his natural gas.

That uninvited limousine ride apparently did the trick. On February 19, 1941, Jones announced that the Reconstruction Finance Corporation would "grant $9,250,000 to Henry J. Kaiser interests for construction of a huge magnesium plant near San Francisco which, when in operation, is expected to double the nation's present output of that metal." Kaiser had asked for $10 million, but Jones balked at $750,000 which was supposed to pay for the carbothermic patent.

At that time various reports came out that Tommy ("The Cork") Corcoran pulled the strings to secure Jones' approval of the loan. Corcoran, who had been an intimate adviser to President Roosevelt, was at that time doing some Washington contact work for a law firm that represented Todd Shipyards Corporation. In early 1941 Kaiser was president of Todd-California Shipbuilding Corporation, and it was this entity that was prepared to stand behind the loan.

Although Kaiser always maintained respect for Corcoran's abilities, he did not concede that Corcoran had played a meaningful role in securing the loan. There is no evidence that Kaiser had ever asked for any assistance. In a hearing before Senator Ball in June 1941 Corcoran highlighted various contacts he had made for the law firm, including some efforts in behalf of Todd Shipyards:

Senator Ball:	You were never retained by Kaiser directly?
Mr. Corcoran:	No.
Senator Ball:	There was a story in <u>News Week</u>, I think, about your having presented a bill to Kaiser for $34,000.
Mr. Corcoran:	I saw that story in <u>News Week</u>. I have never had any direct financial relations with Mr. Kaiser.
Senator Ball:	Did you represent any of the patent holders on this magnesium process?
Mr. Corcoran:	No, I represented the people who were trying to buy the patents.

(It was a nice gesture on Corcoran's part two years later when <u>Fortune</u> magazine of May 1943 quoted him: "Kaiser is one of the great natural resources of a nation at war.")

Kaiser's men were ecstatic. They promised "the boss" they would have the new plant running within five months. They were even predicting their costs would be the lowest of any method the government might consider for other magnesium plants. "It's a thrilling achievement to take a raw material worth four bits a ton and turn it into a metal worth five hundred and forty dollars a ton to the United States Government," gloated Harry Davis, who was superintendent of the cement mill and who was also going to head up the new magnesium project. Davis had a paternalistic interest—he was a next-door neighbor of Hansgirg and brought him in touch with Kaiser.

But alas, the new technique was more difficult than Kaiser and his men had bargained for. From its very inception the venture was trouble-prone. The carbothermic-reduction method had not been completely perfected and the necessary experimentation was slow and costly. Hansgirg, who served as a consultant, was hard to work with; but even his services were lost when soon after Pearl Harbor, the FBI declared him an enemy alien and would not grant him a security clearance. For a time he was in a detention camp in California where he could advise from behind the bars. Subsequently, he was moved into the Midwest with virtual elimination of his consulting services.

That the powdery form of magnesium which the carbothermic process produced would always pose a fire hazard was tragically underscored in September 1941 when three men were fatally burned when a quantity of magnesium burst into flames.

Actually, the first refined magnesium ingot was produced September 20, 1941. At that time the company said the plant was operating at a rate of about 1,200 tons annually as compared with the ultimate hoped-for capacity of 12,000 tons a year. The grim fact remained, however, that production was slow and troubled until 1943. By the time the war was over the company could announce it had produced 20,000,000 pounds of ingot or 10,000 tons—a far cry from early expectations.

Nevertheless, the savings to the Government were considerable. Permanente delivered magnesium ingot at a cost of 33.8 cents per pound while other plants operated at Government expense ranged from 70.3 cents per pound to $1.161.

"Goop" To The Rescue

Goop is an awful-sounding name. How could any chemical compound be given a name like that? It isn't even in the dictionary.

Goop is an awful-looking product. It's an asphaltic-looking, gooey mess. That's why after looking at it somebody came up with the name "goop."

But goop was used to burn out large sections of Tokyo, thereby shortening the war. And goop was produced in large quantities by Kaiser's magnesium plant, thereby salvaging what could have been financial disaster for that corporation.

The story is this: magnesium dust is highly inflammable and almost impossible to put out until it burns itself out. Kaiser's magnesium plant, in its first stage of operation produced finely powdered magnesium dust. Then the dust had to be carefully melted until it became liquefied and could be cast into an ingot—a very expensive process. It was the only magnesium plant in the country that started by producing dust particles. All others smelted the magnesium-bearing ore into liquid for direct casting into ingots. They could not reverse the process and convert ingots into powder.

To control the dangerous inflammability of the powder, someone at Permanente began mixing it with an asphaltic, petroleum paste. Then it dawned on people that this would be ideal for incendiary bombs. By 1944 the Chemical Warfare Service insisted that Permanente abandon all other production in favor of producing goop. In just over a year Permanente produced 82,000,000 pounds (41,000 tons) of this material for bombs which were used against Germany and to burn out the the heart of Japan. This means that in about one-fourth the time Permanente produced four times as much goop as it did magnesium ingots from 1941 through the end of the war in 1945. Of course, allowance has to be made for the weight of the asphaltic base.

In any event, Captain G. E. Dawson, Chemical Warfare Service, United States Army, on August 29, 1945, awarded Permanente the Army and Navy "E" for production excellence and publicly declared:

> The goop bomb was really the fourth and highest step, in the development of incendiaries for the Army and Navy Air Forces. To shorten up a long story, the goop bomb and other incendiaries did so well against the industrial strongholds of Japan that nearly 160 square miles of industrial areas were bombed out. You [he referred to Kaiser workers] helped immensely to shorten the war and save thousands of American lives.

The price Permanente charged the Government for goop was considered by the Army to be very reasonable—an average of 18.3 cents per pound. At the same time, it was highly profitable to Permanente and gave a much-needed financial boost to the company. It could accurately be said that goop saved Permanente from various financial troubles.

The carbothermic process never did end up using magnesite from Nevada. Instead, Kaiser engineers devised a program that involved opening a dolomite quarry and calcining plant at Natividad, California, near Salinas. At the same time an innovative plant at nearby Moss Landing was erected for processing sea water into magnesia. Both plants were financed by an RFC loan. Products from these plants contained magnesium that came into being in the carbothermic process at Permanente. After the war the Natividad and Moss Landing plants were operated at capacity, producing and marketing calcined dolomite, dehydrated and processed lime, magnesium oxide, and many other allied products. Essentially these served as ideal refractory materials. It would take a chemical expert to explain why these products with their magnesium contents would have such high fire-resistant qualities when the magnesium itself in powder form was so dangerously inflammable.

The Ferrosilicon Process

In his zeal to help the war effort, Kaiser went along with Government and industry findings that magnesium could be economically produced by a process utilizing ferrosilicon. He produced the ferrosilicon at Permanente and shipped it to a brand new magnesium plant at Manteca, California. Starting in March 1942 the plant was built by Kaiser for the Government as a Defense Plant Corporation project at a cost of $6,224,000 on a nonprofit basis without a fee. Magnesium was produced three months after the award of the construction contract. In two years of operation it produced over 24,500,000 pounds (12,250 tons) and reached production 15 percent in excess of its rated capacity. The plant ceased operations in June 1944 when most of the Government-owned magnesium projects were discontinued. This was over a year before the war had ended, showing that the Government itself had gotten carried away in its enthusiasm for the "miracle" metal, magnesium.

The extent of the Government's extreme misjudgment can be found in the fact that $370 million was invested in Defense Plant Corporation magnesium producing facilities. Applying that to the actual output of magnesium by those plants, the costs were astronomical. To make matters worse, the Government, after the war, could not sell these plants to anyone planning to produce magnesium. As a result the amount realized was a small fraction of the Government's investment—a total contrast to the loan arrangements made with Kaiser on the carbothermic magnesium plant.

One Hundred Cents On The Dollar, Plus

It was a bold decision that Jesse Jones made in 1941 to loan Henry Kaiser $9,250,000 to build an "untested" magnesium-producing process. But it was a loan which the Government stipulated must be repaid in full. And it was a loan to a man who had demonstrated his remarkable ability to make a success of anything he undertook. And it was a loan that would be backed up by pledges of shipyard earnings. And it did involve a product that was considered to be desperately needed to stem the tide of the Nazis in Europe. Then, not foreseen at the outset, it would involve a remarkably lucrative product, goop.

Along the way, the RFC expanded its loan for the Permanente magnesium plant. Then came additional loans for the Natividad, California, dolomite plant and the Moss Landing sea water magnesia plant, both of which became postwar moneymakers. It was a happy day for Kaiser (and for Jones) when this news release came out November 30, 1945:

> Henry J. Kaiser, president of the Permanente Metals Corporation, announced today that the government had been repaid in full for its RFC loan of $28,475,000 on the magnesium plant at Permanente, located near San Jose, and allied plants at Moss Landing and Natividad, California. In making the final payment on the ten-year-loan, which has been settled six years before maturity, Kaiser said the Permanente Metals Corporation has paid the government an additional $3,500,000 in interest at the rate of four per cent. 'With the ending of the war the time has come to replace government money in wartime industries with private money turning the wheels of private industries wherever private investments are able to carry the load,' Kaiser asserted.

As with nearly everything Kaiser did, the friendship and goodwill and mutual respect which he built ranked high alongside the success of the project. A climate had been created so that within two months when he would start negotiations with the government for war-surplus aluminum plants, he would have relatively smooth sailing.

Kaiser had kept up his personal contacts with Jesse Jones. As far back as June 1942 Life Magazine would write:

> In March Henry Kaiser was talking to Jesse Jones about another technology that enthralls him—the cracking and synthesizing of fuels, rubber, and other strategic materials out of petroleum. Mr. Kaiser likes to speak of planes as made with petroleum and magnesium as their only raw materials. Mr. Jones, perceiving the gleam of another enterprise in Mr. Kaiser's eyes, said, 'Henry, you're no longer a young man. I am not accustomed to putting all my eggs in one basket. What would happen to us if you were to go and die?' 'My boys would finish all your contracts, Mr. Jones,' said Henry Kaiser. 'I would just be sorry not to be here asking for more work to do.'

It was a fitting wind-up—vintage Kaiser—that he would write this letter to Jones at Christmas time shortly after the magnesium loan had been repaid in full:

> Christmas is a time that calls out the best in human relationships. I want to send you a personal greeting for the Season and to express my wishes for a Happy New Year.

We have both lived to see the end of an epoch. We have shared the responsibilities of public service in a time of great crisis. We have learned that there can be no deep or lasting reward other than the inner knowledge that we have done our best.

The memories we share go back nearly fifteen years. They include many undertakings which you gave encouragement and support. A good many years before the declaration of war you will remember I appealed to you for a loan in connection with the development of the Permanente Cement Company. Although this venture finally proceeded under private financing, it is good to recall that you expressed a willingness to provide the needed credit. There is no need to review the many instances throughout the war when you gave me invaluable assistance. With the ships, the magnesium, and the steel there were problems that seemed insurmountable. In the discussion of the necessary loans your cross-examination was severe, but on every contact I came away with the thought that your caution was never destructive and that you were holding firm to the principles and high purposes for which the RFC was formed.

Now that reconversion is well under way the form of things to come slowly takes shape. You will be happy to know that with the aid of a small short-term bank credit, the magnesium loan from the RFC has been paid in full.

Perhaps this is the best Christmas greeting I could bring. Nevertheless, now that the crisis is past and we have all taken the road to peace, I want to send a token which will evidence not only my feeling of friendship but a never failing appreciation for the confidence which was always present when we were working together.

CHAPTER 6

A SHIP A DAY

"Faith, I am convinced, is the key to unlocking limitless powers of the heart, the mind, the soul."

"But where are your shipyards?", the leader of the British delegation asked. He and his colleagues had made a long journey to inspect the shipyards of "a Mr. Kaiser" who had offered to build 30 cargo ships for the British in their hour of peril.

It was November, 1940. Hitler's bombers were pulverizing British cities and his army was massing in France preparing to invade. America was in a position of uneasy neutrality. Western civilization was facing utter darkness if England fell.

The great need was for ships to bring American supplies, and supplies from the British Empire, to England. German U-boats were sinking ships at an alarming rate. Existing shipyards simply could not turn out ships fast enough to keep up with the sinkings, let alone add to the fleet so that England's ever-increasing demands for food and military equipment could be met. This "Mr. Kaiser" was said to be someone who could help. But where were the shipyards they had come to see?

The group was standing on the windswept mudflats of Richmond, California, bordering San Francisco Bay. They were shivering in the wet wind, looking at the overweight, bald man who had brought them there. At an age when many men were thinking of retirement, Henry J. Kaiser was almost boyish in his enthusiasm.

"There are our shipyards," he said with a wave of his hand at the mudflats. "It's true you see nothing but mud now, but within months this vast space will have a shipyard on it with thousands of men and women building the ships for you. This is an ideal place."

If some of the delegation thought the man was a dreamer, no one could blame them. This "Mr. Kaiser" had never built a ship before, and now he was waving at mudflats, promising miracles.

Well, miracles were needed to win the war, and fortunately Kaiser and some of his dam-building partners had recently linked up with Todd Shipyards, a builder of ships with an outstanding reputation. The British were desperate. They said they wanted 60 ships, half to be built in Richmond under Kaiser's direct control, the other half to be built on the East Coast where Todd would carry the responsibility.

Not for one moment did Kaiser consider the possibility that he might be biting off more than he could chew. Hadn't he and his construction partners tamed the mighty Colorado River with Boulder Dam, the largest ever built up to that time; then conquered the raging Columbia River with a dam at Bonneville, and most recently was nearing completion of the Grand Coulee Dam on the upper Columbia which was an even bigger dam than Boulder? These were one-time jobs where engineering and construction techniques had to be specially designed to fit the unique features of the terrain; where large crews had to be assembled in remote areas; and where huge new sources of dam-building materials had to be developed. In every instance his key management people came up with innovative ideas to get the jobs done faster and more efficiently than ever thought possible at the start.

How much easier it would be to build ships, because the engineering designs would be furnished by the British, and the supply of both labor and materials would, at least at the start, be much more readily available than at dam sites. Besides, his nucleus of management people was now made up of young but seasoned veterans champing at the bit to plunge into shipbuilding. Indeed, before the British came shopping, Kaiser and his top construction people had recognized that the era of dam building was past and that shipbuilding would be the ideal business to get into. Various studies, some private, some government, had warned that the United States itself was dangerously deficient in its merchant fleet. And with each passing month it became clearer and clearer that the United States was being drawn closer to war.

Yet, even with these forces at play, and with all his unbounded ebullience, Kaiser could never in his wildest dreams have foreseen just how many ships he would end up building. Nor could he have ever predicted the speed with which his people would learn to turn out one ship after another. The only thing he knew for sure was that the British were prepared to give him an order for 30 freighters calling for the earliest possible delivery, and he and his men were ready to accept the challenge.

The Commission Eyes Kaiser

The United States Maritime Commission had great foresight not only in anticipating the need for more ships but in rousing the interest of the kind of builders who could plunge into shipbuilding and make a success of it. Naturally, they thought of the rugged builders who made up the Six Companies, big western dam builders. In testimony before a congressional committee Admiral Emory S. Land, Chairman of the Maritime Commission, stated:

> Kaiser certainly was one of the key men in Six Companies, and it took us two years to hook him. He came down to my office at least three times, and I

do not know how many times to Admiral Vickery's office, before we could get them mixed up in the shipbuilding business.

Kaiser was at the same time getting his feet wet in an unplanned-for way. He had just completed construction of the country's largest cement mill in Northern California, primarily to supply all of the cement needs for the construction of Shasta Dam. With the extra capacity of his mill, he wanted to ship bulk cement to defense installations in Pearl Harbor and Guam, so he bought two aged ships and had them towed to Seattle for reconditioning in the Todd yards. Through this deal, he met John Reilly, forceful head of the Todd company which had repair yards in several different locations. Reilly foresaw the shipbuilding boom, but regretted that he didn't have the manpower to handle all the business he could get. Kaiser jumped at the opportunity to bring his team of dam builders into a partnership with Reilly.

It was the British requirement for sixty freighters that dictated the direction the partnership would take. It was to be a Kaiser show at Richmond for thirty of the ships, with the Reilly team building their thirty vessels in the shipyard of the Todd-Bath Iron Shipbuilding Corporation at South Portland, Maine.

The contract with the British was signed in New York City, December 9, 1940, almost exactly one year before the bombing of Pearl Harbor. The next day the New York Times reported:

> British representatives signed a contract in New York last night for the construction of sixty new freighters costing nearly $100 million to replace some of the Empire's war losses. The agreement was signed in the offices of Todd Shipyards Corporation at 1 Broadway by John D. Reilly, president of the firm, by Henry J. Kaiser, who becomes president of the Todd-California Shipbuilding Corporation, and by William S. Newell, head of the Bath Iron Works. It was said to be the largest ship order ever placed here when this country was not at war and marked the first time since the World War that ships for the British government had been ordered built in the United States. An important feature of the contract is the fact that it will in no way interfere with other shipbuilding in the United States, in so far as actual shipyards are concerned, although it will naturally make great demands on the nation's steel production.

Hit The Deck Running

The situation was made to order for Kaiser. Here were the British who desperately needed speed of production, and here was Kaiser, who, more than any other builder, was a fanatic on speed.

Within a few days Kaiser had formulated his game plan—he would make Clay Bedford head of his Richmond project. Clay, who was only 37, was one of Kaiser's most resourceful and brilliant engineers since the late twenties when Kaiser put him in charge of finishing the 200-mile Cuban highway job. After that, Clay had top-level responsibilities in the building of Boulder Dam, Bonneville Dam, and Grand Coulee Dam.

At the time, Bedford was directing construction of a huge naval air station at Corpus Christi, Texas. He had been there since June 22, had organized a team of eight thousand workers, and had done $80 million worth of work. Kaiser decided the project was far enough along he could turn it over to Bert Inch.

One call from Kaiser and Bedford was flying to Richmond. At most, Kaiser gave Bedford a general outline of what should be done—a generous use of space so that production of the ships would never be cramped, a program of prefabrication of huge ship sections using massive cranes the way they had proved to be so efficient in building the dams, and the use of welding to replace the old-fashioned technique of riveting. Beyond that, Kaiser would rely on the ingenuity of Bedford and his group of engineers to lay out the yard and to line up the workers.

As Bedford later recalled:

> We designed the yard. The chief engineer was Einar Larsen. The design engineer was Harry Bernat, and the architect was Morrie Wortman. Actually, there was a race between the Kaiser draftsmen and the field people as to whether we could build it first or the engineers and architects could draw it first. We knew what we were doing, so we just went right ahead and built it. We finished the office in thirty-four days, during which it rained heavily every day, to the point where the fibreboard panels in the ceiling got so wet they sagged. I remember going into the office and having to duck my head walking down the hall. Actually, it rained steadily for fifty-three days. We had water six inches deep along Cutting Boulevard resulting from a high tide and a hard southwest wind, yet we kept twenty trucks busy night and day for three months bringing in fill, and dredging the area. It was a miserable time, but we took it in stride because I had a lot of fellows from Bonneville Dam where it rained eighty-four inches a year.

The British order for sixty freighters had brought into sharp focus just how critical the sinking of ships in the Atlantic had become. The time had arrived for the United States itself to plunge into the shipbuilding race. The studies of the merchant ship shortage had convinced Congress, the President, and the Maritime Commission, that the hour was at hand to do something. Early in 1941 the announcement was made— the Maritime Commission would contract for the construction of two hundred Liberty ships, or "ugly ducklings" as they were called because of their simplicity of design which would make for speedy production.

Kaiser was determined to play a leading role in the program. For the previous month or two he had had his son, Edgar, 32 years of age and still in charge of construction of Grand Coulee Dam, slip away for several visits to shipyards around the country to study different techniques. Kaiser was eager therefore, to accept an order for thirty-one of the ships to be built, not at Richmond which had its hands full on the

British order, but at Portland where the land and labor conditions were very comparable with Richmond. Besides, Kaiser had a grand design—he would put Edgar in charge of the Portland shipyard where he and the people of that area could compete against Bedford and the workers from the San Francisco-Oakland Bay Area. Kaiser's long construction experience had convinced him that when workers are given high goals, when they compete with another group, and when they get recognition for their achievements, they are sure to break one record after another. For the next 4-1/2 years the competition between the two shipyard areas would be a constant incentive at all levels of management and in all departments. Without any doubt, each shipyard ended up producing a great many more ships than would have been the case without that competition.

By the time the contract was worked out with the Maritime Commission, it meant the Portland shipyard would be started one month later than Richmond. It was January 20, 1941 when this article was run in the Portland Oregonian newspaper:

> The Oregon Shipbuilding Corporation, recently formed to erect an eight-way yard for constructing thirty-one freighters, rolled up its sleeves today and lit into the big task of getting to work on building the plant which will cost $4,700,000. Edgar F. Kaiser, vice president of the corporation and in charge of the job locally, outlined the company's program when interviewed Sunday. It is thought the first keel will be laid about June 15. Nine construction companies are financially interested in the corporation, Kaiser said. They are Gilpin Construction Company, Portland; J. F. Shea Company, Portland; Morrison-Knudsen Company, Boise; Henry J. Kaiser Company, Oakland; W. A. Bechtel Company, San Francisco; Utah Construction Company, Ogden; McDonald and Kahn, San Francisco; Pacific Bridge Company, Portland; and Todd Shipyards, New York. These concerns are all interested in Six Companies, Inc., builder of Boulder Dam. Charles A. Shea of Portland is president of the Oregon Shipbuilding Corporation. In explaining why Portland was selected, Kaiser said, 'the site is ideal for shipbuilding, there is a great market here for labor, and this is Charlie Shea's home town.'

The Race Is On

Sloshing through rain and mud at both Richmond and Portland, thousands of workers busied themselves with building the shipyards. It was a hectic time assimilating all the workers into functioning organizations. And groundwork had to be laid for opening up a network of suppliers for the enormous flood of materials that would soon be pouring into the shipyards.

At <u>Richmond</u>, it was a memorable day on April 14, 1941 when the keel for the first ship was laid. This was another instance when the act itself preceded the drawings. At 1:30 o'clock in the afternoon, a small group of shipyard workers and British representatives officiated at the ceremonies. Kaiser himself was too busy to participate. Three more keels were laid before April was over, and the rest of the seven shipways were filled by the middle of May.

Just two days after this first keel-laying—on April 16, 1941—the office of production management approved construction of a second shipyard at Richmond, "to build twenty-four ships for the United States Maritime Commission." The goal was set to have this second shipyard in operation by September.

At Portland, the laying of the first keel on May 19, 1941, was celebrated with fanfare. The Maritime Commission, as well as the state of Oregon, wanted the nation to know that ships were on their way. Construction crews stopped operations for 30 minutes while Captain Howard L. Vickery (soon to be appointed Admiral), the shipbuilding expert of the U. S. Maritime Commission, admonished the crowd of 1,000 workmen, company officials, and guests "to build ships well and build them fast in coming years."

He went on, "You fellows are talking of a February launching. Now it's up to you to roll ships out of here at the rate of 45 a year. I know you can do it, and I don't mean to start next February."

Edgar Kaiser responded, "Boys, you've heard what they told us. It's our job and we're going to put this ship out and do it fast. Let's go."

Other pep talks were given by Oregon Governor Charles A. Sprague, the acting Mayor of Portland, and other civic leaders.

The day of May 19 had been chosen because it was the 100th anniversary of the launching of the first sea-going vessel built in Portland, the 53-foot "Star of Oregon." The decision had already been made that this first Liberty ship from the new Portland yard would likewise be named "Star of Oregon."

Two months later, on July 18, about half of the 4,700 Richmond workers, most of them in hard hats, cheered a stirring talk by Lord Halifax, British Ambassador to the United States. Flanked by Henry J. Kaiser, Henry J. Kaiser, Jr., and Clay Bedford, the Ambassador toured the yard before making his talk. His speech was reported in the newspapers:

> What has been done here in the last six months is as near a miracle as any other human thing I've ever seen. It's wonderful. To think that last January this place was a mudflat, and a month from now you are to launch your first ship. If one read about it without seeing it, it would be truly hard to believe. If you do your best, as you will, and if we do our best, as I promise you we will, the joint effort will be good enough to make an end to Hitler. I'm going back home and tell our shipbuilders that good help is coming from California and that in a short time they will feel the effect of it. No job in the whole war effort is more important than what you are doing here.

The big event at Richmond, of course, was the launching on August 16 of the first freighter to be built there, the "Ocean Vanguard." Here are excerpts from newspaper accounts the day before:

Chairman Emory S. Land of the Maritime Commission, and Mrs. Land, will arrive by plane this morning for the launching tomorrow at Richmond of the Ocean Vanguard, first American-built British freighter. Mrs. Land will smash a bottle of champagne on the bow of the vessel as it slides down the way at 5:38 p.m. Her matrons of honor will be Lady Salter, wife of Sir Arthur Salter, head of the British Merchant Shipping Mission to the United States, and Mrs. Edward Macauley, wife of California's only member of the Maritime Commission. Sir Arthur will also attend the launching. He is expected to arrive tonight from Washington. Shipping leaders and celebrities from Terminal Island to Puget Sound will attend the launching. KFRC and the Mutual Broadcasting System will broadcast the launching over a coast-to-coast hookup from 5:15 to 5:30. Paul C. Smith will introduce Sir Arthur and Admiral Land to the radio audience. Only shipyard employees and their families and invited guests will be allowed inside the plant for the launching. Richmond will hold a civic celebration in honor of the event.

A Star Is Born

Portland's turn came a month later on Saturday, September 27, a day officially designated Liberty Fleet Day by the United States Maritime Commission. The agency thought it would dramatize the whole shipbuilding program if twelve new merchant ships could be launched on that one day by shipyards on all coasts of the United States participating. Each yard was asked to arrange a colorful ceremony for the occasion. It was the intention to make Liberty Fleet Day an event of nationwide scope and significance, and the general public was cordially invited by the Commission and the shipbuilders to participate. President Roosevelt made a nationwide address over the radio to underscore how important shipbuilding was to the country.

It was only appropriate therefore, that the wife of the Governor of Oregon should be the one to christen the ship. The program for that occasion, while involving a bit more high-level people because of its historic significance, was essentially the pattern for the launching of all the ships that followed:

Launching Day Program
September 27, 1941
Ceremonies - 3:00 P.M.
Launch - 3:30 P.M.

National Anthem . . . U. S. Army Band, 162nd Infantry

Introduction of Master of Ceremonies, Hon. Joseph K. Carson, by representative of Oregon Shipbuilding Corporation.

Address by the President of the United States (by transcription)

Introduction of youngest workman on the job, Charles Thomas Albert, 16-year-old ship-fitter's helper

Presentation of Bouquet of Portland roses to Mrs. Charles A. Sprague, Sponsor, and Mrs. Charles A. Shea and Mrs. Paul B. Wallace, Matrons of Honor, by Mr. Albert.

Introduction of U. S. Maritime Commission and Oregon Shipbuilding Corporation officials

Address by Mayor Earl Riley

Address by Governor Charles A. Sprague

Invocation by Chaplain C. H. Mansfield, U.S.N.

Christening of Ship by Sponsor

Selection by U. S. Army Band

Welcome to Our Visitors

Pearl Harbor, December 7, 1941

If anyone had insisted that the shipyards in Richmond and Portland could have done a better job in 1941 than they did, there would be 20,000 workers rise up and say, "No way." After all, they were working 24 hours a day with brilliant night-time lights flooding every area of construction activity.

Yet Pearl Harbor worked a special kind of magic. Now everyone in the yards knew he was fighting for his own life, for his family's life, for his country's life. Kaiser knew it called for more shipyards, and the Maritime Commission which had to place the order for ships and to finance the construction of the yards had the President and Congressional backing to go all out. One after another new shipyards sprang up until Richmond had four of them and Portland had three—the original, plus another at Swan Island in Portland plus one across the Columbia River at Vancouver, Washington. At full complement there was a total of fifty-eight shipways in the seven yards.

The Maritime Commission had moved fast. On January 9, 1942 they signed a contract with Kaiser Company, Inc., for a whole new yard—Richmond Number Three—which would be capable of turning out huge C-4 troop transport ships, altogether different from the freighters being built for the British and the flood of Liberty ships which would be built for the United States.

Then eight days later they placed an order for sixty Liberty ships to be built in Yard One by the end of 1943 (in May fourteen more were added).

With the construction pace mounting furiously, it became evident that a more workable arrangement could be achieved by separating the responsibilities of Kaiser and Todd. This was reported in the New York Times of February 14, 1942:

The affiliation of the Todd Shipyards Corporation and the associated companies of Henry J. Kaiser, a West Coast industrialist and shipbuilder, has been dissolved by mutual consent, it was announced here yesterday by John D. Reilly, president of Todd.

Mr. Kaiser is president of the Todd-California Shipbuilding Corporation and is the head of Six Companies, a group of Western industrialists who participated in the construction of Boulder Dam, the Bonneville Dam and other great projects in the West. The two concerns joined forces late in 1940 when they signed contracts with the British Purchasing Commission for sixty freighters at a cost of $100,000,000.

The Todd-Kaiser combination has held government contracts running into millions of dollars for the construction of merchant ships for the Maritime Commission and the warships.

Mr. Reilly said the companies reached an agreement to dissolve their interests after several weeks of consideration and negotiation.

'It is believed that by more intensive concentration in definite areas the individual organizations can more effectively speed up construction programs of the Maritime Commission and the Navy,' he said.

A division of the various shipyards in which Kaiser and Todd held joint interests was arranged at a meeting held at the Todd office at 1 Broadway within the last few days.

The Kaiser group will, in the future, wholly control the four new Pacific Coast construction yards that are now working on a full schedule. They are the Oregon Shipbuilding Corporation, at Portland; Todd-California Shipbuilding Corporation at Richmond, California, the California Shipbuilding Corporation at Los Angeles, and the Richmond Shipbuilding Corporation at Richmond.

(Kaiser's ownership in the California Shipbuilding Corporation of Los Angeles was very minor and he never had any management responsibilities.)

Because of its size, and the fact that it was planned as a somewhat permanent yard, special care went into the design of <u>Richmond Number Three</u>. Though conceived in haste, it became one of the most efficient in the country, with great emphasis on unprecedented spaciousness, so immense sections could be fabricated in separated areas, then brought together for final assembly. It was not laid out in a sea of mud, but this time it required blasting a rocky hill 140 feet above the water's edge. Scarcely five months later, the yard had been leveled, most of the buildings erected, the first hull steel had been lowered into a plate rack on March 17, and the first keel for a huge C-4 troop transport had been laid on May 14, 1942, before the walls were poured or the gates installed.

A unique feature was that the vessels were to be constructed level, in vast concrete drydocks instead of on sloping ways. This level construction simplified the work in many areas of the shipbuilding process. Also, when the time came for launching, the drydocks would be flooded so the ship could be floated away, not slid downhill into the water.

Bedford and his men were extremely proud of the speed with which Yard Three had been built. He moved in to the new administration building leaving other top men located in yards one and two. Just as he was settling down in his new headquarters he received a call from Henry Kaiser in Washington, D.C. "Clay," the boss said, tentatively departing from his usual decisive manner, "the Admiral wants us to build LST's out there. Do you think you could build another yard?" Bedford heaved a mighty sigh, mustered all his courage, and started to answer, "Not a chance." It was entirely out of the question. His men had given their all in finishing Yard Three. There were simply no extra men, equipment, or materials available. That was that.

An hour later, Kaiser telephoned again. "Clay, Admiral Vickery says we are unpatriotic if we don't build LST's. How about another yard?" That did the trick. With Vickery and Kaiser talking about patriotism, what could Bedford say? By June the new yard was begun, with little fanfare, for here were to be built "special craft for the United States Navy," the then secret Landing Ships, Tanks.

Again, Bedford and his crew were put to the task to lay out a yard that would mesh with the available land and that would adjust for the length and characteristics of the LST's. It turned out to be by far the most challenging design of any Richmond yard. So many original and ingenious engineering concepts had to be developed, horrified consultants said it was doomed to fail, yet on October 4, 1942, just four months after Vickery had appealed to Kaiser's patriotism, the first LST splashed into the water.

With all the flurry in the new Richmond shipyards relating to ships for America, there was no let-up in building the original thirty ships for Britain. That historic moment arrived on Saturday, June 27, 1942, when Hull Number 30, the Ocean Victory, was launched amid appropriate fanfare, with Kaiser himself as the main speaker praising the workers for their tireless work and ingenuity, and thanking the British for their unwavering cooperation. It was a portent of greater miracles yet to come, because ship number 30 was delivered five months ahead of schedule.

Portland On A Roll

Because Richmond was next door to Kaiser's headquarters in Oakland, it would seem logical he would spend more time there than in Portland. Not so. He didn't spend much time either place.

The phone was something else. He kept in almost daily touch with progress in each of the yards. He would initiate most of the calls just to keep posted on developments. However, Clay Bedford in Richmond and Edgar Kaiser in Portland never hesitated to call Kaiser when they felt so inclined. On April 12, 1942 the Oregonian newspaper in Portland ran this story:

> By the time these words reach print the keel of the first of Vancouver's ships may already have been laid—less than three months after construction began. Young Edgar Kaiser gives all credit for his successes to the guiding genius of his fabulous father. In typical vein at a banquet welcoming him to Vancouver, Edgar declared: 'There is an unseen guest to whom this banquet is really dedicated—my father. I never make a major decision without conferring with him, by phone, wherever he may be.'

Although Oregon Shipbuilding Corporation in Portland would remain the backbone of ship production in the area because of its emphasis on building Liberty and Victory ships, the two new yards—one at Vancouver, Washington, for which ground was broken in January, 1942, and the other at Swan Island in Portland started in March, 1942—would play an enormously important role because of the kind of ships they would build.

All three yards were destined to win more than their share of awards for speed and quality of production. By February 16, 1942, the newspapers were reporting:

> The Navy's E pennant, insignia for excellence in production was hoisted over the Oregon Shipbuilding yard in Portland as the 15th Liberty ship went down the ways. The Oregon Corporation was the first builder of merchant ships to be given the coveted pennant. The yard leads all others in production.

In Drew Pearson's column, Washington Merry-Go-Round of April 8, 1942, he wrote: "The ace shipbuilding plant in the country is the Portland, Oregon shipyard managed by Kaiser's son Edgar."

A year later, Oregonship received the "Golden Eagle Merit Award" for "unprecedented performance in the shipbuilding industry." It was the first yard in the country to receive this award. Six months after that it received the U. S. Maritime Commission's coveted "Gold Wreath Award"—an honor never granted before. By the end of the war it had earned the reputation as one of the best—"if not the best"—shipyard in the United States.

Vancouver was the utility yard, producing a half dozen different ships, including the historic "baby flat-tops" as described later in this chapter. It, too, gained a reputation as "one of the best of the emergency yards in equipment and layout."

Swan Island had one assignment—to produce huge oil tankers to carry fuel for U. S. ships and equipment around the world. On October 24, 1942, it was proudly announced in the Portland Journal:

> Kaiser Company employees prepared to launch at noon today the biggest ship ever constructed in this area, the 523 foot, 16,500 ton tanker, Schenectady, built to carry the lifeblood of United States war machines to fronts

across the seas. The Schenectady is the first of 56 tankers to be built for the Maritime Commission at the Swan Island yard and its launching follows its keel laying by only 115 days. Oregon Governor Charles A. Sprague was principal speaker at the launching.

Three months later a near disaster struck the Schenectady while it was still tied up at the outfitting dock at Swan Island. It split down the sides at about the middle and sank. As initially shocking as it was, it took less than three weeks to refloat it and repair the damage. It ended up performing a long career of service for the Navy. No other Swan Island tanker suffered a similar problem.

Indeed, by May, 1943, Swan Island received the Maritime Commission's "M Award" for "meritorious achievement." Then in June, Admiral Vickery noted that the rate of production of tankers was higher at the Swan Island yard than in any other yard in the country. The New York Times praised Swan Island for its "extraordinary history of achievement" as "one of the most compact and efficient yards in the world."

The Ten-Day Wonder

Edgar Kaiser and his mushrooming team of shipbuilders in Portland were having so much fun breaking one production record after another they decided to shoot for the moon. Not really. All they decided to do was to build a ship in ten days, which by their own experience and careful planning they knew they could do. Even though no one had ever before built a ship in less than twenty-four days—and most shipyards were still taking two months per ship—they had the nerve to invite President Roosevelt to attend the launching on September 23, 1942 of the Liberty ship, Joseph N. Teal. They went one step further—they invited the President's daughter, Mrs. John Boettiger of Seattle, to christen the ship.

Precisely ten days earlier the keel was laid and the parts began being fabricated and laid out in an orderly manner in preparation for final assembly. If ever there were a human beehive it was the hundreds upon hundreds of workers who, night and day, were doing the thousands of jobs, big and little, in putting the ship together.

Edgar wanted to shock Clay Bedford in Richmond with his incredible feat, so he hadn't told Clay when the keel was laid. The day before the launching itself, Edgar called Clay and asked him to be in Portland for the occasion. Clay said he was awfully sorry but he was too busy at Richmond and couldn't spare the time. "Do you want me to call my father and have him order you to be here?" Edgar asked. Clay got the message, and took the first train that would get him into Portland early in the morning. He recalls seeing the President's special train pull into the shipyard just before the launching ceremony. He was flattered when the President greeted him, "I remember you from Grand Coulee Dam when you were one of the men who showed me around there."

There were 14,000 cheering spectators to witness this record-breaking launching.

President Roosevelt warmly congratulated everyone who had a part in building the 10,500 ton ship. He stressed that it was an historic milestone in the country's rapid build-up of arms. He told the crowd:

> I am very much inspired by what I have seen, and I wish that every man, woman and child in these United States could have been here to see the launching and realize its importance in winning the war.

When it came Kaiser's turn to respond he couldn't restrain his pride:

> Our original contract called for the delivery of ships in about 150 days. The average in the first World War had been more than 200. Many experts shook their heads and said we could not do it. Yet, here beside us is this great craft—only ten days from keel laying to launching; and in a few days she will be on the ocean bearing cargo to our allies and to our soldiers. It is a miracle no less—a miracle of God and of the genius of free American workmen.

"How long will that ten-day record stand?" Kaiser was asked. "I expect that record to go by the boards in the very near future. Never in my long experience have I seen men so imbued with the joy of achievement as these shipyard workers. I have gotten a tremendous lift myself from the manner in which these men have taken hold and responded to opportunity."

Edgar Kaiser was quick to point out the 10-day miracle was no stunt done at the expense of other ship production. He said, "In September, every department has increased its production per man, as well as building and delivering this fast ship." His assistant general manager, Albert Bauer, said that despite the terrific building pace of the Teal she went through:

> ...exactly the same construction and pre-assembly process as any other Liberty ship. We simply program the erection on a faster schedule. More men and equipment are swung into the job and the groups work on a rapid schedule. The record ships get every inspection the regular vessels get. The men themselves wanted the new record. They like to 'ride a winner.' The record is a stimulant and there's a certain amount of schooling for production gotten out of each try. The Teal is the most complete ship ever launched in our yard.

The 34,000 workers in the record-breaking yard wanted to share in the glory, so a company publication of that day, The Bos'N's Whistle, listed all of the other "firsts" the yard had achieved:

First to adopt assembly line methods
First and only maritime yard to receive "E" award of merit
First yard to employ women on ship construction
First yard to inaugurate christening of ships by wives of workmen

First yard to complete initial contract with Maritime Commission
First yard to launch a ship in 26 days
First yard to outfit a ship in 5 days
First yard to deliver a ship in 31 days

And Today
First yard to launch a ship in 10 days

And Next Sunday
First yard to deliver a Liberty ship in 14 days

The workers at Richmond might have challenged two or three of these "firsts," but nothing could detract from the triumph of that day.

A month later Henry Kaiser was at the Waldorf Hotel in New York City when a reporter asked him about the new ten-day shipbuilding record. "Frankly," he confessed, "we could have launched that ship in eight days." "Then, why didn't you?" the reporter asked. "We held it up for two days," explained Kaiser, "so that President Roosevelt could witness the launching."

One-Upmanship
The workers at Richmond had mixed emotions—pride that their counterparts in Portland had stunned the world by building a ship in ten days, and envy that Portland had beaten them to the punch. The sentiment began to mount that Richmond must find a way to outdo Portland.

With Bedford's approval, J. C. McFarland, Superintendent of Yard Number Two, began charting exactly how a ship could be built in five days. The management team looked the plan over and agreed it was workable. Then Bedford sensed a possible problem. What would President Roosevelt's reaction be if a ship could be built in half the time of the ship he had just helped launch in Portland? Bedford took it up with Kaiser, who shared his concern. Kaiser decided the answer should come from the President himself, so he asked James F. Byrnes, the President's assistant, to clear it with the Chief. The President's response was instantaneous, "Build it, and if it can be done in one day, so much the better."

Saturday afternoon, November 7, 1942, the "five-day ship" was strewn all over Yard Two. From the old shell assembly down to Way Six there was practically nothing but Hull 440 lying around like a torn-apart Chinese puzzle on the living room floor. Hunk after hunk of 440, stacked all over: masts, anchor chains, deckhouse.

"Five days!" grinned a chipper. "Hell, it'll take 'em five days to even find the keel."

They did find the keel some way or other. It was already welded to the bottom shell and that helped. They laid down that keel at precisely 12:01 a.m. Sunday, November 8, and by the time the day shift came on the ship looked a week old.

As one worker put it:

The biggest problem that first day was in persuading the guys in the rest of the yard not to wander down where all the action was. No wonder, it was something to see--just one big seething mass of shipfitters, welders, chippers. Ten chippers hacking away on a transverse seam...hose and cable a foot deep. ...I'll be blind and deaf by next week, but it's worth it, I guess.

At 3:27 p.m. Thursday, November 12, Hull 440 was launched just 4 days, 15 hours, and 26 minutes after the keel was laid. Sponsor of the S. S. Robert E. Peary was Mrs. James F. Byrnes. Acceptance by the Maritime Commission of the completely outfitted ship on Sunday, November 15, established another new record of 7 days, 14 hours and 23 minutes from keel to delivery.

Workers at the Portland shipyards couldn't resist getting in the act. They sent a wire to Richmond congratulating them, and then adding, "Now if we cut your record in half, what will you do?" Neither side pressed the challenge.

How did the Robert E. Peary perform? Was it just a showboat or did it do the work expected of it?

So pleased with the performance of the Peary, Admiral Emory S. Land, Chairman of the Maritime Commission, sent this wire on June 4, 1943:

TO THE WORKERS OF RICHMOND SHIPYARD #2:
PERMANENTE METALS CORP.
RICHMOND, CALIFORNIA

Production Communique #16. The Master of the S. S. Robert E. Peary, your own Liberty ship, which you well remember and which America will never forget says this of your ship. Quote. We loaded in record time and were at sea with a cargo fifteen days after the keel was laid. I rather think the Japs and the Heinies would have to hump a little to equal that. We had a very nice trip going out and made better speed for the passage of almost 6000 miles than we expected. The ship behaved fine and handled very well. Nothing serious went wrong at all. We discharged some cargo at our first port. Loaded more at the second and then laid a full shipload down at the third port. Things were rather interesting there. Sometimes a little hot. But when we saw those kids in our Armed Forces, and most of them were kids, it made us damned proud that we were Americans and able to do our little bit. On our return trip we stopped at another port and loaded a full cargo. In loading this cargo, another record was established. 10,500 tons were loaded in 34 hours and 50 minutes. We are almost ready to go again and I sincerely hope we will be able to help set a few more records for the Robert E. Peary. Unquote. Every one of you should be proud of the ship which your sweat and energy built in record time and which now carries on in such splendid tradition. Keep up your good work.

The first master of the Peary was Captain Harold E. Widmeyer of San Pedro, Cali-

132

fornia. His wife gave this interview to the Richmond shipyard employee publication, Fore 'N'Aft in September, 1944:

> In a recent convoy to England, a crack developed in the shell plate of the Peary below the water line, and my husband was irate at the suggestion by crew men that this was due to structural defect. Actually, the ship was in the outside lane of the convoy, and depth charges burst very close by one night just after my husband had hit his bunk. He jumped up, thinking his ship had been torpedoed. It was discovered that concussion had caused the break and water was 25 feet deep in the bilges. My husband didn't want to drop out of the convoy because the Atlantic was thick with subs at that time. Officers aboard the ship calculated that the stability of the ship was such that it would hold together until they made port, if the convoy did not pass through icy waters that might aggravate the crack. Only after two days did my husband report the break to the convoy's commodore. By that time it was obvious that the ship would not slow the convoy down. Also, by that time they had run into waters that were iceberg-infested, but the Peary churned through without mishap. He has always been extremely proud of the Peary's performance.

At about the same time, the War Shipping Administration issued a summary of the Peary's career to date. It said the ship had voyaged more than 42,000 miles to far places in the Atlantic and Pacific. "Masters' and engineers' reports show her mechanical and navigational efficiency equals that of sister ships much longer on the ways. The building of the Robert E. Peary in one week was a feat matched only by her continued sturdy performance."

In terms of its performance, the Peary might be said to be the "flagship" of the Richmond Liberty ships. At different times during the war a news story would touch on the fact that a Richmond-produced ship had a problem at sea. For those who were eager to criticize the front runner, Kaiser, the word would spread that his ships were "cracking up." Some would pronounce themselves experts and proclaim that these pre-fabricated and welded ships simply could not hold up like the old-time custom-built, riveted ships.

Just the opposite. The ships from Richmond became the envy of all the country's shipyards. This was brought out by the findings of the Senate's Truman Committee in July, 1944. Here was the official Truman report:

Ship Yard	Deliveries	Faulty	% to Deliveries
All Shipyards	1756	346	19.6
Richmond Yard One	116	8	6.9
Richmond Yard Two	288	23	7.9
Bethlehem-Fairfield	204	20	9.8
St. Johns	30	3	10.0
Marinship	13	2	15.4
Southeastern	44	7	15.9

The Truman Committee released further findings:

Manhour Champs:
Fifteen yards produced Liberty ships, and those which averaged less than 600,000 manhours per ship were ranked in order:

Oregon Shipbuilding Corporation
Richmond Yard Two
North Carolina Shipbuilding Company
Richmond Yard One
Bethlehem-Fairfield

Dollar Champs:
Yards turning out ships costing less than $1,000,000 each to build (excluding cost of materials furnished by the Maritime Commission, and fees) were ranked:

North Carolina Shipbuilding Company
Oregon Shipbuilding Corporation
Richmond Yard Two
California Shipbuilding Corporation
Richmond Yard One

Wanted: 100,000 Workers

Kaiser's shipyards could get off to a fast start in 1941 because the supply of labor at both Richmond and Portland was plentiful. To a large extent, the workers had enough skills to adapt reasonably well to the kind of work required in ship building. So, for the first year, it was not so much the supply of labor that presented a problem, it was more a matter of training the workers in the arts of shipbuilding.

That situation changed overnight once the Japanese bombed Pearl Harbor. Suddenly, there was a desperate shortage of workers, and suddenly those seeking jobs required a great deal more training to get them ready for shipyard work.

Rulings by the United States Draft Boards forced a lot of people out of non-war related jobs, and that meant many of them turned to the shipyards for work. Likewise, those physically unfit for military service came to the shipyards, and while their contribution was indispensable, still it meant the yards had to give a great deal of attention to cope with their disabilities.

The word went out from both Richmond and Portland that workers were needed, not by the thousands but by the tens of thousands. In the 1840's and 1850's the Oregon Trail saw a steady stream of pioneers wending their way west, and once gold was discovered in northern California in 1848, "the world rushed in." But neither of those westward migrations could compare in numbers with the flood of shipyard workers that would find their way west on their own or would come by the trainloads provided by Kaiser.

The yards issued calls for help through the press regularly which got the message out all around the country. "Help Wanted" ads were published in major areas. The campaign was at its height by the fall of 1942.

One problem had to be ironed out before the desired results could be achieved. Some unions had a ban on allowing membership to negroes. Because of the war emergency, however, and because Kaiser himself was such an outspoken champion of negroes, the ban was soon lifted.

Typical of the news coverage on this employment drive was the story of September 22, 1942, datelined New York City:

> Master builder Henry J. Kaiser, who likes to move in giant strides, stepped into the New York labor market today and hired two trainloads of men to work in his Portland, Oregon shipyards. Out to get 20,000 workers to build ships without lost motion or wasted time, Kaiser's hiring representatives said the first 600 men selected today would probably be bound for Portland on Friday aboard a special train. The second train will pull out early next week, and hundreds of men are already lining up for the next Kaiser special. Company barracks at Portland will house 5,000 men at a minimum living cost of $13.50 weekly. Men are advised not to bring their wives 'right now.' 'If they know one end of a monkey wrench from another, we'll take them as helpers. If they don't, we'll label each end.' The Kaiser company hopes to recruit 20,000 additional men in Indiana, Louisiana, and Texas.

A week later the Portland Oregonian ran this story:

> Aboard the Kaiser Special Train, Spokane, Washington. Out of the east and into the far west rolled the 'Henry J. Kaiser magic carpet' tonight bearing 490 enthusiastic, happy future shipyard workers from New York, the first contingent of a new movement over the new Oregon Trail.

Two other newspaper articles are worth recording:

> 9/28/42 West Coast shipyards, principally those of Henry Kaiser, are attempting to recruit about 35,000 workers from the East and Middle West.

New York City, where there is still an unemployment problem because of the absence of significant wartime plants, is expected to produce from 10,000 to 20,000.

10/2/42 Another contingent of 500 workers including negroes will depart tomorrow from the B&O railroad terminal in Jersey City for Henry J. Kaiser's shipyards on the Pacific Coast. Todd Woodell, in charge of the office, declined to comment on reports from Portland, Oregon, that a union there had sought to bar negroes from jobs in the Kaiser yards. 'We do not ask what their color is,' he said.

At the peak there were 197,000 workers in the Kaiser ship yards. That this huge, motley, raggle-taggle assemblage of shipyard workers ended up doing such a splendid job has to be one of the proud moments in American history. It was a confirmation of Kaiser's conviction that every person has something to offer if given a fair chance and if treated with proper respect. It was a microcosm of America itself—where the blending of different races and different levels of skills produces a strong and balanced economy.

Ever since the shipyards closed down, there have been voices raised that Henry Kaiser adversely affected the social structure of the San Francisco-Oakland Bay Area and the Portland area by the number of blacks and other elements he brought in. I do not share this viewpoint. To begin with, it wasn't Kaiser who brought the people west—it was America itself that, fighting for its life, was grateful for every shipyard worker who could be found. Kaiser was simply the enthusiastic agent who carried out the government policy. In the second place, the fact is that today there is no bigger percentage of minority population in Oakland or Portland than there is in dozens of other major cities throughout the rest of the country. Finally, I look at the Bay Area (and I assume the Portland area is essentially the same), and I see a reasonably balanced economy—though far from perfect—showing the country, and indeed the world, that diverse elements can be a source of strength if groups work together.

Admiral Emory S. Land

It was September, 1942. The war was at fever pitch. Nowhere was there more action than at the offices of the United States Maritime Commission in Washington, D.C.

The chairman of that Commission was Admiral Emory S. Land, a brilliant and dedicated maritime expert. Three years before America entered the war Admiral Land had led the efforts to get Kaiser interested in building ships. He ended up being one of Kaiser's best friends and staunchest admirers, and when Kaiser launched his first ship August 16, 1941, he was careful to have Mrs. Land as sponsor.

On this September morning Kaiser had an 8:00 a.m. appointment to see Admiral Land. He especially wanted to introduce A. B. Ordway to the Admiral. Kaiser had put Ordway in charge of the project to build repair docks at Mare Island, California.

As usual, Kaiser arrived ahead of schedule, this time by twenty minutes. There was no secretary on duty at the time so Kaiser, with Ordway in tow, barged into the Admiral's office, to find him enjoying his pipe and reading the morning's newspaper. Kaiser said: "Admiral, I want you to meet A. B. Ordway, who is in charge at Mare Island. He is my oldest employee in point of service. He has been with me for thirty years."

The Admiral laid down his pipe, squinted at Ordway, and said: "Good God, thirty years with Henry Kaiser and still alive!"

Admiral Land was a great believer in giving praise, regular praise, and often lavish praise, for a job well done. To a large extent he left the needle work up to his right hand man, Rear Admiral Howard L. Vickery, vice-chairman of the Commission.

Whenever the occasion warranted it, Land would visit shipyards to tell the workers firsthand how much their efforts meant in the prosecution of the war. He was so pleased with the record of Richmond Yard Three in building troop transport ships in its first year of operation, he gave this message to the workers there in late May, 1943, at the launching of the General Robert L. Howze:

> Hirohito and Mussolini have said the record you have made was an hallu-cination of the Rooseveltian Administration. You have proved them liars....Two years ago it was said that two ships a day would keep the Ger-mans away. We are now doing five ships a day.... You have proved that you are willing to deliver the goods for the boys at the front.... We may battle back in Washington. We talk too damn much while you do the work. How-ever,...although we do too much talking, we appreciate what you are doing... a swell job. Without you, they can't accomplish results in this, the war of transportation.

Throughout the war Admiral Land maintained a steady program of sending com-muniques to his shipbuilders letting them know of any outstanding performance by the ships they had built. His communiques were always addressed to the workers, not to the bosses. It was his communique number 16 of June 4, 1943 that told the Rich-mond shipyard number two workers of the remarkable performance of the ship they had built in less than five days.

Because the communiques tell something about the man himself, and because they really tell something about the American way of doing things, two of these commu-niques are submitted as being typical:

TO THE WORKERS OF RICHMOND SHIPYARD NO.1—March 22,
   1943 PERMANENTE METALS CORP
RICHMOND CALIF.

Production Communique #5. You have probably seen in the newspaper stories the heroic job one of your own Liberty ships has accomplished. How the O. Henry, a convoy to Malta, was savagely but ineffectually bombed by

German planes, how its guns brought down a dive bomber. How the O. Henry fought its way through, without the loss of a single man, and delivered its cargo of food and munitions to that besieged island fortress. And how enroute her captain loaded her deck with oranges for the children of Malta. I know every worker at your yard will take personal pride and satisfaction in knowing that your ship reached Malta and gave new courage to its brave people in their heroic fight against the axis.

E. S. Land Chairman
U S Maritime Commission

TO THE WORKERS OF RICHMOND SHIPYARD #2—Aug 5, 1943
 PERMANENTE METALS CORP
RICHMOND, CALIF.

Production Communique NM. 19 Your Liberty ship—S.S. George B. Selden, November 4, 1942 at Richmond Yard No. 2 has just returned from North Africa with huge quantities of captured German and Italian war material. This vessel has battled her way successfully through Pacific, Atlantic, and Mediterranean war zones. Her officers asked me to relay these messages to you. Quote the George B. Selden has seen plenty of action in this war. Submarines followed us for days. General behavior of ship was wonderful. Can't be beat for steering: Steering engines worked perfectly. In heavy weather in South Pacific we had to heave for three days to protect deck load of bombers. Speed above average: Engine very economical on oil consumption. My deep appreciation to men and women who built her for this outstanding job of what these days is a rush order. Unquote Master, SS George B. Selden. Quote. Workmanship on Keel and engines as nearly perfect as could be. Bearings never heated up. Boilers used less oil than specified with throttle wide open. We got more than rated speed out of her. My fondest hope is that when I go aboard another ship, she will give the performance that the Selden did. Hope you men will put same effort and care into every ship you turn out. Unquote. First Asst. Engineer, S. S. George B. Selden. This is proof that the men and women of Richmond Number 2 have built strong and good ships. We are proud of it—Keep up the good work.

Emory S. Land, Chairman
U S Maritime Commission

Admiral Howard L. Vickery
Admiral Vickery was a perfect first mate for Admiral Land, chairman of the Maritime Commission.

Land operated mostly with a pat on the back. Vickery was the gunner, the ramrod, the needle.

One of Land's proudest achievements was his "discovery" of Vickery. From the moment they teamed up, they were known as the Siamese twins of Washington. If they ever argued with each other, apparently no one ever heard them.

Vickery, "the shipbuilder with spurs," would jab away at the shipbuilders so sharply and so relentlessly he would have them all up in arms. But he seemed to know just when to let down and give credit. Fortunately, he was blessed with a sense of humor and that softened his attacks.

After he had been made a member of the Maritime Commission in 1938, he began to hear about this man Kaiser "who gets things done." Vickery looked him up. Kaiser had never worked with anyone he didn't like. Neither had Vickery. They met, they sized each other up and down. They liked each other. As recorded in the Saturday Evening Post in 1943:

> At that moment Vickery and Kaiser began a friendship which has become an epic of verbal assault and battery. Kaiser has alternately called Vickery one of the greatest men in America, and the first man he will strangle with his bare hands right after the war. Vickery has maliciously goaded and jabbed Kaiser into setting records which could be put in front of other builders.

It was right after America entered the war that Vickery really turned on the screws. He had been summoned to meet with the President, Winston Churchill, Lord Beaverbrook, Harry Hopkins, and Admiral Land. The Allied Nations wanted 8,000,000 tons of merchant ships built in 1942 and 10,000,000 in 1943. Roosevelt asked Vickery if it could be done.

"Can I get the steel?" The steel was promised.

"Can I select the management of the shipyards without any interference from anyone?" The President grinned. Freedom of selection was approved.

"I'll get you the ships," said Vickery.

His shipbuilders had been planning their 1942 schedule by completing ships in an average of 210 days. He decided ships would have to be built in 105 days.

Here's how Saturday Evening Post records the reaction of the shipbuilders when told they had to build ships in 105 days:

> 'We can't do it!' they exploded. 'It's impossible.' Vickery went to work on Kaiser. For nearly a week Kaiser was bedeviled and insulted and ridiculed. 'Oh, so you're the man who can get things done? So you can build things? So you think you're a shipbuilder?' Vickery had located that one sensitive point. 'All right,' Kaiser said, 'if you think it can be done, we'll try. We'll get you your hundred-and-five-day ships!' Vickery hung up the telephone, rubbed his hands and bit into a fresh, black cigar. Then he placed a

series of calls all over the East. 'Kaiser's going to build hundred-and-five-day ships for me,' he announced. 'I scarcely suppose you fellows could keep up with him, could you?' That hurt. As a shipbuilder Kaiser was only a novice from the West Coast, and his name was already rasping and grating on sensitive prides. The Eastern builders, with their long tradition of shipbuilding couldn't afford to be outclassed. And all over America, from general manager down to the lowest laborer, the heat went on.

By late August 1942 Kaiser was launching his 55th Liberty ship. Vickery was in the audience when Kaiser spoke. Thomas L. Stokes of the New York World Telegram quoted Kaiser:

> I met Admiral Vickery when he arrived and told him I wanted to make a speech, too. I didn't tell him what I was going to say. Well, he made his speech. Then he sat back comfortably on the platform. You should have seen him when I began talking about using shipyards to build cargo planes. He didn't know anything like that was coming.

Then Stokes went on to write:

> But Admiral Vickery, knowing Henry Kaiser's record, got accustomed to the idea quickly. 'If he says it can be done, I'm not going to argue with him. Most of the big names in Washington thought I was crazy when I signed a contract with Henry Kaiser. They pleaded with me to cancel it. Mr. Kaiser didn't merely keep his word. He's the reason why this country is six months ahead of its shipbuilding schedule.'

Then miracle of miracles happened. In September 1942 in the Portland shipyards a vessel was built in ten days. Less than two months later the time was cut in half at Richmond. That was all Vickery needed. He began to ride other shipbuilders mercilessly. 'Kaiser's just built one in five days. Are your ships going to be ready for World War II or World War III?'

"That man's inhuman!" the builders swore. "He expects the impossible. Doesn't he know the problems we have?"

Vickery didn't always treat Kaiser with kid gloves. In testifying before the House Committee on Resolution 30, on November 30, 1943, Kaiser said:

> And I am back to Admiral Vickery. He doesn't pay any attention to launchings. Every time we launch a ship he sends us an insulting telegram and says the ship isn't 'delivered.' Launching means nothing to him. It's only actual deliveries when ships are ready to load cargo, that counts with him.

Typical of the communications Vickery was forever sending Kaiser was this wire of March 20, 1943:

> With the failure of the Richmond Shipbuilding Company to make deliver-

ies, I expect that you will now inform me that the responsibility for this yard is the same as with the California yard, and that you are not responsible. Is it true that Bedford and Henry Kaiser are spread too thin, and is it necessary that Edgar Kaiser carry the entire production load?

A month later Vickery sent a more detailed letter to Kaiser:

April 16, 1943

I am still considerably disturbed over your unsatisfactory performance at the Richmond 3 and 4 Yards. To date this month you have delivered only one LST. This seems a rather pitiful showing when four yards have been actually struggling to deliver these vessels, and as you know, the outfitting of this class of ship is no impossible task, as shown by the work done by Bethlehem Fairfield and the Vancouver Yard. Something must be done regarding this matter.

With reference to the C-4 vessels, I am not satisfied with the progress being made on them. I have just returned from a survey of the Sun Shipbuilding Yard where they have C-4's under construction. They laid the keel of their first C-4 a month after you had launched two of your vessels of the same general type. This yard is completely manned by colored labor which had no experience in shipbuilding. Their first C-4 will be launched in the early part of May and delivered some time in June. From the latest information I have received, you do not hope to get one of your C-4's into commission until July, which is some eight months after you launched the vessel. There undoubtedly is something radically wrong, and I think before this matter becomes the subject of a lot of adverse publicity for you, you should take steps to correct it.

It was on June 9, 1944, just three days after D-Day, the day U. S. troops landed on Normandy Beach, Vickery sent this wire to Kaiser:

Richmond Number One is making the worst record of any yard shifting from one design of ship to another. What are you going to do about it?

Kaiser replied the same day, but that didn't appease Vickery. On June 10 he wired Kaiser:

Reurtel. Can well realize that you have to take refuge behind the weather, as I understand there is no other alibi for your present poor record at Richmond Number One.

In Vickery's "knock-em-down, pick-em-up" style of operating he was always quick to give credit when it was due. In one breath he could be castigating the work of one Richmond yard, and in the next praising the work of another. After chewing on

Kaiser in June for the results in Yard One he made a special trip to Richmond the very next month to commend Yard Three for its work in turning out troop transport ships. His visit was recorded in the shipyard weekly news magazine, Fore 'N' Aft of July 14, 1944:

It was just one year to the day after certain 'little people,' in the words of Admiral Howard L. Vickery—and he really spit out the words—accused Yard Three of 'soldiering.' It was a big day—the day Yard Three workers were given both the Maritime Commission's 'M' pennant and the Vickery Fleet flag, along with merit badges for the individual workers. And what's more they got the awards from the two-fisted, hard-hitting Admiral Vickery himself, vice-chairman of the Maritime Commission, and the guy behind the nation's gigantic shipbuilding program. 'In the period of one year since those criticisms were made,' the Admiral declared, 'you Yard Three workers have delivered into service ships of more troop-carrying capacity than any other shipyard in the world has ever done before in history.' The big guy with the gold braid on his hat thundered it out and left no doubt he meant it. And it brought down the house. The worker-audience was still busy eating their lunches when Clay Bedford introduced Henry J. Kaiser. 'I'm hungry, too,' Kaiser exclaimed and then went on: 'The human heart is always hungry, too, for recognition and that's why Admiral Vickery is paying this visit to us.'

Vickery always played the Richmond and Portland shipyards against each other. Whatever good job one could do he would challenge the other to equal it. Although the records didn't always justify it, he seemed to chew on the Richmond shipyards more than on Portland. Thanks to the sense of humor Clay Bedford had (as well as the sense of humor Vickery had), one of the most memorable experiences for Bedford was his continuous exchange of wires with Vickery. Here are just a few samples:

From Bedford February 16, 1942:

We are sending you under separate cover one of our safety hats. You will note on the side of your hat is an ax ... but a broad ax, the significance of which we are sure you appreciate because of your ability to handle it well.

From Bedford March 24, 1942:

Dear 'Chief,' I received a very nice letter from you about the safety hat with the ax on it. It amazes me how you find time to write to anyone at all. In construction parlance, a construction 'stiff' recognizes the man who swings the big ax as the 'Big Chief.'

From Vickery April 20, 1943 (Re: Shipyard Two):

M C E hulls 1099 and 1100 scheduled for completion April 17 and 19 respectively have not been delivered. What is the trouble? Please advise.

From Vickery April 20, 1943 (Re: Shipyard One):

M C hulls 1003, 1004 and 1007 scheduled for completion April 16, 10 and 15 respectively have not been delivered. Why not? Please advise.

From Bedford April 21, 1943:

Retel Richmond Yards One and Two. At Yard One we delivered Hull 536 at 2:00 p.m.; Hull 1004 is on sea trial today and will be delivered tomorrow. At Richmond Two hull 1007 completed dock trial yesterday; sea trial will be held Friday; and delivery made April 24. Hull 1099 will be delivered tomorrow and Hull 1100 on 24th. In response to your request for reasons for failure to deliver in accordance with our estimated schedule, please be advised that during the first 19 days in April our hires were 6,872, our separations were 10,660, a loss of 3,788. Manpower is our principal difficulty. This is especially true on LST's, on account of our loss of electricians and pipefitters.

From Bedford July 20, 1943:

At 3:15 p.m. yesterday we delivered hull 1587. The delivery of this ship constitutes the 250th emergency cargo ship to be delivered from all the Permanente Metals Corporation Shipbuilding Division Shipyards. Are we now members of your exclusive club?

From Bedford September 9, 1943:

God bless you and good luck on your journey. And if you happen to see any steel, would you mind sending it to the Permanente Metals Corporation at Richmond, California, where we are patiently marking time waiting for an opportunity to show how many Liberties we really can produce and how cheaply.

From Vickery October 2, 1943:

With all facilities and materials you have, it does seem you might be able to emulate Oregon, instead of being a poor third.

From Bedford October 5, 1943:

Welcome home and if we knew how Oregon got all those materials away from you we would most certainly emulate them. As I advised you when you suggested that we slow down instead of shutting down for lack of material, we can run out of steel any time you wish and on short notice. There is so much interest around the Richmond shipyards in taking Oregon on anyway despite the shortage of materials and the lack of an assembly plant that we may not be able to keep the brakes on. So don't be too surprised if we have to shut down anyway before long.

From Bedford October 16, 1943:

We have for rent one very fine shipbuilding way with southern exposure and lots of services available for immediate occupancy. Last customer was launched on Way Four on October 15 and no materials for new customer are available. Convalescents from eastern shipyards taken without extra cost. Big opportunity—don't wait—act now!

From Vickery January 3, 1944

It affords me great pleasure to tell you that you and other shipyards met the Commission's challenge magnificently in 1943.

From Bedford January 11, 1944:

I received your telegram of January 3, and after checking with Western Union to find out if it actually came from you, since such a telegram from you is most amazing, I proceeded to have it printed in our weekly paper publication immediately, before it was withdrawn. I didn't answer your wire because it is my experience that every time I open my mouth, I manage to get my foot in it. So I just kept still and only bragged about it to our 90,000 people.

From Bedford June 9, 1944:

Contract delivery date first Victory ship Yard One is June 20. Only date I can ever remember telling you or anyone else was June 15 and I still don't think we'll miss that more than a week. We are trying to beat Oregon's outfitting record on our first Victory, but it is a tight squeeze. It must be hot in Washington. Can't you plan to come out and spend a little time helping us?

From Vickery August 15, 1944:

With Oregon's delivery you now understand what it means to be in first class competition. Don't you ever get out of the second division?

From Bedford August 15, 1944:

Retel. Only when the bread is buttered on the right side. P.S. The allocation for our second AP 5 is twelfth. Will bet you a hat that we deliver our second ship not later than the eighth AP 5 delivered.

The Vickery saga was one of the most fascinating home front by-plays of the entire war. He was a standout personality. He was a force. He moved men. He moved mountains. He was hated at times. He was respected at all times. Without any doubt the ship production was significantly higher because of him.

It meant a lot to Henry Kaiser to get a personal letter from Vickery at war's end. Vickery was so sure of Kaiser's mutual fondness he took the liberty of sending him an autographed picture, along with this letter:

January 11, 1946

Dear Henry:

At the close of our business relationship, which has been one of the most stimulating and often one of the most tempestuous, I would like to send you a memento which I hope will serve to remind you in future years of our many pleasant associations.

Sincerely yours,

H. L. Vickery

Baby Flat-Tops

Kaiser was seldom discouraged. It might even be said he was never discouraged. Some of his closest working associates would testify to that. They had watched him time and time again come up with a new approach to overcome seemingly hopeless problems. They knew he would always find a way to bounce back. Resilience was his very nature.

His natural buoyancy, however, would be put to the test on June 2, 1942. He and his able Washington, D.C., vice-president, Chad Calhoun, had just come from an "eighteen-minute meeting" with Admiral King and his top aides in the Navy Department. At that meeting, Kaiser had tried to get approval to build 100 small aircraft carriers, or CVE's as the Navy called them. Displaying colorful drawings of the proposed ships, and providing basic engineering data, Kaiser felt sure his proposal would win instant approval. After all, a contract for 50 CVE's, of somewhat similar design, had been given to the Seattle-Tacoma Shipbuilding Corporation, so the Navy had already accepted the concept of small carriers. Kaiser's message was that he could convert his Vancouver, Washington, shipbuilding yard to the exclusive production of the "baby flat-tops," and start turning them out fast enough to give a prompt lift to the war effort. He asserted that within six months after the start of production he would have 30 of the ships in the water.

To his amazement, the Navy "brass" didn't spark to his offer. They had been trained to rely on the might and serviceability of the full-size aircraft carriers, and, besides, they thought they already had enough small aircraft carriers on order. They had reservations as to just how these "tin cans" would stand up in a heavy barrage of bombs and torpedoes. Further, they didn't want to let production of these smaller carriers interfere in any way with the building of the larger carriers, or with the construction of cargo ships. They hastily voted 16 to 0 against his proposal.

Even with this unanimous decision against him, Kaiser didn't for a minute lose faith in his plan. All he could think about was what other avenue might be open for him to overcome the Navy's decision. Call it fate, call it Kaiser luck, as he and Calhoun were walking along the street, they happened to meet Mordecai Ezekiel, an acquaintance of Calhoun's. In the course of the conversation they took occasion to tell him about the turndown they had just gotten from the Navy. Ezekiel asked to see the drawings and the engineering data. They were standing on a sidewalk adjacent to a park, and the most convenient thing to do was to spread the papers on the lawn. For ten minutes the three men were on their hands and knees poring over the material. Kaiser stressed that the ships could be quickly built without serious interference with other ship construction; that the flight deck, 514 feet, was adequate for launching and landing the aircraft; that the ships would have extreme maneuverability, turning on a tiny radius ("practically a square corner"), compared with big aircraft carriers, thus reducing the vulnerability to bombs and torpedoes; that they would serve a dual purpose, not only as a base of operations for as many as 36 fighter planes but as a transport carrier bringing those planes to airfields near a scene of action; that the ships could be equipped with enough armament to defend themselves reasonably well; and that the cost would only be a fraction of the amount required for the large carriers.

Ezekiel took to the proposal immediately. As a personal friend of President Roosevelt, he said he thought the President should hear about the plan as soon as possible. He felt sure that the President, as a longtime Navy man, and as an admirer of Kaiser, would go for the idea. He, therefore, asked Kaiser and Calhoun to keep themselves available for a phone call in their hotel room that night. The hoped-for call did come—Ezekiel had made an appointment for the three of them to meet with the President the next morning.

When they arrived at the White House, they found that the President had asked Admiral King and several of his top aides, as well as Maritime Commission officials, to sit in the meeting. Kaiser was in his full glory. Without any rancor over the turn-down of the day before, Kaiser expounded upon all the advantages of the baby flat-tops. It didn't take the President long to decide. He could see that the small escort carriers could play an important role in winning the war. He thereupon requested Admiral King to get together with the Maritime Commission and work out the contract for Kaiser to build the baby flat-tops—originally calling for 100 ships but later cut back to 50 at the insistence of the Navy. In less than twenty-four hours Kaiser had gone from defeat to victory, a turnabout that might have surprised the Navy, but not those who knew Kaiser well.

Nine months later—on March 12, 1943—Kaiser brought to the White House a glass-encased model of his new aircraft carrier for viewing by the President, and by Vice-Admiral Emory Land, chairman of the Maritime Commission, Rear Admiral Howard Vickery, vice-chairman of the Maritime Commission, and Artemus Gates, assistant secretary of the Navy for air. It was acknowledged that the American carrier force had already been depleted by the sinking of four large carriers—the Yorktown, Lexington, Wasp, and Hornet. Roosevelt was more than ever pleased to see the model of the small carrier and to envision how 50 of them could make a big difference in the war effort. He had already sent a message to the Navy by agreeing to have his wife christen the first of these ships.

Now it was Eleanor's day, and a throng of some 50,000 persons—mostly workers and their families—witnessed the christening. It was reported in the newspapers:

Vancouver (Washington), April 5, 1943. Mrs. Franklin D. Roosevelt, christening her first ship on the Pacific Coast, crashed a bottle of champagne across the bow of the U.S.S. Alazon Bay today and Henry J. Kaiser's first aircraft carrier slipped into the Columbia River. The vessel, a new type of escort carrier being built for the American and British Navies, is the first of a series to be turned out at the rate of six a month. In a press conference before the launching she said, 'The President is greatly interested in this type of ship and has great hopes that it will be a decisive implement in winning the war. He has sent Mr. Kaiser his very best wishes and hellos to the workmen.' She added that the Vancouver Kaiser yard was the 'neatest and tidiest I have ever seen, and everyone seemed busy at his or her particular job. I was pleased that your housing projects haven't forgotten the importance of schools and hospitals. I was particularly impressed with the dormitories (Hudson House) and could see the possibilities of the family center (Vanport City) I just visited.' The Alazon Bay was not the first carrier she had christened. She recalled her sponsorship of both the Yorktowns, the old which became a war casualty, and the new, just beginning its war career. The Kaiser escort carriers are identical, the Navy said, to others which have gone from Pacific Coast shipyards and are now in service, but the others have been converted from cargo hulls while the Kaiser craft was built as a carrier from the keel up.

Kaiser was determined to make good on his promise for quick delivery of the carriers, and so was his son Edgar who was vice- president and general manager of the Portland and Vancouver shipyards. Using their patented technique of throwing out a challenge to the workers, the slogan was adopted, "Eighteen or more by 1944." The production race was on. At the end of 1943 one of the Vancouver workers expressed the pride of all of them:

How does it feel to win a race against time? Every person who worked at Vancouver in December of 1943 knows just how good is the joy of winning. The Kaiser Company shut down operations for Christmas, but the Gambier Bay, the nineteenth ship, was delivered December 28th. It was the bonus ship—our Christmas present to our Navy. We sent it off with our old gang-plank slogan 'THIS IS A FIGHTING SHIP. GIVE IT YOUR BEST.'

Admiral Howard Vickery, Vice-Chairman of the United States Maritime Commission, seemed to know just when to give praise for good work done by shipyards and just when to jab with a sharp needle to demand greater productivity. In the case of the Vancouver yard, he never had to use his needle. Instead, he was quick to praise the Vancouver workers for getting their escort aircraft carriers into production "in such a short time." Later he congratulated the Vancouver yard for spending less manhours building its baby aircraft carriers than most yards spent building the simpler and more standard Liberty ships. The Vancouver yard was credited with building its aircraft carriers in one-third the time that a regular Navy yard would require to build a similar vessel. And later, when critics of Kaiser would search for something to complain about, they would contend he was mainly interested in making big profits. The Vancouver yard conversion would put the lie to that, because experienced shipbuilders knew the earnings from building Liberty ships would have been far greater than building escort carriers. In the end, the Navy and the Maritime Commission proudly stressed that, not including the engines and other equipment furnished by the Maritime Commission, Kaiser's cost of building the 50 carriers was only $5,573,000 each, an incredible achievement.

As dramatic as the escort carrier production was—all fifty of them completed in sixteen months—the real heroics took place in the battle zones. At first, some Navy men made a play on words contemptuously calling them "Kaiser's Coffins." Only two of them were sent to the Atlantic because by the time they were delivered the German submarine threat had greatly lessened. In the Pacific, however, they were in the thick of every major battle. The first ones cut their teeth in the Aleutian Islands and continued through the invasions of the Gilberts, the Marshalls, Hollandia, the Marianas, and the Palau Islands. As reported in Time magazine of September 4, 1944, "Last week a CVE air squadron, Composite Squadron 33, was home after ten months of combat in the South Pacific. Planes and guns of the baby carrier had destroyed 35 Jap aircraft. The little flat-tops had become an offensive weapon."

At Saipan, they broke the world's record for continuous operation by a naval task force inside an enemy area, staying twenty-three days while under almost continuous attack by hordes of dive bombers, until the island was captured. Their planes kept the Japanese submarines away from the transports, they knocked down aerial attackers, they blasted enemy guns ahead of U.S. ground forces, they flew the artillery and infantry observers, they flew the reconnaissance photographers, they strafed the beaches minutes ahead of the landing barges, they ferried out the Army planes as soon as the airfield had been won. They did all this day-after-day, week-after-week, until victory was theirs. Said one Admiral: "Without these baby flat-tops, the U. S. Navy would not be fighting today west of the Marianas."

But it was in the battle of Leyte Gulf in the Philippines that the small carriers reached their highest glory. For five hell-filled hours a handful of these lightly-armored CVE's slugged it out toe-to-toe with the major units of the Imperial Japanese battle fleet. Two of the carriers were sunk, others were badly damaged, but they fought the enemy groggy until larger allied units could move in for the kill. Admiral Thomas Kinkaid said the baby carriers played an "unbelievable" part in the rout of the Japanese. Admiral Vickery in Washington wired Kaiser: "We owe this day to you and to your aircraft carriers."

A few months later one of the carriers, the Ommaney Bay, took on the Japanese practically singlehanded. The drama was reported in the New York Times of February 14, 1945:

> The Ommaney Bay, an escort carrier which in her six months in the Pacific had sunk or damaged the equivalent of a Japanese task force, has been lost in the Philippine area as a result of enemy action, the Navy Department announced today. The ship which had participated in the invasions of the Palaus, Leyte and Mindoro was sunk by Japanese air action. She was caught with all her planes aboard. She was the fifth escort carrier and the tenth carrier of all types lost in the war. The Navy Department said the Ommaney Bay and her planes had sunk one heavy cruiser of more than 10,000 tons, damaged four cruisers, attacked and probably damaged three battleships with torpedoes and bombs, damaged four destroyers, sunk one troop transport, shot sixteen enemy planes out of the air, damaged or destroyed 'many planes' on the ground, bombed scores of enemy anti-aircraft guns, dugouts, trenches, pillboxes, ammunition dumps, oil storages, supply dumps and transport vehicles and wiped out a large number of Japanese ground troops with bombs, rockets and bullets.

The Ommaney Bay, a Kaiser-built 'baby flat-top' of 10,902 tons, was commissioned on February 11, 1944, and got into action in time to support the Palau invasion last September. Her Wildcat fighter and Avenger torpedo bombers softened the beachheads and supported ground troops for twelve days. Once the Avengers caught a heavy concentration of Japanese troops with ten accurate bomb hits.

At Leyte in October the Ommaney Bay helped fight off the Japanese battleship fleet that tried to reach the American beachhead. On October 24, the day of the big fleet battle, her airmen fought two enemy forces.

When the Mindoro invasion came in December, the Ommaney Bay provided air cover for a naval task force.

Two days after the New York Times article Kaiser wrote to his good friend, Henry Luce, publisher of Time magazine:

Dear Henry,

Because I feel as close to you as I do, I always have been distressed about the 'Kaiser Coffin' article, particularly so, because it was in Time magazine. (Thereupon, Kaiser summarized the highlights of the New York Times article listing the war action of Ommaney Bay. Then Kaiser went on to say:) You and I were on the first trial trip of one of these ships. You saw the production organization which we had labored for two years to achieve. Fifty of these carriers were built in sixteen months. Last night, in reading that 1,200 planes from carriers had bombed Tokyo, I could think only of how many of the 1,200 had flown off aircraft carriers built at Vancouver.

Kaiser coffins, indeed. It was more like Japanese coffins. Before the war had ended the Navy knew, and the Japanese knew, that the novel baby flat-tops had played a decisive role in one sea battle after another.

And, with an appropriate measure of pride, Kaiser could look back to the time when some three years earlier, after being turned down by Navy Admiral King, he had gotten on his hands and knees on a Washington, D.C. park lawn, along with Chad Calhoun and Mordecai Ezekiel to study the drawings of the proposed carrier that would be used to open the door for President Roosevelt's approval.

It, therefore, had its own kind of personal meaning to Kaiser when this letter was written to him February 24, 1945:

Dear Mr. Kaiser:

Thanks for your note of February 17th. Needless to say, I am as pleased as you are by the fine battle performance of the escort carriers.

Sincerely yours,
E. J. King, Fleet Admiral, U.S. Navy

I Christen Thee

Production was the name of the game. It was ships alone that counted. Why bother with any fanfare? Why bother with any fancy christenings? Why go to the trouble and expense of formal launchings?

Don't say that to any shipbuilder. He knows that christenings give meaning to all the planning, all the work, and all the materials that go into the building of a ship. To do without a christening would be like constructing a magnificent building without dedicating it. To do without a christening would be to flaunt one of man's proudest traditions.

With the full blessing and encouragement of the Maritime Commission, Kaiser and his people were almost as outstanding in the way they christened ships as in the way they built them. Their biggest challenge was to arrange the christenings as fast as the ships were being built. It was no simple matter to do all the organizing involved in launching 1490 ships in the four short years from the first launching in August, 1941 till the war's end in August, 1945. That figures out to be almost exactly one launching a day, although, of course, there were two different shipyards and seven different shipways over which the launchings were spread.

Just think of the single problem of choosing names for all of the ships. At first, the Maritime Commission specified that it would provide the names. With all the launchings going on around the country they soon had to enlist the help of the shipyards themselves in selecting names. They started out by picking important names in American history, then from history in general, then foreign countries.

Here is a small sample of the range of names that were picked from all walks of life.

The George Gipp   Notre Dame Halfback
The Matthew B. Brady   Civil War Photographer
Michael Pupin   Inventor
Edward A. McDowell   Musician
Joseph Smith   Founder of Mormonism
General Robert L. Howze   Military Leader
Cyrus Hamlin   Missionary
Tecumseh   Indian Chief
John L. Sullivan   Prize Fighter
Henry Bergh   SPCA Founder

Since nearly all Liberty and Victory ships have by now been scrapped, these names no longer ride the waves. Their wartime mission was accomplished; their peacetime services were no longer needed as they grew old and as newer, faster ships came along.

Choosing sponsors for the ship launchings posed an even tougher—though much more pleasant—challenge than selecting names for the ships. All sponsors, of course, were women. It was the inviolable tradition of the sea that sponsors had to be women. Superstition warned that ill fate would befall any ship sponsored by a man.

A big pool of sponsors came from the wives of government officials—from Mrs. Franklin D. Roosevelt, to the wife of the chairman of the Maritime Commission, to the wives of Senators and Congressmen and state officials at many levels. Women in the public limelight were prime candidates, and every such acquaintance of a Kaiser official was invited to christen a ship at one time or another. Wives of company employees were frequently smashing champagne bottles. My wife, Dora, had the high honor of christening the ship, SS Iraq Victory, in Richmond Shipyard Number One on the evening of June 6, 1944—D-Day. During the war, the women who sponsored ship launchings could have formed one of the most representative, and strongest, women's groups in the country.

The invitations to become a sponsor had to be handled on the highest possible level. Kaiser himself extended the invitations to scores of women. Edgar Kaiser and Clay Bedford were constantly involved in making the choices and contacting the invitees.

In addition to the sponsors themselves, nearly every launching included a lady Matron of Honor and a Presenter of Flowers. Then, of course, it was always necessary to have a speaker, or speakers, as well as a minister for the invocation and blessing on the ship.

Programs were always printed up, and an abundance of pictures were taken, which would go to make a fine, bound album to be given later to the sponsor and the other major participants. The champagne bottle was always wrapped tightly in red, white and blue ribbon so that even though the champagne was splashed on the ship, the broken glass caught in the ribbons could be given to the sponsor as a memento.

Transportation arrangements to and from the shipyards were always provided for the main participants, as well as hotel reservations when necessary.

Clearly, this was big business. It not only required forward planning by top company officials, it necessitated full time departments at both Richmond and Portland to keep on top of all that had to be done.

In Retrospect

It was the shipyards that made Kaiser a national hero. His other enterprises commanded national attention, but the shipyards alone gave him national stature.

Dambuilding? Indispensable to western economy, but Kaiser was only one of a team of builders.

Cement production? He had the biggest and most efficient plant in the country, but the impact was largely regional.

Steel manufacture? Unbelievably bold in overcoming so many odds, but only a small percentage of national production.

Aluminum manufacture? Extremely successful and big, but very little pioneering.

Automobile manufacture? A gallant try that came incredibly close to succeeding.

Hawaiian developments? Far more outstanding than the country has ever recognized.

Hospitals and health care? The most successful and enduring of all his enterprises.

But most of all, the public remembers, and history will record, that it was ship-building where Kaiser served his country's greatest needs.

Consider these astounding figures:

Richmond 747

Portland 743

Kaiser built: Seven new shipyards with a total of 58 building ways

1,490 ocean-going ships, 1,383 merchant ships and

107 warships

13 different types of ships

25.73% of total shipbuilding program of the U.S.

Maritime Commission 1941-45

Total dollar volume of Kaiser program: $4,019,256,462

Peak employment: 197,000 persons

Richmond No. 1 yard (Permanente Metals Corp.) built:

30 British freighters

138 Liberty ships

53 Victory cargo ships Total: 221

Richmond No. 2 yard (Permanente Metals Corp.) built:

351 Liberty ships

67 Victory cargo ships

22 Combat transports Total: 440

Richmond No. 3 yard (Kaiser Company Inc.) built:

30 Troop transports

5 Troop carriers Total: 35

Richmond No. 4 yard (Kaiser Cargo Inc.) built:

12 Frigates

24 Coastal cargo

15 Landing ship, tanks Total: 51

TOTAL RICHMOND: 747

Portland, Ore. yard (Oregon Ship Building Corp.) built:

330 Liberty ships

99 Victory cargo ships

34 Combat transports Total: 463

Swan Island, Portland Yard
(Kaiser Company, Inc.) built:
147 Tankers Total: 147

Vancouver, Wash. yard (Kaiser Company Inc.) built:
2 Liberty ships
31 Combat transports
30 Landing ship tanks
20 Troop transports
50 Escort carriers Total: <u>133</u>
TOTAL PORTLAND: 743

TOTAL RICHMOND AND PORTLAND: 1,490

Just how important these shipyards were to the nation is for historians to continue to explore.

In the heat of the battle, Admiral Chester W. Nimitz, Pacific Fleet Commander, sent his picture and this handwritten autograph:

27 May 1943

To Permanente Ship Yards at Richmond, California

American fighting men are on the offensive on all fronts. To keep the initiative until our enemies are beaten we must have an increasing and steadily increasing flow of the materials necessary to successful action. Victory in the Pacific will depend in an important measure on ships built by West Coast yards.

The British military historian J. F. C. Fuller declared that victory in World War II was not decided on the battlefields but, "for the first time in the history of war, battles were as much tussles between competing factories as between contending armies. The production of weapons, more so than the conscription of men, was the deciding factor in battle. God now marched with the biggest industries, rather than with the biggest battalions."

Sir Arthur Salter, head of the British Shipping Mission to the United States, praised the production skills of "men like Henry J. Kaiser who have in the most literal sense the faith that moves mountains. Without his ships, it appeared then, and can be seen even more certainly in retrospect, Britain would have otherwise been forced into defeat."

At the Teheran conference between President Roosevelt, Prime Minister Churchill, and Marshal Stalin, late in 1943, the Soviet leader proposed a toast: "To American production, without which this war would have been lost."

Winston Churchill, the most seasoned of all the gladiators, wrote: "Without the supply columns of Liberty ships that endlessly plowed the seas between America and England, the war would have been lost."

How important were Kaiser ships?

It was not only victory that hung in the balance, it was all the lives that would be saved by shortening the war.

If ten thousand lives were saved, if only one life was saved, the world owes Henry Kaiser, and all the other shipbuilders, and all the shipyard workers, a debt of gratitude. A fitting memorial to all of them might be one of Kaiser's favorite poems:

> We never know how high we stand
> 'till we are called to rise
> And then if we are true to plan
> our statures touch the skies.

CHAPTER 7

A FLING AT AIRPLANES

"It isn't power, it's persuasion that makes things successful. The more we grow in size, the more it will be by persuasion."

Flying Box Cars

The gall of the man. The absolute, unmitigated gall.

Here he was in the summer of 1942, just six months after war had been declared, proclaiming from one end of the land to the other that America should be mass-producing flying box cars, and that he was ready to take the lead. He repeatedly insisted the country could produce 5,000 such planes a year.

He had never manufactured an airplane before. At the outset he didn't have anyone working for him who knew anything about airplanes. But then he hadn't produced cement before he built his own mill from scratch. Nor had he been in the magnesium and steel business, and already he had broken those barriers. Most of all, he knew nothing about building ships, and now a year and a half later, he was the country's biggest shipbuilder, setting new records for speed of production month after month.

He didn't postpone his public pronouncements until he had researched the subject. He just "knew" the planes could be built, so he stuck his neck out, ready to prove to the government, to the aircraft industry, and to the public that his ideas were feasible. Only then did he start hiring some aircraft experts to back up his contentions.

One of the first persons he pumped was the famous test pilot, Vance Breese. For several hours Kaiser talked his scheme out in Oakland with his long-time friend and adviser. Breese thought they were through and went down to Los Angeles to see his family and look into his own business.

At 8 o'clock that night Kaiser turned up at the Breese home. He wanted to talk some more, and did—until 1 a.m., when both went to bed. Breese was awakened suddenly at 4 a.m. by someone whistling outside his window. It was Kaiser. So he got up.

Between that time and 8 o'clock, when the two had to leave for appointments, Kaiser was constantly on the telephone to Washington, talking to Donald Nelson, General Arnold, and other top officials.

Some of Kaiser's stiffest opposition came from the Army. One meeting where he was grilled mercilessly was with Lt. Gen. Brehon B. Somervell, chief of the Army's Services of Supply, Lt. Gen. Henry H. Arnold, chief of the Army Air Forces, and their aides. The strongest objection dealt with the shortage of materials needed to produce the planes. Kaiser responded by telling how he built a magnesium plant which was already in production whereas Henry Ford's magnesium plant was not yet turning out any metal.

"That makes you better than Henry Ford," interjected General Somervell.

"That's plain sarcasm," Kaiser shot back. "I don't think that is worthy of a man in your high position."

Then, according to reports of what happened, the two barked back and forth at each other with some display of heat until General Arnold intervened to restore good humor.

After the luncheon was over, Kaiser grabbed General Somervell about the waist in a bear hug and good-naturedly lifted him clear off the floor, shaking him in his big arms.

"I like a tough fight—and you are going to get one," he told the General with a smile.

In another Washington meeting an Air Force officer chided Kaiser: "You're talking as far ahead of the times as Leonardo da Vinci." Kaiser missed the needle entirely. As he left the room with his Washington man, Chad Calhoun, he turned to him and said, "Have we talked to da Vinci yet?"

By mid-summer Kaiser was really getting up a head of steam. He was popping off to anyone who would listen, and there were plenty of eager listeners. The July 27, 1942, issue of Time magazine ran this story under the heading, "Kaiser Takes To The Air":

> The biggest, most dramatic shake-up in transportation since the Wright Brothers got their flimsy biplane off the sand at Kitty Hawk is just around the corner—that is, if fabulous Henry J. Kaiser has his way. This week Engineer-Shipbuilder Kaiser pulled all the talk about air freighters right down to earth with a concrete proposal to build in 1943 at least 5,000 giant 70-ton flying boats like the Glenn L. Martin Mars. 'These ships could land 500,000 fully equipped men in England in a single day,' he cried. 'The next day they could fly over again with 70,000 tons of fresh milk, beefsteaks, sugar and bombs. No submarines could shoot them down.'

The aircraft industry was not sold on Kaiser's ideas. They not only considered it far too visionary but even if it had some practical aspects they could not see where the materials would come from to build all those planes. As president of Eastern Air Lines, Captain Eddie Rickenbacker, World War I ace flyer and national hero, didn't hesitate to raise his doubts. In a Senate subcommittee hearing he said "there's a hell of a lot of difference between building ships and making airplanes."

Although the aircraft manufacturers were very skeptical of Kaiser's proposal they tried to be open-minded and at least respectful. Phil G. Johnson, president of the Boeing Aircraft company said, "I don't think it is possible to convert a shipyard into an aircraft plant—that is, readily. However, if such a plan were attempted, we would do everything in our power to make it a success."

Harry Woodhead, president of Consolidated Aircraft Corporation challenged Kaiser head-on:

> If he means flying boats like the Mars, why it would be absolutely impossible to put that into production in 10 months. It would take 4 years to put such ships into production. 'And what good would that do to the war effort today,' he asked, quickly answering himself. 'No good at all. Wouldn't it be smarter to put the strength even to experiment with Kaiser's ideas in to producing more and more of the good cargo planes we already have. Four of our B-24's can carry more tonnage than the unproved Mars and it would be cheaper to build four B-24's than one Mars, a good deal cheaper. Then supposing one of the B-24's gets shot down. You still have three-fourths of your cargo-carrying capacity left with the other three. But if a plane like the Mars was sunk, there'd go your enormous investment in one shot. We're still willing to welcome Henry Kaiser the minute we're convinced he really has something to contribute to victory in the air.'

Kaiser was accustomed to this kind of opposition, so it really didn't rattle him. As one news reporter put it:

> One nice thing about Mr. Kaiser is that he doesn't get mad at the men who oppose his ideas. He doesn't believe in going out and blasting at men who tell him he can't do things. But patiently, thoroughly, he starts on a campaign of education to bring these men with different ideas into line with his own. He's an old hand at being told that things can't be done.

The ultimate courtesy to Kaiser took place at the Santa Monica, California, plant of Douglas Aircraft on August 24, 1942, where a meeting of aircraft manufacturers and Kaiser was held under orders from Donald M. Nelson, War Production Board head, "to study and evaluate Kaiser's proposal from a practical manufacturing standpoint." Those in attendance were:

Donald W. Douglas, president of Douglas Aircraft
Glenn L. Martin, president of the Glenn L. Martin Company
John K. Northrop, president of Northrop Aircraft
Grover Loening, War Production Board consultant

A picture of the four industry leaders with Kaiser was carried in newspapers throughout the country. No public statements were offered by the aircraft leaders, but subsequent action by the War Production Board would clearly indicate the industry did not endorse the Kaiser ideas. But as usual Kaiser would speak out, "Everything's fine. We'll do the job. But whether the government wants them or not is another question."

It didn't take long for the government to answer that question. Less than a month later—on September 17, 1942—a letter of intent from Defense Plant Corporation authorized Kaiser and Howard Hughes "to proceed with the design, engineering, and construction of 3 cargo planes (flying boat type) similar to the designs which they had submitted to the War Production Board." The contract was for $18 million and work was undertaken on a non-profit basis without fees of any kind. The 3 cargo planes authorized were to consist of one for experimental purposes and two for flying purposes. Due to the cost, size of the plane, and scarcity of materials, construction of only one was commenced at Culver City, California, under the direction of Howard Hughes in his existing plant which was enlarged to accommodate the project.

The teaming up with Howard Hughes was a last-minute expediency that was only announced the very same day that Kaiser was meeting with the aircraft industry leaders, August 24, 1942. Exploratory discussions with Hughes had taken place just a couple of weeks prior, in a kind of a harum-scarum acquaintanceship, not at all untypical of the dealings Kaiser would experience with Hughes in the years ahead. The first overture was made by Kaiser in a phone call he tried to put through to Hughes. Hughes' right- hand man took the call and dared to wake the 36-year-old Hughes who was sleeping at the time. At first, Hughes declined to accept the call, but when his assistant said that Kaiser was coming to meet with him and was already talking as though Hughes would be producing giant planes for him, Hughes finally condescended to take the call. For the next few days one call after another from Kaiser was shunted aside. Each time Hughes' assistant would promise to have him call back but it would never materialize. However, Kaiser was not to be denied. He finally reached an understanding that he would come from Oakland on a weekend to work out partnership details. He took three assistants with him on the Southern Pacific train to Los Angeles Friday night which would give them all day Saturday and Sunday to meet with Hughes and his people. Saturday morning Kaiser tried to reach Hughes by phone, but to no avail. Again, Saturday afternoon and all day Sunday, no contact. Finally, Kaiser blew his top. He demanded to talk to Hughes and gave him an ultimatum"—"either we get together before I return on the train tonight or there will be no partnership." Hughes at last agreed he would meet Kaiser in the parking lot of the Southern Pacific Glendale station at 7:00 p.m., two hours before the train was to leave. It was a genuine surprise when he actually showed up. Immediately, Kaiser and Trefethen got into the back of Hughes' limousine and within an hour had agreed to team up in the production of flying boats.

Armed with this partnership understanding, Kaiser was in a position to close a deal with Donald Nelson. He could stress Hughes' existing facilities, his know-how, his successful production of other planes, his experience with the use of wood and other substitute materials. It was the springboard to win that first airplane contract, however tiny it was compared to Kaiser's boast of 5,000 flying box cars a year.

Once the contract was signed, it became almost exclusively a Hughes' show. Kaiser had been talking of mass producing planes in his shipyards and now all he had was an order for three planes. Obviously, no attempt was ever made to convert his shipyards into airplane-producing plants.

It was the strangest kind of match—Kaiser, family man, straight arrow, tireless worker, dreamer and doer, mass production expert, greatly overweight, 60 years old; and Hughes, 36-year-old playboy, brilliant aviation engineer, champion speed aviator, scratch golfer, movie tycoon. They seldom sat across the table from each other to go over any manufacturing details. Their contacts were mostly random phone calls touching only on the highlights. From time to time their paths would cross, permitting somewhat unplanned discussions to take place.

Kaiser's indispensable secretary Edna Knuth (Piper) remembers several of these get-togethers, one in particular:

> This was at the Shoreham Hotel in Washington, D.C., and Mr. Kaiser had an appointment with Howard Hughes who was going to be flying in his own airplane. We were to meet in the bar, and Mother Kaiser and I and Mr. Kaiser were there when in walked Howard Hughes in his sneakers and no necktie, but he did have a jacket of sorts on. Sure enough he had a blond on his arm, this time with long hair over one eye. They came in and had dinner with us, and I think Mother Kaiser almost died. But it was interesting because that didn't bother Mr. Kaiser. He was talking business with Hughes and it was a big night for him. He didn't care about the blond.

It could accurately be said the Kaiser-Hughes' program was doomed from the start. Not the least of the problems was that the government mandated that the prototype plane be made of plywood because of the desperate shortage of aluminum and magnesium required by the other plane manufacturers. This wasn't considered insurmountable, because Hughes already had experience in the use of plywood. But the problems piled up and the prototype had not been completed by the end of 1943. It was no surprise, therefore, that on February 11, 1944, Chairman Donald Nelson of the War Production Board called for the cancellation of the Kaiser-Hughes' contract. By March 27 all the details covering the cancellation were carried out and a new agreement provided that only the plane under construction should be completed ready for flight. In view of the fact that Kaiser's original interest was in the mass production of huge planes, he terminated his connection with the project and relinquished his interest to the Hughes Aircraft Company.

There was a temporary flurry regarding conversion of the plane to metal, because plywood had come into shorter supply than metal. However, Hughes stuck to his plans, determined to pioneer in the use of plywood for the monster plane. Actually the costs kept mounting, and before he was through Hughes had been forced to spend an additional $2 million over the $18 million provided in the original government contract. By then the designation of the plane had been changed from HK-1 (Hughes-Kaiser) to H-4, properly reflecting that it had become exclusively a Howard Hughes' project.

It is to his eternal credit that Hughes went to the trouble and company expense to complete the plane. More glamour than ever began to surround the plane, and once it had been named the "Spruce Goose" it had become a household word.

The "Spruce Goose" never took to the air until after World War II had ended, so it never served its original purpose. But, piloted by Hughes himself, it did make a much-publicized short distance flight over water. It was almost a bigger achievement to haul the plane a short distance over land to its final resting place at Long Beach near another transportation leviathan, The Queen Mary. These two majestic relics of glory days have become a sightseeing "must" for visitors to that area—the plane giving everyone an added sense of pride in the industrial might of America.

Was the "Spruce Goose" worth all the breast-beating and furor of the previous three years? Critics of Kaiser would proclaim a resounding "No," but the public wouldn't share that view. People knew Kaiser had performed a valuable war service by sounding his own kind of alarm over the need for more and bigger aircraft. And they tended to forget that the flying box car program never got off the ground, because they kept hearing how the Kaiser shipyards were setting new production records right through to the end of the war.

Even the aircraft manufacturers never saw fit to belittle Kaiser (or Hughes). No doubt they had stepped up their own production somewhat because of the needling that Kaiser gave them.

The proposed "Flying Box Car" program had served the country well in its own way and both Kaiser and Hughes could share in the pride of their efforts.

Oh, What A Beautiful Day

Have you ever heard a businessman start a speech by bursting into song? An unprofessional singer without musical accompaniment? A bald, fat man of 61 years?

Some 7,500 workers at the Brewster Aeronautical plant at La Guardia Airport in New York City did on Sunday, November 7, 1943. They had come to hear the new president of their company tell how, with their help, he was going to work wonders in stepping up production of fighter airplanes.

Just one month earlier Henry Kaiser had taken over the presidency of strike-ridden Brewster at the insistence of the Navy. Now he was addressing 7,500 Brewster employees, management and labor, to try to fire them with enthusiasm and confidence. But he couldn't contain himself:

"I feel so cheerful I could sing to you." Then before his audience could catch on that he was serious, he broke into a song hit from Oklahoma, the last line of which he paraphrased to fit the occasion:

> Oh, what a beautiful morning,
> Oh, what a beautiful day,
> I got a beautiful feeling,
> Everything's going our way.

The newspapers reported that Kaiser later was inclined to take a modest view of his renditions:

> You can't actually say that I sang, because I can't sing, but it was a beautiful morning and it was a beautiful day, and I certainly felt like singing. Seeing all those people there and the planes they helped to make, well, it gives you a feeling of confidence. That's why I couldn't help but do my best in trying to sing.

Kaiser's involvement was an outgrowth from all the clamor he had been raising ever since the war began about the need to mass produce large cargo planes. The Navy decided that with his interest in plane production—and his proven record in mass production of ships—he might be just the man to work a miracle at Brewster, so in March 1943, they asked him to become chairman of the board working hand-in-hand with the newly elected Brewster president, Frederick Riebel, Jr.

It had been a deplorable situation. The war had been going on for nearly a year and a half, and the production of fighter planes at Brewster was pitifully low. Management blamed labor, particularly branding Tom DeLorenzo, local president of the CIO's United Automobile Workers, as dishonest and unpatriotic, interested only in holding the company at ransom. DeLorenzo in turn blamed management for actions that led to all the disputes, slowdowns, and wildcat strikes.

Notwithstanding the new approach that both management and labor had announced when Riebel took over as president, things went from bad to worse. By October the Navy concluded it had no choice but to remove Riebel as president of Brewster and to prevail upon Kaiser to take charge. It was written up in Time Magazine November 1, 1943:

> Frederick Riebel, Jr., was ousted from his $30,000-a-year job as president of Brewster three weeks ago. Testifying before the House Naval Affairs Committee, Mr. Riebel rattled all the Brewster skeletons in public. Sometimes weeping softly, sometimes roaring with rage, frog-voiced Mr. Riebel blamed all the troubles at Brewster on the 'hellish' contract it had with the union. He lashed out at the union's tough, head-strong boss, Tom DeLorenzo, impaled lesser officials as 'punks and heels,' denounced the local itself as that 'gang of forty thieves.' The committee asked, 'In view of all this, could Brewster's new president, Henry J. Kaiser, get Brewster into production?' Riebel replied, 'I say a little prayer every night for Kaiser's success

at Brewster.' But pachydermatous Mr. Kaiser showed no embarrassment, wanted no prayers. He calmly stated that Brewster's failure to produce planes was due to lack of cooperation between labor and management. He promised to end this and get Brewster producing on schedule. Kaiser said, 'You can't cure a patient by whipping him.'

Because fighter planes were so desperately needed by both United States and England, Congress thought it had the right to get to the bottom of Brewster's problems. Even though Kaiser had not asked for the job, and indeed had tried to turn it down, he was treated almost as an adverse witness in day-long hearings on House Resolution 30, November 30, 1943. Congressman Melvin J. Maas from Minnesota was the principal interrogator:

Mr. Maas.	Mr. Kaiser, I notice in your letter to Mr. Gates you said on page 8 that 'the responsible union leaders at the Brewster plant assure management of their desire that we should continue, and give assurance that we will receive the support and cooperation of labor in order to achieve an increase in plane production for the maintenance of the war effort.' They have opposed every other manager, but they do endorse your management. Why? What makes you think that they endorse your management while they opposed every other management at Brewster?
Mr. Kaiser.	I guess I have confidence and faith and trust.
Mr. Maas.	Of course, if you give all the candy he wants, he is for you; isn't he?
Mr. Kaiser.	That isn't what I said. You are making a statement that I am giving them the candy; I am not.
Mr. Maas.	You said that when you had a fight with the union, production went down and costs went up.
Mr. Kaiser.	Do you want to know what I told him?
Mr. Maas.	If you have production up now, is it because you don't fight with them anymore, but capitulate to them?
Mr. Kaiser.	I would love to tell you what I first told Tom. I told Tom this: 'Why should you be concerned with but one thing? You say you are interested in your people, the people you represent. If you are, it is necessary to make them so efficient that six months later, when we are

going into the post-war era, they can exist and live, produce and create in a competitive market and make a living for themselves and their families. Tom, the sooner you start moving in that direction the greater will be your service to your members.'

The interrogation dragged on through the morning hours with Maas constantly challenging Kaiser: "Just what new things are you doing that will turn Brewster around?"

Mr. Maas.	I don't want to know what your staff knows about. I want to know what you know about it.
Mr. Kaiser.	I have just told you I never do the work, I am an executive. I hope that I am building morale. I build men. I hope I take those men that exist and build better men of them. You know that is the way to do it in your own heart.
Mr. Maas.	That is a very nice platitude.
Mr. Kaiser.	They are not platitudes. Thank God they are not platitudes.
Mr. Maas.	They are good platitudes.
Mr. Kaiser.	Do you know how many men I am employing under me? Three hundred thousand.
Mr. Maas.	I merely wanted to know—
Mr. Kaiser.	Do you think I employ that many people by platitudes?
Mr. Maas.	You told me you are an executive, you get other people to do the work.
Mr. Kaiser.	I do, but I have to talk to the other people to get them to do it.
Mr. Maas.	That is what I know, but in a broad way as the president—
Mr. Kaiser.	(interposing) Listen, I talked to them last night after midnight. I got up this morning and talked to them before they even got there, and I had to wait for them to get there to talk to them. I am at it day and night and everybody knows that.
Mr. Maas.	I have just one or two questions and then I'm through, Mr. Kaiser.

Mr. Kaiser.   Thank God.

Thereupon, Kaiser gave a lengthy description of how people had tried to get him to buy Brewster, and how he had turned them down. He ended by saying that the Navy pleaded with him to take over the chairmanship. Kaiser continued:

> I later discussed it with Secretary Forrestal, with Secretary Gates, and with our counsel, and finally after much discussion, the result was they said if you will take the chairmanship of this board we have a man here who has been very successful with the Navy, Mr. Riebel, and you will have no problems other than the chairmanship, it will help the labor position, it will help generally, and Mr. Riebel will do all the work that is necessary; and Mr. Riebel was present and told me how much he could do and what he would accomplish. We need the planes. That was the conversation, that was the situation that existed then and exists today. So I took it and I guess I had blinders on when I did.

Mr. Maas.   I am glad that while your name is being used you are actually going to run the company now.

Mr. Kaiser.   Yes. That is no credit to me. I didn't want to. It was just a tough deal and my conscience would not permit me to give up the production of those Corsairs. It just would not permit me to do it.

Kaiser had been on the witness stand all morning. When the hearing reconvened in the afternoon it was Congressman Hebert who grilled him relentlessly. The questioning kept putting Kaiser on the spot, not so much in criticism of him, but insisting that he was naive to think he could get along with DeLorenzo.

Somehow, Kaiser did find a way to live with DeLorenzo. It wasn't a true love affair, and it never quite reached the heights of production Kaiser dreamed of, but it amazed everyone else. The September output under the old management was four Corsair fighter planes. Under Kaiser's leadership, plane production jumped:

1943	Production of Planes	1944	Production of Planes
October	14	January	60
November	40	February	74
December	73	March	101
		April	123

In September 1943, the manhour record per plane was 24,000; in October it dropped to about 20,000; in March 10,000; in May 8,000. From October to May, personnel was reduced from 21,500 to 11,500.

By May, the monthly rate of production was established at 120 planes, a standard acceptable to the Navy, and Kaiser asked to be relieved, he and his four-man operating committee having served for seven months without fees, profits or remuneration for their services. At no time did Kaiser or any of his associates have any financial interest in the company.

Artemus Gates, Assistant Secretary of the Navy for Air wired Kaiser:

> I wish to thank you for the fine work which you have done at Brewster, and the very real contribution you have made to the war effort. You may be sure the Navy Department is very appreciative of the task performed by you.

Kaiser hadn't asked for the job; didn't want the job; admitted he must have had blinders on when he took the job; but ended up working a semi-miracle.

The Aircraft Side Show

The outbreak of war in Korea June 25, 1950, meant a sudden turn in the road for Kaiser-Frazer automobile company. Too bad that no one could see the chuck holes that lay ahead.

Actually, Kaiser was never one to see chuck holes ahead in any of his businesses, so even though like all Americans he was shocked by the war in Korea, he quickly envisioned what he could best do to help the war effort. Under contract with the Air Force, Kaiser-Frazer had for almost a year been conducting studies in preparation for converting the Willow Run, Michigan automobile plant, to aircraft production. With the groundwork already laid, the Air Force immediately contracted with K-F to gear up for volume production of Fairchild-designed C-119's, or flying boxcars.

Great. A natural for Kaiser. For two years during World War II he had gone up and down the land proclaiming that he wanted to mass produce flying boxcars. Now the opportunity had come his way because the Willow Run plant which had originally been built by Ford to produce bomber planes was two-thirds idle, providing excess space for defense work. Besides, a portion of Kaiser's team of automobile workers could presumably adjust rapidly to the production of the C-119's.

Within six months the company had signed up for $300 million in defense work, two-thirds for C-119 construction and the balance for Wright R-1300 aircraft engines to be turned out at K-F Engine Division plants at Detroit and Dowagiac. To many people this seemed like a godsend for K-F. FORTUNE said it, "seemed almost certain to be profitable enough to offset any conceivable upsets in the auto business for two years or more."

From the start the production of C-119's was fraught with problems—almost total lack of cooperation from Fairchild, continuous, last-minute design changes by Fairchild and the Air Force, inexperience of the Willow Run personnel, and almost constant harassment by government agencies, including long-time, bitter critics of

Kaiser, Senator Styles Bridges and Congressman Alvin O'Konski.

Fairchild's maximum production capacity was 35 C-119's per month. Kaiser's ultimate capacity at the Willow Run was 500 per month, but the maximum contract schedule granted by the Air Force was only 28 per month. In the end Kaiser only produced a total of 159 planes.

In a late June 1953 hearing before Bridges' Senate subcommittee, Kaiser testified:

> Fairchild's bitter opposition has been manifest ever since the C-119 contract was first awarded to us. A Fairchild executive has been quoted as saying, 'We are not interested whether or not Kaiser ever builds a C-119 aircraft.' There was tremendous demand for the C-119's as a result of the Korean crisis, and the Hagerstown, Md. facility of Fairchild was unable to meet the requirements. It made sense for the Air Force to select a plant that had the tremendous 500-plane-per-month capacity of Willow Run. Yet Fairchild dragged its feet in all dealings with us, costing Kaiser Motors and the Government untold sums of money and many months of delay. Cost comparisons between Fairchild and Kaiser are totally unfair. Fairchild had the benefit of a Government-furnished plant, free of cost, with a large portion of its tooling costs and plant rearrangement written off on previous contracts, and Fairchild had the advantage of having produced 800 aircraft of the same basic type over many years.

With the fighting in Korea nearing an end, it was right in the midst of this June 1953 Senate subcommittee hearing that all participants were suddenly and unexpectedly advised that Air Force Secretary Harold Talbott had just cancelled Kaiser's orders for C-119 Flying Boxcars, along with $225 million in orders for 244 assault transports (C-123's) from Chase Aircraft, 49% Kaiser owned. This broke up the hearing abruptly, and brought to a quick end Kaiser's C-119 and C-123 side show, except that Kaiser people would continue to be nagged to clean up all remaining details on their contracts and would, of course, have the time-consuming and management-draining nuisance of disposing of all their aircraft production equipment.

One very important spin-off, however, from the aircraft adventure involved Chase Aircraft, 49% of which stock Kaiser-Frazer had purchased in late 1950. The remaining 51% interest was owned by Michael Stroukoff. Chase had designed the C-123 assault transport plane. Agreement was reached for Willow Run to tool up for the production of 25 of these planes per month, with the first prototype to be turned out at Chase's plant at West Trenton, New Jersey.

In the late spring of 1952 Clay Bedford was named president of Chase. His main office was in Willow Run, but he commuted regularly to Chase's New Jersey plant. Working harmoniously with Stroukoff was no easy matter for Bedford who later recorded:

> I had many battles with old man Stroukoff. I once actually threw him out

of my office in the Chase Aircraft plant in New Jersey because he cussed me out for ordering some work done. I did this in front of all of his people, and you know the Russians—saving face is everything. From that time on, I had less difficulty with him, but still many disagreements.

When the Government cancelled its contract for C-123 planes Chase had completed its prototype at New Jersey, but at Willow Run only four planes were in the process of being completed—from 82% complete down to 41% complete. Obviously, Chase had not turned out to be the money-maker Kaiser-Frazer had expected.

Nevertheless, on August 31, 1953, Willys Motors, Inc., owned by Kaiser-Frazer, purchased Stroukoff's 51% interest in Chase. This did not result in any production of planes but it did set the stage for the manufacture of a whole variety of machines and equipment. Most important, Chase had the organizational structure and experienced personnel that would lead to the formation of Kaiser Aerospace and Electronics, a solid and growing company which, though small, proved to be very profitable throughout the late 50's and into the 70's.

Clearly, the high hopes that Kaiser held for the "mass production" of planes never came close to being fulfilled. And the Korean War knocked the bottom out of the automobile market in the spring of 1951 right when Kaiser-Frazer had come out with its stylish new Kaiser car and the imaginative new compact, the Henry J. All in all, the aircraft side show proved to be diversionary, combative and costly—if indeed not disastrous—to Kaiser's automobile dream.

CHAPTER 8

MOTHER OF INDUSTRIES

"Our main business is building people, building ourselves, and those who join us to take on bigger and tougher jobs, building the courage, the faith, the imagination, the will and joy of work."

The check was in the amount of $91,476,989.92. It was dated November 1, 1950. It was a check of The Chase National Bank of the City of New York, made payable to the Reconstruction Finance Corporation.

That morning Kaiser Steel Corporation had deposited that same amount in Chase. Now Henry J. Kaiser was presenting the cashier's check to RFC Vice Chairman, C. Edward Rowe. Lightbulbs flashed. Kaiser, the man with the perennial smile, had a bigger smile than usual, for he had just paid off all obligations of Kaiser Steel Corporation to the Reconstruction Finance Corporation, principal and interest, twenty years before the last payment was due.

In that one stroke Kaiser was fulfilling all the dreams, all the planning, all the hopes, and all the struggles through which he and his people had been for ten embattled years. And now the slate was clean. He was free to go forward in the kind of expansion that would know no completion as long as he was alive.

Kaiser knew the importance of steel. In all his construction jobs—roadbuilding, dambuilding, shipbuilding—steel was the one product he could not do without. The bigger the steel scrapers the faster the roadbuilding, the bigger the steel cranes, the more efficient the dambuilding, the bigger the volume of steel plates the greater the production of ships.

And he was aware that the production of steel in the West was pitifully low--just a· tiny fraction of steel output in the East and Midwest, and far below the consumption of steel in the West. He hated to be at the mercy of eastern steelmakers; he hated to pay the high freight rates to move the steel into the West.

As early as October 4, 1940, Kaiser submitted his first proposal to the government for the construction of an iron and steel mill on the Pacific Coast, and requested government aid for the project. Why the government? With Kaiser never having been in steel manufacture, and with his being relatively unproved and unknown, there was no possible way private financing could be found. Further, Kaiser felt that just as government money required for the building of Boulder Dam and other big dams in the West played such an important role in strengthening western economy, it would rebound to the government's benefit to have a strong steel industry in the West.

Fortunately, President Roosevelt had become interested in doing something about steel in the West. He wanted to give a shot in the arm to the western economy if he justifiably could. He thought western steel production could conceivably be a healthy offset to what he thought might be an eastern steel monopoly. Then, too, he was worried about the way the war was going in Europe, and he wanted America's steel production to be equal to the challenge.

On April 21, 1941, just four months after Kaiser signed his first contract to build ships, he had a meeting with the President in the White House. As reported in the Wall Street Journal, he told the President he had already talked to the Office of Production Management about a steel project in the magnitude of $150 million, including:

1. A pig iron plant at Mt. Pleasant, Utah, utilizing ore deposits in that area.

2. A high grade steel mill in Bonneville, Oregon, making steel from scrap by using Bonneville's power.

3. A major mill in Southern California, using pig iron shipped from Mt. Pleasant plant and utilizing both gas and electricity in a new process of steel production.

In the rush of events, Kaiser most certainly had not had time to document his proposals by in-depth studies. His statement to the President, "I believe I have had sufficient raw materials studies made to insure the plan," was more hopeful than reliable. As the program actually took shape nine months later, it bore no relationship to the ideas he presented to the President, to wit:

1. The iron ore deposit near Mt. Pleasant, Utah, never proved of sufficient quality or quantity to support a steel mill.

2. No one ended up making steel from scrap in the Bonneville, Oregon, area.

3. The Kaiser steel plant in Southern California never used pig iron from Mt. Pleasant, but instead used iron ore from Southern California and coal from Utah.

No matter. Kaiser had sounded the alarm and had stirred up national interest in the possibility of new western steel plants. By the end of that year sufficient investigations had been made to make it clear—there would be a steel plant at Geneva, Utah, utilizing coal from central Utah and iron ore from Southern Utah (nowhere near Mt. Pleasant), with Kaiser closing in on his plans for a plant in Southern California.

There would be one big difference—a difference so fundamental it would make for ten years of almost constant wrangling and name-calling, but ten years that in the end would produce a leaner, stronger, more competitive steel company than might have come about if the ownership had been different. The difference was this: Through its studies the government had become convinced a steel mill in Utah would be economically sound and would be far enough inland to be safe from Japanese attack. Accordingly, the government was willing to be owner of the Utah steel mill, a so-called Defense Plant Corporation project.

On the other hand, the government was leery of a steel mill in Southern California—the economics didn't seem to add up, the supplies of iron ore and coal were not that well established, and the coast of Southern California where Kaiser favored locating the plant at Port Hueneme was too vulnerable to Japanese attack. The government refused to take the risk on its own.

Undeterred, Kaiser spent three whirlwind months hounding government officials, mostly Jesse Jones, head of the Reconstruction Finance Corporation, who in February 1941, had loaned Kaiser $9,250,000 for the construction of a magnesium plant near San Jose, California. Finally, on March 19, 1942, the RFC approved a loan "upwards of $100 million to construct an integrated steel plant in Southern California."

There is no one, but no one, except Henry J. Kaiser, who could have persuaded the government to risk $100 million for a steel mill in Southern California. Millions of tons of steel later, several large iron ore mines and coal mines later, and tens of thousands of jobs later, the legacy of this one man's efforts, could never begin to be measured. Seldom has one man done so much for so many over so many years, as in this one enterprise alone.

Yet, Kaiser benefitted from two forces, without which he would never have been granted his loan:

(1) War broke out December 7, 1941. It was no time to haggle. The country desperately needed the steel.

(2) Kaiser had successful and growing shipyards, and he was willing to pledge the profits from three of those yards to help pay off the loan. Besides, the RFC would hold a mortgage on all the properties of Kaiser Steel (as well as claim whatever earnings the company might make). If Kaiser Steel failed, and the loan could not be repaid, the government would end up owning the business, which would not be very different from all of the other new steel projects the Defense Plant Corporation sponsored. The government was in a "win, no-lose" situation.

An Inland Location

Right down to the end of the negotiations, Kaiser kept insisting his plant should be located at Port Hueneme, about fifty miles north of Los Angeles. After all, wouldn't it be prudent to be on the water where iron ore and coal could be imported when available, and where, after the war, steel exports to the Pacific Basin could be loaded directly on ships?

The government flatly ruled it out. With the whole Pacific Coast still jittery over the possibility of a Japanese invasion, the government at first mentioned the Barstow, California, area in the Mojave Desert, some one hundred and twenty-five miles inland. When Kaiser protested, a compromise was struck--the plant would be located at Fontana, forty-five miles east of Los Angeles and ten miles west of San Bernardino.

Although Kaiser and some of his executives would later on make passing remarks about the penalty they suffered by not being allowed to locate at Port Hueneme, the truth of the matter is that a better location than Fontana could not have been chosen if months had gone into the selection. The San Bernardino-Fontana area is where three major railroads come together, two of which would be involved in bringing coal from Utah,, and the other would, a few years later, start hauling trainloads of iron ore into the plant. If the plant had been located at Port Hueneme, there was no chance whatsoever of receiving import iron ore and coal while the war was on, and the additional rail freight charges that would have had to be paid on those raw materials at Port Hueneme instead of Fontana would have run into tens of millions of dollars. Even after the war Port Hueneme would have offered no worthwhile advantages. It would take twenty or so years before economic sources of foreign iron ore and coal would open up. As to the sale of steel products after the war, the domestic demand was so strong it left only a tiny fraction available for export.

The Fontana location had many other things going for it. It was a broad-based labor market. Land was plentiful and cheap, so that under Kaiser's mandate, "think big, don't allow operations to be cramped," his people could swiftly buy 2000 acres, mostly hog farms, surrounded by orange groves. It was deemed reasonably free from earthquake risk, but the "Santa Ana" winds called for the planting of large numbers of eucalyptic trees as windbreaks. Even though the Los Angeles Metropolitan Water Aqueduct ran right through the plant property, that water was not available to Kaiser, so the plant had to rely on digging wells for its supply. This required the company to install the most sophisticated water purification and recycling system of any steel mill in the country. By contrast, eastern steel mills had unlimited supplies of river water which, after being contaminated by use, could be dumped back into the rivers.

One problem which was not given extra thought at the start but which became more and more burdensome was the matter of air pollution control. All of the original ovens and furnaces were designed with the same emission controls as the newest steel mills in the East, but that proved not to be enough in the smog-conscious Southern California. However, as troublesome and costly as the problem proved to be, his engineers and operators knew they would always have Kaiser's backing in their efforts to be leaders in the field of air pollution control.

What's A Turbo-Blower?

In the final days of the Washington negotiations that led to the RFC loan, the War Production Board threw up a roadblock. Why should the project be approved in the face of the fact that the principal manufacturer of turbo-blowers was already swamped with priorities? A turbo-blower is a huge piece of equipment in the power-house which blows the air with turbine force over to the blast furnace where it fans the fire that smelts the iron ore, coke, and limestone.

"Why, that's no problem," said Kaiser. "We can build our own." When the meeting broke up and Kaiser was walking along the hall with his Washington vice president, Chad Calhoun, he turned to him and said, "What's a turbo-blower?" Calhoun allowed as how it was probably a turbine and a blower. "Then couldn't we build one at Joshua Hendy?" Kaiser asked.

Joshua Hendy was a manufacturer of ship turbine engines located south of San Francisco. Kaiser had a small ownership interest in the company but was the major customer for the ship engines. Joshua Hendy was called and they wired back, "Regarding turbine blower, can build unit in three to four months." (A turbine was something altogether different from a turbo-blower.)

Without realizing what a serious mistake might have been made, the WPB gave its approval for the building of the steel mill. Fortunately, before it was too late, the WPB was able to furnish a genuine turbo-blower, so that Fontana did not end up—as it might have—with a giant ship's turbine sitting out in the middle of the orange groves.

In a way, the turbo-blower episode symbolized the whole frantic, exciting process of building a steel mill from scratch. In his usual rashness, Kaiser announced an "impossible" goal for himself and his people—to "blow in" the blast furnace by the end of the year.

The vortex for all the swirling activity was the Oakland office of George Havas, Chief Engineer, in the Latham Square Building. Havas was an Hungarian engineer who had joined Kaiser in 1928 during the building of the Cuban highway. He was so brilliant, so thorough, so hardworking, Kaiser would keep piling more and more responsibility on him. By 1942, Havas, whom Kaiser called "the little giant," was ready to take on the challenge of directing the design for a whole new integrated steel mill, even though he had absolutely no previous experience along that line.

It was a sight to behold, seeing the steady stream of engineers coming in and out of his office at all hours during the day and into the evening with bulging blueprints. He didn't take long to approve, or disapprove, or modify, the drawings. With his European mannerism, he sometimes seemed like a dictator, but often enough, his eyes would twinkle and people could sense his warm human qualities. Rarely did Havas bother Kaiser with his questions. If the subject was important enough, he would clear it with Gene Trefethen who would make the decision whether Kaiser should become involved.

The Construction Stiffs

Shouldn't an experienced steel mill builder be put in charge of construction for a plant as large and complicated as the Fontana steel mill? Not if you're the owner, and if your name is Henry Kaiser. A builder is a builder is a builder—as long as you have proved him to be a good builder.

Tom Price was a good builder—a "damn good builder," in the parlance of the construction world. He had joined Kaiser in 1919, the third permanent employee hired by Kaiser. For the next twelve years he proved himself by being in charge of building scores of highways, mostly throughout California. Then in the early 1930's he held very important jobs in the building of Boulder Dam. Now in April 1942 when Kaiser was ready to break ground for the Fontana steel mill, Price was in Panama lining up construction on a major job for Kaiser. One phone call from Kaiser, and Price was flying back to California to take charge of the construction of the steel mill.

The first thing he did was hire men he had worked with and knew their capabilities. It almost looked like Boulder Dam all over again, so many of them had worked with him in building that dam. The key man was Frank Backman.

With all their construction savvy, it was still essential to bring in experienced steel men to work with them—experts in coke ovens, blast furnaces, open hearths, rolling mills. That was not easy, because who would leave a well-established steel company to come with a risky new venture? Money was certainly not the incentive, because both by Kaiser's low salary scales and government ceilings on pay, Fontana was no bonanza. As Tom Price said:

> We did no pirating or buying of men. Most of our men who were hired from other companies came with us at the same salary they had been receiving. With few exceptions the men approached have applied to us because imbued with both the pioneering and the patriotism of the project. They were inspired by Kaiser and wanted to be part of his dream. It was believed to be necessary, the men believed it, government officials believed it. It was a love-child. How could it fail?

The plant was designed while it was being built. Sometimes—as in Kaiser's shipbuilding--construction would get ahead of design. That is the most difficult way to design or construct, but it has one outstanding advantage—it is the fastest way. It is not the cheapest way, but wars are not won on cheapness, they are usually lost. Plans still wet from the blueprinters were constantly being rushed from Oakland to Fontana.

Possibly the outstanding feature of the plant was the layout itself. Most steel plants in the East are necessarily located in narrow valleys on account of rail and water transportation, resulting in a crowded condition. Then, too, most of those plants just "grew." It was impossible to plan them as a whole. Under Kaiser's guiding influence, Fontana was designed in toto on level, rolling ground with plenty of room to grow.

This called for extensive use of conveyor belts, another operating principle insisted on by Kaiser. It proved to be far more efficient than rail car movement used in most other steel mills.

With his fascination in witnessing construction in progress, it was somewhat surprising Kaiser didn't spend more time at Fontana during those hectic days. However, he had so many other balls in the air he could only make it to the steel mill three or four times. Each visit, however, seemed to electrify the workers and to renew their commitment to have the blast furnace in operation by the end of the year.

If the round-the-clock pace had been furious throughout the summer and fall, it rose to a white heat in December. Everyone redoubled his efforts to make good on Kaiser's pledge, not just at the blast furnace but at all locations throughout the plant where workers wanted to show the country that new facilities were rapidly rising in an orderly manner.

It was a beautiful California day on December 30, 1942, when Mr. and Mrs. Kaiser and their son Henry Jr. (the older son, Edgar, was busy turning out ships in Portland, Oregon), along with other dignitaries, walked up on the platform at the base of the blast furnace to begin the ceremonies. More than 8,000 persons, mostly workers, were assembled in the audience.

With Henry Jr. as Master of Ceremonies, the program started at 1:15 p.m. What everyone had been looking forward to took place a few minutes later when he asked his mother to throw the switch igniting a small quantity of coke within the furnace. To give a little drama for the audience the workers had contrived to have some magnesium flares go off, giving the illusion that the blast furnace fires were visibly starting up.

In honor of Mrs. Kaiser, the furnace was officially named "The Bess." She responded, "this is one of the most thrilling days of my life. I have been at scores of projects my husband has built, but most of them have been completed undertakings. This is different. The steel project is an enterprise which will grow with the great Southwest."

Then in his typically emotional, high-flown rhetoric, Kaiser stated:

> For the first time on this side of the Rockies we begin the manufacture of iron, the most fundamental element in modern industry, from ore mined in our own mountains. For the first time metallurgical coke is to be made in the western area by the modern by-product coke-oven method. For the first time on this Pacific slope we have under one complete control the manufacture of steel from the selection of the ores and the other raw materials all the way through to the finished steel products. For the first time in our own West, steel can be made to fit a pattern in a completely integrated plant. A century ago in the 'Roaring Forties' it was gold that lured men west. They sought wealth in its most concentrated form for their individual and personal advantage. Today, we take another, a baser metal and process it for the service of mankind. The westward movement which began so long ago has not come to an end on the Pacific Slope. It is poised now for the next great thrust. The

day of the West is at hand 'Westward the course of Empire takes its way.' Ships are the greatest need of the hour. The shortage of steel and materials is the only thing that stands in the way of vastly increased production. I am now prepared to state that the Oregon Shipbuilding Corporation at Portland and the Permanente Metals Corporation at Richmond, California, will treble their output of ships in the year 1943 if the steel and the materials are made available.

The next important milestone at Fontana took place less than five months later when the first of six 185-ton open hearths was tapped in May of 1943. Blast furnaces produce molten iron, usually called pig iron, but it takes open hearth furnaces to refine the iron into steel, the product with the strength and resilience not to crack under the heavy loads and the beatings that steel is always being put to.

Of course, the payoff is when the steel is rolled or fabricated into the particular shapes needed by the steel user. That day came at Fontana on August 19, 1943, when the first plate of steel was rolled. Kaiser wanted that plate to be welded into the deck of the S.S. Moczkowski Liberty ship at Richmond the very next day, so it was loaded on a truck for the 400-mile haul. Deadlines like this meant everything to Kaiser.

By The Seat Of His Pants

Kaiser was absolutely sure he would come up with sources of iron ore and coal once he needed them for starting up the blast furnace. But he didn't have them when he broke ground for the Fontana plant in April 1942. He was taking a chance that would worry most people to death, but not him. In effect, he was right then flying by the seat of his pants.

Without knowing anywhere near the full details, he had information that there was a large deposit of reasonably good iron ore at Eagle Mountain in Southern California about 15 miles from Desert Center. This was in an isolated area some 50 miles from the nearest railroad, the Southern Pacific. Originally, the property had been owned by the Harriman interests who sold it to Southern Pacific. In the late 1930's Southern Pacific leased the property to Harlan Bradt who in turn subleased it to Edward T. Foley. Foley had ideas the ore might be used for ship ballast, and he nurtured a hope that some steel company might come along which would use the ore in one way or another. However, in his wildest dreams he could not have foreseen that a fully integrated steel mill would rise up in the orange groves of Fontana. When Kaiser went charging ahead with his plant, it gave both Southern Pacific and the lessees a strong bargaining position for their subsequent negotiations with him.

As for the coal, Kaiser knew from the start it would have to come from Utah. There would be some limitations in that regard, because a special kind of coal was required, one that would turn into coke through the by-product oven process. However, a blast furnace at Ironton, Utah, had been converting coal into coke, so Kaiser thought a nearby coal property owned by the Utah Fuel Company would likely have a coking coal. No one claimed that the Utah coking coal would compare in quality with coking coals used by eastern steel mills. There was this further disadvantage— Kaiser's rail haul of 811 miles from Utah to Fontana would be several times longer than other steel mills in the country. Indeed, Kaiser faced the prospect of paying more freight on his coal than the cost of the coal itself.

With the Eagle Mountain iron ore mine being so far away from any rail service, and with the problem of negotiating with both Southern Pacific and the lessees, there was no chance Kaiser could start off using ore from that source. Luckily, his raw material people located a small iron ore deposit at Vulcan, California, that appeared to be available at least for the start-up years. It, too, was remote, being near the Nevada border, some 60 miles north of the Union Pacific Railroad near Baker, California. It would require trucking over a country road to be built by Kaiser, and then a two-line rail haul to Fontana, a rail distance of 181 miles. As the person in charge of building the steel mill, and as one who had spent his entire working career dealing with raw materials (rock, sand and gravel), Tom Price wanted to see where his iron ore would be coming from. He would later record his visit:

Being very conscious of raw materials in general and particularly of a project costing 90 million dollars, I made a trip with Tod Inch as soon as possible to see the Vulcan Iron Mine, which we were negotiating to purchase. Tod and I drove and drove and drove—the last 10 miles being over a horrible desert trail. About a mile from the mine Tod stopped the car and said, 'There she is.' I looked and looked but couldn't see anything. He then pointed out to me a small dark spot on a hill about 100 ft. in diameter. When I was incredulous that it was the mine to supply such a large plant, I couldn't believe it. We turned around at once—rushed back to Fontana. I caught the Lark that night and by 10 o'clock the next day I had asked Mr. Kaiser if he was crazy to build a plant like that with no more ore in sight than Vulcan promised. He very patiently pointed out to me the large number of fine iron mines in the Southern part of the State and assured me we would get them. I was appeased for the present. Little did I know that none of those mines except Eagle Mountain was any good. It, though, was and is a good mine; so I was wrong again.

It was not until 1946 that Kaiser would finally acquire the Eagle Mountain mine. Reaching agreement with the underlying owner, Southern Pacific, was not all that difficult. The railroad wanted the mine to be fully developed because it would mean millions of dollars of revenue each year in the hauling of the ore.

Dealing with Bradt, and particularly Foley, who was temporarily in control with his sublease, was much stickier. It involved negotiations of such importance and such delicacy only Kaiser could handle it. As luck would have it, one of the conditions of Foley's sublease required that he go forward with the mining of the Eagle Mountain property to a specified minimum amount and within a specified period of time. That's where the poker game was played between Kaiser and Foley—how and when could Foley finance and undertake the required mining, and how long could Kaiser count on other sources to meet the needs of Fontana?

Kaiser, who seldom played cards, played a superb poker game. He didn't rush his contacts with Foley. In a wide-open press interview at the Town House in Los Angeles on July 16, 1945, he said Fontana was already getting good quality iron ore from Southern Utah. Then he added significantly: "We have been drilling in an ore field in San Bernardino County where we have come upon evidence that points to a deposit of more than 100,000,000 tons of iron ore within 90 miles of Fontana." Nothing ever really came from that so-called deposit, but Kaiser's men had in good faith been initially hopeful. In any event, it gave Foley something to worry about. Then Kaiser put the screws on, telling Foley, "that the only program agreeable to Kaiser Company, Inc., will be strict compliance by you with all of the terms of the Lease and Sale Agreement," meaning that if Foley didn't start mining and shipping the ore in the amount and by the time specified in his agreement, Kaiser would feel free to deal directly with Southern Pacific.

Foley finally decided it would be better to take the cash amount offered by Kaiser than to face the task of financing and developing a mining operation. He ended up with a great deal more money than he ever envisioned when he first signed his lease agreement.

While Kaiser had been flying by the seat of his pants in terms of his iron ore prospects at the start of his steel venture, he made one of the smoothest landings in the history of the industry. Eagle Mountain turned out to be a bonanza. It proved to have far more ore than even Kaiser had claimed. The company moved ahead rapidly in building a 52-mile railroad from a point on the Southern Pacific at the Salton Sea to the mine. To much fanfare, with members of the California press as guests, the first trainload of iron ore left Eagle Mountain on November 9, 1948, for the short trip to Fontana, Southern Pacific's haul being only 112 miles.

"A Coking Coal Is A Coal That Will Coke"

Few industry experts would ever claim they knew the precise chemical qualities that would make one coal turn into coke in the heating process and another not. And it was coke, not coal, that had to be used in the blast furnace.

Utah Fuel Company had a property at Sunnyside, Utah, with a huge deposit of coal that would coke. It was of marginal quality, certainly inferior to most eastern coals. It was a "high-volatile" coal with more sulphur content than desirable. In time, its coking quality would be improved by blending it with smaller portions of "low-volatile" coal from the midwest, and by "sintering" the coke and iron at Fontana before charging it into the blast furnace.

The Sunnyside coal mine was owned by the Utah Fuel Company, a subsidiary of the Denver and Rio Grande Western Railroad, which served the mines in that area. The president of Utah Fuel was my father, Moroni Heiner. Sometime in April 1942, when ground was being broken for the Fontana steel mill, Kaiser phoned Heiner in Salt Lake City, Utah, to talk about buying coal from Utah Fuel. After two or three phone conversations, in which both parties indicated an earnest desire to work out a contract, it was agreed Heiner should come to Oakland in May to try to agree upon terms. He brought along his son, Claude, who was his executive assistant.

In the evening after the meeting, my father and brother came to my apartment in San Francisco where my wife and I lived with our two baby children. I can clearly recall what my father told me that night:

> It was the strangest kind of negotiating meeting I have ever been in. Mr. Kaiser had a half dozen young men around him who participated in the discussion as actively as he did. They kept pumping me to learn all they could about the coking coal my company owns in Utah which they need for their steel mill. They know very little about the steel business and hardly anything about coal, so they kept trying to pick my brains. Several times during our long meeting, Mr. Kaiser was interrupted by urgent phone calls on subjects totally unrelated to coal. Each time he would ask the young men around him to pick up a phone so they could all participate in the discussion. He never asked me to leave the room, and therefore I overheard conversations on several different subjects.

The next day another meeting was held. On the assumption that Kaiser had his hands full building a steel mill, my father quoted a price for the coal F.O.B. the mine. This wasn't the way Kaiser operated--he wanted to take over the mining, believing he could introduce some mining techniques that would result in lower costs. He actually wanted to buy the mine, but my father refused this suggestion, because he didn't want to take the risk of selling too low. Finally, it was agreed to compromise by Kaiser paying a royalty for each ton of coal mined. Considerable haggling took place until a figure of 35 cents per ton was reached.

The meeting broke up, but my brother remained behind to discuss with Gene Trefethen, George Havas, and others various matters relating to geology, mining conditions, labor supply, housing, railroad service, water availability, etc. As the day wore on, the Kaiser men kept complaining about the 35 cents per ton royalty charge, until my brother conceded that perhaps 30 cents would be acceptable.

When he mentioned this to my father, an immediate call was made to Kaiser for another meeting in the morning. At that get-together, my father bluntly said to Kaiser: "Yesterday, you and I made a deal for a royalty of 35 cents per ton. I will not go forward with the contract at any lower figure." Kaiser never flinched, "I agree you and I settled on 35 cents per ton, and that's what it will be."

Just like with the Eagle Mountain iron ore, it was one of the smartest poker games Kaiser had ever played. Not to have to lay out the millions to buy the mine, and yet to get this precious commodity for only 35 cents per ton royalty, was an almost unbelievable accomplishment. Sunnyside became an absolutely indispensable pillar supporting Kaiser Steel throughout its history.

Purchase Of Sunnyside

Two events brought the Sunnyside coal mine into foremost prominence in 1950:

(1) Kaiser Steel was finalizing a $125 million refinancing plan to pay off the RFC.

(2) The parent company of Utah Fuel, the Denver & Rio Grande Western Railroad, was undergoing reorganization, and was required by court order to sell at public auction its ownership of Utah Fuel stock—the stock having been pledged to secure indebtedness of the old D&RGW. Now was the time for Kaiser to buy Utah Fuel and not run the risk of having an adversary own the coal.

Utah Fuel's ownership was much more than just the Sunnyside mine. It included a second coking coal mine, two nearby domestic coal mines, two mines in Colorado, 246 modern five and six-room houses for employees, company stores, grazing lands, and retail coal yards and sales offices. Some 1300 employees were working for Utah Fuel at the time, with another 300 employed by Kaiser at Sunnyside.

The bidding started April 10, 1950, in the New York office of Guaranty Trust Company. Gene Trefethen, flanked by lawyers, was doing the bidding for Kaiser. Claude Heiner had become president of Utah Fuel after my father's death in 1948. He organized a group of Utah financial interests under the name of Minerals Development Corporation, and was the only other bidder against Kaiser.

The bidding started at $2,750,000. Thirty-five bids later, a top price of $6,625,000 had been reached before the auction was adjourned for the day. Several times during the day as the bid price kept going up, Heiner would phone his associates in Utah to get their approval for raising the ante. Trefethen had no such constriction--he was free to keep raising his price virtually indefinitely.

When bidding was resumed the next day, four additional offers led to the top price of $6,725,000 by Kaiser. Thereupon, Heiner asked for a week's adjournment, hoping to return to Utah to round up additional financing. The referee ruled against the adjournment, and Trefethen closed out the Kaiser bid at $6,800,000.

It really hadn't been a poker game, because Kaiser had all the chips, plus the clear necessity for the coal at issue. Even though for years some Kaiser officials would call Claude Heiner names for bidding up the price, it remained a "steal" for Kaiser to end up with such a valuable property at $6,800,000.

A few years later Kaiser Steel bought a huge coal deposit at York Canyon, New Mexico, containing both coking coal and steam coal. By the mid-1980's when the Fontana Steel plant had been shut down, and there were zero sales of steel, the new owners of the company had sales of coal from its Utah Fuel Company properties and its York Canyon mines in excess of $100 million annually.

"Mr. Kaiser, I'm No Thief"

Why should anything as mundane as rail freight rates be mentioned in a biography about a great man? Because they were a costly expense for his steel company, running into many millions of dollars each year. Because they played an important role in his competition with other steel companies. Because he never hesitated to become personally involved in freight rate negotiations when he could see it was time for him to lend a hand.

It all started when rates on iron ore and coal were being negotiated for the opening of the Fontana plant. Even though it was not a long haul for the rail portion in bringing iron ore from the Vulcan mine to Fontana, it did require hauling by the Union Pacific Railroad for part of the distance and the Santa Fe Railway for the balance. On the much longer coal haul from Utah it involved three carriers—the D&RGW, the UP, the Santa Fe.

By July of 1942, three months after ground was broken for the Fontana plant, requests were made on the carriers for their lowest possible rates on both iron ore and coal. Without any competitive squeeze facing them, the carriers offered rates that would assure them very remunerative returns. As General Traffic Manager of Kaiser Steel by that time, I prepared a study showing how high the offered rates were in comparison with other rates on those same commodities for other movements, and how high they were as compared even to rates on other commodities. When Gene Trefethen saw my figures, he hit the ceiling. He made repeated phone calls to the appropriate top railroad officers, and sent them long, blistering wires demanding they come up with more competitive rates. Although they made slight concessions, it was apparent by early September they were not about to grant acceptable rates for the soon-to-begin movements of iron ore and coal. Trefethen had kept Kaiser posted on the stalemate, when suddenly Kaiser hit on an idea. He told Trefethen to have me prepare a leather-bound, detailed, eight-page report of the rates we needed, and the reasons why we felt we were "entitled" (to use Trefethen's favorite word) to those rates. Once the report was prepared, it was air-mailed to Kaiser in Washington, DC. He had become acquainted with William Jeffers, president of the Union Pacific Railroad, on leave in Washington as the nation's Rubber Czar. Jeffers declined to get into any detailed discussion with Kaiser, but promised to send the report to his vice president of traffic in Omaha, Frank Robinson, asking him to get in touch with Trefethen and "work things out." Then for the next several weeks phone calls went back and forth between Trefethen and Robinson. The other carriers were kept informed, but they were letting UP take the lead. Finally, on November 4, Robinson phoned from Omaha saying the carriers were prepared to offer $4.40 per net ton on the coal and $1.25 per gross ton (2,240 pounds) on the iron ore. These rates compared with the first offer on coal of $5.30 per net ton and on iron ore of $1.60 per gross ton, savings of many millions of dollars. As tenacious and effective as Trefethen's negotiations had been, it was nevertheless clear that Kaiser's contact with Jeffers had opened the door.

The battle over freight rates really heated up after the war. It all swirled around the rail rate to the Pacific Coast on steel from the big new competitor at Geneva, Utah. For a long time before the war the rate from Utah had remained at $12.00 per net ton because there was no steel production there. When the Geneva plant came on the scene, the railroads published a wartime rate of $8.00 per ton, and all shippers were happy, including Kaiser with his shipyards in Richmond, California and Portland, Oregon. At the end of the war, the rate went back up to $12.00 per ton, and this was where Kaiser hoped it would remain because that would provide an umbrella allowing Kaiser to charge more for his steel.

All the steel users on the Coast thought otherwise, of course, and began clamoring for a peacetime rate of $8.00. The Western Pacific Railroad, running from Salt Lake City to the San Francisco Bay Area, wanted to promote business and felt it could make a good profit at $8.00, so it took the lead in publishing the desired rate. Then the Union Pacific which had rail service from Utah to Los Angeles, Portland and Seattle decided it would have to grant its customers in those areas the same rate.

Kaiser thought his Fontana plant had been mortally wounded. Try as he may, however, even phoning each of the railroad presidents, he couldn't get the rail carriers to reverse their decision. Then he decided to appeal to the Interstate Commerce Commission asking them to rule that the $8.00 rate was unreasonably low (noncompensatory) and otherwise discriminatory. Because of the solid, coast-wide support of the rate by steel users, and yet because of Kaiser's loud voice, the Commission agreed to consider the case. After two formal Washington hearings in 1947 and 1948, with the full eleven Commission members hearing the arguments each time, the ruling was made to let the $8.00 rate stand. It couldn't have been otherwise. As a matter of fact, the rate on steel from Fontana to San Francisco was lower, mile for mile, than the $8.00 rate from Geneva. It was recognized by most transportation people as a lost cause, but Kaiser had been determined to fight it to the death.

As usual, his fight and fire paid off—in another direction. He used his frustration to demand some offsetting reductions in his iron ore and coal rates. I well remember his determination to have it out with George F. Ashby who had become president of the Union Pacific. Kaiser had me track Ashby down until I finally reached him on his business car in Las Vegas, Nevada. Kaiser asked me to be on the phone to back him up with facts. Then Kaiser really attacked Ashby for publishing the $8.00 steel rate. Ashby defended his company's action, particularly stressing that once the Western Pacific published the rate to the Bay Area, UP had no choice but to do the same thing for its customers in Los Angeles and the Northwest. Kaiser said, "Why, Mr. Ashby, that's like saying because one of my neighbors is a thief, I can be one." I can still hear Ashby's plaintive reply, "Mr. Kaiser, I'm no thief."

Realizing that he couldn't win in stopping the $8.00 steel rate, Kaiser trained his guns on his coal and iron ore rates, insisting some concessions should be made there to offset the treatment given to Geneva. This gave Ashby the opening to say he would have his people study if anything could be done along that line. Here's the letter Kaiser wrote to Ashby following their conversation:

I was delighted with our telephone conversation and your reaction in regards to the elimination of the injustice that exists on our coal and iron ore rates to Fontana. This is a matter of long standing, and I know you will correct the inequity that exists. Fontana is a great competitive factor in the development of the West, and will be an ever-increasing one, and the elimination of this inequity by you and the other railroads involved will be a step that you will never regret.

I am counting on you to bring this about, as I consider that you are the key to its accomplishment.

It was good to talk to you, and I would like very much to hear from you in regards to the results of your efforts.

Ashby decided to send his two top traffic officials to meet with Kaiser in Oakland—Ambrose Seitz, vice president, and Ken Carlson, general traffic manager, both of whom were good friends of mine. The four of us met in Kaiser's office, and the visitors were visibly impressed by the size and grandeur of the room. Kaiser turned on all his sales charm, foregoing any rough talk or threats. He talked about all his dealings with railroads over the years, then described his dreams that led up to the Fontana steel mill.

The meeting went on for over an hour and then Kaiser invited us to have lunch with him in the Executive Dining Room on the ground floor of the Kaiser Building at 1924 Broadway. Before heading downstairs Kaiser told his visitors he wanted to show them the new dishwasher his Fleetwings company was producing in Bristol, Pennsylvania. There was a small anteroom adjoining Kaiser's office where the dishwasher had been hooked up. As we stood around the dishwasher Kaiser gave a little speech about its advantages, including the fact that the force of the water jet spun the rack in which the dishes were placed. The top was open and Kaiser had his head over it, so he could point out the internal features. Without thinking, he automatically turned on the switch, and a strong spray of water hit him right in the face. It didn't seem to fluster him a bit. He grabbed a towel, wiped off his face and bald head, and went right on talking, but the glances of the visitors indicated they got a kick out of the little mishap.

The significant thing is that shortly thereafter some minor reductions were made in Kaiser's coal and iron ore freight rates. Indeed, as the person in charge of freight rate negotiations, I found for several years thereafter I could get good results because the carriers knew we had been hurt by the $8.00 steel rate from Geneva, and because they knew Kaiser was standing in the background ready at any time to throw his weight around if offered rates could be challenged.

The Showdown Approaches

In three short wartime years Kaiser had done what no one had ever done before—he had built and successfully operated a large, fully integrated steel mill against seemingly impossible odds.

But as imposing as those problems had been, the really big challenge came with the ending of the war:

Could Kaiser expand and diversify his steelmaking facilities to meet the needs of the peacetime market?

Could Kaiser, the builder, who had never sold many products in competition with other manufacturers stand up in the marketplace against the established steel industry?

Was the western steel market likely to prove big enough to take the output of the increased steelmaking capacity the war had brought on?

Could Kaiser ever pay back his RFC loan, which reflected excessive wartime construction costs, especially now that there was no more shipbuilding to contribute its profits to the payback?

Kaiser relished the prospect. Those kinds of problems were "opportunities in work clothes," to use his own overworked counsel. At times, he would bellow, express rage, cajole. He would keep the phone busy in every direction, he would issue a stream of news releases, he would make speeches. But one thing for sure—he would never lose his confidence that he was going to succeed, he would never stop smiling.

The pivotal issue in the whole complex battle was the Defense Plant Corporation's steel mill at Geneva, Utah where the government stood all the risk, as compared with the obligation Kaiser had to make good on his RFC loan. The government people were smart in the construction of Geneva—they asked United States Steel Corporation, the country's largest, to build and operate it for them. In turn, U.S. Steel people were smart—they took the opening given them by the government to install certain equipment that was more expensive and better than Kaiser could afford at Fontana. Even at Geneva's new coking coal mine at Horse Canyon, Utah, near Sunnyside, U.S. Steel was careful to pour in more money than Kaiser did at Sunnyside. Kaiser's steel and coal men were already sensing that U.S. Steel wanted to install the last word in equipment in case it decided to buy Geneva after the war.

With the end of the war, the Geneva plant and its raw materials sources were shut down promptly. The government had no legal basis for operating the plant in peacetime. Kaiser was quick to take advantage of the situation. He called on his men operating the Fontana steel plant to double their accent on efficiency and quality in each department, and he expanded his sales department in an effort to win over as many new customers as possible.

But before that time—early in 1945, Kaiser and Trefethen had decided a change in top management for the steel company was desirable. Tom Price had done a superb job as works manager in building the plant, but he had little background in overall administrative responsibilities, and especially was lacking in sales experience. A. B. Ordway was finishing his work at the shipyards and with his administrative skills in directing numerous Kaiser ventures, it was decided to make him vice president and general manager.

This was a bitter pill for Tom Price, and he took it hard. He had put his heart and soul in the building of the Fontana plant and he was confident he could be equally successful in assuming overall responsibilities. It was a rebuff that remained a sore spot with him throughout his life, but he was loyal enough to Kaiser to hide his feelings and to take on whatever other jobs Kaiser and Trefethen would ask him to do. Like all good wives, Price's wife shared the sting, and, try as she may, she could not always cover up her feelings that her husband had been done wrong by. It was also a source of some hurt that Price was never put on the Board of Directors of Kaiser Steel or any other Kaiser company.

To his great credit, Price concentrated on raw materials problems thereafter. He played a key role in Kaiser Steel's purchase of a large coal mine near Raton, New Mexico; in the tripling of iron ore production at Eagle Mountain; and in every move the company made to increase and improve its raw materials supplies. He was often called upon by other Kaiser companies to counsel them on their raw materials problems.

The payoff for his loyalty came in 1961 when Kaiser Steel was invited by Australian mining interests to explore vast iron ore deposits in the Hamersley Range area of Western Australia. Price was assigned the task of appraising the quality and quantity of the ore, and the prospects for marketing it. After studying the information the Australians had already developed, and after low-flying over the area, as well as tramping around some of the key locations, Price couldn't contain his excitement. He phoned Kaiser, reporting that he found billions of tons of high grade ore, running between 50 and 68 percent iron content; and he confirmed what Kaiser already knew—that the Japanese steel industry was anxious to buy many millions of tons of iron ore annually as soon as the mine could be developed.

In less than year, Kaiser Steel had entered into an agreement with Conzinc Riotinto of Australia to open up the Hamersley Range. It proved to be an enormously profitable venture for Kaiser Steel until the company sold its interest in the 1970's. Kaiser people were always a little amazed they had been invited to participate in something that was so obviously destined to become a big money maker. This was due in large part to the value of having the name Kaiser attached to the project, and in part the expertise Kaiser Steel mining people would bring along. One factor should not be underestimated—Tom Price's enthusiasm for the property, his absolute confidence in the viability of the whole project and his insistence that it should be undertaken at once. His excitement was infectious, not only with Kaiser and his top people in Oakland, but even more so with the Australians. When Australians were later asked why Kaiser Steel had been invited in, they would often reply, "Because Kaiser stood for action, because Tom Price made us believe that. Without Kaiser it would have taken several years longer to open up Hamersley."

The Australians felt that way so sincerely they named the biggest Hamersley mountain in honor of him—Mt. Tom Price. And Price, who had been hired by Kaiser in 1919, who had given his whole career to Kaiser, and who had been hurt when he was not made vice president and general manager of Kaiser Steel near the end of the war, was repaid for his loyalty—and for his competence—when the Australians named a mountain after him.

"My Number One Employee"

Of all the rewarding and challenging jobs A. B. Ordway had held since joining Kaiser in 1912, the one that meant the most to him was being named vice president and general manager of Kaiser Steel in early 1945. He had headed up scores of highway construction jobs along the Pacific Coast; for a while he had been general manager of the big Cuban highway job; he had helped establish, and had been president of, Industrial Indemnity, the insurance firm Kaiser and other builders had formed; he had been vice president of Administration in the Richmond shipyards. Whatever Kaiser asked him to do, he took on willingly and energetically and successfully.

At the same time, Ordway always stood on his own two feet. He was not a "yes" man. And Kaiser respected that. In 1962 Kaiser would say of Ordway: "I've got one employee who in fifty years has never agreed with me on anything. He's invaluable."

Now, in 1945, at age 58, Ordway was being asked by Kaiser to lead out in solidifying the position of Kaiser Steel in the post war, competitive steel market. "Ord" plunged into it on a night-and-day basis. He realized that he didn't know much about steel manufacturing, nor did he know the team of steelmakers at the Fontana plant, so nearly every week over a long period of time he would spend two or three days at the mill. He became the most regular commuter on the Southern Pacific Lark traveling between Oakland and Glendale en route to Fontana. He would go from department to department, or hold group meetings of all kinds, constantly soliciting the ideas of everyone he talked with. It seemed that every night he was at Fontana, following dinner, he would spend two or three hours watching furnaces turn out the metal, or the mills roll out their finished products. It would be no exaggeration to say he not only became well known and well respected, but well loved. Knowing how long and closely associated Ordway had been with Kaiser, the workers could almost feel Kaiser's presence wherever Ordway was.

"Ord" also had a job to do in establishing himself with Kaiser Steel's customers. Jack Ashby, who had done excellent work as an expediter the first year or two when the plant was being built, had been made General Sales Manager, and had gotten a good start in hiring young, aggressive salesmen. He had become well acquainted with the customers, so he and his sales crew made it a point to introduce Ordway to as many customers and potential customers as possible. Still, it was Ashby and his people who were in charge of sales, and Ordway didn't purport to usurp any of Ashby's responsibilities. He certainly didn't throw himself wholeheartedly into sales the way he had into production at Fontana.

Ordway had his hands full with overall responsibilities—overseeing labor relations, iron ore and coal mining, dealings with the RFC, meetings in Los Angeles, Salt Lake City and Washington, DC.

Ordway had been in the saddle for nearly three years and the company was doing well. "Ord" couldn't have been happier.

Then the lightning struck. "Ord" was told by Kaiser that the decision had been made to appoint Jack L. Ashby as vice president and general manager, with Ord to continue as a vice president and a member of the Board of Directors. Ashby was only 37 at the time, and there was no way Ordway, not quite 61, could have anticipated he would be displaced so abruptly.

One of Ordway's finest lifetime qualities was his ability to keep his poise. Hardly anyone would become aware that he was deeply wounded by having the most satisfying job he had ever held taken away from him in his prime of life. From time to time, however, his true feelings would surface, although in the most subtle ways. By contrast, his wife could not always hold back her feelings. Wives of other Kaiser executives heard her voice her resentment more than once. Then when Kaiser three years later married the young nurse, Mrs. Ordway and other wives couldn't hide the fact that they looked upon Kaiser through different eyes.

Most people were at a loss to understand why Ordway had been removed from his post. The only explanation that seemed to make sense was that Kaiser and Trefethen wanted someone who was first, last, and always a salesman. It was peacetime and the thing that Kaiser Steel needed most was to sell an increasing volume of steel in competition with Geneva and the other steel companies. Ashby proved to be a far-sighted choice--for the next twenty-five years he led out in making sales that ran into billions of dollars, including sales of enormous quantities of Australian iron ore and Canadian coking coal. He built a team of loyal and talented young sales people and other key personnel who set the pace in the western steel industry.

All this time Ordway was taking on whatever different assignments were handed to him. When Kaiser Steel bought Utah Fuel Company in early 1950, Ordway became the vice president who oversaw that operation for several years. Once Kaiser decided in the mid-1950s to build a 28-story Kaiser Center in Oakland, Ordway was made vice president and general manager of that project. He remained in charge of that exciting complex for many years after it was occupied in 1960.

On June 14, 1966, at age 77, a little more than a year before Kaiser died, Ordway wrote this letter to him in Hawaii:

Dear H.J.:

I had an interesting telephone call the other night and as a result I am sending you some pictures I am sure will recall some vivid memories.

In the photograph attached to this letter, you may not remember the young man in the driver's seat, but you will never forget the 3-wheeled dump vehicle which was invented by you and proved a great success in our work for many years. The driver was Bill Jost, who was just a kid when this picture was taken. But of all the drivers we had, he could manipulate these things better and faster than any of them. He worked for us around Mt. Vernon and

Seattle and then came to California. When we all went to Cuba he stayed here and has just now retired for age and lives in San Francisco. I gather his health is not too good. He specifically asked to be remembered to you and I know you will recall him because from a young man on he not only was an expert in driving these dumps, but practically drove everything else we owned. He was always good-natured and smiling and a fast operator. The particular picture of the dump truck was taken when it was used on Bothel Road which you will recall was just out of Seattle. . . .

Some time before the summer is over, I would like to visit you some day for a few hours at your convenience so that I can see your pet project and enjoy smelling dirt with you. I would only plan to be there for part of the day with you and a couple of nights in between coming and going. . . .

Then in early 1967, perhaps sensing that Kaiser's health was slipping, Ordway wrote this letter February 6:

Dear H.J.:

I had to make a trip to Sacramento last week to call on the Director of Public Works and it aroused a few nostalgic memories.

You probably recall that it was 46 years ago this month when you and I walked into the general offices of the Division of Highways which was on the 7th floor of an office building just around the corner from the Sacramento Hotel. Now their headquarters is in a large multi-story building just opposite the Capitol and covers about a block. The offices of the Director are very efficient but very tastefully decorated and laid out.

Possibly you recall that the receptionist the first time we called (who was also the switchboard operator) told us her feet were cold, so we promptly went out and bought an electric heater for her, which of course paid for itself many times over in our later business. . . .

A few years back you and several others in the construction business formed an organization called the Beavers, who met only once a year in Los Angeles for cocktails, dinner and the evening. You were one of the first awardees to get their cup under the "management" heading. Edgar has since received the same award. I have gone to the dinners almost every year because it is about the only time I see the many old timers that I used to know who are still circulating. I went this last January and knew very few. . . . Aside from Steve Bechtel, who was there, about the only people I know were our own crowd who go each year, but of course they are all a lot younger. It is a big affair with about 1200 sitting down to dinner at one time. The food is good and well served but it is awfully noisy.

One of the fondest, truest, longest business friendships came to an end when Kaiser died in August 1967. Ordway was like a member of the family, assisting Edgar Kaiser in arranging funeral details, and of course serving as a pallbearer.

If Kaiser's relationship with Ordway had been something unique in American business, it was almost matched by the affection Edgar felt for Ordway. Ord and his wife had tended Edgar hundreds of times when he was a young child. He had carried Edgar on his shoulders countless times. Ord was like a second father to Edgar. Over the years the attachment and affection between the two would continue to grow. In numerous speeches throughout the years when Edgar was trying to define what was unusual about the Kaiser "spirit" he would elaborate on just how much Ordway was the heart and soul of the organization.

It was no surprise, therefore, that when the Kaiser companies would in 1970 build a second towering office building in Oakland alongside the original Kaiser Center, Edgar would choose to name it the Ordway Building. Everyone agreed it was an ideal name. It was a fitting testimonial to a grand, loyal man. And like the Australian mountain which had been named Mt. Tom Price in honor of a person who had remained loyal to Kaiser even though he had been denied the one job he wanted above all, here was a building being named after a man who remained loyal when he had been unexpectedly removed from the most important job he had ever held. There must be a moral to the two stories: no matter how deeply you may be hurt, if you remain loyal to your boss, if you continue to do the outstanding job of which you are capable, you might end up having a mountain or a building named after you.

The First Salvo

No way could Kaiser have predicted it. Here was Benjamin Fairless, president of the mighty U.S. Steel Corporation, writing in early February 1945, six months before the end of the war, to the Defense Plant Corporation offering to buy the Geneva steel mill in Utah and the Fontana steel mill in Southern California.

Buy the Fontana plant? It was owned by Kaiser, not by the Defense Plant Corporation. It was not for sale.

Kaiser came back with a roar. On February 7, 1945, various newspapers quoted Kaiser:

> Fontana is not and will not be for sale. We are at a loss to understand why the United States Steel Corporation writes the Defense Plant Corporation making an offer for the Kaiser Company's property. Certainly, the Kaiser Company would not consider making an offer to the United States Government for any property owned by the United States Steel Corporation. However, since the $200 million Geneva steel plant is owned by the government and will be put up for sale, we are studying the possibility of bidding for its purchase or lease 'exactly as United States Steel has announced it will do.'

From that time on, it seemed like nearly every businessman or politician felt free to get in the act. Certainly, western steel users and suppliers, as well as western politicians, freely voiced their opinions on what should be done.

As a matter of fact, just five days after the newspaper outburst, a large, two-day conference was held at the Hotel Utah in Salt Lake City by the Steel Committee of the Western States Council. Utah interests were determined to find a way to keep the Geneva plant operating after the war and this tended to be the dominant theme of the meeting. Steel users from all over the West were represented and many of them had been invited to give formal speeches. Top officials of western railroads were also there, and several of them were asked to speak. Kaiser Steel was represented by Ordway, Ashby, and me. Both Kaiser Steel and U.S. Steel representatives were listeners only.

By late spring the RFC began breathing down Kaiser's neck. The prospect of Kaiser defaulting on some loan payments led to suggestions that the RFC might have the right to put the Fontana plant up for sale. Kaiser, of course, considered that not only insulting but unlawful. He stepped up his assurances that through additions to the product range of the Fontana plant he could and would make good on the RFC loan. Then in July, almost at the same time he was announcing the formation of an automobile company with Joseph Frazer, Kaiser came up with a grandiose scheme— he would form a syndicate of top industrialists and financiers in the west who would operate combined properties worth more than $350 million including the Fontana and Geneva plants, the Colorado Fuel and Iron Company plant at Pueblo, Colorado, as well as several smaller steelmaking facilities in the west. Kaiser, who was always the staunchest believer in competition, insisted the combine could integrate some operations to advantage, while still fostering market competition on the major products.

Kaiser's plan did not capture public support. It was altogether too complicated, with too many diverse interests. With Kaiser struggling to make good on his RFC payments, he couldn't offer financial leadership that would be required to put the deal together, even though Cyrus Eaton of Otis and Company in Cleveland held out some hopes which soon proved to have too many strings attached.

The issue came right back to the one which had been known all along:

(1) Who would buy and operate the Geneva plant, it having been shut down at war's end?

(2) What plant modifications, what refinancing, would be necessary to make Fontana a strong, viable, low-cost peacetime competitor?

The time had come for the western steel customers to redouble their efforts to work on these two problems. The Western States Council which had called the Salt Lake City conference earlier in the year was headed up by Kenneth T. Norris, owner of Norris Stamping and Manufacturing Company of Los Angeles. He manufactured a wide range of steel products, including automobile wheels, and was Kaiser's biggest customer. Perhaps more to the point, he was a two-fisted fighter. He was a bulldog. He was one person who could slug it out toe-to-toe with Kaiser, which he had to do on three or four later occasions. He was a forceful proponent, willing to spend whatever time was necessary to get the job done.

Two months after V-J Day, Norris led a contingent of industrialists to Washington, DC where they were afforded a meeting with President Truman, western congressmen and senators, as well as with top officials in the Defense Plant Corporation, Federal Loan Administration, the War Assets Administration, the Surplus Property Board, and the RFC. Their message was clear:

1. Find a buyer for the Geneva plant and offer him a low price—the sooner the better.

2. Grant to Kaiser competitive financial terms for his Fontana plant—the sooner the better.

They received a very warm reception in Washington, and returned home confident that real progress had been made. Norris and his group then met with 18 newspaper journalists who were on a "Reconversion tour" trying to arouse public opinion for use of surplus wartime plants. Soon thereafter Norris met with directors of the Los Angeles Chamber of Commerce to rally their outspoken support.

Everything that could be done was being done by the Western States Council—and, of course, by Kaiser. He was extremely grateful that the Council stood shoulder-to-shoulder with him in fighting for better financial terms for his Fontana plant. But still the government sat on its hands, and took no action whatsoever in behalf of either Geneva or Fontana.

As time dragged on, it became increasingly clear that the only company which could realistically be considered a candidate to buy the Geneva plant was United States Steel Corporation. They had built the plant for the government; they had operated it during the war; and they had steel producing and manufacturing plants in Pittsburg, California, near San Francisco, and in Torrance, California near Los Angeles, both of which could use products from Geneva. Further, U.S. Steel had one all-important advantage—they had plenty of cash to pay for Geneva.

Notwithstanding the mounting pressure to get Geneva back into production, U.S. Steel decided to play its own kind of poker. They acted disinterested. At times they would point out that Geneva would have to be greatly modified to turn out peacetime products. They went through this play-acting, even though their president, Benjamin Fairless, had in early 1945 proposed buying both Geneva and Fontana.

Their strategy proved effective. Utah interests, customer interests, and the Defense Plant Corporation came to believe that Geneva was some kind of a "white elephant" which could only survive in peacetime if it could be purchased at a very low price. Then in 1946 when U.S. Steel finally offered $40 million for a plant that had cost $200 million, everyone in the west seemed happy. U.S. Steel was a hero for taking such a "risk," not a company to be criticized for taking advantage of the government. Because of its size, U.S. Steel had no doubt played many poker games before, but this one had to be one of its most skillful.

At first, Kaiser accepted the sale of Geneva as being good for the west. He was never one to complain when the public stood to benefit. And, quite reasonably, he assumed the RFC would scale down his loans on a comparable basis, so that his Fontana plant could manufacture more products at lower prices for the benefit of the customers. But as the months rolled by, it became shockingly clear that the government was determined to enforce a double standard—one for the Kaiser owned plant at Fontana and one for the Geneva plant which the government had just sold.

The Western States Council blasted this unthinkable discrimination. They invited Kaiser to speak to them in Los Angeles so that they could be working hand-in-glove with him. The meeting was set for 2:00 p.m. in the offices of the Los Angeles Chamber of Commerce. Before lunch, Kaiser met in the office of Henry J. Kaiser, Jr. He had with him A. B. Ordway, who was still vice president and general manager of Kaiser Steel, Jack Ashby, vice president of sales, Fred Borden, general sales manager, and me. After lunch had been served in the office, there was over an hour before the meeting with the Council was to start.

For the next 10 minutes, Kaiser put on one of the best and funniest acts any of us had seen. We all knew Kaiser had a streak of the mimic in him. It was his way of bringing a light touch into some business situations. He wasn't one to tell very many jokes, especially not dirty jokes, so once in a while he would turn to mimicry for his laughs.

He was a born actor—very expressive with no inhibitions of any kind. He could pick up facial expressions, bodily movements, and styles of talking, by some of his closest associates and then quietly play them back. It was the subtlety of his mimicry that made it so delightful.

On this day, Kaiser chose to mimic Benjamin Fairless of U.S Steel, even though he liked and respected him. Kaiser picked his chair up, moved it to the center of the room where there was no table to interfere, and began:

Boys, can't you just picture Fairless telling his Board of Directors that they need have no fear of that insect, Henry Kaiser, out on the West Coast? (Thereupon, Kaiser played the role of Fairless and the words he used were supposed to be those of Fairless) 'Members of the Board, I have had several dealings with that insect and I can assure you we'll soon be hearing the end of him. Just to make sure, I'm going to stamp on that insect on the floor.' With that, Kaiser stomped his foot on the floor grinding it and turning it as though Fairless had actually smashed a little insect. Then Fairless went on, 'Kaiser could make a go of it when the government was putting up all the money for his shipbuilding, but he won't be able to make it on today's competitive market. Hold on just a minute, I see that little insect Kaiser has popped up over here.' Then Kaiser literally picked up his chair and moved it a few feet and then began stomping again. 'Well, I got him that time. We won't hear any more from him. Now we can be sure that steel customers in the West will have to depend on us.' He waited for effect, then went on, 'Well, I'll be damned, that insect Kaiser is still alive!' Once more Kaiser picked up his chair and moved it to where the insect was supposed to have been seen. Then Kaiser began stomping and grinding his foot, and Fairless (Kaiser) said, 'I got that insect for sure this time.'

Kaiser went through that mimicry five or six times, putting words in Fairless' mouth and moving his chair each time to stomp out the invisible insect. It was a masterful performance by a master mimic.

It really wasn't done in a smart-aleck way. He wasn't trying to be "cute." He was having fun. The words he put in Fairless' mouth were spontaneous and amazingly like what Fairless could have said. We all split our sides with laughter. And we all got the message—nothing was going to keep Kaiser down. For Kaiser's part, he was now warmed up, ready to give a stem-winding pitch to the members of the Western States Council, where, of course, no mention would be made of Benjamin Fairless.

Outrage In Steel

In retrospect, it is hard to comprehend why Kaiser could not get the RFC to grant him even the tiniest adjustment on his steel loans. Here was Kaiser, the best-known and possibly best-liked industrialist to come upon the high level Washington, D.C., scene in a long time—a man whose salesmanship abilities were quite unparalleled. He was fighting one of the biggest challenges of his life, second only in importance to the battle he was waging at that very same time in his new Kaiser-Frazer automobile venture, and here was the rawest kind of discrimination, with U.S. Steel buying a competing steel plant for only 20 cents on the dollar, while the government was saying to Kaiser: "Pay up one hundred cents on the dollar, plus interest, or we'll take your plant over." To make the comparison even more odious, the government was selling hundreds of war surplus plants at bargain prices far, far below wartime costs. In nearly every instance, the government acted as if the buyers were doing the country a great big favor by putting these plants back into production, whereas with Kaiser the government never gave him any credit whatsoever for keeping his plant in uninterrupted operation.

Kaiser took off his kid gloves. (In reality, he was never known to wear kid gloves.) He harangued RFC officials at all levels. He appealed to his many high-ranking Washington friends to put pressure on the RFC. He kept western congressmen fully informed of his actions, hoping that somehow they would bring a sense of fair play to the RFC.

His rallying cry was: OUTRAGE IN STEEL. In typical Kaiser fashion he produced an attractive 17-page, 8" x 11" brochure presenting all the facts in simple, understandable terms. The brochure itself was titled: OUTRAGE IN STEEL, As Told By Henry J. Kaiser. He wanted "to prove to the American people through congress, the administration, press, radio and every avenue of public opinion," that the government in Washington was:

...menacing a basic steel industry needed by the entire nation, namely the

Fontana steel plant on the West Coast

...Talking lower prices but actually forcing higher prices

...Decrying acute shortages and inflation, yet refusing to permit one plant to expand and help meet the necessity for more production

...Undermining competition and fostering monopoly

...Threatening failure to hundreds of manufacturers

...Blocking use of private funds to expand Kaiser Fontana steel plant

...Refusing to accept a plan for Kaiser to repay the government in full...Holding up Fontana for an excess of $151,907,000

...Forcing Kaiser to pay at least $36.76 for every ton of steel produced at Fontana for 12 years.

At that point, the brochure added: "Actually this will force Kaiser to raise Fontana steel prices by $36 to $130 a ton during steel shortage."

Incredibly, the RFC rejected every proposal Kaiser made to correct the situation. Nor did the RFC come up with any suggestion of its own on how it could assist in keeping Fontana alive.

By this time, even Ken Norris began to wonder if the RFC would ever crack. He suggested to Kaiser that he should allow Fontana to go in default as a form of bankruptcy for the purpose of forcing RFC to write-down the loan. This was something Kaiser would never do. His whole lifetime creed was to pay every loan in full. He was determined to negotiate a voluntary write-down by the RFC, or find some way to make good on his obligation.

Saved By The Market

Kaiser was on the horns of a dilemma—how could he pay off what he called an outrageous debt and at the same time keep talking about expanding his steel mill? Or were expansion and diversification into peacetime products the very way he could service his debt?

The market place provided the answer. Month after month through 1947 and 1948 the shortage of steel became increasingly more severe until every ton of steel Fontana could produce could be sold. Some ingots were even exported to England at a very attractive price for Kaiser. Then for several months ingots were shipped back to the Chicago-Detroit area to be rolled into sheets for the steel starved Kaiser-Frazer automobile company.

Believing that the shortage was sure to become more acute, Kaiser began thinking seriously about an idea he had openly flirted with for some time—why not charge premium prices for his steel? The minute he talked it over with his sales people they were horrified. They argued that the customers would scream to the high heavens and some of them would hold it against Kaiser for years to come. However, after much soul searching, Kaiser—almost standing alone in his decision—brought his management and sales people together in August 1948 and told them a premium of $30 per ton would be added to all Fontana products. As shocked as his salesmen were, he asked them to call on every customer as quickly as possible, and explain why the action had to be taken.

Kaiser felt that because Ken Norris was his largest customer, and because he had tried to be so helpful, it was essential to face the music with him first. Accordingly, Jack Carlson, Kaiser Steel's District Sales Manager in Los Angeles, went to Norris' office and gave him the bad news. At the instant Norris heard mention of a $30 premium he took a large ring of keys out of his pocket and shoved it across his desk to Carlson. "What's that for?" Carlson asked. "Those are keys to my plant. They're no longer any good to me with steel prices like that. Give them to Mr. Kaiser. Maybe he can make a success of my plant with exorbitant steel prices, but I certainly can't."

The reaction of customers ranged from incredulity to outright rage. It was an unprecedented action, and the customers made it clear they would scramble in every direction to find lower priced steel rather than pay tribute to Kaiser. The sales people took awful tongue lashings, and had to struggle to keep their spirits up. This bitter confrontation lasted only about eight months, because the steel market began to soften and Kaiser couldn't hold the line any longer.

However, the timing of the initial $30 premium in August 1948 couldn't have been more fortuitous. The Federal Power Commission had recently granted Transcontinental Gas Pipe Line Company authority to build a 30-inch diameter gas pipe line from Texas to New York City, covering 1,840 miles at a projected cost of $189 million. Claude A. Williams, president of Transcontinental, had been combing the steel industry for the required pipe, but to no avail. The established producers were swamped taking care of their long-standing customers. It looked as though the steel shortage would mean a long, serious delay.

In desperation, Williams went to the extreme measure of talking to Kaiser about producing plate for the pipe in his Fontana, California plant. Kaiser jumped at the opportunity, but made it clear he would have to charge the same $30 premium he was assessing his other customers. Williams could live with that for two reasons: (1) as a public utility he could cover all his costs in the price he would be allowed to charge for his gas, (2) he was up against a government-imposed deadline for the completion of the project, and he couldn't wait for the unpredictable time when some other more economic steel pipe might become available.

Thus, on September 8, 1948, Kaiser and Williams signed a $65 million contract, equivalent to $130 per ton for the 500,000 tons of steel plate. Williams made arrangements to have the plate fabricated into pipe in the Los Angeles area. Soon, solid trainloads of pipe were moving east, reversing the long tradition of steel moving west. From start to finish, Williams gave Kaiser high marks. He was quoted in The Houston Press November 8, 1949: "All the steel Mr. Kaiser delivered to us is above specifications. He has a wonderful organization, and he's an ideal man with whom to deal. The Kaiser interests do everything they contract to do, and more."

This one sales contract was the most important in Kaiser Steel's history because in large measure it funded the transition from wartime to peacetime manufacturing facilities. The company had already completed a new cold rolled strip mill, and a continuous weld pipe mill to produce plumbers' pipe, one-half inch to four inches in diameter. It had opened up the Eagle Mountain mine with a 52-mile railroad. It was building a seventh open hearth furnace. Now, with the huge plate contract, Kaiser immediately announced he would build a second privately financed blast furnace for $17 million, to be followed by construction of a hot rolled strip and sheet mill and an electric weld pipe mill.

As all of these postwar improvements began falling into place—volume production, high prices, new facilities—it began to appear that perhaps Kaiser might not be at the mercy of the RFC after all. He was building a broad earnings base that made financial houses sit up and take notice. That's when he decided to hire Coverdale and Colpitts, one of the country's most reputable consulting engineering firms. They started their work in early February 1949, and four months later in a 279-page report they gave Kaiser Steel a resounding send-off in all aspects of its operations, concluding:

> In conclusion, it is our studied opinion and judgment that Kaiser Steel Corporation is a strongly-constituted and exceptionally well-equipped steelmaking unit. In all fundamental and important respects it is favorably and fortunately situated. Raw materials, plant, diversity of product, location, availability and opportunity of market position are all considerably better than average. Provided with a strong organization and management and operating in a growing territory, there is ample ground for the belief that the operations and earnings of this company will be above those for the industry generally.

With this kind of objective report, and with profits mounting monthly, Kaiser decided it was time to work with a financial institution which could help Kaiser Steel "go public" and raise the private funds to pay off the RFC in full. Happily, George Woods, Chairman of the Board of First Boston Corporation in New York City, had become impressed with Kaiser Steel's remarkable earnings spurt. Then, too, he had worked with Coverdale and Colpitts engineering firm before, and when their findings were so glowing Woods pitched in enthusiastically with Kaiser to chart a refinancing program. Once again, Kaiser had lucked out. Here was one of Wall Street's most respected financiers who not only laid the groundwork for Kaiser Steel's initial refinancing, but who became the financial wizard on Kaiser Steel's Board of Directors for the next 25 years.

Woods' game plan was well-balanced—one that would raise $125 million:

(1)$25 million unsecured loan at 3 percent from 3 banks.

(2)$60 million in first mortgage 3-3/4 percent bonds which would be purchased by 10 major insurance companies.

(3)$40 million from the sale of preferred and common stock.

The borrowings were all lined up in advance, but the stock sale was the one accomplishment that proved Kaiser Steel had "arrived." In twelve major cities throughout the United States, the Kaiser Steel story was told over an over to hundreds of stockbrokers in meetings arranged by First Boston Corporation . Using large colored flip charts (an old-fashioned technique compared with today's video presentations) this management team "sold" Kaiser Steel to the brokers:

1. George McMeans, vice president of operations (age 37)
2. Fred Borden, vice president of sales (age 40)
3. Atwood Austin, vice president, finance (age 46)
4. Jack Ashby, vice president and general manager (age 39)

At age 34, it was my privilege to help prepare the charts and the messages and to be the "flipper" who turned the pages as each speaker went from point to point in his presentation.

It was an interesting closing stretch to ten years of up and down struggling. Kaiser had provided the vision, the fire, the leadership. Backing him up at every turn was a small group of trusted and tried associates, together with thousands of willing workers who somehow believed the project would succeed. And now, without Kaiser's personal involvement, but with his invisible presence in every session, five young men won the confidence of thousands of stock brokers.

Within a matter of a few weeks the stage was set for Kaiser to hand the RFC the check for $91,476,989.92 to pay off his obligation in full, with interest. Most people thought he would never do it. Even he had times he was not sure he could manage it. And today there are too many people who still look upon Kaiser as the coddled darling of the government, when in fact no other steel manufacturer came close to doing for the government what he did.

The first chapter in Kaiser Steel's history had been finished. What lay ahead?

A Whole New Ball Game

There were two vastly different eras in Kaiser Steel's history while Kaiser was alive. The first was the tumultuous, risky 10 years from the time he borrowed money from the RFC until he paid it back, a period when everything revolved around his personal derring-do. For the next 17 years it was an orderly corporate growth era where his influence was always at play but where his management team and Board of Directors shouldered a great share of the leadership initiative and responsibilities. This reflected in part the solid foundation that had been laid, and in part the fact that in 1954 Kaiser got all caught up in the excitement of doing big things in Hawaii. Once he had completed a job he never went back to see it, but was only interested in taking on something new. In a way, therefore, he didn't think Kaiser Steel needed his attention as much as Hawaii did.

One story of how Kaiser operated—bridging both eras—involved construction of a new tin plate mill at Fontana. With the huge food packing industry on the West Coast, particularly California, more tin plate was consumed than almost any other steel product—over 700,000 tons annually. All of this had to be shipped from the Midwest and East to the western can manufacturers because there was no tin plate producing plant in the West. With that kind of wide-open market, wouldn't it be reasonable to assume Kaiser could sell the full output of a 200,000 ton-a-year tin mill at Fontana? He didn't leave it up to guesswork. With three or four of his key people on the lines, he put in a phone call for W. R. Stolk, executive vice president of American Can Company in New York City, by far the biggest tin plate customer on the West Coast. He put it to Stolk point blank: "We're going to build a tin plate mill at Fontana. Can we count on getting a fair share of your business?" Stolk acknowledged his company would be very happy to have this new supplier, but wouldn't commit himself to any particular amount of tonnage. He did set in motion, however, a program for Kaiser's people to visit each of American Can's executives who would be involved in deciding how much would be purchased from Kaiser.

Kaiser then did the same with Hans Eggers, president of Continental Can in New York City, the second largest West Coast tin plate consumer. The response was the same—very friendly, "glad to have another supplier," but "have your people talk to mine and we'll work something out." The third largest tin plate customer was Pacific Can Company, headquartered in San Francisco. Because of the location, Kaiser Steel's vice president of sales, Fred Borden, and two salesmen he had already assigned to be looking into tin plate sales, called on E.F. Euphrat, president of Pacific Can Company. They were given an arms-length, non-committal reception, one that made them very concerned whether they could break into Pacific Can's business.

Soon thereafter, a round-up meeting was held in Kaiser's office to evaluate what the outlook was for tin plate sales once the plant was built. Borden reported on the cool treatment he had received from Euphrat of Pacific Can. Kaiser didn't hesitate. With a half dozen of his people listening in (once again, I was included in the group), he phoned Euphrat, went over his plans for a new tin plate mill, and then asked if he could count on some business from Pacific Can. Euphrat pointed out he felt a strong loyalty to Weirton Steel Company from whom "I have been buying for many years." Kaiser acknowledged that was a good business principle, but stressed that it could be very helpful to Pacific Can to have a western tin plate mill as a back-up source of supply. He described all the planning that had gone into his proposed tin plate mill and the commitment he would be making to serve the western can manufacturers. The conversation went on quite some time before Euphrat happened to mention that his annual requirements were about 100,000 tons. Kaiser then bored in: "Couldn't you still do right by Weirton Steel and yet give us some business as well." After some give and take, Euphrat allowed that maybe 25,000 tons annually was a possibility. Acting as though that might even be a commitment, Kaiser thanked him warmly. When he hung up, he turned to all of us who had been listening and said: "See, boys, it isn't hard to sell tin plate."

Construction went forward on the mill, and by August 1952, the first shipments of tin plate were made. It was such an important facility it was decided to celebrate its opening by inviting top officers of the tin can manufacturing companies to see the mill in operation. In addition, presidents and top officials of banks, insurance companies and railroads, as well as a half dozen publishers of major California newspapers were included. It was the highest level, most select, most restricted group ever "feted" at Fontana—with less than 100 included. Because of the caliber of the invitees it was considered essential to have them stay at the elite Arrowhead Springs Hotel some 25 miles from Fontana, there being no other hotel in the area deemed quite worthy of the guests. As so often happened with Kaiser, his high standards created a problem.

Arrowhead Springs Hotel was owned by Conrad Hilton and had been shut down for several months with no plans to reopen until possibly early 1953. Every effort was made to convince the management of the hotel to open it up at least for this one overnight occasion, but to no avail. It was agreed our only hope would be to call on Hilton personally and ask for his intervention. By that time I had been given the added responsibility of being in charge of public relations for Kaiser Steel, so along with our Fontana public relations manager, Earl Reynolds, I was given the task of appealing to Hilton. We met with him in his ground level, garden court office in Beverly Hills. As friendly as he was, and as much as he wanted to do Henry Kaiser a favor, he made it clear it would be altogether too expensive to open the hotel. Then I showed him the list of invitees. He started out slowly looking the names over. One after another, he found himself repeating: "Oh, I know him, I know him..." By the time he had finished going over the list, it seemed that he knew personally nearly three out of four of the expected guests. That convinced him. He said, "All right, young men, you can tell Henry Kaiser I'll open the hotel for him and all of my friends who will be with him."

By chartered or company planes arriving at the Ontario, California Airport, or by limousines coming from Los Angeles, the guests kept arriving throughout the day of Monday, December 1, 1952. The hotel was spotlessly clean, and with its own kind of Southern California charm, it made a great impact on the visitors. The banquet was lavish, and there was an absolute minimum of gracious remarks by Kaiser, but the highlight of the evening was a surprise to everyone. A relatively unknown piano player was just coming on the scene in Southern California, following a recent performance in the Hollywood Bowl and a Los Angeles television show. His name was Liberace. I didn't even know the name, but Earl Reynolds had heard him perform. Reynolds convinced me it was worth the gamble. We talked to Liberace and found he was available on December 1. He said he would bring along his own piano, his brother, George, together with his candelabra, for a fee of $1,750 (Think what his fee would have been a few years later). At first we balked, but decided it might be well worth it considering who our guests were. We also made another smart decision—not to have any other entertainment.

To say his 1 hour show was a smash would be almost an understatement. He totally captivated the audience. He drew special attention when he played and sang the song entitled September, looking all the time directly at 70-year old Kaiser who had just a year and a half earlier married a very young woman. When the words came out, "One hasn't got time for the waiting game. Oh, the days dwindle down to a precious few," most in the room couldn't keep their eyes off Kaiser either. The businessmen were so enraptured it seemed for years they more often mentioned Liberace than they did the tin plate mill. They could brag to their wives and friends they had first heard Liberace at a Kaiser party when he was a virtual unknown to the rest of the country.

The next day the tour of the steel mill was very individualized with a top person from mill management describing the various operations to small groups of three or four. At one point in going through the tin plate mill itself, there was some concern because no one could find Kaiser. After several company people scrambled about, he was finally located 100 yards outside the building watching workers excavate for a new hot-rolled sheet mill being built alongside the tin mill. As usual, Kaiser was more fascinated by witnessing what was in progress of being done than in what he considered already completed, the tin plate mill.

Kaiser was extremely pleased with the enthusiasm all of his guests had manifested. He knew for sure that with the important customers who had been in attendance he could count on his new tin plate mill operating at full capacity from that time forward. He wrote letters to many of those who had been in attendance, thanking them for their support. He was careful also to write Conrad Hilton on December 12:

> I wish to express to you and your entire organization my deepest apprecia-
> tion for the excellent manner in which you handled the Kaiser Steel Corpora-
> tion party at Arrowhead Springs Hotel on December 1.
>
> Your people were most efficient and courteous and they made all of our
> guests feel very much at home.
>
> I want you to know that we shall long remember the personal attention
> that you gave to this affair.
>
> My very best regards.

Number 1 In Salesmanship

Kaiser thumped the desk for emphasis:

"You have left out the most important Number 1 goal of all. Without it, your whole program is doomed to failure." He waited for his challenge to sink in.

All of the men in the room were dumbfounded. What goal could they have possibly overlooked? They had spent three full weeks in laying plans to launch a new company-wide program aimed at rallying employee enthusiasm to improve Kaiser Steel's operations. In 1954 the steel market had turned down, and competition in the industry had become severe. The company had just completed an $8 million expansion program and was becoming concerned over declining earnings.

It was then that Gene Trefethen hit on an idea. He talked it over with his Vice President and General Manager, Jack Ashby, and other key management people in Oakland. They liked the idea, so immediately a meeting at the Fontana steel plant was set up. About 10 management and top sales people from Oakland were included, along with 15 operating managers from all areas of the Fontana plant, managers of the Eagle Mountain, California, iron ore mine and the Sunnyside, Utah, coal mine, plus the district sales managers from Los Angeles, Oakland and Seattle.

Trefethen started the meeting off by carefully reviewing all ramifications of the problems facing the company. Then he added,

> But I have a solution. One that will work. One that will turn this company around, not next year, but within the next few months. It's such a simple plan you might not believe it will work, but I assure you it will.

> The plan is: Here and now we're going to agree that, working together, we will make Kaiser Steel the Number 1 steel company in the United States. In every department, at every location, we're going to start doing every job more efficiently, more creatively, more aggressively, than ever before. We're going to instill a new pride in all of our employees. We're not going to stop until we have become Number 1 in production costs, in the quality of our steel, in the service we provide our customers. By our total commitment, by our vigorous new efforts, we're going to become Number 1 in every way that measures a company's success, and as we do we're going to start making the profits we anticipated when we took on our expansion program. We won't aim to become the biggest in the industry, but the best.

It worked like magic. Everyone in the room seemed to catch fire. It was like a football team suddenly charged up by a pep talk from the coach. Starting with Ashby, one after another chimed in to say that the plan could work the miracle envisioned by Trefethen.

At the end of the meeting an 8-man committee from operations, sales, and other departments was appointed to formulate the company-wide program and to plan how it could be set in motion. The committee met several times in the next three weeks, and phones were kept busy in between meetings. One of the main responsibilities was to define just exactly what the company intended to become Number 1 in. After exploring all goals, it was agreed that Kaiser Steel should proclaim to all its employees that the company was going to become:

Number 1 in Employee Relations
Number 1 in Customer Relations
Number 1 in Community Relations

Number 1 in Stockholder and Investor Relations

Then to be more specific, to set some goals individual departments could do something about, it was further agreed the people would commit themselves to becoming Number 1 in 19 more specific goals such as:

Number 1 in Quality

Number 1 in Service

Number 1 in New Ideas

Number 1 in Employee Opportunities

In three short weeks, the management people at all locations were so steamed up they wanted to proceed at once with a company-wide kickoff program including special meetings in all departments, posters, bulletins and Number 1 pocket medallions for all employees. One thing was necessary, however, before the splash could be made—the program needed the blessing of Henry Kaiser. The plan had come together so fast, and Kaiser had been so busy in Hawaii (as well as making trips to Argentina to start up an automobile manufacturing plant). Trefethen had never really had an opportunity to fill him in on the proposed program. Finally, the meeting was held in Trefethen's office. He wanted his people to back him up, so he had his Number 1 Committee and top management people in attendance. He carefully outlined to Kaiser why such a program was needed, how everyone had become all fired up, and then he listed the four major goals and the nineteen subsidiary goals that would be sure to make the company Number 1 in the steel industry.

It was at this point that Kaiser had shocked everyone by interrupting Trefethen: "You have left out the most important Number 1 goal of all." After waiting for effect, Kaiser went on:

Number 1 in Salesmanship! That's the only goal that will make your program succeed. What do you mean, Number 1 in Customer Relations? Those are just words—just platitudes. They mean nothing. It's salesmanship and salesmanship alone that counts. It's only when you outsell the other guy that you help your company.

And what's this about becoming Number 1 in Employee Relations? How can you ever do that unless you are Number 1 in salesmanship—in selling yourself to your own people? That's something you boys must learn—a good boss is one who sells himself and his ideas to the people who work for him.

And how can you ever become Number 1 in Stockholder and Investor Relations unless you sell them on the progress our company is making?

Certainly, you'll never become Number 1 in Community Relations until all our employees become salesmen in behalf of the company. If you can find the key to making every employee in our company a salesman in all his dealings, then you'll become Number 1 in Community Relations and your whole program will be a smashing success.

Yes, boys, you're on the trail of something that should help our company, but, remember, it will only work if you and all the other people in Kaiser Steel become Number 1 in Salesmanship."

With salesmanship as the new theme of the whole effort, the Number 1 Program was launched with unprecedented fanfare on October 1, 1954. Few companies have ever rallied their employees so enthusiastically in any campaign. Every employee was made to feel it was his or her opportunity to help the company become Number 1.

The Program gave the company a much-needed shot in the arm. Sales and earnings began to pick up immediately. There was a new sense of teamwork in every department in the company. It was agreed that it should not be a flash-in-the-pan campaign. It was therefore carried forward for several years.

It proved that people working together with enthusiasm can make a measurable difference in results—especially if they are committed to becoming Number 1 in Salesmanship.

Labor's Best Friend

Some years ago I ventured to say that labor relations were nothing more than human relations. As I understand it, humanity is a broad term which means not only mankind as a whole; it also denotes certain virtues which mark man's progress toward perfection: kindness, forbearance, sympathy, and understanding. It is my belief that the Christian faith rests wholly on a humanitarian basis. The rank and file of labor and management accept Christianity, even though they do not always practice it. Nevertheless, the principle should, and does obtain in all human relationships which build, rather than destroy. I know I speak for countless thousands when I say that both labor and management want to build. When we generalize our hopes in the thought that we want to build a better America, we really mean that we want to build a more abundant life for every American. And this, again, is a Christian precept, preserved in the immortal words: 'I am come that ye might have life, and that ye might have it more abundantly.' There is neither secret nor mystery about labor relations. There is no need for a complicated formula, or for cumbersome legislation. The only approach is the humanitarian one: the 'give and take' between men of good will; the wholehearted desire to agree; the will to work together.

Who would utter such high-flown words? A preacher? An academician? A labor leader? A politician?

Who else but Henry Kaiser? He was being given an award by LaSalle College in Philadelphia, April 12, 1944, "for the most conspicuous and constructive service to the cause of industrial peace in America."

To him, his words were not just high sounding. They were not intended for show.

They expressed what he honestly believed. They were the kind of words he had used hundreds of times in talking to people informally. They expressed thoughts that came from his heart. They were his own words, not something worked up for him by a speech writer.

Kaiser was a very fortunate person. Liking people came naturally to him. He automatically accepted people for what they were. He believed in their intrinsic goodness. He had instinctive confidence in their potential. He enjoyed doing what he could to bring out the best in everyone he dealt with.

From this foundation it was an easy transition to learn to get along with labor unions. In his early roadbuilding days unions had not been a factor, but by the time in the late 1930's when Kaiser had his own rock, sand and gravel plants, his own cement company, and his own ships to carry that cement—and with the passage of the Wagner Act in 1938 granting new powers to unions—he accepted the role of unions wholeheartedly. From that time forward he considered that he and unions had a partnership responsibility to do that which was best for the workers and for the company.

Some of his best and most lasting friendships were with union leaders—Phil Murray, president, United Steelworkers of America; David McDonald who succeeded Murray; William Green, president, AFL-CIO; George Meany who succeeded Green; Dan Tobin, president of the Teamsters Union; Harry Lundberg, president of the Sailors Union of the Pacific; Walter Reuther, president of the United Automobile Workers. Whenever any of his companies had contracts with a union he became a warm friend of the leader of that union.

It was no surprise, therefore, that when Dan Tobin held a Teamsters Dinner honoring President Roosevelt on September 23, 1944, Henry Kaiser was one of the main guests. Here are excerpts from the Washington Post article on that dinner:

> At 10 after 8 two Secret Service men walked onto the stage and the orchestra struck up 'Hail To The Chief.' President Roosevelt appeared a moment later, and with him William Green, president of AFL; Daniel J. Tobin, president of the Teamsters, and Mr. Kaiser, the 'miracle man' of shipbuilding. The President attired in a plain blue suit, white shirt and dotted tie, sat between Green and Tobin with Kaiser on Green's right. With Green and Tobin and Kaiser acting as cheerleaders, the teamsters gave the President an ovation that lasted for five minutes or more and finally led Mr. Roosevelt to raise his hand over his head in the Champ's salute. Kaiser's presence at the table, two seats removed from the President, was the surprise of the evening.

Seven months later Roosevelt died, and the new President, Harry Truman, picked up friendships with labor leaders—and with Kaiser—where Roosevelt had left off. One of the surprises the new administration encountered after the end of the war in August 1945 was all the turmoil involved in shifting to a peacetime economy. The United Steelworkers of America—the bellwether union in those days—was determined to negotiate a healthy increase in wage rates, believing the industry could pass along such costs to a steel-hungry nation. Management thought differently, aiming to keep costs in check as much as possible.

As national president of the steel union, Phil Murray directed the negotiations for labor. By January 1946, it had come to the point where industry was holding firm on its offer to go along with an increase of 15 cents an hour, while the union was unyielding in its demand for 18 cents. Kaiser felt the difference was too small to precipitate a strike, so he accepted the union terms. Murray was grateful to Kaiser, convinced that it might set the pattern for the other steel companies. For more background on these negotiations see Chapter 9, "The Near Miss."

The friendship between Kaiser and Murray really blossomed into something warm and personal. Each felt free to keep in touch with the other in matters of mutual interest. If at that period of time Kaiser had been asked to name his closest friends, surely one of them would have been Philip Murray. Likewise, if Murray had been asked to name his closest friends, Kaiser would have been high on the list. When Murray passed away in the fall of 1952, here's the night letter Kaiser sent on November 10th to Mrs. Philip Murray and family:

My deep, heartfelt sentiments are with you at this time when your loved one has gone to rest at the end of his long and remarkable labors. I shall always cherish personally the memories of Philip Murray as a warm-souled man of overwhelming faith—of limitless devotion to the workers, their families and America. Surely his dauntless, kindly spirit will go with you every step of the path ahead, giving you ever-sustaining strength and faith.

A year later David J. McDonald, Murray's successor as president, United Steelworkers of America, was holding a meeting at the Commodore Hotel in New York City for union leaders representing 1,250,000 steelworkers throughout the United States. He introduced Henry Kaiser:

I have a little surprise for you this afternoon—a surprise I know you'll be happy about. In the 1944 Steelworkers' convention in Ohio a most unusual event took place. Phil Murray introduced a speaker whom he characterized as 'The greatest industrial genius of our day.' This gentleman made a remarkable and memorable speech. This gentleman happened to call upon me today on a business matter. I recalled what a hit he made in that convention speech. Of course, he is an industrial genius. But he also has developed into a great sociologist. He has conceived and put into operation one of the finest hospital plans in America. He has built some new hospitals that are absolutely out of this world. They are so completely different from what we have known hospitals to be that I cannot even begin to describe them. You will now hear from that outstanding American—Henry J. Kaiser.

It was an impromptu talk, just agreed upon that day—the kind of talk Kaiser loved most of all to give. (One wonders if Kaiser's business call on McDonald that day was a coincidence, or whether he might have been hoping for an invitation to the meeting.) In any event, he didn't have to search for thoughts, or words, or sentiments, or ideals. They just cascaded forth from him as he paid tribute to Phil Murray, Dave McDonald, union leaders, and American free enterprise. He had been given a rousing ovation when first introduced. When he finished, the audience really let loose in a standing ovation that continued until after he had left the hall.

The Implausible Strike

The strike against Kaiser Steel started July 15, 1959, and lasted until October 26, 104 long and anguishing and enormously costly days.

How in the world could that come about, considering the genuine friendship and admiration that had existed so long between Kaiser and union leaders? Who was to blame? What went wrong? Where did the chain of communication break down?

The strike was industry-wide, affecting all the major steel producers. For the first half of the year teams of negotiators for both sides worked hard to lay the groundwork for a strike-free settlement. It was a time when the union clearly felt a more-than-minimum wage increase was needed and could be afforded by the industry. It was a period when steel leaders thought inflationary forces were threatening the industry, along with rapidly increasing foreign competition. Try as they may, the negotiators weren't close to reconciling their differences, so the union decided it had no choice but to call a strike, although it did delay the strike two weeks beyond the contract deadline of June 30.

It was in that same year that Henry Kaiser had been designated Founder Chairman of the Board, with his son, Edgar, becoming Chairman, and Jack Ashby elevated from Vice President and General Manager to President. In recognition of the continued growth of Kaiser Steel, and with a desire to have its cooperation on all matters affecting the industry, the Board of Directors of the American Iron and Steel Institute had invited Ashby to become a Board member. There were all kinds of benefits that Kaiser Steel enjoyed by being a member of the Institute—working committees in all phases of steel production exchanging information with each other. Ashby became a highly respected member of the Board, and in turn developed the highest regard for the wisdom and integrity of the other Board members.

As the strike deadline approached, it was an uneasy time for Kaiser Steel management. Ashby was clear that the industry position was fair and constructive, and should be supported. Edgar Kaiser did not know industry leaders as well as Ashby did, and he had some misgivings. Besides, he was a very close friend of David McDonald, union president, and Arthur Goldberg, legal counsel for the union, and he tended to lean in their direction. Gene Trefethen, Vice Chairman of Kaiser Steel's Board, relied heavily on Ashby's judgment and began throwing his weight in favor of going along with the industry. This placed the final burden on Henry Kaiser. Should he go it alone, as he had always done in the past? Could he rely on the union leaders to be reasonable in their dealings with industry leaders as he thought they always had been with him? Were the industry leaders he had come to know equal to the challenge of working out a fair and equitable contract?

One situation undoubtedly had a bearing on his decision to go along with the industry. He had been living in Hawaii for several years and was head-over-heels in all of his construction activities there, including some preliminary planning on his concept for a whole new city, Hawaii Kai. He was far removed from the firing line in New York City where all the early skirmishing was going on between management and labor.

No doubt union leaders would have preferred negotiating with Kaiser Steel separately from the rest of the industry, hoping that Kaiser would agree to terms that could be used as leverage against the others. On the other hand, they knew how totally committed Ashby had become to the industry position, so they placed their hopes on the possibility that Kaiser Steel would have some kind of leavening influence on the other companies.

No labor negotiations, before or since, ever had such lengthy and elaborate planning. Each of the twelve companies agreed to have its President in New York City virtually constantly to respond to daily developments. Each company had its top labor relations officer and its top public relations or communications officer in New York at all times in order to make suggestions, and to pass along to employees back home just what was going on in the negotiations. With my responsibility for company communications, I spent almost every working day in New York City from the start of the strike to its conclusion.

The actual industry negotiations were carried on by four individuals, two from the United States Steel Corporation, and one each from Bethlehem Steel and Republic Steel, those being the next largest companies. Conrad Cooper of U.S. Steel was chief negotiator. He had the unqualified backing of all the company presidents. Long before actual negotiations began he had gone into training—analyzing the issues from all sides and actually keeping himself in good physical condition so he would be ready for the grueling sessions.

Once the strike started the negotiators met nearly every working day. When the daily sessions were over, Cooper along with his three aides, would report in detail to the presidents just what had been said by each side. Then in a separate meeting they would go over the same story to the labor relations and public relations people. Main guidance, of course, came from the company presidents, but the other committee was invited to ask questions and make suggestions. It certainly had to be one of the most carefully structured negotiating programs ever undertaken.

For the first two or three weeks each day seemed to be a repeat of the day before— forceful demands by the union, with unrelenting adamance by the industry. Even the passage of time with no apparent progress didn't seem to upset the company presidents. Cooper was doing exactly what the majority wanted him to do. Two or three presidents did, from time to time, mention compromise possibilities, but when Cooper and his aides warned how that might weaken their hand the majority decision was always not to budge.

One of the early points the union wanted agreement on was retroactive application of whatever increases might eventually be worked out. I shall never forget the shock I felt when one day Cooper reported to our group: "I told Dave McDonald and Arthur Goldberg to quit haranguing on retroactivity, for the simple reason we were never going to agree to one penny increase in wages, so there will be nothing to apply retroactively." I knew then it was going to be a long and bitter strike. I venture to speculate that if Henry Kaiser had heard that statement he would have fought vigorously to change the industry position or would have begun exploring how to withdraw gracefully from the group.

As the strike dragged on through August and September and well into October, pressures were reaching the explosion point in every direction. The magnificent Fontana steel plant looked like a graveyard, with all furnaces banked and none of the facilities in operation. It was a haunting, spooky feeling to stand in one of the huge rolling mills, not hearing a sound, not seeing a worker. Try as we did to explain the situation to our employees, few could understand how Kaiser could let his company get embroiled in such a disastrous strike.

As agonizing as it was to him in his new role of President of Kaiser Steel, Ashby never once wavered in his support of the industry approach. On the other hand, Edgar Kaiser—so much like his father in dealing with unions—couldn't endure the stalemate. He went to the committee of presidents and plead with them to find some area of compromise. With Conrad Cooper arguing against Edgar, and with Ashby known to be in support of the industry, the presidents decided to stand by Cooper.

It had been agreed that none of the presidents would deal with McDonald and Goldberg, leaving that strictly up to Cooper. Because Edgar was not officially a member of the president's committee, and because he felt so close to McDonald and Goldberg, he didn't hesitate engaging in exploratory talks with them, which upset the committee, including Ashby.

It was Henry Kaiser who finally couldn't take it any longer. Without dictating the terms, he told Edgar to get together with McDonald and Goldberg and work out an equitable settlement. It didn't take long after that for the three of them to agree on an increase of ll cents per man hour per year. That was to be signed on Monday, October 26, 104 days after the strike began.

Edgar knew this would be headline news, so on Sunday, he decided to explain the rationale for his action to his good friend and trusted reporter, James Reston of the New York Times. The early editions of Reston's story—"Mutiny In The Waldorf," came out Sunday evening.

Ashby had been away for the weekend. When he saw the article on his return late Sunday, he was furious, but had the good sense not to attack Edgar. By this time it was around ll:00 p.m. and several of us, including Ashby, were in Edgar's Waldorf hotel room discussing the article, as well as talking about getting the Fontana plant in operation again. Suddenly, the pressures of the last few days, and the weight of the responsibility he bore for taking his independent action, overwhelmed Edgar both mentally and emotionally, and he broke out sobbing. He left the room. There was nothing for us to do but go to our own rooms to try to get a night's rest.

Eight days later, under the pressure of the Kaiser settlement and direct intervention of Vice President Richard Nixon, the rest of the industry came to terms with the union. The industry felt it had been betrayed, but in turn Henry Kaiser and Edgar Kaiser felt the industry had let them down by being so intransigent. The few years when the Kaisers had been "one of them" were over.

Also, the deep difference between Ashby and Edgar never really healed. Over the ensuing years other differences kept cropping up, so that the two of them never ended up as a truly compatible management team. Indeed, their smoldering dislike for each other seemed to keep growing, an intriguing corporate disaffection that might well merit a study of its own.

In any event, here's a portion of the letter "To Our Stockholders, Employees and Customers" signed by Edgar as Chairman, and Ashby as President, in Kaiser Steel's annual report for the year of the strike, 1959:

> The operations of Kaiser Steel Corporation during the year 1959 can best be examined by dividing the year roughly into two 6-month periods. During the first six months of the year the company had record production and sales. As a result, net sales for the first six months of the year amounted to $147,150,000, and net earnings came to $10,198,000. Shortly following the conclusion of this successful six-month period the largest and costliest strike in the company's history began. The strike lasted 104 days from July 15 until October 26, during which time Kaiser Steel exerted its full energies toward reaching an acceptable industry-wide settlement along with the other major steel companies in the nation. During the latter stages of the negotiations, however, Kaiser Steel management concluded that a general area of agreement had been reached which could lead to a settlement that would be in the best interests of both sides. When it appeared that our employees would be required to return to their jobs under a Taft Hartley Law court order, the company's management decided that independent action was necessary. Therefore, the company signed an agreement on October 26 with United Steelworkers of America extending through June 30, 1961, which will cost the company 11 cents per man hour per year. A major feature of the agreement is a completely new approach to collective bargaining. Two committees have been organized which will work throughout the life of the contract. One will recommend ways for sharing the company's future economic progress equitably among stockholders, employees, and the public, in an effort to eliminate the threat of another strike. The other committee will deal with problems relating to local working practices. As a result of the strike, Kaiser Steel sustained a loss for the second six months of $17,599,000 which more

than offset the earnings of the first six months, and resulted in a loss of $7,401,000 for the full year.

The committee to deal equitably with the company's economic progress was one of the most high-powered ever organized. It was made up of the three top men from the Steelworkers' union: David McDonald, Arthur Goldberg, and Marvin Miller. The company was represented by Edgar Kaiser, Gene Trefethen, and Fred Borden, Executive Vice President. In addition, three of the country's foremost economists and labor consultants agreed to serve on the committee representing the public interest. To add distinction to the group a renowned labor consultant from Harvard University was retained to do research and make recommendations to this so- called "Long Range Committee."

Jack Ashby had been asked to serve on the committee instead of Fred Borden, but his bitterness toward the strike settlement was so deeply rooted, he refused. Ashby always prided himself for standing his ground whenever he believed he was right, but this had to be one of the gutsiest—and most questionable—decisions in his long Kaiser career. It was not surprising that he didn't want to team up with Edgar on the committee, but it was very surprising he would take such a stand in the face of the fact that Henry Kaiser, whom Ashby respected so profoundly, had called for the ending of the strike and later had given his blessing to the Long Range Committee.

The committee met every three months with an agenda as formal as any Board of Directors meeting. Structured as it was, and with a clear goal of cooperation, the committee played an important role in the company's operations well into the 1970's.

It was a noble and well-meaning experiment, and in the end the company was convinced it had served its purposes. In a way, though, it was an over-reaction to the remorse that the strike had brought on. Both Edgar Kaiser and union leaders were so distressed—and almost guilt-ridden because they had not avoided the strike—that they felt impelled to make amends by doing some bold pioneering that might not only help the company and the union but might even become a model for other companies and other unions. They had taken enough criticism from all directions, now they wanted to earn some credit.

There were many, however, who thought the plan was a bit grandiose and a bit top-heavy, with ten (including the Harvard consultant) powerful figures wrestling on such a formal scale with issues that were not always weighty enough to merit so much of their time and attention. Some people looked back with longing to the way Henry Kaiser had always dealt with labor—a good faith approach with just a few people coming to grips with the issues early on. While that era had ended, there was consolation in the fact that Henry Kaiser's spirit was somehow felt in each meeting of the Long Range Committee even though he was not in attendance.

Through it all, Kaiser himself gained stature in the eyes of labor. They didn't blame him for the strike. They thought he had been trapped by the industry. And they were grateful he had given his support to the work of the Long Range Committee.

It was no surprise, therefore, when on May 20, 1965, at age 83, Henry Kaiser was given the labor movement's highest humanitarian citation—the Murray-Green award. Phil Murray and William Green were two of labor's most beloved and honored leaders, both of whom knew Kaiser well. As a highlight of the national convention of the AFL-CIO in Washington, DC, Kaiser became the first industrialist ever to receive the coveted award.

When Kaiser died in August 1967 his son Edgar was deluged with expressions of sympathy. Scores of labor leaders sent their heart-felt condolences, among which were:

George Meany, president of the AFL-CIO

The labor movement has lost a close and cherished friend, and all America has lost a dedicated humanitarian.

Arthur Goldberg, U.S. Ambassador to the United Nations

It seems only yesterday that, at his insistence, you and I worked out a formula which settled the 1959 steel strike. Thus, as always, he showed a warm understanding of the needs of working people. He was truly a liberal industrialist in the best sense of the word.

Walter P. Reuther, president of the United Auto Workers

We can honor his memory by carrying on his work and by giving meaning and substance to the human values and the democratic ideals to which he dedicated his life.

From start to finish, Kaiser had been one of labor's truest and best friends. From start to finish, labor leaders had been among Kaiser's truest and best friends.

What's In A Name?

Except for the 104-day strike in 1959, Kaiser Steel's operations—once the RFC loans had been paid in full in 1950—could have been a model of successful American free enterprise. Two words would come closest to describing the company's success—diversification and growth.

Year after year major additions were made not only to the Fontana plant but to fabricating facilities as well as coal and iron ore mines. Starting with capital expenditures of $15.6 million for the year ended June 30, 1951 a peak of $139 million was reached in 1957. The total assets of the company rose from $190.4 million on June 30, 1951, to $519.1 million on December 31, 1967, a few months after Kaiser had passed away in Hawaii.

Of course, the expansion was only possible because of the solid profits the company kept making. For example, in 1957 net earnings came to $21.4 million; for 1965 and 1966 each years profits exceeded $18 million; and in 1967, the last year we are concerned with in this book, earnings passed the $33 million mark.

These successful post-RFC years didn't reflect any super salesmanship on the part of Kaiser. He had too many other fish to fry. Besides, he had built a management and sales team, fully capable of exploiting all market possibilities. By that time the main value Kaiser represented was in his name. Among his own people, to be a Kaiser employee was to be bold, hard working, persevering. Among customers, the name Kaiser stood for new ideas, good products, good service.

A prime example was Kaiser Steel's entrance into the manufacture of large diameter line pipe for gas and oil. Starting with the 500,000 tons of steel plate Kaiser had sold to be manufactured into 30-inch pipe for a gas line from Texas to New York City, the company went from one big pipe line job to another. Early on, a deal was struck with the Steel Division of Basalt Rock Company, Inc., located at Napa, California to convert Kaiser steel plate into pipe. Soon thereafter, agreement was reached for Kaiser Steel to buy that fabricator. The point to be noted was that the owner of Basalt Rock Company was Al Streblow, a lifelong friend of Henry Kaiser. Here was a situation where Kaiser really didn't do much selling—his name and friendship with Streblow led to one of the most profitable investments Kaiser Steel ever made.

It was in Australia (already mentioned earlier in this chapter) where the name Kaiser opened the door to unbelievable profits in iron ore. Kaiser people did not discover the fabulous Hamersley iron ore deposit. It was the name Kaiser—and the organization behind that name—which in 1961 the Australians decided they wanted. By 1967 the company's annual report could boast:

> During 1967, additional ore contracts were signed, including a $300 million contract calling for an additional 40 million tons of iron ore for Japanese steel mills. Hamersley Iron, in which Kaiser Steel is a 36% owner, now holds contracts approximately $1.3 billion in sales value. Expansion programs now authorized will result in the capacity to produce and ship at an annual rate of 15 million long tons of iron ore and pellets by the end of 1969.

The same situation prevailed in Japan. Henry Kaiser never made a foray into Japan to sell Australian iron ore (or later, Canadian coal), but the name Kaiser was big in Japan. During World War II he had made ships faster than they ever did. His ships had played a big role in crushing Japan. By the 1960's the successful Japanese shipbuilding industry was using some techniques they borrowed from Kaiser.

So when Kaiser was associated with the production of Australian iron ore (and later Canadian coal), the Japanese had a respect, bordering on a reverence, for the name Kaiser. They were far more willing to do business with Australian and Canadian interests than if the name Kaiser had not been involved.

Except for his long-festering dislike of Edgar Kaiser starting with the 1959 strike, Jack Ashby had an outstanding career—mostly of a sales nature—with Kaiser Steel. His build-up of sales during the 1950's was extraordinary. But in a way he reached an all time high in establishing good relations with the Japanese in the sale of Australian iron ore (and later Canadian coal) to them. He was highly regarded and even fondly accepted by Japanese steel industry leaders. It was not Edgar Kaiser, nor Gene Trefethen who stood tall in Japanese eyes—it was Ashby (and the name Kaiser). Japanese even named a ship after Ashby.

While Henry Kaiser never visited Japan on business at that time, he was very careful to keep posted on everything that was going on there. On nearly every trip Ashby and his close associate, Jack Carlson, made to Japan, Kaiser would have them stop by for a visit at the airport in Hawaii, either going or coming, to fill him in on developments. His experienced counsel played an important part in all of the successful dealings that were going on with the Japanese.

The name Kaiser worked magic in Canada just as it had in Australia, only this time it involved coking coal. Thomas Gleed of Seattle, Washington was Chairman of the Board of Crows Nest Industries Limited, owner of a huge, high-quality coking coal property in eastern British Columbia. He knew the Japanese steel industry was searching the world for coking coal, but he didn't have the organization or finances to develop a large scale mining operation at Crows Nest. On a duck hunting trip with Fred Ferroggiaro, President of the Bank of America, in the early fall of 1966, he mentioned how he was struggling to open up a coal mine. Ferroggiaro suggested the name of Henry Kaiser, and became the intermediary to bring the two together.

Kaiser immediately sensed the potential, so he asked Trefethen and Ashby and their raw materials organization to study all aspects of the mining and transportation problems involved. Their explorations revealed proved reserves of 130 million tons and probable reserves of at least an additional 30 million tons of low volatile coal of high quality required in the production of steel. In May of 1967, in one of the fastest mining acquisitions ever accomplished, Kaiser Steel bought the property. With his new holdings of Kaiser Steel stock, Gleed was asked to serve on Kaiser's Board. Within eight months after that, on January 31, 1968, Kaiser Steel had signed a contract for the export to Japan of more than 45 million long tons of coal over a 15-year period beginning in 1970.

Henry Kaiser had not discovered Canadian coal. He had not "sold" himself or his organization to Gleed. All he had done was respond quickly to the opportunity presented to him. It was his name, his reputation, that had made it all possible. He was 84 years old when Gleed had been introduced to him. He only lived a year longer, but it was time enough to see that Canadian coal was well on its way to becoming another enormous profit center, like Australian iron ore.

What's in a name? It's success piled upon success if the name is Kaiser (as long as Kaiser was alive, that is).

I can't end this chapter on Kaiser and his steel company without recounting what I overheard in 1961. Kaiser Steel's Board of Directors was having its quarterly meeting in Kaiser Center in Oakland. That Monday morning the Wall Street Journal ran a long front page article on the Kaiser companies, generally quite favorable. It spent some time describing how Edgar Kaiser was taking over the reins because Henry Kaiser was living in Hawaii "semi-retired." I happened to be talking to George Burpee,

Board member, just inside the meeting room when Henry Kaiser walked in. In his friendly way Burpee said: "Mr. Kaiser, that was a nice article in the Wall Street Journal this morning." Kaiser grunted, not rudely, but enough to show his feelings, "Humpf, semi-retired!" He would not concede that he was even approaching semi-retirement.

I have little doubt that if the Wall Street Journal had run another article on Kaiser mentioning semi-retirement in the summer of 1967, when he was fatally ill just before his death, he would have still grunted, "Humpf, semi-retired!"

CHAPTER 9

THE NEAR MISS

"Life is very simple. There aren't any problems, there are only prospects. Wherever you have bottlenecks, you have opportunities."

Henry Kaiser loved to sprinkle his speeches with poetry—generally inspirational, sometimes corny. One of his favorites was Edgar A. Guest's classic American poem, "It Couldn't Be Done," which he quoted several times when he was getting started in the automobile business. It was ironical that within a few years when Kaiser Motors was faced with shutting down the Willow Run plant, the workers would try to salve their feelings by making a parody out of that poem:

> Somebody said that it couldn't be done,
> But he with a chuckle replied
> That "maybe it couldn't," but he would be one
> Who wouldn't say so till he tried.
> So he buckled right in with a trace of a grin
> On his face. If he worried, he hid it.
> He started to sing as he tackled the thing
> That couldn't be done,
> But, God damn, he couldn't do it.

It would have been more accurate, but no more comforting, if the workers had changed the last line to read: "And, by God, he nearly did it."

For, indeed, Henry Kaiser nearly did it in the automobile business. He came a lot closer to making a success of it than most people realize. Critics have had their field day saying that in the one industry where he had to slug it out toe-to-toe with the big boys in a competitive sales market he couldn't cut the mustard. But automobile experts at that time knew better. They knew he had broken into the country's toughest business with a stronger start than any other company since Chrysler in the 1920's.

They were very surprised he was turning out cars within nine months after leasing the huge Willow Run, Michigan, plant. This was a facility built by Ford Motor Co. to produce bombers during the war which had to be completely remodeled to get it ready for automobile production. Once in operation, it broke all records in the history of the industry for number of new cars produced in the first year. In only 40 months, Kaiser-Frazer turned out approximately 400,000 cars.

There would be many moments of glory during the brief, colorful roller-coaster corporate adventure called Kaiser-Frazer, but none more spectacular or exciting than the premiere showing of the model Kaiser and Frazer cars at the Waldorf Astoria hotel in New York City in January 1946. It was only five months after the company had been incorporated, and it would be another six months before actual assembly line production would begin. But the public couldn't wait. Nor could Henry Kaiser, nor Joseph Frazer.

Here's how the New York Times of January 21, 1946, described the crushing scene:

> 40,000 persons inspected the Kaiser-Frazer cars at the Waldorf-Astoria hotel from 3:00 p.m. to 11:00 p.m. yesterday. Although the premiere hour for the exhibit was 6:00 p.m., so numerous was the throng gathered about the hotel and extending through the lobby that the doors were opened at 3:00 p.m. For more than an hour afterward queues spread to Lexington Avenue despite frigid weather and biting winds. A special detail of police was on duty. So eager were the guests to see the new vehicles that one of the French glass door portals in the hotel was smashed. Almost 40 per cent of the visitors were women. The exhibition will be open today from 11:00 a.m. to 11:00 p.m.

The event held such national interest it was written up in newspapers and magazines throughout the country, as well as being given complete radio coverage. This is the way Business Magazine of February 4, 1946, wrote the story, linking it up with Kaiser-Frazer's second stock issue:

> The big, bald, grinning old roadbuilder, turned dambuilder, turned shipbuilder, turned autobuilder, hadn't yet produced a car to sell, and only a few to show. But in an hour's time the public had oversubscribed an issue of 1,800,000 shares of common stock in the Kaiser-Frazer Corporation at $20.25. The price had doubled since the first issue of 1,700,000 shares in September. In five days 156,000 people, who had waited for hours in all kinds of weather, filed through the Waldorf-Astoria hotel in New York City to see the hand-built Kaiser and Frazer showroom models, and 8,900 signed $11,800,000 worth of new car orders. All deposits, including an offer of $1,500 cash, were declined. Electric recording machines were brought in to speed up order taking after one crowd had broken down a door.

As busy as Kaiser and his production people had been turning out the two model cars, and converting the Willow Run plant into an automobile assembly line, Frazer and his sales people had likewise spent five hectic months lining up a nationwide dealer organization. There was no shortage of men who wanted a Kaiser-Frazer dealership. Indeed, the company was flooded with nearly 12,000 applicants. The job was to sort out 800 of the most experienced and qualified. It was an ideal time to bring these 800 dealers together not only to meet Kaiser and Frazer personally, but to see the model cars and to share in the excitement of the Waldorf-Astoria premiere. In a separate article on the dealer's party, the New York Times reported on January 21, 1946:

> What was scheduled as just a dinner of Kaiser-Frazer automobile dealers at the Roosevelt Hotel developed last night into a series of ovations that approached in enthusiasm those of a political convention, as the top men of the new automobile corporation bluntly challenged the rest of the industry. 'They ask me where we're going to get steel, how we're going to produce motors,' said Mr. Kaiser. 'Well, I'll tell you. The only thing that will limit our production will be our floor space. They tell me I am going out on a limb. Well, that's where I like to be—way out on a limb. I like to be not afraid. We're out to service the nation, the whole world. We're out to produce 13,000,000 cars. If we don't, we'll get darn near it.' The dealers applauded, whistled, banged tables, 'Attaboy, Henry,' they yelled, 'Give 'em hell.' From the very beginning the dinner was charged with enthusiasm. There was a band in the balcony playing favorite songs of many states. Pennsylvania Polka, Dixie, Sidewalks of New York, On the Banks of the Wabash, Deep in the Heart of Texas. When Mr. Kaiser and Mr. Frazer entered it seemed that at any moment there would be a parade of standard bearers. Men rushed to the speakers' dais to get programs signed. Trays of food crashed to the floor. When Kaiser was introduced, the ovation lasted nearly three minutes. It came to another climax when the soft-voiced executive addressed them with, 'Hello, Partners.' After the dinner the dealers were still bubbling with enthusiasm. Standing in long queues for coats they bragged about what they would do to their competitors.

An Instinct For Showmanship

There were many who would say Henry Kaiser was a show off, that he was a grandstander. But they didn't understand his true nature, they missed the real significance of what he was doing. He was a born showman every bit as much as being born to create, to build, to be doing things. He simply was one never to "hide his light under a bushel," good or bad. His life was an open book. He was uninhibited in plunging in to new challenges. He was uninhibited in letting people know what was going on. He could never be accused of covering anything up. He savored recognition but not to bask in it. He didn't want to waste time dwelling on that which had already been finished. He believed that the more people knew about his accomplishments, the more favorable the climate would be for his next undertakings. His overriding interest was always on the job to be finished or the job ahead. If showmanship would help in that direction, he was eager to be the showman.

That's why he was every bit as enthusiastic as the salesman Frazer in planning a spectacular affair to show off the first model cars. The kick-off would have to take place in January, signalling dramatic progress in five months and telling everyone that 1946 was to be the year of the new Kaiser and Frazer cars. It would have to take place in the country's most prestigious setting—the Waldorf hotel in New York City. (Kaiser had for many years maintained a suite in the Waldorf.) And all the forces involved in the new company would have to rally together to give the biggest possible send-off to the occasion.

Production of the two model cars was the responsibility of Henry C. McCaslin who had signed on as Chief Engineer in August just after the company was formed. Although he knew Frazer and had worked for him, he had never met Kaiser before. But it was Kaiser who would stick closest to him as he sweat out the time table for the Waldorf showing.

In his comprehensive book on Kaiser-Frazer, The Last Onslaught on Detroit, written by Richard M. Langworth, Kaiser's dealings with McCaslin are described:

> 'What I remember particularly about the body construction,' McCaslin later said, 'was the great need for speed. I put an organization of 395 people together in 60 days, and we only had 90 days to make a production car out of the design.' Kaiser and Frazer had set the Waldorf show for very early January and when McCaslin found he'd need two additional weeks, it was so important that they called a special meeting of the board of directors to agree to the short delay.

> 'Okay, gentlemen,' said Kaiser, 'from now on until we get these two jobs into New York, everybody's working for McCaslin—including me.'

> According to McCaslin, Kaiser really meant it. 'The next day Mr. Kaiser came over to my office and said, "Okay, Mac, here I am, now what can I do?" I said we needed some aluminum castings in Detroit that we hadn't sent anyone to get. By God, he went down and got 'em in his Cadillac, and he came back carrying one into the office and saying, "Well, here they are, Mac, now what else can I do?" I liked that old guy. He and I got along all right. And he did have his feet on the ground too. If you had a problem you could give him your story, and he'd accept it, but brother you'd better be right.'

Not just at the start, but at every significant milestone of company progress, Kaiser was the first to sense the value of dramatizing it, and the one most eager to maximize the impact. With his uncanny knack for showmanship, he was always searching around for some hook to pay tribute to his workers and to let the public in on the good news. He was particularly proud of how fast the assembly line at Willow Run had gotten into production in the early summer of 1946, less than a year since the company had been incorporated. Then with cars rolling steadily off the line by August he prodded Frazer and Edgar Kaiser to hold a big rally with the workers. To his regret Kaiser had commitments in the west which prevented him from being in attendance, but he was careful to send his wire of congratulations on August 12, 1946, to Frazer who read it to the assembled workers. Copies were later printed and distributed throughout the plant:

I wish I could stand beside you when you talk to our partners at Willow Run today. You and I have seen the first part of a great dream could true.

A new organization is a wonderful thing. The opportunity it gives every man to grow - the opportunity to work and produce to the very top of his ability. To me it's like a clean piece of paper and on it every man who participates writes his own goals and ideals and the sincere purposes of his life. I know you'll say what both of us feel deep down in our hearts, Joe. This is a great battle for the right to serve our nation. What Kaiser-Frazer will be is written right now in the hearts and minds of the people who work with us.

Tell them for me that I'm standing right beside you today a little prouder of being an American, a little surer that men can work together for the good of all, and more determined than ever to prove that America belongs to all of its people.

It's a wonderful day for all of us. We've just begun. Tell every one of those who have joined us the things that you and I have talked about so many times: that the future is greater than we can imagine, and that one thing is certain - whoever regards work as a pleasure can have more fun in this organization than any other place on earth.

A year later when car number 100,000 rolled off the Willow Run line on September 25, 1947, a beaming Kaiser shook hands across the hood with a smiling Frazer. In the background, a horde of happy workers shared in the proud moment. Kaiser always liked people as a backdrop for his pictures. And he was careful to give credit to the union for the role it was playing. The 100,000th car picture was furnished to every possible newspaper and publication in the hope that the public would get the message that good things were happening at Willow Run.

It was less than 6 months later that Kaiser and Frazer could make another boast—with pictures and appropriate fanfare—about car number 200,000, this time a Frazer Manhattan, the more expensive line. Then, within another 5 months, the two would be once more congratulating each other as the first 1949 model Kaiser car came off the line August 28, 1948.

The Moth And The Candle

Kaiser was attracted to the automobile business like a moth to a lighted candle. By the time he was in his late teens the automobile phenomenon was starting to excite America. Over the next few decades it would constitute a revolution—the single most influential force in changing the living habits of the entire nation.

As soon as he could afford it, he bought himself a car. He was one of the industry's earliest and most enthusiastic customers. He reveled in the feeling of freedom it gave him, actually the feeling of being a leader in the community. The mobility it provided was especially appealing because he was always in a hurry.

In his early construction days cars were indispensable. How do you get from one remote job to another without a car? Even when railroad or bus service was available between two major points, he could save time by piling in the car the minute he wanted to leave. When someone was with him they would often drive through the night, spelling each other off for a few snatches of sleep. When hotel rooms weren't available, or when he couldn't afford a room, he did his share of sleeping in a car.

In the October 10, 1929, issue of the daily Chronicle newspaper in Spokane, Washington, there was an article proudly welcoming home the now-famous roadbuilder, Henry Kaiser, and his wife, who had just arrived in their new front-wheel-drive Cord car after a six-day trip from Chicago where they encountered all kinds of road problems along the way. The article pointed out that his Cord was the 30th car he had owned in 22 years.

Kaiser was forever challenging the speed limits. It bothered him to get the number of speeding tickets he did, so he joined in the campaign to pass a law in California requiring that highway patrol cars be painted two-tone, thereby making it easier to spot whether a cop was hovering anywhere near.

His chauffeur, Dick Taylor, could have been a speed car driver he was so handy behind the wheel. He could weave his way through traffic like no one else. Passengers who rode across the San Francisco Bay Bridge with him and Kaiser whistled under their breath how fast the trip was made and yet free from traffic risks or speeding tickets. For most people in the 1930's and 1940's it was a 5-hour trip from Oakland to Lake Tahoe along the two-lane, winding road with the treacherous curves over the Donner Summit. Taylor would do it in an hour less, taking Kaiser to his beautiful new home, Fleur du Lac, on the west shore of the lake. Taylor never had any serious accidents, which helps account for the fact he remained Kaiser's driver throughout the years.

Within a month or two after Kaiser had married the young nurse, Ale, in April 1951, he organized a caravan of five cars for a trip from Oakland to Lake Tahoe where he was planning to open his homes there for summer usage. Kaiser and his wife were in the lead car with Dick Taylor doing the driving. Kaiser's new young assistant, Handy Hancock, was driving the next car accompanied by Kaiser's secretary, Edna Knuth (Piper), and a car full of supplies. Here's how Handy describes the trip which started at 5:00 a.m.:

I have never driven so hard or so fast, trying to keep up with Taylor. I didn't dare drop behind, because you just didn't do that with Mr. Kaiser. He always stopped at a little roadside restaurant on the outskirts of Sacramento for breakfast where they served delicious pancakes. When we raced into the parking lot of the restaurant, everybody scrambled out, hurried into the restaurant, and ordered immediately. Within 10 or 15 minutes Mr. Kaiser was finished and ready to go. I had hardly started my breakfast because I am a slow eater, but with Mr. Kaiser pressing everyone to get going, I literally gulped my food. I will never forget as we walked out the door he looked up at the sky and then at his watch and commented, '30 minutes gone forever.'

Even though Kaiser had appreciation for the aesthetic (the beauty of Lake Tahoe was always luring him), he seldom enjoyed traveling in a car for the sake of the countryside he was driving through. He was too busy talking, or thinking, or planning for his arrival at destination. He would never ask to have the car stopped, or even slowed down, to take in any of nature's marvels.

Because there were occasions when Kaiser had a lot of jobs he wanted Handy to do at Lake Tahoe, he would sometimes ask him to do the driving instead of Taylor. Handy remembers some close calls:

These trips with Mr. Kaiser were the most nerve-wracking I have ever experienced, because all the way he would be pushing me to go faster and faster. If there was a truck on the road he wanted me to pass it. I was a good driver, but not a fast or reckless driver, especially with the precious cargo on the seat beside me. On this particular day, he had been persistently pressing me to go faster to get around the trucks even though it meant passing some of them blind. As we went up one long incline behind a truck, Mr. Kaiser said, 'Pass him, pass him.' I dared to say 'No,' but once again he ordered me to pass the truck. With no other choice, I said, 'O.K., here we go,' hit the accelerator, pulled alongside the truck going up the hill, and suddenly on an unexpected curve came face-to-face with a truck roaring down the hill. We were near the front end of the big truck we were passing, so I couldn't slam on the brakes in time to avoid the oncoming truck. Somehow I did manage enough of a pickup to slide in ahead of the truck going our way. We missed a head-on collision by a hairbreadth, at which point I said, 'Mr. Kaiser, I hope you're satisfied.' From that day on I was never asked to pass another thing.

Kaiser's passion for speed lured him into the boating world. That was one of the reasons he was so much in love with Lake Tahoe—it gave him a chance to take up speedboat racing. As striking as his new Tahoe home was, finished one year before completion of the Boulder Dam in 1936, the thing his neighbors remember most was his boats roaring across the lake with a spray of water that could be seen for a mile.

At most of his plants he had a workshop where new ideas could be tested. In time, he added a central experiment station, his own Hobby Lobby in Emeryville next door to Oakland, so he could keep his fingers on everything that was being tried out. He encouraged his people at all levels to "brainstorm"—to let new ideas pop out at any time from any source. Clay Bedford described Kaiser's wide open approach: "H.J. talked with everyone—cat skinners (tractor operators), shovel operators, foremen, day laborers, mechanics. It was hard to say which ideas he originated and which he picked up from others and expanded."

By the early 1940's the Hobby Lobby was zeroing in on cars. They were having a field day. No idea was too far out to be summarily rejected. They were playing around with different materials hoping to find a replacement for steel. The one that seemed to have the most promising possibilities was fiberglass-reinforced plastic, an offshoot from Kaiser's interest in boats. They were under orders to come up with a low-cost car, one that would excite the public's interest. Kaiser himself kept stressing a front-wheel drive car with torsion bar suspension, a totally different car that would be made in the West. He was no doubt influenced along these lines by the front-wheel-drive Cord he had bought in 1929.

The Hobby Lobby's working materials were dozens of used cars, domestic and foreign. Some of them, like a few front-wheel drive French Citroens were picked up locally from classified newspaper ads. These cars would be completely torn down and the parts used as the starting point for new engineering concepts to be used in designing the car of the future.

By automobile industry research standards this was a tinker toy operation. However, in one way or another many of the things learned at Emeryville would be put into practice at Willow Run. There was nothing particularly secret about the goings on at Hobby Lobby, but of course the automobile manufacturers heard very little about it, and in any event didn't take it very seriously.

However, Kaiser was beginning to get deadly serious. He could look back on his spectacular achievements in dambuilding; his name had become a household word because of the speed with which he was turning out ships for the war effort; his big new steel mill in Southern California was being built in record time; his cement and magnesium plants were operating at capacity.

And in the shipyards hundreds of supervisory personnel were proving their management capabilities by training and directing tens of thousands of unskilled workers in a revolutionary shipbuilding technique—assembling ships from prefabricated parts, a practice not too different from the assembling of automobiles. With their host of expediters spread out all over the country scrounging parts that were in short supply and riding herd on freight trains to keep the material flowing, they were launching ships in ever-increasing numbers. Surely, this team could adapt to whatever challenge there might be in manufacturing cars. The time was now at hand for Kaiser to tell the world he would be in the automobile business after the war. His lifetime fascination with cars was beckoning him on.

He started by challenging the automobile industry to announce its postwar models immediately, taking War Bonds in advance payment. The industry shrugged it off. Except for one self-appointed spokesman. By the strangest kind of irony it was Joe Frazer who blasted Kaiser publicly:

> As an automobile man for thirty years, I resent a West Coast shipbuilder asking us if we have the courage to plan postwar automobiles when the President has asked us to forego all work which would take away from the war effort. Kaiser has done a great job as a shipbuilder, and I'm not depreciating his war effort, but I think his challenge to automobile men is as half-baked as some of his other statements.

Beautiful. Just exactly what Kaiser hoped someone would say. Just exactly the kind of game he liked to play. Not ever dreaming that within three years he would be teaming up with Frazer, he could hardly wait to tell the world:

> If someone didn't call my plans stupid and impractical, it just wouldn't seem right. They said it about our ships, magnesium, our dams and everything else. If Mr. Frazer thinks that the capacity of America has been reached—that our ultimate ability to design has been reached—then he just doesn't think as I do. Planning will give our boys in uniform something to come home to. But what does Mr. Frazer have to offer them? Let him answer that! Any good businessman plans at least two years ahead, and it's too bad that Mr. Frazer won't begin planning today for tomorrow.

A Deal Is Struck

The brief battle of words that had gone on three years earlier between Kaiser and Frazer was quickly forgotten once the two met in San Francisco on July 17, 1945, at a meeting suggested by A. P. Giannini, founder of the Bank of America. The meeting was held in an apartment on Nob Hill belonging to a friend of Frazer. No doubt Kaiser and Frazer shared a bit of good humor recalling their earlier acquaintance through the press.

In any event, World War II was fast winding down (VJ Day was only a month away), and it was no longer time for words but for action. Frazer was convinced by then that Kaiser was for real, that one way or another he was going to burst into the manufacture of cars. Kaiser, always one to take on a partner who could help get the job done, could see that Frazer was the one experienced automobile man ready, willing, and able to get things launched in a hurry. And standing behind them, giving them the kind of encouragement they needed, were the two biggest bankers in the West, A. P. Giannini, and his son Mario.

One week later a news release was issued announcing the formation of Kaiser-Frazer on a $5 million total investment, each side putting up half. The company would produce "a new light-weight, low-priced, front-wheel drive Kaiser car on the West Coast to compete with Ford-Chevrolet-Plymouth, while the conventional rear-wheel drive Frazer car will be assembled in the Detroit area."

The company lost no time in moving ahead on Kaiser's dream for a West Coast plant, leasing a facility at Long Beach, California, from the War Assets Administration. To insure a strong start for the Long Beach plant, Henry J. Kaiser, Jr., and John L. Hallett, a top member of the Kaiser engineering team, were placed in charge. They hired the nucleus of an operating organization and began preparing the plant for assembly line production. But the operation there never really got off the ground. Shortages of materials in the West, lack of a reservoir of experienced auto workers in the Long Beach area, complications in the engineering of a front-wheel drive car, a decline in the market for cars before plant problems could be ironed out, and the compelling demands on top management in getting started in the Detroit area, all combined to keep Long Beach in the background. By late 1946 Hallett had been transferred to Willow Run.

Likewise, Kaiser had long since found his fond hope of producing a front-wheel-drive car to be unattainable. Only two front-wheel-drive chassis were ever built, one with a steel body would be the green Kaiser displayed at the opening show at the Waldorf. The second chassis was fitted with an aluminum body. Both of them were driven to the West Coast and back, one of them ending up covering a total of 70,000 miles. While the roadability was good, they were surprisingly hard to steer, and the gear box made a loud, whining noise. It became clear that major redesigning and special tooling would be required at enormous cost and long delay. Reluctantly, but realistically, the decision was made by May of 1946 to drop the plans for a front-wheel-drive car.

Although Kaiser had his heart set on a West Coast plant when he first teamed up with Frazer, and although he clung to that goal for too many years, it was at Willow Run, Michigan, where Kaiser-Frazer would make its stand. It was a stroke of great good fortune that this huge, modern facility was actually unoccupied and available for leasing. Timing was so critical in the hungry postwar automobile market it would have been a serious handicap if they had had to build an entirely new plant from scratch. The plant had been built in 1942 by Ford Motor Co. to produce bombers, but for postwar automobile production Ford could rely on its River Rouge plant along with its other pre-war auto-making facilities.

Willow Run was on the edge of the automobile world, conveniently located from the point of view of potential suppliers and not very far removed from the trained auto workers in the Detroit area. It was adjacent to the Willow Run airport owned by University of Michigan, later to become the metropolitan airport. The terms of the lease from the War Assets Administration were extremely favorable—$500,000 for 1946, $850,000 for 1947, and $1.2 million annually for the remainder of the lease, with an option to buy the plant outright. The deal turned out even sweeter. By a rare stroke of fortune, Graham-Paige, controlled by Joe Frazer, had a plant the government wanted to lease for storage and display of war surplus. A rent of $500,000 annually, minus maintenance, was agreed upon for the first two years. This meant that

Kaiser-Frazer and Graham Paige were able to lease Willow Run for the first year for literally nothing, and at a cost of only $350,000 the second year.

For the core of his management team Kaiser turned to his West Coast shipyard people. Forty-four supervisory personnel and their families moved from Richmond, California, to Willow Run in the fall of 1945 and early 1946; about thirty more came directly from the Portland area. Probably no other industrial undertaking ever before was launched with that many newcomers to the business, that many transplants from 2,400 miles away. But Kaiser didn't bat an eye. He was offering his "boys" another great opportunity, and he had never been one to worry about moving his people from one job to another.

Not surprisingly, Kaiser himself kept his headquarters in Oakland. After all, the automobile venture was only one of many major businesses he had going at the time. He had maintained his office in Oakland since the construction days of the 1920's, and even though he was constantly visiting the different locations where he had projects underway, he believed he could have a better overall perspective from a distance rather than being caught up in the swirl of day-to-day problems. As was his practice in launching something new, however, he managed to spend a good deal of time at Willow Run in the fall of 1945 and most months of 1946.

Joe Frazer, of course, immediately set up shop at Willow Run. He had been in the automobile business all his life and was prepared to commute every week from his home in Newport, Rhode Island, to Detroit. As president of the new company he plunged in full time to the tasks at hand. He had no diversionary interests except that he would seek to meld his Graham-Paige facilities and operations to the benefit of Kaiser-Frazer. Although his entire background had been in sales and distribution, he could still contribute experience and judgment in guiding the conversion of the Willow Run plant and the start-up of assembly operations. One of his most challenging problems would be to build a good working relationship with all the shipyard people he was suddenly surrounded by.

The third key player was Edgar Kaiser who was made general manager as early as January 11, 1946. Like his father, Edgar was forever on the go. The main difference was that Edgar had kept moving his base of operations—from Boulder Dam to Bonneville Dam to Grand Coulee Dam to the Portland shipyards. Having just turned 37 years of age, it was no big deal for him to move his wife, Sue, and four children (six, very shortly) to Willow Run. It would be like home to him because he knew all of the shipyard people so well. Throughout the life-and-death struggle of Kaiser-Frazer he would be the one top management person who would wrestle with all the problems, night and day, from start to finish.

Next in line to Edgar on the Kaiser team was Clay Bedford who had directed the Richmond shipyards so brilliantly during the war. Because of Clay's record in running the shipyards, it was no surprise that Kaiser would ask him to come back to Willow Run.

One other person should be singled out for special mention—Hickman Price, Jr., nephew of Frazer. He was only 33 in 1945 when he returned from overseas duty to work on Graham-Paige problems and then suddenly found himself in on the ground floor of Kaiser-Frazer. Price was to Frazer almost like Edgar was to Kaiser, a source of family strength. As Executive Assistant to Frazer he became involved in many different aspects of the operation, from dealer contacts to financial counseling even volunteering styling criticisms. At the very first meeting of Kaiser and Frazer in July 1945, he was the one who mentioned that the Willow Run plant might be an ideal facility for manufacturing the cars. He later set up a surprisingly successful export program, at first under the guidance of Frazer, but later with the full backing of the two Kaisers. He organized small assembly operations in Rotterdam, Haifa, Bombay, Japan, Mexico City and Canada. If somehow greater management and financial support could have been provided him, it is interesting to speculate how his overseas successes could have given a significant lift to the fortunes of the company. It was a credit to him and to the Kaiser team that they got along so well through all the crises the company faced.

They Did It With Style

Other than the names Kaiser and Frazer, the main thing the company had going for it in the marketplace was the striking styling of the cars. The Continental engine was never quite up to the competition of the big three auto manufacturers, and, of course, the engineering and assembly of the cars by a whole new team couldn't always equal the work of the going concerns. But from the first models in 1946 to the rakish Kaiser-Darrin sport cars in 1954, it was recognized by many that K-F was setting the pace for styling in the industry.

This was highlighted in the brilliantly-written book by Richard M. Langworth entitled, "Kaiser-Frazer, The Last Onslaught on Detroit,"* This is the only full-length, in-depth book covering all aspects of the Kaiser-Frazer operations. It is laced with innumerable first-hand interviews, backup statistics, and hundreds of pictures of the different model cars, including more than two dozen sparkling color photos. Any person interested in digging into the Kaiser-Frazer saga would be well rewarded to read this book. Because of the research and interviews that went into Langworth's book, it is the only known source for some of the inside stories brought out in this chapter, not all of which are separately attributed to him, but which are used with the permission of the publisher.

Here are a few observations Langworth made regarding the styling of Kaiser-Frazer cars:

> The story of Kaiser-Frazer is largely one of styling; indeed their styling was always unique, often predictive, many times brilliant.

> Kaiser-Frazer built fascinating cars. Of that there can be little question.

* Published by Bitz & Frost, P.O. Box 2010, Sinking Spring, PA 19608, priced at $34.95, plus freight of $2.95.

There is no doubt that the 1951 Kaiser represented one of the great styling landmarks for the industry. Its daringly low beltline and enormous glass area were unequalled by any U.S. rival until Virgil Exner's Plymouth of 1957. Even today, over two decades since its introduction, it is still clean and rakish from every angle. It was a product of the last years of individualism among American manufacturers, when it was anathema for one's car to look like the company's down the street—perhaps the reason so many enthusiasts are collecting cars of this period today.

This imaginative styling was the product of three principal designers. The most important one was Howard A. ("Dutch") Darrin, the creator of some of the more rakish Rolls Royce, Duesenberg and Packard bodies of the twenties and thirties and the designer of the captivating Packard Darrin Victoria. He had done some work for Joe Frazer in behalf of Graham Paige in 1944 before Kaiser-Frazer came into existence. Although he was not engaged by Kaiser-Frazer steadily throughout its years, his imprint was felt on nearly every model the company came out with.

The other two were Kaiser and Frazer themselves. With a lifetime of fascination in cars, Kaiser unhesitatingly fancied himself an expert in what would appeal to the American public.

Frazer, likewise, kept intensely involved in design. His lifetime experience in the selling of automobiles gave him assurance that his design ideas would help the new company. He was not content to leave something as important as styling up to others.

In his free-wheeling, hit-and-run style of management, disregarding organizational lines, Kaiser himself would continue to dabble in styling concepts. One day in July 1948 Edgar Kaiser received a call from his father in Oakland. "I've got an idea. Come on out." Edgar and Dean Hammond, engineering vice president, dropped what they were doing and reported the next day. Kaiser took them down to the basement garage, drawing lines in the dust on a company car to illustrate his concept. He called the idea a "utility car," without knowing more than that it must admit wagon-sized payloads while retaining the niceties of a sedan. "Why not cut a door in the rear and divide it halfway down the trunk lid? Then hinge it here and here, find some way of folding down the rear seat. . . ."

Hammond returned to Willow Run and went to work. It was a lot more complicated than Kaiser had suggested, but that was the way he always operated—get a reasonably practical innovative idea and then turn it over to someone to work out the "details." In this case the "details" involved 200 changes before the basic sedan could be converted to a utility car. The end product became known as the Traveler and its more luxurious counterpart, the Vagabond. The flash idea that Kaiser had sketched out in the dust turned out to be a useful model—more than 25,000 Travelers were sold while 7,400 Vagabonds found buyers. And Kaiser could take credit for doing some pioneering—in one way or another some of the features of the Travelers and Vagabonds influenced the hatchbacks of other car manufacturers.

The Henry J itself was uniquely Kaiser's baby. He had been obsessed with the idea of a really small car since the early 1940's. Not that he was the first or only one to think of a small car or to study it. Nash Rambler came out as a compact in the 1950 model year. GM, Ford and others had often flirted with the idea but had never made the plunge. After the war they were so busy turning out standard size cars for the hungry market they would end up years behind Kaiser in the production of a compact.

So the field was wide open for Kaiser. But he, too, had to get started by making conventional cars. He did turn his "idea" boys loose and they came up with one hand-built compact prototype after another during Willow Run's first three years. However, they never came up with a clear winner, one that Kaiser would be willing to stake his future on.

The moment of truth came in late 1948 when Kaiser opened negotiations with the Reconstruction Finance Corporation for a new infusion of capital. As always in matters of this great importance Kaiser himself made the pitch to the R.F.C., along with some of his key men who could discuss how the funds would be used. Frazer, who would be backing off from active management control within a few months, had no heart for the request and didn't participate in the discussions.

By this time enough warning flags had shown up to make the R.F.C. officials very wary of the outlook. Kaiser decided it would add punch to his negotiations if he promised to have a workingman's car selling for $1195 on display by the summer of 1950. So he bit the bullet and made the commitment. The R.F.C. liked this idea; it helped put the loan across. They made it a provision of the loan, in fact insisting on it, and earmarked $12 million specifically for it. The loans totalling $44.4 million were not finally authorized until October 1949.

The commitment for a compact car having been made, the year 1949 was a busy one trying to finalize all the details of the car and get it into production. The basic design was not conceived by the Kaiser team. Surprisingly, a small outfit in Detroit, American Metal Products, Inc., came forward with a car that appealed to Kaiser both for its simplicity of construction and its styling. When he put the proposition to a vote of all his top people, as he always did, his loyal shipyard men agreed with him. However, the longtime automobile experts who had joined Kaiser-Frazer had sharply different opinions. One by one they ticked off the basic defects of the proposed car. Reflecting the sentiment of this group, Ralph Isbrandt, chief chassis and engine engineer, dared to say, "This idea is so ridiculous I couldn't attach my name to it and have to vote no, emphatically. This car is impractical. We can't even get engineering drawings using it."

But Kaiser, never one afraid to make a decision when all the facts were in and when all the viewpoints had been heard, stuck to his guns. To him the car came closest of any mock-up he had seen to meeting what he had been looking for. Flaunting the unanimous judgment of his experienced automakers, he made the fateful decision to proceed full speed with the compact of his choice—a car ahead of its time in concept but lacking the style and performance capabilities to excite the buying public. Some thought it was the greatest mistake K-F made, a product of Kaiser's misplaced idealism.

By October 1949—the very month the R.F.C. loan was granted—all final touches had been made and the design of the "peoples" car was firmly locked up. Four months later it was introduced to the public with a nameplate reading "Name The Car." A \$200,000 nationwide contest was launched to do just that, even though most of the Kaiser people were convinced the name had already been settled on by Kaiser himself. A flood of suggestions came in with the name, Henry J, so the winner, a Denver housewife, won first prize because of the glowing praise she gave to support her entry. Considering how long he had yearned to burst into the manufacture of cars, it was almost preordained that the fortunes of his company would ride on the two cars bearing his name—the standard size Kaiser and the compact Henry J. The new compact was placed in production in June 1950 and was on the showroom floors by September.

The early response to the Henry J was encouraging. It promptly gained its own identity in the public's mind as the first serious entry in the small car field. And the automotive writers gave it a good sendoff. Said Tom McCahill, the grand old man of Mechanix Illustrated:

> At a quick glance the car resembles a Cadillac that started smoking too young. Like a lot of girls, the chassis looks familiar but you can't quite place the face. This car didn't show the slightest trace of road wander and handled perfectly. I found the riding qualities excellent. If they will just leave it the way it was when I drove it, I feel the Henry J will prove to be one of the most popular buys on the market.

The first year's sales seemed to justify this praise: a total of about 82,000 1951 models were sold between September 1950 and December 1951, fairly evenly divided between fours and sixes.

Then, almost imperceptibly, certainly to the surprise of Kaiser, the slide began. The vagaries of the marketplace, that mysterious force that puts some products into orbit and wipes out others, started taking its toll. Was it the fact that the public, while intrigued with the idea of a small car, was not quite ready to give up the luxury of the larger models, not quite ready to put its money into something as untested as a compact? If General Motors or Ford had come with a small car at the same time as the Henry J, would the public have found it more acceptable to be seen in one of them? In that era of low gasoline prices were the operating savings insignificant by comparison with the pride of ownership of a bigger car? How could the American people be so slow in cottoning up to a small car, considering the flood of compacts that are clogging the highways today?

Whatever the reasons, the days of popularity for the Henry J were numbered. Despite modifications and touch-ups of all kinds, some very expensive, only 16,551

Henry J's were sold in the 1952 model years, plus 7,017 Henry J Vagabonds, actually 1951s reserialed as early '52s. Of the "true" 1952 models which followed, another 16,672 were sold, but by 1953 the sales dropped to 1,123, signalling the sad end of one man's dream.

It was equally baffling to the Kaiser people why the new 1951 Kaiser didn't catch fire with the public. It was far and away the most stylish car of its time. Was its 6-cylinder engine too non-competitive with the V-8's?

Were the lower trade-in values for earlier Kaiser models a warning flag? Were its prices too high in competition with other cars?

Because Kaiser wanted a dramatic change in models, the designing of the 1951 Kaiser had not been a simple matter. All the style experts were encouraged to come up with their suggestions. Even the management people kept getting in the act, freely volunteering their tips.

Standing in the wings was Dutch Darrin who, even though he had left the company in 1946, had been given a contract permitting him to offer his ideas for any future cars before the company finalized any redesign. He had already been toying with some designs at his workshop in Palm Springs, California, when he heard that the project was moving ahead at Willow run, so he returned there immediately. "On my first attempt to visit the styling department they wouldn't let me in. Finally, I persuaded John Hallett to give me a look around, and when I saw the cars they were considering I decided I'd better get to work."

Darrin teamed up with Duncan McRae, a friend from earlier years who was in Kaiser-Frazer's styling department. In their hurry, McRae made a scale drawing on wrapping paper of a one-eighth scale model that Darrin had brought along from Palm Springs. A few days later Darrin was able to show the drawing to Kaiser who approved a full-scale model of the design, with the stipulation, however, that it had to be completed in two weeks.

This, of course, didn't constitute final approval, so the company's styling department redoubled its efforts to come up with the winning design. They even began throwing up roadblocks aimed at sidetracking Darrin and McRae. Finally, in late April 1948 the showdown took place in front of Kaiser and all the heads of his many departments. The company stylists lined up in front of Darrin's model blocking it from Kaiser's view. Darrin decided extreme measures would have to be taken and said to McRae, "Watch this." "Then he loosened his belt, got up, called for both Henry and Edgar Kaiser," said McRae, "and as he walked towards them his pants fell to the floor. After the laughter subsided he held their complete attention. And of course he did a beautiful selling job on his proposal."

Minutes after looking at Darrin's model, Kaiser had made a decision: "Well, this is it." Darrin had won!

A few years later Darrin would once again come up with a startling design, this time for a two-door sports car that would set the automobile world buzzing and would produce a brief hope that it might turn things around for Kaiser. Not only would the styling be breathtaking but it would introduce two outstanding features—fiber glass body construction and the sliding door.

Darrin had been at work for a long time in his new studio on Santa Monica Boulevard in Hollywood, California, when he finally decided in August 1952 that he should show his prototype to the Kaisers. As recorded by Richard Langworth, Darrin described the showing:

> Henry, Edgar, and the whole group came down to my workshop. The new Mrs. Kaiser also attended—Henry's wife had passed away a year and a half before.

> The first thing Henry did was read me out. 'Dutch,' he said, 'what is the idea of this? Who authorized this? We're not in the business of building sports cars. I cannot forgive your audacity in going ahead without our authorization.' I explained to him carefully that the whole project was on my own time and my own money, and this car was a version of what I thought K-F might need. But, I said, if they didn't need it I would build the car myself. I had a sponsor at the time and could have built it. In retrospect, I wish I had.

> At this point Mrs. Kaiser stepped forward. 'Henry,' she said, 'this is the most beautiful thing I have ever seen. I don't understand why you say you're not in the business of building automobiles whether they are sports cars or conventional cars. I don't think there'll be many companies after seeing this car that won't go into the sports car business.'

> That made it another matter entirely. Just those few words from his wife made Henry stop and consider—and he was a very, very acute, perceptive and far-seeing man. By the end of the viewing he had not only bought the idea of a two-passenger sports car with sliding doors, but had ordered us immediately to start a four-passenger car with the same lines using sliding doors going forward and backward."

Once the car had received enthusiastic acclaim at the Los Angeles Motorama in November, there was the problem of naming the car. Should it be Darrin, or just D, or should it be DKF, or DKF-161?

All the heads of the Kaiser companies then met in Oakland to give their independent reactions. Darrin stated that his name was now well known, especially in sports cars, while the Kaiser managers insisted that "Kaiser" or "DKF" was the only acceptable name in view of the car's builders. Once more Kaiser decided to put an important matter to a vote. As each executive let his views be known, it was yes for DKF, no for Darrin. Edgar Kaiser remained silent, and it looked like a landslide, until Henry Kaiser spoke up softly: "I haven't voted."

"Oh, Mr. Kaiser, surely we want you to vote," his people assured him. With a smile at Darrin, Kaiser said, "I vote we call it the Kaiser-Darrin—period." And thus the car was named.

Darrin's beautifully styled 1951 Kaiser standard size cars did get off to an impressive start. Including all the models—sedans, coupes, Travelers—nearly 140,000 cars were turned out. Then, even with a lot of embellishments, only about 30,000 were produced each of the next two years. At that point the roof fell in --only about 7,000 were produced at the Willys Toledo plant in 1954 and a mop-up amount of 1,291 in 1955.

Unhappily confirming Kaiser's initial doubts, the Kaiser-Darrin sports car never really got off the ground. The market, which for sports cars was always a tiny proportion of automobile production, simply never materialized as hoped for. Besides, General Motors had come out with its sporty Corvette and Ford was bringing out its promising Thunderbird. While neither of those cars set the world on fire at the start, they were formidable opposition because of the companies producing them. As Edgar Kaiser often said: "Slap a General Motors nameplate on our cars and they would sell like hotcakes."

Only 435 Kaiser-Darrins were ever turned out, and these were in the model year 1954. Instead of helping a floundering company, they added to its financial woes.

Hell Will Be A-Popping

It hit Kaiser like a thunderbolt. Here was his friend, Cyrus Eaton, head of Otis & Co.—the man who had successfully managed the first two common stock sales of Kaiser-Frazer—suddenly, and at the very last moment on Wednesday, February 4, 1948, announcing that he had decided to back out of selling K-F's third stock issue.

Eaton had been the principal architect of this latest underwriting. He had called the shots on the amount of stock that the market could absorb, the price the stock should be offered at, and the timing of the issue. At his recommendation, a Registration Statement was filed with the Securities and Exchange Commission on January 6, 1948, for the issuance of 1,500,000 shares. All through the month, stock market developments were closely followed trying to decide the most propitious time to offer the stock for sale. Several meetings, and steady phone conferences, were held by Kaiser and Frazer and their top aides with Eaton and his associates and top officials of the other two underwriters, First California Company, and Allen & Company.

Finally, a day-long meeting was held between the top people of all interests on Monday, February 2. Edgar Kaiser asked Eaton several times whether he thought Kaiser-Frazer should market the stock immediately. Each time Eaton replied that K-F should do so. He said he thought the stock was actually underpriced, and that it would make for good public relations if the stock went up after the issue was on the market. During that day, Monday, K-F was selling in the range of $13 to $14 per share. After lengthy discussion, it was agreed the stock should be offered the next day at $13.50 per share with $1.50 commission for the brokers.

Then Eaton threw his final curve at Kaiser. He wanted K-F to "stabilize" the stock, i.e., stand ready to buy enough of the stock to keep the price up. This is a function the underwriters often perform, but rarely the company whose stock is up for sale. But Eaton kept insisting, stressing that it should not require more than 10,000 shares to be bought by the company. While the Kaiser-Frazer executives felt that Eaton's demand was unreasonable and inopportune, they believed another postponement would create considerable confusion and, hence, would not be advisable. Reluctantly, they agreed that if the registration statement was to be made effective on the next day, the company would stabilize the market until 3:00 p.m., E.S.T. In turn, the underwriters, with all principals participating, made a firm verbal agreement to buy and market the full 1,500,000 shares once the stabilization was completed.

Conferences were held uninterruptedly on stabilization day in Kaiser's New York offices in the British Empire Building. All principals participated. To be helpful, Kaiser agreed he would be willing to increase the stabilization by buying up to 15,000 shares. At 10:36 a.m., Eaton placed an order for 15,000 shares at $13.50. In less than 10 minutes Eaton said it might be necessary for the corporation to buy 50,000 shares; by noon he said the corporation should be ready to buy up to 75,000 shares. As the pressure mounted, the company went on to buy 100,000 shares by 1:00 p.m.

Stabilization day experienced the worst stock market nose dive since the preceding May of 1947. A selling raid of mysterious proportions was being unleashed against the stabilization purchasing. Should the company stop its stabilization at 100,000 shares, having invested $1,350,000 in its own shares, and, if so, would it precipitate abandonment of the sale of the 1,500,000 shares?

The underwriters had agreed they would take over the stabilization on the second day, Wednesday, February 4. That morning Eaton told Kaiser, "It's another Kaiser miracle. Yesterday was an historic day in finance. It was your day to show courage. Today it is time for the underwriters to show the same kind of courage. We won't waver. The stock that isn't sold now we can just put on the shelf for a while; we know how good it is. Why, Kaiser-Frazer will be selling later for $25."

Kaiser replied, "I don't see why you should be trying to praise me. I didn't see anything wonderful about yesterday. We only did what you recommended. We had to rely on your advice."

Eaton then stated he believed there would be no trouble in selling the full 1,500,000 shares that day.

But that day, Wednesday, proved to be another stock market disaster. In the morning the underwriters took over the stabilization and bought 44,000 shares at $13. Even with that support, K-F stock closed the day at $11 5/8.

By early afternoon Eaton panicked. He arranged a meeting in Kaiser's office at 3:45 p.m. for William R. Daley, President of Otis & Co., Harold Allen, President, Allen & Company, H. T. Birr, Jr., President, First California Company.

Under instructions from Eaton, Daley said Otis was withdrawing from the stock sale. Kaiser then asked Birr and Allen if they were willing to go ahead. Birr declared, "We are ready to go through on our commitment. We are assured of selling all our stock." Allen said his company would go to market provided Otis & Co. did.

To keep things alive Kaiser proposed a compromise: Would the underwriters bind themselves to take 900,000 shares, and accept an option until Monday, February 9, to purchase the balance of 600,000? At 4:15 p.m., this was agreed to (even by Otis & Co.), the price to be returned to K-F would be $11.50 a share on the 900,000 shares, or a total of $10,350,000; with the company to receive $11.60 a share on the 600,000 shares or a total of $6,960,000.

In less than two hours after that, Eaton was in Kaiser's office where Frazer and other top K-F officials were. "We are in a very bad situation," Eaton began. He said First California had indicated it had sold 400,000 shares, but this now seemed to be slipping away. He stated that Otis and Allen had not sold more than 150,000 shares. He then flatly said, "You have an underwriter's agreement that cannot be carried out." He turned to making threats:

If you force the sale now, you will see Kaiser-Frazer stock driven to $5; there may well be a stop order from the Securities and Exchange Commission preventing sale of the stock because of its effect on present stockholders; there will be various kinds of court actions and investigations; there will be bad publicity against the company.

Then he made his confession,

We aren't good for the 10 to 11 million dollars. We cannot make such a payment. You should face the realities and dangers of the situation. If you want to avoid trouble, you must let the underwriters out of their contract.

Kaiser was dumbfounded. He replied that his counsel advised him it would be nothing short of "an act of insanity" to permit the underwriters to welsh on their agreement. "It would clearly violate the rights and interests of our stockholders."

Then Kaiser looked right at Eaton and said, "If I made a losing contract, I would spend the last day of my life working to pay it off, rather than break my word."

In uncontrolled anger, Eaton brushed those words aside, stormed to the door, turned around, and blasted Kaiser and his associates, "I am warning you—Hell will be a-popping."

By virtue of accepting Kaiser's compromise proposal—to go forward with the sale of 900,000 shares and an option to purchase the balance of 600,000 shares by Monday, February 9—the underwriters had additional time to make good on their commitment. To Eaton, however, it just meant more time to concoct some scheme to break the contract in a manner giving the appearance of a legal out.

His first move was to send a telegram on Sunday, February 8, to Kaiser-Frazer at Willow Run urging "that the 186,200 shares of its own stock purchased on stock exchanges by the company last Tuesday, at a cost in excess of $2,500,000, be purchased by the directors at the company's cost." Even though he was the person who had insisted the company stabilize the stock, he was now inferring the company could be in legal trouble unless the directors personally bailed the company out. (On February l6 he told the press, "Refusal of the directors to restore the $2,500,000 to the Kaiser-Frazer treasury was one of the compelling factors in our decision not to market the stock.")

Eaton's big maneuver came the next day, Monday, the deadline. There was a clause in the underwriter's agreement that Kaiser-Frazer should certify at the closing date "no suits are pending, or to the knowledge of the company threatened, against the company or any subsidiary which may affect any substantial portion of their respective properties or substantially affect their business except as set forth in the Registration Statement." The deadline time for the underwriters to pay the $10,350,000 for the 900,000 shares was 10:00 a.m., Monday, February 9. Cleveland was the designated place to close the transaction. K-F attorneys proferred the stock to the three underwriters, and they in turn stated they had the money in the bank. But Otis and First California attorneys proceeded to haggle, paragraph by paragraph, almost sentence for sentence. They were obviously stalling for time, raising every conceivable technicality. Time dragged on and on.

Otis attorneys, strangely and persistently, kept asking, "Has any suit been filed against Kaiser-Frazer?" They got the K-F attorneys to telephone to Reno, Nevada, where K-F had been incorporated. Answer: No suit. They got another call placed to Frazer in New York. Answer: No suit filed to his knowledge. They demanded an inquiry be made at the Willow Run plant. Incredulously, when the reply each time was no, they would persist, "Are you sure there's no suit?"

Finally, one lawyer for Otis said, "Well, boys, shall we show them this?" He pulled out a Cleveland newspaper that carried a dispatch revealing an eleventh hour suit had been filed in Detroit asking the Circuit Court to restrain the corporation from proceeding with the stock sale. K-F attorneys observed that no one had entered or left the conference room for an hour and three-quarters. So Otis had been playing a cat-and-mouse game and waiting for the first disclosure of a suit that then would be used as pretext for evading the stock commitment. It was more than seven hours after the underwriters were obliged to close the stock purchase!

A Philadelphia attorney, James F. Masterson, filed the suit as a stockholder owning 300 shares. He had had his complaint typed up on Sunday in time for it to be given to Cleveland newspapers for Monday afternoon publication. When late that day the stock sale was repudiated, Masterson was quoted in news dispatches, "We won!"

It was quickly ascertained that Masterson had represented Eaton in other lawsuits. A suit subsequently filed by Kaiser-Frazer against Otis & Co. asserted that Otis, with the intention of avoiding payment for the stock, "inspired, incited and caused to be instituted" the Masterson suit. In any event, it was the Masterson suit that was used as an excuse by Otis & Co. for sending wires that very night all around the country, "The purchase contract between Kaiser-Frazer Corporation has been terminated today, and the offering of Kaiser-Frazer stock is withdrawn. Dealers funds on deposit in Cleveland are being returned."

Frazer had known Cyrus Eaton for more than ten years and had introduced him to

Kaiser shortly after Kaiser-Frazer Corporation was formed in August 1945. Eaton and Kaiser hit it off right from the start because both were bold risk-takers, both were mavericks.

Agreement was quickly reached for Otis & Co. to head the underwriters for K-F's first stock issue September 27, 1945. The other underwriters were First California Company and Allen & Company. As reported in the Cleveland, Ohio, <u>News</u> of September 26:

Heavy Demand Greets Kaiser Stock Offering

Henry J. Kaiser could have $85,000,000 of money from the American public to finance his dramatic entry into motordom if he wanted it, instead of the $17,000,000 he asked. As the registration statement for the $20,000,000 Kaiser-Frazer Corp. stock cleared the Securities and Exchange Commission in Philadelphia, Cyrus S. Eaton, of Otis & Co., underwriters for the stock issue to be sold to the public, predicted that the issue would be five times oversubscribed. 'It is the most dramatic thing that has ever happened in American finance,' commented Eaton.

It was only natural that Eaton was picked to head up Kaiser-Frazer's second stock issue of January 23, 1946. Once again, Eaton was joined by First California Company and Allen & Company. By this time K-F stock had risen dramatically so the underwriters were able quickly to sell 1,800,000 shares for a price of $20.25 per share, less an underwriting discount of $1.10, bringing in a total of $34,470,000 for K-F.

Kaiser (and Frazer) and Eaton were exultant. They were convinced they had launched what would prove to be one of the most successful enterprises in American history. But their jubilance was ill-founded. They had woefully underfinanced the new corporation. The net amount to the company from the two stock issues— $49,600,000—was just barely enough to get the company started. As wags would keep pointing out, it was much less than just the advertising budget of General Motors. With this slim funding, and with the fiasco that shattered the third stock issue in early 1948, Kaiser-Frazer would remain grievously strapped for funds throughout its operating years. It would have to turn to bank borrowings, loans from the Reconstruction Finance Corporation, and investments from the parent Kaiser companies, as well as various financial arrangements with Graham Paige, controlled by Frazer. Without any doubt whatsoever, the fate of Kaiser-Frazer would have been vastly different if the first two stock issues had brought in all that the market stood ready to invest.

Primary blame for this underfinancing has to fall on Kaiser himself, along with his aides, and to a lesser extent on Frazer. Kaiser had run seven shipyards for four years during the war, operating on a minimum of private capital and relying on a steady flow of payments from the Maritime Commission. In starting up his automobile business he (and Frazer) totally misjudged the horrendous costs that lay ahead.

Cyrus Eaton must also share some of the blame. As an experienced underwriter—one who had seen the problems other big companies faced in getting started—he should have warned Kaiser and Frazer to raise their sights, especially when the market was so eager to gobble up whatever shares the company put on the market.

Then, of course, when Eaton pulled the rug out from under Kaiser-Frazer by withdrawing from the third stock issue it was a deadly wound from which the company never fully recovered. It not only shook up the financial world, it seriously shattered public confidence in the future of the company. No estimate could ever be made of the tens of thousands, possibly hundreds of thousands of people who were turned away from buying a Kaiser or Frazer car because of the uncertainties brought on by the stock fiasco. And it would be hard to measure the toll on management time the ensuing lawsuits would take. Except for Ford's early patent fight, no other beginning automobile company had ever been confronted with such a costly, time-consuming and debilitating legal battle.

Vendetta

On February 13, 1948, Kaiser-Frazer filed its suit against Otis & Co. for $7,762,500. Half of this amount was for monies due from Otis & Co. and half was sought for damages on the grounds Otis & Co. induced First California Company to withdraw from the underwriting contract. (Allen & Company did not end up repudiating its obligation under the contract.)

By May 1948, Eaton had "incited" various other small stockholders to file derivative suits supporting the complaints of Masterson. These stockholders held 20, 300, 8, 25, 40, and 80 shares. In July, Otis & Co., with its 10,763 shares, started another suit in Delaware.

The main battleground was the District Court of the United States for the Eastern District of Michigan, Southern Division, before Frank A. Picard, U.S. District Judge.

Under the prodding of Eaton, and taking advantage of hindsight since most of the final court proceedings took place two years after repudiation of the stock sales contract, lawyers for the plaintiffs tried to scrape up every possible grounds for proving mismanagement of Kaiser-Frazer. They cited more than a dozen such instances. They had the gall to contend that K-F management was at fault to "stabilize" the stock the day before it went on the market in February 1948, even though it was Eaton's insistence that it be done. One by one, each of these trumped-up charges had to be painstakingly overcome. The most potentially damaging one involved the charge that Kaiser-Frazer gave away its most valuable asset—the Trentwood, Washington, aluminum sheet rolling mill—to another Kaiser company, the Permanente Metals Corporation. Lawyers for K-F convincingly established that when the company assigned its rights to the Trentwood plant to Permanente, it was doing what K-F had to do under its charter, and that all members of the Board of Directors, except Kaiser himself, demanded that the assignment be made in the best interest of K-F. In early 1945, when the assignment was made, Kaiser stood entirely alone in his belief Trentwood would prove to be profitable.

Naturally, Kaiser was the key witness in dealing with the most critical issues. He was tireless in taking the time and working with the lawyers.

The trial lawyer for Permanente Metals Corporation was Gordon Johnson of Thelen, Marrin, Johnson & Bridges in San Francisco. Here's how he relates the showdown testimony of Kaiser in February 1950 before Judge Picard:

> At the end of Friday's hearing the judge ruled the case would be carried over until the next Tuesday, Feb. 21. Mr. Kaiser left immediately to fly home to be with his wife who was ill. He was forced to land in Reno, because of weather conditions in San Francisco. That meant driving from Reno to his home in Oakland. He had scheduled a return flight to Detroit for Monday, hoping to arrive by late afternoon so he could meet with his lawyers in the early evening. However, he didn't reach the hotel until around 9:00 p.m. at which time he went right to bed with an ice pack on his head to relieve a headache. He did agree to meet me for breakfast at 8:00 a.m. I worked on my notes till after midnight, then went to bed. At 2:15 a.m. my phone rang. It was Mr. Kaiser asking me to come to his room so we could go over the case. He told me he had been busy talking to Edgar (Kaiser) and Gene (Trefethen). I told him I was too exhausted to come to his room. He then said, 'All right, let's get together at 5:00 a.m.' I said I simply wouldn't be any good at that time, so we compromised by agreeing to meet for breakfast at 7:00 a.m.

Kaiser was the principal witness in the court which started at 10:00 a.m. Johnson led off with his planned questioning of Kaiser. Johnson describes what happened after that:

> I was asking Mr. Kaiser to give the background on his interest in aluminum production in the Pacific Northwest. To my surprise, Judge Picard intervened and asked if Mr. Kaiser's production of small aircraft carriers during the war was in the Northwest or in California. That was right up Mr. Kaiser's alley. Did he take off! He told about getting President Roosevelt to override Admiral King of the Navy, resulting in an order for fifty 'baby flattops' to be produced at Vancouver in Washington, across the river from Portland. The judge was absolutely fascinated. He kept pumping Mr. Kaiser for every detail of the production and the record of the ships during the war. This must have gone on for more than a half hour without any interruption in the dialogue between the two. It was evident the judge had been interested in the subject for a long time, and wanted to hear the story firsthand. There couldn't have been a more golden opportunity for Kaiser to display his sincerity, his patriotism, his eloquence. After that, I only asked Mr. Kaiser two or three questions to help round out the point we were trying to put across. He had been about the most persuasive and convincing witness I had ever examined. By

ll:30 a.m. I said I was finished with my witness, and he would be available for cross-examination by the opposition. Their lawyers surprised everyone by saying, 'No questions.' The judge then called a luncheon recess. As we left the courtroom, I happened to be near the opposition lawyer, and I asked him why he had passed up the opportunity to cross examine Mr. Kaiser. He replied, 'Because I didn't want to get my arm cut off by that buzz saw, Kaiser.'

The decision of Judge Picard on August 11, 1950, was a resounding victory for Kaiser. Following is an extract from his 25-page verdict:

. . . .Cyrus Eaton has allegedly sworn a vendetta against Henry Kaiser.

. . . .We have come to the conclusion and hold that in none of these trans-actions has there been any fraud, collusion or attempt on the part of the so-called Kaiser interests to benefit at the expense of Kaiser- Frazer. On the contrary, Henry Kaiser has time and time again, according to the undisputed facts, come to the rescue whenever the Kaiser-Frazer Corporation appeared to be headed for financial disaster. He began early by endorsing bank loans and rather than be condemned in the Permanente case, he and his family should be commended because they took a plunge in the aluminum business that might have proved fatal—partly to be of service to Kaiser-Frazer in the future. We believe his interest in Kaiser- Frazer is more than financial --at times it is almost paternal—and its the paternalism that has gotten him into trouble. He wants Kaiser- Frazer to succeed. Everybody seemed satisfied to trust in Henry Kaiser until February 9, 1948 when the break came between the Kaiser interests and those of Otis & Co. No suit had been filed against these defendants until that day.

Considering the thorough care with which Judge Picard had written his decision, it was open to question why Eaton and the other plaintiffs would appeal the ruling. But appeal it they did, to the appellate court in Cincinnati, Ohio. Even if the chances weren't promising, at least it would mean continued harassment of Kaiser. So it was that it took nearly a year before the appellate court in early July 1951 would uphold the lower court's decision. That meant that for three and one-half years Eaton and his group had plagued Kaiser.

What Business Are We In?

Considering that a shortage of steel supply would prove to be Kaiser-Frazer's number one supply problem, the company couldn't have gotten off to a worse start. The United Steelworkers of America had, throughout the fall of 1945, been calling for a major increase in wages, with the industry determined to keep costs in check as much as possible.

The showdown came in January 1946 when the union was demanding an increase of 18 cents an hour, and the industry was holding firm at 15 cents. The <u>Detroit</u> <u>News</u> of Sunday, January 20, 1946, reported on the confrontation:

> President Truman is considering seizing the nation's steel plants and placing them under the direction of Henry J. Kaiser as a means of cutting short the steel strike which will start at Sunday midnight. Kaiser visited the White House yesterday with Philip Murray, president of the CIO, and steel strike leader. Kaiser announced he had signed a contract with Murray on the President's terms of 18 cents an hour for his Fontana, California steel plant, and issued a blast at the 'Wall Street-connected steel companies for letting 3 cents an hour stand in the way of the welfare of 140,000,000 people.'

It would be hard to describe the rage this caused among steel industry leaders. Imagine the President seizing their plants! (Something he would do a few years later.) Imagine putting Henry J. Kaiser in charge of their industry—a man with a relatively small plant in California, and an avowed friend of labor! It didn't help that the papers ran a large picture of Kaiser and Murray together at the White House.

Fortunately for all concerned, the President did not seize the steel plants, but Kaiser had been squarely established as putting labor ahead of his counterparts in the steel industry.

This antipathy towards Kaiser was a natural carry-forward from World War II days. Steel executives remembered how he had beaten on them for steel all throughout the war, never hesitating to berate them publicly for inadequate shipments. They were disposed to ship to long-time customers nearby, and here was Kaiser pounding on them to ship all the way to the West Coast.

Moreover, it didn't help Kaiser's image as an industry man when he announced tentative agreements with the United Auto Workers (UAW) in early January 1946. <u>FORTUNE</u> commented:

> This was at the height of the General Motors strike, then in its forty-eighth day, when the Ford labor negotiations were apparently stalled, when Chrysler, whose UAW contract had expired, was not even negotiating. This was news. Next day Kaiser-Frazer stock went to 17 and kept on going.

With that kind of start, and with Kaiser-Frazer never having built up a buyer relationship with the steel companies, it was no surprise to anyone except Kaiser and Frazer themselves that their first orders for steel were not immediately filled. But when a month and a half went by without any steel the two partners could see that they would have to come out fighting. The <u>New</u> <u>York</u> <u>Herald</u> <u>Tribune</u> of March 6, 1946, described the company's dilemma:

> Henry J. Kaiser and Joseph W. Frazer charged yesterday that virtually the entire steel industry had discriminated against the Kaiser- Frazer Corporation in failing to supply the company with sheet steel for automobile production,

and demanded that the government restore steel allocations, and take action 'under the law' to rectify the situation. In a press conference both men said they were 'now fighting mad.' They stated their beliefs that settlement of wage issues at Kaiser's steel mill in Fontana, California, and at Kaiser-Frazer Corporation at Willow Run in advance of general settlements in the steel and automobile industries might be in part responsible for their troubles.

While boldness was the one quality that distinguished Henry Kaiser from others, it was his unremitting resourcefulness that could always be counted on to keep things moving ahead. There was simply no situation that "threw" him for a loss for any length of time. No matter what roadblocks showed up in his path it was only an invitation for him to come up with some solution. In the process he nearly always came up with new ideas.

This became an ingrained way of doing business for Kaiser people. They prided themselves that, like the boss, they could always find a way to do the seemingly impossible. It was a pride that would be put to the ultimate test once they started scrounging for supplies to keep the assembly line going. From Day One to the winding down of operations at Willow Run eight years later it was a constant scramble to procure the materials, mostly steel, for the 18,000 parts that went into the cars. During much of that time there were severe shortages and most of the 3,000 suppliers were careful to take care of the established automakers before shipping anything to Kaiser-Frazer. It got to the point where more management attention had to be directed towards securing supplies than to the assembly of cars. The history of the industry had been one of assembling cars from parts that kept flowing freely from eager suppliers to the car manufacturers. Now Kaiser-Frazer was confronted with a problem never really encountered before. At times the employees would have to wonder: Are we in the business of assembling cars or are we in the business of producing or procuring the parts to be used in our assembly?

The situation became so desperate that Clay Bedford was placed in charge of all procurement. Here was a Vice President of Manufacturing, an expert in assembly line operations from the shipyard days, who was now told he was needed more urgently to keep the supplies coming in.

It was a night and day challenge for him and a huge department of people he lined up to help him. He had three airplanes, D-18's, small twin engine prop planes made by Beechcraft, which he and his people kept busy all day long hopping from one supplier to another. He was free to make any deal on the spot—to pay any price he judged to be acceptable, to work out any arrangement that might help the vendor step up its production.

Steel was the biggest bottleneck. Here's how Bedford described a meeting he and Tom Price had with Charlie White, Chairman of the Board of Republic Steel:

> Charlie was a great big tall fellow known for his barnyard language. I told
> him it wasn't quite fair to allocate steel only to former customers, and that he

should allocate at least some proportion of their new production that they had been adding since the end of the war to new businesses, like Kaiser-Frazer. I pointed out that we had acquired certain steel facilities ourselves and that maybe we could even help them out with some of the problems they might be having by swapping steel. Well, his feet came down with a bang and his hat went on the back of his head and he said: 'I'll tell you what my greatest problem is—it's keeping S... O... B's... like your group out of my hair and wasting so damn much of my time.' Charlie, of course, had reasons for his strong feelings. He remembered the shipyard days when Mr. Kaiser bugged the steel companies no end to get enough steel to build ships on the West Coast when they could have sold it at greater profit closer to home. Also, like so many other steel men, he was upset at Kaiser for building his own steel mill in California. However, after Charlie got his feelings off his chest we had a chance to talk things out, and before the day was over he gave us an allocation of alloy bars.

To cope with the continuing steel shortage, Bedford early on appointed his key assistant, William F. Freistat, as manager of the Steel Control Division. Freistat highlights some of his problems:

My department soon had 48 people in it, whereas if the steel could have been obtained at mill prices, 3 or 4 people could have handled it. Nearly every 'deal' we made was different. It was not unusual to have to start by buying steel ingots at Kaiser Steel's plant in Southern California, move them across country to Chicago for rolling into slabs at one mill, then to another mill for rolling into hot bands, then to another mill for conversion into cold-rolled coils, and then to still another mill for conversion into cold rolled sheets ready for use by the automobile plant. Of course, K-F had to pay all the conversion costs and all the freight bills.

One of the most extreme—and costly—actions K-F was driven to by the steel shortage was the purchase of an old, rebuilt blast furnace along with antiquated beehive coke ovens in Utah. During the war an inefficient blast furnace owned by U.S. Steel in Joliet, Illinois, was dismantled and re-erected at Ironton, Utah, by U.S. Steel at the expense of the Defense Plant Corporation. It was operated by U.S. Steel for the government for only nine months during the war and was then shut down. After the war the government could find no buyer, not even U.S. Steel which had just bought the huge modern Geneva steel mill nearby. In its desperation, Kaiser-Frazer purchased the blast furnace in early 1948 hoping to barter the pig iron for other steel products.

Arrangements were made for Kaiser Steel to operate the plant. Production of pig iron reached a far higher rate—800 tons daily—than was obtained in the wartime operations. But because the beehive coke ovens were so inefficient, and because Utah was so far away from the midwest steel mills where the pig iron was to be used, and because the steel requirements of K-F were so erratic at that time, decision was reached within two years to close down the furnace.

It was on a Sunday afternoon in the spring of 1950 that the phone rang in the home of Barney Etcheverry in Berkeley, California, while he and his young family were having dinner. Etcheverry was the head of Kaiser Steel's planning department and was an expert on the economics of the steel industry. His ten-year-old daughter answered the phone and carried on a two-minute conversation with the party on the other end of the line. Finally, the young girl said, "Daddy, it's for you." Etcheverry picked up the phone not knowing who was calling. Without any introduction the voice said, "Barney, what are we going to do with that furnace?" Etcheverry immediately recognized the voice as being Kaiser, but he had no idea what furnace Kaiser could be talking about. Then Kaiser filled him in on the current ramifications of the Ironton blast furnace. For over a half hour the two of them discussed all the possibilities of utilizing or selling the furnace. That kind of phone conversation taking place on a Sunday afternoon, with Kaiser personally probing a subject in depth, was one of his trademarks.

Closer to home, Kaiser-Frazer, in the summer of 1948, leased from the Government a war-time blast furnace and coke oven facility at Cleveland, Ohio. Republic Steel Corporation had built this facility at Government expense ($28 million), and operated it during the war and, under lease, after the war. Republic was demanding to pay less to the Government than War Assets Administration required, and threatened to close the blast furnace at a time when the nation was desperately short of pig iron. War Assets thereupon made a written proposal to Kaiser-Frazer on the plant, and the company accepted it, agreeing to meet the Government's terms and to pay more than the amount that Republic had refused to pay.

Then all hell broke loose. Republic was furious that the blast furnace had been leased out from under them. They invoked all their political contacts to overturn the Government lease. They rallied a group of customers who would be hurt if the pig iron were taken away from them for use by Kaiser-Frazer. Here began another unwanted battle for Kaiser—politically, publicly, legally.

Kaiser came back with his usual roar, as evidenced by these excerpts from a news release dated September 14, 1948:

> Henry J. Kaiser today appealed to the two Congressional committees to re-open investigations immediately and to 'crack wide open the conspiracy by powerful persons and interests to make a scrap of paper out of the Government's binding lease of the Cleveland blast furnace to Kaiser-Frazer Corporation. An undercover conspiracy is breaking astoundingly into the open. It involves the use of underhanded, yes, and highhanded political pressure to bludgeon the Government into violating the sanctity of contracts and into scrapping Kaiser-Frazer's firm lease of the Cleveland iron plant. Republic

Steel Corporation, which ordered the Cleveland furnace closed unless it could club the government into accepting Republic's dictated terms, served written notice on us that it proposed to contest, legally or otherwise our acquisition of the Cleveland plant. Evidence is accumulating that the legal or otherwise measures threatened by Republic are being carried out by means that will profoundly shock the American people if fully disclosed by Congress.

Eventually, a compromise was agreed to by Republic and Kaiser, where Kaiser took possession of the furnace but Republic kept operating it through mid-1949, paying K-F for the privilege—but not as much as K-F was paying the Government in rent. The arrangement worked, leading to a five-year agreement the following year for Republic to supply K-F with automotive sheet and pig iron while retaining its furnace operation and supplying its other customers. One hooker was insisted upon by Republic as part of this deal—Kaiser-Frazer had to build at its expense an open hearth furnace for Republic.

The whole brouhaha was another unfortunate drain on Kaiser-Frazer's management attention. Also, as clear as Kaiser's case was, other steel companies were inclined to side with Republic out of loyalty to the industry. More than ever, Kaiser-Frazer was looked upon as a thorn in the side of the established steel companies.

Kaiser-Frazer continued being victimized by a shortage of steel, so as the company faced the critical time of preparing for the production of its new 1951 model car and the compact Henry J., it was decided to request President Truman to invoke the Defense Production Act of 1950 to insure that the company would receive its "fair share of the available civilian supply" of steel. In support of that position, K-F on October 14, 1950, advised the Government and the steel industry:

Kaiser-Frazer is entitled to purchase steel on a basis competitive with the rest of the automobile industry—both as to competitive price and the obtaining of steel upon the same percentage basis by which the balance of the industry obtains its steel through regular channels from the steel companies. Up to now Kaiser-Frazer never has been sold steel by the steel industry on the same basis of treatment accorded to the rest of the automobile industry. K-F buys only about 3 per cent of its steel requirements on direct allocation by steel companies at mill price. The 97 per cent remainder must be obtained by trade, barter, conversion or investment in facilities at premium prices. The result has been—Kaiser-Frazer, since the beginning of its operations through June, 1950, has been forced to pay in premiums above open market prices in order to obtain steel a total of $18,827,703. The average premium or variance per ton of steel which has gone into Kaiser-Frazer carbuilding has been roughly $53. This is the average cost above market price on all steel used by K-F. The average cost added to the autos produced by K-F by reason of premium-cost steel has been roughly $42 a car.

Kaiser's mother, Mary, in her wedding dress — 1873

Kaiser's grandmother and grandfather in Steinheim, Germany — 1870.
Kaiser's father, with mustache, is on the left.

Kaiser at age 12.

Kaiser at age 18, Lake Placid, New York.

Kaiser at age 19, upstate New York.

Kaiser at age 20.

Kaiser with widow Fannie Nash Noble – Lake Placid, New York — 1902.

Kaiser, 2nd from left, with fellow contractors at Boulder Dam — 1935.

Kaiser, with model of flying box car which he proposed to mass produce
during World War II — 1942.

Kaiser, Mrs. Bess Kaiser, and Reverend
Noel Porter at Lake Tahoe, California,
1943

Kaiser's Portland shipyard launches its first ship, "Star of Oregon",
September 27, 1941, more than two months before Pearl Harbor.
Note the ten prewar shipways.

Kaiser and
President Franklin
D. Roosevelt at
Portland, Oregon
launching of ship;
September 23,
1942, Joseph N.
Teal, built in ten
days.

Kaiser and his two
sons, Edgar, left,
Henry Jr., right —
1948.

Left to right. Henry J.
Kaiser Jr., George
Havas, Gene
Trefethen,
Tom Price, A.B.
Ordway, Kaiser, G.G.
Sherwood, Clay
Bedford,
H.V. Lindbergh,
Robert Elliott —
1949.

Kaiser, right, shakes hands with Joseph Frazer, September 25, 1947.

Snappy 1953 Henry J – forerunner of today's compacts.

1951 Kaiser – the most stylish 4-door sedan of the fifties.

Kaiser planning assault on world speedboat record, April, 1949. Guy Lombardo, orchestra leader, right, was to be driver. Norman Lauterbach, mechanic, left.

Kaiser hands over check for $91,476,989.92 to pay off his R.F.C. loan on his
steel operations — November 1, 1950.

Dr. Sidney R. Garfield and Kaiser reviewing plans for three new
Kaiser Permanente Hospitals — 1950.

Wedding announcement picture of Kaiser, 68, and Alyce Chester, 34 — April 10, 1951.

Kaiser in front of Hawaiian Village Hotel which he built.

Mrs. "Ale" Kaiser
christens new
catamaran as Alfred
Apaka, Hawaiian
singer,
and Kaiser look on
— 1959.

Kaiser, Alfred
Apaka, Hawaiian
singer, and Fritz
Burns, Kaiser's
construction
partner in Hawaii,
make music —
1958.

Kaiser at 80, looking over Hawaii-Kai, the vast resort city he was building — 1962.

Kaiser at his 80th birthday party.

K-F was not only forced to spend a great deal of money (which it did not have a lot of) in producing its own steel, but within nine months after production began the company found itself in the business of manufacturing engines. This had certainly not been planned. Kaiser and Frazer were happy there was a long-established, highly respected independent engine manufacturer named Continental ready to provide K-F with its requirements. It was par for the course, however, for Kaiser engineers to begin pressing Continental for modifications and improvements in the engine. Continental was quick to cooperate and together the engineers of both companies developed more horsepower, changed the valve timing, and upped the compression of the "Red Seal" L-head six cylinder engine. There would be further changes as experience dictated—for example, the problem of vapor lock was not licked until 1952—but Kaiser's fate would be linked to that basic 100 horsepower engine.

Then, as the pressures for volume production mounted, Kaiser engineers, again in keeping with their way of doing things, decided they could do a better job with both quality and quantity by producing the engines themselves. In March 1947, Kaiser-Frazer negotiated a 5-year lease to operate Continental's old engine plant in Detroit. Plans called for 700 engines a day, with Continental itself continuing to supply about 150 engines a day from its Muskegon plant. Production at the Detroit plant never reached 700 per day on a sustained basis, but by March 1, 1951, K-F had bought the Detroit Engine Division from Continental. The tools and dies at that plant were to play an important role in getting Kaiser started in the manufacturing of cars in Argentina in 1956. In retrospect, however, it was both diversionary and costly for Kaiser-Frazer to get drawn into the production of engines. If Continental had been manufacturing a truly competitive engine at a satisfactory rate of production, it could have made a significant difference in Kaiser-Frazer's primary aim of producing and selling cars.

Other Stumbling Blocks

While most people would agree the two biggest handicaps that "did Kaiser-Frazer in" were (1) inadequate financing, and (2) shortage of steel, as just described, there were other problems that stood in the way of a successful automobile venture.

Was one of them a weak dealer organization? With all their initial enthusiasm, the dealers were not the time-tested, street-smart, well-financed outfits like those selling General Motors or Ford cars. There was no way one of the old time dealers for these established lines would want to take on the risk of an entirely new car. With both Kaiser-Frazer and the dealers feeling their way through the untested waters it was inevitable that there would be a lot of lurching. And it didn't help when Joe Frazer, the partner who had lined up the dealer organization, was replaced as President in 1949 by Edgar Kaiser. How could Edgar Kaiser do as good a job in communicating with the dealers and providing leadership for them when he was up to his armpits in all the other problems the company was going through? This was the very time the dealers for the other car manufacturers began a campaign, not necessarily avowed, but nevertheless real, of pulling the curtain down on Kaiser by severely downgrading the trade-in value of Kaiser and Frazer cars, thereby scaring off the public.

Was labor the Achilles heel in the whole operation? Kaiser prided himself on being able to get along with organized labor more amicably than any other businessman. He genuinely believed in the rights of labor. He genuinely believed that when you cooperate with labor you achieve greater productivity at lower costs. And labor responded in kind. They welcomed doing business with Kaiser. That's why a labor agreement was reached in January 1946 that staggered the industry for the speed with which it was negotiated and for the happiness each side expressed over its terms.

But good intentions and carefully worded contract terms are sometimes forgotten in the push and shove that goes on over a long period of time in a massive plant under the pressures of a relentless assembly line. In 1950 Fortune reported:

> The company started with no fixed labor policy except the usual Kaiser policy of trying to do right by the employees. It had two defects: (1) Detroit labor did not necessarily respond to good intentions, and (2) the company's overwhelming aim, correctly enough, was to get the cars out. So . . . it found itself making abnormal concessions to workers to keep them on the job.

No question about it—Kaiser ended up paying a price for its all-out efforts to appease labor. Nevertheless, this was not the controlling factor, only a contributing factor, to Kaiser's demise.

Did Kaiser's competitors have a big cost advantage because their plants had already been partially amortized over the years they had been in operation, and because they had a bigger volume to spread their fixed costs over? As reasonable as Government lease and purchase terms were for the Willow Run plant, Kaiser had to take on a lot of fixed costs for amortization over a shorter period of time and with a smaller number of cars. In an industry where costs (and profits) are measured in dollars per car this was a very real disadvantage for Kaiser, especially when demand dropped off and buyers could shop around for the best bargains.

Did Kaiser go overboard in his faith in his young men from the shipyards? As dedicated and resourceful as they were, did they somehow lack the knock-down, drag-out experience required to survive in the cost-competitive world of automotive assembly? Did they ever acquire the production efficiency of other auto manufacturers? It was one thing to produce 1490 big ships with costs paid for by the Maritime Commission and quite another thing to tighten the screws on costs in the rush of getting established in the manufacture of cars. Overall, the "orange-juicers" from the West Coast did a remarkable job, but too many experienced auto men hired by Frazer were pushed aside to make way for Kaiser's shipyard workers. There was even a bit of lack of cooperation between the shipyard workers from Richmond and those from Portland.

Could Kaiser himself have made a difference if he had spent more time at Willow Run and had taken time to visit the dealers? Throughout all the critical years of Kaiser-Frazer's existence his other major companies—steel, aluminum, hospitals—

were growing so rapidly and facing so many challenging opportunities that they placed heavy demands on his time. Actually, it was the kind of pressure situation that he enjoyed. And right at that time he found new zest for living in his marriage to the young nurse, Ale, in April 1951. In time, this led to his "discovery" of the Hawaiian Islands where he became excited over the prospects for new ventures there. The net effect was that he had little time to sweat out the problems at Willow Run, little time to personally boost the morale of the dealers.

This was not an unusual approach for him. In construction, in the shipyards, and in his other major operations, he always set the program in motion, and then turned an astounding amount of responsibility over to the young men he placed in charge. However, when the problems piled up as they did at Kaiser-Frazer it is fair to wonder why Kaiser did not somehow devote more time trying to solve them. There was a magic in his name—and his forceful personality—at that time, quite unmatched by his son Edgar, and not matched by Frazer. That magic might have made a difference with the dealers, the workers, and even some of the suppliers, if he had been more available to work on the company problems.

Did The Other Auto Companies Put The Squeeze On K-F?

There was a rather widespread impression that throughout its years Kaiser-Frazer was being subjected in one way or another to a "squeeze play" by the other automobile manufacturers. Human nature being what it is, wouldn't it be inevitable that the industry would find various means to stand in the way of K-F, or at least turn its back on this upstart?

Not so, certainly not any of the Big Three companies. Neither Kaiser nor Frazer nor any top company officer would level such a charge against those automobile companies. In part, this acceptance by the industry may have reflected the high regard automobile leaders had for Frazer. Also, many top auto executives had toured one of Kaiser's shipyards during the war and had come away with great admiration for his assembly wizardry. Another possible factor may have been concern that any opposition to this new company would be attacked by the government as monopolistic. Or it may have been recognition that K-F would face enough problems on its own without the industry deliberately adding to them. But in the final analysis, Kaiser and Frazer would hold to the view that industry leaders were simply high caliber people who would not stoop to obstructionist tactics.

One of the important contacts took place when Charlie Wilson, president of General Motors, initiated a phone call to Clay Bedford inviting him for a brief visit to the General Motors' headquarters in Detroit. They had met a few years earlier when Bedford hosted Wilson on a tour of the Richmond shipyards. Bedford recalled:

> That was like being invited to talk with God. Wilson was very generous in his remarks about our progress at Kaiser-Frazer, and in particular he wanted to know how in the world we could get steel while he couldn't. He got so

interested in what we were doing to get steel that we were there for an hour and a half; it made him late for dinner. I said, 'Well, if you want to get some more steel we'll trade you Stack 5 (a blast furnace) in Cleveland for your steel plant in Gary, Indiana. With that steel plant we think we could supply our needs better and more cheaply; and with that blast furnace you can supply pig iron to your steel producers and they in turn can increase their output of what you need.' Wilson considered it very carefully, but it finally didn't work out, because by the time the proposition could be carefully studied the supply of steel was temporarily catching up with the market. Interestingly, we later transferred this blast furnace operation to Republic Steel under a contract for preferential deliveries to Kaiser-Frazer.

Another productive visit with Charlie Wilson and other GM brass took place in May 1951 when Edgar Kaiser had lunch with them, agreeing to produce some car bodies at Willow Run for an undesignated GM product. This get-together was reported in the May 23 issue of FORTUNE:

> He [Edgar] also got a lot of excellent free advice. Recalling Chevrolet's early travail, Wilson advised Edgar to fight it out. On the one hand, said Wilson, don't build more cars than you can sell to the dealers, but on the other, keep production going so that the people can't say you've gone into the aircraft business. More immediately helpful, Edgar got several contracts. Having strapped K-F to acquire steel facilities and assure some steel at mill price through all its expediting years, he now had some important and valuable assets that he had no immediate use for. GM agreed to buy the ingot rights for an Alleghany Ludlum furnace that K-F had built in 1949, and agreed to take K-F's commitment of pig iron from the Republic blast furnace.

At the end of this meeting Wilson graciously walked Edgar to his Kaiser car. Edgar was embarrassed when he went to open the door and the handle came loose in his hand. Wilson smoothed over the embarrassment by volunteering, "When something like that happens with one of your cars, the owner probably blames it on your engineering. When it happens to one of our cars the owner would not likely blame it on our engineering but on our labor."

Over the years GM was generous in its free consultation and advice as well as actually going out of its way to supply needed components to K-F. GM furnished K-F with Hydra-Matic transmission and electrical parts from 1950 on, as well as Buick transmissions when K-F ran short of gearboxes during the 1951 model run.

Perhaps the most mutually beneficial business dealing between K-F and GM—and the one that demonstrated the genuine trust that existed between the two companies—took place as an outgrowth of a tragic fire. In the spring of 1953 GM had proudly completed a brand new Hydra-Matic plant at Livonia, near Detroit. Incredibly, it burned to the ground in July. Kaiser was at his Lake Tahoe, California, home at the time. His assistant, Handy Hancock, came running in with the front page story in the morning paper. Here's how Hancock recalls Kaiser's quick instinct:

> He took just long enough to scan the first two or three paragraphs, then asked me to get Charlie Wilson, GM's president, on the phone. After a brief greeting he said, 'Charlie, I just saw the headlines in the paper. Is it true?'. When told it was, Mr. Kaiser went on, 'Is it as bad as it says?' After Mr. Wilson confirmed it was, Mr. Kaiser said, 'Well, now listen, Charlie, this nation cannot afford to have General Motors shut down. Here's what I want you to do. Have your people start shipping to Willow Run whatever tools and dies you have been able to salvage. We've got more space at Willow Run than we know what to do with. I'll call my son Edgar and tell him to work with your people. Don't worry about any terms. We can work that out later. The important thing right now is for you to get back into production as quickly as possible.'

That short conversation set the wheels in motion. GM took Kaiser up on his offer and started moving equipment into Willow Run at once. By November the terms of the sale of the Willow Run plant were agreed upon, with both sides very satisfied. GM had immediate access to a fine facility that is still the plant for their Hydra-Matic transmission production. Kaiser received $26 million for a plant that cost $15 million, a facility that had become a white elephant. Although there were those who speculated that GM had taken advantage of Kaiser's plight by driving a hard bargain, no one in Kaiser would make such a contention. They were happy to take the $26 million, add $700,000 to it, and send it to the RFC, reducing the outstanding government debt to $18,456,000 as compared with a one-time peak of $74,789,843.

Betting On The Jeep

But, as usual, hopes burned brightly with the Kaiser team. Certainly, their determination to find some viable solution to their problems was only intensified. In this atmosphere it was almost inevitable that they would turn to Willys Overland, manufacturers of the world-famous Jeep. Top officers of the two companies had had many dealings together for several years, especially when Willys became the source of engines for the Henry J. It was somewhat ironic, though, that the glory period for the Jeep—World War II—was at the very time when Joe Frazer was president and general manager of Willys, and now in mid-1953 at the time the announcement came out that Kaiser-Frazer had made a proposal to buy Willys, Frazer was no longer a major factor with the company bearing his name.

Considering the losses the company had been sustaining, it was no small matter to round up the $62,381,175 price tag placed on Willys by its president and chairman, Ward M. Canaday. Voices were raised warning Kaiser not to send good money after bad, but he never really flinched. Once again he would put his money where his mouth was by coming up with $37.6 million from his parent firm, the Henry J. Kaiser Company. Then his two financial allies lined up alongside him—$15 million from the Transamerica Corporation in the form of a stock purchase and a $20 million loan by the Bank of America.

The assets of Willys had a book value of about $15.5 million more than was paid by Kaiser. The facilities themselves were considered efficient and relatively competitive, with the main plant at Toledo, Ohio, and other plants at Maywood, California, Anderson, Indiana, and Pontiac, Michigan.

A major consideration in the deal was the prospect of tax savings through a large tax loss carry-forward. K-F had an accumulated $31.5 million loss in automobile manufacturing, and Willys, with little record of past earnings, had a low tax base for purposes of excess profits taxation. All well and good, but no company can stay alive very long unless it has enough income against which the tax loss carry-forwards can be offset. The burning question therefore would be: Will the market for Willys and Kaiser cars prove strong enough to get the company back in the black?

Once again, an all-out marketing drive was put together to capitalize on the public acceptance of the Jeep and to try to revive public interest in the continuing style leadership of the Kaiser cars. Roy Abernethy, a twenty-five-year sales executive from Packard, was named vice-president in charge of Kaiser-Willys Sales Division. He immediately sought to rebuild the confidence and enthusiasm of the dealers. In one of his first communications to them he closed with a plea, "to keep the orders coming in! We have given you price position on the Henry J. We have increased your gross profit by means of trade-in allowances on the Kaiser line, and to back these programs, we have increased our advertising support. . . . We are depending on you to do your share."

As part of the planned "rebirth," Edgar Kaiser and Abernethy arranged a press conference for July 29, 1953. Abernethy stressed that Kaiser Willys now ranked as America's fourth largest automobile manufacturer, with over four thousand U.S. outlets, assets of approximately $200 million, more than 24,000 employees, and twenty-five plants around the world. Edgar waxed dramatic: "We are stiffening our muscles. Jack Dempsey wasn't great until he was knocked out of the ring. We got knocked out, and we are now coming back in."

To Henry Kaiser himself the most frustrating part of the entire automobile venture was trying to capture the public's mind. If you have a tough engineering problem, you come at it from all sides until you work out the solution. If you are faced with production roadblocks, you can always figure out some way to overcome them. If you are short of supplies, you keep scrambling until you find what you want at the price you are willing to pay. If it's new money you need, you sit down with your banker and prove to him the loan will be secured. If it's a customer who buys millions of dollars of products you take the time to convince him you are his best supplier. But how do you get through to the little guy, those millions of potential customers who keep hearing rumors that your company might soon be going out of business? How do you make contact with that nebulous, ephemeral phantom in the far corners of the marketplace?

Frustrating, indeed, to one who fancied himself as the world's greatest salesman. Kaiser was absolutely confident, and his record proved he was justified in his confidence, that he could sell anything to anyone as long as he believed in it and as long as he could talk eyeball-to-eyeball with the other person. And few who knew him well would doubt that Kaiser Motors would still be a going concern if it had been physically possible for him to talk individually to each potential customer.

Of course, that's the role advertising and a good public relations program must play. Quite naturally, therefore, Kaiser thrust himself into that field, and he did so probably as energetically as any chairman of the board ever has. He pumped his PR people up constantly—his public relations counsel in New York, Carl Byoir and Associates, as well as his own staff—challenging them to come up with stories showing the world that Kaiser Motors was on the move. Every idea that flashed through his mind would be passed along; every program that was proposed by his people would be run past him to glean the benefit of his thinking.

He was equally obsessed with the company's advertising program. The primary agency was William Weintraub and Associates in New York City. Bill Weintraub was a colorful, creative ad man. As was always the case when he worked closely with someone, Kaiser encouraged Weintraub to come up with ideas on how to help the company, not limiting his suggestions to the field of advertising. In turn, Kaiser didn't hesitate in telling Weintraub how to run his business. As sales of cars kept sliding, Kaiser became increasingly disenchanted with newspaper and magazine advertising. He began to think they were too inanimate, too non-motivational. He wanted something that came as close as possible to face-to-face selling—something that would stir the potential buyer into action. It was then he became intensely interested in television which was just starting to become a force in communications. He decided to project himself over television, thinking his personal persuasiveness might arouse the public. Without very much encouragement from his agency or even his own people he went ahead and produced some commercials starring himself. They never really caught on with the public. Was it because they were not professionally enough done? Was it because the public had not become conditioned to television as it has today? Was it because Kaiser had so many balls in the air he couldn't find time to sustain a series of commercials on just automobiles alone? Was it because time was already running out on Kaiser Motors?

Whatever the reason, it is interesting to recall that Kaiser, again ahead of his time, was on the trail of something that could have made a difference in the fortunes of his company. Certainly, thirty years later Lee Iacocca, charismatic chairman of the board of Chrysler, showed how a forceful personal image projected over national television can play a decisive role in turning an automobile company around.

But the Willys passenger car business was soon to experience the same fate as the Kaiser cars. In the 1954 model year production only reached 11,875; in 1955 it was down to 6,564. Nevertheless, Kaiser's faith in the Jeep began to pay off. In 1955 Willys' sales volume totalled over $160 million with a profit of $4,645,708—the first profit from a Kaiser automotive operation since 1948! Commercial vehicles came to 76,000 and the domestic share of these was up 50 percent to 30,000. Willys maintained third place among U.S. commercial vehicle exporters. Thanks to the Jeep, production continued at Toledo until in 1963 Willys Motors became Kaiser Jeep Corporation. By 1966 Kaiser Jeep Corporation was manufacturing a wide variety of sports and compact cars, station wagons, and 'Jeep' utility vehicles in the United States and in 32 foreign countries, as well as producing numerous military vehicles. Kaiser 'Jeep' sales totalled $333 million in 1966, and the two South American companies produced 121,000 vehicles, not counting other 'Jeep' affiliates in more than 30 countries.

Finally, in 1970, Kaiser got completely out of the automobile business by selling the Jeep corporation to American Motors. It had been a roller coaster existence for the twenty-five years since Kaiser and Frazer had agreed to team up in 1945, certainly one of the most colorful chapters in the history of American automobile manufacturing.

(Addendum: As evidence of the timeless market appeal of the 'Jeep' it is interesting to note Renault Company of France bought American Motors in the mid-1970's, and then in 1987 Chrysler Corporation, under the leadership of Lee Iacocca, bought American Motors from Renault for the primary purpose of getting the rights to manufacture the 'Jeep'.)

The Kaisers Never Retrench

For the first nearly three years since teaming up, Kaiser and Frazer got along with each other remarkably well. Here were two captains of industry with vastly different backgrounds who were thrown together (by their own choosing) in what would be best described as a "crash" program. The challenge was to capitalize on the expertise each other could bring to the table and somehow harmonize the inevitable differences in approach. At the outset it was a true "partnership" in contrast to other automobile companies where there was but one "boss" or owner. Certainly both men had to go to extra effort to give support to the other.

One major area of tension involved manufacturing costs. With his long experience in the automotive world, during which time he had to cope with economy drives, Frazer was much more sensitive to costs than Kaiser whose shipyards were more concerned with output than with expenses. As early as November 5, 1946, Frazer wrote a surprisingly detailed summary to Kaiser and son Edgar on how economies could be effected. His proposals included:

1.I will start this economy drive by reducing the amount of money I take for my own salary by one-third.

2.Stop all advertising of all nature whatsoever.

3.Abolish the Public Relations Department entirely.

4.Abolish the Graphic Arts Department entirely.

5.Eliminate all special events programs and Singing Sentinels.

6.Don't pay expenses beyond 30 days for individuals moved from one locality to another. (This brings up the proposed transfer to Willow Run of 35 individuals from Long Beach. It might be better to let them out of Long Beach than bring them here and find them a drain upon us.)

7.Our Air Transport Division should be closed immediately.

8.The company should not furnish cars to executives. Every executive should buy his own automobile and maintain it himself.

9.Every division must drastically cut back its number of employees—plant construction, planning, traffic, export, industrial relations, comptroller, purchasing, engineering, plant cleanup.

Frazer wasn't the only one concerned with serious overstaffing—visitors to Willow Run, as well as employees themselves, were somewhat overwhelmed to see the seemingly endless string of offices, two-thirds of a mile long on two levels, filled with office personnel. Comments were made that if Edgar Kaiser would walk the length of these offices he, too, would wonder what all these people were doing. It's possible that if Frazer's suggestions had been fully implemented they could have made a significant difference in the company's operations. K-F was fast gaining a reputation for extravagance, but the two Kaisers kept their eyes primarily on production.

The default by Cyrus Eaton in the common stock sale in early February 1948 as reviewed elsewhere in this chapter, brought on severe financial pressures that led to speculation about a management shake-up. By April 9, 1948, Frazer was prompted to write Edgar:

As you know, there has been for the past several months a growing rumor that I am to sever my relationship with Kaiser-Frazer Corporation. I am told that such rumor has been reported in the press and numerous dealers and distributors questioned me about it during my recent country-wide tour. I feel that it has had a very bad effect on the morale of the Kaiser-Frazer organization, especially its dealers and distributors. I have given serious consideration, therefore, to the most effective means of finally refuting all reports of this nature.

My considered opinion is that two steps should be taken. First, Kaiser-Frazer and I should enter into an employment contract for a term of years. Second, the Board of Directors of Kaiser-Frazer should be reconstituted so that half of the directors will again be my nominees, which was the understanding between me and your father at the time of the formation of Kaiser-Frazer.

After several conferences regarding my proposals with you, your father and your counsel, you came to me and asked that I temporarily, at least, abandon my request for an employment contract, because such request had been opposed by your father and further pressing of the matter would be very upsetting to him. I naturally acceded to your request, phrased as it was, but assumed that the second proposal would be put into effect at the annual meeting of stockholders in May. . . .

Shortly thereafter, overwork and worry over the foregoing matter, among other things, sent me to the hospital. During my recuperation you have continued to lead me to believe that the change in directors would take place. I am now informed by your counsel that the Kaiser interests in Kaiser-Frazer will not permit any such change. . . .

It was certainly not Kaiser's inclination to welcome any change in relations with Frazer. He had warm regard for Frazer personally, and he recognized it would be in the best interest of the company for the two of them to work as partners. He conveyed these feelings to Frazer, and throughout the rest of 1948 their close teamwork continued. Frazer felt so good about it he wrote this letter in longhand to Kaiser on Beverly Hills Hotel stationery December 16, 1948:

Dear Henry! I feel I must write you a note today and tell you what a great man I think my partner Henry Kaiser is. I enjoyed our two days together this time more than ever and I think our decisions were most constructive—a very Merry Christmas to you and yours and happy New Year.

Affectionately Yours,

s/Joe Frazer

Notwithstanding the best intentions of both men, the days of a true partnership between them were numbered. The crunch came just three months later in March 1949. By this time costs were skyrocketing, and the sales outlook was anything but reassuring. Frazer, in particular, was pessimistic. As recounted in Richard Langworth's, The Last Onslaught On Detroit:

Joe Frazer, canny in the ways of the auto business, had looked ahead and saw that 1949 would not be a good year for a company with mildly face-lifted products. 'Because we didn't have an all-new model for 1949,' he said, 'I decided that we could sell profitably about 70,000 cars and make about $7 million—a considerable cutback from the previous years. I drew up a proposed budget on this basis, and a plan which would save us $3 million a month. But this is the way the auto business has gone, ever since I've been in it, since 1912. Every time you didn't have a new model you had to retrench.' 'The Kaisers never retrench,' said Henry at the climactic meeting. He proposed to make good the loss of capital from the aborted third stock issue by borrowing some $40 million more. 'He wanted to build 200,000 cars in 1949,' Frazer said, 'which I said couldn't be done. I calculated that at that budget we'd lose about $36 million. I had put half the collateral on the first loan ($20 million from the Bank of America in 1948) personally. I refused to go on any more. It was a pretty hot meeting—names were called and a few other things. I said we had to get economy minded. Henry wouldn't see it, so we parted.'

Kaiser's boldness (bullheadedness?) may have been a fatal error. No one will ever know what the history of Kaiser-Frazer might have been if Kaiser had played it closer to the belt while making the transition to new models. Nonetheless, the die was cast—Kaiser-Frazer was now embarked on a program that could best be described as "going for broke."

While Frazer's days of meaningful influence were over, he remained on the board of directors for several years and kept up outwardly respectful relations with the two Kaisers. One evidence of his desire to maintain friendly contact was this letter he wrote to Kaiser May 27, 1953:

I have written Henry Jr. a letter, copy of which I am attaching.

I don't know if you even knew my daughter Aerielle had multiple sclerosis nearly three years ago and that she is now completely cured. I noticed in your office the other day that although Henry seems much better there is still evidence of the disease and I felt that I wanted to tell him how Aerielle was cured, and if he cares to check into this I will be only too happy to arrange it.

I also want to tell you that I think we had a very constructive meeting in Reno. I am heartily in agreement with Edgar's recommendations as to the consolidation of these various activities, and have told him that I will be only too happy to assist him in any way I can in making them effective. I think he conducted a rather difficult Stockholders' meeting very well.

Best regards.

Years later Frazer was interviewed by Richard Langworth for his book, The Last Onslaught on Detroit. By that time Frazer had agonized at length over the events that led to the falling out of his partnership with Kaiser. Perhaps Frazer's feelings were influenced by the fact that Kaiser was still making a go of it with the Jeep, and with the two South American automobile manufacturing plants—and even by the remarkable success Kaiser was having with all of his non-automobile companies. History should not judge either Frazer or Kaiser too harshly for these views of Frazer as recorded by Langworth:

> I was awfully disappointed in Mr. Kaiser. Henry was a great man, and he did a great deal of things, but he was not a good partner, and never has been. He's always for Henry. And that's okay if he wanted it that way. But when we started out I was to lend him my know-how, and he was to lend me his, and we got money from the public to utilize it. I think he was selfish. I don't want to criticize, but he isn't loved by the men I brought into the show.

The Last Hurrah

The Kaiser automobile saga was not to be confined to Willow Run or to Toledo. Once the decision had been made to sell the Willow Run plant, there was an enormous surplus of tools and dies and other machinery, much of it comparatively new and efficient. If it were broken down and sold piecemeal, it would bring only a fraction of its worth. But where would a buyer be found when the big three automakers were steadily increasing their stranglehold on the U.S. market?

This would be one occasion when Henry Kaiser's involvement in so many industries outside of automobiles would not rise up to bite him, but would open an exciting new door. By this time, Kaiser Aluminum was operating two plants in Louisiana. Because of the importance of these operations to the area, Kaiser had become a close personal friend of de Lesseps S. Morrison, mayor of New Orleans who had concentrated on promoting trade with Latin America through his port. He was on first-name-speaking terms with the heads of most South American countries.

One weekend in late July 1954, a year after Kaiser had sold the Willow Run plant to General Motors, Mayor Morrison and his family were guests of Kaiser at his Lake Tahoe, California, home. Morrison mentioned that there were two hundred million people in Latin America, yet there was no automobile industry there. Kaiser's ears pricked up, "Do you think Juan Peron (President of Argentina) would be interested in having cars manufactured in Argentina?" "Probably so," came the answer. Kaiser began to get excited. "We could start one by sending all of our surplus tools and dies there. Let's get Peron on the phone." Morrison said he would be glad to write to Peron once he returned to New Orleans. "That will be an eternity," said Kaiser, "get him on the phone right now." The call went through direct to Peron and within a matter of minutes it was agreed Kaiser should come to Argentina as soon as arrangements could be made.

Always one to see the big picture, Kaiser planned to use his visit to Argentina as the springboard for an industrial development tour into Mexico, Panama, Colombia, Ecuador, Peru, Brazil, Uruguay, and Venezuela. In each country he met with top government and industrial leaders. He openly explored with them what their needs might be, and how his companies might assist them in developing new sources of power, transportation, steel, cement, aluminum. It was almost as though he were speaking for the United States in pointing out the unlimited opportunities that lay ahead for each country. In each instance, he offered to follow up his visit with specific surveys by Kaiser industrial and engineering teams.

The entourage that left for Latin America in early August -- less than two weeks after Kaiser had talked to Peron—included his wife, Ale, with Mayor and Mrs. Morrison, Mr. and Mrs. Bill Weintraub and Mr. and Mrs. Bob Elliott, Kaiser's executive assistant.

The group visited nine countries and seventeen cities in twenty days, saving Argentina for the last. On his stop in Brazil, Kaiser told President Getulio Vargas, "we have the know-how, we have the tools, and, if we locate here, we would want the Brazilians to own the majority of stock in the company." The government was impressed by this unusual approach but it would take two years before car manufacturing operations could be set up in Brazil.

However, the reception in Buenos Aires, Argentina, was enthusiastic. Mayor Morrison of New Orleans, with the help of Bill Weintraub and Bob Elliott, had really primed the meeting with Peron. In his book, Latin American Mission, Morrison described the scene:

> Huge signs at the airport, saying, 'WELCOME KAISER!'; a red carpet stretching from our plane to a reception area; a welcome by high governmental officials; the road to the city lined for miles on both sides by cheering crowds waving small American flags; and when we reached our hotel, the Plaza, another enormous electric sign across the street, saying 'WELCOME KAISER!'.

In just a matter of days the main principles of an automobile plant in Argentina had been agreed upon. But not without incident. In the face-to-face meeting with Peron, it was brought out that Peron expected a relative of his to be designated as distributor, with a commission going to him for all cars sold in Argentina. As interpreter, Morrison detected that, in turn, part of the commission would end up with Peron. Since the distributor would perform no function it was to be a means of skimming automobile sales, or in effect an under-the-table payoff. Morrison pointed this out to Kaiser. There was not an instant's hesitation. Kaiser had vowed while building the Cuban highway in 1927 never to be involved in any payment under-the-table. At the obvious risk of blowing the whole deal in Argentina, Kaiser's face reddened and he stood up: "Gentlemen, I'm sorry, if you will excuse me, I will return to my hotel and catch the afternoon plane out. Let's forget everything we've talked about. I will not be a party to this kind of dealing." He left with his associates. By the time he reached the hotel, there was an urgent message from Peron requesting reinstatement of negotiations with no undercover payments to be involved.

Within a few days, an agreement in principle had been hammered out, including provision for Argentinians to own the majority of the stock in the company. For the next week or two management teams on both sides were busy working out the detailed plans for this unprecedented partnership venture. Then on September 1,

Kaiser went right back to Argentina to insure that the negotiations would be rapidly moved ahead, embracing the terms he thought were essential. Never one to pamper himself, he spun around a third time, taking along with him not only his son, Edgar, but young Jim McCloud who would head up operations in South America the next thirteen years. McCloud had been in charge of Kaiser's engine plant in Detroit which was the source of some of the most valuable equipment to be transferred to Argentina.

This time a preliminary pact was signed for a 40,000-per-year auto factory. The New York Times of October 6, 1954, reported:

> Henry J. Kaiser signed a preliminary contract yesterday to manufacture cars, trucks, and jeeps in Argentina in partnership with the Argentine Government and Argentine private investors. The United States industrialist will invest $10 million worth of machinery, representing about one-third of the capital in the new company for which he will manage the company. Mr. Kaiser's goal is to produce 40,000 units annually in Argentina. He promised to build the plant in one year, start turning out motor cars by the end of the second year, and reach full production in three years.

Notwithstanding this signed agreement, Kaiser made his fourth trip to South America for one week in early November. That was typical of Kaiser—conceive the idea, lead out in all the discussions till clear agreement is reached, then turn the project over to his "boys." Considering his age, 72, his overweight, and the projects he had going in Hawaii in the late summer and fall of 1954, it was indeed a strenuous commitment on his part to make four trips to South America, each requiring from a few days to twenty days.

While for all practical purposes the deal had been struck, there remained the thorny problem of agreeing on the valuation to be placed on the machinery and tools each side—mainly Kaiser—was contributing to the project. It also was a time to line up the myriad vendors who would supply parts for the cars.

Finally, on January 19, 1955, Juan Peron, Argentina's President, meeting with Edgar Kaiser, signed the definitive contract and issued the necessary Government decrees to get the company underway. The annual planned production was announced at 20,000 4-wheel-drive Willys Universal Jeeps; 10,000 Kaiser-Argentina 4-door sedans; 5,000 2-and-4 wheel drive station wagons; and 5,000 1-ton pickup trucks.

It was the sale of stock in the new company that dazzled Jim McCloud. He could never quite get over the day of the stock issue, seeing the people waiting in long lines for the privilege of buying stock in this new enterprise.

By March, ground was broken at Cordoba, in the central part of Argentina, and thirteen months later, the first Jeep was produced in that plant.

Although Kaiser himself never returned to Argentina, he kept in steady touch with all developments because he was determined to do whatever was necessary to make this complex undertaking a success. Every so often he would have Edgar, Jim

McCloud and Steve Girard fly over to Hawaii to fill him in on progress.

The South American foray turned out very successfully. Industrias Kaiser Argentina was Latin America's first and largest automobile manufacturer. By 1956 Willys-Overland do Brazil was organized along the lines Kaiser had sketched for President Vargas two years before—Brazilians owned the majority control of the company, and all plans were directed toward giving the country an all-Brazilian vehicle. WOB quickly grew to become the largest auto manufacturer in Brazil.

When Kaiser sold its holdings in the two companies in 1967, the year Henry Kaiser died, it was, paradoxically enough, because each company had become dominant in passenger car manufacture—an area which Kaiser could no longer augment with models from the U.S. This was precisely what Ford and Renault could do—the former buying out the Brazil operations and the latter taking over in Argentina. Kaiser had been washed out of the automobile business in those two countries, but had left a priceless legacy in the form of two strong, self-sufficient automobile industries that not only bolstered the economy but gave a great sense of national pride to the people.

Looking Back

Nobody in the Kaiser organization would ever disagree with Clay Bedford's verdict regarding the entrance of Kaiser into the automobile manufacturing business: "This is the roughest thing we have ever tackled."

But many Kaiser people would go further. They would say: "This is the one business we should never have tackled in the first place." They would say Kaiser should have realized he couldn't make it in the one industry where well-established giants had so many production advantages and so much more marketing expertise. They would support their judgment by underscoring the heavy losses year after year which necessitated financial backup from Kaiser's holdings in his other companies. They would point to the dedicated management team that was trying to make a go of it, and stress how much had been taken out of the lives of so many. They would call attention to the repeated number of times the automobile troubles spilled over as problems for the other Kaiser companies. They would emphasize how the automobile failure damaged the image of Kaiser in the public mind as being the one person who could always do the impossible. They would say that if only the clock could be turned back they would make every effort to talk Kaiser into staying out of the automobile business entirely.

Of all those who agonized through the trying times, the one person who paid the highest price for his involvement was Edgar Kaiser. Here was Kaiser's 37-year-old son fresh from having successfully directed construction of the Bonneville dam, the Grand Coulee Dam, and the amazing production at the Portland-Vancouver shipyards. Capable, conscientious, fantastically loyal to his father, incredibly hard-working, Edgar would now be locked in a life-and-death struggle for eight years at Willow Run. His father could come and go touching only the high spots, his management team could change many times, but Edgar would be the one on the firing line from start to finish. The exhilaration of the many remarkable achievements (such as they were) would be his to enjoy; the trauma of every defeat would hit him the hardest.

Although no father and son ever worked more harmoniously together than Edgar and his father, they rarely had offices side-by-side in all their years. Their daily contacts were by phone or when Kaiser would visit whatever project Edgar was running. By the time Edgar left Willow Run in the mid-1950's for the Oakland headquarters his father was operating out of Hawaii.

During Edgar's long and uninterrupted absence from headquarters, the responsibility for selecting and directing top management for all the other major Kaiser companies fell on Gene Trefethen. Inescapably, these officers felt a little closer to Trefethen, and even a little more loyal to him, than to Edgar. Their umbilical cord was to Trefethen, not Edgar. For a long time Edgar seemed almost like a visitor to the Oakland office. He could never quite catch up to Trefethen in his knowledge of how to successfully run these other companies.

There was also an uneasy feeling among most of the Oakland executives that Edgar was primarily to blame for the failure of Kaiser-Frazer. This was shared by many outside automobile experts who were closest to the action. Yet, to be fair, it must be acknowledged that Edgar seldom undertook any major program without first consulting with his father. It was often a case of Edgar trying to push ahead too far too fast, with Kaiser failing to exercise the necessary guidelines and constraints.

Sweating out all the problems at Willow Run for ten years, trying to keep pace with the successes of his father, then trying to put the defeats at Willow Run behind him, and finally struggling to win over the confidence of the firmly-rooted Oakland management team, placed strains on Edgar that very few people are ever called upon to endure. In the process something had been taken out of him and the marks would remain with him for the rest of his life. Surely, if he had it to do over again, he would ask to be spared those harrowing years at Willow Run.

The only person who would never cast any backward glances, and, even if he did, would not ask to be spared the trials, was Henry Kaiser. He looked upon business as a game, with all the excitement of both winning and losing. From his earliest construction days he knew there would be some jobs where he would make money, some jobs where he might lose his shirt. The challenge would always be to come up with enough good-paying jobs to help him weather the bad times. As bitter as the losses were in the automobile business he was grateful he could turn to his other profitable ventures to tide him over.

However, in the compassion that was his nature he seemed more concerned about the impact the automobile fiasco had on others than on himself. While he expected his employees to ride out the misfortunes in their own way, he empathized with them and their families far more than most industrial leaders do. Likewise, he often expressed deep solicitude for the suppliers, the dealers, the customers, the stockholders, and anyone else who might be hurt by Kaiser-Frazer losses. Typical of his feelings for others was this account given by his young executive assistant, Handy Hancock, who was driving Kaiser to his Lake Tahoe, California, home in the summer of 1952:

> I had been driving for nearly an hour without any comment from Mr. Kaiser. He was in deep thought, obviously worried about something. Once he dozed off. When he woke up, still noticeably concerned about something, I finally said, 'What is bothering you, Mr. Kaiser?' He replied, 'I'm just trying to figure out some way to salvage Kaiser-Frazer.' I dared to say, 'Why don't you give it up; everybody else says that you should; you're just throwing good money after bad.' He said, 'Handy, I can't give it up. I recently received a letter from a retired railroad conductor telling me he had withdrawn all his life savings from the bank and had invested it in Kaiser-Frazer stock. He didn't ask me for anything. He just expressed confidence that I would somehow make a success of the company. I can't let people like that down. I feel an obligation to make good in behalf of him and all the stockholders as well as the other people who will be affected by what happens to Kaiser-Frazer.'

It was that deep concern for other people that prompted him in 1956 to do one of the most daring things of his lifetime. His automobile company was in its death throes, and he was asking Bank of America to loan him $95 million. The bank told him the loan could not be made unless he pledged as collateral his ownership in all of the other viable companies. His key executives pleaded with him not to do it, because it would be "risking all the family jewels." He responded, "Well, boys, we have our obligations to the people who have supported us—the stockholders, the creditors, the employees. Bankruptcy is out of the question. I have never borrowed money I did not expect to pay back, so we will do it."

With his heart and soul (and money) so completely committed to the success of his automobile company, there is little doubt that, all things considered, Kaiser was glad he had entered the automobile business. After all, would he want to have:

Missed out on the thrill of the spectacular Waldorf opening show for the brand new Kaiser and Frazer cars in January 1946? No way.

Missed out on the excitement of working with Howard Darrin to dazzle the automobile world with new standards of styling? Never.

Not experienced the intense feeling of pride at having a true people's car, the compact Henry J? Not on your life.

Never known the satisfaction that would come from buying the plant and manufacturing rights for the world's best-known car, the Jeep? No, thank you.

Been denied the deep pleasure of personally selling the Argentine dictator and his countrymen on the benefits in establishing that nation's own, self-sufficient automobile manufacturing plant, the first in South America? Wouldn't have missed it for anything.

Never experienced the fulfillment that came from producing a total of 746,000 Kaiser, Frazer, and Kaiser-Darrin cars? Worth all the heartache.

These were fun activities for Kaiser, richly rewarding, very gratifying.

Sure, it was not always a bed of roses—there were plenty of headaches along the way. There would be harassment from banks, from labor, from government, from suppliers. There would be an untimely doublecross by a major investment banker that would severely jolt the company. Most of all, there would be the frustration in not being able to hold the public's confidence after the first few years—and heartache over others whose lives were marred by the company's woes.

But problems are not only opportunities in work clothes—as Kaiser said so many thousands of times—they can be stimulating, they can add zest to the day's work. No one would ever go to a ballgame, or enjoy playing in one, if it were known that the same team would win every time by a wide margin. It's the sweet agony of suspense, the uncertainty of the outcome, the challenge to the players, that excites people and keeps them coming back.

So it was with Kaiser in the big leagues of automobile production. He was playing against the world's best, and he found it exhilarating. He got his share of hits, maybe more than his share of strikeouts, but he kept swinging away, he was never called out on strikes. He found out what every competitor in this world discovers—it is always best to win but it isn't all that bad to lose. And it is sure a lot more fun to be in the game than just standing on the sidelines.

That's why Kaiser took all the bad along with the good. That's why he would never look back and bemoan what everyone else considered a disaster.

Indeed, if some prophet could have positively foretold in 1945 what would beset Kaiser in the automobile business, you can be sure he wouldn't bat an eye in responding:

"It's something I've always wanted to do.

Let's get on with it."

CHAPTER 10

WITH A LITTLE BIT OF LUCK

"Every day is a golden day for hastening the national preparedness with expansion in aluminum facilities."

In nearly every venture Kaiser got into, he had to slay dragons at the start. Battling the entrenched establishment. Building new, sometimes unproven, facilities from scratch. Borrowing heavily. Gambling on market uncertainties. Doing what experts often call foolhardy. Overcoming the seemingly impossible. Hurrying, hurrying, hurrying. When he died at age 85, Time magazine entitled his obituary, "Man Who Always Hurried."

He thrived on it. Every roadblock simply spurred him on. The greater the risk, the stronger the opposition, the more he would enjoy it, the higher he would rise.

Getting started in aluminum was really quite a different story. It was far easier than breaking into shipbuilding, or steel, or autos, or hospitals. It was nothing to compare with the challenge he would face eight years later when as a 71-year old man he would burst upon the Hawaiian scene.

Sure, there was a chorus of voices warning him he would lose his shirt in aluminum. Sure, most experts thought the postwar aluminum market would consume only a fraction of the nation's potential productive capacity. Sure, few could see how a newcomer could survive the competition of the entrenched Aluminum Company of America (Alcoa) which had been producing aluminum since the early 1900's. And, except for two or three individuals, even his own people were too wrapped up in their own challenges to beat any drums for getting into aluminum.

But it was as though people had blinders on. The underlying fundamentals of a sound aluminum venture were there all right. It was nothing less than a "golden opportunity" for those who had "eyes to see," or maybe more accurately "faith to believe." That's the role Kaiser always played, so here was something made to order for him. As events would soon prove, this was the one industry where it could most accurately be said he was blessed "with a little bit of luck."

It was therefore not really surprising that Kaiser would enter the aluminum business. What was surprising was that with one possible exception no other qualified company had either the vision or the courage to take advantage of those same favorable conditions.

The sole exception undoubtedly was Alcoa, the nation's largest producer. Responding to the wartime emergency, Alcoa, in 1942 and 1943, built and operated a host of new aluminum producing and fabricating plants for the Government. Those facilities included a huge rolling mill at Trentwood, Washington, just outside of Spokane, a smelter at nearby Mead, and a plant at Baton Rouge, Louisiana, which refined bauxite ore into alumina, the product used by the smelter.

These three plants incorporated all the advanced manufacturing techniques Alcoa had learned in its long history of aluminum making. They were the most modern and efficient in the world. They were designed to complement one another. The output from Baton Rouge was just what was needed at Mead, and the ingot production at Mead was geared to the capacity of Trentwood. Alcoa had operated the trio very successfully for more than two years during the war.

There were those who would look at the long distances separating these plants, including the fact that Trentwood was far removed from eastern markets, and conclude these integrated facilities could not be operated competitively in a peacetime market. That was actually a superficial evaluation because Alcoa had given a lot of thought in choosing those locations in the first place, with due consideration to postwar economics.

The alumina plant was a short distance up the Mississippi River. It was ideally situated for receiving shiploads of bauxite from the vast and rich deposits just across the Caribbean at Surinam on the northern shores of South America. The smelter at Mead was in the heartland of the Northwest's almost unlimited power supply. Electrical rates were the cheapest in the industry, and making aluminum takes a lot of electricity. With power being by far the biggest cost in aluminum production, Mead had a very significant competitive advantage over other smelters.

And, measured by actual cost, Baton Rouge and Mead were not as far apart as geographical distance seemed to put them. During the war Alcoa had negotiated a remarkably low rail freight rate of $8.00 per net ton to move alumina for the 2600 miles from Baton Rouge to Mead. This was the lowest freight rate the railroads had ever published on any commodity for that length of haul. Among other factors, this showed the carriers had a natural interest in helping make these distant plants economic. It was profitable to the rail lines because the alumina was shipped in boxcars which otherwise would have moved empty from the South and Midwest back to the lumber and paper producing regions of the Northwest.

At each of these three plants, Alcoa had developed a team of management and labor that was skilled in operating the facilities. Most of these experienced people were anxious to take up peacetime operation of the plants. Add to that the fact that if any company could visualize the potential of the postwar market it would be Alcoa. They had been in the business a long time, and were enormously successful at it.

Then why didn't they bid on these war-surplus plants? They would have liked to, and so testified in various governmental hearings in the summer of 1945, but they weren't permitted to under a government antitrust injunction. The government was totally committed to promoting competition in aluminum and preventing a monopoly. It should be acknowledged that Alcoa didn't wish to buck government policy, and later, when Kaiser was in the aluminum business, actually extended help to the new competitor on several occasions.

Reynolds Aluminum was perhaps another contender. It was the country's only other aluminum producer of consequence. It, too, had been commissioned by the government to build and operate some major wartime aluminum plants. It certainly held no doubts about the postwar potential for aluminum. However, the obvious thing for Reynolds was to do what it did—bid on the government plants which it had built and operated itself.

One company which might be said to have missed the boat entirely was Anaconda Copper. During the war they had built and operated a magnesium plant for the government near Las Vegas, Nevada. This put them in the light metals field and they should have become aware of the versatility of the other light metal, aluminum. Theirs was a Defense Plant Corporation facility, and Anaconda could walk away from that operation without any obligation, so maybe they were not thinking about postwar possibilities. On the other hand, Kaiser was on the hook to pay back a government loan he had received to build his private magnesium plant at Permanente, California.

The biggest difference, however, was Kaiser himself. He had come to recognize that magnesium simply could not compete with aluminum for cost and all-around utility. Anaconda did not catch the vision of aluminum's many advantages. Moreover, Kaiser's magnesium team at Permanente was not a transient crew but a group of trained and loyal people champing at the bit to find some way to stay in the metal-producing business. Kaiser was anxious to accommodate them.

Whether or not Anaconda gave any serious thought to bidding on the surplus aluminum plants is not known, but they did not do so. They chose instead to stick with the heavier non-ferrous metals of copper, lead and zinc. Ironically, by the late 1950's Anaconda did start producing aluminum, but by that time Kaiser had left them in the dust.

The country's other big copper producer, American Smelting and Refining Corporation, likewise declined to bid on the government aluminum plants. In 1945, Roger W. Strauss, president of that company was quoted as saying, "Anyone would be heroic to purchase any of the government-owned aluminum plants."

In view of Kaiser's immediate success in the aluminum venture, it is fair to wonder why some company in the mighty steel industry didn't see the same opportunity he did. Somehow, steel executives felt they were so all-powerful they could look down their noses at the upstart metal, aluminum. No doubt they had so many opportunities and challenges in expanding their own production for postwar needs they gave little thought to this lightweight metal in the far-away Northwest. Considering the steel industry's problems today, and the efforts of many steel companies to diversify, it is interesting to speculate what a difference could have been made in that industry if one major company had chosen to bid on the aluminum plants. Apparently, to those companies their involvement in steel was reason enough to stay out of aluminum. To Kaiser, his burgeoning steel mill in Southern California with all its promise for postwar growth had just the opposite effect—it convinced him the future was equally bright for aluminum.

In any case, the government had a hard time interesting any qualified bidders to look at the aluminum plants. The government itself actually scared some people off. It was so anxious to put the war surplus plants to use that it went overboard in stressing the low prices it would sell the plants for in order to compensate for the problems facing a prospective peacetime operator. The government had itself and everyone else believing it was trying to dump "white elephants." FORTUNE magazine reported that the government sent out no fewer than 281 letters and wires offering the plants at bargain prices and got only a few bites.

Kaiser's interest in aluminum was no sudden postwar love affair. As early as mid-1940 he spoke out boldly on the importance of aluminum in answering President Roosevelt's call for the construction of 50,000 airplanes to help England and Europe halt Hitler's conquest. At that time Kaiser made a public plea for an immediate, comprehensive report outlining the materials, the factories, and the manpower required to build that many aircraft—with particular emphasis on the need for vastly more aluminum production. Then again in 1941 Kaiser bombarded Washington with proposals for aluminum plants in the Northwest, spotlighting the availability of low cost power in that area.

This early attention to aluminum had been triggered in part by other actions of the Roosevelt administration. In The Secret Diary of Harold L. Ickes, Secretary of the Interior, published by Simon and Schuster in 1955, this entry was made on Saturday, February 22, 1941:

> We [the President and Ickes] talked again about the Aluminum Company of America and he seemed as eager as I to smash this trust. I reminded him that he had said at the previous Cabinet meeting that we should build a government plant and turn it over to someone to manage. I spoke of Kaiser in this connection and I got no indication that the President's purpose is not to go through to this objective. I said that if we do this, we would cut prices very sharply and furnish competition that would be a curb on Alcoa in the future. The President indicated that he would go along on this.
>
> . . . . [Later] I asked Kaiser whether he would be willing to operate the Government-owned aluminum fabricating plant which, at a Cabinet meeting,

the President had suggested should be built. He said that he would, and that he would have tentative plans in the hands of the Department within a day or two.

Kaiser is one of the biggest contractors in the country. I have had dealings with him and have found him to be a man of imagination and great driving energy. He built Boulder Dam for the Government and he is now building Grand Coulee and Shasta Dams. [Kaiser did not build Shasta Dam; he provided cement and aggregate for it.] He constructed the great bridge from San Francisco to Oakland when other engineers said it could not be done. [Kaiser actually only participated in building the east underwater piers for the bridge.] Later, with my help, he built a great cement plant to supply his needs at Shasta Dam, and then broke the prices of the cement trust. He also has contracts to build a large number of ships for the British as well as for our own Government. I would rather deal with him than with Reynolds because he is not afraid of the Aluminum Company of America and will stand up to that concern.

Meanwhile, a contract has been negotiated with Reynolds to build an aluminum pig mill at Bonneville, but I have ordered that it be not executed until I can see what we can develop with Kaiser. We will want more aluminum than Reynolds can produce. As a matter of fact we want both a fabrication plant and a mill for pig aluminum and it is these two things that we are working on with Kaiser.

These contacts with President Roosevelt and Ickes in 1940 and 1941 had certainly made Kaiser aware of the basic economics in the aluminum industry. Now in 1945, with his confidence in the postwar market, he was getting closer to making the plunge that he had been talking about off and on during the war. He was sure that the Bonneville Power Administration, with its surplus power capacity, would cooperate with anyone who would operate the Mead smelter, because the plant was the biggest single user of power in the Northwest. He also knew the people of that area could be counted on to boost the aluminum plants in every reasonable way. And, of course, he knew there was a large reservoir of trained personnel, management and labor, just standing by for the moment the aluminum plants were fired up.

That's why he was front and center at all the Congressional hearings in 1945 on the disposal of the surplus aluminum plants—Senator Murray's Committee in March, Senator Mitchell's Committee in August, and Senator O'Mahoney's Committee in October. Chad Calhoun, Kaiser's Washington, D.C., Vice President, was the star witness before Senator Mitchell's hearing in Spokane, Washington, on August 22, 1945. On that occasion Calhoun introduced a letter that Kaiser had written August 10, 1945, to W. Stuart Symington, Chairman of the Surplus Property Board (the letter was written at the suggestion of Sam H. Husbands, Director of Reconstruction Finance Corporation), as follows:

> This is to advise you that this company requests the opportunity to nego-
> tiate for the leasing of certain Government-owned alumina, aluminum ingot,
> and aluminum rolling mills, forging and extrusion facilities, and other alumi-
> num and magnesium processing plants. We are actively making a study and
> analysis upon which to base our proposal. Our interest is in the Government-
> owned aluminum ingot plants in Oregon, Washington, and California, the
> alumina plants at Arkansas, and Baton Rouge, Louisiana, the rolling mill at
> Spokane, extrusion forging, and sand casting equipment at various locations.
> We have verbally advised Mr. S. H. Husbands, Director of Reconstruction
> Finance Corporation, of our interest in these plants. We would appreciate
> your advising us of the time when the negotiations for these plants should
> commence and with whom. Also if there is any time limit set for the filing of
> proposals.

>   Permanente Metals Corp.
>   Henry J. Kaiser, President

For the next two or three weeks wires went back and forth between Kaiser, Symington, and Husbands seeking confirmation on particular points, with Kaiser each
time reaffirming his desire to bid on the plants.

In order to lay a solid foundation for this proposed entry into the aluminum business, Kaiser asked his Chief Engineer, George Havas, to direct a study "of the aluminum industry in the Pacific Northwest." Havas assigned his chief electrical engineer,
George B. Scheer, to conduct the study. As qualified as Scheer was, both in his electrical knowledge and his long business experience, this was a questionable assignment. The real issue was not how power rates might determine the economics of an
aluminum venture. The controlling issue was whether the postwar aluminum market
could absorb the output of the new plants, and for this a team of marketing experts
would have been better equipped.

All this time pressure was mounting on the government agencies to finalize a program. Even the Attorney General got in the act. On September 11, 1945, he submitted
to Congress an extensive report on "The Aluminum Industry" highlighting the
situation:

> which confronts anyone bold enough to think of engaging in the business.
> The peacetime market for aluminum is an unknown quantity. Predictions
> range from Jeremiah-like prophecies that none of the Government facilities
> will be needed to glowing promises that every bit of capacity now in exis-
> tence, and still more, will be needed to meet demand. But all these predic-
> tions, no matter how clothed with impressive statistics, are built on nothing
> more substantial than fears or hopes. The odds are so heavily on Alcoa's side

today that no one else, regardless of his efficiency or enterprise, can become strong enough to engage in unrestricted competition within that industry.

A month later Stuart Symington testified before the O'Mahoney Senate Committee:

In our efforts to obtain competition we are faced with proposals made by organizations which do not appear to have responsible financial backing, or adequate marketing organizations capable of operating an aluminum business successfully.

By this time it should have been crystal clear that:

(1)The Government stood ready to offer attractive terms to any responsible organization that would bid on the plants.

(2)The Government would be more than willing to help the successful bidder get launched competitively.

Notwithstanding this obvious backing by the Government, and notwithstanding Kaiser's repeated pronouncements that he wanted to bid on the plants, George Scheer's report for Kaiser Engineers finally came out in the middle of January 1946 with a resounding "no" recommendation. The letter transmitting the report stated that "a new and at present non-existing market must be secured" for successful entry into the industry, and that dependence upon a normal share of the established market would result in "a considerable loss" in the early years of operation. The report mournfully concluded: "Until a positive outlet for aluminum is obtained it is inadvisable to enter the aluminum industry."

It came as no surprise to anyone who knew Kaiser that he promptly brushed aside the findings of the report. He not only had unremitting faith in the nation's postwar industrial growth he had just five months earlier plunged into the automobile business, and he was certain that one way or another, these aluminum plants could play a key role in helping his auto company.

The Die Is Cast

Flushed with the excitement of the spectacular, throng-filled showing of his new Kaiser and Frazer automobiles at the Waldorf Astoria hotel in New York City on Sunday, January 20, 1946, Kaiser called Calhoun in Washington the very next Sunday and asked him to get the ball rolling for the lease of the Trentwood rolling mill. Kaiser had become concerned that his automobile manufacturing might suffer from a steel shortage, especially since the major steel companies were in the midst of a very bitter strike. He thought there would be some possibility he could move steel slabs from his own plant at Fontana in Southern California to Trentwood for rolling into steel sheets that could then be shipped to Willow Run, Michigan. The Fontana plant had no wide sheet mill; the Trentwood rolling mill could conceivably be modified to roll steel sheets.

Kaiser was even toying with the idea of building autos with some aluminum parts instead of steel. If that could be shown to be practical, he wanted the aluminum producing capacity to bring it about.

Calhoun said that the Government was determined to foster an integrated, competitive aluminum operation, and wouldn't allow anyone to lease Trentwood without also leasing the nearby Mead reduction plant. This became the main issue to resolve on the next day, Monday. The other issue involved the question as to which Kaiser company should bid on the plants. All along, it was Permanente Metals that had talked of leasing the plants. Now, suddenly, Kaiser decided it was Kaiser-Frazer that should make the bids, because "Kaiser-Frazer was in trouble and I wanted to help."

Frazer himself was dubious about the need to lease Trentwood and was flatly opposed to leasing Mead—"I do not want to have any part of the Mead plant." Nevertheless, under Kaiser's goadings, and under the pressure of time, Calhoun was authorized on that day to write a letter to War Assets Corporation on behalf of Kaiser-Frazer indicating interest in leasing the two plants.

Frazer's nephew, young Hickman Price, vice-president of K-F, shared his uncle's opposition. He had gone to Washington with a company attorney to meet with Calhoun. While there he phoned another uncle, the president of a bank in Seattle, regarding Trentwood and was told that the plant was a "white elephant." Price relayed this to Frazer and asserted that "leasing Trentwood might mean financial suicide for the company."

Kaiser-Frazer's lawyers, both company and outside counsel, were deeply concerned because K-F had just completed its second public offering of stock under a prospectus which contained no indication "of any intention to engage in anything not directly related to the automobile business" and the adoption, so soon thereafter, of a distinctly new enterprise afforded room for the accusation that "there has not been a full disclosure of the pertinent facts at the time the issue went to market." The lawyers unanimously felt that K-F had been chartered to produce automobiles, not aluminum, and getting into that business could lead to "dangerous complications from a stockholder and director responsibility viewpoint."

Here, then, was Kaiser—as happened so many times in his life—standing alone in the center of the stage (except that, as usual, his son Edgar, as well as Gene Trefethen and Chad Calhoun, would be standing in the wings cheering him on). Notwithstanding the warning of the lawyers, Kaiser finally prevailed upon Frazer to allow K-F to bid on the Trentwood plant, but Frazer wouldn't budge on the Mead plant. Thereupon, Kaiser wanted Permanente Metals to bid on Mead, but there was not sufficient time to secure the approval of Permanente's directors, so the decision was made to have Kaiser Cargo, Inc., fully controlled by Kaiser, make the bid. Accordingly, on February 1, 1946, Calhoun submitted to the War Assets Administration a formal bid for leasing Trentwood by K-F and Mead by Kaiser Cargo. He had to bulwark the proposals with assurances that the two plants would be operated on an integrated basis.

War Assets then advertised the plants throughout the country, and on February 21 issued a press release stating:

> To foster the development of new independent enterprises and promote competition in the aluminum industry in conformity with the objectives of the Surplus Property Act, the War Assets Corporation today announced the lease of the Trentwood aluminum rolling mill to the Kaiser-Frazer Corporation and the Mead aluminum reduction plant to Kaiser Cargo, Inc., subject to the approval of the Attorney General. Options to purchase the plants have also been granted.

While the plants were being advertised, the opposition to the Trentwood proposal was dormant, but after the February 21 press release the lawyers really got up in arms about K-F being in the aluminum business. Finally, the Board of Directors of K-F met on March 12 to consider the Trentwood "problem." Trefethen reported on that meeting:

> Mr. Kaiser told everybody that this was going to be a profitable business, but the position of the Board was that even if it was going to be, even assuming it was going to be, they did not want to use Kaiser-Frazer funds in order to go into the business.

Later, Kaiser testified about his unsuccessful campaign to get K-F into the aluminum business:

> .... I was descended on like that, about getting Kaiser-Frazer into the business; they were all very much opposed including [lawyers] Scott and Ballantine. . . . I couldn't get support from anybody to put Kaiser-Frazer into the aluminum business. I couldn't get approval, and I gave up, because they asked what we wanted to get into the business for; everybody was in argument about it; they were very much disturbed about it. . . . . There were too many objections that appeared sound, because of what our own attorneys were saying and had advised me. Even my personal attorneys were advising me. I even went to them to get some support, but didn't make it.

The upshot of all the discussions was the adoption by the K-F directors of a motion ratifying the leasing of the Trentwood plant, but authorizing the officers to enter into a letter of intent to assign K-F's interest in Trentwood to Permanente Metals, or another satisfactory corporation, in consideration of assumption by the assignee of all liability of K-F, and the execution of an agreement to supply the sheet aluminum requirements of K-F.

Permanente Metals Takes Over

To set the stage for Permanente Metals to take over the leases on the Trentwood and Mead plants, Trefethen instructed Donald Browne, top accounting officer, to make a rush analysis of profit or loss prospects if operations were at 100% capacity, 80%, 60%, and even 40%. The report was finished on the night of March 18 just in advance of Permanente's Board of Directors' meeting the next morning. The report showed that whether Trentwood would be a liability or an asset would depend on the potential market for sheet aluminum. Kaiser thought Trentwood would operate at capacity, which would mean a huge profit; everyone else doubted whether even 40% of capacity could be reached, which would mean serious losses. The vote of the directors was divided, Harry Morrison and Felix Kahn voting no.

The directors then instructed the officers to arrange financing and report back. Fred A. Ferroggiaro, chairman of the Finance Committee of the Bank of America was contacted and given a copy of the Browne report which he in turn assigned to the bank's investment department for analysis. Their negative response concluded with these observations:

> So many new factors face the aluminum industry, including the disposal of huge present day surpluses and other large supplies which eventually will come into the market from the scrapping of military airplanes, that a very complete study of all phases of the light metals industry would seem advisable before an attempt is made to forecast the outlook for any particular unit of the industry. The "Permanente Prospectus" presents a wholly inadequate study of the situation. Until a new and detailed study is made, we believe it would be better for us not to come to a decision.

With these views in mind, Ferroggiaro advised the bank's president that he could not conscientiously recommend the credit proposal of Permanente, but he did suggest a credit line of $15,750,000 supported by a loan agreement and ratable stockholders' guarantees to provide adequate capital to the extent necessary to maintain current assets equal to current liabilities, including the entire bank loan. The bank agreed to this financing agreement principally because of the underlying guarantees from the Permanente stockholders who were also directors and who were successful and wealthy contractors.

On April 11 the Permanente management reported on the bank negotiations explaining the effect of the bank's requirement of stockholders' guarantees. The minutes recorded the following action:

> After considerable discourse, the representatives of all the stockholders, with the exception of Morrison-Knudsen Company, Inc., and Macdonald and Kahn, Inc., agreed to the arrangement, provided that as soon as there was a loss which indicated that the Current Assets were approaching the point where they might be reduced below the Current Liabilities, the stockholders should be called for a meeting and at that time should decide if the company should continue, and also permit any stockholders who did not want to go along with that arrangement to withdraw from the company.

The minutes also showed that the Morrison and Kahn interests not only failed to agree to the banking arrangements, but they offered to sell their Permanente stock (each held 456 shares, about 10%) to the corporation for $1,000 per share. A resolution accepting the offer and retiring the stock was adopted. These stockholders, associated in business enterprises with Kaiser since Boulder Dam, could not see the pot of gold at the foot of the aluminum rainbow and decided to get out of Permanente before their investment was lost. As Kaiser would later say:

> They thought it was very hazardous and they thought we could not compete with Alcoa, and we did not have the experience and all the reasons everybody gives that you should not do something.

Not long after that board meeting Utah Construction Co. had a change of heart. At the Permanente meeting of March 19, L.S. Corey, president of Utah, had voted in favor of entering the aluminum business. At a subsequent meeting of Utah's Board, the other directors compelled Corey to renege on his position. Trefethen described Permanente's reaction:

> We then submitted to all the stockholders their ratable proportion of the Utah Construction Company stock, and the only one that picked up any of it was the General Construction Company, and the two Kaiser companies therefore took up the balance.

This meant that even at that late hour, 30% of the normally bold risk-takers who had made their fortunes in the uncertain world of contracting had blinders on when it came to judging the aluminum industry. The three construction partners who stayed with Permanente—General Construction, Pacific Bridge, and J.T. Shea—would end up finding their investment in Permanente one of the most profitable ventures they ever entered into.

With everything having been shaken down, it was only a matter of working out all the legal documents with War Assets to transfer the leases on Trentwood and Mead to Permanente Metals Corporation. On May 14, Permanente was officially approved as lessee, and the approval of the Attorney General was obtained. It is doubtful if any company had ever before gotten into such a big and prospering industry in such a big way in such a short period of time.

It is worthy of note that the aluminum venture was launched exclusively with private capital. Kaiser's steel venture had required a government loan and the auto venture ultimately did, but Kaiser always looked to private capital when it was available. In all cases, he was always ready to risk his own fortune and reputation in any of his undertakings.

The terms for Trentwood and Mead were indeed attractive. The rental for the first year would amount to only $458,000. While no one contended this was a subsidy—no one else wanted to take on the job—and while it followed the very same formula used in government leases to Reynolds, it was still a very low figure for leasing a rolling mill that just a few years before had cost $47,630,000 to build and a smelter that had cost $22,270,000. Not a bad start for a company that would be grossing $3 billion a year thirty years later.

Did Kaiser really slay dragons in getting into aluminum or did he simply take advantage of the golden opportunity that no one else could seem to see? In pointing out how Kaiser stood alone at that time, FORTUNE magazine would write in 1951,

Rarely have so many wise men been so far off in their predictions.

Completing The Foundation

All well and good. Better than anyone could have expected. But the undergirding was lacking. Mead and Trentwood would be swinging loose in the wind without a supply of alumina, and alumina was a product processed from bauxite. So two more cornerstones had to be laid before the company would be solidly in business.

Up until that time everyone had been so busy with the start-up of the two aluminum plants no one had fully zeroed in on the problem of bauxite and alumina. The obvious facility to produce alumina was the plant at Baton Rouge, Louisiana, because it had been the source of alumina for Mead during the war. Built in 1942 and 1943 by Alcoa for the government, this $25 million plant had operated for only 18 months and had achieved only half of its 500,000 tons-per-year capacity before being shut down in mid-1944.

Dusty Rhoades, vice president and general manager, and Tom Ready, vice president and assistant general manager, took on that challenge. On one of their trips through the east in May 1946 they made it a point to swing past the Baton Rouge plant. While their first impression was that it was a "pile of rusting scrap iron," they soon found out different because it, too, was a new plant that had been "mothballed" by the government. By July, management had decided that negotiations should be opened up for the leasing of the plant. Once again, the government proved cooperative, and by August 16 a letter of intent was granted to Permanente, and the lease itself was signed in September on very favorable terms to the company. On a Sunday morning in mid-October bauxite liquor began coursing through the plant, and two months later the first alumina was produced.

Finding a source of bauxite was an entirely different matter. The government owned no bauxite deposits. Locating and developing a new mine would pose all kinds of uncertainties, delays, and expense, none of which the company could afford at that time. There was no choice but to turn to someone already mining bauxite, which clearly meant dealing with Alcoa, who had vast deposits of bauxite in Surinam on the northern shores of South America. Surinam had supplied bauxite to Baton Rouge during the war. It was a huge mine supplying other Alcoa requirements at that very time.

This called for the big guns to swing into action. Kaiser himself, accompanied by Trefethen, and Calhoun, went hat in hand to talk to Alcoa's primary owner and chairman, Arthur Vining Davis. They had been told Davis was a bit feisty, and they knew he held all the trump cards. They were at his mercy.

Recalls Trefethen:

> He was a small man. He sat behind his desk and listened to our story without cracking any kind of expression at all. We asked for a five-year contract. We didn't know what he was going to say. All of a sudden he stood up, and we thought he was going to ask us to leave. Instead, he said, 'I'd be delighted to. I'll have my people work it out with you.' Well, we were flabbergasted.

Two years later it became a little clearer why Davis had been so quick to offer Kaiser cooperation. Not only did he think it served Alcoa's long run purposes to help a competitor get established, but he seemed to be almost entranced by Kaiser. After two years of buying bauxite from Alcoa, Rhoades was now negotiating with them for a five-year extension of the contract. The terms had already been agreed upon and Rhoades thought it was a simple matter of getting it signed. But Kaiser wanted in on the act. And, interestingly, Davis wanted in on the act. As Ready reported:

> When Rhoades got to New York before going to see Alcoa, there was Mr. Kaiser saying he wanted to go to the meeting. Well, when they arrived at the meeting, sure enough Davis was there along with his people. Kaiser and Davis started talking about everything under the sun except signing the contract. Davis kept pumping him about some of his shipbuilding exploits, which of course, Kaiser enjoyed talking about. In turn, Kaiser was fascinated by Davis's success in building Alcoa and by all of his real estate ventures. All this time Dusty kept hoping the talking would stop so the contract could be signed. It came lunch time and the meeting broke up because Kaiser had another date. Davis said, 'I'll give you a call and we'll settle this.' But the afternoon wore on and Davis hadn't called, so Dusty was getting very itchy. Finally, late in the day the meeting was reconvened, and after some more story-telling by Kaiser and Davis the contract was finally signed. It seemed these two giants of industry were using the contract signing as an opportunity to learn more about each other—and having fun in the process.

Whatever the strategy, the gamesmanship ended up with a reliable source of bauxite. This meant that Kaiser had stepped into Alcoa's shoes all the way from the bauxite to the alumina plant to the smelter to the rolling mill. It was to become a fully balanced, fully integrated operation—almost a carbon copy of Alcoa itself.

It took imagination and boldness, all right, to make that plunge in 1946. Certainly, no other company was willing to do it. Still, Kaiser could hardly have been luckier. It was the only way he could have ever gotten into the aluminum business so quickly on such a large scale with so many favorable economics.

The "Boys" Take Over

It had been a one-man show up until now. One man's vision, one man's boldness, one man's reputation. Without him, his team of "boys" would never have done it, could never have done it.

But now the leases were signed on two modern and efficient aluminum plants, and on an alumina plant, and a source of bauxite contracted for. Start-up financing had been arranged. A board of directors with three powerful construction partners on it had been formed. The stage was set for the "boys" to take over. From this time forward they would do most of the work, most of the planning, most of the building of the business. If Henry Kaiser had suddenly died at that point in time, it is quite likely that the growth of Kaiser Aluminum would not have been too different from how it actually turned out.

Not that Kaiser's influence wouldn't be ever present for the next twenty-one years. His boldness at the outset created a "can-do" climate that would prevail at every stage of the company's forward progress. And his people knew he would be looking over their shoulders, needling them, encouraging them, supporting them. He would reserve for himself a lifetime license to come forward with one idea after another to help the company grow. He wasn't about to administer the company's affairs from day to day, but he wasn't about to cut off his steady flow of prodding.

And as Chairman of the Board of Directors he would always be available for the big decisions. When major new financing plans were presented to him, he would add his judgment to the proposals and then his weight in securing the funds. Whenever new plants were to be dedicated he was careful to play the leading role, giving that extra glamour to the occasion. But the main forward thrust would come from an eager band of young men who, working night and day to build careers for themselves, would keep coming up with new opportunities to expand the company.

The one man who would play the biggest role in that growth was Gene Trefethen, only 36 years old at the time. Already he was Executive Vice President of Kaiser's steel, cement, magnesium, gypsum, and sand and gravel companies. He had not been directly involved in the shipyard operations during the war, and he was not to play a major role in Kaiser-Frazer automobile manufacturing during the first years. However, even at his young age he was Kaiser's alter ego, his one indispensable assistant. It became an accepted fact by the employees, by the directors, and even by outsiders that securing Trefethen's approval was equivalent to getting Kaiser's approval. In all of American industry it would be hard, if not impossible, to find a boss who turned over so much responsibility—and so much trust—as Kaiser did to this young man, twenty-seven years his junior.

It was a clear choice who should become Vice President and General Manager. Donald A. (Dusty) Rhoades, based at Permanente, California, was currently general manager of the cement plant there, plus the two magnesium plants (Permanente and Manteca, California), a ferrosilicon plant at Permanente, and a seawater plant producing magnesia at Moss Landing, California. Ever since joining Kaiser in 1927 after graduating from the University of California, Dusty had acquired a wide range of skills in running plants and handling equipment, so he would find it easy to talk the language of the aluminum experts he soon would be hiring.

Trefethen was quick to sense that Dusty could benefit from having a right-hand man who could always see the big picture. The one who fitted that bill best was Tom Ready who had done an outstanding job for Trefethen in working out some difficult problems in Kaiser Steel. It would prove to be a wise choice because as Vice President and Assistant General Manager, Ready played an important role in every stage of the company's progress, finally succeeding Dusty as president in 1963.

Bert Inch was appointed Vice President of Sales, not because of any long experience in that field, but because his enthusiasm and energy were contagious. With his personality it wouldn't take long to rally a strong sales organization. Also, he would be the ideal one to blaze the trail in opening up the contacts with potential aluminum customers.

The financial duties were taken over by Don Browne, a long time Kaiser man who had worked closely with Trefethen on several projects. When Kaiser Steel was launched in 1942, Browne was made Administrative Manager.

Since aluminum was a whole new field for Kaiser, and since the possibilities for new products were almost unlimited, it was important to have an experienced person in charge of research. The logical choice for that responsibility was Ralph Knight who had been with Kaiser a long time and right then was working for Kaiser Engineers.

One other key executive has to be mentioned—Chad Calhoun, Kaiser's vice-president in Washington, D.C. Calhoun enjoyed remarkable rapport with Kaiser, as well as with Edgar and Gene. Few Washington representatives have ever been in steadier contact with their headquarters; few have ever had the influence on headquarters that Calhoun had. And few ever maintained friendlier and more respected contacts with high level government people than he did.

Here, then, was the top team to get Kaiser launched in the aluminum business:

	Age
Henry J. Kaiser	63
Gene Trefethen	36
Chad Calhoun	46
Dusty Rhoades	43
Tom Ready	36
Bert Inch	37
Don Browne	36
Ralph Knight	36

(Edgar Kaiser, 37, was totally involved in running the Willow Run, Michigan automobile plant of Kaiser-Frazer at that time.)

Rounding Out The Team

Because it was so essential to choose the right men to get the operations started, Dusty and his associates moved quickly to do the hiring themselves, not waiting to set up a personnel department to screen the candidates. Not often in American industry has a major company needed so many key men so fast, and not often has the supply of qualified people been so plentiful. The firm recruitment principle agreed upon by Dusty and Tom was: get the best people possible "and don't quibble about salary." As impressive as that may sound it was somewhat misleading, because Kaiser salaries throughout all the companies at that time were low as compared with industry standards, certainly low as compared with industries in the east. It, therefore, wouldn't be the starting salaries that would attract the new managers as much as it would be getting in on the ground floor of a new company with a bright new future where the top management believed in granting key people more freedom in handling their own jobs than most companies do.

The first important slot to be filled was superintendent of the Trentwood rolling mill. Typical of Kaiser's continuing good fortune, the man who had run that facility for Alcoa during the war, John Meek, was in the market for a job. He could have been cut from the Kaiser cloth he was so bold, so decisive, so optimistic—anything but meek. It didn't take long to agree on terms and one of the first things Dusty wanted to do was have Meek meet Kaiser, not only to let him feel he knew Kaiser personally, but at the same time to let Kaiser know what a gem of a manager Meek was.

Dusty recalled:

> I will never forget, Tom Ready and I took John over to Mr. Kaiser's office on Fifth Avenue in New York City. We kept telling John, 'Just don't be too optimistic about this thing. Mr. Kaiser never forgets anything. Don't stick your neck out and say you are going to do a lot of things. If they don't work out you are in trouble.' So we went into Mr. Kaiser's office there in New York. He was rocking back in his chair, smoking that cigar. He said, 'John, how long do you think it will be before you will have that rolling mill on a profitable basis?' John said, 'Mr. Kaiser, we will have it on a profitable basis the first month.' I almost fell through my chair, but actually that first month he turned a profit.

The next important step to take was to find a qualified works manager for the Mead smelter. Again, lady luck was a friend. As part of an eastern recruiting swing where Dusty lined up nineteen men, he and Ready were in Washington, D.C. Norman Krey, who had been Alcoa's works manager at their Massena, New York, smelter during the war, happened to be in Washington at the same time, and "just dropped in to the Kaiser office on the offhand chance there might be somebody there," remembers Ready. "The receptionist held onto him until we got back to meet him, and we hired him on the spot." Krey, much more soft-spoken than Meek, proved to be an excellent manager for the smelter. Years later he would be appointed as Kaiser's

Northwest representative because of his knowledge of the aluminum industry and the many important friendships he had struck up with the people of that area.

Meek and Krey, with all their industry contacts, could now play an important role in lining up personnel from around the country. Then there was in Spokane an additional reservoir of experienced men who had worked in the two plants during the war. "They had a foremens' club," explained Dusty, "and when the plants were shut down they continued to meet regularly. So that was a tremendous help to us."

Additionally, production men were taken from other Kaiser operations: magnesium, the shipyards, steel, cement. Other eager young men even came from various copper and brass companies, rounding out the hardhat team with an infusion of operating techniques proven in their industries but new to aluminum.

As the men from around the country began converging on Spokane in the spring of 1946 they had only one thought in mind—to get started as quickly as possible in their exciting new adventure, forgetting the past. And no one was more eager than Kaiser to see things get underway. His dreams of a bright future were foremost in his mind, with little regard to what had gone on before, because he seldom looked back.

Still, it must have had special meaning to him that all this was happening in Spokane, because exactly forty years earlier as a young man of 24 he had come west to make his fortune, and the first job he found was working in a hardware store in Spokane. In less than a year he had built his first home and brought his bride Bess across the continent to live with him. Their son Edgar was born in Spokane two years later, and this would remain their home until 1914—until Kaiser was ready to take wings in the rapidly burgeoning roadbuilding business.

Forty years earlier he had applied for the hardware job 13 times, finally having to start on a commission basis. Now his two plants in Spokane would be the fountainhead that would lead to tens of thousands of jobs around the country and later around the world.

Forty years would seem like an eternity to many people but not to Kaiser. He had been so busy during that time, and had accomplished so many outstanding things, the years had rushed by only too quickly. And the spark that had ignited his early ambitions had now turned into a prairie fire spreading in every direction. In 1906 he dreamed of a bright future; in 1946, having already proved that the opportunities in American were limitless, he was dreaming of an even brighter future.

"Those were the days of the Golden West" he told a Spokane audience in 1946, referring to the rugged turn-of-the-century era. "A land of fabulous opportunities. There was still the glamour of the frontier—and men still worked—and ventured in the spirit of the pioneers. It is my belief that there are even greater opportunities today and that the spirit of the pioneers still prevails."

Call it coincidence, call it destiny, there was something portentous in the fact that Spokane would still play such an important role in Kaiser's life though separated by forty years.

Starting up the Trentwood rolling mill was without doubt the easiest major new operation Kaiser had ever undertaken. The modern plant had just the year before been carefully mothballed under contract from the government and weekly standby maintenance had kept all the equipment in good working order.

The plant itself was enormous—52 acres of joined buildings under a single roof. It was so large that workers used battery-powered carts to get from one part of the plant to another. Yet it was only about 1/2 the size of the Willow Run automobile plant that Kaiser at that very same time was frantically converting from a bomber plant to an automobile assembly plant.

The government had built Trentwood for one purpose: to roll sheet for aircraft, so its capabilities were extremely limited. That meant immediate modification would be necessary to turn out the variety of aluminum sheets which could be sold in the peace-time market. Machinery was redesigned in the cold-rolling area, to produce common or soft alloys, which were in great demand for consumer goods, transportation, and building materials. Blanking processes were installed to stamp out circles to be sold to the pots and pans market which began to boom as returning vets married and households tried to catch up on such items unavailable during the war.

Corrugated roofing was another market "that is sure to be a winner," forecast Ready. Not only was aluminum far superior to galvanized steel, but the steel companies had begun diverting their metal away from that product into more profitable lines.

Contrary to the dire predictions a year earlier when the government was trying to sell the aluminum plants, the main problem was not finding a market but stepping up production to meet the skyrocketing demand. By the end of July, the first month of operation, Trentwood had exceeded its quota and by the end of six months was turning out more than its rated capacity. Operations were going so well that Harvey Black, one of the major owners, and Don Browne, controller, who had been asked by the other stockholders to visit Trentwood once a month to check results, stopped going after only six inspection tours.

The start-up of the Mead smelter also went forward very smoothly. In early April, Ready toured the plant with Krey. "How long do you estimate to get Mead into production?" Ready asked. Playing it on the safe side, Krey, a 19-year veteran of potline operations, said six months. "We can't last that long," countered Ready, let's make it three."

Mead was a mammoth installation, covering 234 acres with 101 structures, including 12 potroom buildings. Each potroom housed 64 pots, the containers in which primary aluminum is smelted. Two potrooms made a potline so Mead had 6, making it the second largest aluminum smelter in the country. It had a rating capacity of 216 million pounds of primary aluminum a year. Like Trentwood, it had been maintained in excellent condition since mid-1945.

But there was the problem of the silver bus bars. "In building a potroom," explained Jake Lindemuth, carbon plant superintendent working for Krey, "you need a lot of electrical conductor called bus bar and the metal normally used for bus bar was copper. However, during the war, copper was in very short supply, so the government decided to use silver, which is an excellent conductor of electricity. Hundreds of thousands of pounds of silver, carloads, were fabricated into bus bars."

When Kaiser leased Mead, the silver bus bars were still in place. "That's the first time I've ever seen $50 million in one pile," remembered Henry Kaiser as he gazed across the vast expanse of precious metal. "It looks nice."

As security officers stood guard the silver was removed and replaced with copper. "We were quite relieved," observed Lindemuth in a masterpiece of understatement, "when it finally got all cleared out of the plant." Several years later Mead's bus bars once again made news when copper was replaced with aluminum—an industry first.

Although Kaiser had not yet opened negotiations for leasing the alumina plant at Baton Rouge, Louisiana, there was enough alumina left in Mead's storage bins to get started and to keep a few potlines running for several months.

Mead won its race with time. On July 11, at about 11:30 p.m., potline number one "went on line." A small group of executives and department managers gathered in the plant cafeteria, then proceeded in a body to the potroom where a temporary buzzer, running back to the rectifier, was rigged up.

"It's not a very exciting show for the observer," remarked Lindemuth, recalling the event, "because you don't see anything happen except someone throws a switch. It takes a while for the potline to warm up and a little while for the metal to start collecting."

The Mead pots "baked in" for eight days, and at 9 a.m., July 19, pots 8, 16, 24 and 32 in Building Four of Line One were tapped and 57 aluminum pigs, weighing 50 pounds apiece, dropped from their molds. It was three months to the day from the start of reactivating the plants.

A Free And Easy Style

Kaiser was never one to stand on formality in his meetings. He was totally absorbed in getting at the heart of any matter, so he didn't concern himself with how the meeting should be started or where it should end. And he wanted everyone who could bring something to the discussion to be involved. He wanted each person to speak his own piece whether in agreement with the consensus or not. Experience had told him that out of a wide range of ideas the best solution would begin to emerge.

Of course, where he sat was always the head of the table, even if it was in Trefethen's or someone else's office. This wasn't something he imposed upon the others, it was simply their automatic response to his leadership and to his intense pursuit of any subject.

From earliest days he was always called "Mr. Kaiser" by his own people, even by Trefethen and most members of the boards of directors. When talking among themselves some of his closest associates like A.B. Ordway or Clay Bedford or Chad Calhoun would sometimes refer to him as "HJ," but seldom in Kaiser's presence. Calling him "Mr. Kaiser" never created a gulf between him and his people, never slowed anyone down in speaking out during meetings with him.

At every other level in the Kaiser companies all communications, oral or written, were on a first name basis. Trefethen always identified himself as Gene. Everyone who ever worked for him could expect to see the memos signed, "Gene," never E.E. Trefethen, Jr., although, of course, to most outsiders the more formal name would be used in letter writing. He always wanted people to call him by his first name, and those who didn't simply felt they weren't close enough to take that liberty.

It also helped to have someone heading up Kaiser Aluminum by the name of Dusty. How more folksy could you get? Nobody called him Mr. Rhoades. People throughout the company felt that somehow Dusty was their kind of guy, a person they could talk to on relatively equal terms. Whether they were located in Trentwood, Washington or Baton Rouge, Louisiana, they felt a little closer to headquarters because "Dusty" was a name they could feel at home with.

This open informality may not sound too different or significant in this day, but in Kaiser's time it was a departure from most business practices. It created a climate that helped make each person feel a little more at ease. And it became a way of business life in nearly all departments and at nearly all plants. Without any doubt it helped make employees more creative, more venturesome. It gave the Kaiser companies an extra edge in many situations.

It was certainly an important element in getting Kaiser Aluminum launched. The hundreds of people who were suddenly working for Kaiser never had to stand back in awe or fear of the home office or someone higher up. The opportunities were so many and the challenges so great it was essential to give everyone the authority and the backing to get things rolling.

The pattern of informality was set at the company headquarters, 1924 Broadway in Oakland. Kaiser had purchased this eleven-story building during the war, but no sooner had it been occupied than it was entirely too small for the exploding organizations. Within a short time Kaiser employees were spread around downtown Oakland in nine additional buildings.

Dusty Rhoades, Tom Ready, Don Browne, Bert Inch, and Ralph Knight each occupied a small office on the ninth floor, with Dusty and Tom sharing the same secretary, a customary practice for Kaiser executives. Communication was easy. "When we wanted to say something," Inch recalled, "we would just open the door and yell." It was even a standing joke that Trefethen on the eleventh floor didn't need a phone to talk to them, his natural voice was so booming.

Behind this informal method of operating was a tried and true principle from construction days: choose good men, give them the ball, and let them run with it. By delegating to his men almost complete responsibility, Kaiser motivated them consistently to outperform themselves. As Kaiser himself explained, "You find your key men by piling work on them. They say, 'I can't do any more,' and you say, 'Sure you can.' So you pile it on, and then they're doing more and more. Pretty soon you have men you can rely on absolutely. You have an organization that really can get things done."

As Kaiser saw it, there was no particular virtue in highly specialized knowledge. Unfamiliarity with aluminum, coupled with broad general experience promoted versatility. "There'd be a meeting called, and whoever was there would be in the meeting," recalls Ready who had the responsibility of overseeing the operation of the plants. "It didn't make any difference what your assignment was. Mr. Kaiser didn't want people saying, 'I don't know anything about that.' You were there and supposed to make your contribution, whether you knew that much about it or not. It was a very cohesive group."

Board meetings were equally unorthodox. It was not uncommon for Dusty to stop by Ready's office beforehand and simply ask, "What do you need in the way of capital funds?" Board members seldom demanded comprehensive back-up reports. There wasn't time to prepare them nor previous experience to measure them. It was a kind of seat-of-the-pants way of doing business, relying on the best judgment of some pretty hard-headed people.

"Dusty was a very direct boss who operated without flourish," Ready added, "and so the rest of us did too."

So did the plant managers. Dusty delegated virtually total responsibility for plant operations to the managers, setting each plant up as its own profit center. Each manager kept his own profit and loss statement and, unburdened by mountains of red tape, was free to try anything that would improve production and decrease costs. "Profits are what Oakland wants," was John Meek's primary guideline at Trentwood.

The system was a powerful builder of men. "It was a sink-or-swim situation," recalls Don Browne, "and quite a few people sank and disappeared. The ones who didn't soon took wings and began exercising initiative they had never before enjoyed working for anyone else." It was the birth of the flexible, tough, vibrant personality that has survived to this day.

It was not enough to turn management people loose to do their thing. They had to be given the tools to get things done, the most important of which was the telephone. Letter writing was kept to a minimum—"far too slow, get on the phone, work things out and get going" was the creed. Nobody was ever called on the carpet for the cost of his long distance calls. Results were the only yardstick management was interested in. It was not surprising therefore that by the late 1940's and throughout much of the 50's and 60's the Kaiser companies had the biggest phone bill in the Bay Area—larger than Standard Oil, Bank of America, and other long-established, major companies.

That soon became true of air travel. Kaiser believed that being on the scene could lead to quick decisions and quick action, so people at all locations were free to travel if they felt it would bring about the desired results. Again, management didn't waste time trying to monitor each other's travel expenses. As a consequence, for long periods of time the combined Kaiser companies became by far the largest users of airlines in the Bay Area.

Kaiser even believed that mobility in a given area was crucial to getting things done. He allowed management people—at many levels—to have a company car. While other companies reserved company cars only for the very top people, Kaiser looked upon a car as a tool of management. He had never been one to stint on giving his workers the best tools to get the job done and to him a company car was an indispensable management tool. While the salaries he paid were a bit lower than some companies, the freedoms he granted to management and the "perks" he gave them made them the envy of the whole Bay Area.

Another unique Kaiser attribute in those early days was open acceptance of trade unions. This was a shock to the men new to Kaiser, but it was an accepted way of life to those who had been with Kaiser any length of time. "Labor relations are no more than human relations," Kaiser reasoned. "People want to be treated like human beings. They are jealous of their dignity and self-respect. They resent either being neglected or exploited."

Bonneville Dam had been Kaiser's first all-union project, and from that time forward he maintained a sincere and open friendship with unions quite unparalleled in American industry. To him unions were not adversaries, they were "partners." His critics would blast him for being a pushover for unions, but anyone who studied the situation knew that Kaiser was counting on, and generally got, that little extra effort of productivity that other companies missed.

So it was that Kaiser didn't waste any time in signing up with unions to get started in the aluminum business. To the young, cash-hungry company it meant avoiding slow-downs or costly work stoppages. The union men and the plant managers, "captains of their ships," proved in the very first month the value of this maverick approach as Trentwood's production exceeded projections. Now the skepticism was turned in another direction: "What's going to happen to all this stuff?"

Selling The Stuff

It was a Friday night about midnight when Bert Inch received one of Henry Kaiser's famous late night phone calls. "Bert, we're in the aluminum business, and you're now the sales department." "What aluminum business?" was Inch's reply.

Inch didn't know anything about producing or selling aluminum. But he did know Kaiser. So there was no hemming or hawing. He had himself a big new job, one of many he had been asked to take on during his years with Kaiser.

By Monday he was flying to Trentwood to find out about the new products he was supposed to sell. He learned that aircraft companies would be prime prospects, "so I went out to try to sell an unfamiliar product to aircraft builders I didn't know. Luckily, my first sale was to Glenn L. Martin Co. in Baltimore for 1.5 million pounds of 245 alloy aluminum sheet. That same day Boeing called in an order direct, so the honor of being our first customer goes to them both."

Inch's main qualification was his enthusiasm and confidence—qualities Kaiser always looked for. "Breezy, solid, impatient," Sales Magazine described him. "Extremely energetic, restless and utterly fearless," added a plant superintendent from those early days. "He had no worry at all about going in and asking for an order even though he wasn't sure whether the company had the ability to make it or not."

Inch had his own sales creed:

> We have never yet told a customer we would ship an order that we didn't mean to ship when we said it. This business philosophy goes back 20 years to a statement Henry Kaiser made to me: 'Scare 'em to death, Bert; tell 'em the truth.' We haven't a single individual who doesn't know our principles and doesn't live up to them. I would pit them against any sales department and under any circumstances. I could take this gang tomorrow and sell cheese— and we'd sell a hell of a lot of cheese.

If Inch didn't know much about aluminum he had the Kaiser savvy to surround himself with men who did. Jerry Palmer, a long-time Alcoa veteran, was hired as assistant general sales manager, and John Menz came aboard from Reynolds.

The first district sales office was established in Oakland, followed shortly by offices in Los Angeles and Seattle (both home to major aircraft manufacturers), Detroit, Chicago, Kansas City and New York.

District sales managers, like plant supervisors, were given an unusual degree of autonomy. "If you had any knowledge about the business at all," quipped a member of the original Los Angeles sales force, "if you could read and write and were willing to put forth extra effort, it was pretty hard not to be promoted."

Discovering where and what the aluminum market was turned out to be not as difficult as had been expected. By June 1946, just three months after Kaiser had taken over the plants at Trentwood and Mead, the aluminum glut that economists had so gloomily predicted turned to shortage. Alcoa and Reynolds, deluged with orders, were turning away customers, and many fabricators were simply grateful that they were no longer at the mercy of a single supplier.

One move that helped position Kaiser itself solidly in the industry was the establishment in the spring of 1947 of a system of 24 warehouse distributors in key markets nationwide to handle less-than-carload orders. Within a year distributors accounted for about 25 percent of sales.

By the summer of 1947—just twelve months after production first got underway— Kaiser was a force to be reckoned with, producing 20 percent of the nation's primary aluminum, behind only Alcoa and Reynolds. First year figures were impressive:

primary aluminum production	59,802 tons
sale of aluminum products	78,311 tons
net sales	$45,418,000
net income	$ 5,338,000
number of employees	3,834

But that was only the beginning.

Leapfrogging Ahead

With such dramatic early success the aluminum team was all fired up—casting around for every conceivable production and sales opening that might help the company leapfrog ahead. They hit pay dirt in their own backyard at Tacoma, Washington, where they ran across a small two potline smelter built for the Government in 1942 by Olin Corporation, and idle since the war. It had a rated capacity of 41 million pounds of primary aluminum a year, as compared with the Mead plant and its 216 million pound capacity. By early February 1947 an agreement had been reached to buy the plant from the War Assets Administration on a ten-year installment plan for $3 million, thus becoming Permanente's first wholly-owned aluminum plant. By the fall of 1947 Tacoma was in production, giving Permanente a total annual primary aluminum capacity of 128,500 tons, almost 80 percent of the entire United States prewar capacity.

The next significant acquisition was in a different direction, involving facilities to produce aluminum foil. A somewhat out-of-date German foil mill was acquired for $203,000, dismantled, and shipped to Kaiser's moribund magnesium plant at Permanente, California. After a renovation costing $1.25 million, it became the first foil mill west of St. Louis, and launched the company into the manufacture of its first consumer product. Kaiser was fascinated by foil; it virtually became his "baby." Over the years when his men were complaining it was not profitable enough, Kaiser would spend a great deal of time trying to promote the market for foil and challenging his people to cut production costs.

Lady Luck continued to play in Permanente's favor. Early in 1948 the company ordered a rod and bar mill (which would produce electrical cable), planning to install it in the Trentwood plant. The nearby Bonneville Power Administration would provide a large and ready market. But before the mill could be delivered, another war surplus plant hit the market. Lying idle in Newark, Ohio, was a $23 million rod and bar mill, built in 1943 by Alcoa for the Defense Plant Corporation and operated for only two years by Alcoa. Recalls Tom Ready:

> It was a marvelous buy. Nobody wanted it. Reynolds (which had taken an option on it) had just given it back to the Government. It had this marvelous 38-inch breakdown mill in it, and we knew we could get into the forging stock business with that, and we'd already ordered the rod mill, so we moved that from our prospective Trentwood location to Newark.

The Newark plant was leased in September 1948 and with $4.5 million worth of additional equipment was producing aluminum rod by July 1949. "I've never seen any gang get into gear so fast and stay there," the plant superintendent proudly boasted. Initial operations were so successful Permanente bought the facility outright for another $4.5 million in June 1949.

(To get a focus on just how lucky Permanente was, it is only necessary to compare it with what was going on at the same time with its sister company, Kaiser Steel. To adjust to the postwar market, Kaiser Steel was having to design and construct, at postwar high costs, extensive new facilities of all kinds. By contrast, Permanente was picking up relatively new and efficient plants—a huge, modern rolling mill, two fine reduction plants, an alumina plant, and now a modern rod and bar mill—all at only a fraction of original cost which itself was far below what postwar costs would have been.)

Permanente's growth had become "explosive" as measured by normal American industrial expansion. Then came the unexpected war in North Korea in June of 1950 bringing on a military emergency that called for a crash program to greatly expand aluminum production for tanks, airplanes, and munitions. That was right up Kaiser's alley. He plunged into the challenge with the same exuberance he had shown nearly ten years earlier when he had started building ships for World War II. He proclaimed, "Kaiser Aluminum and Chemical Corporation definitely is prepared to do its part without delay toward meeting the aluminum needs which confront the nation."

Immediately the company announced a round of expansions in every phase of operations: a 30 percent increase in smelting capacity, a 25 percent increase in finishing capacity, and stepped up production of alumina at Baton Rouge. The main question was where to accomplish the increase in smelting capacity. As logical as it seemed to locate another plant in the northwest, the supply of power there was not unlimited. Indeed, reflecting the mood of certain groups in that area, Iron Age asked the question: "Is the Northwest aluminum industry a watt-sucking vampire absorbing power at the expense of other industries which would support more manhours of labor per kilowatt?"

The other logical location for a new smelting plant was in Louisiana, nearby the company's alumina plant at Baton Rouge, where there was a plentiful supply of natural gas at low costs making it possible to produce the vast amount of electrical power required in the manufacture of aluminum pig and ingot. To set the stage, the company purchased 280 acres at Chalmette, a few miles down river from New Orleans, and then successfully negotiated a favorable, long-term contract for natural gas. Armed with these two options—an expansion of the existing Mead plant or a whole new facility at Chalmette—company officials needed final government approval, so they met with Secretary of the Interior, Oscar Chapman. He concluded that the best interests of the country would be served by developing a new area for the production of aluminum. Company officials had already made up their minds in that direction, so it was an immediate "go" situation. It proved to be a very wise decision over the long run.

Constructing the Chalmette plant—in the usual Kaiser hurry-up timetable—was no piece of cake. Because the underground water was so close to the surface, heavy pilings—19,000 of them—were sunk in the Mississippi mud to support the plant. Against the advice of his construction crew, Kaiser demanded that the plant be completed for dedication in early December 1951. Frank Backman, Kaiser Engineers head of construction, panicked. Then suddenly he got a short breather when Kaiser phoned his friend the mayor of New Orleans, de Lesseps Morrison, to be sure he and the governor and other important officials would be available for the ceremony. Morrison pointed out that the dedication plans would conflict with events scheduled for the Tulane-LSU football game at Baton Rouge, one of the biggest celebrations of the year, which meant that no one important could be counted on to attend a plant dedication. That was something even Kaiser couldn't buck, so the date was set back till Tuesday, December 11.

The opening, recalls Jack Watson, who helped coordinate the event, "was a real extravaganza. It was our first plant in the early stages of our rapid expansion and development, and it was also the very beginning of the desire to be recognized, so we shot the works on it."

Five hundred leaders of government, military, business, finance, labor, and the media were flown to New Orleans on eight chartered airplanes. They were honored at a banquet, entertained by a Dixieland band, and toured through the plant, where they viewed elaborate exhibits showing how aluminum was made and used.

The big moment came when the first aluminum was to be poured. The guests overflowed the plant area, with special bleachers erected to accommodate the crowd. Kaiser made his opening remarks, followed by Defense Mobilizer, "Electric Charlie" Wilson who praised Kaiser's extraordinary contribution to the Korean war effort.

Then, as one news account put it, "a hushed silence crept over the big room." Kaiser and Wilson donned safety goggles, adjusted their asbestos gloves, and walked to a huge ladle hanging from an overhead track. The two men reached up, firmly gripped the ladle's handle, and pulled downward. Shiny molten metal trickled from the ladle into the molds beneath. During the long wait at the ceremony the metal had grown slightly cold in the crucible so it only trickled, it didn't gush, but still it was enough for Dusty Rhoades to break the silence: "There she goes."

Fortuitously, right at the same time Chalmette was being built, the company was able to lease a war surplus extrusion plant at Halethorpe, Maryland. Built in 1943 and operated during the war by Revere Copper and Brass Co., it had an initial capacity of 30 million pounds of billet and 12 million pounds of extrusions, vitally needed to fill military requirements for tens of thousands of new aircraft. (Here was another copper company that as late as 1951 had not caught the vision of aluminum's potential, but would by 1955.) A $4 million rehabilitation program began immediately, and on December 14, 1951, three days after Chalmette came on stream, the first Chalmette pigs were trundled to Halethorpe's doorstep. Shortly thereafter, that aluminum emerged as structural shapes for a B-36 bomber, and on January 9, 1952, 27 days after the metal had been poured, the parts were assembled onto a wing bulkhead at an aircraft plant in Fort Worth, Texas. Kaiser loved to challenge his "boys" to come through with crash programs like that.

The Chalmette plant cost $79 million to build and was completely privately financed. It was the first large-scale response to the war emergency and Kaiser Aluminum's first "green site" plant. It boosted the company's primary capacity by 80 percent and was financed by a $115 million loan, involving 8 banks and 23 insurance companies.

Two years earlier the company had negotiated a price of $36 million to buy the Trentwood, Mead, and Baton Rouge plants from the government—plants that had cost $95 million to build a few years earlier. During those two years the company had enjoyed a fortunate break—a new law had been passed by Congress authorizing payment to the government in the form of metal in lieu of cash. Kaiser made its down payment on the $36 million with 12,000 tons of aluminum pig and ingot, agreeing to pay the balance over the next 25 years. Now, thanks to the $115 million private loan, and thanks to strong earnings, the company was able to pay off the government loan in full, 23 years before its final due date.

A New Name

It was only a matter of time until the company would drop the name Permanente. By the late 1940's the name Kaiser was the one that had caught the imagination of the public, not Permanente. It was a time to capitalize on the magic of the Kaiser name for all the companies founded by Kaiser, allowing the success of each company to carry over to the sister companies.

It was no surprise therefore that in 1949 a change in name came about. What was a bit surprising was that the new name became Kaiser Aluminum and Chemical Corporation, reflecting the fact that the company was already breaking into the chemical business. More significantly, if not prophetic, it signalled a commitment of the company to plunge as full-scale as possible into the world of chemicals. That was one of the most far-seeing actions the company would take, because for the next thirty years chemical business of one kind or another would constitute a main source of income.

The seed for the chemical business had first been planted in 1941 when Permanente started up a seawater magnesia plant at Moss Landing, California, near Monterey, to provide the basic material from which the magnesium could be produced. This magnesia also proved to be an ideal refractory, so in 1943 Kaiser began producing his own refractory bricks for his cement-manufacturing kilns. By 1946 a high quality magnesia brick was being turned out for sale to outside companies, mostly steel producers.

From that small beginning, refractory output would continue to grow until in 1955 the company would decide to build a basic refractories plant in Columbiana, Ohio, in the midst of all the steel plants. Soon the refractory, Permanente 165, would become the most widely used proprietary hearth mix in the world for open hearth and electric arc steel furnaces.

With its reputation for high quality refractories now established, the company bought the Mexico Refractories Company of Mexico, Missouri, in 1959. This added four new plants to the Refractories Division plus a wholly-owned Canadian subsidiary.

The company's team of production people proved so resourceful in coming up with so many different chemicals, and the sales department was gaining such a strong reputation throughout the country it meant continued growth for the company. It must be acknowledged, however, that in the chemical division of the company, Kaiser personally was much less directly involved than in the aluminum end of the business. Nevertheless, he could always be counted on for strong support and that meant his "boys" had a continuing hunting license. Certainly it had been a wise decision when in 1949 the name Permanente was dropped in favor of the name Kaiser Aluminum and Chemical Corporation.

Rolling Along

Like the mighty Mississippi, on whose banks Kaiser now had two plants (soon to be three), the company found itself in a business that would just "keep rolling along." While there were temporary slowdowns in the growth of the aluminum market from time to time, the upward thrust kept carrying the company forward. There was a constant pressure to step up output at each plant as well as to modify facilities to turn out different forms of aluminum. Each new facility would call for another one to balance out the production capabilities. It was a happy combination—a surging market and a "go-go" management, fired up by Kaiser himself.

Although each year would see some kind of growth and diversification that would make most other companies envious, there were five major "epochs" during the twenty-one years that Kaiser guided the fortunes of his aluminum company from its beginning in 1946 until his death in 1967:

1. The purchase in 1946 of the original war surplus plants. Kaiser, almost single-handedly, accomplished this.

2. The construction of the huge Chalmette, Louisiana, reduction plant in 1951, followed by other new facilities in that area. This growth was not exclusively Kaiser's idea, but he provided the thrust for its accomplishment.

3. Development of Kaiser Aluminum's own bauxite mining operations in Jamaica to service its alumina plants in Baton Rouge and Gramercy, Louisiana. Kaiser pushed for this self-sufficiency from the start, but his "boys" located the bauxite deposits and then in furtherance of his industrial ideals brought into being one of the most enlightened mining operations anywhere in the world.

4. The construction of a large reduction plant and rolling mill in Ravenswood, West Virginia, beginning in 1954. Again, Kaiser's people would largely be behind this, but Kaiser's inspiration would embolden them.

5. Entrance into overseas aluminum production and marketing. The opportunities were popping up so rapidly and so unpredictably, Kaiser in Hawaii could not possibly keep ahead of them. His main contribution was in the encouragement he kept giving his people and in the magic of his name.

Did any of these "epochs" mean that Kaiser hadn't been keeping his hand on the tiller? Not in any way. It was a basic principle of Kaiser's that his "boys" should be turned loose to do more and more. No founder ever took more delight in seeing what his people could do on their own. He wasn't losing control, he was simply demonstrating his lifelong conviction that each person can rise above himself if given the proper freedom and the proper encouragement.

Jamaica Bauxite

As already described, Kaiser was able to get a quick start in the aluminum business because of the unstinting willingness of Arthur Vining Davis, Chairman of Alcoa, to sell bauxite ore from its Surinam, South America, mining operation. The quality was good, the price was fair, and the supply was reliable. The alumina plant at Baton Rouge was designed specifically to process the quality of ore coming from Surinam.

As cooperative as Alcoa was, however, it was clear the arrangement couldn't go on indefinitely, so in mid-1948 company geologists began explorations in Surinam near Alcoa's reserves and in Jamaica near Reynolds' deposits. Jamaica proved to be the answer mainly because of its proximity as compared with Surinam. By the latter half of 1950 the company had purchased 10,600 acres and optioned 8,000 more. The red, clay-like bauxite lay in relatively thin seams near the surface which made for economic open-pit mining, but it did require unprecedented acreage.

In November 1950 a preliminary mining organization was established, and work begun on a standard-gauge railroad to connect the inland mines with drying and storage facilities adjacent to Kaiser's ocean pier, likewise just getting underway. (There would be a flurry of tidying up to do in early April 1951 when word reached Jamaica that Kaiser would be honeymooning there following his April 10th wedding to the young nurse, Ale.)

While mining and transportation efforts in Jamaica were going full steam ahead, the operators of the alumina plant at Baton Rouge were sweating out how to modify facilities there to process the peculiar qualities of the Jamaican bauxite. It was no easy task, and it took more than two years to work out. Then there was the problem of transferring the new techniques to the plant itself. Construction and production went forward side by side.

The problems piled up to the point where Kaiser himself decided to visit the plant. This became the occasion for a big luncheon with management and employees where Kaiser addressed them. Lloyd Amos, manager of the Chalmette plant at that time, recalled the visit:

> I think most of them expected, quite logically that they were going to be fired, because the plant was in terrible shape. Instead of that he told them about some of his mistakes, like when he built the big conveyor to haul sand and gravel, and the banks all told him, 'You're going to go flat broke. This conveyor is never going to work.' He said, 'You know, the conveyor never

gave one minute's trouble, but we hadn't paid much attention to the gravel plant that was feeding it and that almost broke me.' And then he told about working on the underwater piers for the San Francisco Oakland Bay Bridge, and the many problems on that job.

He told these stories for quite awhile to this group in serious trouble. He said, 'You boys—you haven't made any worse mistakes or gotten into any worse trouble than I have.' He said, 'You look down at Chalmette. Chalmette had trouble for a long time. They're now out of it. They are running beautifully now; they've come out of it, and you boys, I can tell by talking to you and looking around, six months from now, you'll be out of it'—and they were. He had them where they would do anything for him. He had that ability. He always had that ability.

It was on this same visit to Baton Rouge that Kaiser held a press conference. True to form, he was bubbling over with optimism, with particular emphasis on the exciting prospects for "the tremendous market, export as well as import, right here in the Baton Rouge—New Orleans area." He said Kaiser Aluminum had already invested $200 million in the Chalmette and Baton Rouge plants resulting in wages and salaries of $22,500,000 a year. He went on:

This is 50 per cent more than the $15 million purchase price of the Louisiana Territory. That handful of men who made the Louisiana Purchase demonstrated that they had a vision. And, at that time, if anyone had thought that one little firm would invest 13 times as much in two plants as they did in the whole territory they would probably have been remanded to a mental institution.

Reflecting the start-up problems in Jamaica and the change over problems at Baton Rouge, it was not until early 1953 that the first full-scale shipments of bauxite were made. Thereafter, Jamaica entered a long period of continuous growth, providing the foundation for all the company's ever-expanding aluminum production. The volume of shipments became so great it was necessary to build a second Jamaican port on the other side of the island. At each port a beautiful recreation area was provided for the employees as well as the public. And at each port the most modern, sophisticated dust control facilities were installed at the very outset, which stood in sharp contrast to the billows of red dust which for a long time was emitted from the competitor's shiploading operations nearby.

To achieve the bauxite production required, Kaiser people embarked on a "partnership" with the Jamaican people. From the beginning, the patchwork collection of small landholdings had brought the company into intimate contact with the small farmers of Jamaica's interior. Here was another opportunity to bring into play Kaiser's concept of "partnership" in dealing with the Jamaican people. There was no single owner of the bauxite; instead the company had to pick up nearly 5,000 landholdings from farmers averaging less than 5 acres each. Kaiser built new homes for these farmers in resettlement areas where land was more fertile than the bauxite land, provided them with wells (up to then a rarity), community centers, and assistance and training in modern farming methods. Other projects included a technical training school, student scholarships, expansion of a local hospital and subsidization of an employee medical center, an investment loan company (operated by and for employees), and a new police station.

Simultaneously, a land reclamation program was launched to return mined-out land to a higher level of agricultural productivity than it had enjoyed before it was mined. It was a model program, the most thorough and widespread of its kind, and earned high praise from the Jamaican government. Reforestation (for every tree cut by Kaiser Bauxite, more than 1,000 were planted), rehabilitation of traditional crops, renewal of watersheds—all proceeded as part of the fundamental desire to be a good citizen and friend. It stands in sharp contrast to the ravaging of the countryside in the coal fields of Appalachia in the 1980's.

But the Kaiser belief in partnership went deeper than just working together to make money, to provide employment, to pay taxes and royalties, to build roads, harbors, and piers—although those alone were terribly important to the Jamaican economy. Trying to capture the true Kaiser spirit, the company's news magazine wrote:

> Partnership is the sum of a thousand kindnesses performed unthinkingly, without rationalization, without ulterior purpose. Partnership is doing things with people—and for them—because you would never think of doing otherwise.

Jamaica was indeed the foundation of the entire aluminum operation, but it also became a showcase of the high standards Kaiser always stood for. It should become a model for more American businesses.

Ravenswood, West Virginia

It was August 1954 and the Ravenswood "coffee club" that nominally ran the town of some 1,500 people was having a meeting. As one of the more progressive members put it, "Well, gentlemen, we've fished for a long time and hoped and prayed a lot too—we even had a few nibbles—but who'd ever thought we'd land a whale."

He was rejoicing that Kaiser Aluminum had just announced it would build a foil and sheet mill nearby, soon to be followed by an announcement that a huge reduction plant would also be built there. It was a bold and historic decision for Kaiser, entering into production in the very "backyard" of Alcoa and the "frontyard" of the mighty steel industry. (By that time was any steel company kicking itself for not having bid on the war surplus aluminum plants in 1946?) The decision was dictated by two major forces: (1) the surging demand for aluminum in the industrial east, and (2) a new recognition that coal, the supply of which was virtually unlimited in that area, could be an economic source for generating the power needed in the production of

294

aluminum.

Ravenswood had been selected after a careful study of over 40 locations up and down the Ohio River from Pittsburgh, Pennsylvania, to Cairo, Illinois. An important consideration was that alumina could be barged up the Mississippi and Ohio rivers from Baton Rouge (and soon, Gramercy, Louisiana) or shipped by rail at water-competitive rates.

This time the company was under no particular pressure to get into production overnight, so careful planning went into every phase of the construction. By now the management team itself had acquired the experience and expertise from operating comparable plants at its other locations. Also, remarkable breakthroughs in technology had occurred in the industry, and all of these advances could be incorporated in this totally new integrated operation.

The smelter was budgeted at $120 million with an initial capacity to produce 72,500 tons annually but with eventual potential of more than double that. The rolling mill would come in at more than $100 million, and with all the other related facilities the cost for the Ravenswood plant was announced at $280 million. It was to be the largest and most highly automated aluminum rolling mill in the world.

Under instructions from Kaiser himself, the management gave careful and continuing thought on how best to serve the interests of the tiny community the company had descended on. The prime objective was not to make it a "company" town. Instead, in keeping with his lifelong belief in the benefits of partnership Kaiser urged his people to put that principle into practice at Ravenswood with the main guidance coming from the local townspeople, and the company only providing the necessary backup support. "The community had to make its own decisions about what it wanted and where it wanted it to go. We intentionally set out on a program of participation rather than paternalism."

City planning consultants were brought in to design orderly housing construction, to be financed by local money and other private funds. The company built a 20-room elementary school which it leased to the town for $1.00 per year. "And we helped build a hospital, but only after the people voted a bond issue to help finance it."

When construction of the new Ravenswood facilities was far enough along to show the plant off to best advantage, it was agreed a gala dedication ceremony should be scheduled. It was Kaiser's lifelong pattern—let the world know of significant progress, pay tribute to the employees who made it possible, and tip your hat to the community where the operations would go forward. But for all the important non-residential guests who should be honored at the ceremony—customers, financial backers, Government officials—it required all kinds of special travel arrangements to get them to this out-of-the-way location.

One large contingent was to come from Washington, D.C. Kaiser and his son, Edgar, who was no longer tied up with running what remained of the automobile business, were in Washington, D.C., early that Sunday evening preparatory to flying in a company plane to Ravenswood. To Kaiser's dismay someone in his Washington office had invited a senator from West Virginia, whom he did not like, to come along on the plane. Kaiser said he wasn't going to get on the plane, he would have another plane take him. This brought consternation to his people who were standing around in little whisper groups in the Statler Hotel lobby trying to figure out what to do. Finally, Edgar prevailed on his father to get on the plane. The senator sat toward the back. Kaiser was careful to sit up front, where he could eat his box lunch alone.

As Jack Watson remembers:

It was in the summer, it was hot, there were a lot of thunderstorms, the plane was pitching and rolling, the senator got violently sick, throwing up several times. Mr. Kaiser went right on eating his box lunch. He had a cast iron stomach and he loved to eat. When he realized, however, how much the Senator was suffering he changed completely. He went back and sat down by the senator and did everything he could to console him. From that point on he couldn't have been more gracious to the senator.

The next day the press conference and civic luncheon were held in a big tent. Cards had been prepared posing probable questions and suggested answers, so Kaiser was ready to answer any question relating to the new plant. Watson continues:

The first reporter who stood up was a lady from a Wheeling, West Virginia, newspaper. She smiled and said, 'Mr. Kaiser, I'd like to ask you a question.' He smiled and said, 'What is it, young lady?' 'Mr. Kaiser, what ever happened to that jet-propelled dishwasher you were manufacturing ten years ago?' Kaiser's smile disappeared. That wasn't a subject listed on the cards. He glowered at his people. He certainly didn't want to start off an important event like this by explaining why his dishwasher business had failed. He made a short answer, then asked for the next question. It ended up a very glowing press conference. At the luncheon itself, Mr. Kaiser made another of his forward-looking, inspirational talks even tipping his hat to the senator. The people of West Virginia loved him."

It came as no surprise to people who knew him that Kaiser would end up building a warm, personal friendship with the Senator. Time and time again throughout his life Kaiser would go out of his way to make friends with someone after an initial misunderstanding.

Years later Kaiser would make one of the warmest friendships of his life with another West Virginia Senator, Jennings Randolph, who was first elected in 1958, several years after the Ravenswood dedication. Randolph often pointed to Kaiser as the kind of enlightened industrialist this country needs. On May 9, 1982, Randolph was a main speaker at a program in the Kaiser Center in Oakland honoring the memory of Kaiser, it being 100 years since his birth. He elaborated on his earlier description of Kaiser:

Henry Kaiser's business philosophy was unique. He felt that it is more important to build people than to build plants. His vision—and his faith in the people of West Virginia—has created a bright new chapter in our state's industrial history.

Growth Through Private Financing

"Debts are assets," Kaiser often openly declared. "It's through debts that you get the money to meet payrolls and buy the plants and equipment. Then you finish the job and pay off your debts and everybody is happy."

To him, borrowing money was a way of life. "It's not borrowing money that's the tough part of business," he would point out, "you can always find someone who wants to make money by lending to you. The tough part is finding the right persons to run the job to be sure you do make money."

All his life Kaiser had been a borrower. And all his life he paid back his loans to the satisfaction of the lenders. During the 1950's Fred Ferroggiaro, Chairman of the Board of Bank of America, would boast, "I've loaned Henry Kaiser so many hundreds of millions I can't remember the exact amount."

Now in 1948 with the demand for aluminum mushrooming, Kaiser and his construction partners were in need of capital to finance the expansion and diversification of facilities. To Kaiser it was a simple matter of borrowing the necessary funds. But to Gene Trefethen and his financial advisers the time had arrived "to go public." He explained:

> We needed to have a broad base for financing. When we told Mr. Kaiser we would have to sell 15 to 20 percent of the company for so much a share he was horrified. 'What are you giving away the business for?' he said. He understood why his automobile company, Kaiser-Frazer, had had to sell stock two and a half years before to get started, but now that his aluminum company was riding a booming market he just couldn't see giving away part of the ownership of the company when the money could come through borrowing. We tried to convince him this was in order to build some confidence in the securities market and to gain stockholders around the country who would become supporters as the company expanded.

As usual, Kaiser insisted on looking at the proposition from all angles. He made his own independent phone calls to his partners, to his lawyers, and to his financial advisers. His treasurer, Don Browne, recalls one of the phone calls:

> It was a Sunday afternoon. Mr. Kaiser said, 'Don, are you busy?' I said, 'Yes, Mr. Kaiser, I am. My daughter is having a birthday party and I have twenty little girls here.' He said, 'Well, I'll only be a minute,' and then he launched into why we should borrow money instead of selling stock. The party was over and the kids were all gone before I finally hung up.

In the end, Kaiser acquiesced in the sale of 600,000 shares of capital stock at $15 per share, bringing a little more than $8 million into the company's coffers and 3,500 new owners into the business. From that time forward, Kaiser became fully committed to keeping his directors and stockholders informed of every aspect of the company's progress. "This was one of his great traits," Trefethen pointed out. "He had a great sense of responsibility to his stockholders. He would never write off any disgruntled stockholders, and, of course, there were very few because the company kept doing so well. He always tried to get the consent and support of everyone involved whenever we took on something new."

Public ownership had benefits extending far beyond the money raised. Kaiser customers themselves could become stockholders, thereby having a reason to buy more aluminum from the company. Employees had the incentive to work harder once they became stockholders. And the Eastern money market tycoons who had their first taste of Kaiser public financing in handling the Kaiser-Frazer stock issues became aware of the glowing money-making outlook for this new aluminum company. "The problem," explained Chairman George Woods of The First Boston Corporation, which handled the issue along with Dean Witter, "had been to get these boys accepted in Eastern banking and industrial circles."

After that, Kaiser never hesitated to balance his borrowings with funds from the sale of stock. Because of its rapid growth, the aluminum company later had several new issues of stock. By 1967, the year Kaiser died, there were 18,000 common stockholders and 5,700 preferred stockholders. In the early 1950's Kaiser Steel Corporation and Kaiser Cement Corporation also went public, so along with Kaiser-Frazer stock, the Kaiser name had become well-known along Wall Street.

Kaiser The Advertiser

In the early construction days Kaiser was forever tinkering with equipment trying to increase its performance one way or another. He was not a trained mechanic, but he had an insatiable curiosity and a natural aptitude, so no one came up with more ideas on how to improve an operation than he did. If he had thought it important enough, and if he had had more time, he no doubt could have made some operating changes in every one of his aluminum plants.

But at this stage of his life (he was 74 in 1956), and considering the challenge of establishing the name Kaiser as a major force in the aluminum business, he directed whatever time he could devote to that company into promoting its image and increasing its sales (and coming up with new ideas). He had been frustrated in the automobile business by his inability to capture the minds of the public, so he was determined to do some imaginative things in aluminum. In autos, however, he had done just enough television advertising to become excited about its potential. Then in Hawaii he became further persuaded of the "halo effect" of publicity when he got an enthusiastic response from his appearance on a TV charity fund raiser.

The ideal product to promote was aluminum foil, because potentially every household in the United States could be a user. The thought intrigued Kaiser. It left all his other people cold, because they didn't look upon it as a moneymaker and because they couldn't see how Kaiser could penetrate the market in which Reynolds had maintained such a strong position for such a long time. Besides, they kept reminding each other, we have no experience or expertise in marketing a consumer product. Dusty, of all people, had no stomach for the idea, because his bag was in the operation of plants not in selling products. For the next several years he tried to stay as far away from advertising as possible, relying on his advertising director, Jack Watson, to handle the brunt of the dealings with Kaiser.

But Kaiser would not be thwarted. He wanted a winning, hour-long, Sunday night TV show. To kick this program off he decided it would be appropriate for him to appear in person with his upbeat message about aluminum and the future of America. It was a bit long and a bit heavy, but it was vintage Kaiser. Here's a portion of the script he presented:

> Good evening. You are watching the first of a new series of one-hour dramatic shows sponsored by Kaiser Aluminum.

> We know that if these programs serve you in making your lives more interesting and entertaining, you will want to see them each week.

> (Pause)

> What giant strides the American people have taken in the last 10 years! What a limitless future we have before us!

> Playing a vital role in providing people ever greater abundance in their daily lives is the light-weight and versatile metal...... ALUMINUM.

> Ten years ago, there were only 4,500 manufacturers using aluminum. Today, there are more than 24,000. Just think of it! More than 24,000 manufacturers producing new and better aluminum products, many of which were unheard of ten years ago. Aluminum has moved into endless uses...the building of homes, offices, stores, factories...better automobiles, better buses and planes and countless new products of aluminum foil.

> As I said, it is a limitless future I see before us....a future in which our best dreams and goals can be attained...so long as we base our plans and goals on serving people.

> In that future, Kaiser Aluminum and all the men and women of the 24,000 manufacturers using aluminum will play their part....All of us will be producing to serve your needs....to help bring you products made of aluminum that will make your lives more comfortable.

> It has been a privilege to talk with you. Thank you.

The show itself, a weekly live program called the Kaiser Aluminum Hour, highly touted by TV experts, premiered in July 1956 with a then-unknown star, Paul Newman. Watson vividly remembers that first show:

> Paul Newman played the role of a minority Jewish boy in a controversial situation which TV producers thought would stir audience interest. Kaiser didn't like it at all; he never liked anything controversial or violent. He had his family and all his relatives and top people glued to the TV set. Halfway through the show he phoned me expecting me to explain why the actors were doing this or saying that. It was the same nearly every week—he was the armchair expert, second-guessing everything about the show and hounding me. With Kaiser refusing to budge in his judgments, with the TV pros sticking to their guns, I was the fall guy, unable to keep either side happy. It finally got so bad Kaiser insisted that his son Edgar, Gene Trefethen and I join him in a meeting with Robert Sarnoff, Jr., head of NBC, to do something about the 39-week contract we had signed for several million dollars. The upshot was that the live shows were cancelled and some very innocuous Hollywood movies were substituted. This saved money but didn't boost the Neilson ratings.

Thereupon Kaiser rolled up his sleeves determined to find a winning TV show. For several days he sat by Watson's side and others in New York City looking at pilots of shows that had been produced but not sold to anyone. Watson recalls:

> We looked at them practically around the clock. It's funny when you see an endless stream of shows, it almost becomes a blur, trying to sort out the good from the bad. Finally, we had to give up, and Mr. Kaiser returned to Hawaii. Then something unexpected happened. Leonard Goldenson, Chairman of the Board of ABC, called Mr. Kaiser and told him he had seen a pilot film he thought Mr. Kaiser might be interested in. He wanted to show it right away, so he offered to bring it to Hawaii. I was called over to see it also. It was a film spoofing the heroics of the typical western movie. The lead was played by a total unknown, James Garner. Before the film was halfway through, Mr. Kaiser became excited about it because he fancied himself the maverick that was portrayed by Garner. He also approved the name 'Maverick' for the show. It was an education to see how quickly he could tell the show was going to be a good one.

The hour-long, Sunday night Maverick program was an instant success, eclipsing the stiff competition of two blockbusters, Ed Sullivan and Steve Allen. Kaiser was jubilant, convinced that he had established himself as a TV expert, that once again he had shown his "boys" he could still blaze new trails. In his enthusiasm he practically adopted Garner, hosting him and his friends many times at his Lake Tahoe home and in the Hawaiian Islands.

As popular as the Maverick show was, however, it didn't work a miracle in selling foil. Finally, Dusty couldn't remain silent any longer in the face of the large outlay for television with hardly any increase in sales to show for it. He dared to challenge Kaiser, "If you really insist on promoting foil, the best way to do it would be take all the money we're spending on television and hire the Western Union to hand deliver free a package of foil to every household in the United States."

Dusty even went so far as to hire an outside consultant to report on whether Kaiser should be in the household foil business. Once their study had been completed a management meeting was called with Kaiser in attendance. They made a very fancy, comprehensive flip chart presentation concluding with their recommendation that Kaiser should get out of the foil business. At that point the consultant said, "Are there any questions?" Kaiser was the one who spoke up. "Did you bother to find out why we are unable to sell it? Did you talk to the store owners who have foil on their shelves? Did you visit any of the store owners in Hawaii who are doing such a good job of selling it? How many housewives did you talk to to find out how well they know the Kaiser name? Did you point out to them the advantage of our "quilted" aluminum foil?" The questions went on and on.

That was too much for the consultant. He could see he was pursuing a lost cause. He said, "Well, we obviously did make one big mistake. We neglected to talk to the one person who knew the most about the subject—you, Mr. Kaiser."

When Dusty kept up his complaint about the expense of television advertising Kaiser drew his steel and cement companies in the act to help share the expenses, even though neither of those companies was marketing a consumer product.

With several of his companies involved, Kaiser then turned to his manager of public relations, Chan Young, to participate in the search for more effective advertising techniques. He also hired full-time a bright young TV specialist, Richard Block. He even retained two nationally known television and advertising experts, Pat Weaver, former president of NBC, and Mort Werner, later to become top programming officer for NBC. He gave free run of all the Kaiser organizations to them so that they could formulate the best possible promotional programs. His office, and his phone, were open to them at any time, day or night.

Chan Young felt that many of the people in the world of entertainment took advantage of Kaiser's wide-open friendliness. They "conned him," to use Young's words. One time when Young resisted the use of Eddie Albert in a TV commercial, Kaiser fired him. Again, it was the intervention of Trefethen that smoothed things over and kept Young on the team.

For a while Kaiser sponsored the TV show, Hong Kong, starring Rod Taylor, but that never matched the success of Maverick. For several years, however, Rod Taylor was a welcome part of all Kaiser's activities, both family and business. Along the way, Kaiser also became a warm friend of Lucille Ball, but nothing was ever finalized with her shows.

At one point, his TV team became excited about the pilot of a proposed new TV show, Dr. Kildare. They had it flown to Oakland immediately for a showing in the Kaiser Auditorium. They were stunned when Kaiser decided it was not for him because "it was a medical show and people don't want to be reminded of sickness while watching television in their homes." Undaunted, his experts came back with another pilot film, Ben Casey, thinking that its slightly different approach might be acceptable to Kaiser, but again he turned it down. Considering that those shows turned out to be such hits, Kaiser's grades as a TV expert would end up: "A" for Maverick, "C" for Hong Kong, and "F" for turning down Dr. Kildare and Ben Casey. People still wonder how Kaiser could have missed the boat on Dr. Kildare and Ben Casey, since he was so totally dedicated to his Kaiser Permanente Health Program.

While Kaiser had stood alone in championing both household foil and television advertising it was a different story when it came to magazine advertising. He didn't want any part of it. It was too lifeless for him. Nevertheless, his sales and advertising people, working with the ad agency, eventually convinced him there should be a series of double-spread ads in Life magazine promoting the sale of aluminum shades-creen. It was to be tied into a spring promotion with hardware dealers all over the country.

Right at that time Watson's wife was in the hospital expecting her first baby. He spent most of the night at the hospital before returning home for a few hours sleep. At daybreak the next morning he was about to leave home for the hospital when the phone rang. It was Kaiser calling from the Washington, D.C., airport, "I didn't like that ad. Why did you run it?" Kaiser barked. Watson didn't have the slightest idea what ad Kaiser was talking about so he had to say, "Which ad, Mr. Kaiser?" Thereupon Kaiser unloaded on him, "Well, this just confirms what I suspected. You don't even know what's going on in your own department. You don't know as much as I do."

Watson was worried about his wife because the baby was due any minute, but Kaiser didn't know that and kept badgering him, "Why in the world did you run that ad. It's no good." As Watson related:

> That made me mad, so I said, 'Mr. Kaiser how can you say its no good? A lot of people gave a lot of thought to it.' He came back at me, 'I took a survey on the airplane. I showed it to everybody and they all agreed with me that it is no good.' I said, 'Why isn't it any good?' 'Because it is all copy, no pictures, and the logotype with my name is much too small. You no doubt approved that ad, didn't you?' Well, I didn't approve every ad—we were having so many in so many different publications, but I wasn't going to tell him I hadn't approved it. So I said, 'Yes sir, I approved that ad.' 'Well, I think you exceeded your authority to spend that much money and I just don't think you should work for this company. I'm going to call Dusty and ask him to fire you.' So I said, 'Fine, Mr. Kaiser, but right now I've got to go.' This really upset him, 'What have you got to do that is more important than talk-

ing to me?' I told him, 'Mr. Kaiser, if I don't hurry, my first child is going to be born and I won't be there.' I told him about the problem my wife was having. Well, he changed instantly. He said, 'Oh, I'm so sorry. I was only trying to stimulate you. God bless you and your wife. You hurry to the hospital and I'll talk to you later.' Sure enough, he did call me back after the baby was born.

Because of Kaiser's fascination with advertising, and because the aluminum company was the one with the big budget, Kaiser kept harassing Watson, who remembers:

> If he got on the trail of something, he would dig in to the smallest detail. It would either scare us to death or stimulate us to come up with something a lot better. I ended up with the very dubious distinction—all the guys used to kid me about it—as a matter of fact, some of the guys still introduce me as, 'The guy most often fired by Mr. Kaiser.' On at least four or five occasions he said to me either, 'You're no longer working here,' or 'I'm going to call Dusty or Gene and tell them to fire you.' That's when I really came to recognize what a broad-gauge person Gene Trefethen was. After every threat Gene would call me at home, often at nine or ten o'clock, and say, 'I know what you're going through. But don't be worried. Mr. Kaiser is only trying to stimulate you. The time to worry is when he isn't paying any attention to you. As long as he is trying to work with you and change you, don't worry.'

Trefethen's unique ability to cope with Kaiser's every mood and every action came into play at the company's first big event in Spokane in connection with a major expansion of the Trentwood rolling mill. All the members of the Board of Directors were there; the Chamber of Commerce planned a huge community banquet for the evening honoring their "son," and that morning a big press conference was to be held.

Kaiser, Trefethen, Watson, and Bob Elliott, Kaiser's public relations man, had adjoining rooms at the Davenport Hotel with a large central living room. As usual, Kaiser had asked Elliott to think up all the questions the press might ask and then supply the answers. Each question and answer was put on a 3x5 card. Trefethen and Watson had looked over the questions and answers, but Elliott was in charge of the cards.

Early in the morning, too early for breakfast, Kaiser wanted to see the cards. Elliott couldn't find them and suggested that Watson might have them. Kaiser, still in his pajamas, knocked on Watson's door, then walked in, asking to see the cards. Watson recalls:

> I didn't have them. I wasn't supposed to, but Mr. Kaiser got real upset. He said, 'I came all the way up here to your plant. You're supposed to be in charge of these affairs, and now you've let me down again. I can't get any cooperation from you.' He turned around in a huff and left my room, but he

went out the wrong door. He found himself in the hall in his pajamas without a key at 6:30 in the morning.

By this time Trefethen was quietly listening and not intervening, so he opened the door to let Mr. Kaiser in. This little hallway episode, however, made Mr. Kaiser feistier than ever so he said to me, 'I'm just not going to go to the breakfast with the reporters. I'm not going to go there and be embarrassed. You organized it. You forgot the cards. Now you handle it.' I was appalled. Then Trefethen took me aside and said, 'Don't worry about it. Just get dressed. Go to the breakfast. Say a few words. We'll be there.' Sure enough by 8:00 a.m. the room was filled with the press. I was the loneliest guy in the world sitting there at the head table—no Mr. Kaiser alongside me, no Trefethen. About 10 minutes later in they came, Mr. Kaiser with a broad smile, happy as a clam. He took over and did a great job. But the point is, Trefethen always knew how to handle Mr. Kaiser.

And Now, The World

Kaiser Aluminum's first ten years had been a period of rapid growth seldom matched by any other company in any industry, nearly all of it taking place within the nation's borders. Except for the start, it was not a one-man show. True, Kaiser kept prodding his people, he kept coming up with ideas for possible new uses for aluminum, he spent a good deal of time trying to think up ways to promote the sale of aluminum, but his main contribution to the company's success was in stimulating his management team to be bold in their undertakings.

The next ten years would see equally remarkable growth for the company, but this time most of it would be happening overseas. And this time Kaiser's personal involvement would be even less. He was so absorbed in all the exciting projects he had underway in Hawaii that he simply didn't have the time to visit the foreign countries where aluminum opportunities were opening up.

Nevertheless the role he played at the start of the second ten years was crucial. Up until then Kaiser had a deep distrust of doing business in foreign countries. "What changed that," Edgar Kaiser said, "was Kaiser-Frazer." By 1954, the auto manufacturer, in its death throes, had begun to look overseas for some measure of salvation. Kaiser himself hit on the idea of taking his surplus automaking facilities to South America to start up an automobile business. He lead a whirlwind 20-day scouting trip through South America ending up by making an arrangement with Dictator Juan Peron to manufacture cars in Argentina. As Edgar later said:

The trip through South America changed my father's perspective about doing business overseas. He saw we could do business in countries without getting involved in paying off somebody. As long as you could do that, it was fine with him. It was another opportunity.

But it would take a sharp downturn in the domestic aluminum market to jolt management into the necessity of plunging big-time into world markets. That occurred in 1957 when metal began piling up in the plants and prices slid dangerously.

This was the time for the company's tiny export department to come forward. Since 1946 under the expert guidance of Ray Boyd the company had made enough foreign sales to demonstrate that profitable deals can be made overseas. Also, a lot of valuable contacts and experience had been built up.

Rhoades and Ready at first were skeptical. "Dusty, not sales oriented, was argumentative," recalls Boyd describing one of their several meetings to discuss the creation of an international sales division, "seemingly a little irritated because he was burdened with more urgent problems and showing also the well- known Kaiser antipathy to actually operating outside the U.S. But later that evening, while having dinner with Rhoades and Trefethen, I was immensely pleased to see Dusty turn to Trefethen and say, 'Gene, I think we ought to be in the international business' using my identical arguments."

Next it was essential to secure the approval of the Board of Directors. "Domestic prospects were gloomy," recalls Boyd, who made the presentation to the board, "and Dusty suggested I leave the directors with an up note about prospects." Boyd outlined the potential markets abroad, concluding, to the board's delight, "Other companies aren't alert to this yet, but we'd better move fast." This was the kind of talk Kaiser liked, and he let the board know it had his full backing. So now the door was open. The International Division had a hunting license good for any country in the world.

At that time, per capita annual consumption of aluminum in the U.S. was about 23 pounds. Overseas, the industrialized Free World countries used only 9 pounds. In underdeveloped South America, consumption was a mere 8/10 of a pound, and the entire balance of the Free World accounted for only 6.4 ounces per person per year. A more promising market would have been hard to find, but it would take a new kind of resourcefulness from individuals almost totally inexperienced in international affairs.

Sales people were dispatched to different countries to the extent they were available. They were not only to try to sell aluminum but to survey the markets so that sales programs could be mapped out. Boyd took Rhoades and Ready on an extended visit to Europe and they came away convinced the potential was great. Other representatives scoured South America, Africa and India looking for possibilities. At first, sales were picked up directly by these contacts, but soon agents were appointed to represent them. Later, sales offices were established in Zurich, London and Buenos Aires. By December 1960 export sales for that one month amounted to almost 30 million pounds and netted several million dollars. "It was our understanding," remarked Boyd, "that in that year the difference for Kaiser Aluminum was export sales."

. . . Early in these visits it became evident that the company should be looking at manufacturing opportunities in certain countries, not just trying to promote sales of American produced aluminum. The first acquisition was in Spain in 1958. There Kaiser bought into a complex of three plants including a smelter and a rolling mill.

. . . The next opportunity arose in India. This came about as the result of a suggestion by G. D. Birla, one of India's leading industrialists, to Edgar Kaiser, whom Birla knew from Kaiser Engineers dambuilding projects in his country. In August 1959 Kaiser joined with Birla in a partnership to build an integrated primary aluminum facility. At a cost of $30 million it was the largest single U.S. private investment in a venture with an Indian firm.

It was the kind of partnership that Kaiser liked, with Birla owning 73 percent and Kaiser 27 percent but providing most of the technical know-how. By 1962 the smelter was on stream and in two rounds of expansion over the next five years, output was increased to 79,000 metric tons. In 1965 a sheet and plate rolling mill was added, making it a very important factor in India's industrial economy.

. . . With the ink hardly dry on the contracts in India, the company was concluding a negotiation halfway around the globe in Argentina. The location was not a surprise; by 1959 Industrias Kaiser Argentina was the country's largest auto manufacturer. Although it started out to be a partnership with a leading non-ferrous metal fabricator, Kaiser soon bought the company out and then proceeded on its own to build a $7 million hot and cold rolling mill, with additional capacity in extrusions. Kaiser had also hoped to build a smelter in Argentina, but eventually the government awarded that to an Italian firm, so Kaiser had to be content in owning and operating the largest sheet and plate mill, the largest foil mill, and the largest extrusion plant in Argentina.

. . . In England on January 1, 1960, Kaiser paid $14 million for 50 percent of the assets of James Booth Aluminum, one of the country's largest aluminum fabricators. The immediate challenge was to modernize and expand an obsolete plant at Birmingham. A group of top production people from the U.S. went to England to work on the project. At the same time about 40 people from the mill were sent to America to learn how to run hot mills, cold mills, and shearing equipment. It was a model teamwork arrangement that soon turned Booth into a highly profitable organization.

. . . By November 1960 Kaiser was plunging into its biggest foreign partnership of all—a deal with Consolidated Zinc to establish a fully integrated aluminum complex in Australia and New Zealand. The $300 million investment would be shared equally by the two companies. Major projects included developing the massive Weipa bauxite reserves (largest in the world); construction of an alumina refinery at Weipa; expansion of an aluminum smelter in Bell Bay, Tasmania; construction of an electric generating system at Lakes Te Anau and Manapouri, in New Zealand, building another smelter at Bluff, New Zealand; and acquiring fabricating facilities. The new venture was called Commonwealth Aluminum Corporation, Ltd., Comalco for short. It proved to be Kaiser Aluminum's most successful overseas partnership, outpacing all other foreign aluminum ventures in Australia; growing to about half the size of each of its parents. When, in 1969, Comalco offered 10 percent of its stock to the Australian public for the first time, it was immediately oversubscribed.

. . . Probably Kaiser Aluminum's riskiest, and yet in time one of its most successful, ventures was Volta Aluminum Company, Ltd., in Ghana. What began as highly tentative discussions in 1958 between Edgar Kaiser and Ghana's Prime Minister Kwame Nkrumah, developed over years of delicate negotiations into a massive complex of a hydroelectric dam at Akosombo and a five-potline aluminum smelter at Tema. The dam, which began operating in 1966, and the reduction plant, VALCO—owned 90 percent by Kaiser—which came on stream in 1967, are now operated almost entirely by Ghanaians.

. . . By 1967, the year Henry Kaiser died, it could be said that the sun never set on the Kaiser Aluminum family. With almost two dozen enterprises in eighteen countries, one trade magazine observed that "Kaiser Aluminum could become a division of Kaiser Aluminum International." Sales offices in The Netherlands, Germany, France, Italy and England served all of the industrialized and developing areas of the Free World. "We don't merely think as an American company with extensions overseas," reflected Gene Trefethen in his office lined with clocks showing the different times around the world, "we think in terms of a global enterprise, a company of the world rather than of any one country."

Far As Human Eye Could See

One of Henry Kaiser's favorite poems, which he quoted often, was written by Alfred Lord Tennyson:

> For I looked into the future,
> Far as human eye could see,
> Saw the visions of the world,
> And the wonders that would be.

It took vision when Kaiser stood alone in January 1946 with the willingness to bid on two war-surplus aluminum plants in Spokane, Washington. But with all his imagination—with all his irrepressible optimism—there is no way he could possibly have envisioned, nor even dreamed about, "the wonders that would be" in the 21 years he would be around to participate in, and to see, the fantastic growth of his aluminum company. That growth in the United States alone would be so rapid, and would spread out in so many directions, as to totally defy any possibility of accurate prediction in 1946.

As to what lay ahead on the international front, there is not the slightest chance Kaiser gave any thought to that in 1946. Up until then his only overseas experience had been building a road in Cuba, and he developed a repugnance for foreign work because of all the harassment he went through in refusing to make any "under-the-table" payoffs—so he most certainly wouldn't been have been thinking about international markets. Further, he had so many big domestic ventures in full swing in 1946—steel, automobiles, cement, hospitals—there was simply no occasion to be dreaming about opportunities in aluminum around the world.

Of course, it really didn't matter that he couldn't accurately foretell how explosive the aluminum business would turn out to be. All that really mattered is that, like Tennyson, he did see "the visions of the world, and the wonders that would be" clearly enough to make the initial plunge. From that time forward he rode upward on one wave of good fortune after another—just as so many great American companies have been carried upward by economic forces to heights of success their founders could never have dreamed of.

The following figures showing Kaiser Aluminum's meteoric progress prior to his death in 1967 is both a testament to one man and his team of "boys" and to a surging economy, first domestic, then worldwide:

Year Ended	Net Sales (Millions)	Net Income (Millions)	Number of Employees	Number of Plants	
May 31, 1947	$ 45	$ 5	4,000	5	
May 31, 1950	$ 76	$11	5,000	11	
May 31, 1955	$268	$29	15,000	15	U.S.
				1	Abroad
Dec 31, 1960	$407	$23	19,000	29	U.S.
				2	Abroad
Dec 31, 1965	$642	$37	23,000	43	U.S.
				18	Abroad

Did Kaiser have a little bit of luck when he broke into the aluminum business? You bet he did. It was one of the luckiest things that ever happened to him in his more than sixty years of starting up his own businesses. But it was luck he deserved. It was luck he brought on himself. It was luck he was ready for.

By his great good fortune in the aluminum business, he was only demonstrating once more the wisdom behind the adage so many American businessmen have found to be true:

Success in business is largely a matter of luck. Funny thing, the harder I work and the greater chances I take, the more luck I seem to have.

CHAPTER 11

HAWAII CALLS

"We've got almost everything here—perfect climate, perfect people. These islands are going to become the vacation paradise of the world."

Setting course by the sun and stars, by ocean currents and swells, and by the flight of birds, Polynesian mariners sailed their double-hulled canoes 2,000 nautical miles across the South Pacific until finally reaching the cluster of jewels we now call Hawaii. For over 1,400 years they would have this paradise to themselves before "civilization" would come to bless them.

Then British Captain James Cook "discovered" the islands, landing at Kauai on January 20, 1778. "How shall we account for this nation spreading itself so far over this vast ocean?" he asked.

Forty-two years later, in 1820, Protestant missionaries from New England decided the Hawaiian natives needed to be "saved." The repressive form of Christianity they tried to inflict on the Hawaiians threatened to destroy the peaceful existence of the islanders. Fortunately, the innate beauty and goodness of the people, nurtured by the pleasant and salubrious climate, survived this well-intentioned intrusion.

But Hawaii was really discovered in December 1953. Or so Henry Kaiser would claim. That's when he took his young wife, Ale, to the islands for a vacation. Even though he had been to the islands twice before, he suddenly saw it through different eyes—a place to start a whole new life with his young wife, a golden opportunity to plunge personally into construction once again. In that light he had all the excitement of discovery that Captain Cook must have had; that the missionaries must have had; that, indeed, every first-time visitor to Hawaii instinctively has. Soon thereafter, Honolulu would be his principal base of operations, not only from which to direct an uninterrupted flurry of building activities in the islands but to maintain control over the rest of his world-wide interests. The question now facing the islanders would be: Could they survive the onslaught of Henry Kaiser?

Captain Cook was 51 years old when he first landed in Hawaii. Within a year after that, native priests acknowledged him as a God in a ceremony at Hikiau temple. Then a month later he was unexpectedly slain by the natives following a dispute.

Henry Kaiser was 71 when he "discovered" Hawaii in 1953. Over the next 14 years there would be many Hawaiians who would also consider him some kind of God because of the opportunities he provided them; there would be others whose acceptance of him would be tested in one dispute after another as he bulldozed his way not only over precious terrain but over peaceful mores of a tranquil society.

Inauspicious But Important First Visits

Kaiser's first visit to Hawaii in 1940 hadn't caused any stir among the islanders, nor had it aroused any dreams within him about how glorious it might be to live there. It was a combination holiday and business trip, as reported by Frank Taylor in the Saturday Evening Post, June 7, 1941:

> Only once has Kaiser been known to take a holiday trip for pure relaxation, although he and his family have traveled together constantly from his early paving days. A year ago Mrs. Kaiser persuaded him to take a vacation in Hawaii. On the ship there was nothing to make over, no telephone with which to call up somebody. Kaiser plunged into the business of seeing that everyone on shipboard was doing something all the time. Before they reached Honolulu, the other passengers were worn out. He himself was in fine fettle for the vacation, which he spent discovering that the Navy needed more concrete fortification, figuring out how it could be done in double-quick time, and engineering a new group that is now handling the work with cement from his Permanente mill. The discovery made it a perfect holiday for Kaiser.

That first trip proved to be very fortunate for Kaiser and for the country. He decided to install silos in Honolulu to handle bulk cement from his big new plant at Permanente, California, a short distance from the port of Redwood City where bulk ships could be loaded. After the bombing of Pearl Harbor, it was Kaiser's bulk cement that played the major role in rebuilding Navy installations both in Hawaii and in the South Pacific.

Kaiser's second trip to Hawaii—some ten years later—caused more of a ripple, because he had become well-known through his remarkable wartime shipbuilding record and because of all his burgeoning industries, including steel and aluminum production as well as automobile manufacturing, and his rapidly-growing hospital program. Reporters sought him out for his views on the economy in general and the outlook for Hawaii in particular. Here is an excerpt from a newspaper article written by Hugh Lytle April 6, 1950:

> Kaiser is not expected to plunge into great enterprises here to change the

face of the Territory as he did literally in California and elsewhere. His chief interest here is his own Permanente company. But he cannot keep his hands and his mind off the workings of gigantic machinery when he sees it. If he had time he undoubtedly would like to buy a plantation and show the world how it should be run, but there are the 44 other plants and that small car which is about to go into production, to prevent or delay such an experiment.

At a recent meeting of the Hilo Kiwanis Club Kaiser, invited on five minutes notice to speak, asked the club's motto. Told it was 'We Build,' he went on from there, because that is Kaiser's motto too. Members of the club said he left them with enthusiasm and confidence in their own abilities and in their own enterprises. The reason is that some of Kaiser's energy rubs off on everything he touches, but his own supply never runs out.

'There aren't any problems,' he insists, 'just opportunities.'

If there were more of the caliber of that amazing man, even Russia would be no problem, merely an opportunity.

The True "Discovery"

Now it was December 1953, and Kaiser was in Hawaii with his wife, Ale, on a "fun" vacation. With her youthful zest for life, she immediately fell in love with Hawaii and everything about it. Practically every evening after dinner, the two of them would be found at Don The Beachcomber's night club at the International Market Place listening to the talented—and handsome—baritone, Alfred Apaka. Several nights they danced—Kaiser at 250 lbs., Ale, willowy and tall—under the stars at the Royal Hawaiian Hotel in the balmy tradewinds. During the daytime they enjoyed the thrill of catamaran sailboat trips off the shore of Honolulu where they could take in the spectacular views. It was during these exciting times that the romance of the islands, and the romance of their marriage, seized them, and they knew this was to be their future home.

As luck would have it, while he was on this trip, someone hit on the idea that it might be helpful to have Kaiser take part in a TV marathon auction for the benefit of the Kapiolani Hospital Fund Campaign. What a golden opportunity to get known by the islanders! He immediately accepted, and ended up doing a bang-up job. Within twenty-four hours, he received enthusiastic reports from so many sources, he became sold on the power of Hawaiian TV as well as the press in general.

It was no surprise, therefore, that on Kaiser's very next trip to the islands, two months later, he would buy a home—not just an ordinary residence but one that would typify Hawaiian architecture at its best and one that would have high visibility in the heart of Honolulu. With front page banner headlines proclaiming, "Henry J. Kaiser Buys Kahala Home for $187,500," the Honolulu Star Bulletin ran this story Monday, February 22, 1954:

Henry J. Kaiser, West Coast industrialist, has purchased the Kahala beach home of Mrs. Margaret Baker Emerson for $187,500, it was announced today. The property at 4607 Kahala Avenue, was built in 1951 by Mrs. Emerson and covers one and one quarter acres of Bishop Estate leasehold property with a 150 foot frontage. The Hawaiian styled home, designed by Vladimar Ossipoff, was purchased completely furnished. The main house has four bedrooms, four bathrooms, living room, lanai, sitting room and three servants rooms. Also on the property is a three-bedroom, two-bathroom guest cottage and a three-car garage. Kaiser said he doesn't plan to make his new home his permanent residence. 'Mrs. Kaiser and I would like to, but the continuing press of our operations on the Mainland will require me to maintain my legal residence in California. However, with the continuing expansions of our operations here, we plan to be here considerably more than in the past . . . at least we will be back here every bit of the time we possibly can. For years I have loved your lovely islands and admired the warm hospitality of your people. More importantly, I have admired your faith in the progressive future of both your Islands and America.'

It also came as no surprise, at least to those who knew him, that Kaiser would seek to gain early notoriety by sponsoring a public essay contest. His creed had always been "Faith In The Future," so why not throw out this challenge to the people in Hawaii, with attractive prizes for the winners?

He discussed his ideas with Vance Fawcett, head of Vance Fawcett Associates, advertising and public relations counsel. Fawcett had been in charge of public relations for Kaiser in Oakland for several years, but had left a few years earlier under pressure from Kaiser himself. Because of a major ownership position in a Hawaiian stevedoring company which his wife held, Fawcett and his family moved to Honolulu shortly after he left Kaiser. With their stevedoring connections, and with Fawcett's public relations expertise, they soon became highly regarded in Honolulu business and social circles. It didn't bother Kaiser that he had been involved in Fawcett's departure from Oakland. The fact was that Fawcett could open countless doors for him in Hawaii, so Kaiser was eager to appoint Vance Fawcett Associates as advertising counsel for the Kaiser companies in Hawaii. Over the years it would turn out to be a very harmonious and productive relationship.

Just before buying his Honolulu home, Kaiser kicked off his contest with a radio address. He expressed his own optimism, then invited the people of Hawaii to outline in writing why they could see a great future ahead. Always one to seek a benefit for one of his companies, he had talked his top aluminum people in Oakland into financing the contest as a means of promoting sale of Kaiser household aluminum foil.

The timing was ideal—President Eisenhower had just come out with a message to the Congress and the nation stressing that confidence in the future could give a much-needed boost to the economy. Kaiser wrote him a long, supportive letter pointing out in particular the kinds of things his companies were doing. In this letter, dated February 27, 1954, he said:

> Believing with you that this is a time for our people to demonstrate faith—faith in country, in God, in themselves and the future, we have conducted a test public opinion campaign among the people of Hawaii to bring out their thinking on the challenging question, 'Why I have faith in the future.' It is stimulating to discover anew how the people respond to faith instead of fear.

Kaiser had mentioned returning to the Islands in a couple of months, but he couldn't wait. Before the end of March he held a fancy garden party at his Kahala estate for more than 150 guests. Hawaiian torches were everywhere in the yard, entertainment was provided throughout the evening and cocktails and dinner were served. It was a gala affair to show off the home and to make friends with as many Hawaiian leaders as possible—most of whom had been suggested by Fawcett. Only two Kaiser couples were included—Dr. and Mrs. Sidney Garfield and Mr. and Mrs. Tod Inch. Dr. Garfield was head of the Kaiser Health Program and was married to Ale Kaiser's sister, Helen. Inch was a Kaiser lawyer involved in the purchase of the Kahala home.

Two days later Kaiser made another splash that caught the attention of the press. In an appropriate Hawaiian ceremony arranged by Fawcett on Waikiki Beach in front of the Royal Hawaiian Hotel, he launched his new aluminum catamaran, "Ale-Ale Kai," sporting a salmon colored sail. It was only Waikiki's third catamaran and soon became a symbol of Kaiser's commitment to Hawaii.

Two other activities were part of Kaiser's plan to get off to a running start. The first was his willingness to be interviewed by the press at the drop of a hat. Here are excerpts from just one such article by Jack Burby on the front page of the <u>Honolulu Advertiser</u> for February 25, 1954:

> Kaiser is a friendly, eager and candid man who operates sometimes on hunch and always on optimism, and he is as overwhelming with his grand-scale thinking as a bulldozer. When he looks you in the eye and says Hawaii could play host to a million and a half tourists a year if it had enough hotels, you can practically see them pouring onto the beaches. And he has started producing a motion picture built around the theme that Hawaii is both an American community with paved streets and a land of moonlight and palms. As he warmed up to the interview, his toes began dancing a little on the carpet, and soon he was on the edge of his seat, talking about his favorite subjects—production and faith in the future.

As mentioned in the article, the other action Kaiser took to gain attention was to begin production of a movie, "The Hawaiian Incident." It featured his new automobiles and a Kaiser-made military jeep that could operate completely submerged under water. Hawaii's most popular singer, Alfred Apaka, and dancer Queenie Ventura, were starred in the movie which climaxed in a daring rescue in Hanauma Bay of a damsel "in distress and threatened by sharks." She was plucked off the reef by a marine driving the submersible jeep. To celebrate, they all ended up having a Luau on the beach with a gorgeous sunset behind the sea in the background, with Apaka singing the Hawaiian Wedding Song while Queenie danced.

It was a low-budget film produced in a hurry by Kaiser's assistant, Handy Hancock, but even with its corny plot and an over-abundance of Kaiser cars in the background, it ended up getting extensive showings thanks to a push by the Kaiser organization, together with United Air Lines.

Kaiser later had Hancock produce another film, this one aimed at promoting the sale of Kaiser aluminum. The title was a little tricky—"Munimula Eivom," which is "Aluminum Movie" spelled backward. It featured aluminum catamarans, but it was not a captivating movie, nor was it promoted vigorously. After these two ventures into the amateur film-producing business, Kaiser decided there were other, more effective avenues for promoting his Hawaiian projects and his industrial products.

Kaiser's Challenge

Consider the challenge facing this 71-year-old man. No one had invited him to Hawaii. He had no roots there. He owned no property. Most of the people really knew very little about him. Those who did, including the Hawaiian establishment—the Big Five—were less than enthusiastic about someone who might disturb the business balance they had taken so long in structuring, especially someone who was known for being very liberal in his dealings with labor.

What's more, his superb management team at Oakland headquarters couldn't be counted on to help him very much. All his life he had blazed the trail into new ventures, then turned the business over to his "boys." Now the management team had its hands full running the wide variety of major businesses that were already in full swing. Further, none of the Oakland officials had any interest in, or real expertise in, serving vacation land activities. As a matter of fact, many of them thought the boss was once again going too far, that he was likely to suffer another fiasco like the automobile business.

Great. Just the way Kaiser wanted it—essentially his own show. This time he would be his own market survey expert, engineer, construction stiff, real estate salesman, public relations manager. Sure, he would have to turn to Oakland for a healthy supply of money to get things started. He would also need some top-level engineering help from time to time. And in Honolulu he would have to form a new team of architects, engineers, builders, and promoters—although he hoped to have one experienced construction partner to work with—Fritz Burns. At the end of the war in 1945, Kaiser and Burns first teamed up to build West Coast homes primarily in Southern California. By the time Kaiser became enraptured with Hawaii, this firm, Kaiser Community Homes, had built more than 10,000 homes, so Kaiser had full confidence in Burns' business abilities.

In keeping with his lifetime creed, "Find a need and fill it," Kaiser started by asking as many people as possible what Hawaii needed most. At that time there were about a half million people living in the islands with half of them in Honolulu itself. The main businesses were related to sugar, pineapple, food processing, and some tourism.

Kaiser didn't ask the powers that be what Hawaii needed. He asked waiters, taxi-cab drivers, hotel workers, day laborers of all kinds. The one answer he kept getting was "jobs." There were many people who, having jobs, were still being paid low wages. The ups and downs of the tourist industry plagued them—there were only two seasons, and short ones at that, winter and summer. In between, there were heavy lay-offs. Likewise, agriculture was very seasonal. Carpenters, for example, would take a job in a cabinet shop for 75¢ per hour rather than work in the field for $1.25 because the shop was more permanent and the field worker might be busy for three or four months and then have little else to do for the rest of the year.

Kaiser thought he might get a foothold by shipping aluminum, then his newest and most promising industrial product, to Hawaii where he could set up fabricating plants and hire workers to make it into finished form for marketing in the United States and even to some Pacific countries. However, the economic forecasts didn't prove out, after shipping the primary aluminum over and the fabricated products back. In any event it was only tinker toy stuff. It didn't offer the prospect of very many new jobs; it wasn't something that would contribute significantly to the Hawaiian economy. It couldn't keep Kaiser happy for long.

Kaiser thought he saw the opening he was looking for when a large piece of property at the edge of Kaimuki owned by the Salvation Army was put up for sale. He immediately called for his partner, Fritz Burns, to come running. In order to envision the potential development of the Salvation Army parcel they drove to a promontory which gave them a panoramic view. Spread out below them was the newly created Waialae-Kahala subdivision just being marketed by Bishop Estate. In the far distance the extinct volcanoes, Koko Head and Koko Crater, were clearly visible but no one gave them much thought because they were so "far out." That area was virgin except for the new beach community of Portlock, plus a large swampy pond known as Kuapa Pond where mullet was commercially raised, and a few truck and flower farms as well as some squatters and auto junkyards.

Kaiser tried his best to arouse Burns' interest in the possibilities. He described how as a young photographer in Florida around the turn of the century he had failed to take advantage of the land boom everyone was talking about. Then in the depression years of the 1930's when he was involved in building the Los Angeles Aqueduct in the vicinity of Palm springs he didn't catch the vision of what a magnificent resort area that could become. "This time, I don't intend to miss the real estate boat," Kaiser told Burns.

Surprisingly for two dreamers and doers, they decided not to bid on the Salvation Army property. Perhaps Burns wasn't quite ready to get involved in Hawaiian home building. Perhaps he thought the opportunities were better in Southern California. But at least he had gained enough of a feel for the area that not much later he would be ready to join Kaiser in a different form of Hawaiian real estate development. As for Kaiser, this decision was only a temporary delay in his search for the right kind of opportunity.

It was a chance conversation with a Pan American airways official that finally gave Kaiser the idea he had been casting around for. The official quoted a statistic that for each day a tourist dollar was spent in Hawaii it would maintain three local families for a day as it fanned through the Hawaiian economy. Kaiser knew how important tourism could be, but this one statistic alone brought home to him just how important it really could be. Instantly, Kaiser seized on the idea. There was the business that would help Hawaii the most, the kind of business that he could break into! Other than agricultural products, Hawaii had no commercially adequate raw materials, no minerals, no forests, no power, but it did have the one resource more valuable than all else, the best climate in the world. Kaiser's mind was made up—he was now determined to come forward with the very best possible tourist attraction.

It didn't take Kaiser long to make his first commercial acquisition. In a letter to Jack Lessman in New York City, Kaiser wrote on April 13, 1954:

> I am back again from the Islands and returning there again tonight. Fritz Burns is meeting me there together with his architect. We bought the John Ena property (for $750,000) and there is a great deal to do with it—about eight acres which has a 500 foot frontage on the beach. I told you before that Fritz Burns and his crew have the responsibility for this problem. They will eventually determine the kind of project that should be developed there.

This was at best minor league as far as Kaiser was concerned. It certainly wouldn't fulfill his dreams of doing something on a grand scale. Here's the kind of thing he was thinking about, as described in that same letter to Lessman:

> In the meantime, I shall be working on the question of seeing what can be done about securing an option on the so-called Queen Emma property which involves 18 acres in the heart of Honolulu. This property includes the Outrigger Club, which has a lease for 9 years, the Liberty House, Don the Beachcomber, and all the area up and down Kalakaua Avenue for a distance of 500 feet on the Beachcomber side. I have in mind this is really the hotel site, and it could be handled with a 150 foot over pass over Kalakaua Avenue with hotels and business buildings built on the ground floor overpass level with stores underneath. Whether we can secure the property on some reasonable basis is not clear to me at this time.

Nothing ever came from this proposal, because Kaiser was not able to negotiate the kind of terms he thought he could live with. This didn't bother him, since he was sure he would eventually find the opportunity he was looking for.

By late August 1954, Burns announced that the John Ena property would be developed with apartment-hotel buildings offering a total of around 200 rooms, grouped around several swimming pools. He pointed out that his and Kaiser's interest in Honolulu was not limited to this particular property, "but at the moment we think our time is better spent on plans for the improvement of that property, with any additional acquisitions of secondary importance right now."

In a way, Burns was stalling for time in behalf of Kaiser. At almost the identical time Burns was making his announcement, Kaiser had initiated negotiations with Juan Peron, Argentina's dictator, aimed at establishing an automobile assembly plant in that country. This was such an important move for Kaiser-Frazer it required Kaiser's personal handling. As a result, he made four trips to Argentina, and other South American countries, in August, September and October 1954. Not just the time involved in making those trips, but the extreme importance of watching over all the terms and conditions in getting the new automobile company launched, placed heavy demands on Kaiser, so he could not be in Hawaii as much as he wanted to.

It was quite incredible, therefore, that shortly after Kaiser returned to Hawaii after a long absence, the Honolulu Advertiser could run this front-page story:

Kaiser Suggests Plan For $50 Million Waikiki Island

Henry J. Kaiser yesterday asked for, and got, general support for a plan to create a 65-acre island off Ala Moana and turn it into a $50 million tourist resort. Backing, 'in principle,' came from the Tourist Industry committee of the Honolulu Chamber of Commerce, after it met with Mr. Kaiser in a special session. Halfway through the meeting, Mr. Kaiser unwrapped architects' sketches of his project, still scarcely out of the idea stage, and passed them around for the first time. After hearing details of the project, members termed it 'challenging,' 'exciting,' and 'terrific,' and voted to ask the chamber's board of directors to make a thorough study of it. The Ala Moana project, as Mr. Kaiser sees it, could be built atop the reef and named 'Coral Island.' The architects' conception of the finished product held hotels, a shopping center, apartments, an auditorium, a parking lot. A strip of sheltered water, spanned by a covered bridge, and measuring 600 feet by one mile, would separate the island from Ala Moana park. Mr. Kaiser said his idea was born one day while he was visiting George Houghtailing, executive director of the City Planning Commission, who pulled out an old blueprint creating an island off Waikiki.

Along with this story, a six-column picture was published exposing all the sordid commercialism of this proposed manmade island.

The concept was, of course, never approved by the Chamber board of directors, and even if it had been it would never have gotten all the governmental approvals that would have been required. It was really a monstrous idea—to put up a huge island, totally commercialized, blocking the free ocean view of the people on Waikiki beach, and destroying the flow of the waves that meant so much to the swimmers, the surfers, and the outriggers. If it had gone forward, it would have meant that all involved in it—and Kaiser in particular—would have been cursed forever.

Lucky for Kaiser that it died a quick death. Interesting, too, that it was never really held against him. It was enough of a daring idea that Kaiser was accepted as a person with imagination, soon to do something big for Hawaii. For his part Kaiser didn't let one foolish idea, adopted in a hurry, interfere with his search for the right opening. All his life he had been free to champion far-out ideas. If they clicked, he was hailed as a hero. If they did not, they were soon forgotten in the on-rush of his other ideas that did prove practical.

The opening Kaiser had really been looking for came just in time to help people forget the "Waikiki Island" fantasy. As luck would have it, a run-down, termite-ridden collection of cottages known as the Niumalu Hotel, located in a slum area at the extreme edge of Waikiki, far from the center of things, came on the market. Kaiser looked beyond the shoddy condition of the property and envisioned a flourishing tropical hotel with modern accommodations, lush landscaping around pools and lagoons, golden sand beach with tourists basking in the sun, and catamarans sailing on the ocean with his hotel customers. All it would take was money, imagination, and a lot of hard work.

Burns was quick to share Kaiser's vision. Together they began negotiating with the owner, finally agreeing in early 1955 on a price of $1 million. Promptly, there was a flurry of activity at the hotel site. Kaiser was at last a happy man. Residents of Honolulu knew that something important was about to take place.

A Hotel Is Born

It's not a particularly big deal to build a hotel. They're going up every year all around the world. But neither Kaiser nor Burns had built one before. Besides, they were taking a gamble on the location of theirs and on the unpredictability of the tourist business. Some of the executives at the Kaiser headquarters in Oakland squirmed a little over the uncertainties.

A prominent local architect who had designed several Waikiki hotels, Edwin L. Bauer, was hired to help plan the new hotel. A scheme was soon developed calling for all of the old usable and movable hotel cottages to be moved to one end of the property in two clusters in front of and behind an existing night club and restaurant called the Tapa Room. Each of the two groupings would surround a swimming pool. The Tapa Room itself would be completely upgraded with a new kitchen, new bar addition, and a much bigger stage with modern lighting and sound.

The planning all went smoothly until it came to the lanai outside the main dining room. Here, Kaiser and Burns for the first time in their partnership dealings had a disagreement which was nothing less than violent. Kaiser, a very heavy man, who was now 72 years old, had felt the romance of dancing under the stars in the balmy trade winds at the Royal Hawaiian Hotel, and he insisted there should be a dance floor on the lanai. Burns, on the other hand, was familiar with how popular it was in California and Florida for patrons to lounge around a pool in the day and sip cocktails. He argued that a pool would be an important money-maker which a dance floor would not. It was strange to see these two partners battle over something that wasn't really basic to the success of the project, but perhaps they were each testing the other out.

Neither partner would give an inch, until finally Kaiser hit upon a compromise— why not do both? With that, the architect was asked to design a swimming pool over which a motorized, movable dance floor could be rolled in the evening during dance periods and rolled back under the Tapa Room floor during the daytime. Both men had won and were happy. Their compromise remained as a unique feature of the hotel for many years. Incidentally, because of the span of the dance floor, it would become quite springy when a large number of people started dancing to the tune of a good beat, creating the feeling somewhat like jumping on a stiff trampoline.

The long-range plan was that the cottage hotel with 90 rooms would be opened promptly to start generating income, then the area down on the ocean front could be made available for new multi-story hotels, shops, restaurants, and entertainment facilities. The plan also called for getting permission from the city and the state to dredge out the coral in front of the property so that sand could be hauled in to make a big new beach which would be available to hotel guests and Hawaiian residents as well. There would also be an enclosed swimming lagoon adjacent to the yacht harbor which would be relatively shallow and safe for children, likewise surrounded by imported sand. It was not going to be a simple proposition of building just a hotel.

This was the time a young man, Handy Hancock, was going to emerge as the indispensable assistant to Kaiser in Hawaii. After a background of photography and small town newspaper publishing, Handy joined Kaiser Steel at Fontana, California, in June 1942. While there he became an assistant to Henry J. Kaiser, Jr. He was handy enough and eager enough to tackle any assignment thrown his way. He came to Kaiser's attention when he performed some special photography in connection with Kaiser's marriage to the young nurse in 1951. Then he did so many unusual services for Kaiser at Lake Tahoe that no one was surprised when he was appointed Kaiser's full time assistant in Hawaii. Indeed, Handy became almost a member of Kaiser's family, living for various periods of time in the home of Mr. and Mrs. Kaiser in Honolulu. Notwithstanding the long years many executives in Oakland had worked directly with Kaiser, none of them was as close to him on a day-to-day basis, none of them was as aware of his moods and feelings and personal life, as Handy was during the last 13 years of Kaiser's life.

To ride herd on everything that had to be done, Handy, with no formal training as an engineer and with no particular experience in construction, was made construction project manager. His 12-hour working days would suddenly become 16 hours. As soon as architectural drawings were approved, he engaged a house mover to start relocating the cottages. Then a swimming pool contractor was hired to build the three pools, followed by lining up hundreds of carpenters, plumbers, painters, masons, cement workers, landscape architects and earth movers. The goal was to open by Labor Day, 1955, a tight schedule by any standard.

To create a polynesian atmosphere and spruce up the termite-eaten cottages, it was decided to build high-peaked false roofs over the original roofs and thatch them with palm fronds. This required a craft never before dealt with by Kaiser, and one that did not even exist on the mainland. It was important that the thatching be authentic, and the Samoan community on the other side of the island was the only source for weavers in the quantity needed. This meant they had to get up before dawn each day, pile into ramshackle cars and drive the 30 miles to Waikiki on the narrow two-lane coastal road, work all day at their weaving and drive all the way back, not getting home until dark.

Handy was warned: "The Samoans cannot be counted on. They will take off and go fishing at the drop of a hat if they feel like it. You'll never get the thatching done on time."

Nothing could have been further from the truth. The Samoans became caught up in the excitement of working for Kaiser and did not miss a single day of work, not only all summer but for a long time thereafter, because the roof thatching was just the start of much more thatching for decorative purposes as new additions were built.

The workers were always quiet in the early morning but soon they would be laughing and giggling with one another. They would often break out singing some of their Samoan chants, and at noon they would have their lunch of strange-looking food mainlanders would not dare sample. By mid-afternoon they were in high spirits, singing and laughing as they worked until Pau Hana (quit working).

When the time came the thatchers had to be moved to another location in order to develop the area where they had been working, part of their secret was found out. Buried beneath the chaff and waste from the palm fronds was a large cache of gin bottles they had been nipping on all through their work.

Once the broad architectural plans were agreed upon, Burns returned to the mainland leaving his son, Patrick, to represent him and to concentrate on decorations, furnishings, and atmospheric features. Kaiser turned his attention for the time being to the all-important subject of how to promote the project so that a splashy grand opening could be achieved and groundwork laid to assure tourist business.

It was an easy decision for Kaiser—he would build his promotion around Alfred Apaka who with his band and hula dancers was far and away the most popular entertainer in Hawaii. Added glamour arose from the fact that Apaka was a direct descendant of King Kaumualii. There was one minor hitch. Apaka was already engaged at Don The Beachcomber's in Waikiki. That didn't bother Kaiser. He had been an enthusiastic habitue at Don's and he felt sure he would lure Apaka away. He was right. In no time at all, Apaka had cast his lot with Kaiser. Up until that time, Apaka, lacking in business talent, had been taken advantage of by greedy business agents, to the point where he was only getting about 25 percent of what he was paid, the rest going to the agents. Not only was he a gifted baritone but he was extremely handsome. Women would literally swoon when he sang, "My Isle of Golden Dreams." Oftentimes these ladies, not necessarily young ones, would actually come down the aisles between the tables and up to the stage, crawling on their knees with their hands clasped in front of them.

Kaiser practically adopted Apaka. He not only enjoyed his singing, he liked to have him around as much as possible, inviting him regularly to his estate for weekend parties, and always including him on boating trips.

Because of the constant association with the singer, rumors would fly thick and fast that Apaka and Ale, Kaiser's young wife, were having an affair. Both Kaiser and Ale took the gossip in stride. She often said, "At least if they are busy talking about me, they are laying off someone else whom they might hurt, and I really don't care what they say or think." Never at any time did Kaiser let the gossip affect his devotion to his wife or his fondness for Apaka. Handy Hancock, who was so close to the Kaisers and who would know if there were any truth to the rumors, was totally convinced of Ale's fidelity.

Instead of being suspicious of the young singer, Kaiser would do whatever he could to promote Apaka's career, first by having his attorneys get rid of all of his booking agents, then by sponsoring all kinds of special events in Hawaii and sending him on extended engagements to the mainland. He personally became involved in making arrangements with Decca Records to produce several albums of Hawaiian songs by Apaka; he opened the door for Apaka to be the featured singer on the "This Is Hawaii" broadcast series over the mutual network; he intervened with the Cal-Neva Lodge at Lake Tahoe to book Apaka. This kind of support for the darling of the islands, together with the gossip, gave Kaiser the recognition he needed to impact on the islands. Without doubt, it played a major part in building up his hotel business, as well as getting him accepted as an islander himself. Shockingly, this father-son relationship would come to a sudden end when Apaka, at age 42, died unexpectedly in 1960 from a massive heart attack while playing handball at the YMCA.

As the construction of the hotel progressed, the place began to take on the atmosphere the tourist visualizes as the South Pacific, thanks to all the thatched roof cottages, the pools, the tropical landscaping, the sisal and abaca cloth and lahala matting decor. The hotel needed a name and after many ideas were thrown on the table, the name Hawaiian Village was selected, which is still proudly promoted by its present owner, Hilton.

By early summer of 1955 Kaiser could see his construction crew had things under control, so he dared to spend some time on the mainland, part of it in promoting public interest in the upcoming hotel. On June 17 he wrote from Oakland to Riley H. Allen, Editor, Honolulu Star Bulletin:

> You know how my heart is in the plans for Hawaii, which will call forth considerable activity for years to come. Fritz Burns and I recently have worked from Miami Beach to New York—and across the country and at Los

Angeles and Oakland—in advancing the plans for the Honolulu project. We are enthusiastic.

Kaiser also spent several weeks at his Lake Tahoe home. It was not a vacation as such—he entertained an almost constant flow of important visitors, and, of course, he kept in daily touch with construction progress on the hotel.

His absence from the Islands became an invitation for Handy and his crew to redouble their efforts because they wanted to prove they could live up to the Kaiser reputation for whirlwind progress. It is doubtful that Hawaii had ever before witnessed any construction where speed, not cost, was the controlling consideration to the extent it was with the Hawaiian Village.

The challenge was not just construction. Instead of contracting with a hotel chain to take over operation of the hotel once it was built, Kaiser and Burns decided their own people could run it. This meant hiring and training a hotel management team as well as waiters, waitresses, bell boys, room maids, cooks, accountants, purchasing agents, and reservation personnel, not to mention the many entertainers needed to back up Alfred Apaka. Considering the inexperience of both Kaiser and Burns in hotel management, this was almost a bolder undertaking than the construction of the hotel itself.

Where is Everybody?

Although construction had gone forward on an around-the-clock basis all summer, it became evident in early August that the hotel could not be open to the public by Labor Day weekend. Therefore, the date was set two weeks later, Saturday, September 18, 1955. Every detail of the festivities was either suggested by Kaiser, or approved by him, with the help of Burns. Invitations had been sent out to everybody who was supposed to be somebody in Honolulu. Of course, it was essential to have traditional Hawaiian ceremonies for the dedication services. Here's how the events were described in the Honolulu Advertiser the next day:

ELABORATE RITES OPEN NEW HOTEL

Hawaii's newest hotel was opened in elaborate ceremonies yesterday with a prediction by Henry J. Kaiser that the islands would have a 'great place in the world' in a prosperity boom ahead. 'I believe there's a great prosperity ahead, a great place in the sun, a great place in the world, for this area.' He was joined in the optimistic outlook by his co-partner in the Hawaiian Village venture in Waikiki, Fritz Burns. The two men spoke at the climax of a colorful Hawaiian hoopomaikai, or blessing ceremony, in which the pageantry of the Aloha Week court played a part. Also adding to the beauty of the dedication service was the Kawaiahao church choir under the direction of David Kalama. They sang Nui Kealoha O Ke Akua (Great is the Love of God). The Rev. Samuel Keala of Kaumakapili church, gave the blessing in

Hawaiian, followed by the Queen's Prayer which was sung by the choir. F. Lang Akana, who is aliiaimoku or president of the order of Kamehameha was master of ceremonies. Mr. Kaiser and Mr. Burns formally opened the Hawaiian Village to the public by cutting a maile lei across the entrance. Governor Samuel Wilder King and his daughter, Pauline, were the first to cross the threshhold. The wives of the two industrialists, Mrs. Kaiser and Mrs. Burns, cut similar maile leis at the close of the ceremony, opening the Village's court and garden to the public. Some 150 guests were present for the dedication. A reception followed at 5:30 p.m.

The reception turned out to be a rousing Hawaiian celebration. Somehow, the guests seemed to double in numbers, and by early evening the Tapa Room and the grounds were jammed elbow-to-elbow. Everyone wanted to shake Kaiser's hand and to tell him personally how much he meant to the Hawaiian economy. He loved it— just the kind of personal contact he thrived on.

The hilarity of the evening was assured by the free flowing of island drinks and the generous serving of the traditional Hawaiian pupus, or hors d'oeuvres. Kaiser people were a bit shocked not only to see how the guests feasted on the pupus, but how many of them made up packets of food which they put in their purses to take home.

A follow-up celebration was arranged for the next day, with two orchestras and entertainers starting performances at 12:30 p.m. Then an aquacade was presented at 5:30 p.m. with a repeat performance at 7:30 p.m. The highlight of the evening was three shows featuring Alfred Apaka and his troupe. Kaiser and Burns and their wives put in another long day, making themselves available to chat with any and all visitors.

On the next day, itself, Kaiser and Burns and all their management team were there at the hotel with open arms, being careful to stand back far enough so as not to be trampled by the crowd. But where was everyone? The only hotel guests were the ones invited over from the company headquarters in Oakland and from the Burns' organization in Los Angeles, and of course, their tabs were on the house.

The Honolulu elite had apparently had their curiosity and appetites satisfied at the gala two-day opening. Other residents were not sufficiently interested to show up either, so the first day the hotel was open for business came and went with a thud, reminding the Kaiser-Burns team nothing comes easy in the hotel business especially when you are a newcomer operating alone in the field.

It soon became clear that the timing of the opening had been a serious mistake. September is always the time for the summer exodus from Waikiki to the mainland. From then until the Christmas holidays one could shoot a cannon ball down Kalakaua Avenue and not hit a tourist. Only a few wealthy travelers would come and go in between time, and they were dyed-in-the-wool Royal Hawaiian Hotel fans. As it actually turned out for the next three months, the Hawaiian Village Hotel rooms had only about a 10% occupancy, with half of that being complimentary rooms.

This meant an all-out drive would have to be made to build up local trade for the dining room and bar and for such shops as there were at that time. Fortunately, Alfred Apaka and his troupe were the best drawing cards in town, so little by little the restaurant and bar business began to flourish.

Then, as though it was not challenge enough to stir up business from scratch, a serious personnel problem arose. Kaiser somehow sensed that the general manager and others were shortchanging the hotel. Having confirmed this suspicion by studying income and expenses, Kaiser called Handy one night, "Handy, I think our manager is dishonest. I want you to let him go tomorrow morning, and I want you to take over."

As often as Handy had been handed new responsibilities, this one scared him: "Mr. Kaiser, I don't know if I can handle it or not." "I'm sure you can, Handy," was the unhesitating reply. Throughout his lifetime, Kaiser had been recognized for his uncanny ability to pick the right person for any given job, and here he was casting his lot with an ex-newspaperman, now in construction, to make a success out of running the new hotel. In keeping with his practice in all of his other business ventures, Kaiser gave Handy carte blanche. He knew of Handy's resourcefulness and of course he knew of his honesty.

It was no easy matter smoking out which of the employees were dishonest. In several situations employees were in cahoots with each other and it became necessary to rotate personnel to break up these combinations. Gradually, the worst offenders were caught, and the others soon came to realize that Handy was determined to run a tight ship, so the problem subsided.

A more difficult challenge was the overstaffing, with about 20 employees more than were really needed. To make matters worse, the ones first hired were those immediately available and they were the ones least experienced. Yet, under the union contract they had seniority even if it was by only a few days or weeks.

This was the time Kaiser had to be consulted. Arthur Rutledge was head of the Hotel Restaurant Employees and Bartenders Union (AFL-CIO) Local 5 and he had a reputation for being tough. Handy didn't want trouble with the union that could shut the hotel down. Kaiser's advice was simple, "Just take your hat in your hand, go visit Rutledge, and ask him what can be done."

Rutledge started by saying that he was not surprised, that he knew Handy would be coming to see him. He said he knew there would be a problem the minute he heard who the first manager was. He pointed out that the manager had not hired through the union but had been hired off the street, and once hired he had to be admitted into the union because of the terms of the contract. Rutledge said the dregs had been given jobs and now he had to represent them. He added, "I could have told Kaiser, Burns, or you that you were in trouble weeks ago, but no one asked me. You see, I always say management has the right to go broke anyway it sees fit."

Nevertheless, the union leader agreed undesirables could be discharged whenever there was a legitimate reason to do so. But he did want to know in advance who was to be fired, and what the reasons were, so he could be prepared when they came running to him for protection. With that kind of cooperation, it wasn't long before the overstaffing had been corrected.

Some time later Rutledge decided he would try to organize the "Mud Trades" in Honolulu—stone and block masons, wallboard installers, and cement finishers. He approached Kaiser to see if he could get his backing. Kaiser told him he would not require his workmen to join a union but if Rutledge could convince them to sign up he would not oppose it. With that license to hunt, it did not take Rutledge and his organizers long to sign up a majority, following which he suggested a contract be negotiated. Kaiser responded by saying he didn't think any negotiations were necessary. "You go back and draw up a contract that you consider fair to both you and me, and I will sign it," Kaiser said.

A short time later Rutledge was back with copies of a contract, presenting them to Kaiser as Burns looked on. Kaiser started flipping pages and then took out his pen, "What page do I sign on, Art?" At that point, Burns almost went out of his mind thinking of signing a labor contract without even reading it. Rutledge was a little surprised himself and asked Kaiser if he wasn't going to read it first.

"No, Art," Kaiser replied, "I told you to draft a contract that would be fair to both of us, one we both could live with, one we could look each other in the eye and not be ashamed of, and so I will sign it."

This took Rutledge aback, and he said, "Well, Mr. Kaiser, I had better take that contract and review it more thoroughly myself. I had the boys draw it up, and I only skimmed through it so I want to check it out before you sign."

A few days later Rutledge was back. "Here's a contract you can sign, Mr. Kaiser." Without looking, Kaiser turned to the signature page and signed his name, with Burns agonizing on the sidelines.

After Rutledge left, Kaiser tossed the contract to Handy and said, "You better check this out and see what I have gotten us into."

As Handy read it page by page he felt it was a liberal but normal document until he reached the section on arbitration. The arbitration clause did not provide for the usual appointment of an arbitrator from each side who in turn would appoint a third. Instead, it read, "In case of a dispute, Henry J. Kaiser shall be the sole arbiter and his decision shall be final." What finer tribute could Rutledge have paid?

Typical of Kaiser's open friendliness with union leaders was his dealing with Hal Lewis*, head of the operating engineers. In later years when Kaiser was building his Portlock estate he would without notice suddenly "rent or borrow" heavy earth-moving equipment or light mechanical equipment from the Hawaii Kai project. Although Lewis was an admirer of Kaiser, this annoyed him because he couldn't keep accurate track of what men were operating what pieces of equipment and what the pay scale should be.

One morning Lewis met Kaiser on the job site and protested, saying that unless he followed the rules of the contract, he (Lewis) was going to shut the job down, adding

---

*Kaiser had another acquaintance with the name of Hal Lewis—a disk jockey known over the air as J. Aku-head Pupule.

that "I can do it by the wave of my hand." Kaiser responded, "Now, you really wouldn't do that to me, would you Hal?" Thereupon, Lewis waved his hand and all the operators stopped their equipment and started to dismount. With a big grin on his face, Kaiser grabbed Lewis around the throat, playfully shook him and said, "All right, I see you can stop my job with the wave of your hand. Now please wave your hand and start it again," which Lewis promptly did.

Kaiser was not only the first one on the job-site each morning, he was nearly always the last one to go to bed at night. All his life he was notorious for only requiring 4 or 5 hours of sleep, and he didn't change in his seventies and eighties in Hawaii. That made him the most regular customer, non-paying of course, in the Tapa Room. It was the entertainment—and the big meals—he liked most. Although he could carry a good load of liquor without showing it, he was not a heavy drinker. The trouble was that while enjoying what was going on in the Tapa Room he was always figuring out changes he thought would help. If there was a Saturday night sell-out, the next Monday morning he would start another remodeling project to squeeze in a few more tables.

Not because of any particular marketing deadline but because it was Kaiser's way of doing things, the construction tempo really began speeding up, becoming what some people would describe as frantic. It wouldn't slow down until Kaiser's death in 1967. The more activity he could see going on, the more ideas kept popping in his mind for different things to do. To him, more was always better.

By this time Kaiser and Burns had acquired all the nearby land they possibly could, including the slum properties adjacent to their hotel project. Extended negotiations were underway with all the authorities of the City and County of Honolulu, State of Hawaii, and the US. Corps of Engineers for permission to dredge the coral in front of the property and to bring in sand for a huge new beach and lagoon. While certain preliminary maneuvers were left to his team, Kaiser insisted on making personal appearances before these bodies at key times to be sure approvals would be granted in a hurry.

Now that the 90 rooms in the thatched cottages were open for business, Kaiser rushed ahead on plans for a 3-story building, the two top floors to be hotel rooms with the ground floor having a lobby, registration desk, hotel management offices, a number of specialty shops for hotel guests, a new kitchen facility, and a large dining room on the ocean front. This would be an "L" shaped building with a large carp pond and lush tropical landscaping in the center of the "L."

True to form, Kaiser set an almost impossible construction timetable of 3 months—almost impossible because this was a time when items like bathtubs, plumbing fittings, sinks and lavatories, heavy kitchen equipment, and hotel furniture were not stocked in any quantity in Hawaii but had to be ordered and shipped from the mainland.

Simultaneously, he wanted to build a large hall, "The Long House" which could be used for banquets, public meetings, trade shows, and conferences. This structure was to be finished at the same time as the 3-story hotel only it was started a month later. Then within another month construction was started on a 2-story Spa or health club, with the decree that it must be finished in 30 days so that all three of these new units would open up at the same time. Kaiser was convinced that both tourists and local people would come to his health Spa, but, like his Henry J automobile, it was 20 years ahead of its time and never caught on. Now, in the late 1980's, Honolulu is overrun with health clubs.

The area where these three buildings were to be constructed was filled with mature coconut trees, but Kaiser gave the order that no trees could be destroyed. Throughout his life he had an appreciation for the aesthetic, especially the beauties of nature, rarely found in a businessman.

As construction sped ahead at the Hawaiian Village it was no small matter to dig up the dozens of coconut trees 20 to 40 feet tall and replant them in areas where they could be blended into the other landscaping. In three or four cases the roof of the hotel building was constructed with a large hole around the tree trunk allowing the tree to penetrate the finished roof line. In the kitchen of the new hotel, two trees were left in their original locations, probably the first and only kitchen having two coconut trees at each end of the stainless steel make-up tables. The chefs used the tree trunks later as a place to stick their knives when they were not carving with them.

When the building was finished, one day ahead of the 90-day schedule (the Long House and the Spa were also completed on schedule), it soon became apparent that one of the coconut trees which was now growing through a hole in the roof should have been moved. It was too close to the driveway at the entrance to the Porte Cochere and if a car came too close it creased the roof. Signs saying "Impaired Clearance—Keep Away," were of no avail, and the insurance company was getting tired of paying claims. Finally, a letter was received saying no further claims would be paid for the tree damage.

Handy went to Kaiser and told him the tree would have to be removed or damages would have to be paid by the hotel. "You will never cut down that tree," he told Handy. "What shall we do then, we can't leave it there," Handy countered. "Raise it up so it will clear," was his solution.

And thus it was done. The tree was dug up, leaving a big ball of dirt around the roots. It was then lifted by a crane which held it suspended in the air for several days while the stone masons built a huge lava rock planter about 10 feet high and approximately 10 feet in diameter which was filled with soil. The tree was replanted and braced so that the trunk would be centered in the hole in the roof. The tree is still there today, 1988, though the main entrance to the hotel has long been shifted, leaving tourists to wonder why that tree sits in a stone planter, 10 feet above the rest of the landscaping.

With the completion of the 13-story Village Tower, Kaiser wanted to add a gourmet Chinese restaurant to be known as the Golden Dragon Room, and Burns thought it would be a good thing to have more shops for the tourists. Like everything else, when the two partners decided to go with the idea, Kaiser wanted it built yesterday and called in his architect Bauer for lunch. After only a brief explanation the architect was asked to sketch a rough design for the shops which he did on a napkin. Kaiser then insisted he draw a foundation plan for the shops which he turned over to Handy, "Get this started right away."

With nothing more than a rough plan on a napkin, work was started on the footings and the foundations, while Bauer went back to his office to draw them properly, complete the blue prints, and obtain a building permit. Somehow the napkin plan was leaked to the press and became a front page story. Needless to say, it took a lot of explaining to assure the officials in the building department and the Chief Engineer that the construction would comply with city standards. Kaiser couldn't seem to understand why they were so upset; after all, why waste precious time on formalities when the final plans would be approved in due course?

As with all construction activities it was not just a matter of building something, there was the constant necessity of conforming to code regulations or getting approval of governmental authorities for variances. This was particularly critical in connection with the beach in front of the hotel which was largely prickly coral in shallow waters on land owned by the state. Kaiser had offered to dredge the coral at no expense to the state, haul in sand from the north end of the island and create a whole new sand beach for both the tourists and local people. In the process there would also be a lagoon built adjoining the yacht harbor which would be a quiet water area for little kiddies. In return, he proposed that the state should allow the hotel to have a portion of the new beach as a private area for hotel guests, with most of the newly created beach open to the public.

It was touch and go with the legislature. Some wanted it; others thought he would be getting away with rape. As the issue heated up, a state senator who was also a prominent attorney and known throughout Honolulu as a political power, called on Kaiser. After the usual felicitations, the senator said he had the prestige, power and contacts to assure adoption of the necessary legislation, but he felt it would take $5,000 to cover costs and other considerations.

Kaiser studied him for a minute and said, "Isn't that considered dishonest and illegal in this state?" The senator said there would be nothing illegal if Kaiser paid the $5,000 to buy an old barge the senator had anchored down at the harbor. Later on, if Kaiser should decide he didn't want the barge, which was practically worthless, the senator said he would buy it back for $1.

That brought the conversation to an abrupt ending, because all his life Kaiser had an inviolable rule against payoffs of any kind. He politely told the senator that he thought his proposal to the state was fair and was a good thing for the people. If the senator agreed with him, he should vote for the legislation; if not, he should vote against it whether or not he was paid any money. It was not long after that the legislation was approved by a large majority.

Kaiser's antipathy toward payoffs often meant extra expense, including the time when small cottages were being moved from the lower end of the property to the upper end where they could be arranged around the swimming pool. One of the cottages happened to be moved 6 inches closer to the next cottage than the building code would allow. A building inspector came by and discovered the discrepancy. A plea for a variance on the grounds that this was all on hotel property, not in any way endangering anyone else's property, fell on deaf ears. As the discussions went back and forth, it became evident the matter could be settled by a small payment to the inspector. When this came to Kaiser's attention on Friday, he said, "We will never pay him off. Get a crew, hold them overtime, cut off 6 inches from the end of that cottage, put it back together, repaint it, and get it all finished before Monday when the inspector comes back to work."

On Monday Handy told the inspector he must have had a rubber tape measure because there was no violation. The inspector then measured the distance between the two cottages—not once, but several times because he couldn't believe his tape. He finally came into Handy's office and apologized, "I must have been mistaken. I'm sorry." Weeks later he asked Handy what had really happened. Handy described the rebuilding and repainting, and said that everyone around City Hall should know that "Kaiser would do that a thousand times before he would pay anybody a nickel."

Another time the rodent inspector came to the hotel to examine the stone walls which were being built. They were purposely being formed in a very rough, rugged way in order to give a natural appearance. The inspector kept poking his figures into holes saying, "Oh, very bad, very bad. There could be mice nesting in here." Handy countered, "I can take you all around Honolulu and show you places just like that. Besides, we have a rodent and insect extermination contract, so there won't possibly be any danger." Still the inspector kept poking his fingers in the holes, repeating, "Very bad, we must do something."

His manner of speaking led Handy to believe there was nothing wrong that $50 wouldn't take care of. Just then, Kaiser walked up and wanted to know what was wrong. When Handy hinted to Kaiser what the inspector was up to, Kaiser said, "It's very simple, Handy, just get a crew and fill up the holes with mortar."

The inspector was dumbfounded when the crew swung into action. He turned to Handy, "Mr. Hancock, maybe we'll wait and see if we have a problem before you have to go to all that expense." The word soon spread through City Hall, and from that day forward, Kaiser was not hit for a payoff by any inspector.

The frantic pace finally caught up with Handy. He had come to Hawaii at Kaiser's personal invitation in the fall of 1954. He had worked 16 hour days till the Hawaiian Village Hotel had been built nearly a year later. But the pace didn't slacken. Handy continued to be willing to work until he literally dropped. One time Kaiser said of Handy, "I believe if I asked him to go in five different directions at the same time, he would try to do it."

Obviously, this didn't make for a normal family life for his wife and four children. By August 1956, Handy and his wife had made their decision—they would move back to Piedmont, California, where he could work in the company headquarters and where his children could return to school with friends they had there.

He knew that if he told Kaiser he was planning to leave, he would be talked out of it, so he made airplane reservations two weeks ahead and then informed Kaiser of his action. Kaiser's only reaction was, "We'll miss you." Here's Handy's account of what followed:

> From that moment on for the next two weeks I suddenly discovered I had a power I was not aware of—I suddenly was the 'invisible man.' I would walk up to a group of men Kaiser would be talking to and they would all say, 'Hi, Handy,' but Mr. Kaiser would look right through me as if I were not there—I was completely invisible as far as he was concerned. That was the way it was for two weeks. Not once did he call on me for anything, no matter how trivial. After a two-week freeze out I went to his office where I fortunately found him alone. 'I'll be leaving in the morning,' I said, 'and I just want you to know how much I have enjoyed working for you.' He interrupted me, 'Oh, Handy, have you seen the latest occupancy figures for the hotel? They are really picking up.' Then to my surprise he asked me to get someone on the phone for him. That broke the ice, and for the rest of the day he was calling me for information of all kinds and wishing me good luck.

Handy should have known his return to the home office wouldn't last. Nobody there had an opening for him, and the menial tasks assigned to him soon became boring. He, therefore, literally jumped with glee when Kaiser phoned him from Hawaii in the middle of the night in November 1956, and said, "Handy, I've got some problems over here. Could you come over for a short time and help straighten them out?" Handy was so excited he found himself talking with the phone in one hand and packing his bag with the other.

Handy could see it was not going to be a short stay, so he and his wife and family made plans to move to Hawaii as soon as the school year was over. During their eight-month separation, Handy and his wife made several trips back and forth to be with each other. From that time forward, Handy was Kaiser's Executive Assistant until Kaiser's death in 1967. Thereafter, Handy remained on the Kaiser payroll for as long as he was required to help wind down all of the projects that were underway. He and his wife still live in their Hawaii Kai home.

Color Me Pink

Kaiser always had a fascination with colors. He never accepted the dull, the bland. He was always trying to add life to his activities by an unusual array of colors. The color he resorted to most often in the thirties and forties was green, partly because his first wife Bess liked that color and partly because it harmonized with nature and symbolized growth. In the first office building bought by Kaiser in 1945, an 11-story building at 1924 Broadway in Oakland, various shades of green were used in all the offices from top to bottom. One of the features that helped Kaiser-Frazer gain a reputation as a style leader in cars, was the daring use of colors both outside and inside. In one of the models all of the cars were separately identified for marketing purposes by their colors.

When Kaiser decided to build a 28-story Kaiser Center in Oakland in the late 1950's, he made it clear that he wanted to be involved in all phases of its planning. He appointed his life time associate, A. B. Ordway, to be in charge because, "you know better than anyone else what I like."

Each time Kaiser came to Oakland from Hawaii he wanted to see what progress had been made on the plans, as well as to make any further major decisions. A typical session was when he flew in from Hawaii, going directly to the Fairmont Hotel in San Francisco at 10:30 a.m. where Ordway and his assistant Frank Scarr were waiting. He sat down, took off his shoes, and began munching on some fruit from a coffee table in front of him. "All right, Ord, what do you have to show me?" Then item by item he gave his decision—wall panels, ceiling panels, rugs, marble floor tiling—always with a concern for color. Scarr urged white for all ceilings "because it will be more reflective, providing better light in the room." Kaiser quickly ruled that out insisting that the ceilings should have colors to match the rest of the room. After reacting to a whole gamut of colors, Kaiser chose blue, yellow, green and burned orange. One of those four basic colors would be the motif for each separate floor, 3 through 26.

This Fairmont Hotel session ended about noon, with Kaiser dashing off to a studio where he was to star in a television commercial. Ord and Scarr walked him to the car to say goodbye. Kaiser turned to Scarr and said, "I don't know whether I'll ever forget that you wanted all the ceilings to be white." This shook Scarr up, and to this day he hasn't forgotten, but it was only Kaiser's way of saying, "Get some color imagination, don't be stuck with colorless white." Kaiser must have soon forgotten it, because within a few years, Scarr succeeded Ordway as Vice President and General Manager of Kaiser Center. The Kaiser Center ended up as one of the most beautiful office buildings ever constructed.

Kaiser's fascination with colors was very much in evidence a few years earlier when he was frantically finishing construction of the Hawaiian Village Hotel. He was right in the middle of all color selections. In particular, he agreed with his wife, Ale, that the dyed leather for the chairs, couches and dining booths in the lobby and in the restaurant should be coral in color. The restaurant itself was to be known as the Ale Kai room.

The air freight shipment of leather arrived literally just hours ahead of the scheduled opening. The upholsterers were standing by prepared to work all night long to get the job done. When the rolls were ripped open, with Kaiser and Ale eagerly standing by the leather was not coral—it was pink!!!

Ale couldn't restrain her dismay. She said it was horrible. She wanted coral and here it was "Portugee" pink (to use Ale's description).

There was no choice at that hour. Everything had to be upholstered in pink. Kaiser promised his wife that a new dye lot would be ordered immediately and the pink would be replaced with coral as soon as it could arrive. "Ale Kai" in Hawaiian translates to "rough water" and that very aptly described the atmosphere created by the mistake.

However, it was a different story the very next day when the Ale Kai room was opened to the public. The place was flooded with people, and the main thing the customers raved about was how beautiful the pink upholstery was.

Kaiser, never one to turn his back on a winner, immediately began painting other things the same color—railings, trim, even his catamarans. In an amazingly short time "Kaiser Pink" had become a household word. The Honolulu Advertiser, running a front page story on something Kaiser had done, printed the banner headline in pink. Soon there was even a fleet of pink jeeps running around the islands as U-Drive rentals. Needless to say, the order for coral replacement upholstery leather was cancelled. The irony of it all was that the Royal Hawaiian Hotel had been known as the Pink Palace for years, but that was completely forgotten once the Kaiser Pink began being splashed all over Hawaii.

The color pink soon spread to some of the Kaiser operations on the mainland. To the embarrassment of the construction stiffs running Kaiser's rock, sand, and gravel facilities, pink had to be used even on the fleet of ready-mix cement trucks spinning around as they chugged all over the Bay Area. Finally, Robert Barneyback, Vice President and General Manager of the company, got up enough courage to plead with Kaiser to return to a color that would be more in keeping with the "he-man" world of construction. Barney asked Kaiser to walk around one of the trucks, so they could talk about it. They really hadn't got started when Kaiser took him by the hand, walked over to the door of the truck, and said, "Barney, what's the name on that door?" "It's the Henry J. Kaiser Company," was the reply. "Barney, when the name on the door says R. J. Barneyback, you can choose the color. Until then, it's going to remain pink."

Kaiser decided if pink was proving so popular, he would join the parade. He started wearing pink slacks and sport shirts, not only in Hawaii but at his home on Lake Tahoe. It was quite a sight seeing this bald-headed man, weighing about 250 lbs., and standing 5 feet 10 inches—a man in his late seventies and early eighties— spryly bouncing around in his dazzling pink outfit.

Kaiser's own pinkness was not always limited to clothing. One time a painter was standing alongside Kaiser at the entrance way to one of the dining rooms. Kaiser made the decision to color the area pink, then turned to look into the main portion of the room. When he wheeled around to leave he didn't look up, walking smack into a ladder with the painter on top swiping pink paint on the wall as fast as he could. Kaiser was suddenly the pink panther in more ways than one.

It seemed like Kaiser always had painters in action in nearly every stage of construction. In normal construction each subcontractor takes his turn in going into a particular area, followed by the next and the next in an orderly fashion. Not on a Kaiser job. He would ask each sub to get busy at the same time, and it was not at all unusual to have the electricians, plumbers, and carpenters all working around each other in the same area.

This kind of pressure was a way of life with Kaiser. He thrived on it. Others were stimulated, yes, but often the pressure would get to them. The doctors in the Kaiser Permanente hospital in Oakland had long before diagnosed a special condition that the various executives suffered from as "Kaiseritis" and had a special pink pill they prescribed for it known only as Rx5B. When Kaiser inadvertently learned about the diagnosis, he was not amused in the least and the word went out that "Kaiseritis" was not to be used as the name of the affliction—at least not in the presence of Kaiser. It was only fitting, though, that the pill to treat the condition was pink, and there were thousands of them used over the years.

At a later time, the clincher for the color pink, not that one was needed, came in the most unexpected way. When the Kaisers completed building their Portlock estate in their newly developed city of Hawaii Kai, it was first painted a beige color. Shortly thereafter, they took a combined business and pleasure trip to Italy where Ale became enamored with the colors of the buildings in Rome. Upon their return she decided she would like to repaint the estate "the color of Rome."

This was a neat little challenge thrown at Handy—to find out just what that color was and to order the paint. No one was quite sure—decorators, paint manufacturers and dealers, or even well-traveled people. All the books on Rome at the library were scanned to little avail. There was no single color that could be said was Rome—the buildings were of different shades ranging from beiges to pinks. Several of the best pictures were shown to Ale who demurred, "I'm not going to pick the color. I leave it up to you to find it."

Finally in desperation, Handy turned to the overseas office of Kaiser Aluminum who had contacts in Italy, asking them to put him in touch with a responsible Italian paint manufacturer. This company said it could provide a paint that would be representative of the general color of Rome. The order was placed, with the instruction to ship it as soon as possible and in the most expeditious manner possible.

The day the ship arrived in Honolulu Handy was at the dock ready to take delivery. There was one problem, however—the paint was at the bottom of the hold with a lot of freight on top of it destined for Singapore. Despite personal calls from Kaiser, the Captain of the ship refused to unload the whole hold just to reach the paint at the bottom and then reload again. He tried to appease Kaiser by saying the paint would be brought back to Hawaii on the ship's return. That was too indefinite so the captain was asked to transfer the paint at Singapore to the first ship coming back to Hawaii.

There was really no urgency for the paint, but to Kaiser everything was urgent, especially with his wife breathing down his neck. Four weeks later the exciting moment had arrived when the truck drove up to the gate with hundreds of gallons of paint "the color of Rome." Kaiser and Ale were there, the decorator, the painters, the estate staff, and Handy on the truck to be sure it didn't get lost somewhere.

The painter ripped open one of the cartons, removed a 5-gallon can of paint, stirred it well and made a few swipes on the side of one of the buildings. There was a hushed silence. No one said a word. No one dared. The color was pink! What was worse it was pink paint manufactured by DuPont in Italy, which could have been purchased in the United States for much less and obtained much sooner. With destiny riding on the color pink, and with hundreds of gallons of it on hand the estate was repainted, but no one ever referred to it as being pink—it was "the color of Rome" from then on.

Taking On Dillingham

Henry Kaiser and Walter Dillingham could have been cut from the same cloth— rugged, bold empire builders. Dillingham's empire was primarily the Hawaiian Islands and South Pacific islands, although his firm did considerable dredging and construction on the mainland. In the course of their activities their paths often crossed, and they developed a mutual respect. In Hawaii, Dillingham was not considered a part of the Big Five factoring houses, but he was regarded as an even more paramount center of business power because of his enterprises in construction, railroading, trucking, land-holding, and pier ownership.

During the shortage of aluminum due to the nation's defense demands, Dillingham appealed personally to Kaiser to make some aluminum available. On May 23, 1951, Kaiser wrote Dillingham:

It gives me pleasure, Walter, to learn from our men who have been working on your aluminum requirements problem, that they have set up scheduling aimed at making available to you the necessary aluminum roofing and siding to repair and develop the facilities at your Honolulu terminal. Your original letter to me came to my office at the very time of Mrs. Kaiser passing away. I was quite upset when I first learned there had been a delay in writing to you. I know that you as an old and good friend will understand my inability during the troubled weeks and travel out of the city to be in touch with you myself concerning this, since you know the genuine personal interest I would take in being helpful to you in any way I could.

On June 19, Dillingham reciprocated Kaiser's warmth of greeting:

Your welcome letter of May 23, 1951 reached me on the 31st while I was laid up at home with one of my attacks of gout. This was a severe one and kept me in bed for more than three weeks. This is the reason for not acknowledging your letter before now. I am glad to tell you, however, that I think your being able to furnish us with the aluminum ordered contributed much to relieving my pain. I am not surprised that you are willing to take your coat off and go to bat for me, but it was a big uplift to hear that you had taken the interest and accomplished what otherwise might have been impossible. It is damnably upsetting to know that another waterfront strike has been started. It seems to me there ought to be some way of protecting American interests that are on a far flung Island. I have often thought that if we had a man here of your stripe we could do something about preventing a recurrence of these lockouts.

Dillingham had been a major customer for Kaiser's cement from the time Kaiser first built bulk silos in Honolulu just before World War II. In turn, Kaiser's hotels and hospital were built with Dillingham crews subcontracted to drive the piles. It looked like a solid, happy relationship between the two men.

That is, until Dillingham dropped a bombshell by announcing he was going to build a cement plant near the Campbell Industrial Park, using coral instead of limestone as a base. Immediately, Kaiser scrambled to secure a limestone deposit at Maile not far from where Dillingham planned his plant, and announced he too would build a cement plant.

Now the fun began. Each side pulled out all stops to win public approval. The main showdown was to take place at a Monday night meeting at the Waianae high school. At the meeting, Dillingham's son was making a presentation when he described Kaiser as a "malahini" to Hawaii (newcomer), which instantly offended Kaiser. When his turn came to speak he told the young man that someone, "who is not yet dry behind the ears should not be making such loose accusations." Up jumped the senior Dillingham who put his arms around his son and addressed Kaiser, "You can't talk like that about my son who is a real 'kamaina'" (oldtimer).

The two men left the meeting in a huff and for the next few years they refused to speak to each other, or have anything to do with one another in any way, even though in the past they had been such good friends and had even engaged in joint ventures. Now, if they both happened to be invited to the same social event or cocktail party, they stayed on opposite sides of the room. The Dillinghams had always been invited to the Kaisers' lavish New Year's Eve bash, but Kaiser refused to let Ale invite them any more.

The two "old men" stepped up their campaigns to win the Waianae people to their side. Kaiser pledged to build a Kaiser Clinic in nearby Nanakuli if he got their support to build his plant. Dillingham countered by offering to build an overpass for school children so they could be safe when crossing the Farrington highway.

Then Kaiser had a stroke of genius—he would build his cement plant on a ship, thereby avoiding all the delay in getting approval for the land and the time involved in opening a quarry. Cement produced on the water would also eliminate the need for a permit to cross a railroad right-of-way and a highway. He knew that coral was a form of limestone from which cement could be made, and there was virtually an unlimited supply of coral just offshore, which could be dredged into the ship by equipment on the ship itself. The cement thus produced could be moved directly by water to any point in the Islands or to South Pacific Islands. He even envisioned a ready-mix plant on the same ship, with the possibility of sailing it to the South Pacific, dredging coral, producing cement, converting it to ready-mix and pouring it directly onto big Navy runways or other installations.

The other thing that excited Kaiser was that his mainland cement company had already ordered equipment for a plant it was going to build in New Mexico. Kaiser called Wally Marsh, Vice President and General Manager of Permanente Cement in Oakland, and said, "Wally, I've decided we'll build our Hawaiian cement plant on a ship at anchor here. I'm going to need the equipment you have lined up for your New Mexico plant. Remember those LST's we built during the war. We'll get hold of a couple of those, lash them together, and end up with enough deck and below area on which to build a floating cement plant."

It was a Sunday afternoon and within a few minutes Marsh had Vic Cole, Vice President of Kaiser Engineers on the line. Cole responded, "Oh, my God, the kiln we have on order is 450 feet long and those LST's are only 325 feet long. Furthermore, a kiln has to be lined up precision straight with no movement allowed. It would be a disaster to put it on two LST's no matter how firmly they were lashed together."

Marsh called Kaiser back at once and reported what Cole had said. Within minutes, Kaiser had Cole on the line, "If you can't do it on LST's, what can you do it on?" "Well, Mr. Kaiser, we built some tankers that are long enough and perhaps we could find a tanker." "Okay, get busy and find one."

Sunday night and all day Monday Cole tried to track down an available tanker, one with an especially strong bulkhead running longitudinally to provide the necessary strength to support a kiln. Phone calls between Honolulu and Oakland were flying thick and fast. Kaiser was challenging Cole at every turn.

At 2:00 a.m. Tuesday night (midnight in Hawaii) Cole received a call from a Kaiser Engineer in Hawaii who had been working directly with Kaiser. "I'm in a helluva spot. Mr. Kaiser has sworn me to secrecy. He told me not to call you because if I did I would be told only about problems. But I am the one in Hawaii who is supposed to make a decision and come to him at 6:00 a.m. in the morning recommending Yes or No on an aircraft carrier that he has already optioned."

Without talking to anyone else about it, Kaiser himself had gotten an option between Sunday afternoon and Tuesday night on an aircraft carrier, which of course would be long enough and strong enough to hold the kiln. Soon, Cole was able to reach Edgar Kaiser and Gene Trefethen in New York City, it being 8:00 a.m. there. After they talked it over briefly, Edgar called Cole back: "I'll tell you what to do, Vic. Remember up in Washington we built a bridge on floating pontoons, great big, barge-type pontoons, great big, barge-type floats. Why don't you call my dad and tell him you've got a brilliant idea—to fabricate a concrete barge which would avoid a lot of problems an aircraft carrier would have. Then I'll call my dad about a half hour later and try the same idea on him. Without revealing that we know he has an option on an aircraft carrier, maybe together we can get him thinking about a barge."

Cole then called his engineer friend in Hawaii and told him to try to stall Kaiser until he (Cole) could reach him. By 6:00 a.m. Hawaii time Cole was talking to Kaiser: "Mr. Kaiser, I think I've got a great idea." He went on to explain about the barges in full detail. There was silence on the other end of the phone. Cole finally said, "Mr. Kaiser, are you there?" "Yes, I'm here. You know up to this point I was very worried about this project with you involved, but now I know it's a disaster." Then he went on to explain why it was such a terrible, lousy idea. He said he had thought about it a long time ago and had gone down and inspected a concrete barge and had discovered firsthand why a barge would be totally impractical.

This now meant a crash program to establish the feasibility of using an aircraft carrier. The one under option was at the Alameda Naval Base, so Cole got some marine experts to join him in looking the ship over. He was concerned about the absolute necessity of holding the 450-foot kiln within 1/2-inch tolerance from one end to the other. A carrier even though at anchor would obviously always be moving, however slightly, due to waves hitting the ship. Besides, with the sun often on one side of the ship or the other, the expansion and contraction of the kiln would likely throw it off balance. Cole reported this to Kaiser who snapped, "Why those problems are nothing at all. Remember those trusses we had on the Bay Bridge? They were long and straight and they have held the bridge in line. We'll just put the kiln on trusses in the ship and it won't matter what movement takes place. Now what's the next problem?"

Cole then pointed out the difficulty of installing and maintaining the heavy machinery down inside the ship. "That's no problem, either," Kaiser said, "the Navy's got a floating crane over here capable of lifting 200 tons. We'll just buy that crane, so that takes care of that, and now what other problems can you throw at me?"

By Thursday Kaiser had Cole inspect the aircraft carrier again to see if the generators on it were capable of providing the power needed by a cement plant. Cole planned to make his report Friday morning. Instead, at 6:00 a.m. Oakland time, 4:00 a.m. Hawaii time, Kaiser called Cole: "Have you got those drawings, yet?" "Mr. Kaiser, I had expected to complete my findings when I got to the office this morning, and I was going to call you." After some exchange Kaiser said, "I don't know why you can't perform more promptly. You really don't seem to understand this problem properly. People over here are aware that this is a fight between Walter Dillingham and me. We have been debating this in school auditoriums and we have been in the newspapers about it. He is a member of the old-time gang here in Hawaii and I'm considered a newcomer. Everybody is looking to see who will build a cement plant first. Can't you just imagine the reaction of people when we come sailing into Honolulu Harbor with an aircraft carrier, the bands playing, the flags flying? The people would all be with us. You don't seem to understand these things. You've raised so many problems, maybe you'd better find a rock to put this cement plant on."

It had been a whirlwind few days. Cole said he had had to use the specially compounded pink pill Rx5B (for treating Kaiseritis),as did others, but not Kaiser. He reveled in the excitement. Finally, however, he played out his string. Reluctantly, he

338

had to concede the aircraft idea did have too many problems. Not long after he also realized the Hawaiian people didn't want a winner and a loser. They wanted two winners, so approval was given to both plants, and construction went ahead on both.

Once Kaiser received approval for his cement plant he wanted a well-orchestrated advertising program. Everyone agreed he should be the company spokesman, not some trained outsider. When he arrived at the TV station, the station director almost blew the campaign by instructing Kaiser to read the "idiot" cards. If he had said "cue" cards, that might have been acceptable to Kaiser, but no way would he concede he needed "idiot" cards—claiming as his excuse he had forgotten his glasses. Finally, Vance Fawcett loaned his glasses and urged Kaiser to use the "cue" cards with whatever ad libbing he felt like doing. The session turned out great with each commercial only requiring one "take."

Sometime thereafter, a reporter from the Honolulu Star Bulletin asked Kaiser how he felt about the fact there were two cement plants on Oahu. True to his lifetime creed, Kaiser replied: "Thank God there are two cement plants here. Monopoly is not a good thing."

Still, Kaiser and Dillingham refused to have anything to do with one another. It was not until a few years after the feud started that Ale Kaiser, planning for another of her lavish New Year's Eve parties used one of Kaiser's own often-quoted expressions, "That's ridiculous," and called Mrs. Dillingham, saying she thought the two men had feuded long enough, and it was time to make up. Mrs. Dillingham heartily agreed. They decided that Mrs. Kaiser would send the Dillinghams an invitation to the party and neither wife would take "no" for an answer from their husbands.

That New Year's Eve the Dillinghams and the Kaisers sat together at the head table and the two old men talked and reminisced with one another as if they had never had a grudge in the world. They had made up and were close friends once again until their dying day, which unfortunately was not too long thereafter for either of them.

Upward And Onward

With Kaiser and Burns acquiring more and more land around the old Niumalu Hotel site, it was obvious that they would not be satisfied very long with a low-rise and cottage-type hotel operation. Hardly had the 3-story section been completed when they began pushing their architect Bauer to rush plans for a 14-story building close to the beach to be known as Ocean Tower.

This involved another flurry of moving coconut palm trees, which seemed to fascinate tourists. They would take a walk down from the thatched cottages to the ocean, and when they returned a few hours later to find a coconut tree where they had earlier walked, it became a topic of much buzzing.

This time a new element of confusion was added amidst all the construction—pile drivers. This noisy operation was not welcomed by the tourist who came to Hawaii to be put to sleep by the lapping of the ocean waves, now being rudely awakened early in the morning with the "Chug-Pop, Chug-Pop" of the pile driver. Handy tried everything to keep the guests happy and laughing, even concocting a new drink which was sold at a bargain price and called "The Pile Driver," consisting of prune juice and vodka.

When complaints would come too thick and fast, he would go to Kaiser and ask if the pile driving couldn't at least be delayed till 8:00 a.m. instead of 7:00 a.m. His pleas always fell on deaf ears because the cornerstone of Kaiser's construction philosophy, and even his general business philosophy, was always speed. Besides, he loved to watch construction and assumed everyone else enjoyed it as much as he did. He would argue that he was doing the tourists a favor by giving them a show they couldn't see anywhere else.

Not surprisingly, the 14-story Ocean Tower was completed in six months, one of its attractions being an intimate bar where entertainment could be staged. Kaiser thought it would be fun to take it upon himself to line up the entertainment. However, his performers didn't seem to be drawing the crowds, and he wasn't about to pay the high prices asked by stars from Hollywood or Las Vegas.

Then he lucked out. Just a few months before a group of Honolulu businessmen calling themselves the "Honolulu Vikings" had made an exploratory stag trip to Tahiti. Although they had pledged each other to secrecy, word soon got out that they had been wowed by a very sensuous dance that the Tahitian girls performed which made the Hawaiian hula look like a missionary dance.

At that time, there were only two ways to get to Tahiti—Pan Am Airways which made just a few trips a week, or a luxury sailing ship, the TeVega with a four to six week roundtrip. Word got to Kaiser that Spence Weaver, owner of a large string of restaurants, some of which featured entertainment, had just sailed for Tahiti on the TeVega and was going to bring back a troupe of dancers and Tahitian musicians who would knock the people's eyes out in Honolulu, especially the tourists'.

Kaiser quickly got together with his Tahitian boatman, Terii Rua and asked him if he knew any of the good Tahitian entertainers. Terii not only knew some, he knew the best, and they were all his friends. With Kaiser listening in on the phone, Terii called Tahiti and arranged for the best of the dancers and musicians to come to Hawaii on the next Pan Am flight. By the time Weaver got to Tahiti, that island's best entertainers were already in Honolulu performing before overflow crowds at the Hawaiian Village in the newly named bar—what else, The Tahitian Room. The next time Kaiser and Weaver met at a cocktail party, the atmosphere was a bit chilly, even for balmy Hawaii.

Even though Kaiser always reveled in the limelight, no one could ever accuse him of being stuffy or prudish. He always seemed more like an uninhibited child caught up in the excitement of what he was doing and anxious to tell others about it. So he gave the young Tahitians a warm greeting they could not have expected. Since they did not speak English, Terii acted as interpreter. They were put up the first night at a nearby home. When they appeared for breakfast at the Village, Kaiser asked how they slept and were they comfortable. The lead dancer rattled off something in French, and

Terii interpreted it for Kaiser, "She says everything was fine, but because of the storm during the night she got scared and jumped in bed with the boys." Kaiser was like a little kid sharing in the laughter that followed.

Because of a lifetime spent in building things, Kaiser always had a pretty good idea of what something was going to cost—or at least what he felt he could justify spending. When someone would come up with an estimate that seemed out of line to Kaiser, he would beat the person down mercilessly, challenging every line item. On one of Handy's paraboloid estimates, Kaiser couldn't find a thing to take out or reduce from the estimate until he came to "Contingency - 10%."

"What's that for?" he asked.

"It's for all the things that will crop up that I haven't been able to think of," Handy replied.

"Well, what have you left out?"

"If I knew that, I wouldn't need the contingency."

"Well then, you must have thought of everything, so take it out."

At that point the estimate was reduced enough so Kaiser felt comfortable starting the job. Later, Handy made the fatal mistake of showing Kaiser the actual cost of the job and it was almost on the nose of Handy's estimate including the 10% contingency. Kaiser berated him for the "overrun," because he had "run such an inefficient job."

In time, the people who worked closely with Kaiser, including his architects and engineers, came up with two guidelines: "It doesn't matter what it costs as long as the estimate is low," and "don't draw attention to how the final cost compares with the estimate."

Two Young Impresarios

It would be hard to say which activity Kaiser enjoyed more—building things or promoting what he had built. The exceptions, of course, were roads, dams, and ships that he built. Once they were finished there was no occasion for him to promote them, so he never looked back.

Over the years he very literally set a goal for himself of having at least 10 new ideas a day he could be mulling over in his mind on how something he was doing, or something he was interested in, could be done faster, better, differently, or more economically. With so many balls in the air at all times, he was never lacking for those daily 10 new ideas.

It didn't bother him that after analyzing his ideas, he would end up discarding most of them as being impractical. But when he got on the trail of one that he felt worthy of being pursued he would drive everyone around him to distraction doing surveys, cost estimates and market studies to determine its feasibility.

With his love of boats it was inevitable that he would build a 100-foot catamaran just to take tourists from the Hawaiian Village to Pearl Harbor. He couldn't quite see them being all that contented just looking at the beauty of the shoreline, so he produced a short movie to be presented on each trip extolling the attractions at his hotel and trying to coax them to come to the Tapa Room for dinner and show.

His aluminum company was at that time promoting household aluminum foil. Kaiser himself was more excited about the market potential for foil than any other person in his company. It was his idea that they insert in every box of foil a promotional piece on the Hawaiian Village with a coupon attached which would get the purchaser a free Hawaiian recipe book if they wrote in. Then he initiated the idea and went to great lengths to cajole his aluminum company executives into holding a cookout promotion, featuring the use of aluminum foil in cooking, with contests to be held in twenty-five regions of the country, and the finals at the Hawaiian Village with the mainland winners getting a free trip to Hawaii.

This was not only a totally innovative scheme, but a major undertaking. It took a lot of nationwide promotion to sell the idea to the thousands of potential contenders. In the twenty-five regions of the country it took a lot of organization to run the contests and end up with a winner. Then in Hawaii three days were required to carry out the championship cookout.

1. The first day was given over to acquainting the contestants with all aspects of the competition.

2. The second day involved (a) orientation of the judges, (b) shopping for food by the participants, (c) familiarization of everyone with the area of competition. The rules specified:

> The cookout arena will be established in the Ale Ale Kai Gardens of the Hawaiian Village Hotel. With the installation of 25 gleaming grills, tables, charcoal, refrigeration equipment, dry storage lockers, etc., the Garden will become the world's largest outdoor barbecue kitchen. It will be guarded overnight and no one will be allowed to enter the area.

3. The cookout itself was held the third day from 10:30 a.m. to 3:30 p.m. "Finalists will prepare their respective recipes three times, one of which will be evaluated by the panel of judges. At 3:00 p.m. a warning whistle will be sounded to notify contestants that they have 30 minutes in which to prepare their recipe for judging."

The first cookout was held in November 1959. Signifying the importance Kaiser attached to the event is this letter he wrote to Governor and Mrs. Quinn of Hawaii:

> We wish to extend a most cordial invitation to you to be honored guests at the award ceremony and dinner Saturday night, November 14, when the winners will be named in America's first cookout championship. Twenty-five chefs from 11 parts of the United States will compete here in an unusual 'Cookoff' sponsored by Kaiser Aluminum. Mainland writers, as well as camera people, coming here to cover the occasion include representatives of N.E.A., United Press International, Good Housekeeping, Parade Magazine, American Weekly, King Features, Chicago Sun-Times, Movietone news,

Travel Columnist Stanton Delaplane—certain of whom have expressed hope that they may interview the Governor of the new 50th State. Judges of the national finals will be Stan Musial, famed first baseman of the St. Louis Cardinals and restauranteur, and four food editors and writers. James Garner, star of the national television show, Maverick, will be Master of Ceremonies at the award ceremony, which will start socially in the Little Long House area of the Hawaiian Village Hotel, followed by dinner with entertainment at 8:00 p.m. in the Tapa Room. Hoping you will be able to join in this pleasant occasion, and with very warmest personal regards.

Reflecting the fact that most outdoor barbecuing is done by men, the contest was restricted to male entries. The prizes were very generous—not only a free trip with all expenses paid to Hawaii for the twenty-five finalists, but a first prize of $10,000 for the winner, and Jeep station wagons for four runner- up winners.

So successful was the event it was carried forward for many years with continued generous prizes. Each year arrangements were made for national celebrities to make the awards. In the second year, 1960, actress Joan Crawford presided at the awards ceremony—her first visit to Hawaii in 13 years. Not long after Kaiser died in 1967 the cookout competition was abandoned, underscoring the fact that it was uniquely his personal sponsorship that had kept it going.

He was not at all shy about making his own sales pitches either in person or on film. During the early days of the Village when occupancy was running at only 30 percent to 50 per cent, he had a talking slide film prepared starring himself. He then bought a slide-sound projector that could be operated on a desk top, grabbed a handful of airplane tickets and personally called on the largest travel agents in the country from the West Coast to Chicago to New York. It did the trick—the Hawaiian Village became known and an ever-increasing number of tours were booked.

Kaiser kept having so much fun dabbling in the entertainment world, his partner, Fritz Burns, decided to get in the act. Soon they were trying to outdo each other in lining up entertainment. They borrowed the conch shell blowing and luau torch lighting ceremony at sunset from the Coco Palms Hotel on Kauai but added to it a flag-lowering ceremony as well, with Emma Vera singing the Star Spangled Banner, a cappella.

It was Burns' idea to have "Ancient Hawaiian Nights" each Sunday evening in the Tapa Room, featuring the foremost exponent of authentic hula, Iolani Luahine. He then tracked down the famous Hawaiian falsetto, George Kainapau, the one with the diamond-studded front tooth who had moved to the mainland, and brought him back to entertain in the garden outside the Ale Kai Room. Then Mary Ann Sears, who had done aesthetic swimming with Esther Williams, was signed up to put on water ballets in the pool at night. Finally, Hilo Hattie was coaxed into joining the Apaka show. The two young impresarios, Kaiser and Burns, really had covered the entertainment market.

In the end, Danny Kaleikini had the tough chore of filling Apaka's shoes, but he rose to it and later went to the Kahala Hilton Hotel where he was starred for years.

When Kaiser's successful television show, Maverick, had about run its course, his advertising agency tried to get him launched in a television detective series. He liked the sound of the script, but he didn't like the idea that it was to be staged in some mainland city. Before his executives realized what was happening to them he had them talked into staging the detective series in Honolulu, more specifically at the Hawaiian Village Hotel, and even more specifically with much of the key action taking place in the Shell Bar and the Tapa Room. Someone hit on the catchy title, "The Hawaiian Eye," which became very popular and which was the forerunner of other Hawaiian detective television series—Hawaii Five-O, Jack Lord, and today's Magnum, P.I. with Tom Selleck.

It was in those helter-skelter days that Fritz Burns gave poetic expression to his feelings about working with Kaiser. Here's his bit of doggerel exactly as he had it typed up for his partner Kaiser, who was 18 years his senior:

THE KAISER-MAN

I'm one of the famous Kaiser crew
The whole wide world we span.
Spent six months in Hawaii --
But did I get a tan?

Six days we work,
One day we rest
By the Good Book we abide
There are six boats in that harbor
But do I ever get a ride?

For work is fun,
And fun is rest --
That's our phil-o-so-phy
In fact we hardly work at all,
And we are so-o hap-py!

Kaiser Takes To The Air

It should not have surprised anyone that Kaiser would enter the radio and television business. He had become personally involved in producing TV commercials for his automobile company. In Hawaii he had accepted invitations to appear on both TV and radio shows, and was amazed at the widespread public response he received. Besides, he was fascinated with the entertainment world, having so many stars as his friends. He knew there was not only money to be made in both TV and radio, but it would be the best possible way to advertise his hotel. He realized that most rented U-Drive cars had radios in them for the tourists to listen to, and most hotel rooms had TVs in them, so if he owned a radio and TV station, and if the call letters were KHVH and KHVH-TV (standing, of course, for Kaiser Hawaiian Village Hotel) and if at every station break the announcer said something about "This program is coming to you from Kaiser's beautiful Hawaiian Village Hotel, home of the Alfred Apaka Show," it would be sure to build patronage at the hotel.

In keeping with his long-established practice, he knew he had to have a partner—a well-known and popular "pro" in the field. He had already become briefly acquainted with Hal Lewis, known over the air waves as J. Akuhead Pupule (in Hawaiian it means J. Crazy Fishhead), the most popular disk jockey in the islands. Then in early 1957 they chanced to bump into each other at a public function. Kaiser took the initiative, cornering Lewis and suggesting that the two of them launch brand new radio and television stations, with Kaiser putting up most of the money and Lewis paying his share from the advertising he would attract and from his individual performance over the stations. Pupule was flattered, and sparked to the idea immediately. As Handy later said, "both Kaiser and Pupule could sell snake oil," so they were a natural partnership, each one trying to outdo the other in his enthusiasm.

The market surveys and the cost estimates were not too reassuring. Fritz Burns declined to participate. However, one finding of a Certified Public Accounting firm in Honolulu caught Kaiser's fancy. It said that the radio station could be in the black in 5 or 6 months, and the television station would be out of the red within a year and a half. He completely ignored the CPA firm's disclaimer which said in effect, "Our conclusion is based on figures furnished to us by Hal Lewis, and we take no responsibility for their accuracy." When people around him would challenge the plan, Kaiser would turn a deaf ear and point to the forecast, "It's all here in black and white. We'll soon be in the black. Can't you see?"

Lawyers drew up a partnership agreement showing Kaiser with 51 percent and Lewis 49 percent. After all, Kaiser was going to put up the money while Lewis would only bring to the table his public following and his creative talent. Kaiser sent the agreement back to the lawyers, instructing them to make it 50%-50%. "How can we be true partners if one of us has the upper hand," had always been his theory. Partner "Aku" was made general manager of both the radio and television stations.

The existing 8 radio stations tried to block FCC authority for the new station, but to no avail. The 3 television stations, with their NBC, CBS and ABC connections, didn't feel Kaiser could pose serious competition without a national network hook-up, so they didn't enter objections.

Construction of the buildings, facilities, and radio and TV towers was another whirlwind undertaking. It was just hours before the deadline for going on the air or losing the license that KHVH Radio hit the air waves of Hawaii.

Fate played right into Kaiser's hands, because the very next day a tidal wave struck the Islands. The wave was not too destructive on Oahu, but it did extensive damage on Hilo and parts of Kauai. With his keen sense of the dramatic, J Akuhead Pupule pounced on the story with both feet and within a few minutes almost everyone within range was listening to the new station, "the News Station," an idea that Aku came up with in the middle of it all. With the tidal wave as a catalyst, the upstart Kaiser radio station already had command of the audience, and the format had been established—a news station with easy-listening music instead of rock and roll. Actually, the easy-listening music didn't last very long because of audience complaints, but at least people in Hawaii had become very much aware of their newest station.

A colorful disk jockey has colorful tastes, especially when he can count on his partner, Kaiser, to foot the bills. Aku was flying high, wide and handsome, and so were the expenses. Even the new TV station, which started up in June 1957 several weeks after the radio station, soon fell on hard times. Since Aku could not use any programs from the 3 major networks, he opted to buy a $1 million package of old movies to be shown day and night. This did not catch on, and KHVH-TV was a poor fourth place when the ratings came out. Consequently, the advertising was exceedingly poor also. The ink was red and it appeared it would remain so for a long time.

It became more and more obvious that the marriage of Kaiser and Aku had not been made in heaven and would have to be split up. To buy Aku's half of the partnership, which represented mostly his talents but no money, Kaiser paid a quarter of a million dollars, which was reasonable enough. Aku did remain as a disk jockey for a long time and he was rewarded handsomely for his services because he was the best in the Islands and brought in a lot of advertising money.

Furthermore, Kaiser and Aku kept up a warm friendship over the years. With all of his showmanship, Aku issued this decree over the air supported by a fancy, formally printed large scroll given to Kaiser:

Decree

Know all men by these presents, Henry J. Kaiser is 'A Legend In His Own Time' because he is 'alive at such an age' and has used his time with verve, imagination and astonishing industry to produce an empire of achievement and is therefore privileged to join this fraternity in all gatherings in Legendary Halls forever. Given under my hand and the seal of the J Akuhead Pupule Show (KGU-NBC) State of Hawaii, this thirteenth day of December A D 1964

Signed
J Akuhead Pupule
A Legend In His Own Time
Custodian of the Seal

In time, Burns changed his mind and the broadcasting business became a part of the Kaiser-Burns partnership for a while. It later was enlarged as the Kaiser Broadcasting Division of Kaiser Industries with radio and TV stations on the mainland as well. A big step forward was taken in Hawaii by the purchase of the Channel 4 ABC network station. All the while the airwaves in Hawaii kept proclaiming "KHVH and KHVH-TV—Henry J. Kaiser's fabulous Hawaiian Village Hotel," and the tourists came flocking in. In the end, the Kaiser Broadcasting Division turned out to be a good profit center.

One very revealing clue to Kaiser's way of doing business came out of the radio and TV station era in the Islands. In an effort to find a winning combination of disk jockeys and announcers, both broadcasting stations had quite a turnover of talent in a relatively short time. This was not too unusual in Honolulu where talent was constantly playing musical chairs.

A group of unhappy Kaiser stations "alumni" got together and decided to have a dinner, invite the press, vent their spleen on Kaiser, and in the end hang an effigy of Kaiser as a protest publicity stunt. Word of the event got back to Kaiser who at first was anything but amused. Consideration was given to having his attorneys get a court order to stop the event, or even suing for defamation of character. Then Kaiser had a flash inspiration -- "I'll go to the party myself."

His associates thought he was out of his mind to even consider such a move, but he couldn't be talked out of it. On the evening of the affair Kaiser and one of his assistants, Bob Elliott, who had had a lot of dealings with the press, arrived at the restaurant just as the "alumni" were warming up in their private room. Kaiser knocked on the door, and when it opened, he said, "Boys, may I come in and join you?"

What could they say except "Come in," which he did? He conveyed the friendliest kind of feelings, had dinner with them, told them stories about his own successes and failures including the time he was turned down for a job 13 times as a youth, told them of the several times he too had been fired, ending up with a pep talk about going out and spending their energies making good instead of spending time tearing someone down. In that kind of situation no one could hold a candle to Kaiser for warmth and persuasiveness.

Needless to say, no effigy was hung and he left with the "alumni" cheering him.

"Those Dirty Pups"

The timing couldn't have been better from Kaiser's point of view—R. Buckminster Fuller had just developed a geodesic dome, an innovative, low-cost structure that covered a large area without any interior structural columns. The ideal material for the building was aluminum, and Kaiser Aluminum Company's engineers had worked up drawings to promote this use for their product. They were already fabricating these panels at the Permanente, California plant where they had the finest open-ended brakepresses on the West Coast.

Kaiser preempted their production because he wanted to startle the people of Hawaii with one of these striking new structures. He knew it would not only create a lot of attention for the Hawaiian Village but would be an ideal facility for theatrical productions, conventions, huge banquets and meetings of all kinds.

Kaiser Aluminum engineers first sent over drawings for the foundations and footings which were huge—not to hold the dome up but to hold it down, because the aerodynamics were such that in a heavy wind it tended to lift like an airplane wing. Then the carefully numbered panels arrived and were placed around the circular concrete floor for easy, orderly assembly.

To construct the dome there was a temporary tower placed in the center of the floor with 4 cables which passed over pulleys at the top and which were attached to hand winches at the bottom. Using a new pneumatic riveting device known as a Huck Gun, the first four panels which would be the top of the dome would be riveted together, lifted up the central tower to make room for the next ring of panels, then the next and the next—a process of building from the top down. Ultimately, when the last row of panels was riveted to the bottom of the dome, it would be secured to the large circumference of the concrete footings. Until the time it was secured, however, it would hang free in the air on the cables and more and more become a potential swinging bell if very much wind should come up suddenly. It was therefore absolutely critical that it be erected during a quiet period when there would be no trade winds.

What a plaything for Kaiser! He would be like a little child with his erector set. Right at that time, however, he had to be on the mainland for an important meeting. No matter. Every few hours on this Friday, January 18, 1957, he would phone to check on the progress being made in arranging the loose panels. Then when construction was to begin on Monday he would be back in Honolulu to "oversee" the erection. Kaiser Aluminum engineers who had come over to supervise the erection had estimated it would take five days to assemble once everything was in place.

That Friday afternoon after work, cars streamed down Ala Moana Boulevard past the dome site which just looked like an empty lot with junk stored on it.

Because the crew that was hired to assemble the pieces had never done it before, and had never even heard of a Huck Gun, it was decided to bring them in Saturday morning for a short time to let them get the feel of the operation. It turned out to be a perfect morning with no wind at all. The workers started riveting some trial panels, and soon they caught on how much fun it was and how fast the dome was taking shape. With the weather being ideal the crew was kept working for 10 hours, finishing nearly half of the dome. Now it was hanging up fairly high, supported only by the four cables. It would be precarious if a wind should come up and start it swinging like a pendulum.

A call was made to the weather bureau who forecast a calm Sunday, but the possibility of a weather front moving in by Monday. What to do, considering Kaiser's desire to be in on the erection? Handy decided that a two-day record construction would please Kaiser, so he made the decision to call the crew back to work on Sunday. Just to cover his flanks, he told Kaiser's wife, Ale who was in Honolulu, what he was doing. She concurred heartily and said she would not mention it to "The Boss," as she always called him, until he got home.

By Sunday sunset and another 10-hour shift, the dome was completely assembled and securely anchored to the foundations. It had taken only 20 hours to erect what the engineers thought would take 5 days. Needless to say, when the people of Honolulu drove by Monday morning on their way to work and saw the huge dome standing where there had been a vacant lot the Friday evening before, they had a hard time believing their eyes.

When Ale greeted "The Boss" at the airport on Monday, his first words were about the dome. She assured him everything was in order, and he would be very pleased with all he saw, but she wanted him to go home first, freshen up after his long flight, maybe take a short rest before going to the Village, because she knew he would be there the rest of the day. No way. He insisted they drive by and see how "the boys" were doing. Then he started telling her about all the things that had been going on on the mainland and he became temporarily oblivious of anything around him. As they came down Ala Moana Boulevard he didn't notice the dome until he was right on top of it. Then he broke out in a big grin and with obvious pride and affection said, "Why those dirty pups, they did it without me." That evening the newspaper carried a picture and story which commented, "And he was tickled you know what color."

With all the fun Kaiser had in arranging construction of the dome, it was only the beginning of the pleasure he would get out of promoting its use. It would become a real showcase for him. He started by having a grand opening Sunday evening, February 17. With a program title "8 Acts in Symphony-Polynesia" it featured George Barati conducting the Honolulu Symphony Orchestra supported by a cast of Hawaii's best performers. Naturally, a major portion of the program starred Alfred Apaka and the Hawaiian Village Serenaders in a dazzling performance. It was a sell-out crowd of 1500, with Governor and Mrs. Samuel W. King as honored guests.

From that time on the dome was kept busy every week with concerts, home shows, conventions, dances, luaus, school festivals, and other activities serving dozens of different organizations. Kaiser's big coup came that fall when he talked his friends, Michael Todd and his wife Elizabeth Taylor, into using the dome for the mid-Pacific premiere of Todd's Academy Award film "Around the World in 80 Days." It was set for Friday night, November 1, 1957, as a benefit performance for the Oahu Society for Crippled Children and Adults. But, as so often happened with Kaiser, his innovative programming was threatened by a court action of other theater owners in Honolulu who claimed there was no license for the dome to show a Hollywood film. Kaiser roared back, asserting that once again a monopoly was trying to deny him his legitimate rights. He offered to underwrite the expense of a mass meeting in the dome where "the people could be heard." This didn't prove necessary as the Planning Commission soon agreed with Kaiser.

The arrival of Todd and Taylor in Honolulu on Thursday morning before the Friday night show was their first-ever trip to the islands. Along with the other Hollywood celebrities who were with them, it created a real stir among the islanders. Todd was host to a select luncheon group in the Gold Room of the Hawaiian Village Hotel shortly after his arrival where he and Kaiser toasted the people of Hawaii for their upcoming support. The premiere itself was a breathtaking spectacle made possible by costly new projection devices, created and perfected by Todd engineers after many months of painstaking preparation. For weeks thereafter the film was shown in the dome, on a reserved seat policy, every night including Sundays with three matinees weekly on Wednesdays, Saturdays and Sundays.

An HMO Comes To Hawaii

As reported in Chapter 4, The Shining Star, not long after Kaiser became established in Hawaii, the Medical Association appealed to him not to bring his prepaid hospital program to the Islands. In response, Kaiser urged the Association to set up its own program and offered complete assistance in helping them get it launched. They didn't want to get involved in such a program, so they never took him up on his offer. Once this became clear to Kaiser, he didn't waver in his original goal to bring the Kaiser Permanente Health Plan to Honolulu. It was the one venture dearest to his heart. He knew it would serve a real need in the community . The only question was one of timing—how could he get all of his other Honolulu activities under control so he could launch the hospital program properly.

By 1957 he had found the property he wanted on Ala Moana Boulevard, backing up to the Ala Wai Yacht Harbor. He started driving piles in January 1958—and shock waves went racing through the medical community. They had no desire whatsoever to see Kaiser and his "socialized" medicine come to Hawaii.

This was a bit surprising to Kaiser. Not that he was unaccustomed to opposition. It was just that by this time most of the opposition by doctors on the mainland had subsided. He somehow thought that with all the things he was doing to bolster the Hawaiian economy, and with all the friendly relations he had tried to maintain with the Medical Association, even the doctors would now be able to recognize it was just the opposite from socialized medicine and would even be helpful to their practice.

Nevertheless, he encountered the same kind of resistance he had met so many times before—doctors didn't want to jeopardize their standing by going with him. Finally, after many months of searching, five doctors in different fields of medical practice who had been well-respected, agreed to form the nucleus of the hospital team. The words "had been" are necessary, because the moment it became known they had gone with Kaiser they were completely ostracized by their former colleagues. Even their wives, who had been close friends of other doctors' wives, were shunned as if they had leprosy.

The five doctors stuck it out, however, and started building a team of additional doctors, because it was anticipated there would be pre-enrollment of health plan members of about 16,000. But it didn't work out that way. When the hospital and clinics opened in November 1958, there were only 5,500 members. The medical group became a bit disgruntled because this meant their income would not be as good as expected.

Handy had been Project Manager during the 10-month construction of the 10-story hospital. Now Kaiser asked him to be Regional Manager of the health plan and hospital. This wasn't too big an adjustment for him because he soon found out running a hospital was very much like running a hotel. The patients were like tourists, they had to be cajoled and entertained as well as treated. The doctors were the prima donnas instead of the musicians.

These similarities led Kaiser into making an unwise decision. With his hospital rooms vacant following the November opening and the hotels temporarily oversold for part of the Christmas holiday season, he began putting tourists in some of the hospital rooms. They loved it—new, clean rooms with a view, beds that would go up and down, electrically controlled drapes, water by the bed, remote control TV, instant room service, everything deluxe.

With the doctors it was another story. They were livid. "Kaiser is making us the laughingstock of the whole town. How can we ever face any of our former medical associates again?" Because of this and other disagreements, it was only a few months later that the original five doctors left the program, but by then there was a good nucleus of competent doctors on the staff, and the health plan was growing in ever-increasing numbers.

In addition to the skills of the medical group, there were two main reasons for the rapid growth of the program: (1) the hospital and clinics were far and away the most modern and best equipped in Honolulu, and (2) nearly every family could afford the very low monthly fees, especially considering the all-inclusive services offered.

After its shaky start, the health plan kept rolling. In 1988 there are more than 150,000 members in Hawaii. However, no more tourists have been put up at the hospital since that first Christmas.

Building A Whole City

One time when Kaiser was crowding one of his executives to hurry up and get a construction job finished, the executive defensively blurted out, "After all, Mr. Kaiser, Rome wasn't built in a day." "That's because I wasn't there," Kaiser responded.

Kaiser found his chance to build his own kind of Rome in Hawaii when he was in his late seventies. It all began when he was negotiating with the trustees of the Bishop Estate for a seven-acre leasehold at the end of Portlock Road, on which he wanted to build his own last "permanent" home. In the process of negotiating this lease, one of the trustees asked, "Mr. Kaiser, you know that swampy area we call Kuapa Pond? We have run many studies of ways to develop it and still have it be economically feasible. So far we have not been able to come up with anything. Would you have any ideas?"

A challenge made to order for Henry Kaiser—made perfectly to order just for him. Within a very short space of time he not only had negotiated a lease for his 7-acre estate at the end of Portlock Road, but had also negotiated an exclusive development contract for 6000 acres of undeveloped Bishop Estate land ranging from May Way to the southeast end of the island, and from the coastline to the ridge of the Koolau Mountains.

Kaiser invited his partner, Fritz Burns, to join him in the venture, but Burns who had bought back into the Hilton Hawaiian Village thought it was too big a bite to take at one time, so he declined the offer. Now it was up to Kaiser to go it alone, relying on his own resourcefulness, and counting on financial help from his own Kaiser sources and from the Bank of America.

Where do you start in planning how to develop most efficiently and most aesthetically 6000 acres of rugged, raw land with a swamp right in the center of the whole project? Then there were the valleys of Hahaione, Kamilonui, Kamiloiki, and Kalama where homes would eventually have to be built. These valleys and the slopes on either side of them were covered with thousands of tons of huge boulders that would have to be removed and disposed of before buildable subdivisions could be developed.

There were the problems of basic utilities such as sewer, water, electricity, telephones and gas. Although some of these services were in parts of the area, they were only on a limited trunk line basis and were entirely inadequate to serve a community of 60,000 people which was the ultimate goal.

It was enough to scare off anyone but Kaiser. He had spent a lifetime moving earth, stabilizing it, laying solid foundations.

One of the first things needed for the area was a name—a name that would have meaning, public appeal, be easily remembered, easily pronounced with a Hawaiian ring to it. It was for Kaiser himself to come up with the name—Hawaii Kai. It sounded Hawaiian. It was appropriately descriptive since "Kai" means sea in Hawaiian, and it interpreted as "Hawaii by the sea," which it was. Moreover, "Kai" had the beginning ring of Kaiser so there was a logical association. It was a lyrical name easy to pronounce and remember. It helped get the project off to a favorable start.

It was almost mind-boggling just to get started on the planning and engineering. So a whole procession of planners was called on to contribute their skills—not just planners on the Kaiser staff but world renowned planners such as Mamoru Yamasaki, the outstanding Japanese firm based in New York; William Perriera; John Carle Warneke and Associates; and L. Frederick Pack, just to name a few.

Master plans were drawn and redrawn until they met the approval of Kaiser and his staff. Then they were submitted to the trustees of Bishop Estate who had the right of approval. Finally, the plans were submitted to the City and County planners and to the Council, all of whom made suggestions and revisions. The first rough, rough General Plan was prepared for "internal office use only" in June 1959. As preliminary as it was, it was enough to get Kaiser off and running in certain areas of the project. However, because of the almost never-ending refinement in plans, it was not until March 1966 that the final General Plan could be officially adopted to become the

"Detailed Land Use Map for Hawaii Kai," approved by the City and County of Honolulu.

All that time money was being poured into the project by the millions with very little revenue coming in return. Kaiser executives were becoming more and more restless. The Bank of America warned Kaiser there was no open end on the loans they could make to him. While Fred Ferroggiaro, Executive Vice President of the bank, had been the primary contact for Kaiser, Clark Beise, recently appointed President of the bank, inserted himself in the negotiations for Hawaii Kai funds and told Kaiser that $5 million, not $20 million, was the most that could be loaned until greater income from the project could be generated.

It was also a different experience for most of the planners and architects. They weren't free to do their work in the comfort and seclusion of their home offices, but instead had to be on the spot in Hawaii Kai where Kaiser could personally watch and participate in every step. He also was not content with taking the planners' word that their more detailed layouts would look all right aesthetically, once built. He brought in a top flight architectural delineator, John Hollingsworth, gave him the Warnecke plans and requested him to do water color renditions showing how the areas would actually look when built. These renderings took months of work and Kaiser would counsel with the artist several times a day.

From the start Kaiser was determined to build a model city with all the latest amenities and aesthetic features. There would be no overhead wiring, no unsightly television antennaes—the entire community would be served with a television cable system, another first for Hawaii. All new home plans and alterations would require approval of an architectural board. Subdivisions with potential views would have sight line restrictions to preserve views. All subdivisions, whether for expensive or moderately priced homes, would have the same quality streets, curbs, sidewalks, and street lights. Kaiser was bringing into play all his construction expertise and all his sense of good living that he had acquired throughout his long lifetime.

In his determination to build a better but less expensive home, he became upset with the local concrete producing companies because they were charging him a premium to deliver ready-mix concrete supposedly because of the distance. He protested that this was unfair because the distance was not much greater than to Aina Haina as just one example. When repeated attempts to obtain concrete at a price equal to his competitors closer to Honolulu failed, he said "OK, I'll bring in my own ready-mix trucks and make my own concrete." It was not long before the ready-mix companies lowered their price, whereupon he sold them his ready-mix trucks and was happy.

Kaiser played no favorites in the hundreds of suppliers he had to deal with, not even to his own companies. For some reason his Kaiser Gypsum Company which produced wallboard would not deliver wallboard to his job as cheaply as another manufacturer. Kaiser placed orders with his competitors to the complete dismay of his Kaiser Gypsum executives. He made it perfectly clear that if they could not compete in the open market, they had better jolly well find out how to. It was not long until they did.

One of the conditions of the development agreement with Bishop Estate was that trustee approval had to be given before any new work could be commenced. This meant loss of time and Kaiser was often in too much of a hurry to wait. If he wanted to see the view from the top of a ridge so he could do his planning better, overnight he would have a D-9 Caterpillar tractor bulldoze a rough road through the under-brush, and the next morning he would drive up there in his pink jeep and thrill at the view. The trustees kept complaining that this sort of thing had to stop until their approval was obtained.

One day Kaiser received a stern letter from the trustees notifying him that he must cease and desist unauthorized operations, ending with "and furthermore if you con-tinue to do so, you will do so at your own risk." He read the letter with a sober expression until he came to the last line at which point he broke out with a loud laugh. Slapping his hand down on his desk, he said, "They've done it. They've given me permission to do anything I want without their approval—as long as I do it at my own risk." To him it was carte blanche. He kept taking more and more risks.

Sales of homes got off to a disappointing start. Surveys indicated the people liked the houses and thought they were of good quality—but Hawaii Kai "was so far out of town," it was "too windy," there was only a narrow two-lane road, and they feared congestion. Many could not see the potentials of the marina and community through the construction equipment, the trenches, and the rubble.

At about that time Kaiser learned the state was embarking on another expensive "study" on the possibility of widening Kalanianaole Highway to four lanes. It didn't take him long to figure out that for the amount the State was going to spend on the "study," he could actually build a four-lane highway. He contacted the governor, Wil-liam Quinn, with his proposal. The governor liked the idea but of course couldn't just give the job to Kaiser; it would have to be put out to open bid. Kaiser bid on the job and won, and within a few months there were four paved lanes to Hawaii Kai instead of two, and for less than the "study" was going to cost.

With his interest in sales as keen as his interest in construction, Kaiser hit on the idea of inviting the Home Builders Association to have their annual Parade of Homes in Hawaii Kai. Always in the past the parade had been held in locations scattered throughout Oahu. In 1963 he offered the Home Builders a row of lots fronting on Kalananaole Highway and facing the marina at very attractive terms. He also agreed to provide backup lots on attractive terms so they could sell more houses as their Parade homes sold. One stipulation—the Parade of Homes would be exclusively in Hawaii Kai. The Home Builders agreed.

When the parade was held there were more than a dozen homes offered by display side-by-side in one location, easily reached by the new four-lane highway. The Home Builders advertised the show, and Kaiser added extensive advertising featuring Hawaii Kai. The results were almost overwhelming. Large crowds had been expected and prepared for, but instead the people came by the thousands. The highway was packed solid, bumper-to-bumper, for long distances most of the first two days of the show. The Parade was such a success that it was repeated the next year in another Hawaii Kai Marina location. Kaiser had broken the ice. A bright future for Hawaii Kai was assured.

Island Paradise

It is doubtful if any person—resident or tourist—ever loved Hawaii more than Henry Kaiser did during the time he lived there, the last thirteen years of his life.

Yet nothing in his earlier years could have portended that he would end up there. He had never been one to dream about moving to an island paradise. He had never yearned for the time he could lie on the beach and take it easy. He had no friends or family beckoning him to join them there. His entire life had been spent in a whirlwind of activities in the big arenas of the mainland.

More than anything else, the thing that attracted him to Hawaii was the chance to start a whole new life with his young wife where almost single-handedly he could launch one major enterprise after another. He loved Hawaii not because he could take things easy there, but because he could do his own thing in his own way on an almost around-the-clock basis.

His good health contributed greatly to his happiness. When one is feeling good it is much easier to be cheerful. Considering that he was in his seventies and eighties, and that he had allowed himself to get fat, it was quite remarkable that he remained so healthy and had such boundless energy. On the other hand, a good case could be made to prove that he remained healthy precisely because he was so busy and so happy.

On an everyday basis he would be up and on his way to the office by or before 7:00 a.m. He would normally have been awake off and on all night, and by 4:00 or 5:00 a.m. would have phoned to his associates in Oakland, Washington, New York, or other locations. It was rare that he ever went to bed before 11:00 p.m. or midnight. Four or five hours were all he slept, except for little nodding catnaps he would take during the day or while he was being driven in the car.

He had the kind of mind that thrived on challenges. Overcoming problems was his greatest satisfaction. He was not one for small talk, chitchat, or gossip. When he conversed with his wife, or a guest, or an employee, it usually ended with him trying an idea on that person of something he was interested in at the moment. To him this was real enjoyment and relaxation. To others, including his wife, this was often a strain, and only a strong woman with a keen mind, like Ale, could have stood up to it for very long.

He held a social membership in the Waialae Country Club where he would eat lunch from time to time, but he never played golf or cards or dominoes. He did not belong to any other social group or business association because he was too busy doing his own thing. On occasion he would go along for a short fishing trip on his wife's 60-foot boat, but instead of hoping to catch a fish he would spend his time trying to come up with an idea for a motor-powered fishing reel, or for some way to remodel the boat.

Because of his wife's intense interest in raising championship poodles, he often displayed surprising patience at dog shows where both of them reveled in winning blue ribbons. It was quite amazing how much time and money was devoted by Kaiser to support his wife's passion for poodles. They had by far the largest number of kennels in Honolulu, possibly among the largest in the United States. Here was a man who had never paid any particular attention to dogs at any time in his life, yet who now actively encouraged his wife in that direction. While Ale seemed uncomfortable in certain social situations—like being in the presence of wives of longtime Kaiser executives—she could totally lose herself in her own world of elegant poodles. There were those wags who would say, "Kaiser has the two finest homes in Honolulu—his Portlock estate, and his kennel compound."

They were not the least bit interested in the so-called "social whirl" of Honolulu itself, and although they were regularly invited to social functions, they declined as often as they could. They did put on one really big party a year—a lavish New Year's Eve party for some 200 sit-down dinner guests, each eating with the same matched china and gold-washed stainless steel place settings. At the stroke of midnight there would be champagne for all, and at the same time a spectacular noisy aerial fireworks display would be set off over Maunalua Bay, followed by guests helping themselves to fireworks and fire crackers from a big box on the lanai. The entire evening was "Black Tie," and this was one of the few times that any of the "social elite" would be invited in. These invitations were among the most coveted in the community.

Kaiser also went all-out to celebrate Christmas, with his wife, Ale, arranging colorful decorations throughout their Portlock Estate. The center piece was always a 20-foot pine tree that would be set up in the middle of the open lawn, off the lanai-living room and swimming pool, strung with 1,000 or more clear white small lights. Each bulb only gave out seven watts of light, but with so many it was seen all over eastern Honolulu. Indoors there would be beautifully decorated Christmas trees, animated animals, and an animated Santa at the entrance bowing as guests came in, with drives and walkways outlined in colorful Christmas lights. The estate was Honolulu's most talked-about Christmas display.

Throughout his lifetime Kaiser was never one to establish a continuing, lasting friendship with any man except his business associates, mainly within his companies. There was never any one person he would consistently meet for lunch or with whom he would spend his evenings. His life, day and night, was built around his wife—first Bess from 1907 till her death in 1951, then Ale for the last sixteen years of his life. He made business friends, of course, thousands of them, but it was like a passing parade, with feelings of friendship remaining, but with different friends commanding his attention once he took on something new. He would be gracious, warm, and hospitable to each new acquaintance, not in a showy, insincere way but because he instinctively liked people, and because the people he kept meeting were indispensable to the accomplishment of each new enterprise. While he made some enemies along the way, and was often sniped at by people who were jealous for one reason or another, he never harbored past animosities any more than he lingered on past loyalties. It was always "get on with the next job," and accept people for what they can do to make something a success. In that sense he was incredibly "open" to the good qualities of others, always giving them the benefit of the doubt, never wasting any time trying to expose their frailties. He prided himself in bringing out the very best in people, because he knew that would help make each project a greater success.

It was this quality of always looking ahead, never looking back, that made his Hawaiian years such happy ones. To many of his closest associates who knew him so well, it was still amazing that he could transplant his roots from Oakland to Honolulu so abruptly and so permanently. True, he was on the phone to Oakland and other mainland cities nearly every single day, weekends and holidays included. True, he managed to preside at nearly every Board of Directors' meeting of his various companies wherever they were held. True, he was always available to participate in special occasions and dedications on the mainland. Nevertheless, his heart was in Hawaii with his wife and the projects he was working on there.

One thing that added spice to his life in Hawaii was all the celebrities he was able to host. Partly through his involvement in television and radio, including the TV shows he sponsored and the commercials he participated in, he enjoyed the friendship of a great many well-known public figures. He delighted in entertaining them at his Hawaiian Village Hotel and often as overnight guests at his beautiful Portlock home. It is very likely that during his years in Hawaii he hosted more big names than any other Islander.

Although no record has been found of the hundreds of guests who shared his hospitality, the list included such people as Spike Jones, bandleader and his wife; LaRaine Day and husband; Sophie Tucker; Mr. and Mrs. Hugh Downs; Mr. and Mrs. Hugh Auchincloss, mother of Mrs. John F. Kennedy. Following are excerpts from letters of appreciation Kaiser received from just a few of his guests:

From Carlos P. Garcia, President of the Philippines
    July 6, 1958

    If there is one thing that Mrs. Garcia and I will remember for long, it was the very lively and enjoyable breakfast you gave in our honor. For it we would like you to know that we are grateful.

From Mrs. Robert Cummings (Mary)
    December 1, 1959

    Bob joins me in sending our sincere thanks for your wonderful hospitality. It was so marvelous seeing you again. It does Bob and me so much good personally to be in your presence, even for such a short time. We come away feeling nothing is impossible if one just has faith, courage and enthusiasm. We feel we can truly conquer the world!

From Mrs. Eddie Albert (Margo)
August 29, 1960

There are no words to thank you for everything, especially the joy of getting to know you and to love you. This goes for the whole family. For Eddie and me especially. . . and because this is my letter, this time, especially just from me, I love you.

From Mrs. Lloyd Bridges (Dorothy)
May 9, 1962 (Kaiser's 80th Birthday)
[First letters from each line spell Henry J. Kaiser]

Happy Birthday, Mr. Kaiser!
Each year for you is a vitalizer --
No other man could match your pace,
Rejoice more in the good life's race.
Youth like yours is doing, daring --
Just zest for life and a heart for sharing.
Keep seeing that we're on our toes,
Aspiring like the tree which grows
Into ever higher places,
Sunlit faith upon our faces,
Enjoying growth through gain and loss,
Rich in living—like the boss.

From Art Linkletter
September 15, 1965

The Linkletters are still warm in the afterglow of your hospitality! It was a lovely evening—casual, intimate, and sort of 'family'—just the kind of small dinner we like best. Thank you so much for enlarging your small circle to include us for the evening.

Although Kaiser himself probably would not agree, he did pay a price for his total commitment to work. His own family, other than his wife Ale, became almost a part of the passing parade. His youngest son, Henry J. Kaiser, Jr., was not often in Hawaii, admittedly in part because of his affliction with multiple sclerosis. When he died in Oakland in 1961, there were those who were concerned that his father might not take time to come to the funeral.

Even the older son, Edgar, who had been so close to his father all his life, and who had headed up so many major businesses so successfully, was not a frequent visitor to

Hawaii. He would usually come at Christmas time almost as a command performance, but not always with his wife, Sue. Neither Edgar nor Sue ever felt close to Ale. There were almost contradictory relationships between father and son—a deep down hope that Edgar would be capable of taking over the controls, yet a strange unwillingness to turn those controls over to him.

The grandchildren were almost strangers to their grandfather and only got to Hawaii occasionally. He seldom spent time with them as most grandfathers do reminiscing or sharing dreams with them. They were never made to feel their grandfather was counting on them to assume the mantle of family leadership at some time in the future.

In Kaiser's will, signed July 26, 1965, two years before his death, the grandchildren are listed along with son Edgar, followed by this provision: "In the knowledge that they are otherwise adequately provided for, I have intentionally and with full knowledge omitted any provision herein for . . . [them]." The estate was left to the wife Ale and to the Kaiser Foundation. The Portlock mansion was willed to Ale who sold it shortly after Kaiser's death.* As events over the next few years began to unfold, it was clear that Edgar and the grandchildren were not "otherwise adequately provided for," certainly not in terms of maintaining control of the Kaiser companies.

For the thirteen years Kaiser lived in Hawaii he was as happy as anyone could be, as happy as he had been all his life. Maybe none of us could ask for a better measure of what this life should be all about. To others, however, something would be missing without more loving family bonds.

Sunset In Hawaii

Kaiser's move to Hawaii in 1954 hit the Islands like a blazing sunrise. It would be hard to find any other place in the world where one man's coming into a new area had such immediate impact on the economy and on the life of the people. From the start, Kaiser charged from one big project into another. He was quoted extensively in the newspapers week in and week out. He gave one inspirational speech after another. He supported wholeheartedly nearly every worthy community project. In February 1960, he was honored by the Sales Executives of Hawaii as "the individual who did the most to promote and sell Hawaii at home, on the mainland, and throughout the world." He had an almost steady flow of visiting celebrities that must have exceeded even those who called on the Governor. He was hero to hundreds of thousands of Hawaiians. He popularized catamarans as the way to enjoy Honolulu's shoreline and adjacent waters. He introduced a whole new dimension of entertainment through the stars he sponsored and through the programs he presented in his innovative aluminum dome. He made Honolulu the "cookout" competition capital of the United States.

He was still going strong into his 85th year. Why doubt the juggernaut would keep rolling? Even when his health began to slip badly after that, few people gave thought

---

*The September 12, 1988 Fortune magazine reported that the Portlock Mansion had been sold to Japanese interests for "more than $40 million—among the highest prices ever paid for any U.S. home anytime."

to how different things might be once he was gone.

But if his entrance into Hawaii in 1954 had been as sudden and portentous as a blazing sunrise, his death on August 24, 1967, would be the sunset signifying abrupt but this time ominous changes.

Within two days after his death, very fitting memorial services were held in his honor at the Kawaiahao Church, an historical landmark of Hawaii, conducted by Dr. Abraham K. Akaka, pastor of the church and a close friend of Kaiser. No one would stop to think about it, but that would be almost the last time any member of the family would be in Hawaii on matters relating to Kaiser's life there.

In another two days the main funeral services were held in Oakland where his body was interred in a mausoleum. Hawaiians, therefore, would never have a burial site to visit to remind them of what Kaiser had meant to them.

To the surprise and disappointment of many Hawaiians, his widow, Ale, did not return to Honolulu to live in the fine Portlock home where she and her husband had "held court" for nearly eight enjoyable years. Actually, she only returned to Hawaii twice after that, once for two days, once for two hours.

His only living son, Edgar, had no incentive to take up residence in Hawaii, nor to try to carry on the projects Kaiser had underway. Likewise, the grandchildren were so far removed from Hawaiian activities, none of them made an effort to get involved. Nor did any of Kaiser's capable executives seek to pick up where he had left off, because they had so many big and challenging operations underway elsewhere that required them to remain in Oakland.

Kaiser's Hawaiian Village Hotel had already been sold to Hilton in 1961. The radio and television stations found ready buyers. In time the cement mill was sold. An effort was made by a small crew of Hawaii Kai executives to keep that project going, but it was patchwork at best and included selling off chunks of land to other developers. All that eventually remained of Kaiser's Hawaiian "Empire" was his very successful and expanding Kaiser Permanente health and hospital program.

Obviously, Kaiser has not been forgotten by many Islanders, especially the older people who were around when he was doing so much. Stories and legends will persist for a long time to come. And, of course, the things he built, even though now under different ownership, will be linked to Kaiser in the minds of many.

Still, it is a sad commentary on human life that one person so forceful in the lives of so many should not be more vividly remembered and honored. Whatever Hawaiians can do to recall the glory days of Kaiser would add glory to Hawaii itself. Certainly such a life merits studies by school children on the ideals and achievements of the one "malahini" (newcomer) who appreciated the grandeur of Hawaii and who did so much to glorify it.

CHAPTER 12

TWENTY-SEVEN DAYS OF WAITING

"The one person in creation you cannot afford to be a stranger to is—yourself."

Henry Kaiser was in high spirits. He was seated at his desk in his huge office on the eleventh floor of his own office building at 1924 Broadway in Oakland. Sitting alongside him were his sons Edgar and Henry, Jr., together with Gene Trefethen. Nearby were A. B. Ordway, Dr. Sidney Garfield, and Paul Marrin, Kaiser's lawyer. In the room were about thirty other key executives who had been told just a few hours before to come to his office that Friday afternoon, April 6, 1951, for a very important meeting, the subject of which was not known. I was in that group.

Once everyone was seated, Kaiser didn't waste any time. "Boys," he said, "I have told Edgar and Henry, Jr., and Gene, as well as Ord and Sid and Paul, what I'm going to do, but I want each of you to hear my plans firsthand. I have asked Alyce Chester for her hand in marriage and she has accepted. We're going to be married next Tuesday."

Just twenty-three days earlier Kaiser's first wife, Bess, had died after a long illness. Her full-time nurse for over two years had been Alyce Chester.

Kaiser continued,

Those with whom I have already discussed this are happy for Alyce and me, but they feel that out of respect for my dear Bess I should wait a few months before getting remarried. Naturally, I have given this a lot of consideration, but I have concluded no real purpose would be served by waiting. Instead, I am convinced it's in your best interests, and the best interests of our companies, for me to proceed with the marriage.

I'm sure all of you know how happy I have been with Bess by my side these forty-four years. She was all that a wife and mother should be, counseling me and sustaining me in everything I did. She was like a mother to many of you. She contributed greatly to the growth of the Kaiser companies.

I have been deeply grieved to watch her health slip away these past two years. I think you know I did everything humanly possible to keep her alive. Sid (Dr. Garfield) and Cece (Dr. Cutting) worked night and day with her, applying every medical treatment they could think of, and calling on many outside specialists for their assistance. In the end, there was just no way to prevent her death.

For the rest of us, life has to go on, and that's why I am going forward with this marriage to Alyce. As you know, I have never worked alone. I was a better builder, I was a better boss, because of Bess's constant counsel and support. I know the same will be true with Alyce.

Some have suggested that I could still get the benefit of Alyce's support even though we put the wedding off a few months. But it wouldn't be the same that way. Besides, it wouldn't be the honest thing to do. I am in love with Alyce, and I shouldn't have to have secret contacts with her, or sneak in and out of restaurants with her, or slide around corners, while waiting for the formal marriage. I have never operated that way, and I won't do it now.

After all, boys, what real meaning is there in waiting? When I was building the Cuban highway in 1927 I saw a lot of people wearing black bands around their sleeves, signifying they were in mourning over someone's death. Even here in the United States people once wore black bands on their arms, but that practice has almost completely disappeared. It was nothing more than a convention that didn't serve any real purpose. Certainly, it did not help the dead person, and only held back the living from getting on with what they had to do.

The same thing is true with regard to waiting a certain amount of time to get remarried—it's only a convention, decided on by some, but still not serving any real purpose. I showed my true love to Bess all during the years we were married, while she was still alive to enjoy it.

No, boys, the honest thing to do, the right thing to do, is for me to go forward with this marriage since Alyce and I are so much in love. I know it will make me a sweeter, simpler, more useful person and a better boss. And I feel sure that within a few months from now those who criticize me will have forgotten all about it. I'm likewise confident that as you see our companies move ahead even more aggressively than before you will agree it was the right thing to do.

He paused, and then added buoyantly, "Thank you boys for your time. Now let's get back to work. "

He was proud of his decision, he was proud of his candor. He didn't have a single trace of doubt over his action. He was eager to join Alyce for a Friday afternoon and evening of rejoicing.

No one in the room had stirred while he talked. No questions were asked, no comments volunteered. Those who were hearing of the marriage for the first time were visibly sobered. During their years with Kaiser, they had looked upon Mr. and Mrs. Kaiser as having the ideal marriage, a life of devotion with not the slightest hint of anything but true love. They had come to consider Mrs. Kaiser as "mother" because that was the way Kaiser referred to her, not only in informal conversations but in public talks. He had always gone out of his way to make his employees feel they were actually a part of his family. Now suddenly they were hearing that this happily married man, just one month short of his 69th birthday, was in love with a 34-year-old nurse, only three weeks after his wife's death.

As the men silently filed out of Kaiser's office, none felt privileged to make any kind of comment directly to him. No follow-up group discussions were held, but a sense of disbelief and shock was pervasive. Even though it was the middle of the afternoon very few felt like going back to work. Soon, company cars started leaving the parking lot behind the building. As one vice president and general manager of a major company prepared to get into his car, he turned to me and said, "God damn it, Al, Mr. Kaiser is going to destroy our companies just because he can't keep his pecker in his pants."

The men had assumed they were hearing the story before the public would know anything about it. However, the early afternoon edition of the Oakland Tribune was already on the streets with a glamorous picture of the bride and a front page report, "Henry J. Kaiser To Marry Aide." The article quoted a news release issued by the company, "They were brought together in a common interest to provide greater medical, surgical and hospital care for people. They will dedicate themselves to carrying on the work of the foundation to which the former Mrs. Kaiser left the bulk of her estate."

But newspapers stories based on a company news release were not good enough for Kaiser's purposes. He wanted to meet the press himself so he could tell the world how this new marriage would lead to bigger and better things for all of the Kaiser operations in the future. He had therefore asked his public relations people to arrange a press conference for the next morning to be held in the doctor's dining room at the Kaiser Permanente Hospital in Oakland at Broadway and MacArthur.

About a dozen members of the press showed up. Kaiser was bubbling over with excitement. He had broken the ice the day before and now he wanted to play the story for all it was worth. He especially wanted to show his bride off to the press. Without any introduction he greeted each member of the press personally, and then proceeded to go through most of what he had told his own people the day before, only this time he expanded on how his marriage to the nurse would especially mean a bright new future for the hospital program. As one of his public relations men later reported, "He was like a little kid, this rather behemoth of a man, bragging about his forthcoming marriage. He went to great trouble to show the engagement ring to each member of the press individually. He kept saying so many glowing things about his bride, it could have been embarrassing, but she took it in stride because she is such a cool character."

In its main front page story the next day, Sunday, April 8, 1951, the <u>Oakland Tribune</u> ran a large picture of the radiant couple with the caption, "Never Lived According to Conventions, says Kaiser." The article went on to quote Kaiser, "I have never lived according to the conventions . . . . I have defied the conventions all my life. I cannot stand not to be busy, not to work. I cannot work and travel without a companion who understands me. Mrs. Kaiser during her life provided that. No one who knew Mrs. Kaiser and Miss Chester and their association could express disapproval of this marriage. It's not a business proposition. I love the things for which Miss Chester stands. I have never seen a woman with Miss Chester's patience or equal in her kindness to Mrs. Kaiser."

At the start of this memorable week the top management team was all geared up to put its best foot forward with Gilbert Burck, Senior Editor of <u>Fortune</u> magazine, and Eileen Durning, Research Associate, who were planning a major article on the Kaiser companies. They had interviewed dozens of different people from all of the companies throughout the week, including Kaiser himself. Kaiser decided to invite them to sit in on his Friday afternoon meeting where he told his key people about his upcoming marriage.

On the Sunday night following, I met Burck and Durning at the Southern Pacific Lark train in Oakland for the purpose of hosting them on a three-day visit to the Kaiser Steel mill in Fontana, Southern California, and the iron ore mine at Eagle Mountain, not far from Indio, California. As we sat down for a visit in the lounge car, I gained an entirely new perspective when Burck told me, "My interviews this week have shown me how really incredible Mr. Kaiser's achievements are. He is nothing less than an industrial giant. But I had no idea what a truly great man he is until I heard him tell you and his other management people about his plans to marry the young nurse. That was one of the most candid and courageous talks I have ever heard anyone give. I know for sure now that with a leader as honest as that the future of the Kaiser companies is bright."

Three months later, in the July 1951 issue of <u>Fortune</u>, in an article titled, "The Arrival of Henry Kaiser," Burck would write:

"Henry is also candid and guileless with them (his men). Last April, four weeks after Mrs. Kaiser died, Kaiser decided to marry her nurse. He called the men together and told them, 'I haven't time to do what the other average person does, to slide around corners. This is a constructive move and in sixty days I will be a sweeter, simpler, more useful person because of it.'"

Burck had started that article with profuse praise for Kaiser:

"Now that Henry Kaiser has achieved the rank of major industrialist and is widely regarded as quite respectable to boot, where in the whole sensational history of private enterprise is there a success story to match his? No industrialist since Henry Ford has achieved so much in so short a time as Henry Kaiser. And not in all history has any industrial figure successfully got into so many and various projects as Kaiser."

Of course, not all people were as broad-minded and as far-seeing as Gil Burck. With all due respect to their boss, who was sincerely liked and looked up to by nearly all employees, it was inevitable the rank and file would have a little fun with the age difference between Kaiser and his bride. One of the questions that went the rounds with some employee groups was: "How many times does 68 go into 34?"

Another question that got its share of play not only with employees but with many outsiders was: "Did you hear about the California nurse who made a hot rod out of her old Kaiser?"

Still others would pose the question: "Did you hear about Kaiser? He took a turn for the nurse."

Alyce Chester had joined the Kaiser Permanente Hospital in Oakland as a nurse nine years before. Some time after that she divorced her husband, Max Pencovic, choosing thereafter to use her maiden name. Their one son, Michael, whom Kaiser later adopted, lived with her. She worked in the surgery department at the hospital where she became very good friends with Dr. Sidney Garfield, who was head of the entire health program, and with Dr. Cecil Cutting, chief surgeon. In particular, she was a close friend with Millie Cutting, wife of Dr. Cutting, who was in charge of personnel at the hospital. When Mrs. Kaiser became so ill as to require a full time nurse, it was Millie Cutting who recommended Alyce Chester as the ideal person.

Miss Chester, as she was called at the time, had a lot of poise and self-confidence and was a good worker. She was tall, about 5 feet 10 inches, and slender—a decided contrast with Mrs. Bess Kaiser, who was quite fat like her husband. Miss Chester was angular, but athletic and graceful. Few, other than Kaiser, were known to say she was beautiful in the classic sense.

When she first became Mrs. Kaiser's nurse, it was at the time Kaiser was thinking about building a new home in Lafayette, California, about 10 miles from his office in downtown Oakland. He decided the nurse should live nearby to where his home was to be built, so on July 12, 1950, he bought a home for her at 1015 Timothy Lane, two doors from his property, which was at 1025 Timothy Lane. Immediately rumors began to fly. Why would Kaiser be buying a home for her, something he hadn't done for anyone else? The rumors weren't confined to company people. Many neighbors and outsiders became aware of the home for the nurse and began buzzing about the stepped-up attention Kaiser seemed to be paying her. Others began talking about the dresses Kaiser was reported to be buying the nurse.

Less than a month later Kaiser decided it might do his wife good to take her for a weekend to their home on Lake Tahoe, which was her favorite vacation spot. They would travel 4 hours from Oakland to Truckee, California, on the Southern Pacific train where a driver would pick them up for the 30 minute automobile ride to the lake. Early that Friday morning, August 4, 1950, A.B. Ordway asked me to come to his office. He told me that Mr. Kaiser would be leaving in a few hours on the train departing from the Oakland Mole, the end of the line where the train originated and where connections were made with the ferry from San Francisco. Ordway handed me a $20 bill and said, "We have two connecting bedrooms reserved on the train. Roses have been ordered for the rooms. I want you to go to the train two hours ahead of its scheduled departure and check the rooms out to be sure everything is in order. Take this $20 and give it to the porter and tell him to take good care of Mr. and Mrs. Kaiser on the trip. Be sure to stay there until Mr. Kaiser arrives and help him in any way you can until he leaves."

The rooms reserved were in the third car from the rear and were clean and cheerful, with the roses very much in evidence. I discussed Kaiser's plans with the porter and gave him the $20.

About 45 minutes before the train was to leave, a big black Cadillac limousine pulled up at the end of the train. I started toward it, but before I got there Kaiser had stepped out of the car and came bouncing along in a very cheerful, jaunty mood. "Is everything okay, Al?" he asked. "You bet, Mr. Kaiser." "Well, let's go look at it." Together we looked at the rooms. "Everything looks fine, Al. Did you pay the porter $20?"

We then started back toward the limousine. Mrs. Kaiser had just gotten out of the car and was starting to walk, with her nurse on one side and the driver, Dick Taylor, on the other, supporting her and helping her take very short, faltering steps. I was shocked to see how weak and unsteady Mrs. Kaiser was. It seemed like an eternity for her to walk the two car lengths where she was to board the train. At that point it became a real workout because of the high steps up into the car. In one way or another, Kaiser, and the porter joined the nurse and the driver and me in virtually lifting the heavy Mrs. Kaiser onto the train.

Once inside the room, Mrs. Kaiser sat down to catch her breath. She was noticeably concerned with her own ill feelings and said nothing about looking forward to reaching Lake Tahoe. By contrast, Kaiser was in a most buoyant mood and kept trying to tell her how much better she would feel once she arrived at beloved Tahoe. Some fifteen minutes before the train was to leave Kaiser told me I could go, but I remained outside the train until it finally left the station.

Mrs. Kaiser's frail condition haunted me all afternoon. When I got home after work, I told my wife how I had seen Mrs. Kaiser struggle, even with the support of her nurse and driver, to walk the short distance to the rail car. "I am really surprised," I said, "that Mr. Kaiser would take her to Lake Tahoe, with its 6223 foot altitude, considering her high blood pressure and her weak heart, even though she loves it so much. But it sure didn't seem to bother Mr. Kaiser. He was obviously all excited about the weekend he was expecting to have."

Mrs. Kaiser died March 15, 1951. Within a day or two, Kaiser told his two sons he would soon be marrying the nurse, Alyce Chester. From that moment on he never had any second thoughts or misgivings about it whatever. All his life he had prided himself on always looking ahead, never back. People were surprised to learn that once Boulder Dam was completed he never returned to see it again. Now the challenge was to make plans for the wedding and the honeymoon, help the bride round out her trousseau, and speed up the construction of the new home.

In keeping with his natural instinct for showmanship he wanted as many people as possible to know as many good things as possible about his bride. That meant he should have the best possible portraits of her to hand out to the press once he was ready to make the public announcement. But, so that the story would have maximum impact he didn't want his secret to be leaked by hiring an outside photographer. Nor did he think he could rely on his own photographers in Oakland to hold such a story in confidence. It was then that his son Henry Kaiser, Jr., recalled that a young man in his Los Angeles public relations office, Handy Hancock, had done portrait work as well as industrial photography. Immediately, Henry Jr. phoned Hancock and told him to pack up all of his photographic equipment and be in the Oakland office the next morning, prepared to take "the best pictures you have ever taken in your life." Hancock wanted an idea of the kind of pictures he would be taking but Henry Jr. told him, "As close as you and I are, this is one time I can't tell you a thing, it's absolutely top secret, you'll just have to trust me."

Hancock stayed overnight at the Leamington Hotel in Oakland, across the street from the Kaiser building. At 8:00 a.m., two assistants came over to help him carry his 300 pounds of overweight photographic equipment. They went directly to Kaiser's plush office on the eleventh floor. Hancock recalls:

> It wasn't until I was in Mr. Kaiser's office, with the door closed behind me, and with no way for me to escape, that I was finally told I was to take pictures of the bride for release to the international press. I have never been so scared in my life, not even when I got married. Nothing is harder than taking a photograph that will please a woman and especially one where Kaiser was seeking perfection.
>
> At the stroke of 10:00, in strode Mr. Kaiser with his young bride. I hadn't realized he had been a photographer in his early days, so I was a little surprised when he took charge. He let me do the lighting and exposure but he did all the rest. He went to great care showing his bride the various poses she should assume, and he did the final focusing. He was enjoying himself immensely.
>
> After shooting an excess amount of films, he felt sure some of them would be good, so he asked how soon I could have the proofs to him. I told him if I could get a darkroom, I would get wet proofs to him in an hour. I was using the term 'within an hour' as a figure of speech, not realizing that he would

hold me to it. When I mentioned to Henry Jr. that it might take a little longer I was told 'when you say an hour it means an hour and he will expect you no later.' Consequently, I have never developed and printed pictures so fast in my life. I didn't even allow drying time for the negatives.

Just on the hour I delivered the wet prints to him at his apartment on Lake Merritt where he and his bride and two friends were having luncheon. He was ecstatic over the quality of the pictures, especially because he thought they brought out the beauty he saw in her. There is no doubt most of the pictures made her look quite glamorous. In the picture used by the Oakland Tribune on Friday, April 6, she looked like a Hollywood star.

I found out later that what I did that morning played an important part in Mr. Kaiser's decision to bring me to Oakland as one of his assistants."

A few days after Hancock had taken the pictures and returned to Los Angeles, he received another hurry-up call from Henry Jr. to join him in Santa Barbara, California, to assist in making arrangements for the wedding itself. As an Episcopalian, Mr. Kaiser hoped to be married in the church, so he talked to the Rector in Santa Monica, California. The Rector regretfully informed Kaiser the ceremony could not be performed by him because the bride-to-be had been divorced. He volunteered that perhaps The Reverend Doctor C. Eugene Sill of the First Congregational Church in Santa Barbara might be willing to conduct the services. The Rector called Doctor Sill describing the situation and stressing that the groom was a very important man, although he was not free to divulge his name. Doctor Sill said he was agreeable, so within a day or two Henry Jr. and Hancock were in his office in Santa Barbara to make the necessary arrangements. They stressed that they wanted the ceremony to be a very private affair with absolutely no publicity. Considering all the efforts to keep the wedding a secret, Doctor Sill was surprised to see so many people descending on his church the morning of Tuesday, April 10, 1951, especially reporters.

One woman reporter planted herself in the ladies rest room and absolutely refused to leave. Consideration was given to calling the police, but it was decided this would only stir things up. She ended up hearing the ceremony after which she dashed out with her story.

Doctor Sill later commented that his secretary, who had been with him a long time and was very reliable, always wore the plainest of dresses. He was stunned, therefore, to see her at the wedding in an absolutely gorgeous gown, which she took off as soon as the wedding party had left.

Hancock waited at the airport in his company car, a Kaiser, to help drive the participants to the inn where they freshened up for the wedding.

First came the company DC3 in which were the bride and her two sisters, Dorothy and Helen. They were taken to the Santa Barbara Inn. Shortly after, the other company plane, which was a converted bomber, landed with Kaiser, his two sons, Gene

Trefethen, and Dr. Sidney Garfield. To Hancock, it was an exciting time not only because of the people involved, but because there was a low fog at the Santa Barbara airport with poor visibility. He later found out that was the first time so many top Kaiser executives had ever flown in the same plane.

Inside the church there were only ten or fifteen guests. The service itself was short. Kaiser stood, beaming throughout. When it was over, the bride and groom came fairly bounding out of the church, as jubilant as any married couple could be. Kaiser personally handed Doctor Sill a $100 bill for his services. Doctor Sill thought it was most generous, and looked forward to using it on a trip to New England. At that time there was no possible way Doctor Sill could ever dream that 16 years later he would be heading the First Congregational Church in Oakland where he would preside at the funeral services for Kaiser.

After the wedding the group went to the Inn for an hour and a half of partying and then the newlyweds took off for New Orleans in the company plane, where they planned to spend a combination honeymoon and business trip, not only to the New Orleans area, but to beautiful Jamaica where Kaiser Aluminum had a huge bauxite mine.

Hancock had not been invited into the church for the wedding, nor to the party afterwards. On both occasions he sat on the curb outside, waiting to be called into action. He was surprised, therefore, when he returned to the Inn from the airport and Henry Jr. greeted him, "Handy, what in the world did you say to my father today?" Handy replied, "I didn't say a half dozen words to him all day. I just drove the car." "Well," said Henry Jr., "I don't know what you said or what you did, but whatever it was you made a terrific impression, so don't be surprised when the honeymoon is over if my father calls you and brings you to Oakland as one of his assistants." Sure enough, within two weeks Hancock received a call to close the Los Angeles office and come to Oakland.

For his first day there he had bought a new suit and new shoes. He was assigned a desk just outside Kaiser's office, next to Edna Knuth, Kaiser's longtime, trusted secretary. Within an hour a voice boomed out from the inner sanctum, "Knutie, is Handy out there?" She answered, "Yes, he is." "Good, tell him to get ready, we're going."

Various thoughts raced through Hancock's mind as to what his first assignment might be. Would it be a visit to some officer in Bank of America in San Francisco? Suddenly, Kaiser burst from his office and said, "Come on, Handy, let's go." Downstairs they piled into the limousine driven by Dick Taylor who always drove like he was on the Indianapolis Speedway. The car roared out of the garage driveway and into the traffic, but instead of heading west to San Francisco, it raced east toward the Broadway, Caldecott Tunnel until it reached Lafayette where Kaiser was just starting construction on his new home. It had been raining for two weeks and the construction site was a sea of mud. That didn't faze Kaiser, "Come on Handy, I want to show you the project." Within a few steps, Handy's foot got stuck in the mud, his shoe came off, he slipped down on one knee.

Kaiser paid no attention. As they sloshed around, he pointed to a little flag here and a little flag there, saying "that's where the living room will be, that's where the swimming pool will be," until he had diagrammed the whole layout. Then he called his construction superintendent and asked for a set of plans which he turned over to Handy saying, "Okay, Handy, you're project manager."

A typical Kaiser move—dump something on someone whether he knows anything about it or not—even if it is his first day on the job. Here was Hancock who had been raised in the newspaper business, who knew absolutely nothing about blueprints or construction, being thrust in the position of project manager. But he was smart enough to know he would be given all the backing he needed, because Kaiser wanted the home to be finished as quickly as possible for his new bride. He also knew Kaiser would show up on the jobsite nearly every day he was in Oakland, ready to add his experienced judgment at each step along the way.

Kaiser was particularly concerned about the construction of the staircase for the house. It was to be handcrafted in San Francisco by an old country Italian artisan, very few of whom were still around. It was designed as a work of art to be the central attraction of the whole house. Kaiser told Hancock to be sure to ride herd on the staircase because it was critical to the early completion of the house. He also charged Morrie Wortman, principal architect, to expedite the construction of the staircase. In the rush of activity at the jobsite neither Hancock nor Wortman took time to go to San Francisco to see the progress on the staircase. Instead, they relied on regular telephone assurances from the artisan that the building of the staircase was on schedule.

After weeks had gone by, Hancock drove Kaiser to the Oakland Airport. While waiting for the plane Kaiser said, "Handy, have you seen the staircase yet, how is it coming?" Hancock had to admit he hadn't actually seen it, but he tried to reassure Kaiser by reciting the blow-by-blow progress reports he had been receiving from the builder. Kaiser became very upset. "Handy, I have told you and told you to go over and look at the staircase. I don't think it's even being built. I don't care what happens, tomorrow you've got to go over and look at that staircase yourself."

The next morning Hancock found the little shop in a back alley. When he told the owner he had come to see the staircase he was dumbfounded to hear, "You might as well go home, there isn't any staircase." Hancock challenged him, "Come on now, you have been telling me how well you are doing on it, so I'd like to see it." The man replied, "I'm telling you there is no staircase. I've been lying to you, my man has been sick and we just haven't done any work on it, all I've got in back is a pile of lumber."

Hancock panicked. He phoned Wortman who was likewise horrified. Wortman said, "Come on back and we'll call Mr. Kaiser together." When they reached him in Washington and reported the alarming news, Kaiser responded, "I suspected that all along because his progress reports didn't correspond with the agreed construction schedule." Instead of chewing them out, he went on, "Have you boys learned anything from this? As long as you've learned a lesson, we'll somehow get the staircase finished on time."

Every morning that Kaiser was in Oakland he would stop by the jobsite before going to the office. He would not only outline what he thought should be done during the day, but he would order the crews around. "We want to get this trench over here, so get the crew and let's start digging." Then he would go a little farther, "Now we want to put the sprinklers over here, get the crew." Then at another location, "Let's get this foundation going, so bring the crew here." Laborers who started working on the trench were suddenly working on the sprinklers and then as suddenly working on the foundation. Once Kaiser had left for the office, Hancock would try to get the crew settled down to work on one thing at a time. Yet nearly each night when Kaiser came by to check on the progress he would shake his head and say, "It just seems that you don't get any production."

As much as he insisted on speed, Kaiser tried to avoid having to pay overtime. However, he made an exception for Saturdays and Sundays. On those days he would keep the caterpillar tractors busy. He loved big machinery—there was something about the tremendous power and the ability to move large quantities of earth that absolutely fascinated him. He would sit on a box long hours directing the caterpillar operators almost like a maestro directing a symphony orchestra, enjoying every minute of it.

As construction progressed, Kaiser set up a field office which later became his study. He had a phone installed there which also connected to a construction phone downstairs which the various tradesmen used when calling back and forth to their offices and for supplies. Kaiser would often listen in on the conversations just to keep abreast of what was going on. One day Kaiser had been bugging one of his favorite workmen, Lee the plumber, who was behind schedule in his work. Harried, Lee got on the downstairs phone to tell another worker to bring something to him immediately because he said, "The old coot is all over my back." Kaiser heard it on the upstairs phone, turned to Hancock and said, "He called me an old coot."

He said nothing to Lee until several days later when the plumber was sweating hard to solve a problem on the swimming pool pump. Kaiser had pulled up a packing box and was sitting there watching. As usual, he tried to orchestrate the process. "What are you doing now, Lee? Are you sure that's right, Lee? How about trying it this way, Lee?" Lee was squirming. Then during a quiet period, Kaiser said, "By the way, Lee, do you really think I'm an 'old coot'?" Lee almost died, because he had no idea his earlier remark had been overheard. However, he had nothing to worry about because Kaiser liked hard workers and skilled craftsmen, and Lee was one of those.

By September the home was finished with its beautiful tropical landscaping. It was surprisingly modest for a man of Kaiser's wealth and flair for elegance. It was in an unpretentious neighborhood surrounded by inexpensive homes. Roadways in the area were not first class. (By 1988 the Kaiser home, which had been sold several times, had fallen into shocking disrepair, not too unlike what happened to many of the Kaiser companies years after his death.) Its design was an outgrowth of a trip that

Mrs. Bess Kaiser and Miss Chester had taken to the Hawaiian Islands the year before. Mrs. Kaiser loved the tropics and wanted to return, but her condition would not permit it, so Kaiser from the outset had the home designed "to bring the tropics to her."

The home incorporated every electronic device for communications and for automatic control of the sophisticated equipment throughout the house. It was a fun home for Kaiser to be in. His new wife was thrilled with the island style and, like any recent bride, was happy she was the first woman to live in it. Together, she and Kaiser had gone all out in selecting fancy interior decorations and furnishings.

Kaiser could hardly wait to show it off. Even more important he wanted to show his wife off in the setting of the new home, so now his attention was directed toward planning a real extravaganza. It, of course, included a very select list of his key people, (my wife and I had the good fortune of being among them) as well as important business and community contacts. One noticeable difference in his list of invitees was a generous sprinkling of doctors and top administrative personnel of the Kaiser Permanente hospitals, who were friends of the new Mrs. Kaiser.

At the reception, Kaiser was bouncing all over the place—graciously greeting each guest at the door, proudly presenting his wife, then taking most of the guests either individually or in groups on tours throughout the house and out into the garden. He called attention to all the special features in the house, all the gadgets, all the unique things about the home. No host has ever been more cordial, more attentive. No husband has been more gallant.

But the thing that meant most to him was the impact his wife made on everyone. She wore a striking dress which he had helped her pick out. Tall and lithe, she moved about with all the assurance of the most experienced hostess. She accepted her husband's attention and flattery with quiet grace.

When the party was over Kaiser knew his wife had firmly established herself as the new Mrs. Kaiser. And he was convinced people had forgotten that five months earlier he had married this young nurse only twenty-seven days after his first wife died.

Subsequent events proved just how fortunate Kaiser had been to marry "Ale." The most important thing was that he was deeply in love with her, so he found great happiness in being a devoted husband. In turn, she was a lively companion who worked at keeping him stimulated. Their lives together were fun—both business and pleasure. Neither of them had one bit of soul searching or remorse over their hasty marriage.

One early incident did demonstrate that Ale had made up her mind that she didn't want to be overshadowed, or put in awe of, her famous husband. It was their first Christmas in the Lafayettte home. Kaiser had racked his brains for a very special gift that would be sure to please her, a Hammond chord organ which was just then becoming popular. He made the purchase, had it secretly installed, and arranged for a professional organist to be available to play it when he showed it to her. As Ale came down for dinner, the music burst forth in all its richness. She took one look, pulled a face, and blurted, "I don't want it. Take it away. I want a diamond." Kaiser, of course, was crushed. That Christmas Eve dinner was a very nervous and awkward one for Kaiser and his few guests.

After dinner, Handy quietly asked why she hadn't been willing to accept the organ and then get the diamond later. She replied, "I couldn't. I have to stay one jump ahead of him or I'll end up subservient to him like Bess was." That attitude would become a pattern of life for Ale—she would always try to keep him slightly off balance so he would have to court her, not overpower her.

There were, however, some scars that remained. Bess Kaiser had been one of the leaders in the Women's Athletic Club of Oakland. To say her friends there were shocked would be an understatement. Most were thoroughly incensed. They were not about to invite Ale to become a replacement. This really didn't bother Ale, because she was only interested in building a new life with her husband, not in trying to follow in Bess's footsteps, nor in joining a conservative women's organization.

In the Oakland community itself, most married women—particularly the older ones—were outspoken in their criticism. However, this gradually lessened in time.

The most lasting scars were with the wives of Kaiser executives, especially those who had known Bess for a long time and who had come to look upon her as "Mother." These ladies simply could not feel close to Ale. And their attitude toward Kaiser himself was never quite the same again. They no longer felt they were part of his family, as had been the case in the past.

The company executives themselves were more inclined to forgive and forget, but still they never developed a close relationship with Ale. Either she didn't want to, or didn't think it appropriate to try to organize "get-togethers" with the men, and they hesitated to take the initiative.

It was even difficult for Kaiser's two sons, Edgar and Henry, Jr., and their wives, to feel at home with Ale. Neither side made a conscious, continuing effort to get together on a family basis. There were some Christmases when Edgar and Henry, Jr., were invited to be with their father in Hawaii, without their wives or children.

The one exception was Dr. Sidney Garfield who had started and was still in charge of the Kaiser Permanente Hospitals. Ale had worked for him for years and knew him so well she felt at ease with him. Then, not long after Kaiser's marriage, Dr. Garfield fell in love with Ale's sister, Helen. This pleased Kaiser very much and he actively promoted their marriage. After that, Mr. and Mrs. Kaiser and Dr. and Mrs. Garfield took every opportunity they could find to do things together.

Part of the reason Ale never blended in with the rest of the organization, of course, was that within two years of her marriage to Kaiser they moved to Hawaii. It wasn't a situation where the day-to-day events would bring everyone together. Ale and Kaiser were building their own world in Hawaii. The multiplicity of companies, headquartered in Oakland, with their tens of thousands of employees around the world, were enjoying breathtaking growth at that time, so the executives had their hands full without worrying about getting closer to Ale.

As sketchy as the communications were between Ale and the rest of the organization while Kaiser was still alive, the curtain almost completely came down once he died. Ale didn't seek comfort by turning to people in the company. Nor did any of the people feel they should reach out to cultivate new bonds with her.

Quite surprising, Ale left Hawaii for good immediately following Kaiser's death, and arranged the early sale of the Portlock estate where she and Kaiser had lived for nearly eight years. Also quite surprising, she didn't take up residence in the Oakland area, even though she was originally from there, and still had many friends in the Kaiser Permanente hospital organization. Too, her sister Helen with the husband Dr. Sidney Garfield lived in that area. Instead, Ale moved first to one of the Greek Islands where she was married for a short time, and later to St. Croix in the Virgin Islands where she had to make all new friends. Concurrently with her home in St. Croix she has maintained a luxurious apartment in New York City.

There is no doubt that if Ale had retained her magnificent Portlock estate in Honolulu, and had kept contact with all the leaders she had met when her husband was alive, the name Kaiser would not have been so quickly forgotten in Hawaii as it has been.

CHAPTER 13

MORE THAN JUST A BUSINESSMAN

"There is only one time to do anything, and that's today."

A Close-Knit Family

Kaiser and his first wife, Bess, and their two sons, Edgar and Henry Jr., were sentimentalists. Unabashed sentimentalists. Unabashed idealists. Almost maudlin at times.

They showed their affection for each other by effusive words of love they so often expressed. And by unhesitatingly putting their arms around each other on a regular basis.

Kaiser made people feel that whatever he was doing was somehow a reflection of his family's support, his family's togetherness. He sought the counsel and support of Bess on a daily basis. He never hesitated to let his sons in on what he was doing, soliciting their comments and suggestions.

Neither of the boys was athletic enough to be "first stringers" on any high school or college teams. The one sporting event that captivated them was speedboat racing which they soon picked up from their father once he had completed his home at Lake Tahoe, California, in 1935. Even though they were seldom the drivers in the many championship speedboat races Kaiser would enter, they became expert enough to test each of the new boats to the maximum.

It was work that would be the dominant interest in their lives. They learned from their father that work can be the most fun of any sport. To the extent that they didn't cause their parents the usual teenage worries, it was largely because their father kept them involved in what he was doing.

By the time Kaiser turned 53, on May 9, 1935, Edgar had been directly in charge of construction of the Bonneville Dam on the Columbia River for nearly a year. He was only 27 years old. Henry Jr. was 17 and still in school. Bess and the two boys decided that the nicest thing they could do for the father on his birthday was to assemble a record of his accomplishments, and for each to write in longhand a personal tribute to him. The originals of these tributes are in the Bancroft Library at the University of California in Berkeley. Under an artistically drawn letterhead reading, DEDICATION, Bess wrote:

> This summary of your life's activities and accomplishments has been assembled, first for you, but in a large part to the memory of your mother, Mary Kaiser, whose high ideals of true manhood meant character, courage, honesty, loyalty, and above all else, kindness and consideration of his fellow man.
>
> It has been a great privilege to follow by your side and to see you develop into every thing she could have wished for and to know that you in turn have passed on her ideals to the two boys so that they will be able to work and to earn their way to success.
>
> She was a truly fine mother.
>
> Bess.

Edgar expressed his feelings:

> Dad:
>
> I stood on the bank watching the river go by—the sun shone on the cofferdam—no men in view—and on the other shore a new plant starting—men, speed, a new task. I thought of you Dad—the river was gone—I saw you working on a toy train and a toy village, spread on the floor of a tiny living room. You were at the hospital—you said mother was sick, she might even leave us. Then you looked worried; I didn't know you had no work—and even no money. I saw you changing the body from a roadster to a sedan—then you polished the brass radiator. You were so proud—we hadn't had a car for a long time. I saw you standing by a mixer in California saying "That's a world's record today, boys." Then you were in bed. Christmas came, you were very sick. I saw you standing on a boat waving goodbye to Havana. Then I saw you at your desk in Oakland.—No—it was the river I saw—the cofferdam—solid, sturdy pushing the river aside as if it had always been there. I know that cofferdam will be gone soon, giving way to a mighty dam—everlasting of itself—yet furnishing power to carry on far greater achievements. Again, I thought of you Dad—no detail too small—no obstacle too great—never at the end—always striving—always building. Why? That we may go on!
>
> Your son
>
> Edgar

Henry Jr. shared in the emotion of the occasion with these words:

To Dad:

As the years slip by one by one, they bring to me a fuller realization of what a truly fine Dad I have. Since you passed the fifty mark your age annually decreases one each year, but, Dad, since your last birthday I have grown one year older and that year has brought to me clearer and more forceful vision of what a swell Dad you are. The indominable [sic] will and courage which has brought you to your success is to me the great thing. The success and the gains from it mean nothing. The true value lies in the courage and the fight to come thru. I don't want to go on saying what a success you are in business for that is secondary to something. It is secondary to being a father. I have always been able to come to you as a pal and a friend, tell you my troubles, and get your patient advice or help. Whenever I did anything or strived to attain a position I knew that you, Dad, were right behind me helping and pulling for me. That means a great deal. The success in business is not a success in life. You, Dad, have reached the height in both business and life. It is hard to put in words just what I feel and all I can say is that your [sic] the finest Dad any boy ever had. Some day, Dad, I hope I'll be able to earn your pride in me and come thru with flying colors. A great example has been set for me but if I have any of your courage, virtue and honesty, I know I'll come thru. About all I can say, Dad, is- Happy birthday and many happy returns to the finest husband, father, and man that ever walked the face of the earth.

With Much Love,

Henry J Kaiser, Jr.

The two sons would remain throughout their lives a bit more emotional, a bit more idealistic, than most businessmen. No doubt this reflected in part their continuing desire to live up to the high standards set by their father. They were very conscious of the fact that their father was one of the great men of the country, and instead of rebelling against his greatness, as some heirs have been known to do, they constantly strove to be worthy of him.

Edgar was placed in charge of tremendously important undertakings early in life. In each of these assignments he felt it was his responsibility to provide the kind of leadership he knew his father would. He strove to have the same kind of warm and friendly relations with the people who worked for him. He felt his workers would be judging his father by the things he did, and he was determined to live up to their expectations. As a consequence, the image he projected, and the words he spoke, tended to be unusually idealistic.

He was a gifted public speaker. Some people thought he might have been a better speaker than his father. He never hesitated, therefore, to take on a speaking engagement if it was important enough. This talent, together with his natural leanings toward community activities, led him to become one of the most spirited and influential leaders in the Bay Area once he returned to Oakland for his headquarters in the mid-1950's.

One thing in which he outdid his father, for sure, was in the spending of money. He was more than generous with money, he was nothing less than extravagant. His hotel bills, his dining bills, his entertainment bills, his whole life style dazzled most people who knew him well. Next to his father he was perhaps the hardest working man in the companies, so he didn't hesitate to be the biggest spender.

No doubt, Edgar's failure to husband his resources more wisely contributed to the fact that after Henry Kaiser's death there was no true family dynasty. Further, it is significant to note that the estate of Edgar Kaiser did not end up making any contribution to The Henry J. Kaiser Family Foundation, whereas the Foundation did receive $38,293,963 from the estate of Henry Jr.

Henry Jr.'s business career was entirely different from Edgar's. He started out as vice-president of Permanente Cement, but without any particularly heavy duties. Then for a while he worked at the Richmond shipyards, soon transferring to the steel mill at Fontana in Southern California. When the Navy asked Kaiser to take over management of the strife-ridden Brewster Aeronautical Corporation of New Jersey in 1943, he assigned Henry Jr. to be his personal assistant. The Kaiser control didn't last long, so soon thereafter Henry Jr. was appointed vice-president and general manager of a new company to produce ammunition shells in Denver, Colorado and Fontana, California. This did involve overall leadership responsibilities, and it was agreed Henry Jr. had done a good job. With the ending of the war in August 1945, this operation was terminated, leaving Henry Jr. available to head up efforts to start an automobile assembly plant at Long Beach. When this never got off the ground, because a decision had been made to concentrate all automobile manufacturing at Willow Run, Michigan, Henry Jr. was free to open an office in Los Angeles where he would become his father's Southern California representative, primarily promoting the interests of the steel company.

Not long thereafter, Henry Jr. moved his headquarters to the home office in Oakland. From that time forward he was almost exclusively involved in public relations and employee relations work. He loved contacts with the press; he welcomed every opportunity to give speeches; he directed all dealings with state officials, several times hosting the governor and large groups of legislators at outings at Kaiser's estate at Lake Tahoe.

Because he couldn't do all the things his father had done, and all the things his brother was doing, Henry Jr. wanted desperately to symbolize the spirit and soul of the Kaiser companies. He took the highest ideals of his father and his brother and tried to project them to the employees and to the public. Many people felt he did indeed personify the spirit of the Kaiser organization through his heroic struggle against multiple sclerosis and through all the things he did to represent the companies.

When the new Kaiser Center building in Oakland was completed in 1960, he had a beautiful office on the 28th floor near his father and brother, overlooking Lake Merritt. He arranged to have these words of inspiration inscribed in large gold letters on a blue leather plaque mounted over the entrance to his office:

GOD, GIVE ME GRACE TO ACCEPT WITH SERENITY THE THINGS THAT CANNOT BE CHANGED, COURAGE TO CHANGE THE THINGS WHICH SHOULD BE CHANGED, AND THE WISDOM TO KNOW THE DIFFERENCE.

Although Henry Kaiser was forever being inspired by seeing the good in most people, there were five persons who meant the most in his life—his mother, his first wife, Bess, his second wife, Ale, and his two sons. His grandchildren—three daughters and three sons of Edgar; two daughters of Henry Jr. by his first wife, and one son by his second wife—were, of course, important to him but he never took the time to become very close to them. None of them ever became a significant influence in his life.

His key executives, however, were like sons to him. They were all his "boys." There is no doubt Kaiser was actually a stronger and finer man because of the strength he drew from the people around him. But the deepest working bond was with his two sons. He was fortunate indeed that they shared his ideals and strove to the end of their lives to fulfill what he expected of them.

Mostly Modest, But Attractive

Except as a source of inspiration, and as a necessary atmosphere for his wife and him to raise their two sons, homes were not all that important to Henry Kaiser. He never aspired to have the biggest or fanciest home. He never wanted, or had, a family estate like the Roosevelts in Hyde Park, the Kennedys in Hyannisport, the automobile tycoons in Grosse Point, the movie stars in Beverly Hills. There is no home of his that is today lived in by any member of his family.

Actually, Kaiser's first home which he finished building in Spokane, Washington, in 1908 when he was only 26 years old, was a surprisingly large and attractive home for so young a man. Then for several years he lived in Everett, Washington, before moving to Oakland, California, in 1921. By 1925 he had built his own house at 664 Haddon Road on a slight hill a short distance from Lake Merritt, and just a few miles away from his downtown office. This was the home he lived in the longest and the one his people would remember the most fondly. Of this home, Frank Taylor would write in the Saturday Evening Post, June 7, 1941:

He gets as much satisfaction out of doing a little job fast as out of a big job. One of his thrills is his home in Oakland, which he built sixteen years ago before he became a rich man. He and Mrs. Kaiser, who is 'Mother

Kaiser' to the whole Kaiser outfit, are proud of the fact that they still live in the old house in which their sons grew up. But as one of Kaiser's men remarked, 'It's the same old foundation, but not the same house. At least twice a year Kaiser rebuilds, tearing out walls, changing rooms, redecorating, and refinishing. He does this just as he builds a Coulee Dam or a shipyard, with day and night crews.'

This home would really come alive each Christmas. He would always have a reception of one kind or another, primarily for his employees and their families. He didn't limit his guests to his key employees; he tried to include as many as possible from among those he had anything to do with directly. He also wanted his neighbors and the public in general to share in the festivities, so each year he would go to great trouble and expense to decorate his home spectacularly on the outside.

Soon after the end of World War II, the Kaisers decided to take up residence in the Bellevue Staten apartments on Lake Merritt in Oakland, less than a mile from his office. At this apartment, the Kaisers occupied the top floor which provided them with a fine view of the area. As nice as it was, it could hardly be said to be worthy of a man of Kaiser's importance. It was here that Bess Kaiser lived the last few years of her life until her death in March, 1951. During the last few months she was alive, she stayed mostly in the apartment where almost daily she would receive treatments by her Kaiser Permanente personal doctors.

It was while living in this apartment that Kaiser began the construction of a new home in Lafayette, California about 10 miles from downtown Oakland. For the detailed story on this home, see Chapter 12.

Kaiser only lived in this Lafayette home four years because by that time he had transferred his headquarters to Hawaii and had bought a home there.

Lake Tahoe Odyssey

With Kaiser's taste for the beautiful, it was no wonder that he would fall in love with Lake Tahoe once he saw it. He had enjoyed Lake Placid in New York in his younger years, so he was understandably captivated by Lake Tahoe with its crystal clear water, one of only three true Alpine lakes in the world.

For his Lake Tahoe home, Kaiser chose sixteen acres of land fronting on the lake on the California side, about 5 miles south of Tahoe City. It was a swampy area, bordered by Blackwood Creek where willows and quaking aspen trees grew, along with pine trees. To Kaiser the swamp posed no problem because he would deepen and rechannel the creek, drain the land, and bring in hundreds of truckloads of fill to raise and increase the lake frontage. Unfortunately, he didn't realize the magnitude of the problem because at the time he was doing his building in 1935, the level of the lake was at one of its lowest points in history. A few years later when the lake rose, the drainage problem would be seriously aggravated. Further, the Blackwood Creek itself would rise to flood levels at times, so on several occasions some of the homes he built would be overrun with up to a foot or two of water. This periodic flooding, to one extent or another, even occurred after Kaiser sold the property in 1962. The problem was eventually solved, however, and in recent years twenty-two of the most magnificent and luxurious condominiums on the entire lake have been built there.

The actual construction of the Tahoe complex was later told by Chad Calhoun, a Kaiser vice president:

In the spring of 1935, I happened to be walking down a street in Portland, Oregon, when I ran into Mr. Kaiser. I was in Portland, between trains, on my way to California. Mr. Kaiser told me he had been looking for me. He said I needed a vacation and he wanted me to go to Lake Tahoe where he'd bought some acreage. He said I could superintend the transformation of that land into a summer place while I was on my vacation. Vacation? He assembled more than 100 workmen with heavy equipment of all kinds, drained the land, cleared it, working right through the night with bright flood lights, built a main lodge and five chalets, a boathouse, landscaped the ground and, lo and behold, in 28 days there was a beautiful summer place on the lake and five speedboats in the boat house. The equipment made so much noise the neighbors sought an injunction to restrain us at night but before the necessary signatures could be rounded up, the project was finished and the machinery was gone. It certainly wasn't a vacation for me, but at least it was a change.

The entire complex was given the romantic name, Fleur du Lac (Flower of the Lake). Each of the main living units was given its own colorful name—the Lodge itself, then Hilltop, Glocca Morra, Wild Canary, Rain Barrel, Aspen. Smaller living quarters were given the names, Chipmunk, Birch, Willow, Fir, Pine. On three different occasions my wife and I had the thrill of staying in the Cat's Cradle which was a small apartment, just for two people, upstairs in the Harbor House itself, with a spectacular view of the lake.

As busy as he was, Kaiser could always find time to slip up to Lake Tahoe, not for relaxation but for stimulation. There was never a let-up in his attention to his company affairs. He always had a secretary and one or two assistants along with him. Most of all, he kept the phone busy, day and night. While he was there, his long distance phone bill from Lake Tahoe would set an all-time per-day record.

In the 1950's Kaiser began using his Tahoe home for company activities of all kinds. His son, Henry Jr., hosted many outings lasting two or three days for state officials including California Governor Edmund G. (Pat) Brown and dozens of legislators. Quite a few Board of Directors meetings were held at the lake with members bringing their wives. After a sumptuous dinner, guests danced. One evening about 10:30 p.m., Kaiser was dancing with Dorothy (Buff) Chandler, wife of Norman Chandler, publisher of the Los Angeles Times and Kaiser Steel board member. They were dancing vigorously when suddenly they slipped and fell down with a thud, a big thud, because they were both big people. It was quite a sight seeing how quickly they scrambled back to their feet without help from anybody—and then went right on dancing.

Whenever he was at the lake, Kaiser was the perfect host. He seldom sought solitude; rather he was right in the middle of most of the activities. As a lifetime photographer he loved taking pictures of his guests and sending them copies. From the time he fell in love with the color pink in Hawaii he would wear pink slacks and pink sport shirts. Most guests enjoyed seeing this fat man dressed in pink, bouncing all over the place taking pictures.

At times, especially with some of his own key people, he would take part in volleyball games. It was understood by everyone, however, that all he would ever do was serve the ball.

Water skiing was one of the main activities, not only for those who braved the cold water and who might be trying to ski for the first time, but also for those who enjoyed watching the beginners flounder and the experts gracefully skim across the surface of the lake. Kaiser himself, as fat as he was, learned (with help) to water ski in his late sixties, although he really did it only a few times.

Kaiser's young wife, Ale, whom he had married in April 1951, was an outstanding water skier and did a lot of it, not only at Lake Tahoe but later in Hawaii. She also enjoyed driving the racing boats and the sailboats. One time, just three months after she had married Kaiser, a catamaran she was sailing in suddenly flipped over. It was reported in the "Los Angeles Times" of July 4, 1951:

KAISER HELPS SAVE BRIDE AS BOAT TIPS

Industrialist Speeds to Scene at Lake Tahoe When He Spots Accident From Shore

LAKE TAHOE, July 3 (AP)—Driving a speedboat five miles in seven minutes, Henry J. Kaiser raced to the rescue of his bride of three months today after an overturning boat had spilled her and two men into the water.

The wife of the industrialist was with Dr. Sidney Garfield, director of all the Kaiser-sponsored Permanente hospitals, and Dr. Cecil Cutting, chief surgeon at Oakland Permanente.

It was not long thereafter that Kaiser and his wife, with her at the wheel, were putting one of their boats to a speed test making sharp turns, when suddenly he was thrown out of the boat into the water. Judy Murphy, daughter of Phil Murphy, well-known western bridge builder and a neighbor of Kaiser at Lake Tahoe, happened to be driving her boat at high speed immediately behind where Kaiser was thrown into the water. She made a sharp 180 degree turn to avoid hitting him. Kaiser told her later that her quick thinking had saved his life.

Kaiser's Tahoe neighbors, of course, were always curious about all the comings and goings and all the activities at the Kaiser estate. One time in 1946 the neighbors heard an airplane circling over the lake nearby. It was in the late afternoon, so one or two neighbors got in their boats just to watch the flying boat settle down on the lake. When it finally came to a stop, the plastic top of the cockpit was flung open and out popped the begoggled head of Howard Hughes. Then a woman stood up in the plane who the neighbors thought might be Elizabeth Taylor. A few years earlier Kaiser and Hughes had teamed up to build a fleet of flying box cars for the war effort, but the only outcome of this project was the building of the massive wooden "Spruce Goose" by Hughes and his organization.

It was Kaiser's love affair with Hawaii that would eventually spell the end of his Lake Tahoe Odyssey. In late 1953 he fell in love with Honolulu and by February of 1954 had purchased a Kahala beach home. He became so enamored with the beauty of Hawaii itself, and with all the construction work he was doing there—to say nothing of the happy new life he was building there with his young wife—he found less and less time to spend at Lake Tahoe.

Company officials continued to use Fleur du Lac for various important company affairs, but there was never quite the emotional attachment Kaiser had felt. Even his son Edgar had few ties with Tahoe. As a matter of fact, Edgar had come to feel most at home in the Pacific Northwest during the 1930's and 1940's when he was building dams and ships there. It was at that period of time he had purchased property on Orcas Island in the San Juan Straits, not far from Victoria, British Columbia. Year after year he added to his beautiful complex of homes on Orcas Island. It was always there, not at Tahoe, that he and his family sought their recreation.

Henry Jr. was the one person who never lost his love for Tahoe. However, multiple sclerosis was increasingly taking its toll on him and he was forced to cut back on his use of Fleur du Lac. When he finally died in 1961 at age 44, the last link to Lake Tahoe had been broken.

Not long thereafter, Fleur du Lac was put on the market for sale. On the 5th day of March, 1962, John B. DeMaria, of San Francisco, bought it for $387,500. Even making allowance for the change in money values since then, this was an astonishingly low price for one of the grandest properties on the entire lake.

To many Kaiser people who shared in the glory of Fleur du Lac during its twenty-seven years of Kaiser ownership, it was a sad ending. There was added irony in the fact that by the mid-1980's the twenty-two condominiums which had replaced the original chalets, were listing for sale at prices ranging from $2 million to $6 million each.

The Roar Of The Engines

"I am not disappointed," he said easily and with a cheerful smile. "No, I am not disappointed."

Not disappointed? How could that possibly be? What kind of Pollyanna was he? How could anyone find anything to be cheerful about?

For a long time Henry Kaiser had dreamed of setting the world record for speed boats. And for the last six months he was sure the time had come. He had contracted for two specially designed unlimited hydroplanes with the nation's most highly rated speed boatbuilder.

He had carefully planned the timetable, relying on the experienced judgment of the boatbuilder and his other expert consultants. He had chosen the ideal lake for the tests—Lake Placid, New York, which had extra appeal because as a young man he had lived there for several years. He had signed an agreement with his longtime friend, Guy Lombardo, orchestra leader and experienced race boat driver, to do the driving on June 11 and 12, 1949. Two weeks of test runs prior to that would be time enough to get the boats in prime working order to shoot for the record.

Not one to hide his light under a bushel, Kaiser had let it be known he was out to break the world record. The news services, radio, television, newsreel folk—everybody was informed and many were at Lake Placid to report and record. The people around Lake Placid were sponsoring civic events to herald the expected run.

Nothing happened.

That is, nothing happened as expected. What did happen was that Aluminum First, the hydroplane with the big engines driven by Guy Lombardo, all but tore herself to pieces in her effort to make good during the trial runs.

The other boat, Hot Metal, driven by Max Collins, one of Kaiser's own men, reached a speed of 105.571 miles per hour in trial runs before it encountered troubles, so no attempt was made on the world record by it.

Kaiser was not unmindful of the crushed feelings everyone else working with him on the project would have. He tried to buoy them with hope:

> Naturally, I regret the unfortunate turn of events which has temporarily frustrated our efforts. However, it is not for myself in any way that I feel badly. Rather it is for the engineers and the designers, for the mechanics and the drivers Guy Lombardo and Max Collins, that I feel badly. It is upon all of these fine young men that the disappointment falls so heavily. In no way do I look upon our experience here as a failure. To the contrary I consider the very failure itself as a success. This is a young man's world in which we live, and young men learn best through adversity. This has been a hard lesson in adversity which these 'boys' will never forget. It is a lesson for which they will be much better men and citizens in the long run. We are pioneering in this field, and pioneering is the thing on which this country is so well founded. By making possible the construction of these newly designed aluminum boats and the experiments which these young men are conducting with them, I hope that I am providing incentive and inspiration in this particular field of science and engineering. The men who have devoted their time, abilities and energies, and, above all, their confidence and determination, are pioneers in every sense of the word. Their work is for the good of the country, and I am happy to contribute to it.

Lake Placid was just the beginning of Kaiser's boating disasters in 1949. He had planned not only to set the world record on June 11 and 12, but to be ready to:

1. Enter Hot Metal, the 28-foot boat, in the Detroit Gold Cup Regatta, Saturday, July 2;

2. Send Hot Metal, the hoped-for Gold Cup winner, to Lake Tahoe, California to race there Sunday, July 10;

3. Race Aluminum First, the 32-foot boat, in the famed Harmsworth Trophy event, Friday and Saturday, July 29 and 30;

4. Race Hot Metal again at Lake Tahoe August 14;

5. Late in September race Aluminum First, the hoped-for Harmsworth winner, at the President's Cup Regatta on the Potomac River near Washington, DC.

It was not to be. Hot Metal took a sound beating in the Detroit Gold Cup. To the surprise of many, but to the distinct pleasure of Kaiser, his very young friend from Lake Tahoe, R. Stanley Dollar, Jr., came in second driving his own boat, Skip-A-Long. Guy Lombardo drove his own boat, Temper VI, but he was not among the winners.

Showing that his performance in the Gold Cup was no fluke, Dollar went on to win the Harmsworth Trophy, July 30. This was the most coveted victory of all, because the winner qualified to represent the United States in international competition. And it was the toughest race of all on both boat and driver because it involved six times around a 7-mile lap, a grueling distance of 42 miles.

Soon after winning the Harmsworth, Dollar trucked his boat out to Lake Tahoe for the August 14 race. By that time Kaiser had borrowed a special propeller for Hot Metal which he promised to return by air express after the race. Again, something went wrong—the propeller punctured the hull when something gave way and (the propellor) sank to the bottom of Lake Tahoe. Luckily, Kaiser was nearby in another boat and was able to get a line on Hot Metal itself in time to beach her before she sank.

Dollar was not so lucky, Shortly after winning the Tahoe Regatta he was for some reason towing Skip-A-Long not far from Kaiser's estate, Fleur du Lac. There were all kinds of boats speeding around making waves when a particularly large boat raced by, creating a huge wake. Like all racing boats, Skip-A-Long had very little freeboard, and the combined waves swamped her and she started to sink. In one of the saddest moments of his life, Dollar himself had to cut the tow rope and watch his beloved boat sink—an unbelievable ending for America's best racing boat of 1949.

Herb Caen, San Francisco's premier columnist, writing in the Chronicle a few days later, reported:

Henry Kaiser Sr. is this kind of a guy. After Stanley Dollar's Harmsworth-winning, 'Skip-A-Long' speedboat sank tragically in 400 feet of water at Lake Tahoe last Sunday Kaiser immediately offered him his own powerful boat, 'Hot Metal,' to use as his own, any time, any place.

Why Speedboat Racing?

It was only natural—almost inevitable—that Kaiser would end up in speedboat racing. He was such a competitive person, and yet he had no outlet for that in athletics. He did some ice skating and roller skating as a boy and he had his own bicycle. He enjoyed swimming as a young man in Lake Placid, but he never went to high school or college where he might have competed in baseball or football or track. He was much too interested in getting off to a running start in the challenge of making a living.

And speed was an obsession with him. As exciting as sailboat racing is to many people, that would not do for him. Too slow, too quiet. He ended up being the fastest roadbuilder, the fastest dambuilder, the fastest shipbuilder, the fastest steel mill builder, the fastest home builder.

The other enchantment which speed boats held for Kaiser was the opportunity it provided him to experiment with engines. All his life he was tinkering with engines of one kind or another. No matter how many talented engine experts worked for him he could keep up with, or ahead of, them in even the most technical aspects of engine operation. And he loved the roar of engines. His Lake Tahoe neighbors would call his hydroplanes "Thunder boats," because he was always racing them with the throttle wide open.

It was while building his elegant estate, Fleur du Lac, at Lake Tahoe, California, in 1935 that he became enraptured with the excitement and challenge of speedboat racing. The lake was an ideal place to launch his racing career. Not the least of the inspiration was the sheer majesty of the lake—one of the beauty spots of the world. The lake was big enough—12 miles wide, 22 miles long—and so totally free of debris the boats could open up to full speed for long distances without any particular concern for safety. At an altitude of 6,223 feet it required special tuning of the engines, but Kaiser only looked upon that as a challenge to improve their efficiency.

While construction of the home was going forward, Kaiser was already entering Lake Tahoe's summer speedboat championships. Because he spared no expense to buy the fastest boats he could find, he came off a winner in his very first important race.

However, it was a different story in 1936, as recounted in the Oakland Tribune covering the race of July 12:

Tahoe Trembles to Roar of Craft As Dollar Boat Wins

Driving his favorite racing boat, 'Baby-Skip-along,' R. Stanley Dollar Jr. of San Francisco won the lake championship event in the Tahoe Power Boat

Club's annual regatta for the fourth time. Henry J. Kaiser Jr. of Oakland was second, bringing in his, 'Hornet,' 42 seconds behind Dollar. F. T. Barrow, in 'Miss Oakland' was third, and Henry J. Kaiser Sr., who won the event last year, fourth in the 'Bess.'

During the war Kaiser spent a minimum of time with his racing boats. Instead, he was busy turning out ships for war in record time. But that didn't mean any let-up in his dreams of winning some national speedboat championships. By the summer of 1946 he was back at it again. The San Francisco Examiner had this article June 28, 1946:

> With a record number of spectator boats standing by, Henry Kaiser's Silver Shell, driven by Brooks Walker, captured the championship Free-For-All power boat race Sunday in the season's second session of the Lake Tahoe Power Boat Regatta.

It was the summer of 1949 that Kaiser suffered the ignominious performances of his two highly-touted new boats, Aluminum First and Hot Metal. He was determined to pick up the pieces, however, as indicated by a letter he wrote on September 9, 1949, to Leonard H. Thomson, Secretary of the Detroit International Regatta Association, in which he said:

> Improvements still remain to be done in the Aluminum First and Hot Metal to get them to maximum performance, but I guess that part of the thrill of racing is in overcoming the obstacles and difficulties which you mention.

A clue as to how deeply Kaiser kept involved in trying to improve the performance of his boats can be found in excerpts from the daily log or diary of his activities, as written in longhand by one of his secretaries:

> Thursday, February 2, 1950 Mr. Kaiser, Trefethen and Barneyback went to look at the boats

> Monday, February 6, 1950 Mr. Kaiser and Mr. Elliott went to look at boats

> Tuesday, February 7, 1950 Mr. Kaiser looked at the boats

> Wednesday, February 8, 1950 Mr. Kaiser looked at boats

> Thursday, February 9, 1950 Mr. Kaiser looked at boats

> Friday, February 10, 1950 Mr. Kaiser went to the boats

> Saturday, February 11, 1950 Mr. Kaiser went to the boats

> Tuesday, March 14, 1950 Mr. Kaiser, Mr. Barneyback went to look at boats

Saturday, March 18, 1950 Mr. Kaiser, Mr. Trefethen looked at boats

Monday, March 20, 1950 Mr. Kaiser, Mr. Barneyback looked at boats

Friday, March 24, 1950 Mr. Kaiser in the office, and then went to look at the boats

Wednesday, March 29, 1950 Mr. Kaiser and Elliott looked at boats

Friday, March 31, 1950 Mr. Kaiser - Mr. Elliott looked at the boats

Saturday, May 13, 1950 Mr. Kaiser - Mr. Elliott looked at the boats

It was quite amazing that Kaiser could find time to look at the boats so often in the year 1950. This was the year Kaiser Steel was coming into the home stretch in its program to pay off the Reconstruction Finance Corporation; the Kaiser-Frazer automobile company was facing a very rough time both in marketing and in production; Kaiser Aluminum was bursting with growth; the Kaiser Permanente Health Plan was trying to bounce back from its battles with the American Medical Association; and various other Kaiser companies were blossoming out in different directions.

With his flair for things mechanical he could keep coming up with one idea after another on how to improve the boats' performance. Over and above that, it was a chance to break away from the pressures of the office. He never took a vacation, so little breaks like this were a tonic. And without any doubt most of the time he was traveling to and from the boats, or looking at the boats, his unconscious mind was busy coming up with ideas that would help one or more of his companies. Most of the time when he returned to the office he would call a meeting or get on the phone and stir things up.

Try as he may, consult with as many experts as he may, Kaiser could never bring the performance of either Aluminum First or Hot Metal anywhere near their hoped-for potential. Actually, the one he had the highest hopes for—Aluminum First—was never in shape to be entered in races and certainly not equal to shooting for a world record. Neither boat was ever again entered in the Detroit Gold Cup race nor in the Harmsworth Trophy Race.

However, the convenience of the Lake Tahoe was such that nearly every summer Kaiser raced one or more of his boats (never Aluminum First) in the regattas there. The best showing, and the most exciting race, took place on Sunday July 13, 1952. It was written up in the newspaper:

In a nip-and-tuck battle featuring Lake Tahoe's regatta Sunday, won on the last turn of the final lap of the race, R. Stanley Dollar Jr., drove his 1500-horsepower hydroplane, 'Short Snort,' across the finish line in front of Henry J. Kaiser's 'Hot Metal' driven by Max Collins. Collins got off to a substantial lead in the feature race of the afternoon, and held his lead well into the second lap when, with a tremendous burst of speed on the straightaway,

Dollar, driving a magnificent race, pulled up on 'Hot Metal.' As he made the final turn into the straightaway, Collins' boat went into a spin. Collins handled the speeding aluminum-hulled craft beautifully and brought it around, but Dollar, quick to take advantage of the spin, pulled up on even terms with the Kaiser craft and picking up speed bounced across the finish line a length ahead of Collins. Collins wrenched his back as his boat went into a spin and was unable to attend the presentation ceremonies where 4,000 persons in boats or on the beaches at Chambers Lodge gave the popular Dollar a rousing ovation. (Collins later said he had trouble with oil on the pedal, causing his foot to slip.)

As disappointing as that was, it turned out to be a proud day for Kaiser himself. Over the years he had gained the reputation of being a nerveless driver. He could bluff most anyone on the turn and often did it, and he had the trophies to show for it. Now at age 70 he had elected to drive one of his boats, "Lemme Go First," in the 325-horsepower class—and he came in a clear winner. For a fat, bald-headed man wearing a large life jacket, his victory smile, as published in the newspaper, was every bit as broad and infectious as that of the handsome young Stanley Dollar.

It was at the end of the 1952 racing season that Kaiser, at age 70, decided to leave the driving to others. Notwithstanding this decision, Kaiser was not yet ready to let go of his love for fast boats. He had been entered so often in the President's Cup Race on the Potomac River he was determined to keep his boats entered there. In one of those events, just two days before the race, a specially-designed carburetor blew on his boat. Word went out through the companies' nationwide teletype system to find a replacement. Luckily, the Los Angeles office tracked one down in a nearby airplane plant. Time was so critical, a Kaiser employee flew with the carburetor on his lap to Kansas City, while the company plane flew from Washington DC to Kansas City to meet him and carry the carburetor to destination. The crew worked all night making the installation, finishing just in time for the boat to line up for the start of the race, with Kaiser watching very excitedly nearby. The gun sounded, the boats roared off and into the first turn, when suddenly Kaiser's boat coughed and "conked out." It wasn't the carburetor's fault. Incredibly, in all the excitement, nobody had thought to fill the gas tank! Not surprisingly, the chief mechanic and driver disappeared for three days—somehow trying to drown their chagrin.

On another occasion, Kaiser heard of a new Cadillac engine that had just been developed by General Motors which with custom milling could become the greatest thing that had ever been invented for a speed boat. He wanted one right now, so he asked Handy Hancock to get it to Tahoe at once. Working with freight traffic experts, Hancock was to follow the engine every day as it rolled west on a freight train. As fate would have it, there was a fire in a Utah railroad tunnel and the whole train had to be rerouted, making it ten days late. During those ten days Kaiser chewed Hancock up one side and down the other, because "you should have known there might be a fire in a railroad tunnel"—an absurd accusation on the face of it. This went on day after day, but there was nothing Hancock or anyone else could do about it. Hancock's daily apologies didn't appease Kaiser. Let Hancock describe the outcome:

Finally, one day as I was sitting at Mr. Kaiser's desk I cracked and started to cry. I said, 'Excuse me,' and retreated to the men's rest room just outside Mr. Kaiser's office, where my nerves cut loose and I sat blubbering like a baby uncontrollably. First, Mr. Kaiser sent his secretary, Edna Knuth (Canutie), into the men's john to try to get me to come out, but I told her to 'go away, I don't want any part of it, I don't even want any more part of Henry Kaiser.' Soon Mr. Kaiser came in, ostensibly to relieve himself at the urinal. He could hear me sobbing away in one of the stalls and tried to console me, at which point I lashed out and said, 'Leave me alone, get away, I don't want to have any more to do with you, I hate you, I quit,' Finally, after getting my nerves together again, I came back out, only to find him waiting outside the door for me. He put his arms around me, took me in his office, told me he was sorry, asked me to go home early that day, to relax and come back in the morning so we could get going on other things. From that day forward we had a whole new relationship—he would still press for speed, but with more consideration of my feelings, and I would have more confidence because I had tried to resign and had been asked to stay on.

In the 1955 Lake Tahoe Regatta, Kaiser did not have a boat entered. It turned out to be one of the lake's most exciting races. In the main event, the unlimited class race of the huge hydroplanes, everyone was surprised to see a tiny 14-foot hydroplane driven by a complete stranger to Kaiser, Kenny St. Oegger. His small craft was powered by a Chevrolet engine laid on its side to cut wind resistance. Incredibly, St. Oegger, by sheer guts and skill won the race, mainly because he could cut inside the big hydroplanes on the turns, even though he came close to being swamped every time they would come roaring by him on the straightaway. Kaiser was ecstatic—in an instant he made up his mind he must own that boat. Without any introduction, Kaiser leaned over the side of the dock as St. Oegger was climbing up the ladder to come to the winner's platform, and asked him how much he would sell his boat for. Kaiser was looking down and St. Oegger was looking up, and they made a deal right there on the ladder, including an agreement that St. Oegger would come with Kaiser as a driver.

Betting on St. Oegger's driving skill, Kaiser decided to make another run at championship racing. He had a hydroplane racing hull manufactured by the same people who had produced the hull of the boat that was then holding the world record. He named the hydroplane, "Miss Hawaii Kai" and entered it in national cup races on Lake Washington in Seattle where it showed its championship caliber.

Soon thereafter Kaiser was going through a period of poor health in Hawaii. Edgar decided it might raise his father's spirits and his overall morale if they could set a world speed record in Hawaiian waters. Accordingly, the boat was shipped to Hono-lulu where it was tuned up to run at sea level in salt water, and arrangements were made for it to do an official speed record run at Kikei Lagoon.

For several days after the recording equipment had been set up and the speed traps had been positioned, the weather was bad making the water too choppy for racing. Finally, the water was smooth enough one morning to shoot for the world record. St. Oegger climbed in the cockpit, roared down the course in one direction, and the clocking indicated he was easily going to smash the world record. However, to be accepted the boat has to make a run in the opposite direction, with the average of the two speeds being the official time. As the boat reached its highest speed on the reverse lap, the rudder at the stern of the craft suddenly gave way, causing the boat to dig into the water, smashing it into thousands of pieces, and catapulting St. Oegger high into the air before he crashed into the sea. Miraculously he lived, although broken and bruised horribly. It took him months to recuperate, during which time his business of manufacturing store fixtures went down and down and into the red. Typi-cal of Kaiser and his son Edgar, once St. Oegger was back on his feet and able to return to his business, they helped him financially and in every other way they possi-bly could. However, that close call spelled the end of speedboat racing for the Kais-ers, because they agreed world records and trophies just were not worth risking a man's life. It was a clear decision without any lingering regrets but it was weighted with sadness because it meant the end of 20 years of excitement and glory which speedboats had brought into Kaiser's life.

My Heart Leaped With Joy

"There is no there, there," Gertrude Stein once wrote about Oakland. One woman's opinion. Or was it simply one woman's way of trying to say something cute that would be sure to be talked about?

Whatever the motivation, it was a statement that would be repeated over and over many thousands of times. It was a statement that still keeps popping up whenever anyone wants to make light of Oakland.

It wasn't an opinion Jack London would have agreed with. He loved Oakland. It was his base of operation for most of his writing and for all of his Pacific Ocean adventures. It was so much a part of him a large, beautiful waterfront development by the city of Oakland at the foot of Broadway would become famous, known as Jack London Square.

Certainly, Henry Kaiser never agreed with Gertrude Stein. To him, Oakland was not only his proud home for the most meaningful years of his life, but it was the source of most of his inspiration. His deep-rooted attachment for Oakland was elo-quently brought out on the occasion of Oakland's "Henry J. Kaiser Day" Banquet and Award, given by the French Legion of Honor, at the Scottish Rite Temple, Thursday night, June 5, 1952.

After expressing his warm gratitude to all who had planned the gala affair—

including a greeting to "my home-town folks,"—he said:

> Tonight I stopped for a moment outside this Scottish Rite Temple ... looked across Lake Merritt upon the beautiful vista . . . and recollected: It was almost at this spot . . . just about exactly 31 years ago . . . that I drove my car down here from the Pacific Northwest and stopped by twilight, feasting my eyes and spirit upon Lake Merritt and the friendly hills. . . . My heart leaped with joy. . . . This was my home city at last! . . . Here in 1921 I resolved that Oakland would be a grand and perfect place to establish head-quarters for our paving and construction business. . . .

"Feasting my eyes and spirit upon Lake Merritt and the friendly hills. . . . my heart leaped with joy."

Henry Kaiser was a sentimental man—a very sentimental person. Not just for appearance sake. Not just to make an impression. Sentiment was imbedded deeply in his very nature. No matter how hard-headed his business challenges were, there was a sentimental factor that influenced his every decision. Today we tend to identify Kaiser for the material things he accomplished. His memory would be more lasting if we remembered the "feelings" he put into everything he did.

That night he waxed emotional as he traced how freedom had come both to America and to France—a freedom that made it possible for the people of Oakland to do so many worthwhile things. To understand Kaiser better, it is necessary to lift a few quotes from his talk:

> And now tonight—as the 31 glorious years of living and working among you flash their memories—I want to see whether I can add up the three decades of experience and find some underlying, unifying thoughts that might have a meaning to your own lives and philosophies. . . .

> The fact that the distinguished French envoy was going to be with us tonight gave me the key to finding a certain significance that I was hunting. The Republic of France and my home city of Oakland are united in this event—Paris and Oakland almost 6,000 miles apart—yet they are bound together by heritages of ideas and ideals that are as close as brother to brother.

> Over and over I've thought, as tonight approached, about the stories of two parallel revolutions that were of transcendent importance to the whole future of mankind and civilization. . . . The Revolutionary War of the American colonies and the French Revolution went hand in hand in bequeathing to us the most precious values of our lives—the human rights without which none of the things that have been mentioned tonight could have taken place.

> American patriots of 1776 wrote the Declaration—'Life, Liberty and the Pursuit of Happiness'!

The plain people of France in 1789 rose up and cried out 'Liberty, Equality, Fraternity'!

Thus, some 170 years ago, in the hearts of plain folks on both sides of the Atlantic, there burst into flame an idea as old as the teachings of Christ. Jesus had taught the sanctity and worth of the individual—that in every man, there is the divine spark of God, the Father; that the least among us are our brothers, imbued with immortal souls.

Yet—despite Christ's teachings—going down through the centuries, Kings, Emperors and feudal lords, had kept down the rights of freedom, equality and brotherhood.

The American and French Revolutions liberated the spirits of men. Never has there been so powerful a force released upon this earth as the ideas of freedom. Now the dignity—the sanctity—the inherent greatness of the individual human being were given reign. None was born to be crushed and enslaved. Free men could dream, set goals, work and realize to the fullest the amazing powers within them. Indeed, freedom and equality of opportunity were opened up to mankind as never before.

Over the years, Kaiser and his people constituted the most powerful force in Oakland. With his encouragement, Kaiser personnel at all levels played leading roles in nearly every worthwhile community activity—from United Crusade through the Oakland Symphony through the Oakland Chamber of Commerce. Kaiser employees always set the pace in total as well as individual giving.

Then when Kaiser electrified the community by building his magnificent 28-story Kaiser Center on the shores of Lake Merritt, it gave a distinct character to Oakland. Actually, several financial and other business friends had stressed to Kaiser that his companies had grown so big he should move his headquarters to the more prestigious San Francisco, but he never once wavered. Later after his death, his organization would build a companion tower to Kaiser Center in Oakland—the Ordway Building.

It was only fitting that Kaiser would top off his spectacular Kaiser Center with a lavish Executive Dining Room on the 28th floor. In addition, a dozen smaller dining rooms were provided for luncheon sessions where group discussions could be held. Every room had a dramatic view overlooking Lake Merritt and the East Bay Hills. The big dining room also had a full sweep of the Bay and San Francisco itself. No liquor was ever served in the main dining room at lunchtime. It was an ideal place for the executives of the different companies to get to know each other better and to swap experiences. At night the whole spread of dining rooms was made available to outside groups who sponsored Oakland's most important community functions.

Now that the Kaiser companies only occupy a small portion of the Kaiser Center and the Ordway Building, the Executive Dining Room has been leased to a private group known as The Lakeview Club. An entrance fee and monthly dues are charged, but membership is open to everyone of either sex or any ethnic background. The members who belong to the club have access to it for lunch or dinner. There is simply no club in the whole Bay Area with as beautiful appointments or as dazzling a view. Naturally, while enjoying the use of the facility, few members have occasion to think about its origins. However, whenever I am there I find myself musing how the vision and courage of one man are still bringing so much enjoyment to so many.

Seldom in the annals of American history has one man meant so much to one community as Kaiser meant to Oakland. Over and above the payrolls which he brought, he created a spirit and pride that was felt either directly or indirectly by most other businesses in the area. While he was alive, and while his companies were booming, Oakland enjoyed a special kind of vitality. In appreciation the people of the community were always anxious during those times to give Kaiser the credit he was due.

However, once Kaiser moved to Honolulu in 1954, there began a gradual, subtle, almost indistinguishable, falling away of the Kaiser companies' leadership. Then when he passed away in 1967 (he had asked to be buried in Oakland), the strong personal bonds were no longer felt. This void was accentuated as the companies, one by one, began encountering hard times in the late 1970's and early 1980's, until now, there is not a single company that is owned and controlled by anyone from the Kaiser family or by Kaiser stockholders, as was the case when Kaiser was still alive. While most of the operations were able to keep going in one way or another, they came under different ownership and control. (The one exception is the remarkably successful and fast-growing Kaiser Permanente Medical Care Program which is still headquartered in Oakland and which is operating essentially as it was in Kaiser's time.)

The Henry J. Kaiser Family Foundation was first established in Oakland in 1948. It was a bit surprising—and certainly a distinct loss to Oakland—when that Foundation with its more than $400 million in assets available for philanthropic purposes (mostly medical) transferred its headquarters to Menlo Park, California, some fifty miles away from Oakland.

While it's a sad commentary that such a great American as Henry Kaiser could be so quickly forgotten by the American public, it is even more unbelievable that Oakland has failed to honor appropriately its Number One Citizen. True, the city recently renamed its fine, large civic auditorium as the Henry J. Kaiser Convention Center Arena (which was designated in February 1987 as the number one arena in the United States in the under-7,000-seat capacity division by readers of Performance Magazine in its Reader's Poll Awards), but this is far from enough to do justice to Henry Kaiser's memory.

What needs to be done is to have a rebirth of the Kaiser spirit in Oakland. I have no doubt if he were still alive he would personally organize and become the driving force in a campaign to ignite pride in Oakland. He would most certainly tell the community to quit dwelling on what's wrong with Oakland and begin emphasizing what's right. In keeping with his lifetime buoyancy he would no doubt call on all the people, all the businesses, the churches, the schools, labor groups, city and county officials, Chamber of Commerce, and advertising bureaus to unite under the banner, "Pride in Oakland." Once that became the city-wide theme song Oakland would take on a new burst of progress.

As a part of such a campaign the city should develop a professional exhibition facility, either part of the Henry J. Kaiser Convention Center Arena or somehow in conjunction with the Kaiser Center. If professionally planned, with pictures and samples of products turned out by the different companies with memorabilia of all kinds, and with a high class video on the Kaiser story, it could become a "must" visit for students of all ages including the college level. It could also become an attraction for all visitors who come to Oakland. Copies of Kaiser's marvelous speeches could be made available, along with representative magazine and newspaper articles, as well as any biographies that might be written about him. There would be great educational value in having students read all about Kaiser and then come forth with essays on how this one man epitomized all that America stands for.

Unfortunately, people around the country have already forgotten much of the glory he achieved, but certainly the people of Oakland should not. Instead, they should take immediate steps to try to recapture some of the pride that was theirs when Henry Kaiser was at the height of his amazing career.

One great man can help make one city great—if properly remembered and honored, and if the people take pride in their community.

CHAPTER 14

ASK A BUSY PERSON

"I have never felt it means much to earn money for money's sake."

A Close Call

"If only we had pushed a little harder."

That was Judge Samuel I. Rosenman, long-time advisor to President Franklin D. Roosevelt, lamenting the fact that Roosevelt had not chosen Henry J. Kaiser as his running mate in the 1944 election. In a press interview August 1, 1946, Rosenman said that for a short time in 1944 the wartime President "was thinking of Kaiser—a liberal industrialist—as a possible Vice Presidential candidate."

Rosenman was not alone in his belief that Kaiser would add strength to the ticket. He was the most talked-about industrialist in the country with his record-breaking shipbuilding, his daring proposals for massive cargo planes, together with all the other industries he had launched. He symbolized America's growing might in the death struggle with Germany and Japan. His name was a household word that should attract votes. And, of course, he was such a well-known friend of labor he would be sure to strengthen support from that direction.

Under a headline, "Henry Kaiser Dark Horse In Political Race," William K. Hutchison of the International News Service wrote, July 5, 1944:

> High new dealers are persisting today in an effort to persuade President Roosevelt to take Henry J. Kaiser, construction mogul, as his running mate in place of Henry A. Wallace in the coming presidential campaign. Thus far, Mr. Roosevelt has held out for Wallace. The presidential advisers, however, have not yet admitted defeat, despite published reports that Mr. Roosevelt turned down the Kaiser plan. Some left-wingers, reportedly led by Sidney Hillman, head of the CIO's political action committee, favor the switch from Wallace to Kaiser. The Hillman faction says Kaiser would be a better vote-getter among laboring men and would command the respect of the business

world, an asset that Wallace lacks. Kaiser's name was first mentioned as a possible running mate for Roosevelt in mid-April. High new dealers 'sounded out' Kaiser sentiment on Capitol Hill but found the democratic lawmakers lukewarm, because most of them were committed either to Senator Alben Barkley of Kentucky, or Speaker Sam Rayburn of Texas. A few preferred Senator Harry S. Truman of Missouri. Capitol Hill democrats were opposed to Kaiser solely on the ground that they preferred a practical politician on the ticket—a man they knew personally—to a business man whose political background is obscure.

Politically obscure indeed. He had never run for any office. He hadn't been in the ring in any election. He hadn't proved himself to be a vote-getter. Nor was he experienced in the intricacies of power politics. He wasn't a member of the party machine, certainly not part of any inner circle.

Never at any time in his life had he registered as a Democrat, even though his friendship with Roosevelt and other high administration and congressional officials had led people to assume he was one. When the Democrats in his home town of Oakland, California, couldn't get him to contribute to the party in the 1940 election, they "stormed Washington to demand why Kaiser who had been awarded half a billion dollars worth of government work, shouldn't do his bit." Actually, according to Frank Taylor writing in the Saturday Evening Post, Kaiser "went overboard for Wendell Willkie in the 1940 election."

It didn't set well with many Democrats when a "Henry J. Kaiser-for-President Club" was formed in January 1944 by a Republican attorney in Chicago, Vandorf Gray. By mid-February Gray thought he had the makings of a national movement, even though he acknowledged his efforts were "without consent or authority from Mr. Kaiser." As reported in the Oakland Call Bulletin of February 16, 1944, with a Chicago dateline:

Chairmen of Henry J. Kaiser for President Clubs will meet in Chicago April 7 and 8 to mobilize support behind the West Coast shipbuilder as a 1944 Republican presidential candidate. Vandorf Gray, general chairman of the movement, said today that district chairmen already have been established in 24 districts and that more will be appointed as Kaiser support continues. The 'boomlet' for Kaiser as a G.O.P. presidential candidate started early this year and the Kaiser-for-President Club has been incorporated with the secretary of state of Illinois. 'To date,' Gray said, 'Mr. Kaiser has indicated that he is not interested in any political affiliations of any kind, but it is because of this attitude that the American people in great numbers are urging his selection as the Republican candidate.'

With that kind of organization shaping up, Kaiser decided that he owed it to his well-meaning supporters to take an unequivocal public stance. Newspapers ran this story:

> Henry J. Kaiser declared today he would 'never be willing' to be a presidential candidate. Advised of Chicago efforts to boom him into the 1944 race, the 'miracle man' of industry said: 'Every bit of that is news to me. In the first place, I'm not fitted for it. In the second place, I'm a builder—not a politician. My sole ambition of the future is to provide employment and to do my utmost—everything within my power—for the conversion from war to peace and maintain employment.' He added that he could best attain this goal as an employing builder—and not a presidential candidate.

Now it was early July and with the Democratic convention approaching, President Roosevelt had to choose who his running mate would be. It wasn't an easy decision. No clear-cut favorite stood out. Although Collier's Magazine in 1946 reported that Kaiser had been summoned to Hyde Park by the President "to learn that Mr. Roosevelt looked on him favorably for Vice President," this was denied by Kaiser who said at that time:

> Although the late President Roosevelt never at anytime discussed with me the question of my being a candidate, I later learned that he discussed it with others and did consider it seriously. I have had hundreds of letters from members of both parties urging me to become a candidate, but over the past twenty years I have always taken the position that I would be helpful to any Administration which concerned itself with the welfare of the United States. I have never been interested in being a candidate for any political office nor have I any intention of changing my position.

When the final hour of decision arrived, President Roosevelt did what politicians always do—he chose another politician, Harry Truman. Already, history is saying it was a very wise choice. Yet one cannot escape conjecturing how different history might have been if Kaiser had been chosen as Roosevelt's running mate in 1944.

Laying The Groundwork For The United Nations

How many people know that Henry Kaiser was one of the nation's early leaders calling for the formation of a world body that would end up as the United Nations? Yet six months before the United Nations charter was signed in San Francisco in June of 1945, Kaiser was asked to be chairman of the National Membership Committee of Americans United for World Organization, Inc. His acceptance of this post came only two weeks before President Roosevelt would ask him to become National Chairman of the clothing drive.

So here was the busy industrialist Kaiser, eight months before the end of the war, up to his eyeballs in two major nationwide campaigns, each of which could be a full-time job. Following is an article published in the New York Times of January 8, 1945:

KAISER NAMED CHAIRMAN OF PEACE GROUP

Henry J. Kaiser has been named chairman of the Americans United for World Organization national membership committee, Dr. Ernest M. Hopkins, Americans United board chairman and president of Dartmouth College, announced yesterday in New York.

KEEP THE PEACE

Kaiser, accepting the post in California, forwarded the following statement to Dr. Hopkins:

United States participation, in a world peace organization is necessary for its success. A world peace organization, backed by moral and military might of all its members can keep the peace and keep it in a democratic way. I hope that all Americans will get behind this movement to make secure the future of peoples everywhere.

No time was wasted. In less than a month, a large impassioned ad was run in nationwide newspapers, carrying a big picture of Kaiser.

WITHIN THE NEXT FEW MONTHS, WE'LL KNOW WHETHER OR NOT WE'VE SUCCEEDED, says HENRY KAISER

No one is carrying such a heavy burden in the war effort that he can afford to neglect the problems of a lasting peace.

We who have come through this tragedy alive owe it to our dead, and to our children, to do everything possible to make this the kind of a world God wants it to be. It may be our last chance.

This is why we must unite now, to build this kind of peace. And if enough of us want a peace that will prevent another war—we can have it. Our government needs to know what we want.

Americans United for World Organization is a group of people, big and little, who want this sort of peace passionately.

I joined Americans United because the pressure of this important job was greater than I could resist.

Our task is not only to win this war but to prevent World War III by joining an effective world organization. . . .

If you believe with us, that only a lasting peace can compensate our dead for their sacrifice, and the living for their suffering, send us the coupon below. Fill it out now and mail it today. The fate of civilization is in the balance.

Most sincerely yours,

HENRY J. KAISER, Chairman, Membership Committee

Mrs. Eleanor Roosevelt, who would eventually become one of the Founders of United Nations, was intrigued by Americans United for World Organization, and wrote to Kaiser inquiring about it. Knowing the boost her backing could provide, Kaiser quickly gave her the information, to which she replied February 22, 1945:

The White House
Washington

Dear Mr. Kaiser:

Thank you very much for your letter of February 19 in answer to my inquiry about the Americans United for World Organization. I have joined the organization.

Kaiser expressed his gratitude for her support by writing on March 7:

I am grateful for your letter of February 22, and am heartened to know you have brought your support to Americans United for World Organization.

While Kaiser would lend his name and provide the leadership for a membership drive, Mrs. Roosevelt would become one of the principal architects, and one of the strongest moving forces in the founding of the United Nations.

Kaiser was proud of the role he had played in getting United Nations launched. On August 20, 1945, just when he was getting started in the automobile business, he was the guest columnist for Drew Pearson presenting his views on the important challenges which lay ahead for America. He saw fit to include a comment about the United Nations:

It was thrilling, during the United Nations Conference on international organization at San Francisco, to watch our nation's new friends from the world abroad climax their discovery of America by discovering the secret of America's great power. For many of them it was at first difficult to understand how such coordinated industrial might could flow from a system of economic freedom motivated by self-interest. The secret, of course, is the force of competition.

Kaiser's friendship with Mrs. Roosevelt would continue until her death in 1962, although the frequency of the contacts would diminish. On May 1, 1946, nearly a year after the signing of the United Nations charter, Kaiser accepted the invitation of Mrs. Roosevelt for him and Mrs. Kaiser to have lunch with her at Hyde Park. At that time Mrs. Roosevelt was playing the delicate leadership role in bringing about an important amendment to the United Nations charter. There is no doubt whatsoever that the main topic of discussion at that luncheon involved the United Nations.

In the year 1988 it is impossible to look at the United Nations without wondering how far off the mark it has strayed from the dreams of Henry Kaiser, Eleanor Roosevelt, and those other idealists who gave so much of their hearts and souls in getting it launched. Too few people today honestly believe the United Nations can truly bring about world peace. And too many nations, United Stated included, tear the vitals out of the charter, by exercising their veto power whenever it serves their purpose.

Still, isn't it somehow reassuring that there were so many people who dreamed the dream in 1945—so many people in 1988 who continue to believe in the noble dream called the United Nations?

Man With A Heart

As victories on the battlefields gave promise that peace was not too many months away, President Franklin D. Roosevelt wrote this letter to Kaiser January 22, 1945:

> January 22, 1945
>
> Dear Henry:
>
> I am informed by Director General Herbert H. Lehman of United Nations Relief and Rehabilitation Administration that a united national clothing collection is planned for April 1945 by UNRRA and all voluntary war relief agencies.
>
> The people of America will be asked to contribute 150,000,000 pounds of good used clothing for free distribution to needy men, women, and children in war-devastated areas. . . . My recent report on UNRRA revealed that as many war victims have died from exposure and a lack of adequate clothing as have died from starvation, and I agree with Governor Lehman that this problem of securing clothing for war relief needs ranks high in urgency.
>
> I feel assured that this appeal will receive the traditionally generous response of the American people. The importance of the cause demands a leader who will stimulate thousands of our people throughout the land to give vast amounts of volunteer service, as well as inspire all Americans everywhere to contribute all the clothing they can spare.
>
> I am confident your personal leadership will command the nation-wide cooperation needed for success, and I hope very much that you will be able to accept the invitation of Governor Lehman as National Chairman of this project. . . .
>
> Very sincerely yours,
>
> Franklin D. Roosevelt

There was no indecision in answering the President. On the very day Kaiser received the letter he agreed to take the job. As busy as all his companies were in turning out ships and other products for the war, as strongly committed as he was in planning for a strong postwar economy, he wrote the President:

My dear Mr. President;

The humanitarian appeal in your letter of January 22 is one that cannot be denied. I shall therefore undertake to assist Director General Lehman in the service which you propose. . . .

The burdens of your high office and the strength and courage with which you carry them bring all of our efforts into proper perspective. Therefore, I am unable to plead any barrier to fulfilling your request. Please say to Mr. Lehman that I shall be glad to proceed with the assignment whenever he is ready.

Kaiser had never headed up a national campaign before. True, he had served as national president of the Associated General Contractors of America, but that was a relatively small group of builders all having a common interest. And through so many joint ventures he had learned the art of teamwork. But now he had to assume the leadership in putting together a team of thousands of workers from all parts of the country.

He knew, of course, that there would be a spontaneous outpouring of support from the people of America and that it shouldn't be too difficult to find local chairmen for the drive. News releases for newspapers and magazines and radios helped stir up public interest. The War Advertising Council published very persuasive full page ads calling for support.

The kick-off drive was set for Friday, March 9, 1945, with the main luncheon at the Waldorf-Astoria in New York City. The next day the New York Herald Tribune reported:

Thirty million inhabitants of the liberated countries of Europe alone are 'statistically naked,' out of a total of 125,000,000 persons in 'desperate' need of clothing, shoes, and bedding, the first service bulletin of the United National Clothing Collection for War Relief reported yesterday. The nationwide drive for gifts of serviceable used clothing starts April 1. Henry J. Kaiser called the effort to collect 150,000,000 pounds of clothing during the thirty days of April 'a fantastic job.' In the last fortnight, 2,500 local chairmen have been named, with a total of 10,000 to be lined up by the time the drive starts. Mr. Kaiser observed that the drive would crystallize American readiness to aid the world community, and said he had made it his own 'first responsibility,' even while engaged in twenty-five enterprises producing for the war effort.

A few months later, Kaiser was proud to announce that 7,672 local chairmen in cities and towns all over the nation reported collections totally 150,366,014 pounds of used clothes, shoes, and bedding. He called the response 'an inspiring demonstration of democracy in action.' He said the first shipments of contributed clothing had already arrived at their destinations and were being distributed to the needy. Kaiser, the shipbuilder, had proved to be a dynamic, forceful campaigner who could rally public support.

It was only natural, therefore, that President Harry S. Truman would draft Kaiser's services for the same kind of work once the war was over. Less than a week after VJ Day Truman appealed to Kaiser to head up another national clothing drive. Again Kaiser quickly agreed.

In the end, the second national clothing drive proved to be as great a success as the first. The goodwill and compassion of millions of Americans were reflected in the torrent of clothing that was streaming to the war-ravaged countries. And once again, Kaiser had proved he was more than an exciting industrialist, he was a man with a heart.

The Train Engineer

Kaiser was not a trained engineer. He was a builder, a salesman. Yet he knew more about engineering than most engineers did. He hired engineers by the thousands.

In late 1947 he became an engineer of sorts—a train engineer. The people of the United States had taken it upon themselves to organize a program of sending vast food supplies to the people of France. They gave it the name, the Friendship Train. As one of the ways to publicize the program, it was decided to have a long trainload of food move from Chicago to New York City where it would be loaded on a ship for France. Accompanying this train ride was a host of well-known public figures, including Henry Kaiser. It was suggested that along with some of the others he should actually serve as the engineer of the train for a certain distance. He jumped at the chance. He donned an engineer's cap, listened to instructions from the experienced engineer, poked his head out of the locomotive cab window for a picture, and with the engineer looking over his shoulder, took over the controls. With his natural enthusiasm, he was like a kid with an electric train. He enjoyed every minute. Let others worry about his companies' problems, he was out to enjoy the free ride from Chicago to New York. Within a few days he received this letter:

Washington, D.C.
6 December 1947

Dear Mr. Kaiser:

As the USS Leader is about to leave New York Harbor loaded with American food, I want to thank you for the magnificent effort that you have furnished in order to make the Friendship Train possible.

Without your contribution and the encouragement that your backing and your presence on board the train gave to the Committee, this fine gesture of the American people would not have met with such an overwhelming success. I know the personal part you have played in this enterprise and I appreciated your staying on board the train from Chicago to New York, in spite of the strain resulting from your work and the numerous tasks that you were already responsible for.

Please convey my thanks to Mrs. Kaiser for having come to New York in the cold weather and having given to the Committee her help and assistance. I am well aware of your cooperation and I want to thank you in the name of my Government as well as in my own.

With my best wishes,

Sincerely yours,

Henri BONNET,

French Ambassador to the United States

The Speechmaker

It would be a betrayal of everything that Henry Kaiser stood for and did in his life to have a biography written about him dealing only with his material accomplishments, and not try to capture his deeper qualities that made up his philosophy for living. As bold and as spectacular as his industrial ventures were, he stood out from other national leaders just as much for his high-minded yet down-to-earth ideals.

His effervescence was spontaneous, ever-present, contagious. People could not sit in a meeting with him without having some of his enthusiasm rub off on them. Reporters who interviewed him were always impressed that he would not only come forth with all the facts but he would throw in some upbeat comments about the great future of America. Nearly all of his letters were laced with optimistic observations. The personal friends he made found their outlook on life enriched by sharing his wisdom.

Considering how busy he was, it was amazing how many speaking engagements he accepted. Hardly any invitation was ever rejected out-of-hand. He would always search for a way to fit the talk into his schedule. He was rarely selective. He spoke to the full range of audiences—bankers, publishers, advertisers, salesmen, purchasers, engineers, contractors, automobile dealers, chambers of commerce, college students, servicemen, church members, employees, unions, doctors, nurses, service clubs, the Press Club, Newcomen Society, Congressional Committees, and numerous radio and television programs.

He was nearly always showered with praise for the message he brought and the sincerity with which he delivered it. Typical of the thousands of congratulatory letters he received are these comments he received following a talk he gave to the California Newspaper Publishers Association in July 1944:

> I discovered a Henry J. Kaiser completely different from my previous impressions. You have a heart and spirit, besides your amazing ability to accomplish things.

> We go home with a vision of California and the West, given us by a great citizen of the Pacific Coast.

> The impact of your speech keeps growing on me. The more I think of it, the more powerful it becomes.

A year later Fortune magazine took a slightly different, more sophisticated slant:

> Although Kaiser laughs often, in a rumbling chuckle, he never seems far from tears. About him there is a massive sentimentality. His speeches are almost maudlin, sprinkled with hallelujahs and Fourth-of-July oratory. He is so monumentally, so awe-inspiringly corny in his utterances that some sophisticates entirely miss the important thing—his dead-earnestness which saves his speeches somehow.

Most of his speeches didn't need to be "saved." Especially with each passing year they got better and better. Together they comprise a rare collection of lasting wisdom. It would be great to include all of them in this biography, but, of course, space doesn't permit. It may well be that some publisher will find a market for a book composed exclusively of all his talks.

CHAPTER 15

IRON CONSTITUTION

"You can't sit on the lid of progress. If you do, you will be blown to pieces."

Sickly persons have accomplished many incredible things in this life—raising fine families, crossing new frontiers, inventing marvelous and useful products, setting standards in education, writing books, becoming government leaders, and even performing heroic military exploits. The list could go on and on.

Fortunately, most people are not sickly. This gives them that extra freedom to spend more time in doing creative things. And it usually blesses them with extra boldness to be doing creative things. Vigorous good health often leads to vigorous efforts and vigorous creativity.

Henry Kaiser was blessed from birth with an iron constitution. Those who knew him well marveled at how seldom he was sick and especially how tireless his energy was. In a way, this was surprising because he didn't always take the best care of himself. The two primary abuses he put his body to were overeating, together with a failure to get a proper amount of physical exercise. Somehow he seemed to compensate for these abuses by his unabated enthusiasm for hard work which did involve the release of a great deal of mental and emotional energy.

With his gargantuan appetite, he always seemed to be hungry, and he would always eat more than others. Often people would be surprised to see him eat two steaks instead of one. His own personal doctor, Dr. Sidney Garfield, repeatedly warned him to cut back on his eating, but both the pleasure of tasting the food and the good feeling that came from being filled up were such that he couldn't quite accept the necessity of eating less. He often said, "My only affliction is that I suffer from stomach trouble. I never can get enough in it."

In his roadbuilding and dambuilding days he acquired a strong liking for smoking cigars, and he smoked the best, each hermetically sealed in its own aluminum container. At times when the pressures were great he would almost chain smoke them and there was always a big, inlaid humidifier on his desk full of them. From time to time when he had his medical checkup the doctors would tell him they thought he should give up cigars for a while, and he never questioned their advice. He would put the lid on the humidifier and not touch it again until the doctors would say he could light up for a while. During the times he was "off" smoking it did not seem to make any difference in his attitudes and one would never know whether or not it even bothered him. In later years he smoked fewer and fewer cigars and was never seen smoking them in his executive dining rooms or in board of directors meetings or in any other situation where it might interfere with business discussions.

As to cocktails, he could take them or leave them. Often when he was with three or four of his own executives for dinner he was unaware whether the drinks were alcoholic or not because he would become so engrossed in the business discussions. At cocktail parties, especially in his later years in Hawaii, he did have his share of drinks. Partly because his weight could absorb more alcohol than others without his feeling it, and partly because he seemed to know when to stop, cocktails would make him happy but never tipsy. He established an inviolable rule that no alcoholic beverages, beer and wine included, could ever be served for lunch in his executive dining rooms.

He couldn't, or wouldn't, tolerate sickness. Most of the time he would simply ignore it and go right on working. Work was the therapy he relied on more than anything else. However, he found there were certain pills and other medicines that could help in some illnesses, so he always kept handy a black leather bag full of sick supplies. If a doctor recommended a certain dosage, Kaiser would not hesitate to double it just to be sure the medicine would work. The ever-present black bag would leave some people with the impression that he was a hypochondriac, although in truth he was anything but a hypochondriac. He never babied himself.

He couldn't tolerate sickness in people around him any more than he could with himself. Not that he was critical or impatient with them. Instead, he had a compulsion to help them by giving his best advice in their situation and usually by administering some of the medicine from his black bag. Too often he would double the dosage, creating an over-reaction. It got to the point where most of his key men would hesitate to mention any sickness for fear his treatment would make them feel worse than the illness itself.

Joe Reis, one of Kaiser's earliest executives, remembers the black medicine bag well, as does Edna Knuth (Piper), Kaiser's personal secretary throughout the thirties, forties and early fifties. An interview with them went like this:

Reis: Kaiser had this mania for medication to treat anything—sore throat, headache, pains of any kind. He had all these little vials with aspirin, powders, and nostrums of various kinds. He always carried them with him in a little black medical bag like the old doctors used to pack and bring with them when they made house calls.

Knuth: What any of us had, he had the cure for it.

Reis: He was doing this long before the days of the Kaiser Foundation Health Plan—it goes back to my days in Cuba in the late twenties. And, you know, he kept it up almost to the day he died, because I remember Dr. Sid Garfield (founder of the Kaiser Health Plan) and Julian Wiese, who was the Plan's head pharmacist, had to see that that little black bag was always stocked with medicine.

Knuth: Before we went on an extended trip I'd have to go through it, you know, to see if all the right medicines were there. I remember the time—after Mother Kaiser had died, and he was married to Ale—and I'd always had this wart on the end of my nose, and it always annoyed him and annoyed Ale, and it was unsightly, but I had been scared to death to have it cut off. So, unbeknown to me, one day they told me they were going to take me to lunch and that we'd have to go by the hospital to pick up something or other. Well, it turned out that they had made an appointment with the head surgeon. They went in with me to the surgery room and before I could protest my wart was removed. It was a beautiful success! I've been grateful ever since because I was afraid to have that thing taken off.

Apparently as a youth Kaiser had robust health. There are no records of any serious illnesses. The pictures of him at that time of life portray an active boy and later a dashing young swain courting the loveliest of the gentler sex. But as solid as his youthful physical attributes were, and as a remarkably as his physique held up during his eighty-five years, he encountered a few setbacks along the way which could have changed the course of his life if they had been more severe, or if he had given in to them.

In a letter written April 27, 1914, in longhand by Kaiser while still living in Vancouver, British Columbia, he told W. A. Semple, his former boss in the photographic supply business in Utica, New York:

> I nearly lost Mrs. Kaiser about ten months ago at which time I wasn't very well myself, but since then I took some rest and now there is nothing strong enough to hold me.

About nine months later Kaiser was the recipient of a letter from Allen J. Hill, for whom Kaiser had worked in Spokane several years before. After praising Kaiser on a roadbuilding job, "You have done many things, Henry, that make me proud of you, but I believe that this is the best of all, and certainly from the bottom of my heart I extend you my congratulations as I consider it splendid work," Hill went on to say:

> Now you mention about the speed you are developing, and would remind you that last Fall in spite of your splendid constitution and good habits you were down and out with what you thought was a cold, but I know it was nervous prostration—Henry you cannot keep up the gait you are going without taking some relaxation; all the business in the country cannot be done in one year. You are a young man and remember you have many years ahead of you and I warn you not to go as strong as you are, but take it easy even if you do

not get the same amount of business—why dont [sic] you arrange to go to the fair in San Francisco about the last of this month before active construction season begins for a couple of weeks; it will do you all the good in the world and you will be in a much better position to push your work after taking this rest.

By 1924 Kaiser was in high gear constructing highways all over Northern California. He had also been elected President of the Northern California chapter of the Associated General Contractors of America, Inc., a piling up of responsibility which he enjoyed. Then he was stricken with typhoid fever which put him out of action for a time. In the Association's bulletin of February 1925 this happy announcement was made:

Henry J. Kaiser who was re-elected President of the Association at the recent convention while confined to his home with an attack of typhoid fever is, we are happy to say, once more out and about and rapidly regaining his old-time strength and dynamic energy.

In June 1941 Frank Taylor wrote a comprehensive story on Kaiser for the Saturday Evening Post in which he said: "Seldom sick, Kaiser always has at least three doctors when he is. Now and then he takes a day off to rest up. He spends it lying on a couch with a telephone within reach so he can talk to people from New York City to Los Angeles."

One time in New York City in November 1944 Joseph Field, writer for PM, had a good interview going with Kaiser when time ran out. Kaiser had an appointment with a masseuse which he did not want to miss. Kaiser didn't stand on formality. He said, "Why not come along with me? We can continue the interview while I am being massaged." Field later wrote:

The masseuse was a small, energetic, gray-haired woman. I walked inside with Kaiser and waited while he took off his coat off. He lay on the table, wearing his shirt, and sighed in relief as the masseuse started to rub his back. 'This is the only thing that helps me,' he said. 'I've tried all kinds of doctors.' 'Remember,' the masseuse told him, 'get up at least once every half hour in your office and walk around.' 'I'll remember,' Kaiser promised.

Considering how overweight he was, and how little physical exercise he engaged in, it was quite amazing how well his legs held up. By late 1948 he started having some bothersome pains which would continue to flare up off and on to one degree or another throughout the rest of his life. This never became an excuse to slow down, only an invitation to overcome the pains by doing more. It hurt him to have to write this letter to one of his major partners and longtime friend, Jack McEachern, of General Construction Company in Seattle on December 17, 1948:

As I told you on the phone, I was very hopeful of being able to accept the

Seattle Chamber of Commerce invitation to address the January 7th luncheon for the Associated Boys Club.

But for the last few days I have been forced to bed with a painful leg, and Mrs. Kaiser also has not been very well.

So I feel I cannot take the chance of not being able to keep the engagement and, as much as I would like to be there, I should decline.

Eleven days later Kaiser wrote to two of his dearest friends, Mr. and Mrs. Paul de Kruif about his continuing leg trouble. de Kruif was a prolific medical writer who had written a book about Kaiser's Health Plan in 1943—"Kaiser Wakes the Doctors." He was just finishing another book extolling the farsightedness of Kaiser's approach to medicine, "Life Among the Doctors." Kaiser's telegram was dated December 28, 1948:

Just like Paul and Rhea—always working at helping somebody. Thank God for the two of you and the good you do for so many.

Have had exactly ten doctors now on this sciatic leg of mine but still the pain persists and all the doctors have given up science and are living on hope.

Leaving for the east tonight as a first class cripple because the medical science is still in doubt.

The very real purpose of this telegram is to let you know I appreciated your telegram and mother joins me in wanting to see life give you its best in the new year.

Throughout January 1949 Kaiser continued to make references to his sciatica. Then on February 5 he wrote this letter to George D. Woods, Chairman of the Board of The First Boston Corporation who had recently become Kaiser's top financial adviser after Cyrus Eaton of Otis & Company had defaulted in the handling of a stock issue by Kaiser-Frazer:

I appreciate the thoughtful observations you recently sent me regarding the question of listing our stocks on the New York Stock Exchange. Your opinions and recommendations went to all of our interested executives.

I am thinking of you—learning of all our boys visits with you—missing much seeing you.

Someday I am sure I personally will be completely returned to health and reinvigorated but the progress from day to day is microscopically slow, but from week to week good progress is much more evident. Your good friend Paul, with Dr. Shaner, made the greatest contribution.

With kind personal wishes to you and yours and I am looking forward to seeing you.

The "microscopically slow" recovery continued, so there didn't seem to be any slowdown in his activities during the next several years. In fact, his marriage to the young nurse, Ale, in April 1951 added a noticeable bounce to his walk and his overall activity.

The next time written mention was made about Kaiser's health was on September 20, 1954, when it was noted he was "spending the day at home nursing a sore leg." The following summer he wrote: "I am temporarily laid up with some back trouble—in fact, so much so that I do not expect I shall be able to get to the plane Sunday when Ale comes in."

It was at that period of time that Kaiser, Clay Bedford, Gene Trefethen and Bill Freistat made a visit to the new plant of Kaiser Aerospace and Electronics in Palo Alto where, among other things, there was keen excitement over the discovery of a "flat" television picture tube. Bedford was president of the company, Freistat was general manager. Near the end of the tour Kaiser turned to them and said, "Congratulations for the remarkable things you are doing here. Now what I'd like you to do is to find some way to treat my back."

When Kaiser's infrequent health problems did crop up, the word seemed to get around to friends and business contacts. So it was that his friend Dr. Norman Vincent Peale of the Marble Collegiate Church in New York City would communicate with him in January 1956 after Kaiser had injured himself in a fall the month before. Dr. Peale's solicitude was acknowledged by Robert C. Elliott, Kaiser's executive assistant:

> Your kind letter has been forwarded to Henry J. Kaiser in Honolulu, and I know he will be most happy and appreciative of hearing from you.

> Mr. Kaiser is back at work much improved in health. He slipped and fell at home there December 19, suffering a cut on the head. Because intermittent bodily pains continue, he underwent thorough examinations recently, and the consulting doctors determined, fortunately, that he had received no internal injury whatever.

However, Kaiser's low threshold tolerance of pain nearly led to serious consequences some time later. He had developed an arthritic condition in one of his big toes, and spurs developed in the main knuckle joint. It was extremely painful and bothered him no end.

The doctors first prescribed aspirin, but the condition continued to grow worse and more uncomfortable. He asked for something stronger and they gave him empirin and codeine, but in very restricted doses. In keeping with his lifetime adage that if a little will help, more will help more, Kaiser began to double up on the dosages. Surreptitiously, he started taking other pain killers without the doctor's knowledge. This began relieving his pain, but it also started to affect his mind and his decisions. Some people thought senility was setting in.

One night when he could not sleep, but was pretty well loaded with pain killer, he tried to get out of bed, fell and struck his head on a sharp object, gashing his scalp which started him bleeding profusely. Fortunately, he was able to make his way to the side of the room where an inter-com was located in the wall which he used to call for help. In her nearby bedroom, Ale heard his call and came rushing to his aid, finding him lying in a pool of blood. Being a nurse, she could administer immediate aid, after which she called his doctors.

Finally, the truth came out. He had been taking too many pain killers, even getting his supply unbeknown to the doctors. As soon as it was safe, the doctors operated on the toe removing the knuckle joint. Then, following a carefully supervised period of withdrawal, it was not long before he was his own normal self once more and any signs of senility completely disappeared. From then on, he never took anything stronger than aspirin for pain, but the incident did explain some of the strange actions and decisions that were made during that short period of time.

That this experience did not have any lasting effects on Kaiser's abilities is evident from this description of his activities in February 1960, when he was 77 years old, written by his Executive Assistant, Robert Elliott:

HENRY J. KAISER'S TYPICAL WORKING DAY

4:30 - 5:30 a.m.	Rises, shaves, showers and gets out into garden at home overlooking azure Pacific. Telephone conferences with companies' executives in Oakland, California, New York and elsewhere.
6:15 a.m.	Breakfast
6:30 a.m.	Leaves home
Around sunrise	Goes to his latest construction or operating projects. At construction of new resort city of Hawaii-Kai, he inspects and directs earth-moving work and latest operations.
	Coffee in the Ale Ale Kai dining room at Hawaiian Village Hotel—as manager of hotel, hospital manager, some of his construction heads, perhaps architect or interior decorator drop by and sit down and go over with him the current developments, a new idea for construction, Medical Center matters, or hotel operations, day's plans, etc.

Before noon	In his office—lunch across his desk with business associates—steady running stream of conferences....
through lunch	a round of matters concerning Medical Center....Hawaiian Village Hotel.... construction conferences with architects,
and into afternoon	etc., on newest projects—calls from Oakland to New York—conferring by long distance with his executives on affairs of various Kaiser Companies.
Afternoon	Flexible but unremitting schedule: More followups on the morning work.... Conferences on construction of Hawaii-Kai city and new hotels—session with executives from mainland, expeditious run down through his letter writing, business reports, memoranda from his companies, business reading matter, stream of telephone conferences.... Will make another trip around his latest building jobs....
By 7 p.m.	Finishes his business office day
7:30 p.m.	Dinner at home
Evening at home.	Usually some telephoning with mainland or local associates, and quietly viewing TV and chatting with family.
10:30 - midnight	Retires....notebook handy to jot down ideas.

(4:30 to 5:30 a.m.—back to usual daily schedule—usually arriving with a new "sunrise idea," which may run the gamut from a major new project to an architectural change to enhance beauty of a new structure or hotel or hospital or Hawaii-Kai)

Henry Kaiser works a 6-day week—12 to 16 hours a day, or even more in his working day, considering he is thinking, breathing, talking, doing without letup.

12,000-mile mainland flying trips on business made as need arises:

Example of one traveling week—Honolulu, day in Oakland-San Francisco busied with constant conferences and gathering with all Western Hotels' managers; all-night flying—San Francisco, Dallas, New Orleans; three days at Kaiser Aluminum plants at New Orleans, Baton Rouge, Gramercy, Aluminum directors meeting, several speeches, major address and acceptance of Cunningham Award from New Orleans for contributions to Latin America; thence to Washington—on his feet 12 hours from conference; then New

York, round of business negotiations; back to Los Angeles for full day of conferences; overnight flight to Honolulu. Mainland trips the following two months; another 12,000-mile flight around United States.

What does he do for relaxation?

Work! Building something new is the greatest relaxation in the world for Henry J. Kaiser. Putting big dredges to work is sheer fun. Building a catamaran...puzzling on the architectural design of a new structure...master-planning Hawaii-Kai resort city...is recreation to him.

Personal pleasures include boating, emphasis now on catamarans and sport fishing boat, since he has given up high speed boat racing because of the hazards to drivers' lives in getting into the 200-mile-an-hour range...enjoying the poodles which Mrs. Kaiser raises...dropping in on the entertainment at his Hawaiian Village Hotel, hearing records and watching television.

Physical shape? Still driving as hard and at fast pace that he's always done. Rugged.

Even at 80 years, Kaiser enjoyed batting around in a motorized cart. One time it caught up with him, as reported in the Honolulu Star Bulletin of June 2, 1962:

On Memorial Day Kaiser was driving around the grounds of his home in a motorized cart similar to a golf cart when the cart began going faster on a steep incline. To bring the cart to a stop he guided it to a retaining wall and was knocked out. He suffered a cut on his scalp, a scrape on his right arm and other bruises and abrasions. He was treated at the hospital and went home, working Thursday and Friday. Then Friday afternoon the doctors ordered him back in the hospital for the weekend.

Doctors found that a blood clot on his leg was still bothering him, and popped him into the hospital on the theory that it was the only way to force the 80-year-old industrialist to slow down.

The doctor said in very loud tones, you stay right here! 'And she knew about it all the time,' Kaiser said, gesturing toward his wife with an impish grin.

Kaiser is most upset about missing the Islanders baseball games this weekend. He listened to a broadcast of the game Friday night, and yesterday was impatiently waiting for evening so that he could catch the play-by-play.

But even that is not enough. 'I want to see them win,' he said impatiently.

Kaiser is impatient about the work he feels he should be doing.

'I thought I had a lot to do today, but I guess that's out,' he grinned.

People never ceased wondering why Kaiser had not seen fit to trim down his weight. Certainly, in the fifties and sixties the medical world and the public in general were becoming weight conscious. His own doctor, Sid Garfield, repeatedly urged him to reduce, stressing that Kaiser would have fewer leg and back problems if he did. Garfield also tried to convince Kaiser he could add years to his life if he would only lose weight.

It was ironical that it would take another Permanente doctor to finally persuade Kaiser he had to do something about his weight. In November 1963 a writer for the Honolulu Star Bulletin reported:

> Sticking my head in Henry J. Kaiser's office to ask directions to Hawaii Kai's new shopping center, I was invited to sit down for a chat that was most refreshing, stimulating and informative. 'My legs have been giving me trouble,' said Kaiser. 'After consulting a specialist who ran a number of tests, he just pointed to my stomach and said, 'there's the trouble. You must lose 50 pounds.' So now I'm on a diet.'

> As usual, he was bubbling with plans for the future. 'I've been checking into places for retired people. I think we'll be doing something about this at Hawaii Kai.' Kaiser is most thrilled about the progress of his hospitals. 'We have over a million members now.'

By the fall of 1964 Kaiser was bragging about the progress he was making in cutting back his weight. This article was published in the Honolulu Advertiser of October 9, 1964.

Kaiser, 82, Fit;
Diet the Secret

> Industrialist Henry J. Kaiser is trimmer these days, after losing 40 pounds in the last six months.

> Like most weight-watchers, Kaiser, 82, knew his poundage to the ounce yesterday when asked his weight.

> 'It's 213 and three-quarters pounds,' he said.

> Kaiser says 'self-control' is one secret of his successful dieting. The other is 'a good doctor who keeps me on my resolution,' he said.

> KAISER SAYS he hasn't really been going hungry but has just been concentrating on eating such things as steak, which 'gives you lots of protein and energy but not too many calories; pineapple and cottage cheese, and dietetic soft drinks.'

He feels better and 'spryer' now that he is slimmer, he said.

One other feature of his diet was not mentioned in the newspaper article. His doctor had told him that if he got hungry between meals he could eat all of the shark fin soup that he wanted to fill the void in his stomach. With this permission, he would each day order a big kettle of shark fin soup from the Golden Dragon Room at the Hawaiian Village hotel which by then had been sold to Hilton. He would be seen sipping the soup almost constantly throughout the day.

Kaiser had lived such a vigorous life and had conquered whatever illnesses that came his way it almost seemed he was the indestructible. People knew the end would have to come, but still the impression prevailed that this man with the iron constitution would keep going for another few years. Even this article in the Honolulu Advertiser of June 26, 1967, two months before his death was not taken as a portend that the end was near:

Kaiser Uses Ambulance After Flight

Multimillionaire industrialist Henry J. Kaiser returned here from the Mainland yesterday and was taken by ambulance to his home.

A spokesman for Kaiser said the 85-year-old businessman went to Oakland, Calif. June 9 for a series of business meetings. He then had hoped to travel from Oakland to Wisconsin for the wedding of his grandson, Henry Mead Kaiser.

Doctors advised Kaiser not to go to Wisconsin the spokesman said.

He said Kaiser continued his business meetings in Oakland, then left for Honolulu.

'It happened that one of the Hawaii Medical Group was in Oakland for some meetings,' the spokesman said. 'He returned on the plane with Mr. Kaiser.

'The doctor suggested that he might have a better trip if he conserved his strength by stretching out on the plane.

'I understand that he had a fine trip back and that he will return to work soon,' the spokesman said.

Yes, Henry Kaiser had an "iron constitution." How else could he have punished his body so much and still had so much energy? How else could he have remained fat for most of his life and still lived to be 85? His genes must have called for a long life span.

The other thing that had to be as important as his genes was his enthusiasm for life, his power of positive thinking, his irrepressible optimism. That gave him such zest in living he never left an opening for thoughts of illness or death to slow him down. His life should be a testimony to all—live cheerfully, keep busy, if you want to stay healthy.

CHAPTER 16

FOUR SCORE AND FIVE

"What has been true of our past must be doubly true of our future. We must go on building people . . . for the best is yet to be."

"Handy, he's gone," Ale said as she broke into tears at the bedside of her husband, Henry J. Kaiser, that Thursday, August 24, 1967, in Honolulu. Handy Hancock, Kaiser's faithful assistant, was in the room at the invitation of Ale, and along with her heard the final "beep" of the monitor that signalled the end of the heartbeat. Edgar Kaiser, the only living son, was racing from the airport to be with his father but didn't reach the bedside in time to bid his final farewell.

Somehow, it didn't seem possible. For four score and five years Kaiser had astounded everyone who knew him with his unbounded energy. Along the way, he had been warned that he was overweight but no diagnosis ever brought out that he should watch out because of a weak heart. When death came, it was not a "heart attack" as such. It was just that his "time clock" had run out. The magnificent genetic gifts that came into being at his birth had run their course, and death came peacefully.

Word of his death spread throughout the nation—and even the world—instantaneously. News media had updated their files on his life so that front page coverage, and radio and television reports provided facts and pictures in great detail.

Then the condolences began flooding in from all around the world and from nearly every walk of life. Those who knew Mr. and Mrs. Kaiser intimately sent their heartfelt sympathies on a personal basis to Ale. But the great torrent of condolences were addressed to Edgar by all the business people, political figures, labor leaders, employees, and other groups who knew Edgar personally or had had business dealings with him and his father.

Typical of the thousands of tributes was this expression of sorrow from President Lyndon B. Johnson to Edgar:

The entire nation shares with you in mourning the loss of a great American. Henry J. Kaiser embodied in his own career all that is best in our country's traditions. His own energy, imagination and determination gave him greatness—he used that greatness unflaggingly for the betterment of his country and his fellow man. May the memory of his long and creative life and the knowledge of his lasting achievements help console you and your family in the sad moment of loss.

The Kaisers had a deep-rooted family tradition—whenever remembrances were received at the death of someone in the family the others took the time to write letters of gratitude in longhand for the goodwill expressed. When the first Mrs. Kaiser, Bess, died in March 1951, Henry Kaiser, Edgar and Henry Jr. sat down together for more than a day to write their notes of appreciation. When Henry Jr. died in May 1961 Henry Kaiser and Edgar wrote longhand letters of gratitude to all who had communicated their sympathies.

Now it was for Edgar, along with Ale, alone to carry on the tradition. He set aside more than a week in early September to thank everyone who had gotten in touch with him over his father's passing. Once again, he was careful to express his feelings in letters written in longhand. There are five large cartons at the Bancroft Library at the University of California in Berkeley containing communications received by Edgar and copies of his personal longhand responses.

My wife and I happened to be on vacation at Lake Tahoe at the time of Mr. Kaiser's death. In addition to making a special trip to Oakland to attend the funeral, I wrote this letter to Edgar and his wife Sue from Lake Tahoe, August 26, 1967:

Dora and I send you our heartfelt and deepest sympathies on the loss of your beloved Father. I feel privileged indeed to have worked for twenty five years for a man of such great inspiration and dedication. His faith, his imagination, his devotion to work and his concern for the welfare of people will always serve as an ideal. Truly he was one of the great men in the history of America. We know that Kaiser men and women throughout the world will always have a special pride in working for an organization built on the high principles set by your Father.

Very sincerely,

Al and Dora Heiner

We were not surprised to receive this longhand letter from Edgar dated September 12, 1967:

Dear Dora and Al:

The Kaiser family join in thanking you for interrupting your vacation to express your heartwarming tribute to my father—and for holding our hand during the difficult time. You were one of his boys, Al, and throughout your twenty-five years with us, you have helped prove the practical application of the principles taught to us by our founder. He has left us a great heritage of achievement and guiding philosophy. It is now our privilege to continue building together.

Sincerely,

Edgar

It was Edgar who arranged most of the funeral plans. A special service was held on short notice Saturday, August 26, at the historic Kawaiahao Church of Honolulu conducted by the Rev. Dr. Abraham K. Akaka, pastor of the church and a personal friend of Kaiser.

The main service was held two days later at the First Congregational Church in Oakland conducted by the Rev. Dr. Eugene Sill, pastor of the church. By the strangest kind of coincidence, it was Dr. Sill who performed the marriage of Kaiser and Ale in Santa Barbara, California, 16 years earlier.

In making musical arrangements, Edgar turned to his longtime friend Harold Youngberg, Director of Music for the Oakland School System and Conductor of the Chancel Choir of the First Congregational Church. Youngberg remembers receiving a call from Edgar in Honolulu about 1:30 p.m., Friday, August 25:

'This is Edgar Kaiser. As you must know, my father died here yesterday and I am planning the funeral at your church next Monday morning. Will you please try to get your choir together to sing at the service?' I had to think fast. My choir had been on vacation all summer and was not scheduled to return until after Labor Day. I then asked, 'Do you have any special music in mind?' 'Yes, will you sing Onward Christian Soldiers in a real march tempo? My father loved it. And there is a song which has impressed us. It is called The Impossible Dream from a new show, The Man From La Mancha. My father's motto was 'Nothing is impossible.' I replied, 'Nothing is impossible. We will sing.' I then suggested, How Lovely Is Thy Dwelling Place from the Requiem by Brahms, to which he agreed. He ended the conversation by thanking me, adding, 'And since I am exhausted I am now going to lie down for a while.'

On Monday morning the large chapel was filled to overflowing, preponderantly men, many of whom had come from long distances. Honorary pallbearers were heads of the principal companies founded by Kaiser, longtime associates in the Kaiser organizations, and personal and business friends, men of great stature in their own right. Never before or since has the church seen such elaborate floral offerings. There were thousands of orchids and other Hawaiian flora to go along with 800 dozen white roses and 1,000 dozen red roses which completely depleted the supply of roses of all the florists in the Bay Area.

Dr. Sill's tribute to Kaiser and his expression of comfort to the bereaved family were based on the Psalms and other Biblical passages. Noting Kaiser's age, Dr. Sill said that any man who lives eight and a half decades sees many changes. "In the case of Henry J. Kaiser," he declared, "it can be said that he wrought many changes."

Assisting Dr. Sill was the Rev. Abraham K. Akaka from Honolulu who offered prayers and a hymn in the ancient language of Hawaii. Dr. Akaka accompanied himself on the ukelele. He extolled Kaiser as "a man in whom dwelled the power and glory of God himself." He recalled the high esteem in which Mr. Kaiser was held in Hawaii and said the Islanders' reverence for him was best expressed in the term "a man of Aloha."

A moving part of the solemn funeral service was the playing of a recording by the late Hawaiian vocalist, Alfred Apaka of one of Kaiser's favorite melodies, "Beyond the Reef." Kaiser was a staunch friend and devoted fan of Apaka until the young singer's death in 1961.

One of the nicest tributes to Kaiser came from a young lady who was not in attendance at the funeral. She was Denby Fawcett, daughter of Vance Fawcett, who worked for Kaiser in the forties and who later served as Advertising and Public Relations Counsel for Kaiser in Honolulu. In a letter of sympathy to the widow, Ale, Denby wrote from Saigon, September 5, 1967:

....When I was 18 my feelings toward Mr. Kaiser changed. It was because of a long afternoon we spent together chatting in your apartment at the Waldorf. You invited me to spend the weekend with you. I came into the city a little early, killed some time window-shopping and finally, went up to your apartment. Mr. Kaiser was the only one home. I puttered around my room unpacking and some time later, forced myself to go in and say hello to Mr. Kaiser. I was still quite in awe of him and wondered how my conversation could possibly interest him. It turned out to be quite the contrary. He ended up asking me dozens of questions, about my studies at Briarcliff, the school, and my fellow students. We played records and talked about French, God, sociology, Mary Martin, Jackson Pollock, Carnegie Hall, neo-drama, the fascination of building, how he got bored with the Hawaiian Village and the little photo shop he worked in in Florida. I suppose that was one facet of Mr Kaiser's greatness. He was interested in everything and everybody of ages. . . .

Aloha

It's a haunting feeling standing alongside Henry Kaiser's marble crypt in the mausoleum of the Mountain View Cemetery in Oakland, California. His first wife, Bess, to whom he was married for forty-four years, is in another crypt at the other end of the building, some one hundred yards away. The crypts for his two sons, Edgar and Henry Jr., are separated from each other, not far away from their mother.

Kaiser's crypt is on the second level in a prominent location visible for some distance as one walks along the hallway of the first level. However, no effort is made to draw attention to the Kaiser crypt. The body rests in a coffin on the top half of the large crypt, with another coffin already in place on the bottom. Presumably, this is available for his second wife, Ale, but inasmuch as she was married again for a while after his death and has not lived in Oakland since he died in 1967, one wonders if she will actually be interred there on her death. Many people close to the situation believe she will not.

The mausoleum vaults are all marble, thousands of them, and the place is spotlessly clean. The halls, of course, are pervasively silent. From time to time flowers are left on Kaiser's coffin. After all, who would there be to do this on a regular basis, with his two sons having long since passed away, and with his second wife living thousands of miles away in St. Croix in the Virgin Islands? Also, there is nothing unusual in the fact that the few grandchildren who live in the Oakland area feel no inclination to visit their grandfather's final resting place on any kind of a regular basis. And Kaiser himself would be the first to say, "what purpose is there anyway to flowers when there is no more life?"

Life, of course, is much easier to comprehend than death. Yet death is one stage of life; without it there would be no life renewal. What jars a thoughtful visitor is how a person of such enormous energy and creativity as Henry Kaiser should become no different from the rest of mankind in death. Death is truly the ultimate equalizer.

Perhaps Henry Kaiser can be better understood by likening him to the mighty rivers he helped conquer—Boulder Dam on the Colorado, Bonneville and Grand Coulee dams on the Columbia, and levees on the Mississippi. Like those rivers, Kaiser was a powerful force constantly moving, moving, moving—sometimes cascading through canyons of doubt and negativism, sometimes flowing smoothly and gently, as he reached out to help people along the way. And, like those rivers which brought new life wherever their waters touched the soil, Kaiser brought new life and new hope to the hundreds of thousands of people whose lives he touched.

Henry Kaiser will live on in this world in one way or another, certainly through the children who will come along in the Kaiser family as few offspring as there are. Not so much, however, in the giant corporations he created, although his Kaiser Permanente Health Plan is sure to keep expanding. Not so much in all the plants and facilities he built, because those can become obsolete or can be sold off. Not even in the memory of those who knew him personally, for, in time, they too will be gone.

He will live on primarily as a symbol of all that is good and great in America and in our free enterprise system, both of which he loved so dearly. He will live on to the extent we don't lose sight of the inspirational truths he defined so often in the hundreds of speeches he gave and the articles and letters he wrote. He will live on because historians will keep trying to probe the mystery of how this one man could do so much and come forth with so much wisdom in one lifetime.

Yes, the river called Henry J. Kaiser will continue flowing, though only in small streams as compared with the flood waters that could never be dammed while he was yet alive.

AFTERWORD

Henry J. Kaiser was one of the boldest, most spectacular entrepreneurs in American history. Of that, there can be little doubt.

Why, then, is he not better remembered? Why has he not become a meaningful symbol of all that is good and worthwhile in our free enterprise system?

Ironically, part of the blame—if blame there be—must rest with Kaiser himself. In his lifelong obsession to find happiness through hard work he simply did not take the time to lay the careful groundwork that might have helped perpetuate the organizations he had created. The man who throughout his life stood out for always looking ahead and preparing for the future failed to set the stage for the continuity of his own companies.

Incredibly, even in his eighties he had not turned over the full control of his operations to his son, Edgar, who had worked side-by-side with him for over forty years. Somehow, as much as he had relied on Edgar's leadership abilities—in dambuilding, shipbuilding, and automobile manufacturing—he didn't quite perceive that for the strengthening of his son and for the possible good it might do in perpetuating the Kaiser companies it would be necessary to step aside ever so slightly, allowing Edgar to assume top command. Right till his death in 1967 it was tacitly accepted that Henry Kaiser was not only Founder of all the companies but was still the person with the final say-so.

Nor did Kaiser spend any significant time with his grandchildren preparing the way for their future leadership. "He was almost a stranger to us," some of them would later say.

Then, in his will signed two years before his death, he left the "entire rest, residue and remainder" of his estate to his young wife—other than what had already been placed in trust, or what was being placed in trust, for the benefit of the The Henry J. Kaiser Family Foundation. Except for some personal effects that had sentimental value to his son, he excluded him and the grandchildren from any benefits, "in the knowledge that they are otherwise adequately provided for." However, as it turned out, they were not otherwise adequately provided for, because they ended up with neither the stock ownership nor the mantle of leadership that could have led to a family dynasty—in sharp contrast to nearly every other great American industrial family.

Now, in 1988, only twenty-one years after his death, all of his industrial companies have been sold or have gone out of business. Operated generally under the name Kaiser, but with entirely different ownership, many of these companies are reasonably successful. The two major entities that have remained unscathed are:

- The immensely successful and growing Kaiser Permanente Health Program.

- The Henry J. Kaiser Family Foundation which had $80 million shortly following his death and which has grown to over $350 million.

Typical of the travails which have beset the industrial companies are:

- Kaiser Aluminum and Chemical Corporation which sold off most of its chemical operations and huge real estate assets to help offset operating losses, and which is now subject to different ownership, under the name KaiserTech, Inc.

- Kaiser Cement Corporation which, after selling off all except its main plant, now appears to be a viable company under foreign ownership.

By far, the saddest—and most shocking—collapse of all (except for the demise of Kaiser-Frazer automobile company when Kaiser was still alive) has befallen the once-mighty Kaiser Steel Corporation, which was plundered by corporate raiders bringing on bankruptcy in early 1987 and making it impossible for the company to keep up its payments on health insurance, life insurance, and even some pensions for the retired employees who actually built the company.

This shocking disintegration of the Kaiser family of companies is primarily the result of:

(1) Radical changes in the cost of production and market competition for the kind of basic industries Kaiser was into. Many argue that even if Kaiser had stayed alive, he wouldn't have been able to overcome the changing economics, or they contend he might have sold off the companies more quickly and profitably.

(2) Lack of dynamic, forward-looking leadership comparable to that provided by Kaiser himself when he was alive. All his life Kaiser had been astoundingly resourceful, resilient, opportunistic—swiftly adjusting to every new challenge that came his way. Certainly if he had stayed alive in good health, the shape of his family of companies would be entirely different from what it has turned out to be.

Over and above these erosions one wonders if there were other forces that led to the fading out of Kaiser. Has the public forgotten him because he was too good a guy? Was his fate foretold by Mark Anthony's melancholy appraisal of life some 2,000 years ago: "The evil that men do lives after them, the good is oft interred with their bones."

If he hadn't paid back his large government borrowings, if he had turned his back on creditors and stockholders by taking out bankruptcy when his automobile venture failed, if he had been caught in any scandalous infidelity, if he had been like some of the robber barons of the nineteenth and early twentieth centuries, he would certainly be talked about more than he is now. If instead of being a proud, devoted father to his two sons, he had humiliated and crushed them as Henry Ford did with his son, Edsel; or if he had kept a mistress as Henry Ford did; or if he had turned sour on unions and union workers as Henry Ford did; then more people would make it a point to know these things about him, and in the process would actually end up becoming better acquainted with his remarkable achievements. And, true enough, if he had only been finally successful in his automobile business, where he just about made it—if there were Kaiser cars still being turned out in large numbers—those cars would carry the name Kaiser forward just as Ford cars do the name of their founder.

Whatever the reason he has been forgotten so completely our country is the loser. Too bad, indeed, because we need more Henry Kaisers to help our capitalistic system stay in high gear. In a nation where our industrial leadership is being challenged from all sides, isn't it time we glorify old-fashioned principles of integrity and hard work instead of always headlining sleaze and scandal? Why shouldn't we proudly anchor our forward progress on the kind of ideals that helped Henry Kaiser do so much for so many, and in the process do so much for our country?

It's for those industrialists who deeply believe in our free enterprise system; it's for students of history; it's for young people who dream mighty dreams of their own, to keep alive the memory of what he did and how he did it—this man, Henry J. Kaiser, America's bold and spectacular entrepreneur.

INDEX

432

434